ANNALS OF COMMUNISM

Each volume in the series Annals of Communism will publish selected and previously inaccessible documents from former Soviet state and party archives in a narrative that develops a particular topic in the history of Soviet and international communism. Separate English and Russian editions will be prepared. Russian and Western scholars work together to prepare the documents for each volume. Documents are chosen not for their support of any single interpretation but for their particular historical importance or their general value in deepening understanding and facilitating discussion. The volumes are designed to be useful to students, scholars, and interested general readers.

The Leningrad Blockade, 1941–1944

A New Documentary History from the Soviet Archives

Richard Bidlack and Nikita Lomagin

Translations by
Marian Schwartz

Yale

UNIVERSITY PRESS

New Haven & London

Published with assistance from the Louis Stern Memorial Fund.

Yale University Press books may be purchased in quantity for educational, business, or promotional use. For information, please e-mail sales.press@yale.edu (U.S. office) or sales@yaleup.co.uk (U.K. office).

Set in Sabon Roman type by Tseng Information Systems, Inc.
Printed in the United States of America.

Library of Congress Cataloging-in-Publication Data
Bidlack, Richard, 1954–
The Leningrad blockade, 1941–1944 : a new documentary history from the Soviet archives / Richard Bidlack and Nikita Lomagin ; translations by Marian Schwartz.
p. cm. — (Annals of communism)
Includes bibliographical references and index.
ISBN 978-0-300-11029-6 (cloth : alk. paper)
1. Saint Petersburg (Russia)—History—Siege, 1941–1944. 2. Saint Petersburg (Russia)—History—Siege, 1941–1944—Sources. I. Lomagin, Nikita. II. Title.
D764.3.L4B48 2012
947′.21—dc23
2011047638

A catalogue record for this book is available from the British Library.

This paper meets the requirements of ANSI/NISO Z39.48-1992 (Permanence of Paper).

10 9 8 7 6 5 4 3 2 1

Yale University Press gratefully acknowledges the financial support given for this publication by the John M. Olin Foundation, the Lynde and Harry Bradley Foundation, the Historical Research Foundation, Roger Milliken, the Rosentiel Foundation, Lloyd H. Smith, Keith Young, the William H. Donner Foundation, Joseph W. Donner, Jeremiah Milbank, and the David Woods Kemper Memorial Foundation.

To our wives,

Nancy and Anastasia,

for their love, support, and encouragement

Contents

List of Maps   ix

Acknowledgments   xi

Note on Transliteration   xv

Note on the Documents   xvii

Soviet Terminology, Acronyms, and Abbreviations   xix

List of Documents   xxi

Chronology of the Leningrad Blockade   xxvii

INTRODUCTION   1

CHAPTER 1. Leningrad During the Second World War and
Its Aftermath   15

CHAPTER 2. Who Ruled Leningrad?   78

CHAPTER 3. Policies of Total War   184

CHAPTER 4. The Struggle to Survive   262

CHAPTER 5. The Popular Mood   329

CHAPTER 6. The Question of Organized Opposition   368

CONCLUSIONS   404

APPENDIX A. Daily Bread Rations   413

APPENDIX B. Official Monthly Rations for Food Other than
            Bread   414

APPENDIX C. Rations Actually Distributed Other than Bread,
            1 January–31 March 1942, According to
            Leningradskaia Pravda   416

Notes   419

Bibliography of Sources Cited   461

Index   475

Photo gallery follows page   328

Maps

The City of Leningrad   16

The Advance of German Army Group North toward Leningrad,
    22 June–20 August 1941   33

The Front Line on 25 September 1941   37

The German Advance to Tikhvin in November 1941   47

Piercing the Blockade in January 1943   64

Acknowledgments

In this book, I have attempted to write an original comprehensive history of the blockade comprising several perspectives (ranging from the actions of political, military, and security elites in Leningrad and Moscow to the reactions and attitudes of ordinary Leningraders) and based on a wide range of primary sources and scholarly publications. Within that detailed narrative, I have devoted special attention to analyzing a collection of Soviet documents that my collaborator, Nikita Lomagin, and I consider to be particularly important.

I am delighted to recognize and thank those whose assistance has been indispensable in researching and writing this book. Professors Anne and Lowell Tillett of Wake Forest University introduced me to the fascinating city of Leningrad during a summer study tour way back in 1976. At Indiana University, Alex Rabinowitch encouraged me to pursue dissertation research on the USSR during World War II, and particularly on the siege of Leningrad, even before the archives began to open, and he supervised my efforts. Ben Eklof impressed upon me that the heart of social history consists of illuminating the inner world of people's ideas and mentality. While in Bloomington, I was also fortunate to make the acquaintance of Lev Pevzner, who recounted his experience of surviving the horrific winter of 1941–42 and graciously responded to my many questions about life inside the blockade.

Historians rely on the vast knowledge of archivists and librarians, and I am indebted to those who helped Lomagin and me find primary and secondary sources at Indiana University, Columbia University, Harvard University, the University of Virginia, the U.S. National Archives, the Hoover Institution, and the Churchill Archives Centre. In St. Petersburg we were ably assisted at the Academy of Sciences Library, the St. Petersburg State University Library, the Russian National Library, the State Memorial Museum of the Defense and Blockade of Leningrad, and the Museum of the History of St. Petersburg. In Moscow staff members at the Russian State Archive of Social and Political History, the State Archive of the Russian Federation, and the Russian State Library aided our efforts, as did archivists at the Central Archive of the Ministry of Defense in Podolsk. We are particularly grateful to Vladimir Taradin, Irina Sazonova, and Taissa Bondarevskaia at the Central State Archive of Historical-Political Documents, St. Petersburg; to Nadezhda Cherepenina and Mikhail Shkarovsky at the Central State Archive, St. Petersburg; and to Yelena Liubomirova at the Central State Archive of Film, Photographic, and Phonographic Documents, St. Petersburg for their kind assistance in locating many documents and photographs. Sergei Chernov and Stanislav Bernev facilitated our research at the Archival Administration of the Federal Security Service for St. Petersburg and the Leningrad *oblast'*. Betsy Brittigan and Elizabeth Teaff of the Leyburn Library at Washington and Lee University fulfilled numerous interlibrary loan requests. The maps in this book have been reprinted from Leon Goure's pioneering work, *The Siege of Leningrad*, with permission from The Rand Corporation.

This book would not have been completed without generous financial support. It is a pleasure to thank the International Research and Exchanges Board (IREX) for a travel grant to St. Petersburg in the summer of 1999 at the beginning of this project and the Advisory Committee of Washington and Lee University for several summer Glenn Grants. I am deeply indebted to the American Philosophical Society for a sabbatical fellowship during 2003–4.

Over the years, several Russian historians, including Andrei Dzeniskevich and Valentin Kovalchuk of the Petersburg Branch of the Institute of History, Russian Academy of Sciences, have freely and generously shared their scholarship, insights, and opinions on the blockade. Viktor Bortnevsky was a dear friend and young scholar of the Soviet-German War and Russian Civil War, who often put aside his own work to help me with mine. When we first met during the politically dark days of the autumn of 1983, when *Pravda* referred to the U.S. government as the "second fascism," he offered to help my research in any way he could. He opened his personal library to me and welcomed me to his home where I became acquainted with his grandmother (a former baroness) and his mother, Marianna Korchinskaia, both of whom survived the blockade, as well as his wife, Nadia, and daughter, Nastia. Viktor had great promise as a historian, and his untimely death in 1996 was a major loss.

It was through Viktor that I became acquainted with Nikita Lomagin. For over fifteen years, we have shared documents, references, insights, and our writings on the blockade, participated together in scholarly conferences, and contributed essays to edited volumes on the blockade. I have written the entire text of this book, but the careful reader will notice that Nikita's name is the one most cited in notes that reference scholarship on the siege. His numerous publications (not only on the Leningrad blockade) and his broad and deep understanding of Western scholarship in several fields show that the future of Russian history lies with the younger generation of Russian historians. He and his wife Anastasia (a noted scholar of Danish language and literature) exemplify the best of the new Petersburg intelligentsia. I am grateful for their stimulating friendship and warm hospitality.

American colleagues David Brandenberger, Jeffrey Hass, Steven Maddox, Leslie Rimmel, and Jeffrey Rossman have enriched this book through their comments and critiques at various stages, and the detailed reports from the two anonymous reviewers for Yale University Press proved most valuable. Richard Brody gave me issues from the journal *Izvestiia TsK KPSS,* from which I selected several documents for this book, and Evgeny Kogan passed along to me copies of documents when he gave up the study of the Leningrad blockade. Alexis Walker and Ingrid Sinclair-Day translated some German texts, and Marian Schwartz provided professional translations of most of the Russian documents in the book. (I translated a few.) Gavin Lewis, the book's superb copyeditor, untangled my twisted sentences and forced me to rethink ideas and check facts and footnotes. Jonathan Brent and Vadim Staklo at Yale University Press offered their unflagging support for the project from our initial conversations through the book's publication. My wife, Nancy, a veteran IREX spouse from Soviet days, has been more patient than even Jonathan and Vadim, and has allowed the siege of Leningrad to occupy an important part of our lives. Her cheerful encouragement has been constant and unconditional. Our teenage son, Christopher, is intrigued by his dad's obsession with Russia's past and present. His older brother, David, unfortunately, may never be able to read this book, but his innocent and loving smile is a continual source of profound inspiration.

Any merits this book may possess are due in no small measure to those mentioned above. Of course, I bear the responsibility for shortcomings that remain.

RICHARD BIDLACK

Note on Transliteration

In transliterating proper names from Russian to English in the text and documents, and in English wording in the notes, we have used a slightly modified version of the standard Library of Congress (LOC) system. Soft and hard signs have been omitted, and the following changes have been made:

In the final position:

> ii in the LOC system becomes y (Kirovsky, not Kirovskii)
> iia = ia (Beria, not Beriia)
> oi = oy
> nyi = ny

In the initial position:

> E = Ye
> Ia = Ya
> Iu = Yu

Strict LOC transliterations have been used in the citations of Russian-language works in the notes and bibliography, and in Russian words and phrases other than proper names that appear in the text.

Note on the Documents

All of the documents included or referred to in this book are from the archives listed in the bibliography. Russian archival documents are cited and ordered by collection (*fond* or *f.*), inventory (*opis'* or *op.*), file (*delo* or *d.*), and folio (*list* or *l.*, or in plural, *ll.*). Thus, a sample citation would read: TsGAIPD SPb [the transliterated initials of the Central State Archive of Historical-Political Documents, St. Petersburg] f. 24, op. 24, d. 4808, ll. 1–3. The citation system for the archives of the Federal Security Service (FSB) includes a "running number" (*poriadkovyi nomer* or *p.n.*) and sometimes a "volume number" (*tom* or *t.*) between the inventory and file.

All of the reproduced documents are translations from the original Russian. Several are too long to have been reproduced in full. We have inserted ellipses within brackets [. . .] to indicate where material has been excised. Ellipses without brackets exist in the original documents. Authors' explanatory comments within the documents have been inserted within brackets. Russian words from the documents that do not translate well into English have been identified within brackets.

Soviet Terminology, Acronyms, and Abbreviations

apparat	apparatus or administrative organs
A/S	anti-Soviet
com. (English translation)	comrade
FSB	Federal Security Service
Genshtab	General Staff of the Army
GKO	State Defense Committee
gorkom (GK)	City Committee of the VKP(b)
Gosplan	State Committee for Planning
GPU	State Political Administration
ispolkom	executive committee
ITR	engineers and technicians
KBF	Red-Banner Baltic Fleet
Komsomol	Young Communist League
KPK	Party Control Committee of the Central Committee of the Communist Party of the Soviet Union
KPSS	Communist Party of the Soviet Union
krai	territory
KR	counterrevolutionary
KRO	Counterintelligence Department
Lengorispolkom	Executive Committee of the Leningrad City Soviet
Lenoblispolkom	Executive Committee of the Leningrad Regional Soviet
Lensovet	Leningrad Soviet

LF	Leningrad Front
LGU	Leningrad State University
LO	Leningrad Region
LP	*Leningradskaia pravda* (newspaper)
LPO	Leningrad Party Organization
MGB	Ministry of State Security
MPVO	Local Antiaircraft Defense
narkom	People's Commissariat, Commissar
narodnoe opolchenie	People's Militia
NKGB	People's Commissariat of State Security
NKO	People's Commissariat of Defense
NLO	Illegal Leningrad Organization of the VKP(b)
NKV	People's Commissariat of Weaponry
NKVD	People's Commissariat of Internal Affairs
obkom	Regional Committee of the VKP(b)
oblast'	region
OGPU	United State Political Administration
Osobyi otdel	Special Department
Osobyi sektor	Special Sector
otdel	Department
partkom	Party Committee
raifo	District Financial Office
raikom (RK)	District Committee of the VKP(b)
raion	district
raiotdel	District Department
raisovet	District Soviet
RKKA	Workers' and Peasants' Red Army
RKKF	Workers' and Peasants' Red Fleet
sovet	Soviet (council)
Sovnarkom	Council of People's Commissars
SPO	Secret Political Department
SR	Socialist Revolutionary
Stavka	Headquarters of the Soviet Supreme Command
SVB	League of Militant Godless
svodki	Summary reports
TsK	Central Committee
UNKVD	Regional Directorate of the NKVD
VCh	high-frequency radio transmission
VGK	Supreme High Command
VKP(b)	All-Union Communist Party (Bolsheviks)
VMF	Navy
VMN	highest measure of punishment (execution)
VP	Military Procuracy
VSLF	Military Soviet (Council) of the Leningrad Front
VT	Military Tribunal

Documents

1. Reports sent between Smolny and the Kremlin, 22 August 1941   90

2. Report from Molotov, Malenkov, Kosygin, and Zhdanov to Stalin on ten-day evacuation plan for Leningrad civilians, 29 August 1941   97

3. Report from Molotov, Malenkov, Kosygin, and Zhdanov to Stalin on ten-day evacuation plan for industrial workers and equipment, 29 August 1941   97

4. Report from Molotov, Malenkov, Kosygin, and Zhdanov to Stalin on food resources within Leningrad and a plan to increase their supply, 29 August 1941   99

5. Telegram from Stalin to Molotov and Malenkov ordering them back to Moscow and criticizing Leningrad's military leadership, 29 August 1941   101

6. Telegram from Stalin, Molotov, Malenkov, and Beria to Voroshilov and Zhdanov asking whether they have decided to surrender Leningrad and demanding information on military strategy, 9 September 1941   105

7. Report from Stalin and Shaposhnikov to Headquarters of the Leningrad Front replacing Voroshilov with Zhukov as front commander, 11 September 1941   106

8. Report from Stalin and Molotov to Zhukov and Zhdanov announcing that Voroshilov has been recalled to Moscow, 26 September 1941   107

9. Detailed plan to destroy the Baltic Fleet in the event of a retreat from Leningrad, 6 September 1941   111

10. Mandate from the State Defense Committee that orders Merkulov and *gorkom* secretary Kuznetsov to supervise preparation of important installations and bridges for destruction in the event of a retreat from Leningrad, 13 September 1941   115

11. Report from Baltic Fleet Division Commissar Lebedev to Zhukov regarding confusion over demolition signals and low morale among fleet officers, 20 September 1941   119

12. Military Order 0064 from the Leningrad Front to Military Councils (Soviets) of the Forty-second and Fifty-fifth Armies ordering deserters to be executed, 17 September 1941   122

13. Telephone order from Stalin to Zhukov, Zhdanov, Kuznetsov, and Merkulov to fire on civilians used by the Germans as human shields outside Leningrad, 21 September 1941   124

14. Zhukov's terse correction to Kubatkin regarding the military situation at Siniavino, 24 September 1941   126

15. Stalin's order to Leningrad Front Commander Fediuninsky, Zhdanov, and Kuznetsov to launch immediately an offensive to the east to break out of the siege and avoid possible capture, 23 October 1941   127

16. Letter from *gorkom* secretary Basov to Kuznetsov requesting that the Commissariat of Weaponry halt its practice of reassigning skilled defense plant workers from Leningrad to other parts of the country, 30 April 1942   139

17. Letter from Leningrad Front Commander Khozin to Zhdanov accusing VSLF commissar Zaporozhets of slander, 3 June 1942   148

18. Report from the deputy head of the Leningrad NKGB Shvyrkov to *obkom* and *gorkom* secretary Kuznetsov on the anti-Soviet comments of Maria Bakshis, an employee in the *osobyi sektor* of the *obkom* and *gorkom* VKP(b), January 1945   152

19. Report from the deputy head of the Leningrad NKVD Ivanov to *gorkom* secretary Kapustin on the illegal receipt of food and cigarettes by *raikom* secretary Kharitonov, 22 December 1941   157

20. Report from Kubatkin to People's Commissar of Internal Affairs Beria on the suicide of Ivan Lysenko, *gorkom* secretary for transportation, February 1942   162

21. Photocopy of the picture of Lysenko from his party personnel file   163

22. Appeal from Aleksy, Metropolitan of Leningrad, to believers to defend the Homeland, 26 July 1941   168

23. Memo from Council of Twenty Chairman Pariisky of the Kniaz-Vladimirsky Cathedral to the senior inspector of the Administrative Office of the *Lensovet* A. Tatarintsevaia expressing thanks for the provision of wine and flour for communion services, 26 February 1942   172

24. Complaint from Council of Twenty Chairman K. Andreev of the Church of St. Serafim to senior inspector Tatarintsevaia regarding the looting of the church and its conversion to a warehouse and morgue, 29 January 1942   173

25. Report on sums allocated by the Nikolsky Cathedral to the Red Cross Society, 3 November 1941   174

26. Report on the patriotic contributions of the churches of Leningrad for the period 1 July 1941 to 30 June 1945 in rubles   175

27. Telegram from Metropolitan Aleksy to Stalin announcing the collection of 500,000 rubles by the Eparchy of Leningrad for construction of a tank column named for Dmitry Donskoy, 12 January 1943   176

28. Telegram from Metropolitan Aleksy to Stalin stating that the fund drive to build the Dmitry Donskoy tank column continues and that he hopes for "Divine assistance" for Stalin, 13 May 1943   177

29. Stalin's reply to Metropolitan Aleksy expressing gratitude for the fund drive, 17 May 1943   178

30. Report from the head of the organizational instruction office of the *gorkom* VKP(b) Antiufeev and head of the information sector of the *gorkom* Chistiakov to Zhdanov, Kuznetsov, and Kapustin on public reactions to Stalin's meeting with church metropolitans, 10 September 1943   179

31. Report by Antiufeev and the *gorkom*'s War Office Head Pavlov on mobilization for the Red Army and Red Baltic Fleet, October 1941   186

32. Report by the Leningrad NKVD's Deputy Head Ogoltsov on the removal of the counterrevolutionary element from Leningrad, 25 August 1941   205

33. Report from Kubatkin to NKVD Senior Major of State Security Gorlinsky detailing arrests of 958 people for counterrevolutionary crimes from 1 January to 15 February 1942, 19 February 1942   207

34. NKVD plan for the forced resettlement of 95,400 Finns and Germans from the Leningrad *oblast'*, 28 August 1941   209

35. Report from Smolninsky *raikom* secretary Stelmakhovich to *gorkom* secretary A. P. Smirnov on the forced resettlement of Finns and Germans from Leningrad's Smolninsky *raion*, 20 March 1942   213

36. Report by the chairman of the Evacuation Commission for Dzerzhinsky *raion*, Vinogradov, on the forced resettlement of Finns and Germans from that *raion*, 26 March 1942   215

37. German propaganda leaflets dropped on Leningrad on 29 October 1941   216

38. German propaganda leaflets dropped on Leningrad on 10 November 1941   218

39. Report from Antiufeev and office administrator Klebanov to Zhdanov, Kuznetsov, Kapustin, and Shumilov on public reactions to reductions in bread rations, 22 November 1941   229

40. Report from Antiufeev to *gorkom* secretaries Zhdanov, Kuznetsov, Kapustin, and Shumilov on the attitudes of people standing in bread lines, 26 November 1941   231

41. Report from Kubatkin to Zhdanov, Kuznetsov, and Khozin, commander of the Fifty-fourth Army, on the public mood and on food-related crime, 25 November 1941   233

42. Report from Kubatkin to Beria and members of the VSLF on counterrevolutionary activity between 15 October and 1 December 1941, 6 December 1941   236

43. Scathing letter from "Academician Tupolev" to Stalin, 30 October 1941   250

44. Report from Kubatkin to Kuznetsov on the case of "The Insurgent," an anonymous author of anti-Soviet leaflets and letters, 12 December 1943   251

45. Report from Kubatkin to the *gorkom* on the number of people arrested, convicted, and exiled during the war, 1 October 1942   255

46. Report from Antiufeev to Zhdanov on the size of the LPO and the number of new enrollments by month, March 1942   259

47. The fantasy menu of one starving Leningrader, Valia Chepko, during the winter of 1941–42   264

48. The diary entry of a young boy, Valery Sukhov, for 23 December 1941   267

49. Report from Senior *Militsiia* Major E. Grushko to chairman of the *Lengorispolkom* Popkov on the state of the city's morgues, 12 December 1941   269

50. Diary entries of ten-year-old Nikolai Vasiliev from 2 January to 4 April 1942   277

51. Decision of the *Lengorispolkom* to convert the 1st Brick and Pumice Factory to a crematorium, 7 March 1942   282

52. Portion of the memoir of Nikolai Sergeev, head of the raw materials section of the Sausage Factory, during the winter of 1941–42, 3 February 1943   289

53. Report from Military Procurator A. I. Panfilenko to Kuznetsov on cannibalism, 21 February 1942   317

54. Report from Kubatkin to Beria and his deputy Merkulov detailing nine cases of cannibalism, most of which involved murder, 13 December 1941   318

55. Report from Kubatkin to Zhdanov, Kuznetsov, and Khozin on a band of murderer-cannibals in the northern suburban Pargolovsky *raion*, 2 May 1942   320

56. Anonymous letter to Zhdanov asking why Stalin has not addressed the nation on the war, 27 June 1941   332

57. Report from Antiufeev and Klebanov to Zhdanov, Kuznetsov, Kapustin, and Shumilov on a handwritten note found in a bomb shelter, signed by the "Nationality of the Russian People," calling for the surrender of the city, 11 October 1941   338

58. Report from Antiufeev and office administrator Bulgakov to *gorkom* secretaries Zhdanov, Kuznetsov, Kapustin, and A. I. Makhanov on public reaction to the documentary film *Leningrad in Battle*, 22 July 1942   356

59. Report from Antiufeev and Bulgakov to Zhdanov, Kuznetsov, Kapustin, and Makhanov on anti-Soviet public sentiment, 13 July 1942   359

60. Report from Antiufeev and Klebanov to Zhdanov, Kuznetsov, Kapustin,

and Makhanov on public reaction to Churchill's visit to Moscow, 18 August 1942   362

61. Excerpts from a report from Kubatkin to Beria and Merkulov on the "Activists" case involving professors accused of preparing to organize a National Socialist Party in the event that Germany captured Leningrad, 16 February 1942   374

62. Excerpts from the report of the meeting of the *partkom* of the Leningrad NKVD that condemned as unwarranted the arrests of Professors Nikiforov and Gul in the "Activists" case, 12 May 1942   375

63. Excerpts from a report from Kubatkin to Beria, Merkulov, Zhdanov, and Kuznetsov on the "Academicians" case involving distinguished specialists who had previously worked for German firms and were accused of selecting candidates for a government that would work with Germany once the USSR was defeated, 18 October 1941   380

64. Excerpt from a report from Kubatkin to Beria and Merkulov on an alleged "Committee for Public Salvation" consisting of scholars who were preparing to serve as a transitional administration after the Red Army abandoned Leningrad and prior to the formation of a German government, 16 February 1942. (This document and document No. 61 were from the same report by Kubatkin.)   383

65. Report from Kubatkin to Zhdanov and Kuznetsov on the alleged "Committee for Public Salvation," which is described as "an underground center of counterrevolutionary organization that directs all the hostile work of anti-Soviet groups," 15 March 1942   385

66. Report of a meeting of the Party Control Committee of the TsK KPSS exonerating those arrested in the "Committee for Public Salvation" case, 14 February 1958   393

Chronology of the Leningrad Blockade

1941

22 June	Germany invades the USSR without warning. Army groups are directed along the Baltic, toward Moscow, and into the Ukraine
8 July	Fall of Pskov, located 155 miles southwest of Leningrad
18 July	Food rationing introduced throughout the USSR. Workers, engineers, and technicians receive 800 grams (28 oz.) of bread per day; office workers 600 grams (21 oz.); and those in the lowest category, nonworking adults and children, 400 grams (14 oz.)
30 July	Hitler orders the encirclement of Leningrad, but not its immediate capture
10 August	Germany launches an offensive to break through the Luga River defense line
21 August	Leningrad's leaders inform the populace of a direct threat to the city
29 August	Last rail line out of Leningrad severed
2 September	First cut in daily bread rations for all Leningrad civilians. Ration for nonworking adults and children reduced to 300 grams (11 oz.)
4 September	Artillery bombardment of Leningrad begins
6 September	Hitler orders tank and air corps transferred from the Leningrad area to take part in the offensive toward Moscow
8 September	Germany captures Shlisselburg, sealing Leningrad off by land

	from the rest of the USSR to the south. By this time, Finland has cut the city off from the north by advancing to the 1939 boundary in the Karelian Isthmus
	First massive aerial bombardment of the city. Badaev food warehouses destroyed
12 September	Second cut in daily bread rations. Ration for nonworking adults and children drops to 250 grams (9 oz.)
22 September	Hitler issues directive to "erase the city of Petersburg from the face of the earth" through blockade and bombardment
1 October	Third cut in daily bread rations. Most Leningraders receive 200 grams (7 oz.)
late October	First starvation deaths likely occur. First arrests for cannibalism are made in November
8 November	Germans capture the rail junction city of Tikhvin, which necessitates construction of a new road 120 miles long to supply Leningrad across Lake Ladoga
13 November	Fourth cut in daily bread rations. Most Leningraders receive 150 grams (5 oz.). By this time, practically no other foodstuffs are available
20 November	Fifth cut in daily bread rations. Most Leningraders receive 125 grams (4.4 oz.), which increasingly include non-digestible fillers, such as sawdust.
	Three hundred and fifty horses pulling sleds bring the first food into Leningrad across frozen Lake Ladoga
8 December	Traffic on the ice road halted. Between 6 December 1941 and 22 January 1942, reportedly only 36,118 people are evacuated over the ice road
9 December	The Red Army retakes Tikhvin
13 December	First report sent to Moscow documenting cases of cannibalism
25 December	First increase in daily bread rations. Ration for most Leningraders raised to 200 grams

1942

22 January	The State Defense Committee approves a massive new effort to evacuate half a million Leningraders and allocates appropriate resources
24 January	Second increase in daily bread rations. Ration for nonworking adults and children raised to 250 grams
	Lowest temperature of the winter recorded: –40° C
25 January	Due to lack of electrical current, the city's main newspaper, *Leningradskaia pravda,* is not published (the only time that

	happened during the siege), and Radio Leningrad temporarily ceases broadcasting
25–27 January	Very little bread is baked in the city. The city's death toll reaches its peak around this time
11 February	Third increase in daily bread rations. Ration for non-working adults and children raised to 300 grams
22 March	Fourth increase in daily bread rations. Ration for nonworking adults and children raised to 400 grams
27 March	Following earlier attempts, a massive clean-up of Leningrad commences and continues for twelve days
5 April	Hitler orders capture of Leningrad
24 April	Lake Ladoga ice road shut down
26 May	Resumption of evacuation over Lake Ladoga
11 July	General Vlasov surrenders to Germany at Miasnoy Bor south of Leningrad following the destruction of his Second Shock Army
9 August	Leningrad premiere of Shostakovich's Seventh Symphony
23 September	First electrical current received in Leningrad via cable under Lake Ladoga
19 December	Ladoga ice road resumes operation

1943

18 January	Blockade pierced along the southern coast of Lake Ladoga as the Leningrad and Volkhov Fronts link up
7 February	First train arrives in Leningrad from the "Mainland"
30 March	Ladoga ice road shut down
July	Leningrad's civilian population drops to 600,000 from 3,200,000 at the start of the war
September	Artillery bombardment of Leningrad reaches its greatest intensity of the war

1944

14 January	Beginning of the final offensive to end the siege
27 January	Blockade of Leningrad completely lifted

Introduction

The battle for Leningrad and the 872-day blockade of the city by German armies and their Finnish allies during the Second World War rank among the most horrific events in world history. Next to the Holocaust, the Leningrad siege was the greatest act of genocide in Europe during the Second World War, as Germany, and to a lesser extent Finland, tried to bombard and starve Leningrad into submission. No city ever suffered more over a comparable period of time than did Leningrad during its epic struggle to survive.[1] Among the Soviet population, somewhere between about 1.6 and 2.0 million perished within the city and in battles in the surrounding region between 1941 and 1944.[2] The lowest range of this estimate exceeds the total number of Americans, both military personnel and civilians, who have perished in all armed conflicts from 1776 through the current war in Afghanistan. The number of civilians who died from hunger, cold, and enemy bombardment within the blockaded territory or during and immediately following evacuation from it is reasonably estimated to be around 900,000.[3]

The siege of Leningrad is of historic significance for other reasons as well. Leningrad was strategically important for the USSR, especially during the first six months of the Soviet-German War.[4] If the German offensive toward the city had destroyed the Soviet capacity or will to put up resistance, Germany could have linked up with Finland, gained firm control along the Baltic, and committed additional hundreds of thousands of troops to the offensive against Moscow. In turn, had Germany then quickly seized or encircled Moscow with these reinforcements, Soviet resistance might have ended. Germany then most likely would have stripped the USSR of industrial and military resources and turned its attention back to subduing Britain and at a minimum forcing Britain into a peace that would have recognized German hegemony on the continent.

Western studies of Soviet history have recently emphasized the profound and complex influences that the watershed experience of the war had on political and social life subsequently within the USSR.[5] In a general sense, the war's fundamental impact has long been recognized by survivors of the Leningrad siege. For many, it was the defining moment of their lives. How could the death of close to a million inhabitants not constitute a pivotal point in the life of a city? Practically every Leningrader lost a close relative in the siege. Untold thousands of wives were widowed, children orphaned, and lifelong residents of the city relocated thousands of miles away. Seemingly insignificant decisions had a long-lasting impact. Someone who shared a few ounces of bread during the starvation winter of 1941–42 became a friend ever afterwards. In the words of one *blokadnitsa,* the events of the siege were "driven into the life of our generation like wedges, splitting it into two halves: 'before the war' and 'after.'"[6]

In late autumn of 1983, when I was on the IREX academic exchange program in Leningrad, one evening my wife Nancy and I ate dinner in what was then the shabby Oktiabrskaia Hotel on Nevsky Prospect. It was a politically tense time. The Reagan administration had unveiled its Strategic Defense Initiative, NATO was in the process of deploying cruise missiles and Pershing IIs in Western Europe in response to deployed Soviet missiles, and Soviet air defense had recently shot down a South Korean jetliner, killing 269 people. General Secretary Yuri Andropov was convinced that the United States was planning for a nuclear first strike, and *Pravda* referred to the Reagan administration as the "second fascism." When we told the elderly coat check lady in the hotel's nearly empty restaurant that we were from the United States, she suddenly became very agitated, nearly hysterical, and repeatedly asked us through her sobbing why the U.S. government wanted war. She said that war was terrible, and she knew it first-hand. Her behavior was no act. The Soviet press had succeeded in thoroughly scaring a segment of the population, particularly those who had lived through the "Great Patriotic War." In postwar Leningrad, permanent reminders of the war abounded. Some were staggering in their enormity, such as the mass graves at the Piskaryovskoe Cemetery; others small and subtle—the flowers that were refreshed regularly at the simple sign along the north side of Nevsky not far from the Winter Palace that warned pedestrians that it was more dangerous there during an artillery attack than on the other side of the street.

The siege left its political and social imprint on the city in several ways. One's wartime record had a fundamental bearing on one's subsequent career possibilities and advancement.[7] In addition, Leningrad had become ethnically more Russian during the war after residents of German and Finnish descent were deported in 1941–42. Furthermore, it remained a predominantly female city until male evacuees and war veterans returned and people from other parts of the USSR moved in. The rebuilt city was decidedly more provincial and secondary to Moscow in importance, and this trend was accentuated following the execution of Leningrad's top political leaders in 1949–50 in what became known as the Leningrad Affair.[8] Moreover, in the rebuilt city, as elsewhere in the postwar USSR, new security measures were implemented to combat suspected espionage during the Cold War that might precede renewed aggression against the nation. For example, detailed maps of the city were no longer readily available. Maps of Soviet cities that were published for wide distribution after the war were deliberately falsified. Tourist maps of Leningrad from the 1980s distorted the contours of the harbor area.[9] Foreigners traveling to the USSR had to obtain visas for individual cities they wanted to visit, in contrast to less restricted travel that was possible at least up to late 1937.

Blockade Historiography

There is no shortage of books on the siege; however, the great majority of them, approximately four hundred, were published under strict censorship in Leningrad.[10] The first Soviet depiction of the siege was a documentary film from the summer of 1942, entitled *Leningrad in Battle*. This film marks the origin of the divergence between the evolving official view (often referred to as "myth") and popular memory.[11] Leningraders who viewed the film were overheard complaining that it did not sufficiently depict the hardships of life during the starvation winter (Document 58). The film did not lead directly to printed accounts of the siege. In fact, very little scholarly research was published in the Soviet Union on the topic until after Stalin's death. To Stalin and his Kremlin comrades the blockade was likely an embarrassing reminder of their inability to better defend the city, prevent mass starvation, and break the enemy's hold until early 1944. Following the purge of Leningrad's wartime leaders Aleksei Kuznetsov, Pyotr Popkov, and others, their Kremlin rivals and executioners were not about to draw attention to the role they played in the siege or the fate of the city they defended. The most important bit of information about the blockade that came to light prior to 1953 was a summary statement on mortality. At the Nuremburg trials in 1946, the Soviet government stated that 671,635 people had perished in the blockade zone.[12]

As part of his cultural "thaw," Nikita Khrushchev called for the publication of historical works that emphasized the decisive role of the popular masses in winning the war. In the words of historian Lisa Kirschenbaum, individual accounts of courage and suffering were "well suited to one of the chief aims of the state-sponsored war cult: impressing upon the postwar generation the sacrifices and heroism of their elders as well as the legitimacy of the Soviet state that engineered victory."[13] Victory in the war became perhaps the most common theme in Soviet publishing. Between the end of the war and the end of the Soviet Union, an estimated seventeen thousand books were published in the Soviet Union on the war experience, or an average of more than one book per day.[14] During the early Khrushchev years some document collections on the siege in party and state archives were opened to researchers and the first scholarly works appeared. D. V. Pavlov, who was in charge of food supply in Leningrad from the beginning of the siege to the end of January 1942, published *Leningrad v blokade* in 1958, albeit in a small number of copies. Using archival files and his own notes, he described the starvation of the winter of 1941–42, blaming it on mismanagement of food reserves during the summer of 1941, and defended the Nuremburg figure for deaths. (In several later editions of the book, he added further details and stood by his mortality figures against critics who claimed that they were too low.) In 1959 the first general study of the Leningrad blockade based on archival sources appeared: A. V. Karasev's *Leningradtsy v gody blokady, 1941-1943*.

Some of the state and party archival documentation that had been opened during the Khrushchev years was reclassified after his death, and few important archival-based studies of the siege period (with some exceptions)[15] were published in the Soviet Union after the mid-1960s. The most pervasive theme in scholarly works on the blockade as well as in popular accounts and memoirs was that of heroism. *Geroicheskii* was probably the most common adjective in the titles of Soviet-era blockade books. To be sure, true acts of heroism abounded during the siege. If no city ever suffered greater loss of life over a comparable period, perhaps no city ever witnessed more examples of resilience, courage, and self-sacrifice. Memoir literature includes many examples of strangers taking in orphans for the duration of the war. Mothers fed their own rations to their starving children. Svetlana Magaeva, a prominent medical researcher who survived the blockade as a child, described a mother and baby who had been found in a deserted flat: "The mother, emaciated by starvation, had bled profusely, having opened a vein in her arm. She had no milk, but had put her baby's mouth to the wound and it had greedily sucked its mother's blood. Help had arrived in time, and both mother and baby were saved."[16] Such examples could be multiplied many times over. Not long after Vladimir

Putin became Russia's president, he described to journalists his parents' harrowing experiences during the siege, which (assuming his account was accurate) demonstrate several instances of heroism, and probably provide important insights into his own idea of Russian patriotism. He stated that his father's legs were shattered by shrapnel during the winter of 1941–42 away from the city to the north of the Neva River. A fellow soldier who happened to be an old neighbor saved his father's life by carrying him on his back through a battle zone and across the frozen river all the way to a hospital in Leningrad. Putin's mother nearly starved to death around the same time and at one point was presumed dead and actually laid out with the corpses. Her brother fed her his own rations, and Putin's father, while recovering in a hospital, also secretly passed his rations on to his wife.[17] The historian naturally sympathizes with accounts of heroic courage. The image of exhausted, filthy, and desperately hungry teenage girls and boys turning out artillery shells to protect themselves, their families, their partly destroyed factories, and their homeland practically under the noses of the self-proclaimed *Herrenvolk* of the Wehrmacht, who had up to that time conquered every city on the European continent they had set their sights on, has a compelling David-versus-Goliath quality to it.

Blockade heroism is no myth. What is a myth is that all those locked in the blockade acted solely as heroes. Many Leningraders were neither heroes nor villains but simply helpless and tragic victims. Adult Leningraders had been fortunate up to 1941. They had survived the Great War, the February and October Revolutions and the Civil War, the famine of the early 1930s, the Great Terror of the late 1930s, and the Winter War against Finland. Then things got immeasurably worse with the German invasion and the enemy's rapid advance up the Baltic coast.

As a rule, Soviet historians did not falsify information on Leningrad during the Second World War, but they were only permitted to relate part of what happened. The result was an incomplete and seriously distorted rendition, but not one that was inaccurate in detail. Many of the most important topics were off limits for research and publication, such as people's reactions to the Soviet-German Nonaggression Pact of 1939, as well as the pact's secret protocols which the Soviet government denied existed until 1989; the impact of the Winter War on Leningrad's economy and popular attitudes; detailed descriptions of the city's political leaders and their policies before and during the siege; any meaningful description of the security organs; relations between Leningrad's leaders and Stalin and other Kremlin officials; religious belief and practice; widespread criminal activity, particularly during the first winter of the blockade; expression of anti-Soviet and pro-German opinion; as well as the postwar Leningrad Affair. Nevertheless, Soviet accounts of the blockade published between the late 1950s and late 1980s were not without merit. Historians of the siege were generally more interested in revealing specific information than in formulating controversial theses that might be censored. It was possible, therefore, to reinterpret the data that they uncovered and combine them with Soviet published document collections,[18] complete runs of newspapers and journals from the blockaded city, as well as diaries, memoirs, and oral accounts by survivors who later left the Soviet Union, to support alternative theses.[19]

A single work from the late Brezhnev years that in retrospect was a forerunner of Gorbachev's glasnost was a collection of the notes and narratives of several hundred people compiled and transcribed by Ales Adamovich and Daniil Granin, entitled *Blokadnaia kniga*. This landmark book was published in 1979, and an expanded and revised edition appeared in 1982. Although some accounts dealing with the darkest aspects of blockade life, such as cannibalism, were excised by Soviet censors (and published as an article in 1992), this collection contains a wide range of human responses to blockade conditions from the selfless to the unscrupulous, and it describes in detail the extreme deprivations and suffering that Leningraders endured.

In general, the four years of glasnost under Gorbachev (late 1987 through the end of 1991) were too brief for detailed studies of the blockade to be researched, written, and published. A greater impediment to scholarly research in this interval was the fact that the major effort to declassify ("desecretize" in Russian) party documents on the blockade did not begin until 1992. However, some formerly top secret documents concerning the blockade were published in the journal *Izvestiia TsK KPSS* in 1989–91 (Documents 2–6, 8). In addition, the first account of the Leningrad Affair and the first (and only) serious biography of Stalin published in the USSR, which included description of his relations with Leningrad's leaders during the blockade, appeared in this period.[20] Both accounts relied heavily on declassified archival documents.

During the first post-Soviet decade, Russian historians found themselves in an ironic and frustrating situation. On the one hand, the first few years after the collapse of the USSR constituted a halcyon period for researchers as state and party archives were largely opened. Most Russian historians, however, were so impoverished by the hyperinflation of the early 1990s that they could not afford the luxury of conducting research in poorly heated and dimly lit archives and of writing articles and books. They had to hold two or three jobs just to make ends meet, and a decent ballpoint pen for taking notes was often beyond their means. By contrast, this period was an exceptionally good time for foreign scholars. The plummeting ruble made it affordable for even financially strapped American and West European graduate students to spend considerable time in Russia, and comb through the newly released materials. In research trips I took to St. Petersburg in the early 1990s, I was impressed by the fact that despite the hard times, Russian historians and archivists whom I met retained a collegial spirit and were helpful in responding to my research questions. To make matters worse for Russian historians, most state-owned publishing houses were in dire straits and publishing few books, while others, such as Lenizdat, went out of business altogether. New private publishers generally demanded that authors cover costs up front, and few historians could afford that expense. Nevertheless, some very determined Russian historians took advantage of the new research opportunities of the first post-Soviet years. Not knowing how long that window would remain open, they were keen to publish formerly top secret documents. The most important contribution to blockade historiography during this period was the publication in 1995 of 228 declassified documents under the title *Leningrad v osade*. The collection was compiled and edited by Andrei Dzeniskevich, the most prolific scholar of the blockade, whose life had been shaped by the war: in the summer of 1941, he was evacuated from Leningrad with other children, but tragically German fighter aircraft spotted their train and strafed it.[21] Dzeniskevich is an unusual example of a prominent Soviet historian who successfully bridged the great divide of 1991 by later publishing several carefully documented books on original topics. This present study contains many references to his meticulous scholarship. During the Soviet era his options for research and publication were limited. For example, in the early 1980s he published a book with the Academy of Sciences on Leningrad's factory workers between 1938 and 1941 that included no reference to the purges.[22] In October 1983, I presented him with a rare copy of a Russian translation of Harrison Salisbury's monumental account of the blockade, *The 900 Days*, the original English version of which was available in Leningrad only in the restricted "special holdings" of one or two libraries and on the black market. After he read the book, he told me then that his only major criticism of it was that he strongly doubted the veracity of its few brief descriptions of cannibalism. When the archives opened, however, Dzeniskevich found and published in *Leningrad v osade* a detailed report (Document 53) that includes a demographic profile of the 868 people prosecuted for cannibalism in besieged Leningrad through 15 February 1942.

During the late 1990s, the feared reaction to the opening of the archives began to materialize as many document collections were reclassified.[23] Yet, during the eight years of the presidency of Vladimir Putin, which coincided with robust growth in the Russian economy, life for Russian historians and their options for publishing improved somewhat. Blockade research proceeded in two directions. Those working in archives continued to publish document collections as quickly as they could.[24] The other avenue of

research was the collection of first-hand accounts from elderly siege survivors. A group of scholars connected with the Center for Oral History at
the European University in St. Petersburg published a collection of interviews with blockade survivors and children of *blokadniki* together with
essays on how official Soviet interpretations and popular memory of the
blockade were formed.[25] Specialized monographs take longer to write but
have begun to appear on such topics as the maintenance of political control
during the blockade and morale among civilians, as well as factory workers
and the city's medical industry.[26]

In recent years, a renewed emphasis on viewing Russian and Soviet
history through the lenses of heroism and patriotism and on squelching
scholarship that emphasizes Soviet abuse of human rights has been promoted several times at the highest levels. In 2007, President Putin's administration commissioned the publication of a handbook for history teachers
that advocated instilling in Russian students pride in the Motherland.[27]
Then in December 2008, armed officers from the Russian General Prosecutor's Office confiscated the entire computer archive of the St. Petersburg branch of the organization Memorial, which since 1989 has been in
the forefront of the effort to document the crimes of Stalin.[28] On 19 May
2009, President Medvedev created a "Commission to Counteract Attempts
at Falsifying History to Damage the Interests of Russia," which included
the head of the Russian archival administration, V. P. Kozlov, as one of its
members. The alleged falsifiers of history have not been named.

During the past two years, however, Russian officials to a certain extent
have reversed course and allowed greater access to wartime records. The
best example of this renewed openness is the publication online of documents related to the massacre of Polish officers in 1940. With regard to the
Leningrad blockade, in late 2010, archival authorities in St. Petersburg declassified files of the city party committee (*gorkom*) for the war years, which
are featured prominently in this study.

The first Western account of the blockade was written by Alexander
Werth, the BBC and London *Sunday Times* wartime correspondent in the
Soviet Union, who had been born and reared in St. Petersburg. Werth traveled to his home city during the final months of the blockade in September
1943 and the following year published a short, impressionistic work based
on his trip, which included description of his visit to the mammoth Kirov
factory a few miles behind the front lines.[29] In 1962, Leon Goure, a senior
staff member of the RAND Corporation, published the first comprehensive Western study of the blockade based in part on the works of Karasev
and Pavlov, captured German documents housed at the U.S. National Archives, and seven unnamed siege survivors who had left the Soviet Union.
Goure contended that the populace remained loyal and obedient through-

out the siege ordeal largely as a result of "Soviet administrative and political control systems [that] sought to control and direct the behavior of each person . . ."[30] Goure's "control systems" included *sovet* and party structures, the police (*militsiia*), the People's Commissariat of Internal Affairs (NKVD), and military leadership of the Leningrad Front. He concluded his book with the statement: "It appears that in general the administrative and control system in Leningrad was effective even under extreme conditions . . . when firm leadership and habits of disciplined behavior were combined with patriotism, they produced a degree of steadfastness and devotion to duty that astonished not only the leadership but even the Leningraders themselves."[31] The implication was that without coercive control from above, the city would have sunk into anarchy and chaos.

In 1969, Salisbury's *The 900 Days* appeared and quickly became a best seller. Like Werth, Salisbury had been a wartime journalist in Moscow, and for a quarter-century after the end of the Leningrad blockade he gathered information on it. He wove together information from published Soviet document collections, memoirs, scholarly studies, and interviews he had conducted during the war and afterward with the city's political, military, and cultural elites (including later victims of the Leningrad Affair) into an artful tapestry of a blockade narrative. Salisbury's lengthy and richly detailed account[32] placed more emphasis on heroism and patriotism as reasons for the city's steadfast defense than Goure had done, but also included a chapter entitled "Not All Were Brave." Salisbury also focused attention on the relationship between the Kremlin and Smolny (Leningrad's political and military headquarters) and suggested that Malenkov and Molotov may have favored giving up Leningrad in order to undermine their rival Zhdanov, whose political fate was tied to the city.[33]

Western scholarship on the blockade remained almost at a standstill until the archives opened.[34] Retired U.S. Army Colonel David Glantz, the world's top authority on the battlefronts of the Soviet-German War, published in 2002 a magisterial military history of the Leningrad region, which explains the course of the prolonged battle in terms accessible to the nonmilitary specialist (which includes practically all Western blockade scholars).[35] Although he did not work in Russian archives, he did thoroughly scrutinize Soviet and post-Soviet secondary accounts and the German materials in the National Archives. Glantz draws attention to the numerous attempts by the Red Army to lift the siege in 1942 and 1943 and thereby puts to rest any suspicion that Stalin was unconcerned about Leningrad's fate. Our work relies heavily on Glantz's research for the military context of the siege. British historian Michael Jones has recently published a synthesis of the blockade intended for the general reader based on a wide range of published accounts and on diaries and letters from the Blockade Museum in

St. Petersburg, as well as interviews with siege survivors.[36] Recently, Anna Reid published a similar but longer work.[37] Kees Boterbloem effectively mined Zhdanov's personal papers from the Russian State Archive of Social and Political History to write the first full-length biography of Leningrad's wartime party leader.[38] John Barber and Andrei Dzeniskevich edited a collection of essays by Russian historians on aspects of the medical history of the blockade, including the scale of the famine and death, long-term health effects on the survivors, and how healthcare professionals assisted the starving population and conducted research on saving lives.[39] Cynthia Simmons and *blokadnitsa* Nina Perlina, in their edited collection of diaries, letters, memoirs, prose, and oral accounts by female survivors, have developed the idea that women, who made up the large majority of civilians in the city after the starvation winter, had a distinctive way of remembering and recording the siege. Simmons asserts that women's "accustomed position on the periphery, in the private realm, emboldened them to write more openly than the men who also bore witness. They not only wrote of the private side of war. They exercised the relative freedom that they had sensed within the home, even at the height of the Terror . . ."[40]

German historians have only recently been drawn to the topic of the blockade.[41] The first archival-based German account of state and society in the blockade is Jörg Ganzenmüller's *Das belagerte Leningrad*, which focuses attention on German and Soviet military strategies, the industrial evacuation, the wartime mobilization of factories that remained in the city, the ways that individuals found to survive the starvation winter, and the deportation of ethnic Germans and Finns from the blockaded territory.

The Scope of This Study

Any co-authored book requires an explanation. This one is truly a collaborative project. Nikita Lomagin of St. Petersburg State University, who was born twenty years after the blockade was lifted and whose early training was in Soviet counterintelligence work, and I have been colleagues since 1993 and have frequently exchanged ideas on the blockade, research tips, source citations, and documents that we have found in Russian archives and elsewhere. We each wrote essays for books on the blockade that were published in St. Petersburg in 1995 and 2009[42] and have discussed our research findings in panels of the annual convention of the American Association for the Advancement of Slavic Studies in 1997, 2005, and 2009. I contributed documents, insights, and ideas for the basic structure of Lomagin's two-volume study of the siege published in Russia in 2002.[43] He unearthed several of the documents contained in this present study (especially the ones from the Federal Security Service archive in St. Petersburg), and his publications are cited frequently here. I made the final selection of documents for the book, translated a few of them, edited them all, and wrote the entire accompanying text.

This work covers civilian life in wartime Leningrad and is based primarily on archival sources. We focus largely on the first year of the Soviet-German War, because that was when the city's fate was decided and mortality and morbidity rates were the highest. Once the pivotal battle for Stalingrad took shape in September 1942, neither side made Leningrad a top priority. Germany lacked the means to renew an offensive to take Leningrad, and although the Lake Ladoga supply route was fortified and the Red Army pierced the blockade south of the lake so that a makeshift rail line could be extended to the city in February 1943, Soviet supply to the Leningrad sector proved insufficient to liberate Leningrad until January 1944. We have tried to summarize succinctly yet comprehensively the crucial events of Leningrad's war experience in Chapter 1 and to situate them between the transformations and upheavals of the late 1930s and the postwar Leningrad Affair. Subsequent chapters cover the blockade from both "state" and "society" perspectives. Chapter 2 analyzes the complex and often frayed relationship between Stalin and his Kremlin comrades on the one hand, and Smolny's leaders on the other, and delineates power relations among Leningrad's party, military, and NKVD elites. This chapter also includes description of relations between the Leningrad Party Organization (LPO) and the Russian Orthodox Church during the siege, which has been an almost entirely neglected topic in previous studies. Chapter 3 describes the extraordinary and unprecedented efforts made by Leningrad's leaders to mobilize and propagandize the civilian population and compel as strict obedience as possible. Our research on the maintenance of political control in wartime Leningrad is the first exploration of that topic in English since Goure wrote his pioneering study over forty years ago without access to Soviet archives. Chapters 4 and 5 turn to "society" by portraying how ordinary Leningrad civilians attempted to devise means to survive the extreme cold and hunger (words which appropriately rhyme in Russian) of the first siege winter and how they reacted in conversations and correspondence to siege conditions and Soviet policies of total war. Assessing the popular mood of a large city during a prolonged survival struggle is a very difficult undertaking, because people's attitudes are often complex, nuanced, and subject to change. In the obvious absence of objective polling data, we have relied heavily on declassified summaries of secret informant reports to the LPO and the Leningrad branch of the NKVD, both of which were vitally interested in comprehending the popular mood, as well as on published and unpublished diaries and memoirs and occasionally on German intelligence reports. Describing Leningrad's popular mood in critical periods such as the start of the blockade and the starvation winter is an important topic, because mass attitudes were of great consequence: they could determine whether Leningrad's defenses held or the city collapsed in demonstrations and riots. The popular mood early in the war up through the first weeks of blockade was more of a barometer of Leningraders' attitudes toward Soviet officialdom than later on when the populace suffered from the enemy's prolonged blockade and bombardment. As the siege continued, the enemy's barbaric tactics played a larger role in shaping the popular mood. Chapter 6, which is based on party and NKVD files, addresses the issue of opposition to Soviet authority. Studies of resistance during the Stalin years have attracted considerable attention recently. The general interpretation of Stalinism put forward by Stephen Kotkin in his detailed examination of the construction of the massive Magnitogorsk steel plant, which stresses creation of a new Soviet civilization as the populace over time largely internalized the official ideology as they learned to "speak Bolshevik," has been challenged more recently in other studies of Stalinist industrialization and, especially, of the collectivization of agriculture.[44] In this chapter we attempt to measure the extent to which anti-Soviet or "counterrevolutionary" attitudes were translated into organized activity designed to subvert Soviet control.

Discussion of anti-Soviet sentiment is enhanced through use of NKVD files, which are essential for addressing the question of whether there was conspiratorial opposition to communist authority in wartime Leningrad and if so, how extensive it was. However, inclusion of materials from Leningrad's security organs may also be the most controversial aspect of this study. It has become possible in recent years to publish collections of NKVD/KGB documents from the Stalin years in part because during the late 1990s, the Federal Security Service (FSB) transferred to the more accessible State Archive of the Russian Federation (GARF) approximately 100,000 legal investigative files from the Stalin era. The most important publication from those materials is the seven-volume collection of documents entitled *Istoriia stalinskogo GULAGa*, which appeared in 2004–5 and elicited wide praise from scholars, including the best-known revealer of Gulag crimes, Aleksandr Solzhenitsyn.[45] The FSB itself in recent years has authorized publication of document collections from the war;[46] yet the FSB archives in St. Petersburg and other Russian cities remain closed to most scholars. Relatives of victims of "repression" are allowed to submit specific requests for information from FSB archives, and selected Russian scholars and a very small number of foreign researchers have gained access to their collections but without use of indexes or finding guides. By severely restricting access to security archives and selectively publishing document collections, the FSB regulates what is known of its past (aside from the files transferred to GARF) and, thus, would seem to be trying to portray that past in a favorable light and keep many of its skeletons hidden. However, the portrayal of the security organs that emerges in our study based on documents we have used is decidedly mixed. While it is undoubtedly true that most Leningraders supported the security organs in their efforts to defend the city, extinguish incendiary bombs, arrest cannibals, and assist families of servicemen, we have also found in NKVD files evidence that hundreds of civilians were executed for simply having reportedly been overheard criticizing official policies, that harsh sentences were meted out to prominent scholars based on convictions that were later overturned, and that enormous resources were allocated to tracking down a small number of people who produced anti-Soviet leaflets. The NKVD could be viewed as a heroic defender of Leningrad if it could be shown that most of the time it conducted good police work that eliminated real anti-Soviet threats and maintained order and only occasionally victimized innocent people through hypervigilance and the conjuring up of nonexistent conspiracies. Our evidence cannot substantiate such a positive view of the NKVD, though it does not disprove that the NKVD carried out several tasks that enhanced the city's security. In addition, we are not trying to make the case that the NKVD saved Leningrad by crushing incipient political opposition, which if it had been left to develop would have sparked widespread anarchy and rebellion that in turn would have encouraged and facilitated German occupation of the city. At the same time, we acknowledge that the NKVD's draconian policies intimidated some people from expressing their discontent and convinced them to remain loyal to Soviet power, but it is impossible to measure how many people that might include. Finally, it is also worth noting that the FSB may have allowed the publication of documents that describe arrests and convictions that were later shown to be groundless, and whose victims were rehabilitated, in order to gain respectability through such disclosure.

Another sensitive issue regarding use of NKVD files is that the NKVD's assessment of criminal activity has been presumed to have been biased. One prominent historian commented on an NKVD report found by Lomagin that identified sentiment in favor of surrendering Leningrad by stating: "Security police reports would, of course, tend to exaggerate such rumors: that is what their authors are paid to do."[47] In chapter five we compare several NKVD and party surveys of the popular mood from late autumn 1941 (Documents 39 to 42) and show that the NKVD was indeed more likely than the party at that time to classify critical comments as "anti-Soviet." NKVD reports also included more examples of overheard speech that criticized Soviet policies and leaders, but such criticism surfaced in party reports too. Other first-hand observers, such as siege survivors who later left the USSR, have also testified to the existence of anti-Soviet sentiment in Leningrad. Throughout this study, we have tried to corroborate all important finds, especially from NKVD files, with evidence from a variety of types of sources.

CHAPTER 1

Leningrad During the
Second World War and Its Aftermath

On the Eve of Operation Barbarossa

A traveler who happened to return to Leningrad in the spring of 1941, after having left the city at the start of the First World War, at the time of the October Revolution, or even as late as Stalin's rise to power in the late 1920s, would have found it vastly changed. Although building façades in the core of the city, including those of famous historical landmarks, were much the same, almost nothing else was. Most dimensions of life in Leningrad, from political power to the economy, education system, mass media, culture, religious practice, and family relations, had been radically altered by revolution, civil war, rapid industrialization, forced collectivization, purges, and the start of the Second World War.

Almost from the moment that the Bolsheviks came to power, they relied heavily on forced allocation, or mobilization, of materials and personnel to meet their goals. War Communism helped carry the Communists to victory in the Civil War, although in 1921 it gave way to the less coercive New Economic Policy. During the first Five Year Plan and the collectivization of agriculture, which commenced in 1928–29, the USSR built a command economy, in which the state gained control of almost all of the means of agricultural and industrial production. Leningrad occupied an integral part in Stalin's industrialization drive and defense planning, and the city's transformation in the first three Five Year Plans played an important role in shaping how it later responded to the ordeal of the siege. The most significant development was that the city grew substantially; its population doubled from 1.6 million in early 1927 to 3.2 million at the start of 1941. The largest increase was in the industrial work force. By the start of the Soviet-German War, Leningrad employed 1.9 million people,

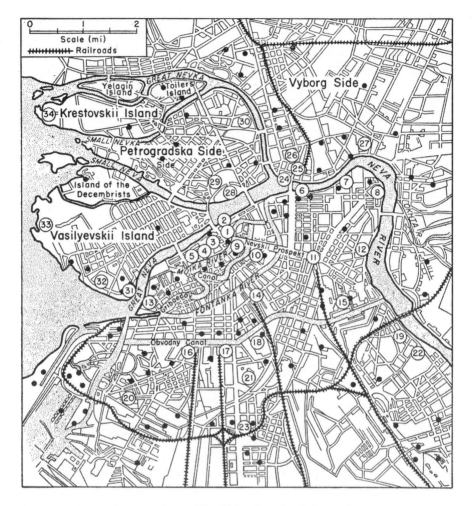

Map 1. The City of Leningrad.

Leningrad: (1) Army headquarters. (2) Hermitage. (3) Admiralty. (4) St. Isaac Cathedral.
(5) Main post and telegraph office. (6) NKVD headquarters. (7) Main waterworks. (8)
Smolny Institute. (9) Kazan Cathedral. (10) Gostiny Dvor. (11) Moscow Railroad Station.
(12) Power station. (13) Marti shipyards. (14) Vitebsk Railroad Station. (15) Power station.
(16) Baltic Railroad Station. (17) Warsaw Railroad Station. (18) Main gas works and power
station. (19) Kirov flour mill. (20) Kirov works. (21) Badaev food warehouses. (22) Lenin
machine building plant. (23) Electrosila works.
Vyborg Side: (24) Liteiny Bridge. (25) Finland Railroad Station. (27) Military Medical Academy.
(27) Stalin metal works.
Petrograd Side: (28) Peter and Paul Fortress. (29) Zoological Garden. (30) Botanical Garden.
Vasilievsky Island: (31) Baltic shipyard. (32) Electric power station. (33) Army food storage.
Krestovsky Island: (34) Stadium.
Black dots indicate some areas of major damage from German air and artillery bombardment.

of whom 740,000 worked in factories. Some 608,000 of the industrial employees were classified as workers (*rabochie*), up from 250,000 in 1928. About 200,000 new laborers, mainly peasants who had fled starvation and loss of their land in the collectivized countryside, entered Leningrad during the shortened first Five Year Plan, which ended in 1932.[1] In 1941 Leningrad, second only to Moscow as the largest industrial center in the USSR, had approximately six hundred factories, which produced about 10 percent of the nation's industrial output. Plants built after 1928, some of which incorporated Western technology,[2] accounted for well over half of what Leningrad produced. Soviet data (which were likely inflated because of pressure to fulfill the industrial plan) show that the level of factory output in Leningrad in 1940 was approximately nine times that of 1928 and roughly one and a half times that of the entire Russian Empire in 1913. In one of the most industrialized parts of the city, Moskovsky *raion,* fifty-three factories were constructed between 1928 and 1941.[3]

The defense sector of Leningrad's economy grew the quickest in the 1930s, making the city one of the largest producers of weapons and ammunition in the world, while the local economy received less than one-third of the city's industrial production. By 1941, close to half of the city's factory workers were employed in metallurgy (steel production in particular) and metal-based manufacturing and construction (diesel engines, turbines, construction cranes, tools, ships, submarines, tanks, artillery guns, ammunition, railroad cars, and tractors). Leningrad built about one-third of the USSR's industrial machinery and most of the nation's power-generating turbines. The city also manufactured approximately half of the USSR's large warships, especially battleships and submarines.[4]

Ironically enough, as Leningrad's population and industrial output grew rapidly in the 1930s, the city became more subservient to Moscow, in part because national centralized planning elevated the capital over all other regions. Moreover, Stalin appears to have harbored a special antipathy toward the former imperial capital city, or, as he called it (Document 1), the USSR's "second capital," which reflected a mentality from centuries past. During the age of Muscovy, grand princes and tsars had continually worried about the security and political reliability of the northwestern borderlands of the realm. Ivan the Great punished Novgorod in the 1470s with a prolonged and bloody sack after it sought the protection of Catholic Lithuania. Almost exactly one hundred years later, Ivan the Terrible repeated the feat when he became convinced of a treasonous plot in Muscovy's second largest city. Leningrad can be likened to Ivan the Terrible's Novgorod in that Stalin continually saw threats to his power emanating from the city. Moreover, Leningrad was a source of humiliating memories for Stalin. Thoughts of the glorious revolutionary year of 1917 must have made him wince. Although he had been the first prominent Bolshevik to arrive in Petrograd after Nicholas II's fall from power, Lenin rebuked him upon his own return to the city in April for supporting the Provisional Government in *Pravda*. Even worse, the summer of 1917 reminded Stalin of Trotsky's arrival in Petrograd, his rapid conversion to Bolshevism, and his meteoric rise within the party to the level of Lenin's chief lieutenant. Stalin, the long-time and loyal Leninist, played a relatively minor role in the Bolshevik seizure of power. On the tenth anniversary of the Bolshevik Revolution, Grigory Zinoviev had tried to turn the commemorative street demonstration in Leningrad (where he had served as party leader until 1926 when Stalin had forced him out of that position and his seat in the Central Committee) into a protest against Stalin. Stalin may or may not have ordered the murder of the darling of the Seventeenth Party Congress, Sergei Kirov, who had been Zinoviev's replacement as Leningrad's party leader. In either case, Stalin used the murder, which occurred on 1 December 1934, as the excuse for a witch hunt in the Leningrad party and security organs. This operation appears to have been one of several catalysts for the Great Terror of 1937–38, which claimed in Leningrad alone up to forty thousand victims, whose corpses continue to be unearthed in mass graves near the city.[5] In the process, Stalin thoroughly purged and reshaped the Leningrad Party Organization (LPO) in his own image.

Stalin installed Andrei Zhdanov as the replacement for the slain Kirov as first secretary of the Leningrad city and *oblast'* party committees (*gorkom* and *obkom*) (Figure 1). Zhdanov was an Old Bolshevik from 1915 and a loyal Stalinist who had served as leader of the Nizhegorod (Gorky) party committee from 1924 until he was elevated to the Central Committee in February 1934 immediately after the Seventeenth Party Congress. A year later Zhdanov became a candidate member of the Politburo. A beneficiary of the party purges, he acquired full membership in the Politburo in 1939. Many considered Zhdanov to be Stalin's likely successor. Seventeen years younger than his patron, Zhdanov occupied an almost filial role, a reflection of the extent to which Leningrad became increasingly subordinate to Moscow in the 1930s. Zhdanov's second in command in Leningrad was Aleksei Kuznetsov (Figure 2). Nine years younger than his boss, and in considerably better health, Kuznetsov had joined the party in 1925. Although he also had served early on in the Nizhegorod party organization, he built his career in Leningrad's district (*raion*) party committees (*raikomy*) and therefore knew the city better than Zhdanov. In September 1937, during the height of the party purge, Kuznetsov rose to the position of second secretary of the Leningrad *gorkom* and *obkom*. Other Leningrad political leaders had also advanced rapidly in the city's party organization and escaped the party purge. For example, Yakov Kapustin signed on at

Krasny Putilovets in 1925 at the age of twenty-one and became a metal-worker and riveter. In 1935–36, the factory sent him to England to study production of steam turbines. By 1938, he served as secretary of the *part-kom* of the factory (which by this time was renamed for Kirov) and the following year was promoted to secretary of the Kirovsky *raikom*. He became a *gorkom* secretary in 1940.[6]

Still others who had received their industrial training in Leningrad in the 1930s had advanced quickly by 1941 to important government posts in Moscow. Aleksei Kosygin's career climb was a spectacular example. In 1937, two years after completing studies at Leningrad's Textile Institute, he became director of the Oktiabrskaia textile plant. In October of 1938, he was named chairman of the executive committee of the Leningrad city *sovet* (*Lengorispolkom*) and fourteen months later moved to Moscow to take the post of people's commissar (*narkom*) of the textile industry and commence a tenure of forty-one years in the Central Committee. A talented organizer, he was named deputy chairman of the *Sovnarkom* in the spring of 1940. Dmitri Ustinov's professional advancement was as striking. He was graduated from Leningrad's Military Mechanical Institute in 1934 and from 1938 to 1941 advanced from engineer to director of the massive Bolshevik arms factory. Less than two weeks before the German invasion, he replaced the arrested Boris Vannikov (see below) as *narkom* of weaponry. Another prominent national leader who had held a key post in Leningrad, but did not serve as a factory director, was Nikolai Voznesensky. An economist who was transferred to Leningrad following purges after Kirov's murder, he occupied the post of deputy chairman of the Leningrad *ispolkom* from June to November of 1937. His career path closely tracked Kosygin's. By January 1938, he was named head of *Gosplan* in Moscow and acquired the post of first deputy chairman of the *Sovnarkom* in March 1941. During the Soviet-German War he would enter the State Defense Committee (GKO) and serve as chairman of *Gosplan*.[7]

The expansion of Leningrad's military-industrial sector was directly tied to Soviet foreign policy and concerns over German rearmament and expansionism. Soviet investment in defense industries, which had grown rapidly from the time of the first Five Year Plan, accelerated in the closing years of the 1930s. The refusal of the Western democracies to confront German and Italian forces that intervened in support of General Franco in the Spanish Civil War was cause for concern for the USSR, which sent matériel and combatants to aid the Republican side. In addition, the Anti-Comintern Pact of 1936 raised the possibility that the USSR might find itself at war simultaneously with Germany and Japan, which had already occupied Manchuria. Indeed, Soviet and Japanese forces skirmished along the Soviet-Manchuria border in the summers of 1937 and 1938. Germany's annexation of Czechoslovakia's Sudetenland in 1938 following the Munich Conference, to which Stalin was not invited, alarmed the Kremlin by raising suspicions that Britain and France, in pursuing politics of appeasement vis-à-vis Germany, were content to let Hitler drive eastward. German intelligence during this period was keenly interested in Leningrad, especially the program that commenced in 1938 to build more battleships, minesweepers, and cutters in the city's shipyards.[8] On 24 July 1938, German airmen photographed all parts of the city and focused their lenses in particular on the sea canal, the harbor, and the Kronstadt naval base, which was located about fifteen miles west of Leningrad in the Gulf of Finland. Then, during the early morning of 15 August 1939, another German overflight occurred, which produced about a hundred photos of the city that featured the harbor, the Kirov factory, and pharmaceutical and chemical factories.[9]

As Soviet and Japanese forces fought at Khalkhin-Gol along the Mongolian-Manchurian border, employing the largest number of aircraft and tanks ever in history up to that time, the Soviet government diminished at least temporarily the danger of having to fight a two-front war by stunning the world with the announcement on 23 August 1939, that it had signed a nonaggression pact with Germany in Moscow. The agreement effectively terminated the Anti-Comintern Pact but did not serve to lessen Soviet armament production. The Kremlin viewed the accompanying trade agreement, which consisted of the Soviet Union sending raw materials and foodstuffs to Germany in exchange for German weaponry and technological expertise, as a way to accelerate the Soviet military buildup. Neither side was willing to trust the agreement to continue indefinitely, despite the fact that the pact's secret protocols divided east-central Europe into Soviet and German spheres, with the Soviet sphere consisting of eastern Poland, Finland, Estonia, Latvia, and the Bessarabian part of Romania. (Lithuania was later consigned to the Soviet sphere in compensation for Germany taking more Polish territory than originally agreed upon.)

The Nonaggression Pact led directly to Germany's invasion of Poland on 1 September. Sixteen days later, the Red Army began to drive two hundred miles into eastern Poland under the pretext of defending Belorussians and Ukrainians, and, in fact, a large portion of the ethnic minorities living in eastern Poland welcomed the Red Army's advance. On 1 October, three days after the USSR and Germany partitioned Poland, the Politburo decided to incorporate eastern Poland into the Belorussian and Ukrainian Soviet Republics. Zhdanov was deeply involved in exerting Soviet control over the annexed territory, as reflected in the fact that on the same day he was put in charge of a commission that was to determine the fate of Polish POWs. One of Zhdanov's main assistants on the commission was Lavrenty

Beria, chief of the People's Commissariat of Internal Affairs (NKVD). In April and May of 1940, the NKVD executed 21,857 members of the Polish elite, including military officers, policemen, mayors, priests, and others. They were shot at several locations in the western part of the Russian Republic, including the site in the Katyn Forest, which German forces discovered in April 1943. In the words of historian Kees Boterbloem: "Zhdanov thus became guilty of what were legally defined as war crimes in the Nuremberg trials in 1945 (although at that point the Katyn massacre was cynically pinned by the Soviet prosecutors on the Nazis.)"[10]

The Red Army encountered relatively little resistance in occupying eastern Poland or in taking the other territories between the Baltic and Black seas that were consigned to the Soviet sphere in the secret protocols. Finland proved to be the remarkable exception. The Soviet government sought to enhance Leningrad's security and demanded from Finland territory in the Karelian Isthmus just north of Leningrad and the Hangö naval base that guarded the mouth of the Finnish Gulf. It offered to give Finland in return larger, though far less important, territory in the north along their common border. The Finnish government realized that acceptance of the Soviet proposal would leave Helsinki dangerously exposed and suspected that Moscow would demand further salami slices of Finnish territory. When Finland rejected the land swap proposal, the Red Army invaded on 30 November. Leningrad served as the Red Army's arsenal and staging ground for the Winter War that lasted three and a half months. Zhdanov, as the party official in charge of the region, was deeply involved in planning the invasion and served as the chief of the Regional Military Council during the war.[11] The USSR's victory and annexation of the entire Karelian isthmus and the northern coastline of Lake Ladoga came at a very high price. According to Soviet military documents revealed only in 1993, 127,000 Soviet combatants were killed or went missing in action, in comparison to about 25,000 Finnish war deaths. (Soviet Commissar of Foreign Affairs Viacheslav Molotov acknowledged in 1940 that approximately 49,000 Soviet troops had perished.)[12] The Soviet Air Force lost about 1,000 aircraft. More important, however, was the impression that the war conveyed abroad. Soviet military weakness had been exposed, which served to embolden Hitler and helped confirm him in his belief that Germany could easily defeat the USSR, and Finland looked for a way to regain the 25,000 square miles of territory that it had lost, as did inhabitants from other areas that the Soviet Union annexed in 1939–40. The Soviet military's high losses and dismal performance against the determined and well-equipped Finns compelled Stalin to quicken the pace of production of war matériel, as did Germany's unexpectedly quick defeat of France in a six-week blitzkrieg in the spring of 1940. Within two days after German troops marched down the Champs-Élysées, Soviet troops occupied Estonia, Latvia, and Lithuania, and toward the end of June, Romania had to cede northern Bukovina, which had not been included in the Soviet sphere in the secret pact with Germany, as well as Bessarabia. A new Special Baltic Military District was headquartered in Riga, and the Baltic Fleet moved its home base from Kronstadt to Tallinn. Stalin's willingness to come to terms with Germany in 1939 had been based on the assumption that an ensuing war between Germany and France would last a long time as in the Great War, which would provide the USSR with ample time to prepare for a possible confrontation with Germany. The USSR would need until 1942 or 1943 to move its defense fortifications forward into the annexed territory, and some of its weapons programs, such as fighter aircraft assembly in Leningrad (see below), were scheduled to go into full production only in 1942. When Germany invaded the USSR, Soviet defenses along the 1939 boundary had been dismantled, but the new forward line, located close to German positions, had not been completed. In several ways, therefore, the USSR was actually better prepared for war with Germany in the summer of 1939 than it was in 1941.

Stalin's defense doctrine presumed that no enemy would be able to penetrate far into Soviet territory. The border military districts were supposed to be strong enough to repel an enemy attack; hence, interior defense was deemed largely unnecessary.[13] Consistent with this policy, the USSR had no plans for massive evacuation of war industries or population groups in the event of a foreign invasion. The Special Baltic Military District, which protected Baltic coastline from East Prussia to as far east as Narva, approximately seventy miles from Leningrad, was only weakly fortified in depth. No plan to defend Tallinn had been worked out. Several weeks before the start of Operation Barbarossa, army engineers did begin constructing a fortification line in the Ostrov-Pskov region along the Velikaia River some 180 miles southwest of Leningrad near the old Estonian and Latvian borders; however, work had not been completed by 22 June. Almost all of the forces in the Leningrad Military District, which extended from Narva to Leningrad but also included the Murmansk *oblast'* and land that had been annexed from Finland, were deployed north of Leningrad to protect the city in the event of renewed hostilities with Finland. Virtually no troops were deployed south or west of Leningrad on the day Germany invaded.[14]

Soviet historians generally portrayed Leningrad as a peaceful city that was jolted into the realities of "putting the economy on a war footing" on 22 June 1941.[15] This distorted view derived largely from the fact that the Soviet government did not acknowledge the existence of the secret protocols of the Nonggression Pact until 1989 and, thus, Soviet historians were barred from researching the history of Soviet military occupation of territory of its six western neighbors between 1939 and 1941. Materials declassified from Russian archives after the collapse of the USSR show that Leningrad's defense industries grew rapidly and haphazardly at the expense of the local consumer and service economy during this period. By 1941, several of the *gorkom*'s sixteen departments, including military, defense and aviation industry, machine construction, shipbuilding, and electricity and electronics, dealt primarily with matters pertaining to defense and war. Similarly, a number of people's commissariats that had a presence in Leningrad were important to the military sector: defense, navy, weaponry, chemical industry, aviation production, shipbuilding, ammunition.[16] The latter three were spun off from the Defense Commissariat in January 1939 and began in early 1940 to replace several industries in Leningrad, including the manufacture of radios, sewing machines, various industrial instruments, and streetcars.[17] Changes in production at the massive Kirov plant, which with thirty-nine thousand employees by 1941 was one of the nation's largest factories, illustrate Stalin's rushed and erratic campaign to boost production of war matériel. In May 1940, two months after the costly war with Finland had ended, the factory began manufacturing the sixty-ton KV tank (named for Marshal Kliment Voroshilov, who in fact was fired from the post of defense commissar that very month for his failures in the Winter War), which carried a 76-millimeter gun also produced at the factory. In early 1941, Stalin, Marshal Grigory Kulik, who was chief of the Main Artillery Administration, and Zhdanov decided to replace the 76-millimeter gun with a 107-millimeter one, mainly because they felt that the larger gun had performed well in the Civil War. However useful the 107-millimeter gun may have been for artillery use, it was not practical for tank use. Boris Vannikov, *narkom* of weaponry, told Zhdanov that he was disarming the Red Army by replacing the 76-millimeter gun. Vannikov was arrested on 7 June for his protest but reemerged as deputy head of the weaponry commissariat in August 1941. Conversion to production of the larger gun had not been completed at the Kirov plant prior to the start of the German invasion. On 12 July 1941, the GKO ordered the factory to resume production of the 76-millimeter gun as soon as possible.[18] Over a month of production had been lost at a critical time.

The attempt to accelerate the pace of production of fighter aircraft spawned similar confusion. The expansion of air power in Leningrad was a project so secret that Soviet historians subsequently were never allowed to write about it. On 26 July 1940, the Central Committee and *Sovnarkom* decided to produce the Iliushin-2 (*Shturmovik*) fighter in Leningrad, and the newly formed aircraft production commissariat proceeded over the next eleven months to build fourteen new facilities in the city, including two for manufacturing aircraft engines and six for assembling the planes. During the same period the USSR attempted to obtain from Germany through their trade agreement examples of every type of aircraft that Germany manufactured. In May 1941, the Kirov factory produced its first M-40 diesel aircraft engines; the same month the first *Shturmoviks* came off the assembly lines. But the forced tempo of production resulted in material shortages, production snafus, and high turnover of managerial personnel, and the new aircraft factories did not come close to meeting their very ambitious production targets. Two of the new factories, which are designated only by secret identification numbers—380 and 381—assembled only seven fighters prior to the start of the war. According to the prewar plan, they were to turn out fifteen hundred in 1942.[19]

Many of the new fighter aircraft were to be based in the Leningrad *oblast'*. According to an NKVD report of 28 May 1941, 15,300 laborers were building eleven new airfields, which were to be completed by September. The NKVD requested a work force of 24,000 by the beginning of June and 34,000 by 10 June.[20] This effort was part of a national aviation campaign, which was carried out in a Stalinesque blizzard of confused activity. The NKVD, which coordinated construction using its vast supply of slave laborers, ignored warnings from the military command against trying to build and refurbish too many airfields at once. When Germany attacked, many of them were still under construction, leaving large numbers of aircraft clumped together on the few fields that were operational. This left the Soviet Air Force dangerously exposed, as did the fact that some of the new fields were located near the frontier. About 1,200 Soviet aircraft were destroyed in the first several hours of Operation Barbarossa.[21] The Kremlin vainly continued to hope that the airfields could be completed after the invasion began. On 6 July, the State Defense Committee charged the NKVD with the impossible task of finishing construction on fifteen airports in the Leningrad *oblast'* within twenty days.[22]

Waging war and militarizing the economy between 1939 and 1941 resulted in numerous shortages throughout Leningrad. For one, the military draft and the fact that the purges claimed far more men than women had left Leningrad with a shortage of men: at the beginning of 1941 the city's civilian population was 56 percent female, and the proportion of the industrial work force that was female was about the same. Women were the large majority of workers in the food processing and textile industries and made up about one-third of the workers in metalworking factories. About three-fourths of all women between the ages of sixteen and fifty-nine were employed.[23]

As Leningrad's military industries expanded during the first two years of the Second World War, the large influx of women into the workplace could not compensate for acute labor shortages, which existed throughout the USSR. According to data from Leningrad's factories, in 1941 prior to the German invasion the city lacked more than 43,000 factory workers. Several attempts were made to raise worker productivity. The Stakhanovite movement, a campaign to get more work out of the labor force ostensibly through introduction of more efficient work routines, had been introduced in 1935. It reached its peak in Leningrad in 1938–39, when just under half of the city's factory workers were supposedly implementing Stakhanovite techniques.[24] In addition, harsh labor decrees were enacted to raise productivity. In December 1938, work booklets, which summarized employees' employment history, were introduced nationwide to reduce job flitting by forcing applicants to present a brief history of their work performance to prospective employers. The idea was that those who had performed poorly or who had changed jobs repeatedly would be less likely to be hired. At this time, stiff penalties were imposed for absenteeism and reporting to work more than twenty minutes late. On 26 June 1940, these infractions became criminal offenses with correspondingly stricter punishments, and all employees were barred from seeking new employment without permission from the director of their workplace. Furthermore, the working day for most laborers was lengthened from seven to eight hours and the work week to six days. A survey of 195,296 Leningrad workers from fourteen commissariats shows that during January 1941, 2,574 (1.3 percent) were brought up on charges of violating the labor code, mainly regarding absenteeism.[25] By 1 March 1941, the remarkably large number of 142,738 Leningraders (on average 578 people per day) had been sentenced to corrective labor for up to six months under the decree of 26 June 1940. Included among the incarcerated were women who took off from work to take care of their sick children. In some cases the children were sent with them to work camps or prison.[26] Some of the convicts may have been sent to build the new airfields in the Leningrad *oblast'*.

In early 1941, Leningrad's economic accounting administration prepared a lengthy report for Zhdanov on worker productivity that stated that unproductive use of labor was resulting in a "colossal loss of working time." It claimed that vast "hidden" reserves of laborers, numbering about 30,000 or about 4 percent of the total industrial labor force, had been uncovered in a number of sectors, especially transportation, communication, and construction. The report also called for drawing still more women into the work force.[27]

The nation's aggressive foreign policy and rapid industrialization resulted in other shortages. Housing, especially in the city's southern industrial *raiony*, was very cramped as little new stock had been built in the early 1930s for the burgeoning work force. By late 1934, over half of all Leningrad factory workers had less than five square meters of living space (an area about seven feet by seven feet) in communal apartments and barracks, which generally lacked running water.[28] The general standard of living appears to have reached its nadir in 1935 and then risen slightly by 1941.

There were critical shortages of fuel. Parts of the city experienced a blackout on 19 November 1939, just prior to the invasion of Finland.[29] The Winter War overloaded the already burdened transport system and prevented coal from reaching Leningrad, causing further power outages. In February 1940, many factories had to halt production temporarily just as they had occasionally been forced to do during the 1930s. After the Finnish war ended, the forced pace of production continued, which resulted in oil shortages. In the spring of 1941, several major defense plants ran very short of oil, including the Kirov plant and Bolshevik, as well as the Izhorsk factory, which produced steel, ships, and tanks in Kolpino located about twelve miles south of Leningrad. Leningrad's power plants also lacked fuel.

The war industries grew at the expense of parts of the economy that served local needs. The number of Leningraders employed in several local sectors declined between 1939 and early 1941.[30] Much of Leningrad's transport network was in the process of being transferred to the military. On 7 May 1941, the head of the auto transport administration wrote a letter to the *gorispolkom* and the military department of the *gorkom* protesting an order to transfer 225 buses to the Red Army and another 130 to army hospitals, leaving the city with only 150. "In this way," he wrote, "the city of Leningrad in present conditions will be fully deprived of city bus transport." He warned that bus transportation would be important to the city's inhabitants if war were to occur: London, he claimed, had 8,000 buses.[31] Leningraders followed events of the London blitz through the newspaper accounts of the TASS correspondent there.[32]

Supplies of food and consumer goods were low in Leningrad and their prices high. By 1941, Leningraders were spending almost 60 percent of their income on food and more than 20 percent on clothing.[33] There were long bread lines in Leningrad during the Winter War. Grain exports to Germany helped keep food reserves low into 1941. City leaders scrambled to find ways to alleviate these shortages. Part of the solution was to confiscate needed items from the annexed Baltic states, especially nearby Estonia, to which Zhdanov was quickly dispatched to introduce Soviet policies. The area was a particularly good source of dairy products. According to Nikolai Rakhmalev, director of the First State Milk Factory in Leningrad, which was one of the USSR's largest dairies, the city received large quantities of milk every day from Estonia in the spring of 1941.[34] In April 1941, *gorispolkom* members Motylev and Ponomarev petitioned *Sovnarkom* deputy chairman Kosygin to allow Leningrad to secure the "cooperation" of Estonian officials in allowing Leningrad to take possession of those consumer goods in Estonia that had been produced by private firms in Europe and the United States.[35]

Hence, prior to the start of the German invasion, Leningrad's civilian economy was already under siege. One gains a better appreciation of the cost of the city's wartime sacrifices by realizing how burdened and fragile the civilian economy was prior to June 1941. It would prove difficult to find additional ways to militarize the economy after 22 June and then to survive the extreme deprivations of the blockade.

At the same time, hardships that Leningraders endured between 1929 and 1941 to a limited extent had an opposite effect of providing some specific preparation for the ordeal of total war. Conditions spawned by the Five Year Plans, collectivization, and Baltic annexations bore similarities to situations that would emerge during the siege, and responses that the authorities and population at large devised to cope with the difficulties of the earlier period sometimes became the basis of emergency campaigns adopted during the siege. Thus, in some instances the harsh conditions prior to the war with Germany provided Leningraders with unintended or "hidden" lessons for the siege period. The failures of collectivization, for example, prompted the Soviet government to impose food rationing between 1929 and 1934 in Leningrad (starting in 1930 in most of the rest of the nation). A similar rationing program would be imposed nationwide in July 1941. Both systems divided the population into classes and gave workers (*rabochie*) the largest allotments. In besieged Leningrad, the difference between life and death for hundreds of thousands depended on how well the rationing system functioned, and practical experience from the 1930s no doubt was of some benefit, although it had numerous shortcomings. Another way that the people of the USSR, including Leningraders, helped make up for food shortages in the 1930s was by planting their own private gardens and collectively tilling large factory "subsidiary farms" (*podsobnye khoziaistva*) on the outskirts of cities. Many proficient but starving peasant farmers who had found refuge as factory workers in Leningrad during the early years of collectivization reverted to gardening and farming during the war. In the summer of 1942, planting gardens and working on the subsidiary farms became the single most important life-sustaining activity for many Leningraders.[36]

During the war with Finland, Leningrad's work force had to assume many new responsibilities. The city met many of the needs of the Red Army, and factories had to coordinate prompt deliveries to the front. Skilled workers also had to form special teams to go to the front to make emergency repairs, which also provided an opportunity for civilians and soldiers to engage in mutually beneficial barter transactions. They would perform all these functions again in 1941–44. Shortages of coal in the city in 1939–40 prompted a search for local replacement fuels. Locating sources of peat and shale around Leningrad and organizing their procurement proved instructive for 1941–44 when greater shortages occurred. At least one major war plant, Bolshevik, enlarged its capacity to generate power on its own premises to compensate for shortages from city electric plants.[37] Those factories that could generate some of their own electrical power according to a predictable timetable in the winter of 1941–42 were better able to transform their workshops into self-supporting enclaves and maintain limited production for the front than those that depended solely on the city's one central power plant that limped along and could not maintain a regular transmission schedule.

The rapid militarization of Leningrad's industry had prompted the city's political leadership on the eve of the German invasion to plead to the Kremlin for relief and to protest industrial conversions. On 21 May 1941, Kuznetsov appealed to *Gosplan* chairman and former Leningrad colleague Voznesensky regarding the city's oil shortage. He asked Voznesensky to order the oil commissariat to send Leningrad a 25 percent advance on its allotment of oil. The commissariat had previously denied Leningrad's request.[38] On 14 June, Kuznetsov joined with fellow *gorkom* secretary Kapustin to seek Voznesensky's help in another matter: to reverse an order to transfer Leningrad's one remaining factory that manufactured and repaired streetcars to the quickly expanding aviation industry. Streetcars were the main mode of transportation for most of Leningrad's more than three million inhabitants. On 19 June, Kuznetsov complained to Zhdanov (who boarded a train that day for a vacation in Sochi) and Voznesensky that too many of the city's industries were being converted to war production. He called on Moscow "to cease further efforts at removal of local industry and industrial cooperatives of Leningrad, which are needed for the local population." The same day Kuznetsov wrote directly to Stalin protesting the conversion of a major food processing plant to production of ammunition. He flatly stated that Leningrad's party leaders did not agree with the transfer and asked Stalin to reconsider the decision.[39] Germany's invasion of the USSR three days later became a post facto vindication of the Kremlin line; however, the point here is that prior to 22 June, Kuznetsov had concluded that the militarization of Leningrad's economy had taken such a toll that he had to confront Stalin over the matter.

Access to declassified Communist Party and NKVD documents, especially summaries of informants' reports of overheard conversations, has made it possible to sketch, though not quantify, Leningrad's popular mood. Dissatisfaction with official policies was increasing throughout the city during 1939–41, according to the party's secret informant reports. The shortages and other hardships resulting from the Winter War, the buildup of defense industries at the expense of the local economy, and the export of foodstuffs to Germany sparked angry and vocal criticism of the authorities and a host of rumors. Sarah Davies has demonstrated, for example, that losses in the Winter War spread panic in Leningrad by mid-December 1939.[40]

Over the period of the second and third Five Year Plans (1933–41)—and probably for most of the rest of the Soviet era—the most common complaints overheard and recorded by the secret informants revolved around difficulties in obtaining food (mainly bread) and essential consumer goods. Another object of criticism emerged in 1938 and 1940 with the introduction of the draconian labor laws. In some ways, workers seem to have been affected more by the labor constraints than by the Terror of 1937–38. As the large majority of party members were *rabochie*, arrests for absenteeism and tardiness included thousands of party members. At this time, some party organizations appear to have given up the struggle to justify the arrests or counter growing anti-Soviet attitudes.[41]

A common thread in the overheard criticism was the perception of a huge gulf between ordinary people ("us") and those on high (the *verkhi*, "them").[42] Political identity and loyalties derived to a large extent from one's immediate social and material circumstances. Those expressing critical views might wish for a return to the more "egalitarian" period of the first Five Year Plan or hearken farther back to the quasi-market economy of the NEP years or to the tsarist past. As the economy grew during the 1930s, the upwardly mobile (*vydvizhentsy*) in Leningrad rose out of the ranks of ordinary *rabochie* and office workers (*sluzhashchie*) and became technicians and engineers (*inzhenerno-tekhnicheskie rabotniki*, or ITR) at the same time that salary differentials between *rabochie* and *sluzhashchie*, on the one hand, and the highly trained personnel widened considerably. The ending of food rationing on 1 January 1935, accentuated the growing economic divide, because the ration system had favored *rabochie* over other groups. When rationing ended, food prices rose more sharply for *rabochie*. For these economic reasons, the *vydvizhentsy* were often viewed with contempt by others. Party composition reflected the changing society. Although around 70 percent of party members in Leningrad were *rabochie*, candidates in party and *sovet* elections in the late 1930s tended to come from the technical and managerial elite. Hence, while the *verkhi* to someone outside the party could include all party members, within the party *rabochie* often saw the better-skilled and higher-paid party leaders as a separate group.

There were ethical and religious dimensions to this divide. Those in power also tended to be viewed by ordinary folk as craftily living off the labor of honest and diligent workers. Seen in this light, it is not surprising that a sizable portion of the working population, ordinary party members and nonparty personnel alike, appears to have either supported arrests of party higher-ups in the Great Terror or remained indifferent. Furthermore, the fact that, according to one survey from the 1930s, about one-third of Leningraders retained religious faith at a time when all forms of religious belief and practice were either subject to outright assault or placed under tight restrictions by the authorities naturally distanced believers from the ruling atheistic elite, especially when persecution was intense.[43]

Another means for assessing the popular mood is to analyze the hundreds of thousands of letters Leningraders wrote to city authorities, especially Zhdanov, and to *Leningradskaia pravda* seeking assistance in everyday matters (*byt*). Zhdanov's secretariat kept meticulous records on the letters sent to him. In 1939, he received 62,866 letters (varying between 4,400 and 7,000 per month, or on average 172 per day), over half of which were requests for more or better living space, for residency permits, or for material assistance. In contrast to private conversation among friends and work colleagues, very few of the letters were of a political nature, and only seventy-one were deemed to contain anti-Soviet content. (Political dissidents were unlikely to document their views in writing to the city's party boss.) This pattern of letter writing persisted up to the German invasion: 5,383 letters were sent to Zhdanov in May 1941. In early June 1941, a construction worker at the Stalin metal works sent a litany of grievances to *Leningradskaia pravda*. Among his complaints were that twenty to forty workers had to live in one room, that many basic consumer items were not available, that heavy drinking was common, and that tremendous amounts of materials were being wasted at construction sites.[44] Letter writers often appropriated the official political rhetoric and implied that redressing their grievances would further lofty state goals. The letters were taken very seriously, scrutinized, and forwarded to various agencies for action. Of the 4,515 letters sent to Zhdanov in December 1939, the largest number (1,341) were forwarded to the *sovety* at the *okrug, gorod,* and *raion* levels. Only 225 were forwarded to the Leningrad NKVD, while 110 were not investigated at all.[45]

In addition to increased public grumbling during the 1939–41 period, informants and NKVD investigators in the spring of 1941 claimed to have detected signs of organized political dissent and to have uncovered isolated planned acts of treason and sabotage. According to one report, members of the Trotskyite Fourth International were planning a mass singing of the Internationale on May Day. During the first twenty-four days of April thirty personnel of the Leningrad Military District were arrested for the following crimes: voicing counterrevolutionary sentiments (fourteen arrests), betraying the Motherland (eight), engaging in terror activities (five), espionage (one), belonging to a fascist underground group named "Streltsy" (one), and for committing an unspecified crime (one). Secret caches of weapons were also reportedly seized. Three of the arrestees were said to be planning to defect to the Germans. On 21 May, Deputy Head of the Commissariat of State Security (NKGB) for Leningrad Sergei Ogoltsov reported on a foiled attempt to blow up an ammunition factory. Two junior NKGB officers reportedly discovered an underground cellar packed with explosives at the Number 5 Ammunition Factory. A copper cable connected the explosives to a transformer booth 450 meters away. Twenty-seven-year-old Pyotr Vaganov, who had no apparent motive or previous criminal record, was arrested for the crime. No evidence pointed immediately to a larger conspiracy. During this period, minor acts of sabotage were also reported in Leningrad's aircraft factories.[46]

By the spring of 1941 Leningrad was a city gearing up for war, yet, ironically enough, it was very poorly defended in the direction from which the lethal threat would come. Investment in munitions production was rapid to the point of being chaotic and diminished the availability of food, consumer goods, and city services for the civilian population. These shortages, combined with a new and extremely strict labor code that reduced the work force essentially to a state of industrial serfdom and with the continued restrictions on public expression, including religious practice, made for an austere existence. Through their network of informants, the authorities were aware of the steady stream of verbal discontent that emanated from the city's more than three million inhabitants but which rarely surfaced in an open and organized way. Leningrad's political leaders protested the Kremlin cuts in local services. On the eve of the biggest challenge the city had ever faced, Leningraders had few reserves with which to protect themselves, aside from the munitions they were manufacturing, and a significant undercurrent of discontent was emerging.

The Great Patriotic War

The Enemy's Rapid Approach

Stalin refused to believe the more than a hundred separate warnings he received in early 1941 from domestic intelligence sources along the border with Germany and from elsewhere, including his well-placed spies in such capital cities as Tokyo, Berlin, and Warsaw, that Germany was preparing to attack the USSR. Perhaps the greatest irony of Stalin's dictatorship was that although he continually suspected conspiracies when they did not exist, he would not acknowledge by far the most potent threat to his country, his regime, and himself. He did not believe that Hitler would actually use the three and a half million troops amassed along the Soviet-German border to invade. Stalin ascribed too much reason to Hitler's decision-making process. Stalin seems to have been convinced that Hitler would not risk war with the USSR while Britain remained at war with Germany. Moreover, an attack so late in the year, as Napoleon had learned in 1812, was a risky undertaking, and why would Hitler resort to war when he might get what he wanted through sheer intimidation? Stalin appeared to be expecting from Hitler the kind of ultimatum that the USSR had delivered to Finland in October 1939 prior to an attack, and all indications are that Stalin would have acquiesced to German demands. Stalin desperately wanted more time to build up Soviet defenses. Germany's military mobilization was not kept entirely from the Soviet public. On 21 June, the Soviet government had felt compelled to respond in its own newspapers to a claim by the British government that Germany was poised to invade the USSR. Buried in the TASS statement, which appeared in *Leningradskaia pravda,* was the admission that "a concentration of German troops for some reason is actually taking place." Nevertheless, Germany achieved the element of surprise it desired when it commenced Operation *Barbarossa* between 3 and 4 A.M. on 22 June all along the frontier between the Baltic and Black seas. Stalin added to the German success by refusing to concede at the very beginning that a general offensive had begun, preferring to think that various insubordinate German commanders had acted on their own.[47]

This initial German success, combined with the facts that Soviet front line defenses were incomplete, that defenses in depth were almost nonexistent, and that Germany was able to capitalize on anti-Soviet sentiments common among Finns, Balts, and Ukrainians, enabled the Wehrmacht to drive far and fast into Soviet territory. Hitler's strategic objective at this time continued to be that which he had outlined in his Directive No. 21 from 18 December 1940: "the establishment of a defensive barrier against Asiatic Russia running along the general line of the Volga to Arkhangelsk." In the north, Leningrad and the naval base at Kronstadt were to be captured within a month. Hitler's desire for Leningrad went beyond its military and industrial power. To him the city symbolized the intrusion of Slavdom onto the Baltic seacoast, that former Germanic domain of the Teutonic Knights and the Hansa, and the cradle of revolutionary communism. In the first three weeks of the war, the Wehrmacht drove steadily in a three-pronged attack toward Leningrad, Moscow, and Kiev. Army Group North, under the command of Field Marshal Ritter von Leeb, who had commanded an army group that attacked Poland in 1939 and defeated France in Alsace-Lorraine in 1940, drove quickly through the former Bal-

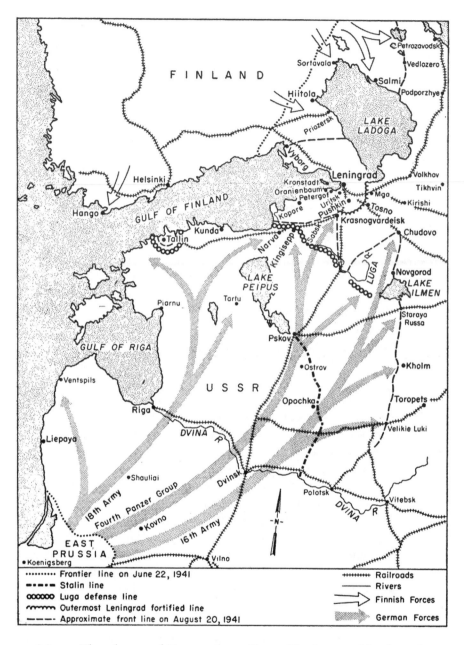

Map 2. The advance of German Army Group North toward Leningrad,
22 June–20 August 1941.

tic states. After sixteen days of fighting, his army had advanced 280 miles (17.5 miles per day) and taken Pskov. Von Leeb was only 155 miles from Leningrad and thus was well on his way to completing his mission.[48]

The two months between the fall of Pskov on 8 July and the fall of Shlisselburg on 8 September can be divided into several periods. Von Leeb immediately followed up his victory with an offensive toward the Luga River, which was quickly being fortified. The German blitzkrieg slowed down but Army Group North managed to reach the Luga area by 8 August. During the period, Hitler modified his designs on Leningrad. Führer Directive No. 34, issued on 30 July, ordered the encirclement of Leningrad, not its immediate capture. The plan was to seal off Leningrad and bombard it. While waiting for its inevitable capitulation, Germany would commence the all-out offensive on Moscow.[49] Meanwhile, the GKO, which was created on 30 June and headed by Stalin, responded to the fall of Pskov by creating the new Northwestern Direction (*Napravlenie*). Voroshilov was named commander of the Northwestern Direction, which comprised the Northern and Northwestern Fronts (the equivalent of German army groups) and the Baltic and Northern Fleets (Figure 4). He had no formal military training but had been a close associate of Stalin since the defense of Tsaritsyn in 1918. Although he had been fired as defense commissar at the end of the war with Finland, he was back in Stalin's good graces within a year as evidenced by the fact that he was an original member of both the GKO and *Stavka*. Voroshilov arrived in Leningrad from Moscow on 11 July, and two days later, when the GKO adopted the policy of assigning party commissars to all military commands, Zhdanov was appointed commissar of the Northwestern Direction. Their mission was to protect the approaches to Leningrad.

The second critical period occurred between 10 and 25 August, when Army Group North broke through the Luga Line. The fighting was intense, and the Germans advanced at an average rate of only about one mile per day. During the last week of August and first week of September, German forces continued to press on to the Gulf of Finland and Lake Ladoga. On 4 September, their artillery shelled Leningrad for the first time. Four days later German aircraft started bombing Leningrad in a massive attack that severely damaged, among other things, the Badaev Warehouses, where much of the city's food reserves were stored. On 8 and 10 September, German bombers dropped seven hundred incendiary bombs on Badaev, which burned thirty-eight storerooms of food and eleven other buildings.[50] It was remarkably irresponsible of city authorities not to have better dispersed the food supply. The first massive air raid did not come as a surprise. In late July *Leningradskaia pravda* had informed its readers that German planes had bombed Moscow, and warnings of impending German air attacks on

Leningrad had been printed in several issues of the newspaper prior to a dramatic announcement by Zhdanov, Voroshilov, and Popkov on 21 August that the enemy might try to seize the city in the near future.[51] On 8 September, German troops took Shlisselburg on the east bank of the Neva River where it flows out of Ladoga and thereby sealed off any land route out of Leningrad. The blockade had begun, and Germany kept it in place until January 1943 by holding a narrow corridor of territory along the lake's shore.

Finland joined Germany in its attack on the Soviet Union; however, its objective was essentially limited to recovering territory seized by the USSR in 1939–40. By the end of August, Finnish forces had retaken pre-1939 Finnish land north of Leningrad and east of Lake Ladoga. Finland blockaded Leningrad from the north. At that point, Germany vainly implored Finland to push on to Leningrad and strike south across the Svir River east of Ladoga to link up with German troops and thereby cut off Ladoga as a supply route by encircling the lake. Finland rejected Germany's appeal, though by the start of winter its troops advanced southward to the Svir River and for security reasons seized the Russian cities of Petrozavodsk and Lodeinoe Pole. In December 1941, the Soviet ambassador in Stockholm Aleksandra Kollontai offered to Finland through neutral Sweden terms for a separate peace and relief for Leningrad where deaths by starvation had already occurred. Finland rebuffed the Soviet offer, because, according to Finnish Field Marshal Karl Gustav Mannerheim, Finland was too dependent on food imports from Germany.[52] At the same time, Finland refrained from attempting to advance along the southeastern coast of Lake Ladoga largely out of fear of provoking the Western powers. Britain and the United States had warned Finland that it would be treated as a hostile power if it advanced further into Russian territory.[53] The lake, therefore, remained the only surface link that Leningrad retained to the "Mainland," and when it froze solid it was used as a military highway.

Even without greater support from Finland, von Leeb probably could have taken Leningrad at the beginning of autumn of 1941 had its capture been Hitler's primary objective. However, during the summer Hitler had indicated repeatedly that he did not want to occupy the city. Franz Halder, chief of the General Staff, noted in his diary on 8 July: "It is the Führer's firm decision to level Moscow and Leningrad and make them uninhabitable, so as to relieve us of the necessity of feeding the population during the war." On 6 September, Hitler ordered key tank corps and the Eighth Air Corps to be transferred to Army Group Center by 15 September in preparation for launching Operation Typhoon against Moscow on 2 October. Hitler's decision produced an ironic turn of events. Right when the Luftwaffe's massive bombardment with incendiary and high explosive bombs commenced, its force was reduced, and when the city's defenders considered a ground assault to be imminent, Hitler decided not to attack the city with ground troops. Deliberate genocide through blockade-induced starvation and massive bombardment would destroy the city and its inhabitants soon enough, or so he thought. On 22 September, Hitler issued the following directive: "The Führer has decided to erase the city of Petersburg from the face of the earth. I have no interest in the further existence of this large population center after the defeat of Soviet Russia. . . . We propose to closely blockade the city and erase it from the earth by means of artillery fire of all calibers and continuous bombardment from the air." Through Alfred Jodl, his chief of the Operations Staff of the German High Command, Hitler informed Army Commander in Chief Marshal von Brauchitsch on 7 October "that a capitulation of Leningrad and later Moscow must not be accepted, even if it is offered by the enemy. . . . No German soldier is allowed to enter these cities." The fact that Germany did not offer surrender terms to Leningrad supports the idea that Hitler did not want to occupy the city. Germany had a difficult enough time feeding its own troops on Soviet soil; it did not have the resources to feed millions of Leningraders. Moreover, Hitler appears to have feared that his troops would be vulnerable to resistance fighters, booby traps, and epidemics if they entered the city.[54]

Hitler's refusal to launch a ground assault on Leningrad, however, did not diminish the city's strategic importance for the Soviet Union in late 1941, nor did it render insignificant or irrelevant Soviet attempts to defend the city. As long as the Leningrad Front was able to mount active resistance and attempt to eradicate the siege, Germany had to keep several hundred thousand troops deployed around the city to maintain the blockade. If the Leningrad Front had been destroyed or subverted from within, Germany could have transferred larger numbers of troops from the north toward Moscow. Then, if Moscow had been surrounded in a crippling siege, the war might have ended. In addition, if Army Group North had been able to complete a tight inner encirclement of Leningrad west of Lake Ladoga, practically everyone within the city would have starved to death. Germany could then have entered the necropolis unopposed in the spring or summer of 1942 to strip it of military and industrial materials for use elsewhere in the war. Finally, it is also possible that if the start of the blockade, air blitz, and mass hunger had prompted an offer to surrender the city, Hitler might have subsequently changed his mind and decided that the city's military assets and war plants were worth capturing after all. In fact, in 1942 Hitler planned to capture Leningrad but lacked the forces to achieve that objective. In 1941, von Leeb was eager to lead the assault on Leningrad as he wanted to go down in history as the conqueror of that city.[55] If the city

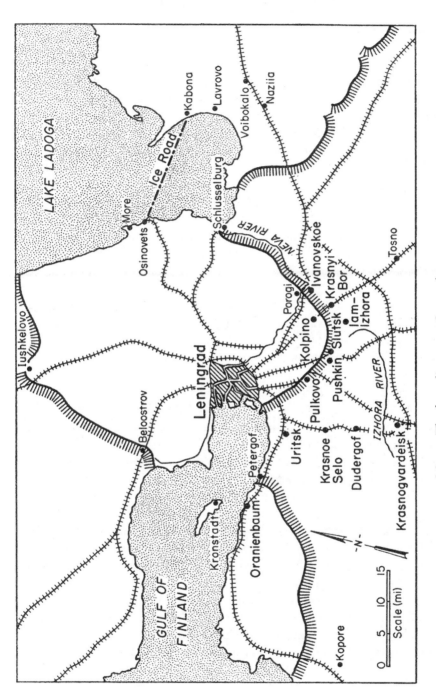

Map 3. The front line on 25 September 1941.

had been captured, Germany might have tried to drive all but able-bodied males to the east, perhaps over Lake Ladoga, to keep from having to feed them. In sum, it was vitally important for the Leningrad Front and Leningrad's inhabitants to continue to fight back against the enemy, even though Hitler had decided not to attempt to occupy Leningrad, at least for the time being.

Enemy bombardment of Leningrad was most intensive during September 1941, and the number of resulting casualties the highest for the war. That month 7,188 Leningraders were killed or wounded by enemy fire, and the high explosive bombs were far more deadly than the artillery shells.[56] Throughout the siege period, 148,478 artillery shells, 102,500 incendiary bombs, and 4,638 high explosive bombs were fired at or dropped on the city, according to Soviet tallies. All told, 16,747 Leningraders were killed and another 33,782 wounded in the bombardment.[57] The prolonged siege reduced many homes to rubble. A total of 3,174 buildings containing 35.5 million square feet of living space were destroyed. Another 23.7 million square feet of space within 7,143 buildings were so severely damaged as to be uninhabitable. In addition, approximately 9,000 buildings were dismantled for firewood (Figures 29–32).[58]

Had Hitler opted for a direct assault on Leningrad in mid-September or later, a massive battle most likely would have ensued. Stalin was determined to defend Leningrad, but at the same time he harbored serious doubts that it could be defended. He ordered the mining of ships of the Baltic Fleet, which would remain bottled up between Kronstadt and Leningrad for the duration of the siege, and of key installations in the southern part of the city, so that if the city fell, the enemy would seize little of military value. Vsevolod Merkulov, Beria's assistant, was dispatched to Leningrad to coordinate with Leningrad NKVD chief Pyotr Kubatkin and Kuznetsov the placing of explosive charges. Nevertheless, General Georgy Zhukov, a former tsarist officer and hero of the Soviet victory against Japan at Khalkhin-Gol in 1939, whom Stalin sent to Leningrad within days of the fall of Shlisselburg, was prepared to defend the city street by street (Figure 5). If von Leeb had managed to take the heavily defended city, the cost to Germany would likely have precluded a follow-up offensive for Moscow. As it turned out, however, the cost of keeping the blockade intact was also very high as it kept several hundred thousand German and allied troops occupied and unable to assist in Operation Typhoon.

Mobilizing for War in the Latter Half of 1941

All accounts indicate that with the exception of top-level military commanders and *gorkom* secretaries, Leningraders, like most of the rest of the

Soviet population, had no inkling that their nation was at war until Molotov broke the news over the radio at noon on Sunday, 22 June. He stated that German troops had "attacked our frontier in many places, and bombed from the air Zhitomir, Kiev, Sebastopol, Kaunas, and some other places." He added that "Similar air and artillery attacks have also been made from Rumanian and Finnish territory."[59] Most Leningraders were off from work and treated the summer solstice weekend as a holiday. Many slept in late that morning having spent the previous night strolling past famous city landmarks during the whitest of the White Nights. Thousands of others, like Zhdanov, had left Leningrad to start vacations or were spending the weekend at dachas in the nearby countryside.

The military and industrial mobilization campaigns in Leningrad between 1939 and 1941, though intensive, were small compared to what the city achieved in the first six months of the Soviet-German War. Barbarossa threw Leningrad's leaders, with Kuznetsov initially in charge of the city's party organization, into a cyclone of activity. A state of martial law was immediately declared for the Leningrad Military District, and on 23 June, the *gorkom* ordered employees in the city's defense plants to work up to three hours longer each day. This resolution preceded by three days an identical one issued by the Supreme Soviet for the entire nation. The military mobilization decree recalled to active duty reservists born between 1905 and 1918. They joined those born between 1919 and 1922, who were already in the armed services. By the start of October, 298,700 had been mobilized in Leningrad, and most were at the front (Document 31). During the war, those who remained in Leningrad participated in numerous fundraising campaigns and collection drives to support the troops.

In addition, during just the first week of the war another 212,000 Leningraders who had not been drafted volunteered, or were pressured into volunteering, for what eventually became known as the People's Militia (*narodnoe opolchenie*). Leningrad was the first city to form civilian divisions separate from the Red Army, and they became the model adopted by the Central Committee for other cities to follow. Most of the Leningrad *opolchentsy* were men, although the military command, the Military Soviet of the Leningrad Front (VSLF), officially encouraged women and teenagers to volunteer in a resolution issued on 25 August. All told, by the beginning of October, 128,800 volunteers were considered eligible and fit to serve and were hastily formed into ten divisions and many supporting battalions that fought alongside regular army formations. Women made up roughly a quarter of the selected volunteers and served mainly in medical and communication services.[60] The *opolchentsy* came primarily from city defense plants, and a high percentage were party members. Many had no previous military training and received little or no instruction before being sent to the front. Their weapons were primitive and included hundreds of thousands of bottles filled with flammable liquids. (The term "Molotov Cocktail" was coined by Finnish troops who used gasoline bombs against Soviet tanks in the Winter War. It does not appear in Soviet documents from wartime Leningrad.) In the words of A. A. Gusev, a political commissar in the Second *opolchenie* Division: "Our people are poorly trained and insufficiently armed. We fight more from the soul and heart than from military training."[61] Their mission was to stop the advance of the armored divisions of German Army Group North. Some were taught to conceal themselves in slit trenches and hurl their grenades or gasoline bombs from close range at vulnerable parts of the German tanks (Figure 20). German armor shredded the *opolchenie* divisions and battalions, resulting in extremely high casualties. Those who survived were inserted into regular army divisions in the autumn of 1941. However, individual German commanders after the war gave high marks to the *opolchentsy* defending the approaches to Leningrad. One senior officer in the Sixth Panzer Division of the Forty-first Motorized Corps stated that his soldiers were "partly faced by troops recently organized among Leningrad civilians, for example, the 1st Proletarian Workers' Regiment which consisted exclusively of fanatical communists and compensated for its lack of training with that much greater ferocity." Another high-ranking officer commented on fighting that took place several days before the siege commenced: "The enemy had been reinforced. He was no longer just a nuisance, but started to become outright dangerous. We encountered the first worker formations, composed of Leningrad's factory workers, and the first brand new tanks."[62]

Moreover, in one of the largest mobilization efforts, roughly half a million civilians were drafted to complete fortifications in the Ostrov-Pskov region and to build another line along the Luga River about sixty miles southwest of Leningrad. Able-bodied males aged sixteen to fifty years and females from sixteen to forty-five were subject to the draft. The original resolution on compulsory labor that was issued on 27 June did not envision sending many fortification workers far from the city, because it stated that employed *rabochie* and *sluzhashchie* were obligated to build defenses for three hours after their work shifts. In addition, all labor conscripts were initially guaranteed at least four days off after not more than seven days of fortification work. However, as the situation at the front rapidly deteriorated, those limits were ignored. Some of the labor conscripts were teenage boys and old men, but most were women, because workers in defense plants, with their high concentration of men, were not drafted until later in the summer. Women in the last eight weeks of pregnancy or in the first eight weeks after giving birth, as well as nursing mothers, were exempt from the compulsory labor.[63] When the enemy broke through the

Luga Line, fortifications were built much closer to Leningrad and finally within the city itself. Laborers dug huge tank trap ravines and built other defenses without adequate tools during the long summer days. They were provided with little food (generally bread and thin soup) or water and often had no shelter against the elements or enemy fighter aircraft, which strafed their anthill-like construction sites. The accomplishments of the compulsory labor (*trudovaia povinnost'*), however, were massive. The land mines, antitank ditches, barbed wire, pillboxes, and barricades along the Ostrov-Pskov and Luga Lines slowed the enemy advance and thereby gave Leningrad and its closest environs valuable time to build defenses. Soviet officials seemed almost obsessed with quantifying all kinds of activities during the war (cubic meters of firewood cut, square meters of gardens planted, number of enemy bombs and artillery shells that hit the city, and so forth). If totals for fortification work are even remotely accurate, they significantly help explain why the German offensive toward Leningrad slowed in August. During the summer around 500,000 civilians per day built fortifications, working on average between two to four weeks each. By the end of the year, the labor conscripts reportedly furnished the following defenses between (and including) the Luga Line and Leningrad: 626 kilometers of tank traps and barriers, 406 kilometers of escarpments and ditches, 306 kilometers of timber obstructions, 635 kilometers of barbed wire, 935 kilometers of communication lines, 15,000 prefabricated pillboxes, and 2,300 observation points. In addition, some 22,000 firing positions and 35 kilometers of barricades were constructed entirely within the city.[64]

German commanders who fought in the Leningrad area testified after the war to the effectiveness of the hastily constructed defenses. One compared Russians to gophers in their ability to dig themselves quickly into the ground. The dehumanizing metaphor cloaks a grudging admiration for the defenders' accomplishments: "[The Russian] is a master of camouflage, entrenchment, and defense construction. With unbelievable speed he disappears into the earth, digging himself in with unfailing instinct so as to utilize the terrain to make his fortifications very difficult to discover. When the Russian has dug himself into his native soil and has molded himself into the landscape, he is a doubly dangerous opponent."[65] Another German officer who served in the Leningrad area stated more simply: "Interconnected antitank ditches, extended minefields, heavy defensive fire from numerous bunkers and also from armored cupola rendered the offensive [of the Forty-first Motorized Corps] extremely difficult."[66]

Leningraders performed several other functions that supported the armed forces and helped protect the city against possible attack early in the war. City leaders realized that Leningrad might be subjected to air raids within days of the start of the war, and in fact the Luftwaffe did conduct extensive high-altitude aerial reconnaissance over Leningrad as early as 27 June.[67] On 23 June, *gorkom* and *ispolkom* leaders ordered the formation of 10,000 local air raid precautions (*mestnaia protivovozdushnaia oborona, or MPVO*) crews to protect all factories and houses from aerial bombardment. With air raids expected at any time, buildings were to be watched at all hours and blacked out at night, although they would still be visible from the air in early summer due to Leningrad's far northern location. Flammable materials were ordered removed from the vicinity of buildings and from their attics. Water and sand were to be stored on the top floors of all buildings as a safeguard against incendiary bombs. The city did not fulfill its ambitious MPVO quota; however, by September, 3,500 crews were reportedly in operation, comprising 270,000 men and women.[68]

On 24 June, in response to a *Sovnarkom* resolution, the *gorkom* ordered factory workers in every *raion* to form combat (*istrebitel'nye*) battalions to secure defense plants, shipyards, government and party offices, and other important locations in the event that enemy paratroopers appeared and to thwart possible spies and saboteurs within the city. The NKVD commanded the operation and selected personnel from male military volunteers, most of whom were party or *Komsomol* members. By 5 July, the battalions had at least 17,000 members. Many were eventually sent to the front.[69] The NKVD also sent 8,613 Leningraders, most of whom were men, as partisans in seventy-three detachments behind enemy lines in the first three months of the war.

Within three to four days after the war began, most Leningrad children who were attending summer Pioneer camps in the surrounding countryside had returned home. Massive evacuations of children then began on 29 June (Figure 15). They were sent to parts of the Leningrad *oblast'* and, as the front approached closer to Leningrad, were relocated to the Yaroslavl, Kirov, and Sverdlovsk *oblasti*. By 7 July, a total of 234,833 Leningrad children, including 105,964 of preschool age, had been sent out of the city. On 18 July, at the Lychkovo station in the southern part of the Leningrad *oblast'* German planes bombed and strafed a train full of children. Forty-one children were killed, including twenty-eight from Leningrad. Many others were wounded. The horrifying spectacle of dead and maimed children being returned to Leningrad was the first direct contact with the war for many Leningraders. News of the disaster spread rapidly by word of mouth and made many Leningraders terrified of leaving the city or sending their children out. In fact, by 1 August, some 115,000 children had been reevacuated to the city, though others continued to leave. By the end of August, 175,400 evacuated children had returned to Leningrad.[70]

On 13 July, the *gorkom* attempted to raise the level of military preparedness by introducing universal military training (*vseobshchee voennoe obu-*

chenie or *vsevobuch*). The program, which preceded by two months a similar national initiative, obligated all able-bodied working men, not already part of a military unit, to enroll in a sixteen-hour military training course after work hours. The purpose was to train reserves for the *opolchenie* and regular armed forces as well as to prepare a home guard should the need arise to defend the city. It does not appear, however, that training programs were widely implemented before the latter half of August. Most men were occupied with a host of far more pressing matters. The training sessions were poorly attended, and practice rifles, grenades, and bayonets were in short supply. Consequently, only about one-third of the 151,294 people who were supposedly eligible for *vsevobuch* completed the program.[71] One component of *vsevobuch* was the creation of worker detachments (*rabochie otriady*) at factories, which were to transform their workplaces into armed bastions. However, few detachments were actually formed before the end of August (Figures 24 and 25).

Industrial employees who remained in the city had to boost rapidly production of war matériel and learn to manufacture many new types of weapons and ammunition. Others were charged with dismantling machinery for evacuation to the east. To carry out these assignments, tens of thousands of new workers had to be found to replace those who went to the front. However, production was hampered by the fact that Leningrad ran short of coal and oil before the start of the blockade. Starting on 8 August, city power stations began adding special boilers to enable them to burn peat and wood, which would be harvested within the blockade zone. Thousands of Leningraders were mobilized to dig peat from nearby bogs and fell trees for fuel.[72]

Despite the mobilization activity and numerous official warnings that Leningrad could be attacked at any time by enemy aircraft, *Sovinformburo* (the Soviet Information Bureau), which controlled publication of news on the front, did not describe the threat Leningrad faced from the enemy's ground offensive until city leaders made their dramatic announcement on 21 August. For many Leningraders, the main source of front line information was retold accounts by refugees from occupied territory who reached the outskirts of Leningrad and by soldiers who returned home on leave. The mass media's failure to report accurately on the situation at the front created an environment for alarmist rumors to circulate. Refusing to acknowledge military defeats early in the war, *Sovinformburo* confined its reporting on the front in the summer of 1941 mainly to isolated accounts of soldiers' heroism and included only vague and sketchy references to the larger military context. When *Sovinformburo* announced that a battle had taken place "in the direction" of a particular city, the city was often already behind enemy lines. Pskov fell on 8 July; yet *Leningradskaia pravda* reported on 24 July that fighting for it was continuing. Similarly, the newspaper did not announce that Tikhvin had fallen until the Red Army had retaken it. On 11 December, the paper stated that Tikhvin had fallen on 3 December, when in fact it capitulated on 8 November.[73]

In late August Stalin became very concerned over Leningrad's predicament. He was alarmed to learn that Voroshilov and Zhdanov had secretly formed a Leningrad Military Defense Council (*Voennyi Sovet oborony Leningrada*) to coordinate defense within the city but had not appointed themselves to the body. On 22 August, there occurred a dramatic exchange of several cables between the Kremlin and Smolny (Leningrad's party headquarters) in which Stalin expressed his fear that the absence of the city's two political and military leaders from the new council would be interpreted by the public as a lack of commitment to defend the city. In his last cable on that day, Stalin forced Voroshilov and Zhdanov to join the council. Stalin's doubts regarding whether Leningrad could be successfully defended, which grew in the ensuing several weeks, appear to have begun at this time.

Stalin sent a team of GKO officials to Leningrad to examine its defenses and organize the immediate evacuation of massive amounts of military-industrial machinery and hundreds of thousands of civilians. On 29 August, the same day that the GKO representatives drew up their evacuation plans, the last rail line out of Leningrad was severed. Many working people and around one million nonworking dependents were left trapped in the city. Evacuations had not been completed for several reasons, aside from fear of traveling into or through enemy-patrolled territory. Due to the official line that any invading force would be quickly repulsed, no comprehensive industrial evacuation plan existed prior to the war. Preparatory logistics took time to work out. As early as the end of July, enemy forces severed all but one rail line out of Leningrad, and the remaining one had to be shared with the military. Although the means to leave the city were limited, more nonworking people would have evacuated if the political leadership had divulged the dimensions of the threat facing the city at an earlier date. Furthermore, there was a natural tendency to postpone dismantling and evacuating machinery from important defense giants, such as the Kirov plant, because their output was integral to the war effort at the start of the war. For those factories that converted to war production, the process often took most of the summer. Having invested the time to retool, industrial planners wanted to reap the dividends. It proved difficult to opt to evacuate a plant that was just coming on line in August.

At the same time that many were reluctant to leave Leningrad and became trapped within it, thousands of others were forcibly exiled. The so-called "social-foreign element"—former nobles, White Army officers, kulaks, and the like—was rounded up and sent to various locations east of the Urals. In addition, mainly during the first week in September 1941 and again in March 1942, there were mass deportations of ethnic Finns and Germans, some of whose ancestors had resided in and around the city for many generations. By the end of the summer of 1942, the NKVD had exiled eastward a recorded 58,210 Germans and Finns (mainly the latter).[74]

Leningrad's situation grew desperate after the start of the blockade. Enemy aircraft and artillery bombarded and burned the city, which received very little in terms of food, fuel, or raw materials from outside the blockade zone. German gun spotters could peer right into Leningrad from hills south of the city. They and the bomber crews used two main sources for identifying targets. As noted above, German spy planes had photographed key installations on at least a couple of occasions in 1938 and 1939. They resumed overflights of the city after the start of the war. On 26 June, at least two aircraft assembly plants and factories that manufactured electric generators, machine tools, and radios were photographed. Early the next morning another approximately one hundred aerial photos of parts of the city were taken. On 7 July, pictures were taken of the Treugolnik (Triangle) rubber plant and the Kirov plant. Over time, photography and identification of key installations became more sophisticated as the photograph of the Kirov factory from 15 September 1942 indicates (Figure 9). German intelligence also made good use of Soviet maps. In 1935 and 1936, detailed maps of Leningrad, which identified most of the city's war plants, had been published in 5,000 and 10,000 copies, respectively. A German war map of Leningrad made in April 1941 was merely a copy of the 1936 Soviet map with several installations added that had been omitted from the Soviet map, including the Badaev food warehouses, the Stalin metal Works, two aircraft plants, the city airport, and various army barracks (Figure 7).

Food supply in Leningrad ran low early in the war, in part because the USSR since 1939 had been exporting massive amounts of foodstuffs to Germany to pay for industrial and military imports in accordance with the trade agreement that accompanied the Nonaggression Pact. Although rationing was introduced nationwide early in the war, on 18 July 1941, Leningrad had less than one month's supply of many kinds of food when the siege commenced. Three mistakes had worsened the situation. The first was that bread and livestock were actually sent out of the Leningrad region during the summer of 1941. Another mistake was the failure to disperse food reserves from the Badaev complex prior to the start of the enemy bombardment. The third error was that food continued to be sold in Leningrad outside the rationing system in some cases until November 1941.

The food rationing scheme was designed to feed best those who were most important to the war effort, but also to feed people roughly according to their needs. *Rabochie* in "hot" workshops, such as steel smelting, received the largest rations. The other three categories, in descending order of the size of their rations, were: *rabochie* and ITR; *sluzhashchie*; and nonworking dependents. The rationing system, however, projected an illusion. When rations were significantly reduced, other factors became more important in determining who survived, and survival rates varied tremendously throughout the city. A poorly paid bakery clerk, who was in the low ration category of *sluzhashchie*, had a much better chance of survival than did a higher-paid defense plant *rabochie* who received the largest rations. Rations were cut several times during the autumn. Supplying the city with food became most precarious between 8 November and 9 December, when Germany temporarily held the rail junction city of Tikhvin and thereby forced Soviet food convoys to lengthen their circuitous supply route to Leningrad over Ladoga by constructing a road over 120 miles long. The capture of Tikhvin was part of an attempt to link up with Finnish forces east of Lake Ladoga and thus seal off the lake as a route of resupply and escape for Leningrad.

Starting on 20 November, the top category of rations was cut to 375 grams per day of bread, which was the only food that was regularly available. Filler such as wood cellulose was added to the bread to make rations seem larger. At the same time, the ration for *sluzhashchie* and dependents was slashed to 125 grams, or slightly more than a quarter-pound, of the adulterated bread. Infants and the elderly were the first to starve to death. By year's end, roughly 50,000 had perished. Among adults, the large majority of early starvation victims were men.

Stalin never sanctioned a large-scale airlift of food into blockaded Leningrad or of starving people out of the city. His main concern regarding Leningrad during the autumn of 1941 was the condition of the four Soviet armies and the naval personnel inside the siege ring (rations for military personnel were approximately double those of civilians), their arms, ammunition, and ships, and the means for producing war matériel. Civilians in general and nonworking dependents in particular occupied a much lower priority for Stalin. His main objective during the autumn of 1941 was the defense of Moscow, and he ordered resources from the entire nation, including Leningrad, sent there regardless of the sacrifice involved. The GKO demanded that Leningrad's war plants produce as many munitions as possible and send a large portion of them to Moscow. Some of the arms and raw materials were airlifted from Leningrad in Soviet versions of Douglas transport planes.[75] As starvation set in and the enemy bombardment continued, Leningraders had to maintain their "storming" work routines, logging shifts of eleven to fourteen hours while subsisting on steadily

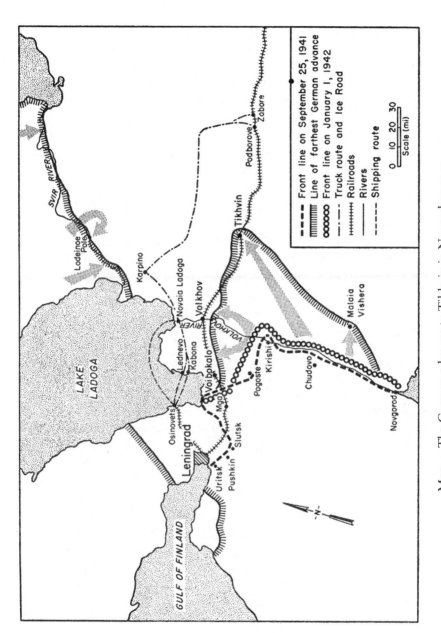

Map 4. The German advance to Tikhvin in November 1941.

Front line on September 25, 1941
Line of farthest German advance
Front line on January 1, 1942
Truck route and Ice Road
Railroads
Rivers
Shipping route

0 10 20 30
Scale (mi)

LAKE LADOGA
GULF OF FINLAND
SVIR RIVER
VOLKHOV RIVER

Lodeinoe Pole
Karpino
Novaia Ladoga
Volkhov
Tikhvin
Podborove
Zabore
 Lednevo
Kabona
Osinovets
Voibokalo
Mga
Leningrad
Uritsk
Pushkin
Slutsk
Pogoste
Kirishi
Chudovo
Malaia Vishera
Novgorod

shrinking food rations. According to one study, toward the end of November over half of all factory workers under the age of thirty were still achieving at least double their work norms (Figures 26, 27, and 28).[76] Leningrad's factories continued to retool for war production and to manufacture as many artillery guns and mortars and as much ammunition as possible until the city's one remaining power plant, operated by Lenenergo, practically ran out of coal in December. Workshops of some enterprises closest to German lines were relocated to regions out of range of German artillery. Some employees who did not relocate reorganized their work space so that they spent much of their time in sections of workshops that were less exposed to artillery fire. Likewise, as the city's population dropped as a result of mobilization and evacuation, as well as death by starvation in the first siege winter, families moved into empty rooms on the lower floors of apartment buildings. They preferred flats facing toward the north, which were less likely to be hit by German artillery located south of the city.

The Hungry Winter

December was a month of rapidly unfolding mass horror interspersed with emerging signs of longer-term hope for those who might survive the ensuing grim winter, which was extraordinarily cold; only rarely did the temperature rise above freezing. Essential services ceased functioning. With coal supplies practically exhausted, only one city power plant barely continued functioning. In December trams quit running, homes and most enterprises lost electricity, and heating pipes froze and burst (Figure 34). Most of the peat and timber that had been harvested in the autumn had gone to factories, which left homes without heating. As few food deliveries reached the city, death by starvation (which was referred to as *distrofiia* in Soviet documents) became widespread. The NKVD made its first arrests for cannibalism in November.[77] Yet over the course of a few days in the first half of December, Leningraders received welcome news. They learned that German armies had been forced to retreat before Moscow, that Tikhvin had been liberated, and that Germany had declared war on the United States following the Japanese attack on Pearl Harbor. Hope for an end to the siege in the near future surged with announcement of the Red Army's victories but proved illusory by late winter. At the same time, the myth of German invincibility had been shattered, which raised the prospect of a longer-term war that the USSR and its Western Allies would eventually win. On 25 December, food rations were increased for the first time. Further increases in the bread ration followed in each of the next three months, and other foods, including groats, meat, sugar, and dried fruit reappeared in late January and February (see Appendixes A, B, and C).

It was also in December, when defense plants were idled due to lack of generating power, that Leningrad's leaders finally turned their main attention to the city's emergency needs. During that month and in January 1942, the first self-standing metal stoves (*burzhuiki*) and power generators were manufactured, and public baths, laundries, heating stations, and convalescent centers (*statsionary*) opened. In late January, *Leningradskaia pravda* introduced a regular column entitled "More Attention to the Everyday Needs of the Population," which focused attention on how cafeterias, food shops, public baths, laundries, barbershops, and other service enterprises were functioning. People were exhorted to apply their creativity to help themselves and others survive. The party attempted to "mobilize" people to become more innovative, and in the process, Leningraders acquired a measure of personal freedom in matters pertaining to survival, which extended through the first half of 1943.

However, for many the increase in food rations at the end of December 1941 and greater attention paid to essential services proved to be too little, too late. Almost two of every five Leningrad civilians who were not evacuated would perish in the city from hunger and cold in the first winter and spring of the siege. The period of highest mortality was in late January and early February. According to the manager of the Piskaryovskoe Cemetery, where perhaps half of the city's civilian victims of the blockade were buried, on individual days in February up to 10,000 corpses were brought there for burial.[78] Many corpses, however, were not discovered or delivered for burial or cremation until March and April. By the end of the spring, the death rate was rapidly declining, although half of all workers still remained at home on sick lists.

Evacuation provided the best hope of survival for Leningraders. Ice on Lake Ladoga froze thick enough by 22 November for sleds to be used to bring food to the city. Russia had a long history of traversing frozen lakes, gulfs, and rivers going back to Aleksandr Nevsky's famous defeat of the Teutonic Knights on Lake Peipus (Chud) in 1242. In 1710 in the Great Northern War against Sweden, Peter the Great's troops crossed seventy-eight miles of frozen gulf from Kotlin Island to the Finnish coast to besiege Vyborg. In fighting Sweden almost a century later in February and March of 1809, Russian forces attacked over the Gulf of Bothnia. Every winter from 1892 to 1913, railroad track was laid across the Volga River near Kazan. The Red Army crushed the uprising on Kronstadt Island in March 1921 by launching an infantry assault over the Finnish Gulf. During the Winter War, a Soviet infantry division crossed the frozen Vyborg Gulf. During the first two months of the Ladoga ice road only 36,118 Leningraders were reportedly evacuated over it, mainly because Moscow provided little logistical support. However, starting in late January, Mos-

cow began to send considerably more vehicles and personnel to the eastern end of the ice road, so that by the time the road was finally closed on
24 April, 4,035 vehicles of various types were in use there, and approximately 19,000 people were working on it (Figure 38). Over half a million
Leningraders, mainly nonworking dependents, escaped the siege during
the first winter over the frozen lake. When the number of people who were
evacuated from the start of the war up to the opening of the ice road is
added, a total of 1,295,100 people, including wounded military personnel,
were sent out of the blockaded territory by 15 April 1942, according to the
city's evacuation commission.[79] In the words of Russian historian Valentin
Kovalchuk: "It is difficult to overestimate the significance of the Ladoga ice
road for besieged Leningrad."[80] Tens of thousands of the refugees, however, were in such an emaciated state that they died during the evacuation
or shortly thereafter. Others were killed by German aircraft that patrolled
the ice road, especially in December and January, just as they had attacked
Soviet ships traversing Ladoga in the preceding autumn.[81] Truckers traveled in the dark, but some fell through holes in the ice. As the temperatures warmed in March and April and the ice road began to melt, there
was a concerted effort to evacuate as many people as possible for as long
as possible. In extraordinary acts of courage and endurance, more than a
hundred drivers completed four and in some cases five round trips in one
day. In April, 163,400 refugees were driven over the lake. In the last days
that the road existed, trucks increasingly crashed through the melting ice
(Figure 39). During the entire time the ice road was in operation in the first
two winters of the siege, a total of 357 vehicles broke through, and in 143
cases, vehicles were entirely submerged in the frozen lake.[82] So many died
crossing Lake Ladoga that the route was often referred to as the "Road of
Death" rather than the "Road of Life," the name that gained popularity
with Soviet historians after the war. In his memoirs, the famous Russian literary scholar Dmitry Likhachev, who survived the blockade, wrote: "The
story was told of a mother who lost her mind: she was traveling on the second lorry with her children in the first, and before her eyes it sank beneath
the ice. Her lorry quickly went round the hole in which her children were
struggling under the water and roared on without stopping. How many
people died of starvation, were killed, fell under the ice, froze or vanished
without trace on that road! God alone knows!"[83]

A basic fact of life of the blockade was that the food rations by themselves were generally insufficient to sustain life, particularly during such
a cold winter (Figure 33). Some extra source of food and/or warmth was
needed. Many blockade survivors have noted in their diaries and memoirs that the generosity of others—a relative, a friend, or even a stranger—
enabled them to survive. As Adamovich and Granin put it in their memoir

collection, "each had a savior," such as parents who saved their own food rations from work to give to their starving children.[84]

There were other keys to survival. It would seem that nearly everyone relied to some extent on black-market transactions. At the city's central markets during the worst of the winter people would exchange a gold watch for a handful of turnips or a Persian rug for a couple of chocolate bars.[85] Although private trade remained illegal, starving people selling a few personal items for food were rarely bothered by the *militsiia*; at worst they paid a small fine. Those trying to sell state property or making a business of private trade were charged with criminal offenses. Private trade flourished between civilians and the several hundred thousand soldiers stationed inside the blockade area. Soldiers swapped their larger food rations with civilians for clothing and other items. Leningraders sought out opportunities to visit troops near the front in any sort of official capacity, such as part of a factory's "goodwill delegation" or an entertainment group. Although there were instances of starvation among the troops of the Leningrad Front, in general the soldiers generously shared their food with the civilians who came to visit them. Leningraders also took advantage of special privilege or influence to find a way to leave the city or to obtain more food if they remained in it. For instance, factories often had "closed" cafeterias and a "directors'" cafeteria, which provided a little extra food. Starvation rates among Communist Party members and officials of the NKVD administration were significantly lower than for the general civilian population.

For ordinary people with no privileged position, the most desirable jobs were in enterprises that worked with food: bakeries, candy factories, other food-processing plants, cafeterias, buffets, and hospitals. There was fierce competition to get on their payrolls, and the starving begged for food on their premises. These places became excellent havens for their employees, and their starvation rates were very low; at several food plants no one died. Some food-processing officials were even significantly overweight. Despite the hundreds of thousands of starvation deaths, there were Leningraders who were very well fed during the starvation winter.

According to the rationing scheme, *rabochie* and ITR received considerably more bread per day and other foods, including groats, meat, fat, sugar, candy, and fish, when they were available, than did other employees and dependents. The reintroduction of food rationing during the war returned *rabochie* to the higher position within the social hierarchy that they had occupied when food had been rationed in the early 1930s. Some city defense plants also provided soup and other hot food in addition to the higher ration. Those in the *sluzhashchii* category often tried to secure the higher *rabochii* and ITR ration or even to convince city authorities to grant them *rabochie* status just for rationing purposes. Factory employment provided other benefits. The largest defense plants received access to special stockpiles of food and also were allowed to dispatch their own trucks across frozen Ladoga to obtain food and deliver it directly to their employees. Many factory workshops became large mutual support centers where workers pooled their strength to carry out essential chores. Some took up living round the clock at their workplaces. Workers formed brigades to clean living space in workshops, mend torn clothing, repair shoes, and set up laundries, baths, showers, and warming stations. It was primarily girls and women who comprised these brigades, which also took food to those too weak to come to work, cleaned their apartments, attempted to place orphaned children in homes, set up childcare centers in their factories, and arranged for burial of corpses.

Many diaries and memoirs attest to the fact that a basic and important key to survival was maintaining the will to endure and not lapsing into a state of lethargy. Sacrifices that parents made for their children, such as giving them part of their own food rations, were partly offset by the powerful determination to survive in order to continue to be caregivers. For many Leningraders that will to survive included rigorous mental discipline. During the starvation winter, city authorities encouraged the population to maintain a positive self-image, to focus on practical survival tasks, and to repress as much as possible fixating on food shortages by channeling one's mental energies elsewhere. One factory posted the following rules:

1. It is permitted to speak about food only during meal time.
2. All men must shave.
3. Everyone, not just service personnel, must gather firewood, carry water, and clean rooms. This is to be established on a rotating basis.
4. All people must occupy themselves with some specialized reading material. Art and literature are recommended.[86]

Leningrad's large and prominent intellectual community showed extraordinary dedication to its scholarly and cultural work during the bleakest periods. During the hungry winter many of Leningrad's institutes and libraries remained open. Every day the main reading room of the city's public library attracted readers. Doctoral dissertations continued to be written and defended during the winter in air raid shelters and basements. Daniil Granin, co-author of the oral history *Blokadnaia kniga*, observed that "morale was one of the major characteristics of the heroic battle for Leningrad, not patriotism, but rather the perseverance of the intellect, the protest against the humiliation of hunger, against the dehumanization."[87] One of the best-known examples of cultural creativity and determination during the siege was the composition and performance of Dmitry Shostakovich's Seventh Symphony. Shostakovich finished the third movement of his famous work dedicated to Leningrad in the late summer and early autumn of 1941, when he also worked as a fireman during the air blitz. In early October, after having repeatedly refused to leave the city, he finally obeyed a command to evacuate. He completed the score in Kuibyshev, where the symphony had its premiere on 5 March 1942. It was first performed by emaciated musicians in Leningrad five months later on 9 August, and broadcast by radio to the world.[88]

The dire conditions of mass starvation and enemy bombardment brought out the extremes of human nature. Untold thousands dedicated themselves to saving others, especially children. Their heroic commitment gave them a reason to live, a will to endure greater deprivation and suffering than they could have otherwise borne. Selfless behavior, however, was also self-destructive. It entailed willingly and quietly sacrificing oneself to provide as much food, warmth, and shelter as possible for the other. Such heroes deliberately and quietly sacrificed their lives leaving few traces of their heroism. At the same time, the siege produced extraordinary acts of selfishness and cruelty. There were those who would commit any crime to survive and even to try to make a profit in the process. Theft of food in small and large amounts was widespread. Starving teenagers snatched rations in and around dark and crowded bread shops. On occasion armed bands looted shops. Workers and administrators in bakeries and food stores systematically stole large quantities of food. During the winter of 1941–42, police recovered 455 metric tons of stolen bread, grain, groats, and sugar.[89] Enterprising and starving thieves alike were generally punished severely and swiftly. *Gorkom* secretary Kuznetsov stated in April 1942 that people were shot for stealing as little as a single day's ration of bread, but the threat of execution often did not deter desperate people.[90] Murder and cannibalism became a significant problem. According to recently declassified Russian documents, during the siege approximately two thousand people were arrested for cannibalism, that is, consuming human flesh, which was classified as a "socially dangerous" crime, similar to "banditry," under article 16-59-3 of the criminal code (Document 53).[91] Most of the accused were young, unemployed women, with no prior convictions, who had been born outside of Leningrad and therefore may not have possessed ration cards.[92] They were simply starving people using any means possible to feed themselves and their children.

Propaganda, Political Control, and the Popular Mood

During the 1930s, official Soviet ideology selectively rehabilitated heroes and values from Russia's prerevolutionary past as useful models for building socialism. As Robert Tucker has observed, "the propaganda of Soviet patriotism" can be dated from June 1934, when the concept of "betrayal of the homeland" (*izmena rodine*) was codified into law.[93] Right from the beginning of the German invasion, however, the emphasis put on traditional Russian patriotism in official rhetoric and propaganda at the national level and especially in Leningrad increased significantly and supplanted to a large extent the theme of communist internationalism. The shift toward more traditional values appears to represent an attempt by the leadership to gain wider support for national defense (Figure 67). When Molotov announced the German invasion in his radio address on 22 June, in a text that he said was prepared by "the Soviet government and its head, Comrade Stalin," he portrayed the struggle as a patriotic or fatherland (*otechestvennaia*) war.[94] That name for the war stuck and continues to be used by Russians today. In drawing a parallel to Napoleon's famously failed campaign of 1812, the statement virtually ignored ideological differences as a reason for Germany's invasion or as a reason to defend the USSR. The announcement placed the war in the historical context of Russia yet again defending its homeland against an aggressive European national foe. The reference to 1812 also implied that the struggle could be a protracted one, not the quick defeat that Soviet prewar propaganda claimed awaited any enemy aggressor. The shapers of public opinion very quickly served up inspiring historic examples of failed enemy invasions. Sergei Eisenstein's film from 1938, *Aleksandr Nevsky,* which famously portrayed the prince's defeat of the Teutonic Knights, had been banned from screening following the signing of the Ribbentrop-Molotov pact, but it was taken off the shelf and shown in Leningrad on the evening of the first day of the war. The Soviet press avoided interpreting the war in Marxian terms. The enemy's invasion was not portrayed as an attack on communism per se, nor was it depicted as the beginning of an inevitable Armageddon-like struggle between the forces of capitalism and communism.[95] The standard prewar rhetoric that predicted that any future war would be short and victoriously concluded on the enemy's soil was quickly dropped. After about a week of war, *Leningradskaia pravda* quit expressing hope that the USSR might soon defeat the enemy because German soldiers and workers would not long support the invasion of the world's first socialist nation. When Stalin directly addressed the nation for the first time during the war on 3 July, his lengthy radio speech included only one reference to the Communist Party.[96] Starting on 28 June, *Leningradskaia pravda* commissioned noted historians to write articles comparing the present war to past wars with Germany. Military history was altered to depict Russians as consistently routing Germans over many centuries. On 9 July, the newspaper printed an article by the historian V. Mavrodin that chronicled Russian victories over Germans from the time of Aleksandr Nevsky through the battle of Grunwald in 1410, in the sixteenth-century Livonian Wars and the eighteenth-century Seven Years' War, as well as the victory over Napoleon and his reluctant German allies in 1812–14. Mavrodin also praised General Brusilov's victory over the Austro-Hungarian army in 1916, and in a display of creative revisionism claimed that the nascent Red Army had defeated German interventionists in 1918, thereby sparking revolution among workers in Germany. In the weeks to come, several similar articles appeared. When the enemy crossed the Soviet western borderlands into the Russian heartland, the invocation of past Russian heroes became more prominent. During the crucial period in the battle for Leningrad, the press emphasized the city's heritage of freedom from foreign domination more than any other theme to rally its defenders. For example, on 18 September, *Leningradskaia pravda* published a letter from female workers at the Red Banner clothing factory exhorting their husbands and brothers to defend their city, which they referred to as "our very own *Piter*" (*rodnoi Piter*—as the city was colloquially called, from the historic name *Peterburg*). They pointed out that it had never succumbed to foreign conquest. Stalin, whose presence in *Leningradskaia pravda* diminished early in the war, particularly during the weeks when the battle for Leningrad was being decided, reinforced the trend to extol heroes from Russia's prerevolutionary past as worthy of emulation in his speech from Red Square on 7 November on the twenty-fourth anniversary of the Bolshevik Revolution: "In this war, may you draw inspiration from the valiant example of our great ancestors— Aleksandr Nevsky, Dmitry Donskoy, Kuzma Minin, Dmitry Pozharsky, Aleksandr Suvorov, Mikhail Kutuzov."[97] The following year new military orders named for Nevsky, Suvorov, and Kutuzov were introduced, and medals for other prerevolutionary national heroes were created in 1943 and 1944. There were protests among some Soviet historians against the valorization of military figures from Russia's imperial past, some of whom had acted in a clearly "counterrevolutionary" manner; however, through the course of the war, the Russocentric line became more pronounced.[98] A survey of 328 titles of propaganda articles for brochures and articles in newspapers and journals, which often served as the text for "agitation" speeches, printed in the Leningrad journal *Propaganda i agitatsiia* between December 1941 and January 1943 reveals that only 13 focused on the role of the party or on political ideology. The most common titles dealt with, in order of frequency: exploits of the Red Army, German atrocities, life inside the blockade zone, and activities of the Western Allies.[99] A list of titles of propaganda brochures published in *Propaganda i agitatsiia* near the start of the starvation winter, on 16 December 1941, shows that only one of fifteen directly concerned the party. When thousands of agitators were sent to city factories in the summer of 1942 their lectures took on a more patriotic tone, emphasizing distinctly Russian achievements. Representative titles of factory agitation lectures from that period included: "On Russian Culture," "On the Motherland," and "Leningrad—the National Pride of the Russian People."[100] Right before the siege was finally lifted, on 13 January 1944, the *gorispolkom* announced that many avenues, streets, and squares would revert to their precommunist names. For example, Twenty-fifth of October Prospect once again became Nevsky Prospect.[101]

Official wartime rhetoric at the national level and in blockaded Leningrad represented, in the words of Jeffrey Brooks, an "opening of the press to the feelings and experiences of a wider public," in an obvious effort to garner corresponding wider support for the war effort. Reviving the memory of heroes from Russia's distant past and praising acts of individual heroism at the front in defense of fellow soldiers and the Motherland appealed to "humanistic values" outside the scope of communist ideology.[102] The dilemma that the LPO encountered in the critical first year of the war was that it tried to broaden its appeal among the populace at the same time that it was rapidly shrinking in size due to the massive transfer of party members to the front, and that it and the NKVD were vitally concerned with maintaining strict public order. The security organs defined "counterrevolutionary" (KR) activity broadly and sought to repress as effectively and completely as possible all forms of expression that criticized the authorities and official policies. It was somewhat difficult for the general public, however, to understand what constituted a KR offense when the party's self-image was in flux and when the policies of cooperation with Nazi Germany during 1939 to 1941 had so obviously failed and official promises of national security made during that period had proved worthless.

Through use of recently declassified party and NKVD documents and by comparing them with independent eyewitness accounts, historians can now assess much better how the party and NKVD attempted to control the populace and how Leningrad's inhabitants reacted to the deprivations and terror of war, the enemy and his siege tactics, and the inability of the Soviet armed forces and political leadership to protect them better. The Party and NKVD employed separate armies of informants in each *raion* to monitor public expression, with the aim of controlling and shaping it. The most critical period of Leningrad's defense was mid-September 1941, when demolition experts under NKVD supervision mined the warships of the Baltic Fleet and many plants and other key installations in the city's southern districts with the intention of destroying them if the city appeared to be on the verge of capitulation. Stalin clearly had his doubts about whether Leningrad could be defended, and informant reports reveal that many in the city (how many is impossible to ascertain) believed that Leningrad would fall and, if that were to occur, party and security personnel as well as the city's large Jewish population would be eliminated. Opinions were divided over what would happen to the remaining inhabitants. Some Leningraders were not alarmed at the prospect of German occupation, and a small minority boldly voiced their hope that the city would fall. Hand-scrawled swastikas occasionally appeared on courtyard walls. Anti-Semitic outbursts (such as, "Beat the Yids!") were overheard on occasion and were generally prosecuted as KR crime. Diaries and memoirs sometimes contain derogatory generalizations about the city's Jewish population. Whatever the level of anti-Semitism in the city, it appears to have increased in the first weeks of the war and to have peaked in September when Leningrad's defense was most in doubt. German propaganda leaflets dropped over the city included crude and vicious anti-Semitic themes, and they likely helped stir up sentiment against Jews in Leningrad. Such leaflets, however, were not dropped prior to the September crisis.

As food rations were repeatedly cut in the autumn of 1941, party and NKVD informants noted a correspondingly sharp rise in criticism of the authorities. One of the most important determinants of political loyalty for Leningraders throughout the war years was how well the authorities pro-tected them, and providing enough food was a key component of protec-tion. Official agitators were taunted and heckled when they had to explain why rations were being reduced. On several occasions small groups of em-ployees refused to work overtime without additional food. Party leaders also received a number of anonymous letters demanding the surrender of the city to save its population. The number of arrests for KR crimes, mainly anti-Soviet "agitation" or overheard speech, was highest for the entire war during the summer and early fall of 1941. Altogether, between 1 July 1941, and 1 July 1943, a total of 3,799 Leningrad civilians were convicted of KR crimes, of whom 759 (20 percent) were executed.[103] The rest were impris-oned, which during the first nine months or so of the war often amounted to a death sentence, given conditions within the blockaded territory. NKVD reports state that there were pro-German conspiratorial groups, but solid evidence for their existence is lacking. At no time did opposition sentiment coalesce into an organized and formidable threat to the authorities. The danger was more potential and latent in nature.

As the level of public criticism increased, the LPO experienced its own crisis. It shrank dramatically, because the number of new recruits did not come close to making up for the large numbers that went to the front. Right from the start of the war, the party actively sought to replenish the membership; yet, despite these efforts, the number of new entrants reached a low point precisely at the time it appeared that the city might fall.[104] At this critical juncture, party personnel often tried subtly to dissociate themselves from the party without severing ties altogether or drawing direct attention to themselves. Candidate members let their candidacies lapse, and full members often refrained from paying dues. When the city's fate hung in the balance, loyalty to the party among its members could not be taken for granted. Only in the latter half of 1943 were the city's party structures rebuilt and communist ideology revived.

Contrary to the hopes and expectations of the German leadership, Leningrad did not collapse into chaos either in the fall of 1941 or during the starvation winter. The percentage of letters that were censored by the NKVD for containing "negative mood," however, did increase sharply as the starvation rate reached its peak and temperatures plunged in late January. Much of this correspondence was sent to soldiers at the front by their starving family members. Yet the rate of arrest for KR offenses at that time was not as high as it had been when the siege began. Order was preserved for a number of reasons. It would appear that most Leningraders despised the enemy's genocidal siege tactics and greatly feared the consequences of German occupation. Leningrad became the first place in the Soviet Union that suffered devastating enemy attacks but was not occupied. During the initial weeks of blockade and bombardment, it became evident to most Leningraders that German troops had not arrived as liberators. As a result, Leningrad became the first Soviet location where a firm desire for revenge was widely articulated. A thirst for vengeance appeared in most of the rest of the USSR only in 1943 and 1944, when the Red Army liberated occupied parts of the USSR and publicized the German atrocities they uncovered. Other reasons for the lack of major political unrest in Leningrad included the widespread desire to support friends and relatives at the front and the ongoing hope that the city would soon be liberated, especially after the Red Army's counteroffensive outside Moscow commenced and Tikhvin was recaptured in early December. Conversely, the realization that German forces blockading Leningrad were on the defensive going into the winter of 1941–42 and hence were unlikely to try to capture the city in the near future discouraged those who held pro-German sentiments from articulating their views. Furthermore, the fact that Leningrad's leaders during the winter adopted many measures to protect the general population probably also played a part in maintaining residents' loyalty, although naturally there was significant dissatisfaction over the authorities' inability to provide more food. Finally, the daily rigors of trying to survive the winter tended to numb and mute expression of political dissent.

A number of studies of the Soviet home front during the war have shown that authorities encouraged spontaneous initiative, not ordered and co-ordinated from above and not always collectivist in nature, and that there existed a greater freedom of expression (but not including anything remotely resembling political dissent) largely because state and party organs were preoccupied with matters directly linked to waging war and lacked resources to deal with less urgent matters.[105] This theme applies well to Leningrad, particularly from the time of the hungry winter through late 1943. The brigades described above that organized emergency services at factories are an example of increased local initiative. The Russian Orthodox Church is a prime example of an institution that took on new social responsibilities and gained additional freedoms. Although only a very small number of churches continued to be permitted to function, they held daily services that were well attended. Official atheistic propaganda ceased at the start of the war as did practically all persecution of Russian Orthodox priests. Orthodox churches contributed generously to several fund drives to aid soldiers at the front. Church activity increased as the city's population declined, and only one church was closed, temporarily, during the war's first winter, although the city *sovet* reserved the right to commandeer church space and confiscate property. Churches tried as best they could to assist their parishioners during the starvation. In 1943, the year that Stalin allowed the Church to reinstate a patriarch, Leningrad's churches raised funds for a tank column and an air squadron.

Continued Adaptation to Siege Conditions

As the starvation winter wore on, city authorities became concerned with other matters pertaining to survival. They worried about the possibility of infectious diseases due to the accumulation of refuse, excrement, and unburied corpses. Starting in late January, the city *sovet* issued several appeals to clean up the city; however, Popkov admitted on 3 March in *Leningradskaia pravda* that most people had not begun to clear refuse from their homes. He announced that those who refused to clean up apartments and stairways could be imprisoned for three to six months, but the threat proved ineffective and does not appear to have been carried out. Sunday, 8 March, which happened to be International Women's Day, was designated a special work day (*voskresnik*) to clean the city (Figure 48).[106] The end of March, when the temperature finally rose above freezing, was a time of particular concern. The number of cases of spotted fever jumped from 15 in February to 379 in March; instances of typhoid fever increased from 42 to 113. For twelve days starting on 27 March, hundreds of thousands of Leningraders, mainly women who were practically walking skeletons, cleaned up much of the city, and the only form of mass transportation, the trams, started running again on 15 April. Widespread epidemics never materialized, although during the spring of 1942 the rate of infection continued to rise, and through the entire year there were 3,516 cases of spotted fever and 1,939 of typhoid fever. Mass inoculations and the fact that city authorities cremated over 100,000 corpses in 1942 helped keep incipient epidemics in check.[107]

At the same time, a citywide gardening campaign was launched. Seeds, seedlings, and tubers were distributed for the population to grow cabbages, tomatoes, potatoes, and other vegetables throughout the city. Cleared excrement was used as fertilizer. Those who were fit enough to dig in the dirt, weed, and water plants greeted the program with enthusiasm. Farmland in outlying parts of the city and in blockaded sections of the *oblast'* was cultivated by workers from city enterprises, though most people preferred to work on their own gardens. The produce grown within the blockade zone was an important part of the reason that by November 1942 Leningrad had amassed a four-month supply of food.

From the spring of 1942 through the rest of the year, Leningrad continued to adapt to the blockade. Evacuation across Ladoga of nonworking people resumed on 26 May. By the end of the year, the city's population had been pared down to 637,000, of whom a recorded 82 percent were employed.[108] A VSLF resolution of 5 July stipulated which sectors of the economy would continue to function and set limits for the number of employees in each:

Defense industries	117,000
Food production	25,000
Textiles and light industry	29,000
Power generation	6,800
Peat and firewood preparation	21,000
Local and cooperative industries	44,000
Rail transport	18,000
Other industries	14,000

All other enterprises were to be shut down.[109] These goals, however, were not attained, as goods and services for the city's residents retained a high priority through the first half of 1943. Between July 1942 and July 1943, a period in which the ongoing evacuation cut the city's civilian population by almost half (from 1.1 million to 600,000), the number of people working for the local economy dipped by only 5 percent to 219,000. The number of workers in defense plants, however, declined by 26 percent to 86,000.[110]

Several programs were implemented to help prepare the city for a second siege winter, and, in particular, to augment fuel supplies for homes and industry. A pipeline was laid under Ladoga to access fuel from the "Mainland." In addition, some 10,000 Leningraders, mainly women, were assembled in June and July to dig peat for industrial fuel. A resolution of 11 June required every able-bodied laborer to cut at least four cubic meters of firewood for the coming winter, half of which the individual would keep and the other half going to the city administration. Back in August and September of 1941, when a top priority had been production of war matériel, only about one railroad car of wood per day had been chopped. In July 1942, when city leaders were more concerned with the welfare of the local population, workers filled on average 106 cars each day with firewood. To increase electrical power in the city, fourteen miles of electric cable, which had been produced at the city's Sevkabel factory, were laid along the bottom of Lake Ladoga, beginning on 8 August. On 23 September, the first current was received from the Volkhov power plant outside the siege ring. As a result, the amount of electrical power available in Leningrad was four times as great in the winter of 1942–43 as it had been during the previous winter, when the population had been much larger.[111] Leningrad was much better prepared for the second blockade winter.

Another pressing concern in the spring and summer of 1942 was the prospect of a renewed German offensive to take the city. In fact, on 5 April, Hitler ordered Leningrad's capture. Meanwhile, Stalin's objective in the north was to end the siege in 1942. Neither side, it turned out, deployed the resources necessary to dislodge the other. Both were well dug in and strongly fortified. Stalin's offensive of the preceding winter and spring had been overly ambitious. By April of 1942, the offensive had ground to a halt. The Red Army was exhausted, overextended, and too many of its reserves had been committed to action. The Soviet Second Shock Army had advanced too far westward. By spring, it was located northwest of Novgorod, about ninety miles from Leningrad, and was threatened on three sides. Lieutenant General Andrei Vlasov was named commander of the Shock Army on 20 April. At first he tried to defend his position against the developing encirclement as he was not permitted to withdraw. When he was finally ordered to break out to the east, it was too late. By late June Vlasov's forces had been destroyed in the most important Soviet defeat in the north since the start of the Leningrad siege. General Vlasov himself was captured, and he later agreed to form a Russian Liberation Army that fought against the Red Army alongside Germany, thus becoming the most notable Soviet turncoat of the war.[112] During the summer of 1942, as Hitler decided in Operation *Blau* to bypass Moscow and drive to the southeast toward the Volga River and the oil of the Caucasus, Stalin tried to end Leningrad's blockade by ordering the Volkov and Leningrad Fronts to fight toward each other through the German-held neck of territory south of Lake Ladoga in what became known as the Second Siniavino Offensive. The fighting was intense and costly. According to recent research, the Red Army suffered 113,674 casualties.[113] The offensive failed to lift the siege but kept Germany from attempting to capture Leningrad in 1942.

The destruction of the Second Shock Army and initial success of Operation *Blau* held dire implications for Leningrad and the rest of the USSR. Leningraders became increasingly worried that a collapse of Soviet defenses in the south would be followed by a renewed attempt to capture their city. Indeed, on 23 August, the day German aircraft commenced carpet bombing of Stalingrad, Hitler directed Colonel General Erich von Manstein to link up with the Finns to level Leningrad to the ground.[114] However, the Red Army's staunch defense of Stalingrad and the ensuing brilliant encirclement of Paulus's Sixth Army prevented Germany from shifting significant resources back to Army Group North. Nevertheless, German artillery continued to fire on Leningrad at close range. A reported 42,000 shells hit the city in 1942. The Luftwaffe curtailed its raids on Leningrad after May yet still managed to drop 760 bombs on the city over the course of the year.[115]

During the summer and fall of 1942, the evacuation of nonessential civilians continued, and Leningrad completed its transformation to a frontline military city (Figure 54). Security measures, such as an 8 P.M. curfew and nighttime blackout, were enforced. Panic mongers and those spreading lies and "provocative rumors" continued to be treated as enemy accomplices. In June, the *gorispolkom* ordered 45,000 Leningraders, mostly women, to complete construction of defense fortifications started in 1941.[116] Defense plant workers were exempt from the labor draft; however, they strengthened city defenses by forming new armed detachments. Most of the workers in the auxiliary military units formed in 1941 had either been funneled into the army or evacuated with their factories.[117] By 9 October 1942, 232 detachments with 19,000 workers had been assembled. During the rest of the autumn, an additional 8,600 workers joined the detachments, which were transformed into fifty-two battalions under Army command. Almost all workers in the southern, industrial *raiony* were assigned firing positions in their workshops.[118] Leningrad prepared once again to become a battle zone (Figures 51 and 52).

During the summer, dozens of defense plants in Leningrad resumed manufacturing millions of artillery shells, bombs, and mines and thousands of small arms. The city's work force had become predominantly female. By the end of 1942, women made up 76.4 percent of all of the city's industrial employees and 79.9 percent of factory *rabochie*. In light industry and textiles, about 95 percent of *rabochie* were female. Most of the women were new to their jobs since the start of the war. Men, however, continued to predominate in more skilled jobs. They comprised about two-thirds of engineers and technicians at the end of 1942. Men also accounted for about two-thirds of the members of the worker battalions (Figure 61).[119]

In October 1942, the Leningrad Front began receiving reinforcements, including tanks and artillery, from outside the blockade zone and increased its size from three to four armies. On 2 December, *Stavka* under Stalin's name informed the commands of the Leningrad and Volkhov Fronts that it had worked out a plan, codenamed *Iskra* (Spark), for the Fronts to fight toward each other along the southern shore of Lake Ladoga. Voroshilov was sent back to Leningrad on 24 December to coordinate *Iskra* and thereby redeem himself for failing to prevent the blockade in 1941. On 3 January 1943, using the *nom de guerre* of Efremov, Voroshilov reported that the ice on the Neva River ought to be thick enough to support tanks—thirty to forty centimeters—by 12 January. A couple of days prior to the start of Operation *Iskra* on 12 January, Stalin must have had renewed doubts about Voroshilov, because he dispatched Zhukov (under the code name for communication purposes of Konstantinov) to the Volkhov Front to report on last-minute preparations for the offensive and to take over the coordination of the two Fronts.[120] Hence, the hero of the victories at Moscow and Stalingrad supplanted Voroshilov in Leningrad just as he had replaced him as Leningrad Front commander during the fight for the city's survival in September 1941. *Iskra* was an important success, but an incomplete one. The two Fronts linked up on 18 January and opened a corridor into Leningrad along Ladoga's shore that was a little over nine miles long and five to six miles wide. The same day Zhukov was promoted to the rank of marshal. As with most of Zhukov's victories, this one came with heavy losses. The Red Army suffered 115,082 casualties, which included almost 33,940 killed, captured, and missing.[121] At 10:09 A.M. on 7 February, the 517th day of the siege, and five days after the Soviet victory at Stalingrad, the first train pulled into Leningrad's Finland Station having passed through the narrow corridor and crossed the Neva River on tracks laid across the ice. Its arrival marked the beginning of the last stage of the siege.

The land blockade was pierced, but the siege remained largely intact for almost another year. Siniavino remained in German hands until September, and Mga was retaken only during the final offensive that smashed the blockade of Leningrad in January 1944. In 1943, 3,105 trains ran the gauntlet of the "corridor of death" (also called the "road of victory"), which German artillery continually shelled at short range. Work crews repaired sections of track some 1,200 times in 1943. The volume of cargo that arrived on trains fluctuated depending on German artillery fire. Despite heroic attempts to keep the line open, during the first months of its existence too few trains reached Leningrad. For example, in April, only about a quarter of the number of trains needed to supply the city with fuel arrived, which forced the *gorkom* to close down thirty factories.[122]

Although the second siege winter was warmer than the first, Lake La-

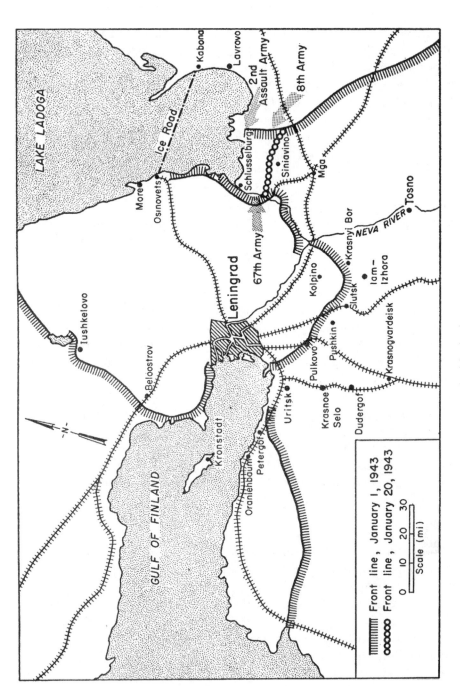

Map 5. Piercing the blockade in January 1943.

doga had ice thick enough to support vehicular traffic from 19 December 1942 to 30 March 1943. There was also an effort to lay rail tracks over the ice, but it was abandoned before it was half completed on the day Soviet forces pierced the blockade. Despite the fact that there were far fewer people to feed in Leningrad during the second winter than the first and that for part of the second winter food was brought into Leningrad over the ice road and by rail, people still starved to death. On 17 December 1942, Aleksei Yevdokimov wrote in his diary: "Nightmare and horror! . . . People are again beginning to fall, people are swelling up and dying . . ." On 11 January, feeling the effects of starvation himself, he noted: "I want to gorge like a wolf."[123] The number of starvation victims, however, was much lower than in the first blockade winter. During March 1943, for example, the NKVD recorded 489 cases of death by starvation and another 280 in April. There were also a few isolated arrests for murder with the intent to consume human flesh.[124]

In 1943 Leningrad began to resemble a safer "rear" city, even though it remained under artillery fire. The rail connection allowed more food, raw materials, and fuel to enter the city and more people and manufactured products to be sent out. Cattle were brought in to build up livestock herds. To increase the food supply further, Leningraders continued to devote as much time as they could to growing vegetables. There were about as many factory-run subsidiary farms as in the previous year, but they functioned more efficiently, and aggregate crop yields rose by 50 percent. Private gardens reportedly made even greater gains as people continued to prefer their own plots to the factory-run farms. The number of registered gardens in 1943 rose by 60 percent over 1942, and even though fewer people were cultivating them, the weight of the total harvest reportedly increased by 128 percent. One specific improvement was that *raionnye sovety* managed to make a wider assortment of seedlings available at an earlier date than in 1942.[125] By the end of 1943, per capita food consumption in Leningrad was close to the national average. About 20,000 Leningraders died in all of 1943, which was less than the number that had perished in one week during parts of the first blockade winter. Toward the end of 1943, for the first time since the start of the siege, Leningrad's birth rate surpassed the death rate (an accomplishment that Russia recently has not been able to claim).[126]

During the latter half of 1943, Leningrad experienced its own "return to normalcy." The city largely reverted to the role it had played prior to the mass starvation winter as industrial supplier to other areas of the nation. Industrial production in the city accelerated. Work norms in some cases had not been raised from their low levels of 1942, so workers could easily overfulfill them. The norms were reviewed and raised in 1943. Leningrad began to manufacture large turbines, generators, and other machines needed to rebuild industrial regions, such as the Donbass, that the Red Army had recently retaken (Figures 58 and 62).[127] At the same time, artillery shells and other ammunition were produced and stockpiled in Leningrad as commanders Govorov and Meretskov of the Leningrad and Volkhov Fronts planned the offensive that would finally smash the blockade.

The Communist Party behind the front lines, including in Leningrad, also revived. On 14 January 1943, the Central Committee ordered primary party organizations (PPOs) around the nation to hold elections and resume regular activities. In May the PPOs in Leningrad held their first elections since the fall of 1941. By the end of 1943, 346 PPOs, representing a quarter of the city's party members, were elected.[128] In the spring of 1943, articles in the press began to feature more prominently themes on communist ideology and the contributions of the party to the war effort, and references to Stalin appeared more frequently.[129]

These changes occurred as the enemy stepped up its bombardment. German bombers returned to Leningrad in 1943 and flew over two hundred sorties, and enemy artillery fire reached its greatest intensity of the war in September, when 11,000 shells from mainly long-range, large-caliber guns reportedly hit the city (Figures 8 and 60).[130] Leningraders viewed the bombardment as an expression of futile vindictiveness. Most seemed to realize that the end of the siege was not far off, because by this time, the Red Army had already retaken most of pre-1939 Soviet territory, and Soviet troops had crossed the old border with Poland. Leningrad acted as the elbow upon which the forearm of the Soviet offensive swung.

In the USSR's first summer offensive of the war in 1943, Army Group North was not as massively attacked as were the other German army groups. German troops, therefore, were transferred from the north to other sectors where they were more urgently needed. Those that remained encamped around Leningrad continued to build fortifications in anticipation of a long-awaited, and feared, breakout offensive. By the start of 1944, the Leningrad and Volkhov Fronts greatly outnumbered Army Group North in troops, tanks, aircraft, and artillery. According to one Soviet historian, the Leningrad Front deployed more artillery for the offensive than the entire Russian Army had possessed in 1915.[131] On 14 January 1944, both Fronts unleashed a ferocious artillery barrage. Within a few days, they had fired half a million shells. By this time, some 1.75 million Leningraders had been evacuated since the start of the war, leaving only 575,900 in the city. Many of them scrambled onto rooftops to watch with pride the awesome and terrifying spectacle of artillery shells screaming over their heads. The last German shell hit Leningrad on 22 January, as the remnants of Army Group North retreated. Five days later, no enemy forces were within sixty-five kilometers of Leningrad. The siege was over, and a massive celebration took place in Leningrad (Figures 63 and 64).[132] By the end of the war, more than a million Red Army soldiers had been killed, captured, or had gone missing in the Soviet northwest, mainly in the Leningrad *oblast'*. When the wounded and those incapacitated by illness are factored in, total Soviet military casualties in the region were just short of four million.[133]

The Red Army refrained from launching a simultaneous offensive north of Leningrad against Finland. Instead, the Soviet government in February secretly offered Finland peace terms and proceeded to bomb Helsinki to pressure the Finnish government into accepting its offer. In negotiations that proceeded intermittently during the latter part of the winter of 1943–44 and into the spring, the Soviet government spelled out its harsh terms. They included Finnish recognition of Soviet territorial annexations during the Winter War, a huge indemnity, and the reduction by half of Finland's armed forces, among other things. Finland, which was under heavy German pressure not to sign a separate peace, at first refused to comply. On 9 June, three days after the Western Allies invaded Normandy, the Soviet Union employed over a thousand aircraft and a pulverizing artillery barrage in a surprise attack against Finnish positions on the Karelian Isthmus. By 19 September, Finnish Field Marshal and President Gustav Von Mannerheim accepted the Soviet peace terms. In return, what remained of Finland avoided Soviet occupation and retained its democratic government and market economy, although its foreign policy would essentially be controlled by the Soviet Union.

The Leningrad Affair

For Leningrad the war years occurred between periods of political purging: the Great Terror of 1937–38 and the Leningrad Affair of 1949–53. During the siege Leningrad's party leaders and prominent intellectuals had acquired a measure of autonomy from Moscow. After the war, Moscow sought to regain tighter control over Leningrad's political and cultural figures and went after the intellectuals first. In August 1946, upon Stalin's initiative, the Central Committee passed a resolution that criticized the city's journals *Zvezda* and *Leningrad* as well as its leading satirical writer Mikhail Zoshchenko and its most famous poet Anna Akhmatova, both of whom had resided in Leningrad for at least part of the siege. The writers were charged with having come under "decadent" Western influence and departing from the Socialist Realist norms established in the 1930s, and were expelled from the Writers' Union. Stalin ordered Zhdanov, who had moved to Moscow after the blockade was lifted to take up the role of the nation's chief ideologue in the Central Committee, to continue the cultural assault in addresses to party and literary elites in Leningrad. Zhdanov's attack on Akhmatova was misinformed, insulting, and crude: "The range of her poetry is pathetically limited—the poetry of a crazed lady, chasing back and forth between boudoir and chapel. . . . Neither nun nor whore, or rather, both whore and nun, whose lust is mixed with prayer."[134] Although Zhdanov was closely linked to this cultural purge (indeed, it is often referred to as the *Zhdanovshchina*), one effect of his criticism was to weaken temporarily his own protégés in his former stronghold, the Leningrad *gorkom*, which had approved publication of the works of the censured authors.[135] Nevertheless, the careers of the city's wartime party leaders advanced quickly in Leningrad and beyond in the immediate postwar years (Figure 66). Kuznetsov took over Zhdanov's former post as first secretary of the Leningrad *gorkom* and *obkom* in January 1945.[136] Fourteen months later, at the relatively young age of forty-one, he became a Central Committee secretary and member of that body's organizational bureau. Popkov, who had served as chairman of the *Lengorispolkom* during the blockade, replaced Kuznetsov as head of the LPO in 1946. Popkov's assistant in the *gorkom* was Kapustin. I. S. Kharitonov, the first secretary of the Primorsky *raion* party committee during the war, was promoted to the post of chairman of the *Lenoblispolkom* after it was vacated by N. V. Solovyov, who became first secretary of the Crimean *oblast'* party committee. Two other former clients of Zhdanov who had not served in Leningrad during the war occupied high-level posts. Voznesensky, who had worked in Leningrad from 1935 to 1937 and briefly held the post of deputy chairman of the *Lengorispolkom* in 1937, by 1948 was a Politburo member, deputy chairman of the Council of Ministers of the USSR, and chairman of *Gosplan*. Mikhail Rodionov, who had served under Zhdanov when Zhdanov headed the Gorky party organization, became chairman of the Council of Ministers of the Russian Republic in 1946.

Zhdanov and his protégés, therefore, were on a fast track within the Communist Party and government hierarchy, although by the summer of 1948 some had suffered setbacks over the accusation of inadequate oversight of Leningrad's cultural periodicals and intellectuals. Zhdanov's reputation was also damaged as a result of a speech that his son Yury, who was head of the Central Committee Secretariat's Science Department, gave in April 1948 that criticized views on genetics held by Academician Trofim Lysenko, the neo-Lamarckian who had Stalin's favor.[137] The elder Zhdanov, who had suffered poor health during the blockade, checked into a sanatorium in July 1948 with symptoms of heart failure and stroke. He had two heart attacks and died suddenly on 31 August. Although rumors persisted that Zhdanov had been the victim of a medical murder, there is no hard evidence to support that view.[138] Within a year, arrests of Zhdanov's protégés had begun. By the end of 1951, 214 people with connections to

Leningrad, including family members of those directly accused, were convicted of forming an "antiparty group." Twenty-three of them were executed, including Voznesensky, Kuznetsov, Popkov, Kubatkin, Kharitonov, Solovyov, Kapustin, and chairman of the *Lengorispolkom* Petr Lazutin.[139] Two died in prison before their trial. Eighty-five others were given long prison terms, 105 were exiled to distant parts of the country, and one was sent to a psychiatric hospital.[140] Altogether, at least two thousand Leningrad officials, and possibly many more, were fired from their jobs through 1952. Some of them, in addition to those named above, may have been executed.[141] Hundreds from many other cities were jailed during this purge.

The origins and precise dimensions of the ultrasecret Leningrad Affair, which was not publicly disclosed until after Stalin's death, remain partly obscure due to a lack of documentation. Kuznetsov's party file was destroyed, perhaps by Malenkov who checked out many documents connected with the case in 1957 and never returned them. In 1988 during Gorbachev's glasnost reform, the Central Committee's Party Control Committee produced a summary report on the Leningrad Affair, published in 1989, which indicated that some pertinent materials remained classified.[142] A few more documents on the case have since been published, and several scholars have recently uncovered details from other documents in various archives.[143] For decades researchers have speculated about the reasons behind the purge and why for the first time since the late 1930s Stalin resorted to executing high-level political officials. The predominant interpretation contends that the purge was a product of Kremlin cabal politics—what Harrison Salisbury described as "Florentine" conspiracies—involving the struggle over who would eventually succeed Stalin, whose health was in decline, especially after his heart attack in October 1945. Zhdanov's rivalry with Malenkov and Beria predated the Soviet-German War, and during the war Zhdanov rarely communicated with his rivals in the Kremlin. Kuznetsov handled correspondence with Beria. In the immediate postwar years, the Zhdanov group appeared to have the upper hand. In April 1946, Kuznetsov became head of the Cadre Administration of the Central Committee, a post that Malenkov had held for over a decade. The following month, Zhdanov took over chairing meetings of the Secretariat from Malenkov, who lost his position there until July 1948.[144] Included in Kuznetsov's new Central Committee responsibilities was oversight of the security ministries, which threatened Beria. Although Beria had given up his post as head of the NKVD in early 1946 to concentrate on the Soviet atomic bomb project, he continued to exert some oversight of security matters as a deputy chairman of the Council of Ministers and within the Politburo, of which he became a full member in March. Yet Beria's replacement at the helm of the NKVD, Sergei Kruglov, was not his protégé, and in the summer of 1946, Beria's loyal subordinate Vsevolod Merkulov was replaced as head of the Ministry of State Security (MGB) by Viktor Abakumov, whom Beria feared. Kuznetsov may have supported Abakumov at this time.[145] However, Zhdanov's sudden death on 31 August 1948, rendered his patronage network immediately vulnerable, and Malenkov and Beria managed to get Stalin on their side against the ascendant Kuznetsov.

Leningrad posed unique threats to Stalin. The city had after all served as the capital of Imperial Russia for over two hundred years. The Communists had moved the capital to Moscow for security reasons in 1918. At the end of the Second World War, there was no conceivable foreign threat to Leningrad; hence, as long as the wartime alliance with Britain and the United States continued after the war, an argument could be made to move the capital back to Peter the Great's Baltic city. Salisbury heard a rumor of support for such a proposal during his visit to Leningrad a few days after the siege ended. An article that he wrote for the *New York Times,* which he later said was "an open plea that Leningrad again be Russia's capital," was blocked by Soviet censors.[146] Of greater concern to Stalin was the fact that during the 1920s and 1930s, Leningrad had been the base for Zinoviev's opposition to him and for the party's rising star, Kirov.

Despite Leningrad's isolation during the blockade, city leaders and the populace at large tended to view the city within a broad international context. In 1942, an informant reported a rumor that negotiations involving the United States, Britain, Germany, and the USSR were taking place to save Leningrad by turning it into an international port.[147] Another rumor that appeared in several informant reports that year claimed that the USSR was arranging to lease Leningrad to Britain and the United States for ten or twenty-five years to pay for Allied assistance in the war.[148] Although Leningraders expressed some distrust of the Allies' motives and trustworthiness, most probably viewed Britain and the United States favorably during the war. In a report on the popular mood in the city submitted immediately following the Yalta Conference, which was forwarded to NKGB headquarters in Moscow, an engineer named Sharyov at the Kirov factory was heard saying, ". . . we have established firm contact with England and America for a long time. Life soon will be very good."[149] As a result of the monumental suffering Leningrad endured, it emerged from the war literally a shell of its former self but with the aura of a hero from one of history's greatest epic struggles, and unlike Moscow, Leningrad could (and did) boast of having never succumbed to any foreign conquest. The city deserved a future to match or surpass its wartime loss. The elections to the Supreme Soviet in 1946 provided an opportunity for leaders to define their visions of postwar Leningrad. Zhdanov returned to Leningrad prior to the elections and gave an address in which he advocated, in the words of Blair Ruble, "policies designed to improve the quality of life of Leningrad citizens. The new Leningrad economy, Zhdanov argued, would be based on consumer-goods production, extensive trade with the West, and a disproportionate claim to postwar reconstruction funds. He thus linked Leningrad's resurgence to particularly volatile leadership struggles in Moscow over the Soviet Union's peacetime relations with wartime allies and, ultimately, to his own fate."[150] State-security informants noted at this time that a portion of the city's population wanted a liberalized economy along the lines of NEP, guarantees of freedom of conscience and religion, and close relations with the wartime allies.[151]

Kuznetsov also gave a public address prior to the elections. On 16 January 1946, Leningrad's political leader delivered a rousing and emotional speech in which he praised the city's inhabitants for their heroic defense during the siege and proudly predicted that the city would regain its former stature and again furnish the nation with political, scientific, and cultural talent and leadership.

> They say about us, that we Leningraders are great patriots for our city. Yes, we are patriots, we love and cherish it. . . .
> Could you indeed not love such a city? How could you not love your city, on which no enemy's foot has ever trodden from the moment it was founded! A Red Banner city bearing the Order of Lenin, the hundreds of thousands of participants in its heroic defense hold as a sign of courage and selfless determination the medal "For the Defense of Leningrad," a city which was the first to stop the enemy, which withstood twenty-nine months of siege and destroyed the Hitlerite hordes in front of its walls; a city whose praise overshadows praise of Troy!
> Could you indeed not be a patriot for this city!

Perhaps deliberately making a pun on his own name, Kuznetsov added that as in the past Leningrad should "spread science and culture around the country . . . like a smithy (*kuznitsa*) of cadres . . . so that new cadres of people of science, party and *sovet* leaders would go forth from Leningrad to the entire country, that in the future we would produce remarkable scholars, musicians, doctors, teachers, architects, and others, that Leningrad would become a treasurehouse of talent."[152] Around this time, Kuznetsov and Popkov presented to the Kremlin an ambitious reconstruction plan for Leningrad's "renaissance."[153]

On the eve of the purge, not only Beria and Malenkov, but Stalin as well had reason to consider Kuznetsov a worrisome adversary. The party's watchdog over the security organs was young, energetic, and politically well connected. In late 1947 or early 1948, his daughter Alla became engaged to Mikoyan's son Sergo.[154] As the speech from 1946 clearly indicated, Kuznetsov personified the steadfastness and heroism of wartime Leningrad. He had played a more important role in running the city's party organization than Zhdanov, who had been ill during much of the blockade. Moreover, Kuznetsov possessed first-hand information from the siege years that could severely compromise the Kremlin's wartime leaders. He could demonstrate that Leningrad had been inadequately defended prior to the German invasion, that Stalin had blocked his request to assign more cargo planes to fly food into Leningrad and hungry people out of the city in the fall of 1941,[155] and that Stalin had waited too long to support the Ladoga ice road. He might also contend that Stalin had "panicked" in ordering preparations to blow up the city and the Baltic Fleet in September 1941. Kuznetsov could also contrast the looting and panic that seized Moscow for several days in mid-October 1941 with the relative calm that prevailed in Leningrad. (At the same time, the Kremlin may have possessed its own *kompromat* on Kuznetsov from the war years, particularly an allegation that at least one *raion* secretary, Kharitonov, had stolen food at the beginning of the starvation period and a report of a thorough denunciation of Stalin and his policies by Maria Bakshis, who was a member of the special security sector of the *gorkom* and who allegedly expressed her views to a subversive political group but was not arrested.)[156] Kuznetsov could also revive discussion on the explosive topic of the murder of his former boss, Kirov. Using his authority as Central Committee secretary in charge of the secret police, he reportedly accessed top secret documents on the murder and allegedly told Stalin sometime after 1946 that the investigation of Kirov's murder had not revealed those behind the crime.[157] The comment was bound to infuriate Stalin even if he had not orchestrated Kirov's murder, because untold thousands had been purged in the highly publicized hunt for Kirov's killers. The combination of the heroic image of Leningrad seeking to rise proudly and nobly from the ashes of war, of sentiment within the city in favor of continuing the wartime alliance, and the elevation of the city's dynamic and outspoken former first secretary into the secretariat of the Central Committee was impressive and, evidently, perceived as a major threat by his rivals.

The purge commenced with a seemingly harmless event. An all-Russian wholesale trade fair was staged in Leningrad, with the participation of organizations from other union republics, on 10–20 January 1949. Although the central Ministry of Trade had approved the fair beforehand, Malenkov charged while it was in progress that Leningrad's leaders had not received requisite authorization from the USSR Council of Ministers. (Another accusation was that Leningrad's leaders in December 1948 had falsely claimed that a party conference had elected them to their posts by unanimous vote.)[158] Malenkov and Beria may have suggested to Stalin that the trade fair was intended to bolster Leningrad's claim to become an international trade center. The fair took place as the Cold War reached a peak of tension. The Marshall Plan was in effect, the USSR was blockading Berlin, and NATO was being formed. It was an opportune time for Malenkov and Beria to play on Stalin's fears of disloyalty in the USSR's geographically exposed "second capital" by greatly exaggerating and distorting any violation of established rules that may have occurred in organizing the fair. Even the slightest expressed desire for an international role for Leningrad could easily be portrayed as evidence of a foreign plot.

Stalin took a direct interest in the trade fair. He summoned Popkov, Rodionov, and a few others to attend a meeting of the Politburo on 12 February, during which he sharply criticized their actions.[159] Three days later the Politburo issued a secret resolution, which is the most revealing document on the origins of the Leningrad Affair that has so far emerged from the Russian archives: "The Politburo considers that . . . Comrades Kuznetsov A. A., Rodionov, and Popkov have [demonstrated] a sick, un-Bolshevik deviation, which is expressed in demagogic overtures to the Leningrad organization, in unfair criticism of the Central Committee, which allegedly does not help the Leningrad organization, in attempts to present themselves as special defenders of the interests of Leningrad, and in attempts to erect a barrier between the Central Committee and the Leningrad organization, and thereby alienate the Leningrad organization from the Central Committee . . . ." The resolution stated further that Popkov "does not inform the Central Committee about the state of affairs in Leningrad" and sometimes forms "self-seeking (*rvacheskye*) combinations channeled through various self-styled 'patrons' (*shefy*) of Leningrad like Comrades Kuznetsov, Rodionov, and others."[160]

The resolution implicated another primary target of the unfolding purge, Voznesensky, who was the Politburo's youngest member, in addition to being the head of *Gosplan*. Voznesensky had reportedly offended his older colleagues with his arrogance, and it has been suggested that his lack of involvement in the Great Terror made him untrustworthy as a continuer of the Stalinist legacy.[161] The resolution stated that in 1948 Popkov had approached him to act as Leningrad's patron. Although Voznesensky claimed that he had rejected the proposal, he was criticized for not reporting immediately to the Central Committee the "antiparty overture to be Leningrad's 'sponsor'." Such "unparty methods have to be nipped in the bud for they are an expression of antiparty grouping . . ." In an ominous portent, the resolution compared the current case to Zinoviev's antiparty and anti-Leninist scheming. The resolution also removed Rodionov, Kuznetsov, and Popkov from their posts and reprimanded them. One week later Malenkov convened in Leningrad a plenum of the *gorkom* and *obkom* and charged Kuznetsov, Rodionov, Popkov, and Kapustin with belonging to an antiparty group.[162] He stated that the Leningrad leaders had "placed discipline in their group higher than party discipline" and that they had "taken the path of group formation and opposing themselves to the Central Committee."[163]

The resolution shows that Stalin could not abide even the suspicion of a patronage network outside of his control that extended into the Politburo.[164] At this time Stalin was likely informed or reminded of an earlier act of "betrayal" by Voznesensky. In his memoirs, Mikoyan states that during Stalin's ignominious retreat to his dacha and two-day funk at the end of the first week of the German invasion when Minsk was falling, Voznesensky blurted out to Molotov in front of other members of the Politburo (including Malenkov and Beria), "Viacheslav, you lead, and we will follow you," which was interpreted as a call for Molotov to lead the nation if Stalin remained incapacitated much longer. According to Mikoyan, no one endorsed Voznesensky's suggestion.[165]

The international dimension to the developing purge emerged in the summer of 1949 when documents fabricated by MGB head Viktor Abakumov tied Kuznetsov, Rodionov, and Leningrad's party leadership to KR activity. On 21 July, Abakumov informed Stalin that Kapustin was under suspicion of being a British agent, in connection with a trip to England in 1935–36, and that Kubatkin had authorized destruction of the incriminating documents. On Stalin's orders, Kapustin and Kubatkin were arrested. Through "application of illegal means," Kapustin gave testimony that linked the others to criminal activity. On 13 August, Kuznetsov, Popkov, Rodionov, and a couple of others were arrested without a prosecutor's sanction in Malenkov's office in Moscow.[166]

Stalin may also have suspected that the Leningraders had been conspiring against him with the support of the Yugoslav leadership, although relations with Yugoslavia were not raised in the Politburo resolution or in the Party Control Committee's report of 1958. In January 1948, Stalin requested that Yugoslav Politburo member Milovan Djilas come to Moscow to discuss a range of issues. According to Vladimir Dedijer, Djilas and the military delegation that accompanied him sought military assistance from Stalin in connection with the Greek Civil War. Following the negotiations, they dined at Stalin's villa with several Politburo members including Zhdanov and Voznesensky. Becoming impatient while waiting for a response to their request, the Yugoslavs decided to visit Leningrad, where they remained for several days. They were warmly received by Popkov, who turned a villa over to them. An NKVD major remained with them as well. One of the members of the Yugoslav delegation, perhaps Djilas, spoke fondly of Leningrad to a Central Committee member who escorted them: "Somehow, in Leningrad one feels different than in Moscow. It is the atmosphere of the city where the October Revolution started, it is the atmosphere of the city which fought bravely in the last war."[167] Upon returning to Moscow, the delegation continued to wait for a couple more weeks and had yet to receive a response when, on 29 January, *Pravda* issued a statement condemning the idea of a Balkan and East European federation, which had been suggested by Bulgarian Prime Minister Georgi Dimitrov during a trip to Romania. Tito aspired to be the leader of the Balkan nations, and Stalin's conflict with him over this matter and others was developing rapidly. On 4 May, about a month before the rupture became public when the Yugoslav Communist Party was expelled from the Cominform, Stalin wrote to the Yugoslav leadership that Djilas had gleaned information on party and state matters from Leningrad's authorities during his visit. He added that when the Soviets had collected similar information in Yugoslavia, the Yugoslavs had considered them to be spies.[168]

David Brandenberger has revived interest in the origins of the Leningrad Affair by suggesting that an important ideological dispute likely lay at the heart of the matter.[169] Unlike the other union republics, the Russian Republic (RSFSR) did not have its own party organization. Brandenberger contends that discussions regarding the formation of a bureau for the RSFSR within the All-Union Central Committee and, more boldly and significantly, a Russian Communist Party (RKP[b]) alarmed Stalin by raising the specter of a possible confrontation between either body (especially an RKP[b]) and the All-Union Communist Party (VKP[b]). He theorizes that although Soviet political culture had been infused with Russocentrism since the mid-to-late 1930s, calls for new administrative structures for the RSFSR went beyond the bounds of extolling Russian national culture for the purpose of solidifying the USSR through the VKP(b). Stalin understood that creation of a RKP(b) in particular could be dangerously divisive and decided that the idea and its proponents had to be destroyed.

Brandenberger's theory may have merit; however, the evidence for it, especially regarding discussions by Leningrad officials on creating a RKP(b), is fragmentary and not firmly documented. The charge that Leningrad's leaders advocated creation of a RKP(b) has generally been viewed as a fabrication leveled at them during interrogation by their Kremlin opponents. If Kuznetsov, Popkov, and others favored the establishment of a Central Committee bureau for the RSFSR or even a RKP(b), that would fit into the pattern of ways that Leningrad's leaders hoped to raise the city's status and boost their own careers in the postwar USSR, and it is likely that their rivals Malenkov and Beria interpreted reports of such discussion in that way. While the possibility that ideology may have played some role in the matter cannot be discounted, the preponderance of available evidence suggests that the target of the purgers was the rapidly emerging bloc of powerful Leningrad associates themselves more than their purported advocacy of new administrative structures for the RSFSR. If Stalin had been so concerned over a potential Russian challenge to the unity of the VKP(b), it would seem that he would have immediately quashed the idea of creating a Central Committee bureau for the RSFSR when Rodionov proposed it in a letter to him in September 1947, instead of waiting almost a year and a half. Alleged discussions about forming the bureau or an RKP(b) were invariably linked to Zhdanov's protégés, who purportedly proposed that either administrative body would be headquartered in Leningrad, and all of the purge victims had a direct connection to Leningrad or Zhdanov. Shortly after Zhdanov died, thirty-six of his protégés, members of the Leningrad *gorkom* and *obkom* and *sovet* executive committees, were convicted.[170] If the Leningraders were actively supporting the creation of a RKP(b), which Stalin saw as a threat to the cohesion of the VKP(b), they would have been naïve not to enlist support from other party secretaries in other regions of the RSFSR. Further revelations from Russian archives might some day clarify the precise motives behind the Leningrad Affair.

Toward the end of the blockade, in December 1943, the VSLF ordered the establishment of an exhibition about it, which in 1946 became the Museum of the Defense of Leningrad. Its collection of artifacts, letters, diaries, and war trophies, among other things, grew quickly to include many tens of thousands of exhibits that covered at least twenty thousand square meters. It was a national showcase that attracted over 150,000 visitors in its first three months. Around the time of the arrest of the Leningrad leaders, the museum was closed without warning, its materials scattered among other museums, and its director was arrested and sent to a Siberian labor camp, which further suggests that the Leningrad Affair was connected to concealing the city's wartime fate. Some items from the exhibition were lost and others may have been destroyed. The attempt to erase the memory of the blockade spread to the pages of *Pravda*. After 1949 the newspaper, which had devoted one to two pages to the event each year on 27 January, the date of the lifting of the Leningrad blockade, ignored the anniversary.[171] The "renaissance" rebuilding project for Leningrad envisioned right after the war was never implemented. Thus, in the postwar years, the Kremlin sought to squelch the history of the siege, to thwart the desire of those who envisioned Leningrad becoming a world-class trading port so that over the decades it became an increasingly provincial city (until President Putin burnished its image), to stifle its renowned cultural figures, and to eliminate its political leaders. To some extent, the Kremlin succeeded in silencing what the cold, hunger, and enemy bombardment of the blockade had not been able to suppress. At least the writers could regain their reputations, and some of their works were published in the Soviet Union after Stalin's death. A new blockade museum was opened in 1957, but it contained only a small fraction of the contents of the original museum. In 1989 what was left of the original collection was reassembled, and the museum finally reopened. The most prominent victims of the Leningrad Affair were rehabilitated in the mid-1950s and posthumously reinstated in the Communist Party under Gorbachev.[172]

The history of the siege and its aftermath is still being written.

CHAPTER 2

Who Ruled Leningrad?

The process of making major decisions regarding Leningrad was complicated. That Stalin's word was absolute in the wartime USSR is beyond dispute, and almost without exception Stalin had the final say in important matters affecting Leningrad—but sometimes not before those executing policy in Leningrad had sharply differed with the *vozhd'* and his associates in the Kremlin. A great deal of tension also existed within Leningrad's power elite. Party, military, and security organs were all part of the decision-making process, and each of these three branches acquired a stronger or weaker voice depending on the type of crisis facing the city.[1] Each branch was also able to check to some extent the power of the other two.

Smolny and the Kremlin

Zhdanov arrived in Moscow from his vacation retreat on the Black Sea on 24 June 1941, two days after the Germans attacked. Stalin's appointment book shows that he met with Zhdanov in his Kremlin office that evening from 8:55 to 9:30 P.M. Molotov was present for that entire meeting, and several others, including Voroshilov, sat in for part of it.[2] Shortly after the meeting ended, Zhdanov departed for Leningrad. The decision that Zhdanov would be the political leader in charge of Leningrad's defense had been made very quickly and was based on Zhdanov's familiarity with the Soviet forces already deployed in the area. The fact that Zhdanov was also appointed as adviser to the chief of the *Stavka*, which was formed on

23 June, indicates that Zhdanov was not expected to remain in Leningrad indefinitely.[3]

From the moment Germany invaded the USSR, Stalin valued Leningrad for what it could contribute to the war effort. Of primary importance were the weaponry and manpower of the army and the Baltic Fleet, followed by the city's military industries. The well-being of ordinary civilians was his least concern. They became more valuable in his eyes if they could be trained to manufacture munitions, dig trenches, or fire guns. Stalin understood Leningrad's vulnerability from the first days of the war as he was aware, probably more than anyone else, of the poor state of the city's defenses to the southwest. He did not express great confidence in Leningrad's defense and immediately began to relocate several of its factories to the east. On 23 June, Isaak Zaltsman, director of the Kirov plant, and his chief engineer were ordered by the Kremlin to fly immediately to Cheliabinsk in the Urals to explore the possibility of transferring production of the KV tanks to the tractor plant there. After only several hours in Cheliabinsk, they flew on to Moscow, where from 4:20 to 5:05 on the afternoon of 24 June, Zaltsman met with Stalin, Voznesensky, Nikolai Kazakov (who had been director of the Izhorsk works, located outside Leningrad, from 1938 but had assumed the national post of *narkom* of heavy industry on 6 June 1941) and a few others, including Beria, who joined the group toward the end of the session. Stalin reportedly proposed evacuating the Kirov factory and commented: "You'll not be able to work [in Leningrad] anyway once the air raids and shelling begin." Zaltsman, however, opposed relocation and won Stalin over for the time being. This decision resulted in what was Leningrad's first major factory order of the war. On 25 June, Moscow directed Zaltsman to commence mass production of the KV tanks at the Kirov works immediately.[4]

Stalin made the opposite decision regarding production of military aircraft. On 27 June, the Politburo ordered equipment and personnel from six airplane factories in Leningrad and seven in Moscow to be sent eastward. The Leningrad installations (Krasny Lyotchik, Maxim Gorky, Pirometr, Krasny Oktiabr, and two unnamed plants) produced trainers, sea planes, Iliushin-2 fighters, aircraft engines, and gyroscopes, and they were to be sent to Kazan, Ufa, Novosibirsk, and Nizhny Tagil. Most of these evacuation orders were carried out at least in part by the start of the blockade. The fate of one of the factories, No. 380, which had no name, illustrates the juggling of industrial facilities that was taking place at this time. It was converted from railway car to aircraft production in August of 1940, then was shipped from Leningrad to Kaunas in occupied Lithuania the following March. The machinery then returned briefly to Leningrad before being sent on to Nizhny Tagil. It managed to assemble only one Iliushin-2 fighter prior to evacuation to the Urals.[5] In mid-July the Kremlin sent more than five thousand workers from the unit at the Kirov factory that produced diesel aircraft motors to Sverdlovsk, where they were put to work manufacturing tank engines.[6]

In public, Leningrad's leaders expressed no doubt that the city could be defended; however, several of their decisions reveal that substantial doubt existed from the start of the war. The voluntary evacuation of Leningrad's children commenced on 29 June. The main reason for their evacuation was not fear that Leningrad would fall to the enemy but concern over air attacks. The Soviet press had provided some coverage of the blitz of London, and at the start of the war many Leningraders feared that a similar attack on Leningrad might be imminent; the surrounding countryside would be much safer. Most of the children did not go very far; only about fifty thousand were sent beyond the boundaries of the Leningrad *oblast'*. When the blitz did not quickly materialize, and following the German air attack on trains carrying the children, many parents brought their children back to Leningrad.[7]

Secret actions of Leningrad's leaders suggest uncertainty over Leningrad's security. According to information from highly classified materials in the *osobyi* (special) section of the party archives, many city leaders sent their families eastward in the first few weeks of the war. (See below, pp. 285–86.) In addition, the party began secretly to burn documents from its archive on 27 June. Further burning sessions took place on 5 and 7 July and continued during July and August. The destroyed materials do not appear to have been particularly important.[8] A resolution adopted by the *Sovnarkom* and the Central Committee on 5 July "permitted the NKVD of the USSR to evacuate the most important documentary materials of the state archival collection of the USSR located in central state archives in Moscow and Leningrad to the cities of Chkalov and Saratov," while ordering the evacuation to Ufa of the archives of the Central Committee, *Sovnarkom*, and other national bodies.[9] However, it does not appear that archival materials from Leningrad were evacuated this early. Destruction of NKVD materials deemed to be of lesser importance also commenced shortly after 5 July. On 15 July, a commission of eight individuals was established to sort through files of Leningrad factories to determine which of them were not of vital significance and would be destroyed. The reason for destroying state, party, and security documents during the first month of the war seems to have been to pare down their collections to make them easier to move in case they had to be evacuated later on. In the event of an enemy invasion of the city, the holdings of at least the NKVD were to be destroyed on the spot.[10] The situation at the front indeed worsened the following month.

On 11 August, as Army Group North reached the Luga River defense line, *gorkom* secretary Kapustin and others signed a secret order to evacuate the *gorkom* and *obkom* archives and the NKVD's archive to Cheliabinsk within two days.[11]

At the same time that Stalin ordered the first evacuations from Leningrad as a precaution in case the invaders might advance rapidly toward the city, he also sought to impose the strictest security regime possible in that region. On 26 June, he sent a telegram to Zhdanov that ordered the securing of communication routes, the clearing of refugees from designated evacuation routes, arrest of deserters, and "liquidation of saboteurs" in the military rear.[12] In his radio address of 3 July, Stalin described in slightly more detail the security measures that he demanded be imposed at once: "There should be no room in our ranks for whimperers and cowards, for deserters and panic-mongers. Our people should be fearless in their struggle and should selflessly fight our patriotic war of liberation against the Fascist enslavers. . . . A merciless struggle must be undertaken against all deserters and panic-mongers. . . . We must destroy spies, saboteurs, and enemy paratroopers. . . . Military tribunals should immediately try anyone who, through panic or cowardice, is interfering with our defense, regardless of position or rank. . . ."[13] The Presidium of the Supreme Soviet of the USSR and the newly created State Defense Committee (GKO) on 6 July 1941, codified Stalin's speech by decreeing that anyone who "spread in wartime false rumors that excited alarm among the population" would be "immediately isolated and sent to the Military Tribunal."[14]

Leningrad's security forces responded to these directives by arresting anyone who expressed any sort of opposition to the war effort. A top secret report from one of the city's prosecutors named Popov to *gorkom* secretary Kapustin from 22 July summarizes 167 arrestees whose cases had been sent to the city's Military Tribunal of the NKVD, which was the only body that could impose the death penalty. Eighty-five of them were charged with anti-Soviet agitation (article 58-10). This "counterrevolutionary" offense, which consisted of calling for the overthrow or weakening of Soviet authority, generally carried a jail sentence of at least six months. During wartime, under part 2 of the article, the maximum penalty became execution.[15] The second most common charge (thirty-five arrestees) was malicious hooliganism and resistance to governmental authority (articles 74-2 and 73-1), which included drunk and disorderly conduct. The third largest group, numbering fifteen people, was charged with violating blackout regulations, which had been introduced by the second day of the war when the entire European part of the USSR was placed under martial law. The report contains brief descriptions of some of those convicted. A. I. Afanasiev, a fifty-five-year-old baker, was convicted of anti-Soviet agitation and sentenced by the Military Tribunal to "VMN" (the initials for "highest measure of punishment," which was the bureaucratic euphemism for execution by shooting). He had allegedly called upon his co-workers to overthrow communism. A. P. Nikiforov, an unemployed and homeless thirty-nine-year-old, was shot for the same offense. While drunk and "occupied with counterrevolutionary agitation," he had called for the overthrow of Soviet power and the Red Army. V. I. Yartsev, a forty-four-year-old cafeteria cook, received a ten-year sentence for advocating the overthrow of Soviet power and its leaders, while F. A. Nemkov, a thirty-eight-year-old civil defense worker, got eight years for "systematically conducting . . . counterrevolutionary agitation by slanderously describing the situation of workers under Soviet rule." Whether there was a clear distinction in these cases between offenses that resulted in execution as opposed to a long period of incarceration is not evident.

The report also contains a few examples of convictions for non-KR offenses. A. G. Kalnin was sentenced to four years for not masking two windows of his room and turning on a light for an hour, thereby revealing a military evacuation hospital located in the same house. V. V. Afanasiev got a ten-year sentence for refusing to mask his windows and turning on his lights after having been repeatedly warned. G. V. Liubimtsev, a chauffeur, was drunk and had made lewd comments to women passing by. He cursed and punched a policeman in the face who attempted to detain him. He got eight years.[16]

Having misjudged Hitler's intentions, Stalin was extremely busy during the first week of the invasion. His appointment book shows that he had twenty-nine meetings on the first day of the war. He consulted with many advisers and military leaders, generally during the evenings and late at night, up through 28 June, when he seems to have become depressed over the fall of Minsk. He paid a visit to the Defense Commissariat, where he had a heated conversation with the head of the *Stavka*, Semen Timoshenko, and the chief of the army's General Staff (*Genshtab*), Zhukov, who gave him a frank assessment of the situation. As he left his two commanders, he reportedly commented: "Lenin founded our state, and we've fucked it up."[17] There are no entries in his appointment book for 29–30 June, when he went into a mysterious seclusion at his dacha at Kuntsevo outside Moscow. During the afternoon of 30 June, several Politburo members drove out to the dacha and asked him to head an emergency cabinet, the GKO. Stalin returned to the Kremlin around 4 P.M. and officially established the committee. He remained firmly in control of all major decisions throughout the rest of the war.

The other original members of the GKO were Foreign Commissar Molotov, Politburo member Malenkov, Marshal Voroshilov, and Commissar of Internal Affairs Beria.[18] The GKO coordinated all aspects of the war effort. It assumed control over "the appointment and replacement of higher-ranking military commanders; the preparation of reserves for the army in the field; the solution of important military-strategic questions; the adjustment of the work of industry, transport, and agriculture to the conditions of wartime; the supply of the population and the army with produce; the procurement of fuel, the preparation of labor reserves and the allocation of labor among the various industrial units; and the battle against enemy spies."[19] The GKO was superimposed upon party, military, and commissariat and *sovet* structures and often bypassed their chains of command in order to promote flexible decision making and centralized control.[20] On 1 July, Zhdanov established at party headquarters at Smolny his own Commission for Questions of Defense, which included, besides himself as chairman, Kuznetsov, second secretary of the *obkom* Terenty Shtykov, chairman of the *gorispolkom* Popkov, and chairman of the *oblispolkom* N. V. Solovyov. The commission, or the "Big Five" as it was often called, was Leningrad's version of the GKO. It mobilized human and material resources for the war in and around Leningrad and issued declarations in the names of the party committees and *sovety* represented by its members. The commission reported directly to the GKO.

By 9 July, Army Group North had captured Pskov, and only the Luga Line remained between it and Leningrad. On 10 July, the GKO created the Northwestern, Western, and Southwestern Directions. Voroshilov was named commander of the Northwestern Direction, which comprised the Northern and Northwestern Fronts and the Baltic and Northern Fleets. He arrived in Leningrad from Moscow the following day and was charged with setting up defenses between the city and the Luga Line. Hundreds of thousands of Leningrad civilians, the majority of whom were women, were quickly and desperately mobilized in July and early August to assist the army in fortifying the region. On 13 July, when the GKO adopted the policy of assigning commissars to all military commands, Zhdanov was appointed commissar of the Northwestern Direction.

On 9 July, Leeb's Army Group North continued its advance toward Leningrad. Hitler and the German High Command saw no reason to augment Leeb's armies as they believed that he would make further steady progress and capture Leningrad within several weeks. (At the end of July, Hitler opted for encirclement of the city.) By the first week in August, Army Group North had reached the Luga Line. In response, on 25 July, the command of the Northwestern Direction created a Special Defense Works Commission under A. A. Kuznetsov, which combined army units and the civilian labor conscripts from Leningrad, and ordered it to construct three defense zones between the city and the Luga Line. According to Dmitry Pavlov, who was GKO representative in charge of food supply to Leningrad from 8 September, "Stalin more than once gave Kuznetsov direct instructions on building the fortified belts and preparing the population for the defense of the city."[21] However, as military historian David Glantz explains: "Even the new construction effort was inadequate, primarily because Voroshilov objected to building defenses so close to the city and instead insisted that defensive work be concentrated on the Luga line. Dissatisfied with the defensive effort, on 30 July Stalin summoned Voroshilov and Zhdanov to Moscow, where he sharply criticized them for their 'lack of toughness' in conducting operations in the Northwestern Theater."[22]

On 8 August, Hitler gave top priority to the northern region by shifting large armored forces and an air corps to Army Group North with the hope that it would quickly smash through the Luga defenses, encircle Leningrad, and link up with the Finns who were advancing southward through the Karelian Isthmus and along the eastern coast of Lake Ladoga. In mid-August a Soviet counteroffensive failed to halt the German advance. On 16 August, German infantry troops took the western part of Novgorod, seized the city of Kingisepp east of Narva, and forced five divisions of the Soviet Eighth Army to retreat. By 20 August, German troops had taken the city of Chudovo and severed the rail line that ran from Leningrad to Moscow. They had also reached Soviet defense fortifications near Krasnogvardeisk (formerly Gatchina), only twenty-five miles south of Leningrad, and the Finnish army had advanced to within eighteen miles of the city on the Karelian Isthmus.[23]

Within Leningrad itself, the GKO's main priorities during July and the first three weeks of August were to evacuate more defense plants to the Urals and destinations farther east and to convert many of those that remained in the city to producing war materials. On 11 July, the GKO ordered the evacuation of eighty Leningrad factories and a large portion of their work force. By 11 August, however, workshops from only six large defense plants, and relatively few workers, had been sent away. Most of the nearly half a million people who were recorded as having left the city between 11 July and 11 August were children and nonworking adults who had evacuated voluntarily, as well as refugees who had poured into Leningrad after the start of the war.[24] The failure of Leningrad's leaders until 21 August to publicize the danger that faced the city may have stemmed from a false sense of optimism[25] and/or from a fear of inciting panic. Reluctance to reveal the threat suppressed people's desire to leave the city.

On 20 August, Voroshilov and Zhdanov briefed the city's party *aktiv* on the dire situation along the front. They also secretly created the Leningrad Military Defense Council and signed a decree that called for the creation of a total of 150 detachments of 600 workers each, and the combining of detachments into worker battalions, to defend Leningrad. Formation of worker detachments had begun on 13 July, and the *gorkom* had ordered every factory to assemble its own detachment, conduct military drill, and fortify factory premises.[26] This mobilization effort, however, had not made much headway prior to 22 August. The new Defense Council would supervise and accelerate the work of the detachments. The decree specifically called for including women in them. Youths were to be organized in the detachments as well, but not to serve in direct combat roles. Instead, they were to conduct reconnaissance, relay messages, and carry food and water. Factory directors were to be appointed detachment commanders, and district party committee secretaries were to become political commissars. Arms would be distributed to the detachments, and those who did not receive military rifles would be supplied with hunting guns, grenades, pikes, sabers, daggers, and/or bottles with flammable liquid. City workers, together with Army, Navy, and NKVD units, were to defend Leningrad street by street if necessary. Starting the next day, all worker military formations went on round-the-clock alert and were not allowed to leave factory grounds.[27]

On 21 August, *Leningradskaia pravda* carried a dramatic appeal from Voroshilov, Zhdanov, and Popkov addressed to "Comrades, Leningraders, dear friends," a salutation similar to the intimate one used by Stalin in his 3 July radio address. Leningrad's leaders stated that "The direct threat of attack of German-fascist troops hangs over our native (*rodnoi*) and beloved city. The enemy is trying to break through to Leningrad." The appeal, which was also read over the radio and plastered along the streets, promised eventual victory but only after much sacrifice: "We will be steadfast to the end! Not sparing lives, we will fight the enemy, we will smash and destroy him. . . . Victory will be ours!"[28]

Stalin could have had few illusions concerning the capabilities of Voroshilov and Zhdanov by this time. In May of 1940, Stalin had removed Voroshilov from the post of defense commissar, which he had held for six years, following his poor performance in the war with Finland. Moreover, reports that Voroshilov lacked confidence in Leningrad's defense had probably made their way to Stalin. On 16 August, the head of government security of the Leningrad NKVD Antonov notified Kuznetsov that a technician named E. A. Fisak who worked at Smolny had said that on 26 or 27 July an electrician by the name of Petrov had asserted that Voroshilov had told an assembly of the party *aktiv* that Leningrad might have to be abandoned because of the cowardice and desertions of front-line troops. Petrov reportedly added that Voroshilov had said that Soviet commanders were guilty of treason.[29] What Kuznetsov did with this hearsay information is not known, but since he was the conduit between the Leningrad *gor-kom* and NKVD central and its chief Beria, this particular report of Voroshilov's alleged comments may have been sent to the Kremlin.

The Kremlin was deeply troubled over the creation of the Leningrad Military Defense Council and the decree on the organization of Leningrad's internal defenses of 20 August. At 1:20 A.M. on 22 August, Stalin, Molotov, Mikoyan, and unnamed others sent an urgent cable to Leningrad's leaders in Smolny that sharply criticized the latter's actions.[30] Portions of the remarkable exchange of messages that ensued have been described briefly by historians many times since the matter was first revealed in 1958 by Dmitry Pavlov, who had been the GKO representative in charge of food supply to Leningrad from September 1941 through the end of January 1942.[31] However, Document 1 represents the first time that the entire transcript of the cables has been published.[32] The topics discussed in the seven messages were considered to be extraordinarily sensitive during the Soviet era. For thirty years up to the Gorbachev glasnost era, Soviet historians merely paraphrased the one paragraph of description from Pavlov.

There can be no mistake that Stalin dictated the transmissions on the Kremlin's end, while Pavlov believed that Voroshilov took the lead in Smolny. The second Kremlin message lapses into use of the first-person pronoun three times, which suggests that that person was in charge of the others. That could only have been Stalin. The time that the exchanges occurred was during the portion of the day when Stalin typically presided over meetings and contacted his subordinates in other cities. The choice of words and the overall tone are unmistakably Stalin's. In the initial salutation, he mysteriously referred to "others" being present in the Kremlin. In the second message he was deliberately vague in stating ominously that Moscow knew about the Krasnogvardeisk fortified zone from "other sources," and added that Moscow had learned of Leningrad's "plans and initiatives . . . by accident." Undoubtedly, one of the "others" present with Stalin was Beria, and the "other sources" and the "accident" were references to the security organs. The paternalistic and berating tone of the Kremlin's second message ("You simply are not organized men and do not feel responsibility for your actions, in view of which you are acting as if you were on a desert island") and the beginning of its third exchange ("There is no need to pretend to be naïve") could only have come from the *vozhd'*. Moreover, the professed rejection of the role of *batiushka*, or "little father" ("You are not children and well know that you do not need forgiveness") cleverly served to let the Leningraders know that in fact he clearly viewed them as subordinates.

The standard interpretation of the controversy over formation of the Leningrad Military Defense Council, which derived from Pavlov's initial description of it and was repeated by Goure and Salisbury, is sympathetic to Zhdanov's and Voroshilov's stated intention to form a body that would function as "a purely auxiliary organ for Leningrad's overall military defense" but would not be led by them as they would remain "in charge of the entire defense as a whole."[33] This version contends that by insisting that Voroshilov and Zhdanov join the new council, Stalin essentially undermined it, because Voroshilov and Zhdanov could not both retain general strategic control over the Leningrad region and simultaneously plan in detail the city's internal defenses. A careful reading of the messages, however, shows that the two parties were communicating at cross purposes. Stalin was more concerned with appearances than organizational efficiency. He had a justified concern that if news leaked to the public that the new council did not include the city's top military and political leaders who had signed the dramatic public appeal of 21 August, "the workers" would conclude that Voroshilov and Zhdanov did not believe that Leningrad could be defended and might have fled the city or even gone over to the enemy. Stalin's accusation that the Leningraders had no authority to create the council in the first place and that they might "think up something similar again" suggests strongly that he did not trust their motives. Stalin might have been receptive to Voroshilov and Zhdanov serving on the council in a symbolic capacity. It wasn't the input of their expertise that he valued most of all; indeed, by that time Stalin was losing confidence in their leadership abilities. He knew that Kuznetsov, not Zhdanov, had been in charge of defense fortification work between Leningrad and the Luga Line since the end of July, and he had summoned Voroshilov and Zhdanov to Moscow to criticize their poor performance. However, no one proposed finessing a solution to the proposed new council by including Voroshilov and Zhdanov in it as essentially figureheads. Stalin's will prevailed. On 24 August, when the resolution on the creation of the Leningrad Military Defense Council was published, it listed Voroshilov and Zhdanov as its first two members. Six days later, however, the council was disbanded, because its function nearly duplicated that of the new Military Council of the Leningrad Front (VSLF), which *Stavka* created on 23 August when it divided the Northern Front into the Karelian and Leningrad Fronts. In a broader sense, the disagreement over whether a separate but subordinate defense council should exist for the city was decided by the rapid development of events as Army Group North continued its advance and imposed the blockade on 8 September. Defending Leningrad proper could no longer be considered an "auxiliary" function when German troops were located only three miles south of the city. The city, its suburbs, and the Kronstadt naval base were all that remained to defend.

Another topic discussed in the messages, which arguably was more sig-

nificant, was the formation of worker detachments and battalions. Creation of military units from the ranks of workers was a logical proposal,
since a large percentage of Leningrad's population was factory workers,
and Leningrad's southern districts, where fighting would take place if
Germany attempted to seize the city, contained many of the city's largest
defense plants, including the massive Kirov factory. In his first message
Stalin objected to the election of the battalions' commanders. Voroshilov
and Zhdanov ignored the matter in their reply, as Stalin pointed out to
them in his second message. In their second reply, the Leningrad leaders
made a startling frank admission when they asserted that although they
had "proceeded in the question of elections incorrectly," their "sad experience" had been that when commanders of the *opolchenie* and regular army
"ran away," the remaining soldiers had elected their own commanders. In
a sentence infused with democratic sentiment, they added that election
of leaders would enhance camaraderie within worker detachments. Their
explanation prompted a sharp and categorical rebuke from Stalin. He insisted that "absolute commanders" were needed, not ones who would be
subject to the whims of voters. What was worse in Stalin's view was the
inevitable pernicious ripple effect: election of worker battalion commanders "will immediately spread to the whole army, like a contagion." It is difficult to imagine that at that moment Stalin did not have in mind the effect
that the Petrograd Soviet's "Order Number One" had had on the Russian
Army in 1917. The election of soldiers' committees that represented their
interests to the officer corps had helped accelerate disintegration within
the army, which had played a crucial role in the Bolsheviks' overthrow
of the Provisional Government. Stalin likely also recalled how Kerensky's
government had been seriously weakened when he distributed weapons to
paramilitary groups of workers in Petrograd in response to the threatened
Kornilov putsch in the late summer of 1917. Those workers had organized
themselves as militia detachments and come largely under Bolshevik control. Stalin had no desire to replay history in the role of the toppled Kerensky.

The goal of filling detachments and battalions with 90,000 workers was
probably not attained. By 28 August, 36,658 workers were officially registered in some seventy battalions. These workers were mainly those who
were exempt from the regular armed forces, the *opolchenie,* and defense
fortification work. Women, teenagers, pensioners, and workers in poor
health made up a large portion of the battalion ranks.[34]

The largest and best organized battalions were located on the premises of large defense plants along the city's southern boundary. The Kirov
factory assembled the largest battalion with 6,500 workers, the battalion
from the Lenin factory had 1,500 workers, and the one at the Bolshevik
plant somewhere between 580 and 1,200.[35]

The Kremlin-Smolny exchange of 22 August does not reveal that Stalin opposed handing out arms to workers; however, he wanted the civilian units to be firmly under the control of the NKVD. On 10 September, Voroshilov and Zhdanov issued a top secret order for the distribution of five hundred carbines to the "party, *sovet*, and economic *aktiv*."[36] This would appear to be the first distribution of firearms to the civilian population. Published Soviet accounts support the view that workers received arms for the first time only in mid-September when the threat of direct German attack on the city was greatest.[37] On 16 September, *Leningradskaia pravda* published an appeal for youths to take up arms ("K oruzhiiu, molodezh' goroda Lenina!") and for the creation of "fighting detachments of *rabochie* and *sluzhashchie* for defense of enterprises, streets, and apartments against the enemy." Up to that time, workers had access to weapons only at training sessions. Aside from the five hundred carbines, it is not clear what kinds of weapons workers were given. One source states that in addition to a limited number of rifles (probably the carbines) and machine guns, workers received some ten thousand shotguns and twelve thousand small-caliber and training rifles and bottles with flammable liquid and grenades for use against tanks.[38]

Another noteworthy aspect of these 22 August telegrams is the lack of communication between Leningrad and Moscow over an important fortified area, which is indicative of the high degree of uncertainty, confusion, and fear that existed in the top levels of the Soviet decision-making apparatus at this critical time. Stalin and *Stavka*, despite their "other" sources, appeared to be unaware of the latest developments around Krasnogvardeisk. Smolny apologized for not "inform[ing] you in a timely fashion about all the work that has been done over the last month" and then went on to admit that the "fortified area designated to shield Leningrad is inadequately equipped with armed military power." In its third message Smolny was forced to acknowledge that although "the main line of the Krasnogvardeisk fortified region has not been breached anywhere," the enemy has "wedged his way in at Predpol'e." They could not guarantee that Soviet forces could retake that settlement or defend the fortified area as a whole. The weakening of the Krasnogvardeisk fortified area, coming on the heels of the loss of Kingisepp and Novgorod, appears to have been what prompted Zhdanov and Voroshilov to form the Leningrad Military Defense Council.

Finally, the first two responses from Smolny show that Voroshilov and Zhdanov were willing to disagree with Stalin up to a point, despite their overall weak position and the fact that several generals from the overrun Western Front had been executed on Stalin's orders in late July for their alleged failures. Twice Voroshilov and Zhdanov defended their creation of the Leningrad Military Defense Council without including themselves

as members. They agreed to join the council only when Stalin unequivocally ordered them to do so. On the question of election of officers in the
workers' battalions, Voroshilov and Zhdanov responded to Stalin's assessment that elections were "wrong organizationally and harmful politically [and] must be corrected" first by ignoring it and then by defending
their original decision. Again, they caved in only when Stalin gave a direct
order to "rescind the election principle." Stalin eventually got his way on
all points but only after an extended argument.

· Document 1 ·

Reports sent between Smolny and the Kremlin, 22 August 1941, RGASPI f. 77,
op. 3, d. 126, ll. 98–104.

———————

[KREMLIN]

22 August 1941, 1:20

    Coms. VOROSHILOV, ZHDANOV, KUZNETSOV, AND POPOV AT THE
APPARATUS.

    Greetings! STALIN, MOLOTOV, MIKOYAN, and others here.

    1. You have created the LENINGRAD Military Defense Council. You have to
understand that a Military Council can be created only by the government or
by Headquarters at its instruction. We request once more that you not permit
this violation.

    2. Neither VOROSHILOV nor ZHDANOV has joined the LENINGRAD Mili-
tary Defense Council. This is wrong and even harmful politically. The workers
will think that ZHDANOV and VOROSHILOV do not believe in LENINGRAD's
defense, that they have washed their hands of it and handed the defense over
to others below them. This matter must be rectified.

    3. In your order on the creation of the Military Defense Council you pro-
pose choosing battalion commanders by election. This is wrong organizationally and harmful politically. This too must be corrected.

    4. According to your order on the creation of the Military Defense Coun-
cil, it comes out that LENINGRAD's defense is limited to the creation of worker
battalions armed more or less poorly without special artillery defense. Such a
defense cannot be considered satisfactory, if one bears in mind the fact that the
Germans have artillery. We think that LENINGRAD's defense must be an artillery defense above all. You need to occupy all points of elevation in the area of
PULKOVO and in other areas and to establish there a serious artillery defense,
by which we mean naval cannon of 100 and 130 mm, six-inchers, and so forth.

    LENINGRAD, as you know, is an artillery district. If there is not enough
army artillery, we could remove the artillery from ships and mount them all
around LENINGRAD. We could put the *Kronstadt* and coastal artillery in mo-
tion. On the basis of this kind of artillery defense, the worker battalions could

play a major role. Without this kind of base, the worker battalions will be slaughtered. It may be that your plan of defense, if you have one, takes artillery defense into account, but the government and Headquarters know nothing about this. We are demanding that VOROSHILOV and ZHDANOV inform us without fail about their plans for operations. They are not doing this, unfortunately, they have decided not to proceed by the book and are making mistakes that reflect on the quality of LENINGRAD's defense.

That is all. Since that is all we have, respond.

[SMOLNY]

From everything said above, we see that a great misunderstanding has come about due to our own fault.

1. The creation of the LENINGRAD Military Defense Council does not to any degree exclude, but merely supplements, the overall organization of the defense of the city of LENINGRAD.

2. Both VOROSHILOV and ZHDANOV are responsible, above all, for the entire defense of LENINGRAD.

3. We understood the LENINGRAD Military Defense Council as a purely auxiliary organ for LENINGRAD's overall military defense.

4. We thought it would be easier to create a solid defense for LENINGRAD with a special organization for the worker community—military detachments.

5. LENINGRAD has a special fortified zone which begins at the Gulf of KAPORSK and continues southerly of KRASNOGVARDEISK and another that joins up with the NEVA, with an overall length of about 130–140 km. On this border, in addition to field fortification, long-term defensive points have been created, numbering 178. In all for artillery, 379 weapons of various calibers have been placed in this fortified strip. Placed in this area in addition are 48 antiaircraft cannon, which will be firing both in the air and against tanks. In addition, the system of this fortified district includes the shore batteries of the Baltic Fleet, as well as warships, including battleships, which together give us an additional 89 weapons of various caliber, including 16-inch ones.

We beg forgiveness that as a result of the great overload of work and our failure to think the matter through we did not inform you in a timely fashion about all the work that has been done over the last month.

6. We consider it our duty to inform you that the indicated fortified area designated to shield LENINGRAD is inadequately equipped with armed military power. Despite an excellent supply of artillery, the KRASNOGVARDEISK, UR [fortified area] is poorly equipped with automatic machine gun firepower. At the given moment, the UR includes just three divisions, of which only one is of the standard new formation, No. 291. Another is a division created from LENINGRAD workers and is almost entirely untrained. On the 19th, we were forced to place a third worker division in the UR, only half armed with rifles. In addition, the UR has 14 infantry machine gun battalions, of which not one is fully armed with machine guns, and 25–50 percent have rifles.

7. We urgently request to be given at least a couple of good infantry divisions and the necessary quantity of machine guns and rifles for the UR. We are not speaking now of the needs for arms or of the replenishment of field troops. That is all.

[KREMLIN]

We know about the existence of the fortified zone, not from you, of course, but from other sources. We are learning about the makeup of the forces of this fortified zone for the first time, although even now you seem not to have given us a complete picture. This fortified zone, however, seems to have been breached already in the area of KRASNOGVARDEISK and it is precisely for this reason that Headquarters is posing the question of LENINGRAD's defense so urgently. Therefore, I am talking not about the fortified zone but about the creation of another additional zone of defense for LENINGRAD. Inasmuch as the main zone has not proven to be very reliable, it has seemed to me that you would pose the question of another additional, narrower zone of defense, and it is in this connection that the question arose about the creation of the Military Defense Council.

With respect to the questions I have raised, you have not answered one of them plainly. You have created a Military Defense Council without having the right to do so. Military Councils are created only by the government or Headquarters. We have no guarantee that you won't think up something similar again that does not fit within the framework of normal relations.

You have introduced the principle of elections to worker battalions. We cannot reconcile ourselves to this, and you did not even answer this question. You yourselves, ZHDANOV and VOROSHILOV, have not joined the Military War Council. We consider this a grave political error, and you didn't even answer this question. We never knew of your plans and initiatives. We are always learning by accident that you have contemplated something, or planned something, and then a breach has resulted. We cannot reconcile ourselves to this. You are not children and well know that you do not need forgiveness.

Your reference to an overload is ridiculous. We are no less overloaded. You simply are not organized men and do not feel responsibility for your actions, in view of which you are acting as if you were on a desert island and not reckoning with anyone.

Regarding your demands for assistance with divisions and arms, report about them more clearly so that we can understand which plans you need new divisions and equipment to carry out. That is all.

[SMOLNY]

First—In organizing the LENINGRAD Military Defense Council, as an auxiliary organ of military defense, we not only were not thinking of violating the generally established order or laws, but in general we had no idea that this could serve as a cause for the kinds of conclusions which we have just heard.

This decision of ours has not been published anywhere, and it was issued as a top secret order.

Second—We may have proceeded in the question of elections incorrectly; however, on the basis of the sad experience of our era, when not only in the worker divisions but also in individual instances in the regular divisions, after the commanders ran away, the fighters elected their own commanders. We felt that the worker battalions, which are improvised formations, would be more tightly bonded around their commanders if their commanders were not only appointed but also elected by them themselves from among their own.

Third—VOROSHILOV and ZHDANOV, although we have already reported this, have not joined the LENINGRAD Defense Committee solely because we thought that they were both in charge of the entire defense as a whole.

Fourth—With respect to your concern that we might think up something else of the kind that does not fit within the framework of regular relations, then we, VOROSHILOV and ZHDANOV, do not entirely understand what we are being reproached for, what we have done that could merit such a harsh accusation.

That is all.

[KREMLIN]

There is no need to pretend to be naïve. Read the tape and you will understand what you are being accused of. Immediately rescind the election principle, for it could destroy the entire army. An elected commander is a mark of anarchy,[39] for in the event of pressure on the voters another will be elected in an instant. Whereas we, as you know, need absolute commanders. No sooner is the election principle introduced for worker battalions than it will immediately spread to the whole army, like a contagion.

ZHDANOV and VOROSHILOV must join the LENINGRAD Military Defense Council. LENINGRAD is not CHEREPOVETS or VOLOGDA; it is our country's second capital. The LENINGRAD Military Defense Council is not an auxiliary organ but the guiding organ of LENINGRAD's defense.

Present a specific plan for LENINGRAD's defense. Will you create a line apart from the main fortified line, a narrower fortified line? If so, then how?

Can you confirm that the main fortified line has indeed been breached by the enemy in the area of KRASNOGVARDEISK?

Today, convey your specific requests for the help you need from MOSCOW in men and arms. At the same time, the requests must be not bare demands but substantiated, sufficiently explained, and tied to a plan of defense.

That is all.

[SMOLNY]

1. The election principle will be rescinded.
2. VOROSHILOV and ZHDANOV will join the LENINGRAD Defense Council.
3. A second, narrower zone of defense has not yet been but is being created.

4. The main line of the KRASNOGVARDEISK UR has not been breached anywhere by anyone, in two places the enemy has small groups of tanks and motorized infantry. Two days ago he wedged his way in at PREDPOL'E, which, unfortunately, had not been occupied by anyone. We think that we will be able to eliminate him here.

5. We will send you not naked but substantiated requests additionally and without delay.

That is all.

[KREMLIN]

We may divide the Northern Front into two parts, the KARELIAN part, from LADOGA to MURMANSK, with its own front command, and a southern part, the LENINGRAD part, actually, which should be called the LENINGRAD Front.

Our motives are well known. Since the Finns occupied the northern shores of Ladoga, it has become impossible to administer the northern part of the Northern Front from Leningrad.

Discuss this issue, and make up your mind.

That is all.

During wartime and other national emergencies, all governments from the most authoritarian to the most democratic acquire greater decision-making power in order to confront crises as quickly and effectively as possible. One advantage that the Soviet government had on the eve of the German invasion was that it already had a centralized and militarized command structure that could rapidly mobilize enormous quantities of natural and manufactured resources and many millions of people. At the same time, the main Soviet weakness in fighting a total war was that its decision-making process was *overly* centralized. There was no formal check on Stalin's power, and when he blundered, as he did in spectacular fashion on the eve of the war and repeatedly during its first year, no one in the Kremlin hierarchy (with the possible exceptions on occasion of Zhukov and Marshal Boris Shaposhnikov, who succeeded Zhukov as head of the *Genshtab* in early July 1941) could restrain or alter his will. Stalin's miscalculations were an important part of the reason that Germany managed to penetrate so deeply into Soviet territory. In addition, the system loathed spontaneous and creative initiative and resisted delegation of authority. If Stalin and the GKO were all-powerful and quick decision makers, they were also ineffectual micromanagers, or more properly, microcontrollers. A minor, but revealing, example of Stalinist control of minutiae occurred on the same day that the dramatic exchange of cables between Smolny and the Kremlin took place. Stalin sent a separate telegram on 22 August to Zhdanov and the rest of the Leningrad *obkom* containing instructions on curtailing publication of newspapers. Daily papers were henceforth to be published only three times per week.[40] No doubt someone other than

Stalin had drafted this message, copies of which were sent to many parts of the nation, but Stalin still had to take the time to approve it. Prior to the start of the war, the print matrixes for each issue of several central newspapers, including dailies, were flown to Leningrad. This practice continued throughout the blockade period for *Pravda, Izvestia,* and *Komsomolskaia pravda,* except during the first week of the war and for a short period in January 1942.[41] Considerable resources were devoted to maintaining centralized control over dissemination of information. Microcontrol was not only wasteful but also counterproductive. As noted above, a popular criticism of the Soviet mass media in general during the war was that reporting from the front, especially during the first year, was lacking in detailed and reliable information. As a result, all kinds of rumors circulated, and the ill-informed public tended to make poor decisions. As the war continued, the Soviet leadership was forced to encourage spontaneity and the establishment of self-help programs in those areas that it could no longer control. This was one of the important keys to the eventual Soviet victory.

For a month following the Kremlin-Smolny exchange of cables, the crisis deepened for Leningrad. Hitler made it a top priority to surround the city in alliance with Finland, preferably in a close encirclement to the west of Lake Ladoga, and then to bombard and starve Leningrad into submission. The Germans never achieved complete encirclement of the city; however, on 8 September, when they captured Shlisselburg, Leningrad no longer had land access to the rest of the USSR. Its only surface link was across Ladoga. Soviet efforts to defend Leningrad during this time became increasingly desperate, and tensions between Smolny and the Kremlin correspondingly escalated. In the middle of September, when the prospect of a German ground assault on Leningrad appeared greatest, Stalin's priorities regarding what was worth preserving in Leningrad came into sharp focus.

The actions by Voroshilov and Zhdanov during 20–22 August convinced Stalin that Leningrad might be on the brink of collapse. He immediately dispatched a large GKO mission, consisting of Malenkov, Molotov, air commander in chief Pavel Zhigarev, chief of artillery of the Red Army and deputy commissar of defense Marshal Nikolai Voronov, and commissar of the Soviet fleet Admiral Nikolai Kuznetsov to Leningrad to plan its defenses. GKO representative and deputy chairman of *Sovnarkom* Aleksei Kosygin had been in the city since July. On 26 August, Stalin signed a GKO mandate empowering by name the six members of the commission to "examine and decide, jointly with the Military Council of the Main Command of the Northwestern Direction [which would be abolished three days later] and with the Military Council of the Leningrad Front, all questions of the defense of Leningrad and evacuation of industries and the population of Leningrad."[42] In this way, Moscow gained direct control over all important decisions made in Leningrad, at least for the time being. The wording of the mandate discloses Stalin's priorities in Leningrad. The fate of civilians was his lowest priority. The delegation remained in the city for about one week. One of its first actions was to enhance Moscow's control over security in Leningrad by installing Pyotr Kubatkin, who had headed the NKVD for the Moscow *oblast'*, as Leningrad's new NKVD chief on 24 August (Figure 3).[43]

Stalin's frustration increased during the last week of August, as the situation grew steadily worse. His actions became more desperate. He made several sweeping and at times inconsistent decisions regarding personnel and policy, none of which prevented the enemy from laying siege to Leningrad. As noted above, on 23 August he created the Leningrad Front out of the remnants of the Northern Front. Lieutenant General Markian Popov, who had commanded the Northern Front, was selected to be Leningrad Front's commander, but he would serve in that capacity for only a week. On 28 August, the same time that Soviet naval vessels abandoned Tallinn for Kronstadt and *Leningradskaia pravda*'s main headline screamed, "Fight for Leningrad to the Last Drop of Blood!" Stalin and Shaposhnikov sent Popov an angry reprimand of three paragraphs. The first few lines accused him of using "blackmail" techniques by scaring the central military command with accounts of enemy breakthroughs and other horrors. "Of course, if you will not do anything about this by making demands of your subordinates, but will only be a supernumerary (*statist*) who conveys complaints to the army, in several days you will then have to surrender Leningrad . . ." The message concluded with a sharp scolding: "Headquarters demands that you finally quit being a supernumerary and specialist in retreat and assume your proper role of commander who inspires the army and raises the spirit of the troops."[44]

The twenty-ninth of August was an eventful day. Having carried out their investigations, GKO members Molotov, Malenkov, and Kosygin, together with Zhdanov, sent three separate telegrams to Stalin at 10 A.M. containing their recommendations on evacuating people and machinery and on food rationing. Three of those cables are presented below as Documents 2, 3, and 4. (Another cable, Document 34, sent on 28 August, which dealt with the planned forced relocation of ethnic Finns and Germans, is discussed in Chapter 3.) The recommendations assumed that a rail link with the rest of the nation would remain open for at least another ten days. In fact, shortly after the messages were sent, the last line was severed. Two trains carrying evacuees left Leningrad early in the morning of 29 August. They managed to slip through the Mga rail station, twenty-five miles southeast of Leningrad, even though the station had already been hit by German bombers. At 2 P.M., however, German bombers cut this last line out of Leningrad, which ran through Mga eastward toward Volkhov.[45] No train would enter or leave Leningrad from outside the region until February 1943. On 11 August the GKO had accelerated the evacuation. It ordered some 400,000 mothers and children to leave the city. A few days later as the situation at the front deteriorated further, the executive committee of the city *sovet* considered it necessary to raise that number by another 700,000.[46] By 29 August, a recorded total of 636,203 people (including 147,500 refugees who had fled into Leningrad from the southwest) of a prewar population of around 3.2 million had left the city since the start of the war. About a quarter of those who left did so after 11 August. The hurried calculations and plans of the GKO team were to no avail. Some 216,000 Leningraders who had been slated for evacuation by the city's district *sovety* were left stranded on 29 August.[47] Many of them and several hundred thousand others would have to remain in Leningrad until at least the latter part of the coming winter when the Ladoga ice road was established, if they could survive that long.

· Document 2 ·

Report from Molotov, Malenkov, Kosygin, and Zhdanov to Stalin on ten-day evacuation plan for Leningrad civilians, 29 August 1941, *Izvestiia TsK KPSS*, 1990, No. 9, 211–12.

Top secret
Transmitted over high frequency on 29 August at 10:00 A.M.

MOSCOW

To Com. STALIN
Copy to Com. SHVERNIK[48]
We report that we have approved decisions to evacuate from Leningrad, over the 10-day period from 30 August to 8 September, 250,000 women and children and 66,000 men from the front line zone, based on an average daily supply of 790 train cars.

MOLOTOV
MALENKOV
KOSYGIN
ZHDANOV

· Document 3 ·

Report from Molotov, Malenkov, Kosygin, and Zhdanov to Stalin on ten-day evacuation plan for industrial workers and equipment, 29 August 1941, *Izvestiia TsK KPSS*, 1990, No. 9, 211.

Top secret
Transmitted over high frequency on 29 August at 10:00

MOSCOW

To Com. STALIN

Copy to Com. SHVERNIK

We report that we have approved a 10-day evacuation plan for several of Leningrad's most important enterprises.

The plan has been drawn up in accordance with the decision previously approved by the Defense Committee on the evacuation of Leningrad enterprises.

In all, 12,313 train cars have been scheduled for the removal of equipment and workers.

MOLOTOV

MALENKOV

KOSYGIN

ZHDANOV

By this time, a recorded 59,280 freight cars of industrial machinery and equipment had already been evacuated; however, by 15 September, almost three weeks after the last train had left the city, 2,177 freight cars loaded with industrial goods were left standing in city rail yards. Some of the materials stayed there a long time. For example, machines from the Elektrosila plant remained crated at one station until March 1943. P. I. Senichev, director of part of the Zhdanov shipyards located on the grounds of the Kirov factory, recalled in September 1943 the confusion that surrounded the industrial evacuation in the summer of 1941: "The evacuation proceeded rather haphazardly and with anxiety. An order would come to evacuate such and such machinery and then it would be canceled. Because of the anxiety . . . at this time part of our machinery is in Tashkent, other parts in the Urals, and so forth."[49]

Document 4 shows how low food reserves were in Leningrad prior to the start of the blockade. The political leadership made several blunders over the summer that would prove tragic later on. At the start of the German invasion, livestock from Soviet-occupied Estonia and Latvia as well as from the Leningrad *oblast'* was evacuated temporarily to Leningrad[50] but was reevacuated farther east later in the summer. According to Mikoyan, at the very start of the war many trainloads of food destined for western parts of the USSR had to be diverted elsewhere. He wanted to send them to Leningrad, but Zhdanov convinced Stalin that all of the warehouses in the city were full. Mikoyan claimed that he tried to persuade Stalin that space could be found for the food in the city's sport complexes, museums, shops, and even palaces, but Stalin refused.[51] On 28 June, the Military Council of the Northern Front ordered all food reserves in the path of the German advance to be destroyed or evacuated. Several bakeries in and around Leningrad were sent eastward.[52] Another mistake was made when Molotov on 17 July ordered the Leningrad *gorkom* to evacuate food reserves to the eastern part of the *oblast'* "and the farthest depths of the country."[53] His order may have been connected with a decision by the Central Committee the same month to evacuate eastward some 1,292,000 tons of bread from all threatened regions of the country. During the first twenty days of July, 2,000 tons of bread were shipped out of Leningrad *oblast'*.[54] Then, on 15 August, the executive committee of the Leningrad *oblast'* ordered the evacuation of tractors and cattle to eastern districts of the Vologda and Kirov *oblasti*. By 10 September, 54,000 head of cattle, 30,000 sheep, and 3,400 pigs had been sent or were in transit to other regions of the country.[55]

To make matters worse, policy within the city deprived Leningraders of incentives either to produce food or reduce consumption. On 1 July, the city *sovet* introduced a supplemental tax on proceeds from private gardens, which discouraged people from selling their own produce in the private markets.[56] One of the biggest mistakes was the way in which food was distributed and sold. Leningrad had experienced food shortages during the Winter War; city authorities should have anticipated considerably greater supply problems right after 22 June. Although rationing was introduced throughout the nation on 18 July, the system did not conserve nearly enough food in Leningrad. Moreover, cafeterias, restaurants, city markets, and seventy-one special commercial shops sold food outside the rationing system in unlimited quantities. Rations should have been lowered in August and distribution or sale of food outside the rationing system ended. The bread ration for *rabochie* through the month of August surpassed the nation's estimated per capita bread consumption in 1940; Leningrad's metal workers and others in "hot" workshops received almost two times the prewar consumption level (see Appendixes A and B).[57]

· Document 4 ·

Report from Molotov, Malenkov, Kosygin, and Zhdanov to Stalin, 29 August 1941, *Izvestiia TsK KPSS*, 1990, No. 9, 212.

Top secret
Transmitted over high frequency on 29 August at 10:00

MOSCOW

To Com. STALIN
Copies to Coms. MIKOYAN and KAGANOVICH[58]

We report on the supply of basic food goods in Leningrad:

The remainder, in days, as of 27 August consists of: flour, including grain, 17; groats 29; fish 16; meat 25; herring 22; animal fat 29.

We consider this situation abnormal, as not providing for the continuous supply of food for Leningrad.

We propose creating in Leningrad by 1 October a month and a half's supply of food goods, for which, calculating from current consumption, we must by that date ship the following: 72,000 [metric] tons of wheat flour, 63,000 tons of rye flour, 7,800 tons of groats, 20,000 tons of meat, 4,000 tons of fish, 3,500 tons of herring, and 3,000 tons of animal fat.

We ask that responsibility be placed on Mikoyan and Kaganovich for the timely shipment and movement of the indicated foods to Leningrad.

For purposes of the food economy, we submit the following suggestions:

first—stop commercial trade in food items in Leningrad;
second—ration the distribution of tea, eggs, and matches.

As of the first of September, set the monthly tea ration for workers and office workers at 25 grams, for dependents and children at 12.5 grams, 10 eggs for workers and children, 8 eggs for office workers, and 5 eggs for dependents; 6 boxes of matches for workers and office workers and 3 boxes for dependents.

MOLOTOV
MALENKOV
KOSYGIN
ZHDANOV

As far as is known, Stalin sent only one telegram (Document 5) to Leningrad on 29 August. Although the time of transmission was not included, it would appear that he sent it after receiving the three messages from the GKO commission, because none of the transmissions from Leningrad responded to Stalin's instruction to Molotov and Malenkov to return immediately to Moscow. Stalin did not react to any of the specific proposals offered by his subordinates. His mind was on another matter. He had just learned that the city of Tosno, located thirty-three miles southeast of Leningrad, had fallen. German advances there and at Krasnogvardeisk and Chudovo enabled Army Group North to surround several Soviet divisions. The Germans estimated that the Red Army lost thirty thousand men in the encirclement.[59] Stalin's frustration, anger, and alarm, so evident in the message to Popov from the day before, continued to grow. Stalin's telegram was not relayed through Zhdanov but through his deputy Kuznetsov, which indicates that Stalin had not regained confidence in Zhdanov after the exchange of messages of 22 August. Stalin had decided that Kuznetsov was more capable than his boss. By the end of the day on the twenty-ninth, the GKO abolished the Northwest Direction, which had been commanded by Voroshilov and had coordinated the Fronts in northern Russia. Its remnants were merged with the Leningrad Front, which together with the Karelian Front would henceforth come under direct GKO control. The GKO appointed Voroshilov to command the Leningrad Front and made Popov his chief of staff.[60]

Stalin remained committed to trying to defend Leningrad; however, in this telegram he expressed greater anxiety than previously over the city's future.

At the beginning of the message he stated that he "fear[ed] that Leningrad will be surrendered in an idiotically foolish way" and concluded it by stating that he was "quite alarmed" by the situation. As in the message to Popov, Stalin adopted a mocking tone ("They are busy searching for new frontiers for retreat"), and he raised the dark suspicion that Popov and Voroshilov might be guilty of treason ("Don't you think that someone is purposely opening the way to the Germans . . . ?"), but this text is less coherent than Stalin's earlier messages. Stalin posed a series of accusatory questions that rambled from tactics, to equipment, to personal assessments of Popov and Voroshilov, but then abruptly ended the message by ordering Molotov and Malenkov to return at once to Moscow.[61] Stalin's eight questions read as almost rhetorical ones; he did not expect Malenkov and Molotov to provide detailed responses based on further investigation. It would seem that Stalin had already made up his mind to replace Popov and Voroshilov and/or that in light of Soviet defeats south of Leningrad he actually feared that the GKO members might become trapped in the city if they did not return quickly. Stalin abolished the Northwest Direction, with Voroshilov as its commander, the same day he wrote this telegram.

Another revealing aspect of this message is that Stalin's only concern over the prospect of surrendering Leningrad was "all the Leningrad divisions . . . falling into captivity." To be sure, the context of the brief telegram was the rapid deterioration of Soviet defenses; nevertheless, the telegram shows clearly that at this point Stalin expressed no concern over the fate of the civilian population.

· Document 5 ·

Telegram from Stalin to Molotov and Malenkov ordering them back
to Moscow and criticizing Leningrad's military leadership, 29 August 1941,
Izvestiia TsK KPSS, 1990, No. 9, 213.

Top secret
Encoded

LENINGRAD

To CITY PARTY COMMITTEE SECRETARY KUZNETSOV for MOLOTOV and MALENKOV

I have just been informed that Tosno was taken by the enemy. If things are going to continue in this way, I fear that Leningrad will be surrendered in an idiotically foolish way and all the Leningrad divisions risk falling into captivity. What are Popov and Voroshilov doing? They are not even reporting on the measures they are thinking of undertaking against this danger. They are busy searching for new frontiers for retreat, which is where they see their mission. Where does this abyss of passivity and purely peasant-like submission to fate come from in them? What kind of men are these, I can't understand it. In Leningrad there are now many KV tanks, lots of aviation, and RSs [rocket systems]. Why aren't these important technical means functioning in the Liuban-Tosno sector? What can an infantry regiment deployed by the command without these technical means accomplish against the Germans? Why isn't Leningrad's abundant equipment being used in this decisive sector? Don't you think that someone is purposely opening the way to the Germans in this decisive sector? What kind of man is Popov? What is Voroshilov actually doing and in what is his assistance to Leningrad being expressed? I am writing about this because I am quite alarmed by the incomprehensible inaction of the Leningrad command. I think that on the 29th you should go to Moscow. I ask you not to delay.

STALIN

Although Stalin had not responded to the specific requests made by his representatives in Leningrad, the Kremlin attempted to implement the recommendations on food distribution. On 30 August, the GKO adopted a resolution on transporting cargo to Leningrad that called for allotting 108 barges, tugboats, and tankers to bring supplies to the city across Lake Ladoga.[62] The resolution, however, was essentially meaningless given the military situation and the fact that Leningrad did not have sufficient port facilities to handle a massive supply effort by boats and barges across the lake. The amount of food reaching the city continued to decline. On 2 September, Leningrad's daily bread ration, which had been the same as in the rest of the USSR, was reduced for the first time since rationing was introduced in mid-July by 200 grams per day for all employed people and by 100 for dependents (see Appendix A). On 8 September, the GKO sent Commissar of Trade Dmitry Pavlov to Leningrad, apparently on Mikoyan's recommendation, to administer food distribution and carry out further reforms.[63] On 12 September, he reduced the bread ration by another hundred grams per day for employed people and fifty grams for nonworking dependents. Then on 1 October, he lowered the bread ration again by the same amount. Rations for other foods, including groats, meat, fish, fat, and sugar and candy were also cut in September, though eggs were never rationed as the GKO team requested (see Appendixes B and C). Pavlov also ordered the closing of commercial food stores and forbade the sale of food outside the ration system in early September. Cafeterias attached to state institutions were to demand ration cards for the meals they served.[64] Significant loopholes in the rationing system would nevertheless continue to exist for a couple more months. For example, fifteen commercial restaurants operated outside the ration system into late September, and the open sale of food in cafeterias and restaurants without ration coupons ended altogether only on 11 November.[65]

The imposition of the land blockade severely reduced deliveries to Leningrad, and the city did not receive the quantities of food requested by the GKO delegation. To make matters worse, a significant portion of the food reserves within Leningrad was destroyed on 8 September in the first aerial bombardment of the city. Zhdanov ultimately was to blame for the fact that foodstuffs continued to be concentrated in the old, flammable Badaev warehouses. Thirty-eight of their storerooms burned when they were hit that day and on September 10 by German incendiary bombs. Following the attack on the Badaev complex, remaining food reserves were dispersed throughout the city.[66]

On 20 September, the GKO issued Resolution No. 692 "On the establishment of an air transport link with the city of Leningrad," which assigned top priority to supplying the needs of the military. Explosives, artillery shells, other forms of munitions, motors, communications equipment, and military spare parts were to be flown into Leningrad, while military hardware and communication systems manufactured in the city, such as tank guns, aviation instruments, radio stations, and telephone and telegraph equipment were to be sent out. The head of Red Army Logistical Services Andrei Khrulev was in charge of determining the cargo lists for the flights. One hundred metric tons of cargo were to be flown in and out of the city each day. On 1 October, the quota was raised to 150 tons.[67]

On 9 November, the day after the Germans seized Tikhvin, Zhdanov talked with Stalin and requested an additional thirty Douglas transport planes and ten TB-3s to bring food into Leningrad and fly out manufactured military materials.[68] Later the same day the GKO issued Resolution No. 871 which directed not less than 200 metric tons of food per day to be flown to Leningrad, but only for five days, from 10 to 14 November. The daily delivery was to consist of 135 tons of wheat kasha and pea soup concentrate, 20 tons of smoked pork and smoked sausage, 20 tons of cooking oil, 15 tons of butter, and 10 tons of powdered eggs and powdered milk. The shipments were to be flown in fifty Douglas aircraft.[69] (With a civilian population of approximately 2.4 million, the completed deliveries would provide about three ounces of concentrated food per person per day if no food was lost or stolen.) In his memoirs, Mikoyan claimed credit for managing to assign "about fifty Douglas bombers" to airlift food to Leningrad. However, Mikoyan also claimed that when Stalin challenged his decision by asking, "What are you thinking? Why are military planes being used not as intended?" he had to redirect many of the planes elsewhere. On 13 November, Zhdanov complained to Malenkov that he did not know where any of the Douglas planes allotted to Leningrad were. Malenkov replied that eighteen had flown to Leningrad the preceding day and that another seven would fly there the following day. Mikoyan further recalled that Aleksei Kuznetsov had a long phone conversation with Stalin's secretary Aleksandr Poskrebyshev, hoping through him to convince Stalin to assign more planes to fly food to Leningrad. Stalin refused. By the end of December, according to Mikoyan, "almost all of the planes" had been reassigned.[70] On 11 December, head of air shipment for the VSLF Petrov submitted a report to VSLF leaders in which he implied that the GKO quota of two hundred tons of food per day was still in effect, but that the mandate was not being ful-filled mainly because of a lack of airplanes. Petrov had at his disposal only twenty-eight Douglas planes instead of fifty and only fifteen TB-3s instead of a promised thirty-six. Petrov also complained that there were "a large number of bosses and authorized personnel" from numerous agencies, including the Air Force, the Red Army Rear Services, the VSLF, and the Leningrad *ispolkom,* among others, attempting to coordinate the operation. He characterized their efforts as a confused "bureaucratic muddle" (*nerazberikha*). Petrov stated that the loading and unloading of the planes was poorly organized and that the planes' crews and employees of the army's Rear Services were stealing some of the food. (These latter comments were underlined in Zhdanov's copy of the report.)[71]

In sum, food supply to Leningrad by air in the fall of 1941 had a low pri-ority and was conducted inefficiently. Thirty of the planes that brought food to Leningrad were used to evacuate civilians and military personnel. The effort was modest and applied only to specific groups. During October and early November, about 30,000 defense plant workers (including 11,614 from the Kirov works and about 6,000 from the Izhorsk plant in Kolpino, twelve miles southeast of Leningrad) were flown to factories in the east, and another 7,000 civilians, most of whom were very ill, were airlifted out of the blockade zone. Parts of two infantry divisions and about a thousand sailors were also evacu-ated by air.[72]

Mikoyan also claimed that he helped organize convoys to ship food over Lake Ladoga in the autumn of 1941, but that the amount delivered was insuf-ficient to feed the population. Only about half of the cargo (898 out of 1,791 rail cars) that was shipped over Ladoga and then sent by train from the Ladoga rail station to the city in October and November consisted of food. Ammuni-tion and fuel oil accounted for most of the other half, which further attests to the high importance Moscow assigned to the armed forces in Leningrad and the city's defense industries. (During the starvation winter, the portion of in-coming supplies, as measured by weight, that was food for people and fodder for army horses rose to 75 percent.) Attacks by German aircraft on boats and barges on the lake hampered shipping as did poor weather in November. The supply effort was restricted further during the month that the Germans held Tikhvin. Between 10 October and 30 November, on average only thirty-six rail cars per day of cargo reached Leningrad.[73]

Prior to the start of the blockade, as the military situation was deteriorating, Stalin directed more men and matériel to the Leningrad Front. Up to 26 Au-gust, all of the 180 sixty-ton KV tanks (the monthly quota) that were manufac-tured at the Kirov and Izhorsk factories were sent to the strategic reserve near Moscow. On that day Stalin agreed to permit KVs that were assembled over the next four days to be delivered to the Leningrad Front. Twenty-seven KVs were driven straight from the assembly line unpainted to the front. In addition, four aviation regiments and ten battalions were sent to bolster Leningrad's defenses.[74] The following day the *Stavka* began to deploy two newly formed armies under the command of Marshal Grigory Kulik and Lieutenant General

Nikolai Klykov along the Volkhov River to prevent a junction of Finnish and German forces southeast of Leningrad.

These emergency reinforcements did not halt the German advance. On 3 September, the VSLF began fortifying six defense sectors within the city in anticipation of defending Leningrad street by street.[75] The following day, German artillery moved to within range of Leningrad and began firing on the city. Popov's twelve-day command of the Leningrad Front was abruptly terminated on 5 September. As noted above, Army Group North made the land blockade of Leningrad complete on 8 September when it took Shlisselburg. When Stalin learned of the loss of the key city the next day not from the command of the Leningrad Front but from a German report,[76] he fired off a telegram (Document 6) to Voroshilov and Zhdanov. As in his telegram of 29 August, this one consists of a series of taunting indictments in the form of an interrogation. Again, he raised the suspicion of treason. ("Have you perhaps decided in advance to surrender Leningrad?") The menacing tone of the telegram is emphasized by the inclusion of Beria's name among the senders.

· Document 6 ·

Telegram from Stalin, Molotov, Malenkov, and Beria to Voroshilov and Zhdanov asking whether they have decided to surrender Leningrad and demanding information on military strategy, 9 September 1941, *Izvestiia TsK KPSS*, 1990, No. 10, 217.

Top secret
Encoded

LENINGRAD, to VOROSHILOV and ZHDANOV

We are disturbed by your conduct, which is expressed in your reporting to us only merely about our loss of a given location, but usually you do not report a word about what measures you have undertaken to put an end, at last, to the losing of towns and stations. You reported just as disgracefully about the loss of Shlisselburg. Will there be an end to the losses? Have you perhaps decided in advance to surrender Leningrad? What have you done with the KV tanks, where have you positioned them, and why has there been no improvement whatsoever at the front, in spite of the abundance of KV tanks you have? No single front, after all, has even a half-share of the number of KVs you have at the front. What is your aviation doing? Why is it not supporting the actions of our troops in the field? Kulik's divisions have come to your assistance. How are you making use of this assistance? Can we hope for any kind of improvement at the front, or will Kulik's assistance also come to naught, as the tremendous assistance from KV tanks came to naught? We demand that you inform us two or three times a day about the situation at the front and about the measures you are taking.

STALIN, MOLOTOV, MALENKOV, BERIA

In fact, Stalin probably had no intention of reading further reports from Voroshilov. Perhaps Beria had picked up on various rumors that were circulating in Leningrad at that time that Voroshilov had lost his nerve. War correspondent Alexander Werth later on heard an implausible rumor from these crucial days: "The dramatic story I heard from several people in Leningrad in 1943 was that about 10 September, when there was practically complete chaos at the front, Voroshilov, believing that everything was lost, went into the front line, in the hope of getting killed by the Germans."[77] On either 9 or 10 September, Stalin ordered Zhukov to fly immediately to Leningrad to replace Voroshilov as Front commander.[78] Zhukov wrote in his memoirs that Stalin told him prior to his departure that the official order on his appointment as commander of the Leningrad Front would be issued only after he arrived in the city. According to Zhukov: "I realized that these words reflected concern that our flight might end badly."[79] Zhukov flew together with Major Generals Ivan Fediuninsky and Mikhail Khozin, who had served under him at the Battle of Khalkhin-Gol in 1939, with a fighter escort and had to evade German Messerschmitts patrolling Lake Ladoga. Khozin was very familiar with the Leningrad region, having served in the Leningrad Military District in the 1920s and 1930s. Arriving unannounced, the three generals went directly to Smolny where a VSLF meeting was in progress, and Zhukov took command of the Leningrad Front.[80] According to several accounts, Zhukov handed Voroshilov a handwritten note from Stalin relieving him of command and ordering him to return at once to Moscow. Thus ended abruptly Voroshilov's four or five days as Front commander. As planned, Stalin and Shaposhnikov transmitted the order replacing Voroshilov with Zhukov on the evening of 11 September after Zhukov had informed the Kremlin of his safe arrival.

· Document 7 ·

Report from Stalin and Shaposhnikov to Headquarters of the Leningrad Front and Commander of the Reserve Front replacing Voroshilov with Zhukov as Front commander, 11 September 1941, TsAMO f. 132, op. 2642, d. 30, l. 35, in *Voenno-istoricheskii zhurnal*, 1992, No. 6–7, 17.

---

19 hours, 10 minutes
1. Marshal of the Soviet Union Comrade Voroshilov is relieved of responsibilities as Commander in Chief of the Leningrad Front.
2. Army General Comrade Zhukov is named Commander of the Leningrad Front and is relieved of his responsibilities of commanding the Reserve Front.
3. Comrade Voroshilov is to hand over matters of the front, and Comrade Zhu-

kov is to accept them within 24 hours (the marking of time having already begun) from the hour of Zhukov's arrival in Leningrad.

Lieutenant General Khozin is named Chief of Staff of the Leningrad Front.

STALIN, B. SHAPOSHNIKOV

Five and a half hours before the announcement of Voroshilov's removal was transmitted, Voroshilov and Zhdanov had cabled a report to the Defense Commissariat, which attempted to address the concerns raised by Stalin in his 9 September cable and to explain their failures. They admitted that the *opolchenie* divisions of July and August were "completely untrained and weakly armed with automatic weapons" but that it was necessary to employ them to stop the enemy. They asserted that they were not preparing to surrender Leningrad and urgently needed assistance, especially military aircraft and weaponry. They claimed that the front had only 275 airplanes, of which just 50 were bombers. A significant portion of the fighter aircraft could not attack enemy positions as they were needed to defend Leningrad against the massive German air blitz. The Leningrad leaders added that they knew nothing of any assistance from the divisions of Kulik's Fifty-fourth Army east of the blockade zone: "Comrade Kulik has not communicated one word to us about his activities." They requested that Kulik keep in continual contact with them.[81]

Although Voroshilov and his staff left Leningrad the day after Zhukov assumed command, they did not proceed directly to Moscow. On Stalin's orders, they went first to Kulik's headquarters and apparently remained there until both generals were recalled to Moscow on 26 September.[82]

· Document 8 ·

Report from Stalin and Molotov to Zhukov and Zhdanov announcing that Voroshilov has been recalled to Moscow, 26 September 1941, *Izvestiia TsK KPSS*, 1990, No. 11, 190.

LENINGRAD. To ZHUKOV and ZHDANOV

Top secret
Encoded

Today Voroshilov recalled to Moscow. 54th Army subordinated to Leningrad Front, Kulik and Antoniuk recalled to *Stavka*. We hope you are using 54th Army to strike enemy's rear and establish contact with Moscow.

STALIN, MOLOTOV

According to Salisbury, Kulik, who had known Stalin since the Battle of Tsaritsyn in 1918, was "as great an incompetent as the Red Army boasted."[83] On 10 September, the Fifty-fourth Army had launched an offensive westward toward the key city of Siniavino, located north of Mga in the neck of territory that Germany held south of Lake Ladoga that kept the blockade intact. Ten days into the campaign, Stalin pressed Kulik to take Mga and asserted that the commander had enough troops to capture the city twice over. Kulik replied that his army had suffered ten thousand casualties over the preceding four days and that without reinforcements, he could not take Mga. At Zhukov's insistence, Kulik was replaced as commander of the Fifty-fourth Army on 26 September by Khozin, who continued the failing campaign, which became known as the First Siniavino Offensive, through October. It would take five more offenses before Siniavino was finally retaken in late 1943.[84] The repeated offensives, which resulted in an enormous number of casualties, show Stalin's resolve to break the blockade; however, the Red Army's chances of success would have been greater in 1941 and 1942 if it had concentrated its forces farther north near Shlisselburg right along the southern coast of Ladoga.[85] This is where the siege was eventually pierced in early 1943.

One can only imagine the frame of mind of Voroshilov, Kulik, and Antoniuk (the head of the operational group of the Fifty-fourth Army) as they arrived in Moscow, or the reaction of Zhukov and Zhdanov to the terse announcement from Stalin and Molotov. In the words of historian Otto Chaney, Stalin "had shot greater men for less."[86] In October 1941, Stalin would order the execution of at least twenty-nine military leaders, including two generals who were Heroes of the Soviet Union, Grigory Shtern and Dmitry Pavlov (not to be confused with the GKO representative in Leningrad). Pavlov had commanded the ill-fated Western Front at the beginning of the war.[87] But Voroshilov was not shot or arrested, most likely because of his long association with Stalin and the fact that Leningrad ultimately did not fall. He found himself in a situation similar to that of April 1940, when Stalin had relieved him of the post of Defense Commissar. Voroshilov's departure from Leningrad in 1941 predictably sparked rumors, which were overheard by party informants, that Stalin had in fact had Voroshilov shot.[88] Later in the war Stalin made further use of Voroshilov. In the fall of 1942, he held the largely symbolic post of commander in chief of the partisan movement, and then in January 1943 he coordinated the Leningrad and Volkhov Fronts as they fought through to each other and punctured the blockade. Kulik, after his failure to take Mga and Siniavino, was appointed *Stavka* representative in Crimea. After it was overrun by the Germans, he was court-martialed, demoted in rank, and stripped of his military orders.[89] Zhdanov meanwhile continued to serve throughout the blockade as the political chief of the VSLF. His political future, and likely his very life, hinged on whether Leningrad held out or fell to the enemy.

In recent years the surviving sons of Stalin's subalterns have written about their fathers in what has become a post-Soviet cottage industry. Their narrowly informed and biased recollections not surprisingly have produced conflicting accounts, which act as additional filters through which the historian observes and evaluates the Soviet saga. Lavrenty Beria's son Sergo claimed that "Malenkov proposed that Zhdanov be court-martialed. Zhdanov's hatred of Malenkov dated from this incident, which he never forgave. Stalin was going to agree, but my father, despite his hostility to Zhdanov, advised against it."[90] A. G. Malenkov contends that when his father arrived in Leningrad, he found Zhdanov in a luxurious bunker, "gone to pieces" (*opustilsiia*), unshaven, and drunk; however, upon returning to Moscow, he did not inform Stalin about Zhdanov's state.[91] Despite his son's statement, it is very difficult to imagine that Malenkov did not take advantage of the opportunity to besmirch his rival before Stalin.

The reports that Stalin received on Leningrad and its principal leaders likely deepened his pessimism. Zhukov recollected that prior to his departure for Leningrad Stalin held out little hope that Leningrad could be defended: "I remember that he even used the word 'hopeless.'"[92] The head of the Soviet Navy Admiral Nikolai Kuznetsov also recalled in an essay published in 1965 that Stalin lacked confidence in Leningrad's defense. "It may be necessary to abandon it," the Soviet leader told him in the first days of September. He further noted that Stalin ordered him to cable the Baltic Fleet command to mine the fleet. "Not one warship must fall into the enemy's hands."[93] The *vozhd'* added that if an order to scuttle the fleet were not carried out, those responsible would be severely punished. Not surprisingly, however, no one wanted to sign a document that could lead to the fleet's deliberate destruction. Kuznetsov refused on the basis that in the chain of command the Baltic Fleet was subordinate to the Leningrad Front, not the Navy, and since that Front was under the control of the GKO, an order to scuttle would have to be issued under Stalin's signature. Stalin then modified his order: Kuznetsov would discuss the matter with Shaposhnikov, and the two of them would transmit the order. But Shaposhnikov wanted no part of the decision, claiming that it was strictly a naval matter. Finally, according to Kuznetsov's account, he and Shaposhnikov decided to submit a draft of an order to Stalin for his signature. Stalin agreed to this arrangement. However, Kuznetsov and Shaposhnikov managed to avoid actually affixing their signatures to the order. That task was left to Kuznetsov's deputy, Admiral Ivan Isakov, who on 6 September signed the draft of the plan for the complete destruction of the Baltic Fleet, civilian ships, and their support facilities "in the event of a forced retreat from Leningrad." Stalin countersigned the order on 13 September (Document 9),[94] the same day that he had one of his seven meetings that month with Admiral Kuznetsov.[95] The document shows that Stalin remained determined to try to defend Leningrad but believed that the ships might have to be sunk to prevent them from falling into German hands. The order applied not only to Kronstadt Island, the headquarters of the fleet, but also to Oranienbaum across the Gulf of Finland from Kronstadt, as well as to three regions in Leningrad: the commercial port, the mouth of the Neva River, and the shipyards. By this time, there were more battleships and cruisers in Leningrad than at Kronstadt.[96]

Stalin's top concern regarding Leningrad remained the preservation of military personnel and keeping important military assets from falling intact into the hands of the enemy. He wanted to be able to extract troops from the Leningrad Front and sailors from the Baltic Fleet, which together numbered 497,000 at the start of the blockade, if they were threatened with annihilation or capture.[97] It is not clear what events would have prompted Stalin to start withdrawing troops from the blockade zone; however, it is logical to surmise that he wanted to retain a land link to Lake Ladoga, since the lake was the only surface connection to the "Mainland." If enemy forces appeared to be on the verge of completing a tight "inner" encirclement of Leningrad, that is, to the west of Lake Ladoga (or possibly even an "outer" encirclement along the entire eastern coast of the lake), he likely would have ordered a rapid, Dunkirk-like evacuation across the lake of as many soldiers and sailors and as much matériel as possible. Document 9 shows that provision was made for a quick, simultaneous destruction of all of the identified items in the three defined regions in Leningrad as well as at Kronstadt and Oranienbaum, which would coincide with the "forced retreat." Transmission of the code word "Chrysanthemum" would signal the start of the general destruction process. Stalin, however, also envisioned the prospect of fighting within the city, of moving ships from areas within Leningrad that were "under direct threat of capture by the enemy" to safer regions. Each region was assigned its own flower name that would serve as the coded signal for sinking ships and destroying other items. "In case it is impossible for them to remain in Leningrad," ships were to relocate to their last bastion, Kronstadt Island, located about ten miles from the city. Herein lies a contradiction, or at least an ambiguity, within the document. If the city were to fall, would "Chrysanthemum" be transmitted, or would the remnants of the fleet be ordered to relocate to Kronstadt? Was there a difference between the "forced retreat" that would prompt the mass scuttling and the "impossibility of remaining" in the city that would lead to evacuation to Kronstadt? Commanders, of course, were not thrown into a state of confusion by these nuances in meaning; they had only to follow their direct orders. However, the fact that the general plan was open to different interpretations reveals a lack of clarity or completeness of thought on Stalin's part. It may be that he simply wanted to issue an order that covered all conceivable unwanted eventualities, ranging from a quick and overwhelming enemy attack on the city and Kronstadt to a more grinding, street-by-street assault. In any case, the document does not reflect a dictator in a state of panic. It does show that Stalin had grave doubts about the prospects for defending Leningrad (which if expressed by anyone else could have led to charges of "defeatism" and arrest for counterrevolutionary agitation), but also that he would react swiftly and ruthlessly to preserve his armed forces and not let the enemy realize material or military gain should the city fall. As noted above, the GKO order of 20 September created a limited airlift to transport military supplies as well as military and military-industrial personnel. The fate of the rest of the civilian population and the casualties that would have resulted from demolition of ships, factories, bridges, and trains were not part of Stalin's calculation. On 2 October, *Leningradskaia pravda* printed a statement of three sentences, perhaps uttered by Stalin himself (indeed, the first sentence has been attributed to him), that succinctly summarized Soviet officialdom's view of the situation: "War is war. It demands large sacrifices and severe testing. But it is nothing in comparison with what the fascists bring to the city."

· Document 9 ·

Detailed plan to destroy the Baltic Fleet in the event of a retreat from Leningrad, 6 September 1941, Tsentral'nyi voenno-morskoi arkhiv f. 2, op. 1, d. 546, ll. 1–4, in Knyshevskii et al., *Skrytaia pravda voiny*, 140–45.

[On the title page of this document there is a note that reads: "Approved. 13 September 1941. I. Stalin."][98]

PLAN FOR MEASURES FOR SHIPS TO BE TAKEN
IN THE EVENT OF A RETREAT FROM LENINGRAD

Top secret
Of special importance
I. General Provisions

   A. In the event of a forced retreat from Leningrad, all naval ships, as well as merchant, industrial, and technical ships, are subject to destruction.

   B. Destruction shall be carried out in order:

   1. to keep the enemy from using them;

   2. to rule out the possibility of the enemy sailing in the Kronstadt-Leningrad area and using the harbors, canals, waterways, and so forth.

   Destruction shall be carried out with the maximum degree of devastation for possibly a long period.

Destruction and sinking shall be carried out strictly according to plan from the moment the Main Command gives the signal.

II. Preparations

A. Preparations are being made for the following districts:

1. Kronstadt District (including Kronstadt itself, the naval port, Oranienbaum, the Northern Waterway, and the Morskoy Channel from the Petergof buoy inclusive).

2. Leningrad naval port (incl. the Morskoy Channel from the Petergof buoy, the enclosed section of the Morskoy Channel, the Zhdanov Plant's defined waterway, the Commercial Port, and Gutuevsky and Konenersky islands, to the mouth of the Neva R.)

3. Mouth of the Neva R. (incl. the Elaginsky Waterway, Petrovsky Waterway, Korabelny Waterway, Bolshaia Neva, Malaia Nevka, Sredniaia Nevka, and Malaia Nevka).

4. Shipyards (nos. 190, 189, 194, 196, 5, 205, 263, and 270).

B. In the indicated districts, all vessels, regardless of their departmental affiliation, are being readied for destruction.

C. Facilities on shore (warehouses, cranes, moorings, and approach routes) shall be destroyed by the respective departments, according to the instructions and plan of the VKP(b) City Committee.

D. Depending on the operational circumstances, the destruction will be undertaken in a district that is under direct threat of capture by the enemy.

In addition, provision will be made for removing the ships from any endangered district to a safer one. In particular, provision must be made for the possibility of moving the ships to Kronstadt, in case it is impossible for them to remain in Leningrad.

E. All preliminary preparations shall be carried out by the Staff of KBF [Red Banner Baltic Fleet] in conjunction with the Leningrad Naval Defense staff (in secrecy).

All executive documents are being drawn up in advance.

Preliminary instructions are being issued.

As they become ready, the documents shall be issued immediately to the principal executors.

III. Senior executors

A. Responsibility for and general supervision of the destruction and sinking of the fleet's ships and the destruction of vessels and ships at the shipyards shall be assigned to the commander of the KBF, Vice Admiral Tributs.

B. Responsibility for sinking all the ships of the fleet and destroying the shipyards, as well as blocking the channels and waterways and immobilizing the dredges is assigned as follows: [. . .]

IV. Demolition techniques

A. Ships shall be destroyed by the following means: scuttling, blowing up the hull, wrecking the machinery and furnaces by explosion, setting fire to the ship, and destroying valuable radio equipment.

Ships in slips and at docks shall be blown up.

V. Preliminary instructions

Are as follows:

A. Obtain and deliver VV [explosive substances] to the sites or to the demolition district in accordance with the calculations of each district's senior executors.

B. Draw up instructions (compile lists of demolition and mining specialists).

C. Place the ships according to the plan.

D. Supply tugboats for placing the ships.

E. In the instructions on removing the crew of the ships—carry the main crew away and remove the demolition squad from the ship.

F. Allocate to the district the number of launches required for the demolition crews.

VI. Notification and communication procedure

After the decision of the Main Command, the order shall be transmitted:

A. Over the telephone by agreed signal, with confirmation.

B. Duplication by telegraph.

C. Duplication by express delegate.

Attached: 1. List of main sites (1 page).

2. Communications schedule (1 page).

> Deputy People's Commissar of the Navy
> Admiral ISAKOV
> ATTACHMENT No. 2

COMMUNICATIONS SCHEDULE

[. . .]

SIGNALS

Common for all districts

"Dandelion"—open packet No. . . . .

"Mignonette"—start placing targets

"Chrysanthemum"—start destroying and sinking targets

For each district

"Rose"—district 1—start destroying and sinking targets

"Cornflower"—district 2 " " " "

"Orchid"—district 3 " " " "

"Gillyflower"—district 4 " " " "

Common for all

"Tulip"—abort [*otmenitel'nyi*]

For each district

"Lilac"—district 1—abort

"Forget-me-not"—district 2 "

"Violet"—district 3 "

"Poppy"—district 4 "

Note: Senior district officials must have a communications schedule worked out with the targets.

It is not clear whether plans to abandon Leningrad and destroy the fleet predated the document above. Dmitry Volkogonov contended that "In the first days of September 1941 . . . the commander of the Leningrad Front K. E. Voroshilov and member of the Military Soviet of the Front A. A. Zhdanov appealed to him [Stalin] for permission to mine the ships of the Red Banner Baltic Fleet and to scuttle them if Leningrad's capitulation appeared likely [*pri ugroze sdachi Leningrada*]. Stalin agreed. And by 8 September Voroshilov and Zhdanov signed the corresponding order."[99] However, Volkogonov did not cite the source of this information, and no documents have come to light to support his assertion. There are reasons to surmise that the proposal actually originated with the Kremlin, because Popov, Voroshilov, or Zhdanov would have been most reluctant to raise the prospect of abandoning Leningrad after Stalin's several severe reprimands between 22 August and 9 September. Stalin had already accused them of not keeping Moscow informed of their decisions and implied that they were guilty of treason. They would not want to give the leader grounds for accusing them of defeatism as well, and none of them ever was so accused. The members of the GKO team that traveled to Leningrad in late August may have presented the proposal for retreat to Stalin.

If Stalin displayed a lack of confidence in victory at Leningrad, his concerns were mirrored by Winston Churchill, who had an obvious interest in the fate of the Soviet Baltic Fleet. Churchill requested that the ships be destroyed rather than to be captured intact by the Germans. On 12 September, British ambassador to the USSR Sir Stafford Cripps delivered to Molotov a memorandum offering British compensation after the war for destruction of the ships. Three days later Stalin replied. In the same letter in which he stunned Churchill with his desperate plea (or was it feigned desperation?) that Britain send "twenty-five to thirty divisions" to the USSR, Stalin confirmed that "There could be no doubt that such a course [scuttling of the Baltic Fleet] will be adopted should the necessity arise." Stalin added that Germany, not Britain, would pay for the damage. Churchill concurred in that judgment on 17 September.[100]

On the same day that he signed off on the contingency plans for destroying Leningrad's ships, Stalin issued a mandate through the GKO for Beria's deputy Vsevolod Merkulov to coordinate the mining of factories, power plants, and bridges in Leningrad (Document 10). Containing language very similar to that in the order concerning the fleet, the mandate stated that the demolition of important structures would occur "in the event of the forced retreat of our troops from the Leningrad area." The intent was to deprive the enemy of any military-industrial capacity and to trap enemy soldiers and tanks in the debris. Merkulov arrived in Leningrad on or about the date of the GKO mandate and remained there for at least one month. S. D.

Voinov, who was the brother of Aleksei Kuznetsov's wife Zinaida and Kuznetsov's wartime aide, later asserted that Merkulov arrived in Leningrad
with no advance notice and that Moscow had already decided that Leningrad could not be defended and would fall into enemy hands. Merkulov
proceeded right away to prepare factories to be blown up.[101]

The mandate on Merkulov's mission is also noteworthy for its omis-
sion of any reference to Zhdanov. There were several reasons that Merkulov worked with Kuznetsov rather than with Kuznetsov's boss. Since the
end of July, Kuznetsov had been in charge of fortification work between
the Luga Line and Leningrad and was better acquainted with the large factories in Leningrad's southern districts near the front. Moreover, Zhdanov and Beria were adversaries, which is reflected in the fact that during
the war, while Zhdanov always signed correspondence to Stalin, Molotov, and others, Kuznetsov's signature was on documents sent to Beria and
Malenkov.[102]

The most important reason, however, that Merkulov worked with Kuznetsov was Stalin's general loss of confidence in Zhdanov. Voinov recollected that Stalin wrote a letter to Kuznetsov, which was hand-delivered
by an NKVD general (a likely reference to Merkulov). The letter stated
that Voroshilov and Zhdanov were exhausted and had "fallen to pieces"
and needed to rest. In matters of defense and force mobilization, Stalin
would rely on Kuznetsov.[103] (The fact that Voinov's depiction of Stalin's
characterization of Zhdanov in the letter to Kuznetsov, as related by historian Afanasiev, bears strong similarities to the condition in which Malenkov reportedly found Zhdanov suggests that, contrary to A. G. Malenkov's account, his father did furnish a very negative report on Zhdanov to
Stalin.) Several of Kuznetsov's associates knew of the letter. His son Valery
said in an interview several years ago that the handwritten note included
the sentence, "The Motherland will never forget you."[104] Stalin's personal
endorsement of his thirty-six-year-old protégé and Kuznetsov's working
relationship with Beria and Merkulov during the crisis of the fall of 1941
becomes highly ironic when viewed from the context of the postwar Leningrad Affair. Kuznetsov's political dossier was destroyed after his execution
in 1950. The Kremlin in fact went to great lengths to forget him.

· Document 10 ·

Mandate from the State Defense Committee that orders Merkulov and *gorkom*
secretary Kuznetsov to supervise preparation of important installations and bridges
for destruction in the event of a retreat from Leningrad, 13 September 1941,
RGASPI f. 644 (GOKO).670ss, d. 9, l. 100.

STATE DEFENSE COMMITTEE
Mandate

Issued to USSR NKVD Deputy Com. V. N. Merkulov, in that he is the Commissioner for Special Affairs of the State Defense Committee.

Com. Merkulov is ordered, together with Leningrad Front Military Council member Com. Kuznetsov, to carefully verify the matter of preparations for blowing up and destroying enterprises of important installations and bridges in Leningrad in the event of the forced retreat of our troops from the Leningrad area. The Leningrad Front Military Council, as well as party and Soviet workers of Leningrad, are obliged to render Com. V. P. Merkulov every assistance.

Contingency planning for demolition of important installations may have preceded the GKO mandate.[105] No evidence has been found in Leningrad's NKVD files that any sites were mined prior to 13 September; however, there is reason to suspect that as early as late August Stalin was contemplating the possibility of destroying important objectives in Leningrad as a prelude to abandoning the city. On 23 August, the day after the row between the Kremlin and Smolny over the proposed Leningrad Military Defense Council, the GKO named Kubatkin head of the Leningrad NKVD and sent him there from Moscow.[106] The following day the GKO ordered the creation of a three-month supply of explosives in Leningrad.[107] It is unclear whether the explosives were intended for ammunition or for mining the city. If Stalin and Beria were beginning to plan for Leningrad's possible fall this early, it would support the interpretation that Stalin's pessimism regarding the prospects for defending the city set in right after the dispute with Voroshilov and Zhdanov, even before Stalin dispatched the GKO team to Leningrad and almost two weeks before the city came under direct enemy fire.

St. Petersburg's FSB archive contains two large volumes of materials on the mining of factories, bridges, and other important structures. The NKVD referred to the operation (which did not include the Baltic Fleet) as Plan "D," and it was supervised by Merkulov, Kubatkin, and A. A. Kuznetsov.[108] Each *raion* had a *troika* in charge of laying explosives that consisted of the first secretary of the *raikom*, head of the *raion* NKVD, and an expert engineer appointed by the VSLF. Similarly, in each factory there was a demolition *troika* comprising the factory director, the head of the factory party committee, and the head of the *sekretnyi otdel* (NKVD). To maintain contact in the event that communications broke down in the city, Merkulov and Kuznetsov recommended that the *gorkom* form "a group of at least ten couriers, who know very well the localities of all the city's *raiony.*"[109]

The GKO mandate of 13 September was only partly fulfilled. During the third week in September, a total of forty metric tons of explosives (which would not quite fill one freight car) had been distributed to Kirovsky, Moskovsky, Volodarsky, and Leninsky *raiony* in the heavily industrialized southern part of the city. As historian Andrei Dzeniskevich has convincingly demonstrated, this amount was a minuscule fraction of what would have been needed to destroy all important installations in Leningrad. To illustrate his point, he described an explosion (the precise cause of which was not determined) of a huge cache of ammunition contained in seventy freight cars at the Rzhevka train station along the eastern outskirts of Leningrad on 29 March 1942, which destroyed completely only the cars themselves and up to twenty buildings in the train yard and in the immediate vicinity. Another forty freight cars and about four hundred buildings within a two-kilometer radius of the explosion experienced some damage. A far greater mass of explosive material would have been needed to destroy hundreds of factories, bridges, and train stations. Dzeniskevich also pointed out that despite the fact that Germany bombarded Leningrad with thousands of tons of explosives during the siege, the city's buildings were not leveled. The forty tons of explosives were used in September 1941 to mine important defense plants within the likely path of a German strike, such as the Izhorsk plant in Kolpino, which was mined on 19 September, and the Kirov factory as well as train stations and bridges. (By 25 September, German intelligence was vaguely aware of the plan to mine all important buildings and factories in the city and of the fact that explosives had already been placed in the Kirov factory.) Mining operations remained confined to the city's southernmost districts.[110]

At 4:45 A.M. on 20 September, Merkulov sent Zhdanov and Kuznetsov a detailed report that listed shortcomings in the mining operations, which were euphemistically called "special measures." He cited a general lack of materials, such as detonator wires, and lack of proper instruction in laying mines, and he ordered a one-day course in use of explosives for leaders of demolition teams. Merkulov also noted deficiencies in carrying out evacuation orders. The Kirov factory, for example, needed about five hundred rail cars to remove machinery, but on 17 September had only ninety-four. Over the next two weeks, he worked closely with the city's district NKVD heads and wrote numerous detailed reports, mainly to Kuznetsov, about delays at individual enterprises in carrying out the special measures and evacuating important materials.

Many of the explosives that were set in factories remained in place through September 1943 or even until the end of the blockade in January 1944. A report on the special measures signed by Kuznetsov and Kubatkin on 20 August 1943, indicated that contingency plans still existed for disabling 58,510 installations in the city's fifteen *raiony*, including 220 enterprises and 160 electric stations and substations. In the event that the city fell, 4,921 of the installations were to be blown up; 53,589 would be destroyed by mechanical means. However, most of Plan "D" existed only on paper.[111] The explosive materials proved far more valuable at the front.

During the September 1941 crisis, the plan was to defend important installations in the southern districts as long as possible. Only if they were about to be seized would they be destroyed and their defenders retreat deeper into the city. In September parts of the work force and some machinery were relocated from large defense plants that were under heavy artillery fire, including the Izhorsk and Kirov factories, to other plants in the northern part of the city. Even before Zhukov's arrival, the leaders of the Kirov plant who had remained at the factory had publicly expressed their intention of fighting to the end. On 6 September, *Leningradskaia pravda* published a letter from plant director Zaltsman, secretary of the factory's party committee M. D. Kozin, and chairman of the trade union committee L. N. Solovyov entitled, "We Will Die, but We Will Not Surrender Leningrad."

Zhukov claimed that plans to prepare for scuttling ships prior to abandoning Leningrad had not progressed far by the time he arrived in Leningrad. He wrote that by the end of the VSLF meeting that he had interrupted upon his arrival, "it was decided to defend Leningrad to the last drop of blood."[112] He asserted that early in his visit he countermanded Stalin's order to mine the Baltic Fleet. "I forbid the blowing up of the warships. There are forty full battle complements on them." He instructed the Baltic Fleet Commander Vladimir Tributs: "As Front commander, I forbid this. In the first place, order the ships to be cleared of mines so that they themselves are not blown up. Secondly, bring them closer to the city so that they can fire with all their artillery."[113] Zhukov further wrote: "Why blow up the warships? Maybe they were going to be sunk, but if so, it should only be in battle, firing their guns. When the Germans were advancing along the coast, the sailors fired on them and they simply ran away. And so they would, from sixteen-inch guns! Imagine the power!"[114] Stalin did not react to Zhukov's reversal (or perhaps suspension) of his order, which Zhukov probably interpreted as the supreme leader's implied consent.

Document 11, however, raises doubt over whether Zhukov had unequivocally and irrevocably terminated all plans to scuttle ships. The author of this message to Zhukov, Division Commissar V. A. Lebedev, assumed that the "special operation" was still in effect on 20 September but complained that it was being implemented in a disorganized manner. The resolutions included at the end of the document show that coded signals for mass demolition (included in Document 11) remained in effect through at least the first week in October, when Zhukov returned to Moscow to shore up its defenses, because on 4 October, the emergency signals were changed to eliminate confusion with other signals. If Zhukov once and for all had terminated plans to destroy the fleet, there would have been no need to keep any demolition signals.

Part of Document 11 is open to interpretation. Lebedev described confusion between the new emergency signals and existing signals for artillery fire. Each set employed the code word "Tulip" but conveyed different instructions by it. Lebedev stated that "Tulip" was transmitted on 18 September. Shortly thereafter it was determined that the artillery signal book had been used for this transmission, so "Tulip" in this case meant "cease fire." However, if "Tulip" was supposed to have been interpreted according to the new signals, it would have countermanded all preliminary orders on deploying explosive charges, which in effect would partly substantiate Zhukov's later assertion that he reversed Stalin's order. What may have happened is that Zhukov on 18 September intended that "Tulip" would be interpreted according to the new signals as an order to halt the demolition planning but not to remove explosive charges already set in place. Such a course of action would have allowed Zhukov to retain the option of restarting the demolition program on short notice. The fact that the emergency demolition signals were retained supports this interpretation of Zhukov's actions.

The document also shows that Lebedev contended that the demolition plans constituted too blunt an instrument as they lacked provisions for destroying objectives by sector within districts. His letter of protest further revealed that the preparations for destruction of the fleet had devastated morale as evidenced by the morbidly defeatist comments attributed to a destroyer captain and the deputy chief of staff of the Baltic Fleet.

· Document 11 ·

Report from Baltic Fleet Division Commissar Lebedev to Zhukov regarding confusion over demolition signals and low morale among fleet officers, 20 September 1941, Tsentral'nyi voenno-morskoi arkhiv f. 161, op. 1, d. 6, l. 7 in Knyshevskii et al., *Skrytnaia pravda voiny,* 145–47.

No. 172661
Leningrad
Top secret
To the Commander of the Leningrad Front
Army General Com. ZHUKOV

Preparations for the spec[ial] operation to destroy fleet vessels and battle units are proceeding in a highly disorganized fashion.

The system of signals, set up on a district-by-district basis, has no flexibility and takes away the right to destroy targets sector by sector [*po uchastkam*]. Thus, explosions and losses might begin before they should, in places where they are not needed, endangering targets (bridges, plants, construction sites) adjacent to this district.

The very organization of the signalization is creating the prerequisite for hindering or prematurely destroying military units.

Characteristically, on 18 September, unexpectedly, the signal "Tulip" was given to the fleet, which according to the TUS [table of prearranged signals] established for the special operation means to cease [*prekratit'*] destruction measures. Soon afterward it emerged that the signal had been given from the table of artillery signals and means to cease firing immediately.

For one thing, the measures being taken to prepare the special operation were reassigned to inferiors in most instances; thus, for the special operations detachment, [they] were being carried out by Coms. Yanson and Klitny, while the command in the person of division commander Captain 2nd Class Maslov and Yevdokimov chose to stand aside. For another, the measures became widely known.

As a result, negative moods have been noted, prefiguring a sad outcome for Leningrad's defense.

Thus, for example:

On 16 September 1941, while on the destroyer *Strogy*, Captain 2nd Class Maslov stated:

"Yes, I've brought you bad news. They're getting ready to surrender Leningrad to German fascism. They've already given the destroyers *Stroiny* and *Strogy* up for lost. The top leadership is making off from Leningrad in airplanes."

Captain 2nd Class Zozulia, KBF dep[uty] ch[ief] of staff, said pessimistically:

"What are we waiting for? We might as well put a bullet in our head."

Head of the KBF 3rd Division
Division Commissar LEBEDEV

Notes on the document:
To Com. Isakov
1. Immediately investigate and arrest the provocateurs.
2. Report why such important work is being done with such criminal ineptitude. ZHUKOV
To the KBF Military Council
Conduct an investigation.
Report to the Military Council that the shortcomings and errors have been taken care of in the final plan. 24 September 1941. ISAKOV

To Rukovsky
Monitor the change of arranged signals. 28 September 1941. ISAKOV
TUS has been replaced. 4 October 1941. RUKOVSKY

Zhukov has been called the "savior of Leningrad," for his decision not
to abandon the city (though he had not entirely ruled out that option) and
for the effective measures he adopted, although his detractors charge that
he wasted far too many lives in ill-conceived attempts to break the blockade.[115] To the Soviet defenders the likelihood of a direct attack appeared
greatest on 16–17 September, although by that time Hitler had settled for
laying siege to the city for an indefinite period as his primary attention had
shifted to the battle for Moscow.[116] The banner headlines of *Leningradskaia pravda* from 16 September read, "The Enemy is at the Gates!" and
"We Will Fight for Leningrad to the Last Heartbeat!" The press broadcast
clearly the message that the city would not be surrendered, though it did
not consistently guarantee that it could be defended. If German land forces
had attempted to occupy Leningrad in mid-September or later, it appears
almost certain that they would have been met by the same type of tenacious
resistance that Stalingrad mounted the following year. Zhukov put into
effect an improved version of a plan for the city's defense that the VSLF
had formulated before his arrival on 4 September. That plan divided the
city into six defensive sectors that were clustered around important factories, bridges, rail lines, and canals. In those six sectors twenty-six regular
divisions were deployed. Zhukov ordered barricades built throughout the
city with antitank ditches dug in front of them and antitank guns covering
them. Leningrad's antiaircraft defenses were also strengthened. Moreover,
two new *opolchenie* divisions were created consisting of 36,000 volunteers,
mainly factory workers, and the number of Leningraders who were working on fortifications increased from 43,000 to 90,000 by 1 October. By
the end of the year, the city reportedly had over 22,000 rifle positions,
3,600 machine gun nests, 570 artillery batteries, 21 miles of barricades,
and approximately 70 naval guns mounted on rail cars. In the Kirovsky,
Moskovsky, and Volodarsky *raiony* no more than 100 yards separated any
two firing points. About half of the fleet's warships were anchored in the
Neva in sections closest to German lines.[117]

Of the 141 factories in the city's six defense sectors, the Kirov works
was the best defended. Although the 6,500 members of the plant's military detachment started building fortifications only shortly before the siege
began, and a unified defense staff for the plant was not created until 12 September, by the sixteenth they had reportedly constructed almost a mile of
scrap-metal barricades, 18 artillery batteries, 27 dugouts, and 13 mortar
emplacements on the 370 acres of factory grounds. Workers also placed

47 machine guns within the factory walls. However, the factory's detachment of 6,500 workers was lightly armed with only 615 rifles. Some of their weaponry they manufactured themselves when they were not busy with other production orders, occupying defense positions, or taking cover from heavy enemy fire. From positions two and a half miles distant, German gunners could hardly miss the half a square mile of factory grounds. During the month of September, over 300 artillery shells, about 800 incendiaries, and 35 high explosive bombs reportedly hit the factory's grounds and buildings. (Figure 9 is a German photo reconnaissance image of the factory from September 1942.) The worker detachment was charged not only with defending the factory's premises but also with assisting the *opolchenie* and the Twenty-first NKVD Division in defending the villages of Avtovo and Alekseeva south of the factory, a section of Stachek Prospect (a main road that ran south to the front), and the city's harbor.[118]

From the moment Zhukov took charge of the Leningrad Front, he implemented very harsh disciplinary measures, which appear to have had the effect of stiffening Leningrad's defenses. An immediate problem that he had to confront was desertion from army and *opolchenie* divisions. Between 16 and 22 August, 4,300 people were detained in Leningrad on suspicion of desertion from the front; 1,412 of them were from the *opolchenie*. From 26 August to 5 September, another 7,328 were detained in the city and its southern suburbs for not having appropriate identity papers; 3,020 of them were handed over to military authorities on suspicion of desertion. Then, during the tense days of 13–17 September, still another 3,567 were detained. In response to the mass detentions and arrests, the VSLF implemented a new registration procedure for military personnel. Those not registered would be considered deserters, and civilians harboring deserters would be handed over to the Military Tribunal.[119] On 17 September (Document 12), the VSLF decreed that all military personnel who left their posts without written authorization would be shot.

· Document 12 ·

Military Order 0064 from the Leningrad Front to Military Councils of the Forty-second and Fifty-fifth Armies ordering deserters to be executed, 17 September 1941, TsAMO f. 217, op. 1221, d. 220, l. 387, in *Voenno-istoricheskii zhurnal*, 1992, No. 6–7, 18.

To the military councils of the 42nd and 55th Armies
FROM LENINGRAD FRONT HEADQUARTERS
   1. Because of the especially great defensive significance of the southern seg-

ment of the Leningrad boundary—Ligovo, Kiskino, Verkh. Koirovo, Pulkovskie Heights, and the area of Moskovskaia Slavianka, Shushary, and Kolpino—the military council of the Leningrad Front informs all command, political, and rank-and-file personnel defending said boundary that all commanders, political workers, and soldiers leaving said boundary without a written order from the military council of the front and army are subject to be shot immediately.

2. The present order shall be announced to command and political staff against a written receipt. Rank-and-file personnel shall be broadly informed.

3. Report execution of the order in code by 12:00 18 September 41.

> Troop commander of the Leningrad Front
> Hero of the Soviet Union
> Army General ZHUKOV
> Member of Military Council LF
> TsK VKP(b) Secretary ZHDANOV
> Member of LF Military Council
> Division Commissar
> KUZNETSOV
> Chief of Staff of the Leningrad Front
> Lieutenant General KHOZIN

As if anticipating the decree, *Leningradskaia pravda* on 16 September bluntly warned the populace that any coward who abandoned his post in the "difficult hour" would be shot. On 26 September, the newspaper called for maintaining strict public order and apprehending deserters. It described one deserter who fled to Leningrad and caused a commotion outside a shop by trying to jump to the head of the queue. The severely distressed soldier ended up throwing a grenade into a group of people. On 30 October, *Leningradskaia pravda* published another article about a group of army deserters who fled to Leningrad and were hidden by their parents. The AWOL soldiers purportedly organized food thefts and looted apartments during air raids, when their occupants sought safety in shelters. Upon their arrest, some of the soldiers were shot and others received ten-year sentences. Those who hid them (presumably including the parents) got five years in jail.

On 18 September, the VSLF ordered the Leningrad NKVD to improve control over the city's exposed southern districts, and it designated areas within the blockade zone for housing refugees. The document also ordered "the handing over to the NKVD of all people who were found to have been on territory occupied by the enemy."[120] Stalin's order of 21 September (Document 13) is the quintessential example of his merciless defense doctrine. Having received reports, most likely from the NKVD ("People are saying . . ."), that the Germans were advancing behind Russian human shields, Stalin ordered the defenders to fire on "the enemy and his accomplices, free or not . . ." What particularly perturbed him was that his sources were reporting that there were "some Leningrad Bolsheviks who do not believe weapons can be used against delegates of this sort." In Stalin's view, such people were "more dangerous than German fascists." The specter of German divisions walking unopposed into Leningrad behind collective farm workers must have loomed in Stalin's mind. While Stalin may have thought that Zhdanov and Kuznetsov needed to be warned not to "get sentimental," his instructions probably seemed superfluous to Zhukov and especially Merkulov, who had supervised the mass murder of Polish officers and arrests and deportations in the Baltics in 1940 and would return to conduct purges after the war in the reannexed Baltic territories.

· Document 13 ·

Telephone order from Stalin to Zhukov, Zhdanov, Kuznetsov, and Merkulov to fire on civilians used by the Germans as human shields outside Leningrad, 21 September 1941, Leningrad, TsAMO f. 132, op. 2642, l. 38, in *Voenno-istoricheskii zhurnal*, 1992, 19.

People are saying [*govoriat*] that the German scoundrels, as they march on Leningrad, are sending delegates from districts they have occupied—old men and old women, women and children—ahead of their troops asking the Bolsheviks to surrender Leningrad and make peace.

People are saying that there are some Leningrad Bolsheviks who do not believe weapons can be used against delegates of this sort. I believe that if there are Bolsheviks like this, then they have to be destroyed first of all, for they are more dangerous than German fascists.

My response: Don't get sentimental. Smash the enemy and his accomplices, free or not, in the teeth. War is implacable, and those who show weakness and allow hesitation are bringing defeat above all. Whoever hesitates in our ranks will be primarily to blame for Leningrad's fall.

Give the Germans and their delegates a thorough trouncing, no matter who they are. Abuse [*Kostite*] our enemies. It doesn't matter whether they're free enemies or not. No mercy for the German scoundrels or their delegates, no matter who they are.

Please bring this to the attention of the commanders and commissars of the divisions and regiments as well as to the military council of the Baltic Fleet and ship commanders and commissars.

I. STALIN

21 September 1941

4:10
Dictated over the phone by Com. Stalin at 4:00 on 21 September.

B. SHAPOSHNIKOV

Germany intercepted this transmission as well as the response from Zhukov, Zhdanov, Kuznetsov, and Merkulov. The latter stated that they were at once ordering all army and naval forces "to open fire immediately on all people who approach the front line and to block their approach to our positions. Conversations with the civilian population will not be tolerated."[121]

Zhukov was also concerned with instances of fraternization with the enemy. In the latter part of September, small groups of Red Army soldiers talked with German troops, after which they crossed over to the German lines. During the month of October, 967 troops of the Leningrad Front deserted to the enemy. Realizing the growing trend, the VSLF on 5 October issued an order to open fire on all fraternizers, to arrest all commanders and commissars of units in which fraternization took place, to arrest family members of "traitors to the motherland," and to destroy as "accomplices of the enemy" all who tolerated traitors. This order echoed the Defense Commissariat's Order 270 from August that surrendering troops would be considered traitors and enemies of the people and their families subject to imprisonment. The number of deserters from the Leningrad Front dropped to 552 in November and 120 in the first half of December. The head of the political administration of the Baltic Fleet had already imposed harsher punitive measures on 28 September when he ordered the immediate execution of families of naval personnel who defected. That directive, however, was declared illegal and abolished in early 1942.[122]

There can be no doubt that for the almost four weeks that he was in Leningrad, Zhukov held supreme authority as Stalin's representative. He was under extreme pressure to produce results. In a postwar interview Zhukov claimed that two days before he was dispatched to Leningrad as Front commander, Molotov threatened him with a firing squad if he failed to halt the German offensive.[123] Zhukov had considerable leeway in formulating his defense strategy. As the example of de-mining warships of the Baltic Fleet shows, he could even rescind, or at least partly overturn, an order from Stalin. After the reprimands that Stalin had delivered to Zhdanov, Leningrad's party chief was in no position to challenge Zhukov's decisions. We have few glimpses into Zhukov's relationship with Kubatkin; however, the terse and dismissive tone that Zhukov adopted toward Kubatkin in Document 14 strikingly reveals the subordinate status of the Leningrad NKVD head. In 1937–38, many of Zhukov's fellow senior officers had been arrested and shot during the army purge, and he himself had been slated for execution in the summer of 1939 but his assignment to Khalkhin-Gol to confront the Japanese had saved his life.[124] Two years later, the general had the upper hand over the NKVD. On 24 September 1941, during the first failed offensive for Siniavino, a secretary of the VSLF sent the following report to Kubatkin.

· Document 14 ·

Zhukov's terse correction to Kubatkin regarding the military situation at Siniavino, 24 September 1941, Arkhiv UFSB RF po SPb i LO f. 21/12, op. 2, p.n. 43, d. 2, l. 23.

SECRETARIAT OF THE MILITARY *SOVET* OF THE LENINGRAD FRONT
TO THE HEAD OF ADMINISTRATION OF THE LENINGRAD NKVD
Commissar of state security of the third rank
Com. KUBATKIN
I am conveying a statement from General of the Army Comrade Zhukov in response to your special report No. 9295 from 23 September 1941 on the question whether on 19 September the adversary was dislodged from Siniavino.
"To Com. Kubatkin. This does not correspond to reality. Zhukov."
Secretary of the Military Soviet of the Leningrad Front
Battalion commissar   [signed] Borshchenko

Kubatkin handed on the rebuke to his chief of staff Tsyganov in an equally laconic note scrawled across the statement: "Com. Tsyganov. It is necessary to verify better before writing. Kubatkin."

In fortifying Leningrad's internal defenses, Zhukov gave specific assignments to Kubatkin. On 18 September, he entrusted him with organizing the middle of three defense lines in the southern part of the city and ordered him to conduct daily security sweeps in the city and to patrol the main roads, rail lines, and defensive positions.[125]

The tone of the relationship between the VSLF and the NKVD remained unchanged after Zhukov returned to Moscow on 6 October. Borshchenko sent Kubatkin a message on 15 March 1942 informing him that from 8 March "it is forbidden to go to the VSLF with notes and reports on questions of current work that exceed 3–5 typed pages." Borshchenko stated (with a detectable note of sarcasm) that the NKVD *apparat* must not have notified Kubatkin about the new regulation, even though a statement about it had been sent directly to Kubatkin on 10 March. Borshchenko requested that Kubatkin rework according to the new regulation an eight-page NKVD report from 14 March that repeated material from an earlier report and included many comments written in pencil.[126]

Zhukov was not able to lift the siege with the offensive toward Siniavino; however, the Leningrad Front stabilized during his tenure as its commander. His draconian policies likely strengthened Soviet defenses, but Hitler's decision of 6 September to make Moscow his main target and transfer large portions of the Fourth Panzer Group and the Eighth Air Corps to Army Group Center by 15 September probably played a larger role.[127] Toward the end of Zhukov's stay in Leningrad, relations between the Kremlin and Smolny improved somewhat. On 4 October, Stalin cabled orders to Zhdanov and Kuznetsov to evacuate to the Urals all machinery used in manufacturing the KV and T-50 tanks and the skilled workers and engineers involved in tank production, especially from the Kirov and Izhorsk factories and a secret facility simply identified by its number, 74, a tank production plant named for Voroshilov. The exchange of messages was matter-of-fact, as the Leningraders agreed to carry out all of Stalin's instructions. Stalin concluded his transmission with the words: Very well. Goodbye. I shake your hand. That's all." The Leningraders reciprocated: "Goodbye. We firmly shake your hand."[128] Yet, by 23 October, as the Siniavino offensive was in its final, failing days and following four days of uncontrolled looting in Moscow, when it appeared that the entire central government was evacuating to Kuibyshev as the German Operation Typhoon gained momentum, Stalin's mood again darkened. Not only did he realize that the siege of Leningrad would not soon be lifted, he feared that the city's defenses might collapse. On Stalin's orders, deputy chief of the army's General Staff General Aleksandr Vasilevsky sent the following late-night message:

· Document 15 ·

Stalin's order to Leningrad Front Commander Fediuninsky, Zhdanov, and Kuznetsov to launch immediately an offensive to the east to break out of the siege and avoid possible capture, 23 October 1941, RGASPI f. 77, op. 3, d. 126, l. 10.

Judging by your slow actions, one can conclude that all of you still have not realized the critical situation that the troops of the Leningrad Front are in.

If in the course of the next several days you do not break through and restore a firm link with the 54th Army, which connects you with the rear of the country, all of your troops will be taken prisoner.

Restoration of this link is necessary not only to supply the troops of the Leningrad Front, but especially to give an exit to the troops of the Leningrad

Front for retreat to the east in order to avoid captivity in case it becomes necessary to give up Leningrad.

Bear in mind that Moscow is in a critical situation, and it is not in a condition to help you with new forces.

Either in the next two to three days you will break through and give your troops the chance to retreat to the east in the event that Leningrad cannot be held, or you will be taken prisoner.

We demand from you decisive and quick action.

Concentrate eight or nine divisions and break through to the east.

This is necessary whether Leningrad will be held or given up. For us the army is more important. We demand from you decisive action.

Stalin 23 October 3:35

Transmitted by Vasilevsky 23 October 4:02

A few hours later, Vasilevsky ordered the commander of the Fifty-fourth Army, Khozin, who three days later would be ordered to exchange commands with Leningrad Front commander Fediuninsky,[129] to provide all assistance possible for the breakout offensive. He added: "I ask you to consider that in this case the question is not so much saving Leningrad as it is saving and extracting the armies of the Leningrad Front. That's all."[130] These are the clearest expressions among the many statements from the late summer and fall of 1941 of Stalin's priorities concerning Leningrad.

In the weeks to come, the Leningrad Front did not succeed in linking up with the Fifty-fourth Army; in fact, Leningrad's situation became more perilous after the Germans took Tikhvin on 8 November. New roads had to be built through forests and swamps to reach Ladoga, and stormy weather reduced shipments across the lake. The German eastward offensive also raised anew the possibility of Germany linking up with Finnish forces on Ladoga's eastern shore. Stalin's relations with Leningrad's leaders again became strained. On the day Tikhvin fell, Stalin conversed with Zhdanov and Khozin. Once again, Stalin exhorted them to launch an assault to the east to break out of the blockade immediately. If they did not, they would be taken prisoner and Leningrad would fall: "If in the course of several days you do not break through to the east, you will fritter away the Leningrad Front and the population of Leningrad. . . . You must choose between captivity, on the one hand, and sacrificing several divisions, I repeat, to sacrifice and carve out a way to the east in order to save your front and Leningrad. You argue as if there were a third way. No such third way exists. Either captivity and downfall of the entire front or not to stop short of any sacrifice and carve out a way to the east. . . . I repeat, there is little time left. To sit and wait for something to turn up is not reasonable."[131]

After a follow-up conversation on 9 November, Khozin and Zhdanov did not converse directly with Stalin until 1 December. By that time, food rations in Leningrad had reached their lowest levels of the entire war as Tikhvin was still in enemy hands. Stalin, accompanied by Molotov, began the exchange with deadly serious criticism regarding the failure to remain in closer contact. The Leningrad leaders had not successfully carried out Stalin's repeated orders to break out of the encirclement to the east, which could be construed by Stalin as constituting major dereliction of duty. Stalin cloaked his criticism in jocular sarcasm:

> It is extremely strange that Comrade Zhdanov does not feel the need to come to the telegraph machine and make requests from one of us for reciprocal information in so difficult a moment for Leningrad.
>
> If the Muscovites did not summon you to the telegraph machine, perhaps Comrade Zhdanov would forget about Moscow and the Muscovites, who could render aid to Leningrad.
>
> One might suppose that Leningrad together with Comrade Zhdanov is located not in the USSR but somewhere in the Pacific Ocean. Report what you are working on, how things are with you and how you think you will get out of the present situation . . .

Stalin signed off by saying:

> Don't lose time, not just each [day], but hour is dear. The enemy has gathered against Moscow all of his forces from almost all fronts. All of the remaining fronts, including yours, now have a favorable opportunity to strike the enemy. Use the opportunity before it is too late. I repeat, don't miss the opportunity. That's all.[132]

Khozin's Leningrad Front had launched an offensive on 9 November, which lasted into December. Its goal was to cross the Neva River in the Moskovskaia Dubrovka region and attack toward Mga in order to link up with the Eighth and Fifty-fourth Armies outside the siege ring. Khozin's attacks had failed miserably. German chief of staff Colonel General Franz Halder barely took note of them in his diary and on 19 November dismissed them with the entry: "On the Leningrad front, the usual attack was repelled."[133] In the conversation with Stalin and Molotov, Zhdanov and Khozin claimed some success in moving tanks to the east bank of the Neva River but then deflected blame for the failure of the operation from themselves toward the commander and the commissar of the Eightieth Rifle Division, Colonel I. M. Frolov and K. D. Ivanov. This division was the former First Guards *opolchenie* Division, which had been badly mauled in the Kingisepp sector in August. Frolov had commanded the division from its inception as a poorly equipped volunteer unit.[134] The scapegoating charge of Zhdanov and Khozin consisted of the following:

This operation thanks to the cowardly-traitorous conduct of the 80th division (Frolov is the commander of the division) was disrupted three hours before it began. The operation was put off until the next day and then carried out, but the element of surprise was destroyed. We direct to you a declaration with the request to authorize that the commander of the 80th division Frolov and the commissar of the division Ivanov be tried and shot.

The Military Council must wage war against cowards and panickers, most of all when they are among the high command staff.

Stalin did not object to Zhdanov and Khozin requesting the court martial of the two high-ranking officers and predetermining the verdict. Stalin simply replied: "Without fail, shoot Frolov and Ivanov and announce this in the press."[135] On the following day, the Military Tribunal of the Leningrad Front sentenced both to be shot. No appeal was permitted. The verdict stated that on 21 November, Frolov had been ordered to attack but that three hours before the start of the operation, he and Ivanov had complained to two representatives of the Front command that they did not believe the operation would be successful. Their objection had disrupted preparations to attack.[136] Assuming that the information in the verdict is accurate, one can imagine their state of mind at that time. Frolov had witnessed the slaughter of his *opolchenie* division, and Soviet losses during the fighting in the late autumn of 1941 were also frightfully high, especially along the Neva River where, according to one estimate, during the course of the entire war as many as a quarter of a million Soviet troops were killed.[137] In November and December 1941, 300,000 Soviet troops fought in the vicinity of Tikhvin and in the failed offensive to break the siege. Some 80,000 of them were killed, captured, or went missing, and another 110,000 were injured for a casualty rate of 63 percent.[138]

The last three months of 1941 were equally critical for Leningrad's civilian population. Food rations declined to starvation levels, and the enemy bombardment remained intensive. Leningraders continued to build fortifications and undergo military training. Workers and industrial machinery in exposed areas were transferred within the city to *raiony* that were less frequently bombed and shelled, and some continued to be evacuated to the east. Workers in defense plants and in factories that were converted to produce weaponry continued to put in long shifts. With the start of the German offensive against Moscow on 2 October, Stalin sought to mobilize the rest of the nation to supply the capital with as much war matériel as possible. In mid-October, Stalin sent Marshal Voronov, a native of St. Petersburg and a veteran of the siege of Madrid in the Spanish Civil War, on his third trip to Leningrad since late August. As GKO representative, he carried orders to increase the city's production of artillery, mortars, and ammunition and to make sure that a significant part of the matériel was flown to Moscow. Over the summer, many of Leningrad's factories had completed retooling for producing a variety of weapons, including artillery, antitank guns, and Katiusha rockets. Voronov immediately ran into opposition from Zhdanov, who demanded that the GKO send the Leningrad Front more munitions to help it break out of the siege. Voronov subsequently claimed that when he told Zhdanov that Leningrad's factories ought to produce not less than one million artillery shells and mines in November, the party chief vehemently protested: "A million artillery shells and mines in a month is crazy! It's a bluff. It's ignorant. You simply do not understand the organization and technology of producing ammunition!"[139] Voronov remained in Leningrad through 5 December, and his orders prevailed, although he did not succeed in procuring as many munitions from Leningrad as he had wanted.

Voinov related a similar conflict between an unnamed Moscow envoy and Kuznetsov. The envoy had arrived in Leningrad (when exactly is uncertain) to collect construction materials, including state-owned furnishings from the homes of Leningraders who had been killed in the war, to be shipped over Ladoga and on to Moscow for the construction of homes for *Sovnarkom* employees. When Kuznetsov learned of the matter, he immediately countermanded the order and demanded that the envoy be expelled from Leningrad within twenty-four hours.[140]

The rifts between the Leningrad leadership and the Kremlin representatives, of course, did not enter into the Leningrad press. During the autumn, the official line remained that the city must produce as much military hardware as possible. On 13 November, *Leningradskaia pravda* printed a new appeal from Stalin for Leningrad to produce more weapons, including tanks and shells. On 20 November, the GKO adopted Resolution No. 927 "On the production of mortars in Leningrad," which required Leningrad to produce 3,700 mortars and ship half of them to Defense Commissariat reserves near Moscow.[141] The assigned quota was unrealistically high given the growing hunger in the city and the fact that most factories had lost electrical power by mid-December. Nevertheless, between October and mid-December, Leningrad's factories sent to Moscow 452 76-millimeter guns (55 percent of all manufactured in Leningrad in this period), 913 mortars, just under 30,000 shells for the artillery, and large quantities of mines, communication equipment, and other supplies. Most of the guns were sent by air; the artillery shells were sent out by ship or barge over Ladoga.[142] The GKO demands meant that through December tens of thousands of factory workers had to continue logging shifts of eleven to fourteen hours while subsisting on shrinking food rations. According to one study, toward the end of November over half of all factory workers under the age of thirty were still achieving at least double their work norms.[143] In return, these workers received between eight and twelve ounces of bread per day, which often contained inedible additives, and on rare occasions a few ounces of groats, meat, sugar, and fat. Even during the month that the enemy occupied Tikhvin, the GKO did not scale back its demands on Leningrad's defense plants.

In retrospect, the GKO's demands on Leningrad in the summer and fall of 1941 were excessive in that the damage done to Leningrad and its ability to fight a prolonged war was greater than the benefit derived from the munitions produced and sent to the GKO's stockpile. If the armies in the Leningrad area had been allowed to retain more of the weaponry (especially the KV tanks) manufactured in city in July and August, perhaps Shlisselburg could have been better defended and the blockade prevented. Stalin's modus operandi during the war, which was highlighted in his policy toward Leningrad, was largely the same as it had been in the 1930s: identify a goal—whether collectivization of agriculture, building Magnitogorsk, or defending Moscow after Hitler launched Operation Typhoon—and mobilize as many people and material resources as possible to achieve, or even overfulfill, the objective without paying much heed to the cost. The Soviet counteroffensive that took place between December 1941 and April 1942, and stretched from the Leningrad *oblast'* in the north to Briansk in the south, exemplifies Stalin's wartime maximalism. It would appear that at the end of 1941, Stalin was thinking in terms of 1812: the tide of the war would be turned at Moscow, and the enemy would be sent reeling relentlessly in retreat to his homeland. Reserves from all over the USSR, including starving Leningrad, were effectively gathered and deployed near Moscow. The fact that the Red Army pushed back the Wehrmacht 200 miles in some sectors along a 560-mile front shows that the amassed reserves were huge. By late January 1942, no German troops were within 100 miles of Moscow as Stalin tried to execute a grand pincer movement that would encircle Army Group Center.[144] But Stalin wasted his reserves by committing too many of them to action and pursuing the counteroffensive too far. Germany regained the initiative rather easily in the spring of 1942, and bypassed the overextended Red Army in its drive through the Ukraine to Stalingrad and the Caucasus.

The war materials produced in Leningrad at great cost and sent to Moscow were not critical to Moscow's defense. To be fair to Stalin and the rest of the GKO, this judgment is rendered in the relative clarity of hindsight. At the beginning of December 1941, Moscow's fate was as uncertain as Leningrad's, with German troops only some twenty miles from the Kremlin, and the capital was strategically more important than Leningrad. Hence, the argument for gathering as many resources as possible for Moscow's defense was a formidable one. However, those who directed the Soviet war effort could have and should have realized after the initial success of the Soviet counterattack west of Moscow that munitions, other supplies, and personnel needed to be conserved and some of the resources shipped to the Leningrad Front or the newly created Volkhov Front.

It is now evident that Leningrad and the entire nation would have been better served had one of two alternative strategies been pursued from as early as October 1941. The first was to have directed those munitions that were sent by Leningrad to Moscow instead to the Leningrad Front to help it break through the siege ring. David Glantz's exhaustive research has shown that the *Stavka* continually tried to liberate Leningrad, including during the starvation winter, and the one significant victory in the Leningrad area was the retaking of Tikhvin on 9 December. Stalin never lost interest in Leningrad during the blockade period; however, if an extra thousand mortars and heavy guns and some of the KV tanks that were shipped to Moscow just prior to the start of the siege had instead been given to the armies of the Leningrad and Volkhov Fronts, they might have tipped the balance in the Red Army's favor. Liberating Leningrad in late 1941 or early 1942 would have saved the lives of hundreds of thousands and enabled the city to resume its role as one of the nation's top munitions producers. Even if the siege could not have been lifted at this time and German forces driven back out of artillery range of Leningrad, a Soviet offensive fortified with the materials that instead were sent to Moscow might have succeeded in regaining control of the narrow stretch of land along Lake Ladoga's southern coast that Germany held and reestablishing a rail link with the "Mainland" as was eventually done in February 1943. In the event that such an offensive had been attempted but did not succeed, it might nevertheless have weakened German defensive positions so that a follow-up attack in the last weeks of 1941 or in 1942 could have enjoyed further success.[145]

The other alternative was to produce fewer munitions during October and November in favor of preparing Leningrad for a winter under siege. A "hunkering down" strategy would have prevented much of the waste that resulted from chaotic efforts to produce as much as possible for the front. Leningrad was unprepared for a harsh winter with frozen water pipes and little electrical power. If the city had produced more metal stoves, pails, sleds, warm clothes, and boots, and chopped more firewood, lives would have been saved and human productive capacity preserved. With the continuation of the blockade through the winter, many thousands would have starved and frozen to death whether or not production had been shifted earlier to the needs of the civilian population; nevertheless, the excessive burdens put on Leningrad's industry to produce for the front in the autumn of 1941 made the city's plight that much more difficult.

In sum, if different strategies had been pursued, Moscow could have been defended at the same time that the Leningrad siege was either ended or weakened, or the city preserved in better shape under siege. From Stalin's strategic vantage point, however, the situation that prevailed was far from desperate. Leningrad's continued resistance kept Germany from consolidating its position along the Baltic and forging a stronger alliance with Finland. Hundreds of thousands of enemy troops were tied up near Leningrad and therefore could not be used in Operation Typhoon in October and November. It would be an exaggeration to claim that the Soviet-German War reached its turning point in the winter of 1941–42; however, the *Stavka* and GKO for the first time since 22 June had reason for a measure of hope, despite Leningrad's wretched condition. Time was on their side. If the USSR could stay in the war through the fall of 1942, industrial production would likely increase as many of the 2,593 industrial enterprises, including 1,523 large factories, that were evacuated eastward would be back in production.[146] Relocated factories would be supplemented by mining and manufacturing industries already established in the east. And what the Soviet Union could not mine or manufacture on its own, it might receive from its new and powerful ally, the United States, which in time would also open fronts against Germany in North Africa, Italy, and France.

When Leningrad lost most of its capacity for generating electricity by the start of the third week of December, the GKO's demands on city industries correspondingly diminished. The *gorkom* and *ispolkom* directed more attention to the city's immediate survival needs and, when Lake Ladoga froze, to evacuating hundreds of thousands of civilians who had been trapped in the city since late August. On 15 November, shipping across Ladoga halted due to ice formation, although a convoy of three ships did manage to avoid ice floes and cross Ladoga bringing the last shipment of flour and ammunition to Leningrad on 29 November.[147] On 20 November, with ice on Ladoga measuring 18 centimeters thick in places, the first experimental ice convoy, consisting of 350 horses with sleds, set out across the lake toward the southeastern shore and returned with sacks of flour. This was also the day that bread rations were cut to their lowest levels. On 22 November, sixty trucks headed out across the ice for the town of Kobona and returned the following day with thirty-three tons of flour.[148] While the convoy headed toward Kobona, Smolny requested permission from the GKO to create an auto road over the frozen lake for delivering large amounts of food to Leningrad. Right around this time, the Leningrad NKVD informed Beria about the first cases of death by starvation in Leningrad,[149] and by 13 December, Beria knew that cannibalism had reared its ugly head there (Document 54). Mikoyan claimed that he immediately supported the ice road proposal and drafted a letter to Khozin and Zhdanov, which stated that 400 tons of flour, 150 tons of groats, 100 tons of kerosene, and 200 tons of ammunition could be sent daily to Leningrad over the road. He sought Stalin's permission for the project, which was given but with major reservations. According to Mikoyan: "Thereupon I approached Stalin and asked him to sign the letter that was sent the same day [22 November]. Although Stalin sanctioned the proposal, he did not understand the vital importance of the road, and that's why at the end of the letter he added a postscript: 'I warn you that this entire business affords little hope and is not of serious significance to the Leningrad Front.' But he was mistaken."[150] Stalin's warning served as a thinly veiled threat to the Leningrad leaders and perhaps to Mikoyan as well should the ice road not produce results. But the VSLF at this time was gripped by the hope that the ice road would end the most pressing supply problems and provide a safe exodus from the city for the starving. On 24 November, Khozin, Zhdanov, and Kuznetsov issued a resolution that had very optimistic goals. They ordered the assembling within one day of 500 vehicles from Leningrad for service on the ice road, plus another 1,000 from the army within two days. The order, however, was unrealistic as trucks and cars in running order were very scarce. Approximately 15,000 vehicles had already been sent to the armed forces from the city and *oblast'* by October.[151] The resolution also gave the head of the October Railroad, I. V. Kolpakov, one week to muster enough locomotives and rail cars to evacuate 7,000 people daily from the Finland Station to Osinovets on the western shore of the lake.[152] In actuality, the operation brought little food into Leningrad and carried few refugees out of the city during its first weeks of operation, despite the fact that the temperature remained below freezing almost all of the time.[153] While Tikhvin remained under German control, food convoys depended on rough, improvised roads to reach Ladoga. There was insufficient antiaircraft defense on the lake and few warehouses to store food along the way. Mikoyan recounted that he had become so alarmed by 7 December that he and the head of the Main Administration of Logistical Supply Khrulev directed Zhdanov and GKO representative Pavlov to reorganize the ice road to make it more efficient. In particular, they called for better protection of the cargo and improved military defense, as well as for more Leningraders to be evacuated on the trucks during their return runs. For reasons that remain unclear, traffic over the ice road was suddenly halted on 8 December, which was followed four days later by a formal decision from the VSLF to suspend operations.[154]

Despite Mikoyan's claims to the contrary, changes made in December did not significantly improve the road's functioning. The VSLF set a new goal of evacuating five thousand people per day starting from 22 December, but that hope, which was scaled back from the more ambitious objectives set forth in the 24 November resolution, was not realized primarily because of lack of organized transport. Between 6 December and 22 January, only 36,118 Leningrad refugees reportedly traveled the frozen lake's military highway. An unknown number of people secretly bribed truck drivers to take them across the lake. Some crossed Ladoga illegally on foot.[155]

The major turning point in the operation of the Road of Life occurred in mid- to late January. On 11 January, the GKO ordered a rail line of about twenty-one miles constructed from Voibokalo to Kobona and to Kosa a little farther north along Ladoga's shoreline. When the track to Kobona opened on 20 February (and to Kosa on 6 March), it shortened the supply route by twenty miles and brought trains right to the lake. Some 3,000 Leningraders helped build the line.[156] On 19 January, the GKO sent Kosygin, who was second in command to Mikoyan in the national evacuation committee, back to Leningrad along with seven other high-ranking officials to improve the functioning of the ice road. Kosygin would remain in Leningrad until July. On 21 January, he requested from Stalin the evacuation of half a million people from Leningrad to be conducted as quickly as possible. The following day, the GKO approved his request and committed far more resources to the operation. Forty buses and 360 trucks were sent to Leningrad from Moscow, Yaroslavl, and Gorky, in addition to vehicles from other cities. The first evacuation convoy assembled from these vehicles left Leningrad on 2 February.[157]

Had Stalin decided earlier to fortify the Ladoga lifeline, far fewer Leningraders would have perished. More people would have been evacuated earlier, and more food would have been sent to the starving city. Stalin was aware of the dimensions of Leningrad's dire food shortages prior to his conversation with Kosygin on 21 January. On 5 December, Zhdanov observed in a letter to Stalin that "the worst is that the hunger is spreading."[158] As Documents 42 and 54 indicate, Beria received much detailed information on 6 and 13 December that Leningraders were starving to death, that food stores were being ransacked, and that instances of murder and cannibalism had occurred. Even if Beria withheld some of the information from Stalin, the *vozhd'* learned about Leningrad's food shortages from other sources, including conversations he or his secretary had with Mikoyan and A. A. Kuznetsov.

Organizational problems remained after the GKO's decision to increase traffic over Ladoga, and the largest numbers were evacuated only in March and April, when the ice road was beginning to break up. All told, between 22 January and 15 April, 554,186 civilians reportedly left Leningrad. (During the entire period that the ice road was in operation in the first winter of the war, seven infantry divisions, two marine brigades, and one tank brigade also left the blockaded territory by crossing the lake.) Of the 360,000 tons of cargo brought into Leningrad over the ice road, 270,900 tons were food. The rest was primarily fuel, oil, and ammunition.[159]

Exactly why Stalin, who had previously shown little concern for civilians not employed in defense sectors, became convinced of the need to authorize a massive supply and evacuation operation and why he finally did so on 22 January are not entirely clear. It may have been that following the liberation of Tikhvin on 9 December, Stalin was counting on a quick end to the siege, after which food could flow easily and safely into Leningrad. In that scenario, a large-scale evacuation, which would draw supplies from other important areas, would be rendered unnecessary. On 11 December, Stalin convened a conference in Moscow, which Zhdanov attended. Marshal Shaposhnikov confidently outlined the plan for smashing the blockade, which was to begin on 20 December. The Leningrad and Volkhov Fronts would strike against the German forces between them.[160] This optimism may explain why traffic on the ice road was halted on 8 December and why the VSLF shortly thereafter suspended the operation. As late as 13 January, *Leningradskaia pravda* stated that the siege would soon end; however, the failure to fulfill that prediction, combined with the accelerating death rate in Leningrad as the coldest weather set in, may have helped convince Stalin to enlarge the Ladoga operation to rescue hundreds of thousands of civilians and relocate several army divisions. Moreover, the simultaneous success in repelling the enemy before Moscow may have persuaded him that he could afford to send more vehicles and other supplies to the ice road. What this evacuation narrative reveals is that Stalin was motivated first and foremost by military considerations; however, he was not entirely devoid of concern for the plight of nonworking Leningraders.

Soviet forces continued the offensive to break the siege until April of 1942 with great loss of life. A German counteroffensive trapped and cut off the Second Shock Army of the Volkhov Front, which had crossed the Volkhov River and driven too deep into German territory. Repeated attempts to relieve that army failed as did later offensives in 1942 and 1943 to lift the Leningrad siege.

Leningrad entered the bleakest period in the city's nearly 240 years of existence when starvation peaked in late January and February of 1942; nevertheless, at this time Smolny's relationship with the Kremlin improved slightly. Although the breakout offensive was failing, the recapture of Tikhvin had made it easier for the "Mainland" to get supplies to Lake Ladoga, and Stalin's consent, even though it came very late, to devote far more resources to the ice road significantly improved Leningrad's situation. Moreover, the cessation of mass production in the city rendered moot most GKO production orders for matériel, and thereby enabled many plants to redirect dwindling human resources to manual production of goods and services desperately needed within the city. Unfortunately for hundreds of thousands of Leningraders, the positive developments occurred too late.

Few Leningrad factory workers carried out GKO orders in January or February. In January thirteen tanks were repaired at the Kirov factory. Workers at the Skorokhod footwear factory produced 8,300 pairs of army boots and shoes. Some of the plant's workers brought in sewing machines from home and operated them by foot treadles.[161] The GKO ordered increases in the production of small arms and ammunition in March, because by then coal supplies needed to generate electricity had grown as a result of rising imports over the ice road. On 9 March, Kuznetsov summoned all *raikom* secretaries and directors of major factories to Smolny to discuss new production targets. He ordered nine factories to start manufacturing mines and artillery shells. On 17 March, the amount of electrical current defense plants received rose markedly when the new coal supply enabled a huge boiler at the city's Krasny Oktiabr power plant to resume operation. The boiler had been dismantled for evacuation months earlier, then reassembled. Mainly as a result of the March upturn in production, the city's workers managed to produce metal parts for over 200,000 grenades, mines, and artillery shells and repair over 1,000 artillery pieces in the first quarter of 1942. The Kirov works and Stalin metal works stepped up repairs on tanks and heavy guns. On 11 March, the Ordzhonikidze and Zhdanov shipyards began work on a GKO order to construct ten metal barges, each capable of carrying 600 tons of cargo. The Mashinostroitelny factory and the Stalin metal works repaired damaged ships, and the Elektrosila plant received orders to assemble 500 engines for ships of the Baltic Fleet.[162] Efforts were made to provide more food to workers in important defense plants.

Renewed GKO demands on Leningrad's industries in the first month of 1942 do not appear to have fueled much renewed tension between the Kremlin and Smolny. However, by spring a new source of friction had developed. The NKO and NKVD, without the advice or consent of Leningrad's *gorkom,* were drafting employees from the city's defense plants and sending them to factories in the east. Leningrad's industrial and political leaders had welcomed the evacuation of industrial personnel during the winter as a way to save lives; yet, by spring with the resumption of intensive German aerial bombardment and artillery fire from 4 April, which targeted war plants, and with GKO orders mounting, further removal of workers, technicians, and engineers made it very difficult to meet production targets. *Gorkom* secretary Mikhail Basov, who was in charge of several areas of defense production, sent Kuznetsov the memo below (Document 16). He complained primarily about Dmitry Ustinov, the commissar of weaponry, who was a former Leningrad factory director.[163]

· Document 16 ·

Letter from *gorkom* secretary Basov to Kuznetsov requesting that
the Commissariat of Weaponry halt its practice of reassigning skilled
defense plant workers from Leningrad to other parts of the country,
30 April 1942, TsGAIPD SPb f. 25, op. 13a, d. 33, ll. 43–44.[164]

TO MEMBER OF THE MILITARY COUNCIL, SECRETARY OF THE
LENINGRAD *GORKOM* VKP(b), *COM. KUZNETSOV A. A.*

A mass of telegrams from Comrades Ustinov, Riabikov, Mirzakhanov, Kostygov, and Karasev from the Commissariat of Weaponry are arriving to your name, to other *gorkom* secretaries, and also directors of factories about the commandeering from Leningrad of workers and engineering-technical personnel.

Up to this time, considering it necessary to help personnel in Leningrad, Leningrad's factories and the *gorkom* sent workers out of Leningrad in response to summonses from the Commissariat of Weaponry. Since December 1941 in response to summonses from the Commissariat and a request from Com. L. P. Beria to factories of the Commissariat of Weaponry, 1,066 workers and engineering-technical personal from Factory No. 349 named for the OGPU, over 800 from Factory No. 7, about 1,300 from the "Bolshevik" plant, and about 400 from the Stalin factory were sent to the interior of the country. It is impossible to send off more workers from these factories. The factories are active enterprises and are fulfilling industrial assignments for the Leningrad Front and are themselves experiencing critical shortages in qualified workers.

Evidently, as a way of helping other factories at the expense of Leningrad's factories, Com. Ustinov in a series of telegrams demands the relocation of the entire technical leadership of the "Bolshevik" factory [. . .] and the last optics specialists from the OGPU factory [. . .] without considering whether the Leningrad factories could fulfill industrial assignments of the Military Council of the LenFront and *gorkom*.

From the Commissariat and the rear factories letters are written directly to the workers of the Leningrad factories summoning them from Leningrad and threatening them with being charged under the Edict of 26 December 1941.[165]

The practice of the irresponsible pulling out of personnel from Leningrad's active enterprises took brash and very pronounced forms precisely in the Commissariat of Weaponry, which not only does not direct and does not help Leningrad factories, but, evidently, does not even consider itself responsible for their work and existence.

If the leadership in Leningrad enterprises in other commissariats in this or that measure is realized through deputy commissars or representatives of the commissariat, who are located in Leningrad (for example, shipbuilding, ammunition, mortars), then for the Commissariat of Weaponry there is none.

I consider it necessary to end further commandeering of personnel from active Leningrad enterprises in the Commissariat of Weaponry.

I ask you to send to Com. Ustinov the enclosed telegram.

Gorkom secretary for defense industry (BASOV)

30 April 1942

The telegram to which Basov referred has not been accessed, and how Ustinov and Beria may have reacted to Basov's complaint is not known. After the war, Basov rose to the position of first deputy chairman of the Council of Ministers of the Russian Federation. In 1950 he, like Kuznetsov, was executed in connection with the Leningrad Affair.

Over the next year, the military situation was transformed. By the summer of 1943, the Red Army was in the process of regaining considerable territory in southern Russia. After Germany lost the Battle of Kursk, the largest mechanized battle in world history involving one thousand tanks, in the summer of 1943, it was only a matter of time until the Wehrmacht would be driven out of the Soviet Union. As soon as mines and industrial areas, such as the Donbass, were retaken, the GKO wanted to revive production as quickly as possible. A few days after the Kursk victory, the GKO ordered Leningrad to manufacture large turbines, generators, and other machines needed to rebuild the Donbass. The GKO directly controlled production processes at several of the city's largest factories. Thus, as in the fall of 1941, during the latter half of 1943, Leningrad's industries were ordered to put the needs of another part of the nation before the city's own needs while still under siege and suffering the heaviest artillery fire of the war. During this time Leningrad was also producing most of the ammunition that would be used by the armies of the Leningrad Front in January 1944 in the breakout offensive.

Repairs were needed at several factories before they could accept new production orders. Reconstruction work began first at the Elektrosila factory, because it assembled the electric generators needed to rebuild other industries. The GKO dispatched three hundred specialists to Leningrad to help make repairs at Elektrosila, which more than doubled its GKO assignment. After completing repairs there, the GKO ordered the rebuilding of fourteen other major factories that manufactured generators as well as munitions. In August the Bolshevik plant made the city's first steel since the fall of 1941.[166]

On 23 July 1943, the *gorkom* summoned the directors and party secretaries of major industries to a conference and presented to them the new production orders. An immediate concern was the one that had emerged in the spring of 1942, when the GKO had first tried to revive Leningrad's defense industries—where to find more workers. The effects of the forced relocation of thousands of the city's skilled workers by the NKO and the NKVD in 1942 were felt anew. To make up for the shortage, some 12,875 members of city civil defense groups and employees from fifteen enterprises that had been serving the local economy were transferred to defense plants. Later in 1943 the VSLF allowed the city labor redistribution commission to draft a limited number of soldiers and sailors for factory work, and toward the end of the year, most defense plants employed some military personnel. Idle sailors in the bottled-up Baltic Fleet were used as replacement workers in shipbuilding industries. They came to number close to 2,000 of the city's 10,000 shipbuilders in 1943. In addition, factory workers who had left the city began to trickle back in the last three months of 1943. For example, between 11 and 13 December, about 600 workers received permission to return and resume factory work.[167]

Shortages of industrial machinery, lost to the city through the evacuation and enemy bombardment, were the other formidable obstacle to restarting large-scale factory production. In October Zhdanov wrote a letter to Stalin that began with a comprehensive list, broken down into fourteen categories, of enterprises, machinery, and raw materials that had been evacuated from Leningrad since the beginning of the war. The list included 70 complete enterprises, 70,319 pieces of equipment, 58,000 electric motors, and 156,000 tons of metals, among other things. Zhdanov made his specific request in the last sentence: "In order to guarantee successful fulfillment by industry of the state assignments, I request the adoption of a resolution on the full cessation of evacuation of equipment and materials from Leningrad."[168] Zhdanov wanted the means of production to remain in Leningrad. It is not certain, however, that he actually sent the letter, because the only copy that exists in the Zhdanov collection in the former central party archive in Moscow is a preliminary draft that contains his handwritten revisions. Regardless, at the end of 1943, shortly before the siege was lifted, the exodus of industrial equipment from Leningrad ended.[169]

In sum, through the end of the siege period, Smolny and the Kremlin were repeatedly at loggerheads over policy regarding Leningrad's military defense, industrial production, and evacuation. With a few exceptions at the beginning of the war, Stalin consistently displayed a steely and ruthless determination to win at whatever the cost. He recognized Leningrad's strategic value to the Soviet war effort, but deemed Moscow's security to be more important. Like other parts of the country, Leningrad, despite being blockaded, would be forced to make a massive material contribution to the defense of Moscow in the fall of 1941. For Stalin, Leningrad's significance lay in its army, navy, and defense industries, and its geographical position between the German and Finnish armies. The city's military and industrial resources were to be exploited as needed by the center. The needs of the civilian population not employed in defense plants were of far less importance to him. Despite his determination to win the war, Stalin harbored serious doubts that Leningrad could in fact be held, which appear to have been somewhat exaggerated by his recurring fear that cowardice and treason lurked in the "northern capital" (which in turn may have been fed by reports from the GKO team that visited Leningrad right before the start of the siege). If Leningrad were to fall, Stalin wanted to ensure that its warships and other weaponry and the factories that produced them would be destroyed first. Leningrad's leaders had a different perspective. While endeavoring to defend their city militarily and supply the front, they placed a higher priority than did Stalin on preserving the city's social and economic infrastructure and protecting the general population. Disagreements between Smolny and the Kremlin were most intense and the accompanying rhetoric most inflamed, especially on Stalin's end, between 2 August and the recapture of Tikhvin on 9 December 1941. The preserved wartime correspondence between Moscow and Leningrad dispels any notion that Stalin ruled as an unchallenged autocrat during the war. Even though Stalin's will generally prevailed in the end, Zhdanov and Kuznetsov disputed policy with him and offered alternatives. The accusations, threats, and sarcastic taunts that Stalin heaped on the Leningrad leaders, however, did not result in any form of harsh punishment, at least during the war. No member of the VSLF was recalled to Moscow to be imprisoned or shot, although the wartime disagreements probably figured prominently in the Leningrad Affair. If Leningrad had been captured, there can be no doubt that Stalin would have placed the blame squarely on the military or party leaders of the VSLF, or both, despite the fact that his own prewar strategy that proscribed defense in depth was largely to blame for Germany's rapid advance on Leningrad. Stalin would have held Leningrad's leaders accountable, if the Germans did not get them first.

Tensions among Leningrad's Leaders

Declassified documents from Russian archives also provide revealing insights into the strained relations among key members of the military, political, and security elite within Leningrad during critical periods. This is not to say that most relationships among the leaders in these areas were conflictual but that mutual suspicions and discord were widespread and persistent. Tensions ran high between political and military leaders, although it is important to note that the party and the armed forces were not neatly separated; indeed, their boundaries were blurred. Russia's prolonged and exceedingly violent revolutionary upheaval from 1917 had produced by the start of the Second World War a political system that was both rigidly militarized and militant as well as a military structure that contained many nonprofessional Old Bolsheviks. There were party leaders who had extensive military experience and military commanders such as Marshal Voroshilov, who had been a founding Bolshevik from 1903 and had risen rapidly within the Red Army at its inception but had no formal military training. The intrusion of the party into the military was accentuated by the imposition of political commissars into the military command structure, creating a "dual command" during times of crisis, such as the Civil War, the military purges of the late 1930s, and the Winter War. Commissars were once again reinstated in July 1941.

As demonstrated in Basov's letter to Kuznetsov (Document 16), city party leaders feared losing control over Leningrad's factories to the NKO starting in December 1941. This concern increased in the spring of 1942 as a result of a fundamental military reorganization. On 21 April, Stalin granted Leningrad Front commander Khozin's request to put the Volkhov Front under his command in order to centralize and unify military control in the Leningrad area. The Volkhov Front was renamed the Volkhov Group of Forces, and the former Leningrad Front became the Leningrad Group of Forces. Both Groups had Military Councils and were subsumed under an enlarged Leningrad Front commanded by Khozin.[170] The new chain of command prohibited the Leningrad Group of Forces from communicating directly with the army's General Staff, the *Stavka*, or the NKO; in matters pertaining to defense and defense industry, communication between Leningrad and the Kremlin was to go through the VSLF. The problem for Leningrad's leaders was that members of the VSLF were scattered. Zhdanov and Kuznetsov were in Smolny, while Khozin and his staff were encamped at Malaia Vishera, east of the Volkhov River and the beleaguered Second Shock Army some ninety miles southeast of Leningrad. The military officials in the VSLF and military commanders and the NKO in Moscow were deciding important matters among themselves. Leningrad's party leaders became deeply concerned that they had not only lost control over the city's human and material resources but were not even being kept informed about major decisions. The isolation of Leningrad's leaders occurred during an important time of transition. German aerial bombing and artillery shelling had resumed. Concerns were growing that the enemy might try to take the city in the coming months, which prompted a renewed effort in the summer to strengthen defenses along the city's periphery. Production of small arms and ammunition was increasing, and starting in the last week in May when the ice on Lake Ladoga melted enough to permit boat traffic, a massive evacuation of people not essential to the war effort recommenced. On 31 May, Zhdanov and Kuznetsov sent a letter to Front commander Khozin and his subordinates, Aleksandr Zaporozhets and P. A. Tiurkin,[171] describing their grievances:

> Are they proposing to us Leningraders that we sever ties with the central institutions? It turns out that that's the case. But this is politically and in principle a most flagrant mistake. . . . [The part of the] VSLF located outside Leningrad cannot take unto itself all current matters. . . . Indeed the Front administration sitting outside Leningrad assumes all responsibility for the everyday leadership of Leningrad?! . . . We, members of the Military Council of the Front, working in Leningrad, consider it incorrect when the most important principal documents and proposals are directed to the center without our knowledge. . . . In view of Leningrad's severe difficulties and the attempts by the enemy to sever our communications with the country, we insist that all borrowing of Leningrad's resources is to be decided on the basis of prior consultations in the Military Council. It is known that in this respect Leningrad has always given all that it can.[172]

Three days later the Front commander responded in a personal letter to Zhdanov (Document 17) that affords a fascinating view into the machinations of laying blame for a major defeat. The proper context for understanding Khozin's letter of 3 June is not so much the issues raised by Zhdanov and Kuznetsov but rather the biggest military crisis for the Leningrad region since the enemy had taken Tikhvin the preceding autumn: the imminent loss of the remnants of the trapped Second Shock Army, including the army's commander, Andrei Vlasov.[173] Vlasov's army would lose altogether 66,000 troops killed, missing, or captured. The *Stavka* had foreseen the threat to the exposed and overextended army as early as 17 March, only two days into the German counteroffensive that aimed at the eastern base of the Second Shock Army.[174] On 21 May, the *Stavka* sent its final directive to Khozin ordering the Second Shock Army to break out to the east. However, the German command detected the subsequent Soviet troop movement, and on 30 May two German army corps attacked the base of the Second Shock Army pocket about five miles west of the Volkhov River. The evening before he wrote the letter to Zhdanov, Khozin had informed *Stavka* that an enemy corridor one and a half to two kilometers wide had completely severed supply to the Second Shock Army. Preparations were being made for a final lunge by the desperate remnants of the Second Shock Army as Khozin took the time to defend his personal conduct.[175]

Khozin had a distinguished career in the Red Army going back to 1918. In 1939, he had become the head of the Frunze Military Academy and early in the war served as deputy chief of the *Genshtab*. He arrived in Leningrad in September 1941 as Zhukov's protégé. Khozin developed a reputation for bluntness and employed colloquialisms in his writing. He started his letter of 3 June to Zhdanov in a courteous and deferential way, addressing Zhdanov by his first name and patronymic. He acknowledged receipt of Zhdanov's letter and conceded outright the validity of his complaints regarding the impairment of command and communication caused by the military restructuring. He admitted that he had not "plumbed the essence of the proposed draft resolution" but then blamed Zaporozhets, who had made his career during the purges of the army, and Major General Grigory Stelmakh, the chief of staff of the Leningrad Front, for developing the restructuring plan. Using this criticism as a segue, Khozin turned attention squarely to his main concern: the infighting with Zaporozhets. In their letter of 31 May, Zhdanov and Kuznetsov had revealed that they were aware of a conflict: "We demand an immediate end to the discord in relations and work among Khozin, Zaporozhets, and Tiurkin, which is incomprehensible to us, and which interferes with their work and establishment of normal businesslike relations among them."[176] Khozin did not indicate exactly how and when he had learned that Zaporozhets had denounced him. Perhaps the message from Zhdanov and Kuznetsov was the initial tip-off, or he may have heard about it from the *Stavka*. Khozin proceeded to tell his side of the story. He rejected Zaporozhets's charge that he had engaged in "degenerate behavior" by repeatedly inviting female telegraph operators to his apartment and by purchasing large quantities of vodka. Khozin felt compelled to defend his social life and drinking habits in detail. He claimed that his relations with the female staff who operated the telegraph machine were friendly but proper and that though he drank "before lunch and dinner sometimes two or three shots of vodka," he had never been drunk. He portrayed Zaporozhets as a petty-minded, vindictive man, who had harassed and fired the telegraph operators because of a most trivial breach in protocol and who tried to ascribe political significance to their exceedingly minor errors. He concluded that "after all these slanders" he could no longer work with Zaporozhets. Khozin then inserted the potentially lethal accusation that Zaporozhets was the "organizer and inspiration behind the opposition to Leningrad" presumably because of his unfounded denunciations of the military commander during the time of crisis.

Khozin also denounced N. D. Melnikov, the head of the *osobyi otdel* (special department) of the VSLF. The special sectors or departments, in the words of historian Robert Tucker, represented "the nub of power." Still poorly understood today because many of their files remain classified, they served as the liaison with the security organs, maintained extensive personnel files, and controlled and transmitted the most secret information.[177] Melnikov's career path was similar to Kubatkin's, and they may have been associates before they were sent to Leningrad. Melnikov was a senior major, which was a special rank in the NKVD one grade below Kubatkin's rank of Commissar of State Security of the Third Rank. Prior to his assignment in the VSLF, Melnikov had served as first deputy to Pavel Sudoplatov[178] in the NKVD's Fourth Directorate, which supervised the NKVD's role in partisan warfare behind enemy lines.[179] Khozin lambasted the NKVD's top official in the VSLF; he depicted Melnikov as no more than Zaporozhets's sidekick, who similarly took great offense at the slightest sign of disrespect. Khozin compared Melnikov unfavorably to Pavel Kuprin, who had been Melnikov's predecessor as head of the *osobyi otdel* and before that the chief of Leningrad's security organs.[180] Khozin's dismissive attitude toward Melnikov was similar in tone to the stance which Zhukov had adopted toward Kubatkin in the example noted above from September 1941. Khozin intensified the severity of his criticism of Melnikov when he implied that his petty obstructionist behavior was diverting him from his principal mission—the hunt for the many spies and saboteurs in the area.

The unstated subtext of Khozin's letter is assignment of blame for losing the Second Shock Army. Khozin must have been enraged at the attack on his personal life and the need to defend intimate details of his behavior, especially during the height of the effort to extricate tens of thousands of soldiers of Vlasov's army. But Khozin understood the very serious implications of Zaporozhets's allegations (assuming that he accurately described them): they were the basis for charging him with dereliction of duty in a time of military crisis, which at a minimum would result in his removal from command and could lead to his execution. He had been an eyewitness of the removal of Voroshilov in October 1941 after the latter had reportedly suffered a nervous breakdown of sorts as German troops had advanced on Leningrad. Khozin sought to expose, as he saw it, the slanderous scheming of the insecure and mean-spirited incompetents in the VSLF. Khozin's deference toward Zhdanov suggests that he realized that Leningrad's political leaders, even though they had been cut out of the communications loop by the reformed command structure, were still prominent national figures who might cast the deciding vote, if Moscow were unsure about whom to blame over the loss of the Second Shock Army.

The fact that Khozin's letter did not mention Leningrad's situation or plans for breaking the siege shows that the city's predicament was far removed from his thinking. The Leningrad Front had halted operations to lift the blockade as all available personnel and supplies had been sent to the Miasnoy Bor area, located some twenty miles south of Chudovo and five miles west of the Volkhov River, to help rescue Vlasov's army.[181]

On 5 June, Khozin issued a desperate request to *Stavka* for an immediate infusion of at least three Yak or MiG fighter groups to counter German aerial bombardment of the Second Shock Army and the Fifty-ninth Army that was trying to rescue it.[182] A day or two later Khozin reported his failure to open a safe corridor to Vlasov's forces, and at 3 A.M. on 8 June, the *Stavka,* above the signatures of Stalin and *Genshtab* commander General Aleksandr Vasilevsky, sent Khozin the expected order of dismissal. Up to that time, of the five generals who had commanded the Leningrad Front, Khozin had served the longest; yet even he could not have hoped to hold onto the post following a major defeat. Khozin's replacement was Lieutenant General Leonid Govorov, who remained the Front's commander through the end of the blockade, after which he commanded a Front in the Baltics (Figure 6). It is not known what role, if any, Zaporozhets's denunciation of Khozin or Khozin's declaration that he could no longer work with Zaporozhets played in Khozin's dismissal or its timing. The directive that fired Khozin also named him as the new commander of the Western Front's Thirty-third Army. During the rest of the war, Khozin held several important posts, including in 1943–44 commander of the Special Group of Forces of the Northwestern Front. He continued to serve in the Soviet armed forces until retirement in 1963 and received numerous orders. In 1966, Khozin published an appraisal of the loss of the Second Shock Army that was remarkably candid for the Brezhnev era. He cited shortcomings at all levels, but emphasized in particular lack of troop reinforcements and insufficient quantities of artillery, tanks, and other equipment. Khozin died in 1979.[183]

Zaporozhets continued to be listed as commissar of the Volkhov Front through 1 October 1942. Later that month, he was demoted to member of the Military Council of the Sixtieth Army near Voronezh in southern Russia. In February 1943, he was sent to the North Caucasus but later in the war returned to the Leningrad area. After the war, he held various positions in the military but none were in the higher echelons of the army's political organs. He died twenty years before his rival Khozin.[184] Tiurkin was removed from the VSLF by the *Stavka* directive of 8 June that fired Khozin, and Melnikov's fate is unknown aside from the fact that he died in 1944.

The exchange of letters between Zhdanov and Khozin and the fate of the Second Shock Army also reveal the failure of the strategy of uniting the Leningrad and Volkhov Groups of Forces under the Leningrad Front. Khozin and his staff could not efficiently communicate with, and coordinate, both Groups. Secondly, the complaint of Zhdanov and Kuznetsov that the dispersal of the VSLF had left the leadership in Leningrad incommunicado had merit. Stalin implicitly acknowledged the first error in the message of dismissal to Khozin on 8 June. The text of the cable announced the abolition of the two Groups of Forces and the reestablishment of separate Leningrad and Volkhov Fronts before it ordered Khozin replaced by Govorov.[185]

· Document 17 ·

Letter from Leningrad Front Commander Khozin to Zhdanov accusing VSLF commissar Zaporozhets of slander, 3 June 1942, RGASPI f. 77, op. 3, d. 133, ll. 1–4.

Dear Andrei Aleksandrovich!

I send greetings and best wishes. I received your personal letter and your letter with the slap for taking an incorrect position regarding the Leningrad group, addressed to the four of us. All this is correct and this happened because, as they say, I had not plumbed the essence of the proposed draft resolution that was worked out by Zaporozhets and Stelmakh.

Now I want to write you the following:

I know that Zaporozhets telephoned you and sent a proposal to you as well as to Moscow to investigate the Commander's conduct and accused me of degenerate behavior. That at home, he says, I entertain in my apartment Travina the telegraph operator and another whose name I myself don't even know. Yes, two or three times we went to the movies in the presence of other people. And I see nothing in this that resembled degeneracy even a little.

As you know, these young women in Leningrad have always worked in military communications, as well as another, Nadia. They are good workers and of course I have always regarded them favorably.

It turns out that if you treat the small workers like human beings, according to Zaporozhets, it's unethical. At the very least, it's low and base whoever lets it happen. How actually did the matter start? Here's how. Once in one of our talks Travina did not observe the order of rank and transmitted that Comrades Khozin, Tiurkin, Zaporozhets, and Kochetkov were at the apparatus, whereas she should have said Comrades Khozin, Zaporozhets, Tiurkin, and Kochetkov. Zaporozhets elevated this "mistake" into politics and without my knowledge issued an order: "I'd better not see these girls doing politics over the phone here." I think you will understand the total lack of principle in that way of stating the issue . . .

After this they began dragging these young women from big commissar to small. I believe that this is incorrect and wrong. I'm guessing that the head of the *osobyi otdel*, Melnikov, who spends most of his time with Zaporozhets, whom he's always conferring with, has taken the wrong line in this matter [. . .] At one Military Council when we were discussing operations issues, Melnikov came and opened the doors. I told him politely: "Com. Melnikov, wait a few minutes. I'll finish the meeting and then I'll call you in." Obviously he didn't like this and after this he took the bit between his teeth and for a long time wouldn't come to see me at all. And in his work this man isn't any better than Kuprin—if not to say more.

There are lots of traitors to the homeland in the units, and when someone is caught, he intercedes. In the rear, there are lots of spies and saboteurs, and the appropriate struggle has not been organized. The second issue of degenerate behavior, that the Commander consumes a lot of vodka. Personally I have never said anywhere that I'm not a drinker. I have a drink before dinner and supper, two, sometimes three shots, and, well, if someone's here I offer it, too. I have always believed this to be a normal phenomenon and never in my life have I been drunk, nor will I be. All this taken together raises a question to me: What's going on? If I'm not good as a Commander, then I should be judged for my practical qualities, and if it's true, then in the interests of the homeland I'm always ready to go to a less responsible job and cede my place to someone more capable, for I have no intention of remaining any longer in that kind of position. I cannot work with Zaporozhets after all these slanders. Believe me that in my eyes he has lost all authority. If it suits you, after all this baseness and intrigue I don't want him around me and I can't look at him calmly. Especially since he is the organizer and inspiration behind the opposition to Leningrad. This is all I wanted to write to you, and get your advice and help. You can at your discretion show this letter to A. A. Kuznetsov and Shtykov.

With Communist greetings,
Respectfully yours M. S. Khozin
Malaia Vishera

Isolated remnants of the Second Shock Army continued to fight on for several more weeks. During the month of June, German forces captured 48,000 Red Army troops around Miasnoy Bor. According to data released by the Russian Ministry of Defense in 1993, total Soviet casualties from the start of the Soviet offensive westward across the Volkhov River on 7 January to the very end of attempts to free what remained of the Second Shock Army on 10 July were 403,118.[186]

The relationship between the leaders of the party on the one hand, and the NKVD and the People's Commissariat of State Security (NKGB)[187] on the other, in wartime Leningrad was complex. While they shared the general goal of promoting mass loyalty to the party-state and maintaining order and security during the siege crisis, the NKVD was charged with uncovering the opposite—of unmasking and apprehending the disloyal and destabilizing elements. A large majority of the operational staff members in the Leningrad Regional Directorate of the NKVD (*Upravlenie* NKVD or UNKVD) had worked for the NKVD for more than three years, which means that as a group they were well acquainted with organizing the mass terror operations of the late 1930s.

In a formal sense, Leningrad's party leadership controlled the secret police. The NKVD was practically a subset of the party. Only 31 of 1,217 staff members of the Leningrad NKVD in December 1942 were not affiliated with the party, and all wartime replacements up to that time came from party ranks. The party committee of the Leningrad NKVD supervised the operations of the security organs and could launch investigations to correct abuses.[188] The party's formal supremacy over the NKVD is further reflected in the fact that the VSLF was the entity within Leningrad charged with deciding all questions pertaining to the defense of the city, and several *gorkom* secretaries, including the top two secretaries Zhdanov and Kuznetsov, shared power with the Front's military commander within the VSLF throughout the siege period. Although UNKVD head Kubatkin was appointed to the VSLF, he was outnumbered and overshadowed by the prominent *gorkom* officials. It should also be noted that NKVD personnel were at times monitored by secret party informants. (For an example, see the first description of overheard speech noted in Document 39.)

The UNKVD, however, exercised a great deal of autonomy. For instance, it essentially controlled advancement within its own ranks. The *gorkom* had to sanction key appointments within the UNKVD, but this process during the war was really a formality. The security organs were also able to curtail somewhat the party's authority through the *osobyi sektor* and the *osobyi otdel*, which were the loci of power of the NKVD within the Leningrad *gorkom* and VSLF, respectively, although not all members of the *osobyi* units were employed by the security organs.[189]

The NKVD exerted an important check on the party by conducting surveillance on party officials. An example of such activity is contained in a report by Antonov, the head of government security of the Leningrad NKVD, to Kuznetsov from 28 June 1942, informing him that VSLF members Shtykov and Kapustin and chairman of the Leningrad *sovet* Popkov had made a mysterious trip outside Leningrad on the night of 14 June. Antonov claimed that they had categorically forbidden security to accompany them.[190] A month later, on 29 July, NKVD official Shashkov wrote to Kuznetsov requesting that he fire his (Kuznetsov's) chauffeur, Evgeny Ivanov, who was said to have a "panicking" attitude. Ivanov reportedly had said that he would not serve in the military if drafted. The driver's uncle was also being watched and was allegedly heard making profascist comments.[191] If Kuznetsov's chauffeur was under surveillance, chances were that he himself was too. Further evidence of NKVD surveillance in close vicinity of the party leadership is found in another report that Antonov wrote to Kuznetsov. On 29 October, he warned that workers at Smolny were spreading defeatist rumors. An informant named N. M. Shishkarev had reported that storeroom workers in party headquarters had said that Leningrad could not hold out for more than another month.[192]

The conviction of a former high-level party accountant on KR charges in the spring of 1942 may have prompted the NKVD to keep closer tabs on the party leadership. On 8 April, fifty-year-old Vasily Amerlchenkov, who had been a party member since 1919 and served as chief bookkeeper of the financial sections of the Leningrad *gorkom* and *obkom* from 1937 to 1940, was arrested for sending a series of anonymous letters of anti-Soviet content to city leaders over a period of several months. The security organs devoted enormous resources to apprehending secret letter writers. (See below, pp. 251–54, for a detailed example.) Amerlchenkov, who worked as the head of the savings bank of the Primorsky *raion,* was sentenced on 29 April and subsequently shot.[193]

An example of NKGB monitoring of the highest level of the LPO that may have led to serious and widespread repercussions occurred in January 1945 when Colonel Shvyrkov, the deputy head of the Leningrad NKGB, sent a report to Kuznetsov denouncing a member of the *osobyi sektor* of the *gorkom* and *obkom* for committing serious KR crimes (Document 18). Maria Bakshis, an ethnic Lithuanian, was accused of a lethal troika of offenses: lambasting Stalin, Soviet policy, and morale in the Red Army; conspiring with a Lithuanian KR group; and assisting an English writer who was suspected of espionage.

Little else is known about Bakshis, aside from the fact that she was not in the employ of the NKGB or NKVD. It is not even certain that she espoused the views ascribed to her. As a Lithuanian, she may have been an innocent victim of ethnic animosity a few months after Red Army troops had occupied and reannexed Lithuania; however, no evidence to support that view has surfaced. The accusations were alarming. The *osobyi sektor* was the most trusted and responsible department within the Leningrad party organization. It was privy to the most secret information; its members were most knowledgeable about Soviet failures and shortcomings in Leningrad and in the nation as a whole. The *osobyi sektor* also controlled the best communication equipment in the city. The prospect that one of its members was relaying top secret information to a subversive nationalist group with a presence in Leningrad and possibly also in territory that the Red Army was in the process of pacifying and annexing was cause for state security to be deeply concerned. In one sense, anti-Soviet dissent appeared to pose a greater threat in Leningrad in early 1945 than in 1941–42, because during the siege anti-Soviet utterances or actions that weakened support for Leningrad's leaders had automatically strengthened the enemy's prospects for conquering the city. The fact that during the siege there was no third option inclined many dissatisfied Leningraders to remain loyal to "the devil they knew" rather than assist the foreign enemy who was trying to pulverize and starve them into submission. With Germany's eventual defeat a near certainty in early 1945, Leningrad's possibilities for the future were numerous. When Leningrad was no longer threatened, many felt that repressive policies should be relaxed, and there was palpable support among the city's inhabitants for continued good relations with Britain and the United States.

The fear that Bakshis might have accomplices cast suspicion on all members of the *osobyi sektor,* as well as on Kuznetsov, who handled communication with the security organs within the *gorkom* and who the same month became the *gorkom*'s first secretary as Zhdanov had gone to Moscow after the siege ended to work in the Central Committee. Shvyrkov's denunciation, therefore, was dangerous for all who were even remotely associated with Bakshis. The shadow of suspicion probably extended to the entire *gorkom* and *obkom.* Kuznetsov had to react to Shvyrkov's report by choosing either to arrest her or attempt to protect her. Arresting Bakshis would reveal KR activity but would also be an attempt to contain it; however, the arrest could have the opposite effect on Stalin. He might conclude, based on this case and other reports he was receiving of political and social discontent in Leningrad, that Bakshis had in fact not acted alone, that the Leningrad party organization was riddled with potential enemies and needed a thorough purging. It would appear that Kuznetsov chose to hush up the matter and protect Bakshis, because there appears to be no evidence in the FSB archive in St. Petersburg of a criminal case having been launched against her in 1945. Squelching Shvyrkov's report, however, was potentially an even riskier course to pursue, because Beria and Stalin might learn of the Bakshis affair from Shvyrkov, or Kubatkin (assuming he know about it), or others. Information on a matter this serious would have been accepted in the Kremlin from lower-ranking Leningrad officials outside of normal channels. Anyone with knowledge of the report would have been afraid *not* to forward it to Moscow out of fear that reluctance would be construed there as conspiracy if someone else sent on the information. It is not known whether the report reached the Kremlin. If it did, it may have played a role in the arrests of Kuznetsov, Kubatkin, and others in 1949–50. Or, the Bakshis case might have been used as a pretext for a purge already in the making.

· Document 18 ·

Report from the deputy head of the Leningrad NKGB Shvyrkov to Leningrad *obkom* and *gorkom* secretary Kuznetsov on the anti-Soviet comments of Maria Bakshis, an employee in the *osobyi sektor* of the *obkom* and *gorkom* VKP(b), January 1945, Arkhiv UFSB RF po SPb i LO f. 21/12, op. 2, p.n. 57, d. 5, ll. 25–26.

REPORT about the materials on Maria Stepanovna BAKSHIS, a Lithuanian, VKP(b) member, working in the *osobyi sektor* of the VKP(b) Leningrad OK and GK

During the cultivation of an anti-Soviet nationalist group of *Lithuanians*, it was noted that various provocative, anti-Soviet rumors have been coming in systematically from the group's participants about a supposed impending change of leadership in the VKP(b) and Soviet government, subterranean "unrest" in the party, and so forth.

Further cultivation established that the group's participants were periodically visited by M. S. BAKSHIS, who works at Smolny and who is the source of several provocative rumors being spread by the group's participants.

About the views expressed by BAKSHIS that are hostile to the leadership of the VKP(b) and the Soviet government, our agent reports:

". . . BAKSHIS believes that due to the improper leadership of the 'totalitarian sovereign,' the 'all-Union autocrat,' who no longer inspires confidence in anyone, other than hidden hatred and fear, the country has been subjected to an unforgivable war. . . .

"BAKSHIS accuses him of Asiatic treatment of the people and the state, a lack of measure and tact, excessive narcissism and a self-deification never before seen in the world, and of distorting the rates of collectivization and industrialization, which supposedly have yielded lamentable results, and of totally violating the party's program and charter and the teaching of Vladimir Ilich. . . .

"BAKSHIS thinks that if any opportunities remain for saving the party and the Soviet system, then they involve rapid replacement of the supreme leadership and the country's entire foreign and domestic policy."

BAKSHIS has spoken out negatively about the Red Army as well, stating:

". . . The new levies of soldiers are fighting badly and have no desire whatsoever to make war. They're dissatisfied with the government, which has subjected them to such a terrible war. They're dissatisfied with their commanders, who in a moment of danger are the first to bolt from the front. They're perishing in silence by the hundreds of thousands, and meanwhile there's essentially no reason for them to be dying and nothing for them to defend but the starving existence on the kolkhoz, without a personal future or confidence in the coming day."

BAKSHIS also says that the VKP(b) is in a period of rebirth, which, as she states, "began a long time ago, on the day of Lenin's death, you might say." In this connection, BAKSHIS said:

". . . Our party has clearly ceased to exist as the party of Lenin. Only the name has been preserved. And now we can expect our hymn to be replaced on order from 'The ONE' [*litso*]."

In one of conversations, speaking about the popularity of S. M. KIROV, BAKSHIS said:

". . . And you believe that he was killed by all those Trotskyites, Zinovievites, and Bukharinites, and whatever else they called them."

At the present time, BAKSHIS is maintaining ties with the writer WINCOTT, an English subject who is suspected of espionage.

BAKSHIS, for example, has promoted WINCOTT's application to be awarded the medal "FOR THE DEFENSE OF LENINGRAD," lent him money, and through Smolny's doctor, EIPSHITS, got WINCOTT's wife into the hospital. Through Com. FRANTSEV, a worker at the VKP(b) City Committee, she attempted to arrange a trip to Moscow for WINCOTT on personal matters.

BAKSHIS's son, Mstislav Vladimirovich BAKSHIS, a sergeant serving in a sapper unit, also expresses anti-Soviet moods.

Thus, speaking about the barbarities inflicted by the Germans, M. V. BAK-SHIS stated: "The Bolsheviks shouldn't be all that surprised at how brutally the Germans are behaving since they've been plenty brutal themselves."

NKGB LO ADMINISTRATION DEPUTY HEAD
Lieutenant Colonel of State Security
(SHVYRKOV)
January 1945

The tension between the party and security organs can also be seen in the struggle to survive the starvation winter of 1941–42, which included competition to control scarce food resources. While food was distributed by shops and other agencies subordinate to the city *sovet*, it was the VSLF (especially its members from the *gorkom*), in conjunction with Dmitry Pavlov, the GKO's special representative for food supply, that set the food rations. Party officials at the *raion* level, in the *gorkom,* and in the VSLF had the authority to direct special food allotments to various institutions, such as important defense plants. Corrupt party officials could abuse their authority to confiscate food for themselves and their associates. The NKVD was dependent upon the party for its food rations, and the NKVD staff ate comparatively well, even though they officially received only the ordinary *sluzhiashchii* rations. Only about 6 percent of the UNKVD staff in Leningrad died of hunger during the siege, although the rate of starvation among the city's police (*militsiia*), which was institutionally part of the NKVD, was higher.[194] By comparison, 15 percent of party members and candidate members who were in Leningrad at the beginning of 1942 perished by the start of summer.[195] (See below, pp. 284–328, for discussion of comparative mortality.) One can imagine that security officials consumed at least part of the food they seized from thieves and black-market traders. If the party fed the NKVD, the NKVD's advantage was that it policed the party's distribution of food, which may in part explain why the NKVD was relatively well fed.

Document 19 illuminates an example of tension between the party and the NKVD over food reserves. The report, sent by deputy head of the Leningrad NKVD Ivanov to *gorkom* secretary Kapustin on 22 December 1941, concerns a case of relatively small-scale and unimportant theft, which, however, given the extraordinary shortages that existed in the siege's first autumn and winter, could have been grounds for severe punishment. By September 1941, all of Leningrad's public food outlets were supposed to cease dispensing food outside the rationing system. Primorsky *raikom* first secretary I. S. Kharitonov hatched a criminal scheme to obtain food from a particular cafeteria (No. 13) in his district without having to use ration coupons. Just prior to the 7 November holiday, Kharitonov demanded various delicacies that were extremely scarce. The cafeteria director provided most of them but refused Kharitonov's request for additional chocolate. Kharitonov also arranged to obtain food directly from the cafeteria trust, bypassing cafeteria No. 13.

The events described in the Kharitonov case occurred mainly at the beginning of November and earlier, but Ivanov did not notify Kapustin until 22 December. It is not clear when Ivanov learned of the matter, but it appears that he waited over a month to file the report. Ivanov claimed not to be concerned about the requisitioning of food without coupons early in the war "when there was enough food in the city," but reported the criminal activity "now when the food situation . . . is quite grave . . . [and] we cannot give our children a pastry." The document's penultimate paragraph provides the key to Ivanov's ire. It was not the theft of state property per se that prompted Ivanov's denunciation but the fact that Kharitonov had upset the established order for dividing up scarce goods among the elite. He had refused to share a thousand packs of cigarettes either with the *raikom* apparatus or with the group that Ivanov was most concerned to protect — the district NKVD. An unstated but obvious assumption underpinning the document is that party and security officials had a right to provisions (in this case tobacco) not available to the population at large. The whistle blower in this case could have been any of a number of people: the cafeteria director; an administrator in the cafeteria trust, which was not paid for the food it provided to Kharitonov; or some member of the *raikom* or district NKVD who did not get his allotment of cigarettes. Ivanov was faced with a dilemma. He probably feared that exposing Kharitonov's actions might prompt a reform of the distribution system that could end the NKVD's preferential treatment. However, as supplies of food (and tobacco) steadily diminished in late autumn and death by starvation became common, Ivanov likely concluded that the threat to the district NKVD posed by Kharitonov's selfish scheme outweighed the risk of reform. Ivanov may have come under increasing pressure from the district NKVD or others to expose Kharitonov.

Other Leningraders were executed for actions similar to those of Kharitonov. For example, *Leningradskaia pravda* on 6 December 1941 announced that an enterprise director had been shot by decision of the Military Tribunal for doling out gifts to his friends outside the ration system. But Kharitonov had protection; he was a rising star at the district party level. In 1939, he had become a secretary of the Primorsky *raikom* and the following year its first secretary. The report presented here did not announce Kharitonov's arrest. Ivanov opted for a more subtle approach. Ia. F. Kapustin was NKVD chief Kubatkin's closest ally in the *gorkom,* and in fact Kubatkin would later be drawn into the Leningrad Affair through his protection of Kapustin. The report appears to have functioned as a confidential warning, a form of professional courtesy, between two associates (even though the document was sent not by Kubatkin but his deputy) regarding a serious breach in accepted practice among the elite that was indeed also a serious crime. The arrest of an important party official such as Kharitonov might prompt the *gorkom* to retaliate by curtailing the NKVD's privileged access to food and other things. Moreover, news of Kharitonov's arrest would probably be reported to Moscow, which would further complicate the case. Kapustin considered carefully how to respond. After interviewing Kharitonov, he decided to quash the matter. Kharitonov was not arrested during the war or even demoted from his party post as a result of this incident. Kapustin did not respond in writing to Ivanov, and it appears that the whole matter was dropped when he ordered Ivanov's report sent "to the archive." Kapustin's handwritten note did not contradict Ivanov's report in any obvious way; yet, the *gorkom* secretary tried to minimize the significance of the misdeeds of his district party secretary by noting that Kharitonov stated that he had ceased requisitioning food two months previously. In addition, Kapustin did not deny that Kharitonov demanded a thousand packs of cigarettes for himself, but rather that the accusation could not be substantiated.

Kharitonov retained a high public profile. In his capacity as Primorsky *raikom* secretary, he published an article in *Leningradskaia pravda* on 24 October 1942 on the poor level of training of teenage youth working in his district's factories. Kharitonov's career in the party continued to advance. In 1944, he was elevated to the *gorkom,* and then in July 1946 was elected chairman of the *Lenoblispolkom.* Kapustin's fortunes were as bright. In January 1945, he ascended to the post of second secretary of the Leningrad *gorkom.*

At the same time, Ivanov's accusations against Kharitonov remained as dangerous compromising material in the archives of the party and NKVD. It is doubtful that Kubatkin sent a copy of the denunciation to Merkulov or Beria because Kharitonov was not arrested. However, if Moscow found out about the case from some other source, all those involved might be accused of covering up a serious crime. Whether Ivanov's report was ever used is unknown; it may have played some sort of hidden role in the Leningrad Affair. Kharitonov, Kapustin, and Kubatkin were among the first officials executed in the autumn of 1950 in that purge.[196] Practically no mention was made of Kharitonov in Soviet published research on the blockade, and his role in the Leningrad Affair has not been clarified in post-Soviet scholarship.[197]

· Document 19 ·

Report of the deputy head of the Leningrad NKVD Ivanov to *gorkom* secretary Kapustin on the illegal receipt of food and cigarettes by *raikom* secretary Kharitonov, 22 December 1941, TsGAIPD SPb f. 24, op. 2v, d. 5515, l. 34.[198]

Kapustin wrote on the document: "To the archive. Comrade Kharitonov was instructed on this issue. According to Comrade Kharitonov, he stopped all this two months ago, and the matter concerning the cigarettes was not substantiated."

Top secret

With the onset of war, the secretaries of the Primorsky RK VKP(b) and Chairman of the *raiispolkom* organized 2 illegal groups for the illegal receipt of food without ration cards at Cafeteria No. 13 of the *raiispolkom*.

During the first months of the war, when there was enough food in the city, the existence of such groups of 5 or 7 people did not arouse any harsh condemnations or interpretations; but now, when the food situation in the city is quite grave, the existence of these two groups would seem inadmissible.

Since November, the one group of 7 people receiving food without ration cards was eliminated, but the group of 5 remains in existence to the present time.

RK VKP(b) Secretary Kharitonov has given instructions for Commandant Sergeev to obtain food without ration cards directly from the cafeteria trust himself, and not from Cafeteria No. 13, which is what he is doing.

According to information in our possession, we know that before the November holidays the cafeteria trust released, especially for Cafeteria No. 13, 10 kg of chocolate, 8 kg of grain caviar, and canned goods. All this was taken to the RK VKP(b), and on 6 November there was a call from the RK VKP(b) to the cafeteria director, Viktorova, demanding that she provide more chocolate, but the latter refused to meet their demand.

The illegal receipt of food is going on at the state's expense, for which 2,000–2,500 rubles a month are being spent monthly, while in November 4,000 rubles were spent.

The bill for 4,000 rubles was presented by the cafeteria trust to *raiispolkom* Chairman Belous for payment. The latter refuses to pay, but wants the sum of 5,000 rubles taken out of the special funds account.

Approximately 1,000 packs of Zefir cigarettes were received by the director of Cafeteria No. 13 for the entire RK VKP(b) apparatus, including employees of the RO NKVD. Kharitonov gave the director an order not to give them out to anyone, stating, "I'm going to smoke them myself."

Right now we cannot give our children a pastry, but in early November of this year Belous telephoned Taubin: "Get him 20 pastries." The latter carried this out. This is being reported for your information.

Deputy head of the UNKVD LO Ivanov

Relations within the *Gorkom*

Among Leningrad's political leaders, the most important relationship was between the *gorkom*'s first secretary Zhdanov and second secretary Kuznetsov. At the beginning of the war, Zhdanov was an ascendant star in the Soviet firmament and seen by many as Stalin's eventual successor. Having become a Bolshevik at the age of nineteen in 1915, he rose to the post of secretary of the party committee of Nizhny Novgorod (renamed Gorky after the writer's death) in 1924. At the conclusion of the 17th Party Congress in February 1934, he was selected to be a Central Committee secretary and member of the Orgburo. Ten months later, immediately following Kirov's murder, Zhdanov was sent to Leningrad as his replacement. In March 1939, he became a full member of the Politburo. Although Kuznetsov was nine years younger than Zhdanov and had joined the party only during the "Lenin Levy" in 1925, he had deeper roots in the Leningrad party organization and had worked under Kirov. From 1932, he rose quickly within the Leningrad party and became head of the *partkom* of the Dzerzhinsky *raion*, within which were located the headquarters of the security organs. Kuznetsov's close ties to the OGPU/NKVD were likely formed at this time. His rapid ascent continued during the party purges; in September 1937, he was named Zhdanov's main assistant as *gorkom* second secretary. Two years later, at the youthful age of thirty-four he became a member of the Central Committee.[199]

Prior to the German invasion, Zhdanov's prominence in the national leadership kept him mainly in Moscow. Confirmation of this fact comes from an unexpected source. On 27 March 1943, Kubatkin wrote to Merkulov requesting additional security personnel, mainly for Zhdanov. He started his request by observing that prior to the start of the Patriotic War, the number of Zhdanov's personal guards had been cut from 125 to 56. "This was due to the fact that the protected person almost all of the time was located in Moscow."[200] (Sergo Beria contends that part of Zhdanov's large personal protection force, which he was allotted by virtue of being a Politburo member, was used to keep his father under surveillance after he arrived in Moscow in 1938.)[201] As noted earlier, Zhdanov did not return to Leningrad until 25 June. In his absence, Kuznetsov took several bold initiatives, including ordering the population to prepare for air raids by digging trenches, carrying water and sand to the top floors of buildings, and camouflaging important installations. Kapustin ordered select factories to change over to producing war materials. On 23 June, the *gorkom* began to take over control from industrial commissariats of coordinating supply of some materials, fuel, and labor, and ordered workers, especially in defense plants, to work up to three hours longer per day. It was not until 26 June that the Presidium of the Supreme Soviet lengthened the working day by the same number of hours for the entire nation. Kuznetsov and his colleagues also supervised the mobilization of military reserves and the mass volunteering for what would become the *opolchenie* divisions. On 24 June, the *gorkom,* in accordance with a Politburo resolution of the same day, ordered factory workers in every *raion* to form "combat battalions" to protect defense plants, shipyards, government and party offices, and other important facilities from possible attack by enemy paratroopers and spies and by saboteurs within the city.[202]

Kuznetsov was a healthier and more dynamic leader than his boss. Operation Barbarossa had interrupted the beginning of Zhdanov's doctor-prescribed therapeutic vacation, and his heart disease progressed during the war. By contrast, several Soviet leaders, including Zhukov and Mikoyan, testified to Kuznetsov's hard work and determination to defend the city. It has already been observed that Kuznetsov, not Zhdanov, was in charge of critical functions such as defense fortification and liaison with the NKVD, that he occasionally shared meals with Kubatkin, and that when Leningrad's defenses were most vulnerable, Stalin sent Kuznetsov a note indicating that he placed confidence in him over Zhdanov, because the latter's nerves were shot. Zhdanov suffered from a series of health problems during the blockade, despite the fact that Smolny was well provisioned with food, and Zhdanov himself, according to various reports, received regular shipments of sausages and fresh peaches, flown into Leningrad.[203] He may even have had his own cow. In late January 1942, he contracted influenza, from which he recovered slowly, and during most of April he was incapacitated with bronchitis. In July he suffered from migraines and again came down with influenza. He was also prone to sleepwalk, which his doctors interpreted as evidence of a restless unconscious. He took ill again during the winter of 1943. A medical report in late March indicated that the left side of his heart was enlarged, and blood circulation to his heart was poor.[204] In his letter of 27 March 1943 to Merkulov, Kubatkin requested thirty-nine additional personal guards and forty-four more agents to secure important roads based largely on Zhdanov's frequent trips to his dacha:

"The main person who is protected, in connection with a poor state of health, often goes to the dacha outside the city." Kubatkin also noted that more leaders were being protected and making trips to the front, implying that others were filling in for Zhdanov.[205] In April he had false symptoms of appendicitis and had further illnesses in August and October of 1943.[206] Kuznetsov posted guards at Zhdanov's home when he was incapacitated, chaired the *gorkom*'s inner circle, the *biuro,* in Zhdanov's name, and conversed directly with Stalin. On 26 April 1943, Kubatkin requested from Merkulov another eight security personnel, two each for VSLF members Kuznetsov, Shtykov, and chairman of the *Lenoblispolkom* N. V. Solovyov, as they were traveling frequently to the front. (Interestingly, he also asked for two guards for Kirov's widow, who was in Kazan.)[207]

In light of Zhdanov's superior title but frequent incapacitation, one might suspect that his relationship with Kuznetsov was tainted with jealousy, animosity, or mutual suspicion; however, evidence of such is practically nonexistent. Kuznetsov's aide and brother-in-law Voinov contended that in 1944 Zhdanov refused to support one of his own "assistants" who had become the head of the *osobyi sektor obkoma,* after Kuznetsov sharply scolded the individual over some unidentified matter and "threw him out of a cafeteria." Voinov claimed that "everybody knew" that the *osobyi sektor* head, whom he called a "modern model of a worker of the Big House" (NKVD headquarters) was "deathly afraid of A. A. Kuznetsov." Voinov suspected that Zhdanov as well felt intimidated by the more capable Kuznetsov. However, Voinov can hardly be considered an unbiased source. In fact, Zhdanov continued to function as Kuznetsov's political patron up to his death in 1948, and Kuznetsov never directly challenged his boss. When Leningrad was most threatened by the German advance, Kuznetsov reportedly told Voinov that Voroshilov was to blame for the sad state of affairs, but he refrained from criticizing Zhdanov, who indeed shared some of the blame.[208]

The extreme shortages during the hungry winter sparked profound and widespread dissatisfaction, a proliferation of crime, and dissension among members of the *gorkom.* Although the volume of traffic across the Ladoga ice road increased dramatically after Stalin fully backed the project on 22 January and frigid temperatures thickened Ladoga's ice, the additional foodstuffs brought to the city proved insufficient to save hundreds of thousands of starving and freezing Leningraders. At this time, on the black market three hundred grams (about eleven ounces) of bread, less than a day's ration for many in the city, could purchase a warm winter coat. Only a trickle of electrical current flowed from the city's one functioning power plant, which severely hampered bread baking and other food production processes. On 26–27 January, electricity generated in the city amounted to less than 1 percent of that produced on the eve of the war. It had dropped to its lowest level since 1917. Bread lines began to form as early as 2 A.M., and some contained seven or eight hundred people; yet, due to the extreme cold and lack of electrical power, many bakeries lost their running water and quit operating for those two days. To make matters worse, transport vehicles were in short supply, and when they broke down they often could not be repaired. As winter progressed, food-related crimes of theft, murder, and cannibalism became more common. Occasionally, bread shops were ransacked, and party and NKVD informants overheard an increasing number of complaints against the authorities. *Ispolkom* chairman Popkov gave a public speech that was printed on 13 January in *Leningradskaia pravda* as a "conversation" in which he raised public hopes by promising that the blockade would soon be lifted, but morale inevitably plummeted when reality proved otherwise. At the end of the month, in another article in *Leningradskaia pravda* Popkov called for a mass clean-up of apartment houses within five days. Informants overheard housing administrators complain in response that due to lack of tram service and other transportation, such a plea was unrealistic. Some said that Popkov was out of touch with reality, and his appeal elicited practically no response.[209]

Given the extreme circumstances, the transport of food to Leningrad was inevitably plagued by widespread inefficiency and corruption. If the drivers of the military trucks traversing frozen Lake Ladoga were known for their exemplary heroism, some of them also engaged in considerable theft and bribe taking. From mid-December through the first half of March, 818 people were arrested for stealing cargo (mainly food) from the trucks; 586 of them (72 percent) were military personnel. Altogether during this time, over thirty-three metric tons (almost thirty-seven U.S. tons) of stolen food were confiscated from those arrested. Drivers often demanded bribes from people they evacuated from Leningrad and on occasion stole their possessions. One driver was arrested for accepting bribes totaling 14,875 rubles from one group of evacuees.[210]

Similar problems existed in the thirty miles of single-track rails that connected Leningrad with Lake Ladoga. The line was overburdened with freight and was attacked 356 times by German planes during the autumn of 1941. Coal supplies were nearly exhausted, and shortages of spare parts hampered repair work. Workers for the October Railroad, as Leningrad's rail network was called, were starving like everyone else, which led to theft, and there were few able-bodied people to clear the tracks of snow. By the start of January, on some days not one train reached Leningrad.[211]

In his 13 January newspaper article, Popkov, who was also chairman of the city's evacuation commission, stated that Leningrad's most difficult period lay in the past when Tikhvin had been in enemy hands and that since its liberation, the supply route had been shortened, which had made possible larger food shipments. At that point in the article he attempted to deflect blame for Leningrad's enduring food shortages away from himself:

> I must say that the improvement of food supply to the city depends largely on the work of the October Railroad, which is headed by Comrade Kolpakov. It must be acknowledged that the railroad works poorly and is unprepared to carry out its sacred obligation of guaranteeing uninterrupted food deliveries. The comrade rail workers and their economic, party, and trade union leaders must completely and precisely comprehend the entire degree of responsibility which rests on their shoulders.
>
> We are obligated also to take the most decisive measures in the fight against any sort of disorganizers of supply and against thieves and marauders, who resort to all kinds of tricks to steal food and enrich themselves at the expense of the people's needs. Thieves, speculators, and marauders will be ruthlessly punished according to the wartime laws.[212]

Popkov did not exactly accuse I. V. Kolpakov, who had been the head of the October Railroad since at least the beginning of the war, of theft or any other crime, but clearly implied that there were criminals among and around those who operated the rail line between Ladoga and Leningrad. A report filed in January by the railroad's NKVD head Bezhanov states that eight top administrators for the railroad, but not Kolpakov, were convicted by the Military Tribunal of criminal activity. One was shot, five got ten-year sentences, and one each received eight-year and seven-year prison terms.[213] (For all of 1942, 359 railroad employees were convicted of stealing over four and a half metric tons of food. Sixty-eight of them were executed; 139 were imprisoned for ten years.)[214] The person in charge of transport in the *gorkom* was Ivan Lysenko. As the following terse report from Kubatkin to Beria shows, Lysenko committed suicide on 3 February over the transportation debacle.

· Document 20 ·

Report from Kubatkin to People's Commissar of Internal Affairs Beria on the suicide of Ivan Lysenko, *gorkom* secretary for transportation, February 1942, Arkhiv UFSB RF po SPb i LO f. 21/12, op. 2, p.n. 19, d. 1, l. 18.

On 3 February, in apartment 17, at 19 Michurinskaia Street, Ivan Kuzmich LYSENKO, Transportation Secretary of the City Party Committee VKP(b), committed suicide by gunshot from a revolver.

Left was a suicide note of the following content:

"My nerves couldn't take it, I worked *honestly* day and night. I'm having to pay for our leaders' incompetence.

"I asked for KOLPAKOV to be removed, KUZNETSOV and KAPUSTIN knew about this. They, especially KAPUSTIN, were demanding more responsibility from me for road work than even from KOLPAKOV.

"Public transport operates criminally badly, but they only try to fix it by swearing at me, as KAPUSTIN does, and this cannot be set right."

The individuals LYSENKO refers to in his note: KOLPAKOV is head of the Oktiabrskaia RR; KUZNETSOV and KAPUSTIN are City Party Committee secretaries.

We are conducting an investigation.

KUBATKIN.

HEAD OF THE NKVD LO ADMINISTRATION
State Security Commissar 3rd rank
KUBATKIN

As Sheila Fitzpatrick has shown, Soviet officialdom ascribed special meaning to suicides: "In Bolshevik revolutionary tradition, suicide was an honorable way of registering a moral protest or exiting from an impossible situation; it had a heroic ring." Yet, by the mid-1930s, the authorities had hardened their position and refused either "to publicize political suicides or represent them as cowardly or despicable acts."[215] Lysenko's suicide was not announced, and no Soviet historian ever wrote about it. The only documentation on Lysenko that was presented to the authors of this study by the administration of the former Communist Party archive in St. Petersburg was the picture from his party file/Document 21.

· Document 21 ·

Photocopy of the picture of Lysenko from his party personnel file,
TsGAIPD SPb f. 1728, d. 196646.[216] [See Document 21, p. 164]

Kolpakov held his post until at least 19 February, when he was ordered by the VSLF to assemble more trains to transport refugees from the Finland Station to Lake Ladoga.[217] However, by 7 March 1942, he had been replaced as head of the Oktiabrskaia Railroad by B. K. Salambekov, who would continue to occupy that position until 1946.[218] Popkov's published criticism of Kolpakov and his attempt to link Kolpakov with criminal activity prompted Salisbury to guess incorrectly that "Probably he was shot."[219] Kolpakov's career in fact rebounded. He served as head of the Severnaia and Kalininskaia railroads from 1944 to 1952, and in February 1945, a special decision was made to award him the medal "For the Defense of Leningrad," which had been established by an edict of the Supreme Soviet on 22 December 1942. (Some 1.5 million people received the medal.) The honor served as at least a partial vindication of Kolpakov's performance as head of the October Railroad.[220] It would appear that

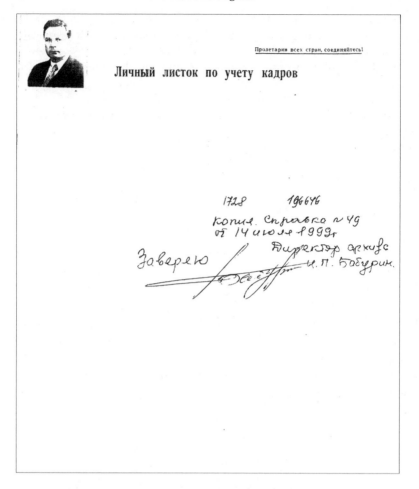

Пролетарии всех стран, соединяйтесь!

Личный листок по учету кадров

neither Kuznetsov nor Kapustin was reprimanded during the war in connection with Lysenko's complaints in his suicide note. It turned out that Lysenko took his life just as food deliveries to Leningrad and evacuation of refugees over the ice road had begun to increase. On 11 February, the bread ration was raised again and from this time all other ration foods were regularly available (see Appendixes A and C). Another reason for the improved supply was that starvation had significantly reduced the population.

The Church's Reemergence

Discussion of the Russian Orthodox Church in a chapter on ruling elites may seem oddly misplaced and exceedingly ironic given the fact that by the start of the Second World War, the USSR had carried out history's most pervasive and brutal persecution of all forms of religious belief and practice up to that time.[221] Of the 54,923 Russian Orthodox churches and 953 monasteries that existed in Russia in 1914, only 1,744 churches remained officially open by the beginning of 1939, of which perhaps 200 to 300 were actually functioning.[222] By the end of the 1930s, as many as 80,000 Orthodox clerics, monks, and nuns may have perished at the hands of the communist authorities.[223] The Church appeared to be quite literally a dying institution. The priesthood was not being replenished, because seminaries were closed, and children were not allowed to receive religious instruction or attend worship services. Nevertheless, the fact that the Russian Orthodox Church had been an important pillar of support for the tsarist system and that it remained the most significant and recognizable autonomous institution within the USSR, despite its subordination to the state in 1926, makes the topic of Church-state relations an important one. Among historians, interaction between religious believers and the atheistic state in the 1920s and 1930s has drawn much attention in recent years,[224] though archival-based research on the Second World War period, including the Leningrad siege, is only just beginning.[225]

Although persecution of believers was the predominant theme in Church-state relations in the 1930s, there were important shifts in official policy. The fierce attack on religious practice, which played a significant role in the initial wave of farmland collectivization and in the rapid construction of new industrial centers, subsided somewhat in 1934. Two factors, however, convinced the state to renew repressive policies a few years later. Believers were emboldened by article 124 of the Soviet Constitution of 1936 that guaranteed freedom of religious worship, and some believers attempted to field candidates in the 1937 elections. In addition, the census of 1937 revealed that despite two decades of atheistic policies, 57 percent of the Soviet population over the age of sixteen identified themselves as religious believers, primarily Orthodox Christians. The results of the 1937 census were officially nullified, and a new census was taken in 1939 without the question on religious belief.[226] More churches were closed in 1938 and early 1939. When it seemed as though the last active churches might be closed, the campaign relaxed again. As Nathaniel Davis has observed, the "Ribbentrop-Molotov pact . . . rescued the institution of the Russian Orthodox Church," because the number of functioning Orthodox churches nationwide rose by 3,500 to 4,000 when the Soviet Union annexed territory in east-central Europe in 1939–40. The Soviet government "understood that the Russian Orthodox Church could be an instrument of assimilation and of Soviet control."[227] However, in the rest of the USSR repression of religion, especially Orthodoxy, ameliorated only slightly prior to the German invasion.

These national trends were reflected in Leningrad. Prior to the Bolshevik

Revolution, there were 498 Orthodox churches of various sizes and functions in Petrograd and its immediate environs. The large majority of them were closed by the end of the 1920s. In 1935, the authorities decided to shut down all remaining churches. At the beginning of 1937, fifty churches were active in Leningrad; by Easter of that year the number had dropped to thirty-three. The following Easter only five remained open. A significant portion of all female purge victims in Leningrad at this time were church personnel. By far the largest single category of employed women who were executed between August and October 1937 "were former or active religious personnel, mostly nuns but also a few individuals who were recorded as church elders or psalm readers."[228] Churches belonging to Old Believers, Lutherans, Baptists, and Seventh Day Adventists as well as a mosque and a Buddhist temple were closed in Leningrad between 1938 and January 1941. (One synagogue remained open in Leningrad throughout the war.) Seven churches held Easter services in Leningrad in 1941, another six in the surrounding towns and villages, and nineteen more in the Leningrad *oblast'* (eleven of which were in and around Pskov and Novgorod). By contrast, on the eve of the atheistic offensive during the Cultural Revolution there had been over a thousand working churches in the area. Leningrad churches also fell victim to construction plans for a city metro, which were first drawn up in the late 1930s. The prominently located Znamenskaia Church was demolished in 1940 to build what would become after the war the Ploshchad Vosstania metro station. At least two other churches were destroyed after the war to make way for cavernous stations, which with their ornate mosaics, statues, and other artwork would serve as surrogate secular cathedrals of the political religion of communism.[229]

Despite the fierce persecution of religion, huge crowds flocked to working churches for the most important Christian holidays in the latter half of the 1930s. On Easter Eve of 1936, seventeen thousand people gathered within and outside the Kniaz-Vladimirsky Cathedral; fifteen thousand were drawn to that church for Christmas services in 1937. The plan to close Leningrad's remaining churches was gradually dropped in 1938, perhaps in part over apprehension of possible public opposition.[230] A secret surveillance report from late April of 1941 written by members of the League of Militant Godless (SVB)—the agitators for atheism whose organization was originally founded in 1925 with the adjective "militant" inserted at the start of the massive assault on organized religion in 1929—provides a demographic profile of the congregations. The report covers size (a total of between thirty thousand and fifty thousand worshipers at Easter services at the seven working churches in Leningrad and one church each in Pushkin and Kolpino and about six hundred for Passover in the lone functioning synagogue that was about two-thirds full); sex ratio (80–85 percent female in the churches); age (60–70 percent "older than 40 and 50 years"), and percentage of children in attendance (1.2 percent). The monitors also watched closely to see if any sermons would be preached and for manifestations of "religious ecstasy," neither of which was observed in any of the churches or the synagogue. Worshippers who showed up late for work on Easter morning were liable to be charged with violating the labor code of 1940 and sentenced to hard labor. The SVB report on the 1941 Easter and Passover services concluded that: "People go to church out of force of tradition and habit. Religion needs to be seen only as a vestige of capitalism in the consciousness of a certain segment of Leningraders." It called for more agitprop work against religious belief.[231]

Right from the very start of the German invasion, the Russian Orthodox Church was allowed a larger public role, and the Church was quick to accept it. On 22 June, Sergy, the metropolitan of Moscow and Kolomenskoe and acting (*locum tenens*) patriarch, issued an appeal to believers to defend the homeland (*rodina*), which was read in Leningrad's churches. Throughout the war he would issue many such statements calling on the faithful to support the war effort. On 23 June, Aleksy, metropolitan of Leningrad and Novgorod, began a campaign to collect money and valuables for defense needs and the Soviet Red Cross.[232] Raising charitable funds was a new departure for the Church in Soviet times as such activity had been banned back in January 1918. On 26 July, Aleksy issued a statement similar to Sergy's that was as noteworthy for what it contained as for what it omitted (Document 22). His statement was inserted into the church liturgy.[233] He depicted the defense of the homeland as a "holy cause" in contrast to fascism which "holds nothing sacred and has no ideals . . ." He directed his message specifically to the "Russian" people, and promised that whoever "[lays] down his life for the people of his blood, for his homeland . . . follows in the wake of the martyrs to an imperishable and eternal crown." The invader can expect only "heaven's curse." Taking a cue from Molotov's address of 22 June, Aleksy compared Hitler to Napoleon, thereby implying that the nation might suffer major defeats in a long and bloody war before victory would be won. During the first months of the war, special victory prayers would be inserted into the liturgy. In the statement of 26 July, the metropolitan, however, did not pledge to support, nor did he even acknowledge, the Soviet government, communism, the Red Army, or Stalin, although he did refer in passing to the "formal" freedom the Church enjoyed "under our Soviet laws." The effect of Aleksy's statement was an implicit and subtle offer of a new social contract: the Church's obedience and full support in the war in exchange for the state significantly diminishing the force of atheistic communism.

· Document 22 ·

Appeal from Aleksy, Metropolitan of Leningrad, to believers to
defend the homeland, 26 July 1941, *Russkaia Pravoslavnaia Tserkov' i Velikaia
Otechestvennaia voina: Sbornik tserkovnykh dokumentov* (Moscow, 1943), 50–54,
in Dzeniskevich, *Leningrad v osade*, 490–92.[234]

"THE CHURCH SUMMONS YOU TO DEFEND OUR HOMELAND"

A message from Metropolitan Sergy to the pastors and parishioners of the
Russian Church has summoned all believers, in the ominous hour of danger
looming over our Fatherland, to the unanimous defense—from each according to his full ability—of our great homeland. In the name of the Church this
message states that she, the Holy Church, "blesses the all-national effort with
a heavenly blessing." This voice of the first arch-pastor of the Russian Church
was not "a voice crying out in the wilderness"! All believers responded to this
appeal. In a moment of common danger, everyone united without distinction
for status, as citizens of one great Union [*Soiuz*], in a single desire—to help no
matter what, to participate in the common work for the defense of the Fatherland. Not only our young boys not yet called up for military service, but also
our elderly, and our old men, have volunteered for the front as for a great deed,
fully prepared to lay down their life for the integrity, honor, and happiness of
our beloved homeland.

Our services in the churches and our pleas for the gift of victory to the Russian host have found a lively response in the heart of every praying person, who
now has one thought, one prayer—God grant that it defeat the cunning and
malicious foe and crush fascism, which has brought grief and ruin to all mankind, and that it return us all to a bright life and joyous creative labor.

The believers of the various churches have expressed their wishes that the
sums held in reserve in the churches—in some, quite large sums, several hundred thousand rubles—be given to the state for the defense fund, for war needs.
Separate mites and donations from believers have also been coming in for these
needs.

Recently, in one church in Leningrad, the following incident occurred. Certain unknown devotees brought a packet and placed it by the icon of Saint
Nikolai, and the packet turned out to contain about 150 gold ten-ruble pieces,
possibly of prerevolutionary minting. They were immediately removed to the
bank, for defense needs.

Doesn't all of this speak to the fact that everyone's love for the motherland
has been wounded, that everyone feels identically the ominous dangers that
fascism brings with it, that all have mustered their entire force for a single
goal—to save the homeland at all costs.

The Russian people have seen and learned from the example of Germany,
which has been enslaved by fascism, and other countries suppressed by the
bondage to which fascism has relegated them, that fascism is the ruin of
everything mankind as a whole has achieved through ages of labor, everything

bright, everything creative. And now they are seeing with their own eyes and feeling the full horror brought by the pitiless foe who has traitorously assailed our land and attempted to ravage and destroy the property we have gained through tremendous labor.

In truth, as the psalmist expressed it, the "untruth of the proud," which could not look calmly upon the victorious might of our fatherland, risen up against us, and judging for itself, did not want to believe our truth and conceived against us suspicions and accusations and opened a way for itself that will be its ruin—attempting by arms and bloodshed to weaken and subdue us.

There is no need to speak at length about what we all see right before our eyes, about the barbarity with which our foe acts, about the purely Teutonic cruelty with which he attempts to frighten us by any means. Many pastors and believers who have fled the horrors of fascism speak of this. These living witnesses have told us about how in seized regions Hitler has organized the extermination of women, children, and old men; he shoots the gravely wounded, fires upon field hospitals, trains carrying civilians, and homes. All this is a special form of psychological warfare, a base, dehumanized form of struggle.

We who are especially hateful to him not only as Slavs but as bearers of a culture that has been eradicated by the fascists and of progress in all spheres he is attacking with special ferocity. And he covers up all his bestialities and horrors with a false and perfidious slogan—"crusade"—failing to notice that by his cruel extermination of everything the nations he has already enslaved both in the material and spiritual sphere hold dear and sacred, he has long since shown the world that fascism holds nothing sacred and has no ideals other than universal deceit and universal enslavement.

On the example of his treatment of the Church—of Orthodoxy (in Yugoslavia), Catholicism, and representatives of the various confessions in the enslaved countries—we can judge what his treatment would be of the Orthodox Church in our country, which is especially hateful to him. This would mean the total destruction of the Church's entire essence, that is, precisely that wherein up to this time it has been not only formally, under our Soviet laws, but also in its essence, perfectly free.

It is not new in world history for madmen to appear who dream of subjugating the entire world to themselves. "Pax Romana" as the self-styled Roman state called itself, strove to realize this proud dream over the centuries; on its side it had strength, art, power, education, population, cruelty, pillaging, and enslavement: everything became a weapon for conquering the world. But how did this dream end? The world was not conquered, and the "Pax Romana" turned to dust. Nor is an attack by a foe dreaming of subduing us anything new for our homeland. Napoleon dreamed of this and was apparently close to his goal, having defeated Russia's heart—Moscow. It was here, however, that he was destined to find not victory but ruin, ultimate ruin, since the entire nation rose up against the foe. And so it is now: our entire nation is fighting, and victory is guaranteed. It is guaranteed by the universal will for victory and the unselfish valor of our soldiers—to the point of total contempt for death, the readiness of each to lay down his soul for the fatherland, and the unshakable-ness of his faith in the conquering power of a just cause.

War is a terrible and ruinous matter for anyone who undertakes it without need or truth, with a thirst for pillaging and enslavement; on him lies disgrace and heaven's curse for the blood and misfortune of his own people and others.

War is a holy cause, however, for whosoever undertakes it out of neces-sity, in defense of the truth, and accepting his wounds and sufferings, and lay-ing down his life for the people of his blood, for his homeland, he follows in the wake of the martyrs to an imperishable and eternal crown. Therefore the Church blesses these deeds and everything each Russian person does for the defense of his fatherland.

The undoubted successes of our troops, which even our foes have recog-nized, in the struggle against our powerful but already weary foe speak to the fact that our faith in victory has not been in vain. It is an immutable law that whosoever takes the sword unjustly will perish by the sword, and in truth the sword of Damocles hangs over the head of criminal fascism. The time is near when this punishing sword will be lowered upon our foe with the full weight of inevitable fate and will crush him.

The Church calls unceasingly for the defense of the motherland. Filled with faith in God's help for a just cause, she prays for ultimate and final victory over our foe.

Aleksy, metropolitan of Leningrad

The characterization of the nation's defense as a "holy" war was adopted almost immediately by political and military authorities, even before Alek-sy's statement was published. On 24 June, a poem entitled "Holy War" was published in *Izvestia* and *Krasnaia zvezda* and was sung by the Red Army Chorus three days later at the Belorusskaia metro station in Moscow for soldiers departing for the front. The song became an anthem of the war when Soviet radio adopted it as its signature tune each morning as it went on the air.[235] On 17 September 1941, when it appeared that German troops might try to fight their way into the city at any moment, *Leningradskaia pravda* declared: "To defend the city of Lenin, to smash and destroy the enemy is our holy obligation before the fatherland."

No closed churches in Leningrad were reactivated when the German invasion commenced; however, from the first week of the war the few that continued functioning were full of worshipers, many of whom prayed for family members and loved ones who had gone to the front. An SVB report of 18 December 1941 on the first six months of the war shows that from as early as August 1941, daily services were held in Leningrad's Orthodox churches. The numbers of child baptisms and worshipers taking commu-nion were on the rise. At one church four priests and two deacons gave communion simultaneously to three separate groups during the summer of 1941. Similar situations prevailed in other churches.

Despite the enhanced role that the Church played in public life from the start of the war, religious believers, including Orthodox Christians, were included in a round-up of "untrustworthy elements" that was conducted in Leningrad as German troops approached the city. An NKVD report of 25 August (Document 32) indicates that twenty-seven clerics and parishioners from the Orthodox Church, Catholic Church, and mainly Protestant "sects," were to be arrested and thirty-eight others exiled. One of the highest-ranking clerics arrested was Archpriest Nikolai Iliashenko of the Nikolsky Church at the Bolsheokhtenskaia Cemetery, who on 28 August 1941, was charged with a KR offense. His arrest, though, may have saved his life. On 4 September, he was evacuated across Lake Ladoga and sent to the prison in Novosibirsk. However, his case was terminated for lack of evidence in July 1942, and he was freed. He survived the war and returned to Leningrad in 1946.[236]

Church attendance dropped around the start of the massive aerial bombardment in September, but after a brief lull attendance rose again, and churches were overflowing with worshipers, even though almost all of the churches were eventually hit by enemy fire. Metropolitan Aleksy regularly carried an icon around the Nikolsky Cathedral, even during air raids. In the starvation winter, when all but one of the churches continued to function, Aleksy would have to celebrate the liturgy alone after the city's last remaining deacon perished. During the fall of 1941, people came to the churches to pray for saintly intercession, and the number of worshipers in military uniform increased. Later on, leading officers of the Leningrad Front, led by their commander General Govorov, were present at several services at the Nikolsky Cathedral.[237]

What remained of the SVB during the war was reinvented in its first few months. The SVB had always been more of a busy façade than a dynamic destroyer of religious belief, and its national membership had dropped from a peak of 5.5 million in 1932 to just a few hundred thousand in 1937, before climbing back to 3.5 million in early 1941. The league's public activities ceased immediately with the German invasion. Its Central Council in Moscow stopped publishing journals, and only minimal league functions continued in the larger cities.[238] The Leningrad branch of the SVB officially boasted 30,397 members in 883 cells at the start of the war in addition to another approximately 20,000 members in the *oblast'*; however, the author of the 18 December 1941 report observed: "It is impossible at present to say whether these organizations exist and conduct any work. Information about this is missing."[239] In that report the SVB compiled a new set of nine themes for propaganda lectures "which respond to the contemporary demands of strengthening the defense of our country." The SVB lecturing staff, which had shrunk from thirty-five members at the start of the war to just five by December, had given sixty-seven lectures during the war to some 10,000 people in military hospitals, army units, and elsewhere on the new themes, which included patriotic topics, such as the "heroic military past of the Russian people" and "the great Russian commanders Suvorov and Kutuzov." One of the three most commonly read lectures—"Freedom of conscience in the USSR and religious persecution in the fascist countries"—established the Godless League's ironic new identity as champion of religious freedom. The other two most common topics were "The Patriotic War and Our Tasks" and "Fascism Is the Enemy of Science and of All Advanced and Cultured Humanity." The report included another example of the SVB's abrupt about-face when it noted that the SVB had used the Kazan Cathedral, which before the Bolshevik Revolution had been one the city's most prominent churches but in 1932 had been turned into a Museum of the History of Religion and Atheism devoted to antireligious propaganda, to mount a photo exhibition on the topic "Fascism Is the Enemy of Culture and the Suppressor of Freedom of Conscience."[240]

The radical change in the SVB's propagandistic mission was accompanied by a near cessation in arrests of Orthodox clerics after August. However, the picture of priests being given greater freedom should not be overdrawn. The secret political department of the NKVD, which sought to unmask political oppositionists through its network of agents and informants, maintained a separate unit that monitored all working churches and zeroed in on small groups of Orthodox Christians who were considered to be politically unreliable as well as "sectarians." Both groups were targets for arrest during the blockade. In April 1942, the department kept a watchful eye on churches' preparations for the Easter holiday.[241]

Another change, which would have had only symbolic political importance had it taken place in less dire circumstances, was introduced during the winter of 1941–42 and further improved relations between Church and state. As thousands perished daily from hunger, the city *sovet* began regularly to provide Orthodox churches with wine and flour for communion services.[242] In the document below the description of allotments of wine and flour as "extremely necessary" seems to have deliberate dual meaning.

· Document 23 ·

Memo from Council of Twenty Chairman Pariisky of the Kniaz-Vladimirsky Cathedral to the senior inspector of the Administrative Office of the *Lensovet* A. Tatarintsevaia expressing thanks for the provision of wine and flour for communion services, 26 February 1942, TsGA SPb f. 7384, op. 33, d. 209, l. 156 in Shkarovskii, "V ogne voiny," 282.[243]

The Kniaz-Vladimirsky Cathedral acknowledges the receipt on 23 February of this year from the Leningrad Trade Department of allotments of wine and flour for religious observances and expresses to you deep gratitude for the assistance you rendered in the procurement of these extremely necessary products.

Council of Twenty Chairman Pariisky

At the same time, however, as is shown in Document 24, city authorities continued to dispose of church property and valuables, including wine and flour used for communion, in any manner they wished without prior consultation of church officials as they had been doing since 1917. The acts described in Document 24 were not uncommon prior to the reestablishment of the patriarchate and other changes that would occur in Church-state relations in 1943. For example, several churches were used as emergency morgues.[244]

· Document 24 ·

Complaint from Council of Twenty Chairman K. Andreev of the Church of St. Serafim to senior inspector of the Administrative Office of the *Lensovet* A. Tatarintsevaia regarding the looting of the church and its conversion to a warehouse and morgue, 29 January 1942, TsGA SPb f. 7384, op. 33, d. 213, l. 117-117ob. in Shkarovskii, "V ogne voiny," 282.

I hereby inform you that as of 22 January 1942, the building of the Church of St. Serafim has been seized by the *raisovet* of Primorsky *raion* for a warehouse and distrib[ution] center for the dead brought from the city and for their eventual burial. By order of Chairman Com. Belousov,[245] without me or a member of the Council of Twenty, the church was opened up and all the property, implements, and so forth were piled near the altars. I do not have access to the building. On 29 January, with the help of the militia, I was able to get inside, moreover it was obvious that the handle had been broken as well as the locks to the entrance doors, and there are wine, flour, oil, candles, and other things missing that had been kept in the treasury in small quantities. The chapel was all smashed up inside and the entire reserve of firewood — approximately 10 loads — had already been burned by order of Com. Belousov.

I beg your instructions on the further fate of the building and the property inside it, for given this state of affairs I cannot be responsible for the further protection and integrity of the property.

Council of Twenty Chairman K. Andreev

During the starvation winter, active churches received heart-rending appeals for assistance from starving parishioners and furnished whatever scarce food, firewood, candles, and cooking oil they could scare up. For instance, on 18 January 1942, Evgeny Radeev, a choir member of the Spaso-Preobrazhensky Cathedral, wrote to the administration of his church: "From my entire soul and heart I thank you for the 150 rubles and the bits of bread sent with Lavrov. . . . You saved me from death. I am feeling better. I bought firewood at the market with your money . . . Radeev." (According to a church report, Radeev in fact subsequently died but up to the end thought that he would regain his strength.)[246]

Churches and their parishioners also responded very generously to Metropolitan Aleksy's appeal to collect supplies and money for the war effort, even though churches were exploited at will by local officials as shown in the above document. Altogether, Leningrad's churches raised over sixteen million rubles of the total of 150 million collected nationwide by the Church during the war.[247] Most donations were probably freely given; however, varying types and degrees of pressure may have been exerted on churches to contribute, and it cannot be excluded that an estimated ruble value of the ten loads of firewood that were confiscated from the Serafimovskaia Church and burned on the order of the *raisovet* chairman Belousov was included in the church's official contribution to the defense fund.

Document 25 records the Nikolsky Cathedral's donations to assist the wounded over a two-month period starting the day after Leningraders were notified that their city was directly threatened.

· Document 25 ·

Report on sums allocated by the Nikolsky Cathedral to the Red Cross Society,
3 November 1941, TsGA SPb f. 7384, op. 33, d. 62, l. 69, in Shkarovskii,
"V ogne voiny," 276.

By resolution of the expanded presidium of the Council of Twenty of the Nikolsky Cathedral dated 14 and 23 August 1941, the following sums have been allocated out of the cathedral's ready money and put at the disposal of the city committee of the Red Cross society to help the wounded:

22 August	−200,000 rubles
1 September	−100,000 rubles
26 September	−25,000 rubles
27 October	−30,000 rubles
Total	−355,000 rubles

The State Bank has credited these sums to the current account of the city committee of the Red Cross Society. They have been deposited with the district office of the Red Cross Society.

For this, Com. Bubnov, chairman of the Oktiabrsky *raion* Council, has expressed his personal gratitude to the general plenipotentiary for cathedral affairs, P. L. Smirnov.

General Plenipotentiary for Cathedral Affairs—signature

Document 26 summarizes church contributions during the war.[248]

· Document 26 ·

Report on the patriotic contributions of the churches of Leningrad for the period 1 July 1941 to 30 June 1945, in rubles, TsGA SPb f. 9324, op. 1, d. 22, ll. 10, 12, 20, in Shkarovskii, "V ogne voiny," 308–9.

No.	Church name	Defense Fund	Red Cross	Gifts for troops	For children and families of military personnel	Total
1.	Nikolsky Cathedral	3,955,832.90	2,765	75,000	670,000	4,703,597.90
2.	Kniaz-Vladimirsky Cathedral	1,628,714.09	1,093,441	25,000	838,172	3,585,327.09
3.	Spaso-Preobrazhensky Cathedral	1,896,600	425,550	68,000	699,000	3,089,150
4.	Nikolsky Church of the B. Okhtenskaia Cemetery	1,622,000	650,091	40,000	395,000	2,707,091
5.	Iovlevskaia Church of the Volkhovskaia Cemetery	655,000	146,167.66	80,000	150,000	1,031,167.66
6.	Sviataia Troitskaia Lesnovskaia Church	281,000	22,250	5,000	30,000	338,250
7.	Serafimovskaia Cemetery Church	108,000	64,505	–	29,264	201,769
8.	Kolomiazhskaia Dmitrievskaia Church	109,000	48,250	750	29,000	187,000
9.	Clergy	358,125	–	500	72,500	431,125
Total		10,614,271.99	2,452,020.66	294,250	2,912,936	16,274,477.65

Despite the outpouring of support for the war effort by churches, limits continued to be imposed on the type of charitable activity in which they could engage. In general, churches were not allowed themselves to offer the services for which they raised funds. In early August 1941, an offer by the Kniaz-

Vladimirsky Cathedral to allocate 710,000 rubles to opening and supporting an infirmary for wounded and ill soldiers as churches had done in the First World War was turned down. The Church was restricted essentially to contributing to state-run programs. On the other hand, the Spaso-Preobrazhensky Cathedral took the initiative, without official pressure, to set up and run a bomb shelter in its basement. That facility accommodated five hundred people and offered hot water and some medicines.[249]

From the winter of 1942–43, as the Red Army turned the tide of the European war at Stalingrad, the Church stepped up its contributions. In response to the appeal of Acting Patriarch Sergy, churches in Leningrad agreed to help raise funds for a tank column to be named for the Muscovite Grand Prince Dmitry Donskoy, who had defeated the Golden Horde outside Moscow in 1380 and was later canonized. Funds were also raised for an air squadron to be named for another early Russian hero and saint, Aleksandr Nevsky, prince of Novgorod, who acquired his sobriquet two hundred years after his victory over the Swedes along the Neva River in 1240.[250] As Steven Miner has noted: "The choice of names directly linked the cause of church and state and identified the current war with the most emotive events in Russian history."[251] Metropolitan Aleksy formally described the collection campaign for the tanks in a telegram to Stalin (Document 27) in which he used the deferential form of address of first name and patronymic. In contrast to his public appeal of 26 June 1941, which employed patriotic vocabulary (motherland, fatherland, homeland), Aleksy by this time praised the Red Army, the "Soviet" people, and defense of the USSR. Most remarkable was the phrase from the last sentence, "we earnestly pray to God to assist You in Your great historic calling," which implied that the Church considered Stalin's role as the national leader to be ordained of God. At the same time, the metropolitan continued to sketch in a few words, as he had done in June 1941, his vision for a new Russia by stating that the ultimate object of his prayer was the defense of the "honor, freedom, and glory of our native land." The metropolitan's plea was that Stalin's leadership would be the means to that end.

· Document 27 ·

Telegram from Metropolitan Aleksy to Stalin announcing the collection of 500,000 rubles by the Eparchy of Leningrad for construction of a tank column named for Dmitry Donskoy, 12 January 1943, TsGA SPb f. 7384, op. 17, d. 693, l. 3, in Shkarovskii, "V ogne voiny," 280–81.

Moscow. The Kremlin. To Iosif Vissarionovich Stalin.
The Russian Orthodox Church, along with all the peoples of the Great Soviet Union, burn with but one desire—to do everything possible to help the attacking Red Army. The Leningrad Eparchy—clergy and believers inspired by the patriotic movement of the entire Soviet people—since the first days of our

homeland's Great Patriotic War against the hated German-fascist aggressors, has supported the military-political efforts aimed at constructing and strengthening the defense of the USSR and our front-line city, which has heroically defended its integrity. Under my supervision, the Leningrad Eparchy, which is under blockade to this day, has contributed to the country's defense fund 3,682,143 rubles ready money, as well as donations of valuable objects. Guided by the appeal of Patriarchal *Locum Tenens* Sergy, Metropolitan of Moscow, the eparchy is contributing 500,000 rubles toward the construction of a tank column in the name of Dmitry Donskoy. The collection of funds continues with invincible faith in the imminent victory of our just cause over the bloody insanity of fascism, and we earnestly pray to God to assist You in Your great historic calling to defend the honor, freedom, and glory of our native land.

Aleksy, Metropolitan of Leningrad.
Cathedral of St. Nicolas, Ploshchad komunarov, Leningrad
Metropolitan Aleksy

Four months later, after the signal Soviet victory at Stalingrad and as both sides prepared for battle at Kursk, Aleksy wrote again to Stalin with the news that the campaign for the tank column was continuing and had garnered more than three times as many rubles as he had reported earlier (Document 28). The metropolitan's emphasis on patriotism and the deference he accorded Stalin are reflected in his appeal for God's help "for You and the Russian [not Soviet] host under Your supreme leadership."

· Document 28 ·

Telegram from Metropolitan Aleksy to Stalin stating that the fund drive to build the Dmitry Donskoy tank column continues and that he hopes for "Divine assistance" for Stalin, 13 May 1943, TsGA SPb f. 7384, op. 17, d. 693, l. 116, in Shkarovskii, "V ogne voiny," 281.

Moscow. The Kremlin. To Iosif Vissarionovich Stalin.
The Leningrad Eparchy, in fulfilling the promise it gave you to make every effort to continue its assistance for our valorous Red Army, and in carrying out your appeal to do everything possible to strengthen the defense capability of our homeland, has collected and donated, in addition to the previously transferred 3,682,143 rubles, another 1,769,200 rubles and continues to collect funds for a tank column in the name of Dmitry Donskoy. The clergy and believers are filled with firm belief in our imminent victory over malevolent fascism, and we are all hoping for Divine assistance for You and the Russian host under Your supreme leadership, which is defending the just cause and bringing freedom to our brothers and sisters who have fallen temporarily under the

foe's heavy yoke. I pray to God to grant our fatherland and You His victorious power.

Aleksy, Metropolitan of Leningrad

Stalin acknowledged the contribution almost immediately and expressed his thanks to "the clergy and believers of the Leningrad diocese." Although Stalin's brief response did not mention the metropolitan, it was clear that relations between the Kremlin and the Church hierarchy were steadily improving.

· Document 29 ·

Stalin's reply to Metropolitan Aleksy expressing gratitude for the fund drive,
17 May 1943, TsGA SPb f. 7384, op. 33, d. 209, l. 156, in Shkarovskii,
"V ogne voiny," 281.

Please convey to the Orthodox clergy and believers of the Leningrad Eparchy, who collected in addition to the previously contributed 3,682,143 rubles an additional 1,769,200 rubles for the construction of a tank column in the name of Dmitry Donskoy, my sincere greetings and the gratitude of the Red Army.

I. Stalin.

Even though Stalin's telegram was published in *Pravda,* the dramatic rapprochement between the Church and state that took place in early September 1943 came as a surprise to the Soviet people. On 4 September, the USSR's three surviving metropolitans—Sergy, Aleksy, and Nikolai of Kiev and Galych—were escorted to the Kremlin for a meeting with Stalin, Molotov, and NKVD Major General Georgy Karpov that lasted just under two hours. The idea for the meeting seems to have originated with NKGB chief Merkulov in early July, and there is no indication that the metropolitans were given much, if any, advance notice of it. On 5 September, *Pravda* reported on the unprecedented event and announced that Metropolitan Sergy would convene a church council (*Sobor*) to elect a patriarch. The news release added that Stalin was "sympathetic" to the proposal. The following document from the Leningrad *gorkom*'s chief surveyor of public opinion shows how ordinary Leningraders as well as party agitators were confused and disoriented by the news.

· Document 30 ·

Report from the head of the organizational instruction office of the *gorkom* VKP(b) Antiufeev and head of the information sector of the *gorkom* Chistiakov to *gorkom* secretaries Zhdanov, Kuznetsov, and Kapustin on public reactions to Stalin's meeting with church metropolitans, 10 September 1943, TsGAIPD SPb f. 24, op. 2v, d. 6259, l. 94.

SUMMARY REPORT

[. . .] Lately, in connection with the publication of a report about Comrade Stalin receiving Metropolitans Sergy, Aleksy, and Nikolai, there have been many discussions of the state's policy toward religion.

Agitators ask whether or not antireligious propaganda has been taken off our agenda now.

Rodionova, a worker at the Skorokhod factory, asked this: "Aren't they going to hang the bell up now, and won't they be ringing it when the church service is over?"

Workers at the 2nd GES [hydroelectric station] have been discussing the fact that soon believing workers will be able to perform church rituals freely, that religious seminaries and monasteries are going to be organized in the near future.

Com. Kaliada, a worker at the 2nd GES and VKP(b) member, had discussions about "the restoration of the Red priests."[252]

To these questions, agitators often do not give precise and clear answers.

> Head of the Organizational Instruction Office,
> Leningrad *Gorkom* VKP(b) Signature Antiufeev
> Head of the Information Sector of the Leningrad
> *Gorkom* VKP(b) Chistiakov

Eleven archbishops and five bishops were hastily flown to Moscow to join the metropolitans to form the *Sobor,* which proceeded to elect a Holy Synod consisting of the metropolitans and four of the archbishops. The synod on 12 September chose as patriarch Sergy, who was seventy-six years old and who survived only until the following May. He was succeeded in February 1945 by Aleksy, who served as patriarch until his death in 1970 (Figure 59). By October 1943, the Soviet government announced that the patriarchate would resume publishing its journal, which had been shut down in 1936, and that a Council for Affairs of the Russian Orthodox Church had been created with Karpov as its head. The latter move was a clear indication that church functions would continue to be closely supervised by the security organs. In 1944, a pastoral school and theological institute opened in Moscow to train the future priesthood, and a small number of church clergy and hierarchs was released from prison.

The changing domestic and international situation prompted Stalin to revive the patriarchate. As Soviet troops advanced rapidly westward into Ukraine following the decisive victory at Kursk in July, they were encountering a religious revival in the many Orthodox churches that the Germans had allowed to reopen. A reestablished Russian Orthodox Church hierarchy in a "Moscow Vatican" (Stalin's phrase) would facilitate the task of reintegrating into the USSR Orthodox faithful in Ukraine and Byelorussia and could dampen the desire to form a religious underground. The Kremlin also used the Russian Orthodox Church against the Ukrainian Autocephalous and Ukrainian Autonomous Churches. Moreover, as the USSR reannexed territory it had originally taken in 1939–40 and extended its borders beyond, such as into Transcarpathia, the Orthodox Church helped the USSR counteract the influence of Uniates and Catholics. By late 1943, Stalin had also set his sights on the Balkans with their own Orthodox traditions and realized that a resuscitated Orthodox presence in Moscow would likely lessen opposition to the Red Army's advance. In addition, a recognized Church hierarchy was designed to broadcast the image of Soviet religious freedom to the Western allies. The archbishop of York led an Anglican mission to Moscow exactly one week after Sergy's election and was favorably impressed by the change.[253] More importantly, Stalin most likely also had in mind the positive effect that the reform could have on the prospects for continued Lend Lease aid as well as on Western recognition of expanded Soviet borders at the end of the war.

The USSR *Sovnarkom* on 28 November 1943, issued a resolution on procedures for opening churches, and by August 1945, the number of active churches in the USSR had risen dramatically to 10,243. Most of the churches that were established or revived during the war were on territory that had been occupied by the enemy, and over 70 percent of them were in the non-Russian western borderlands. No churches in Leningrad and only a few in the surrounding *oblast'* were reactivated during the war.[254]

As Metropolitan Aleksy acquired a public voice in support of the war effort and official recognition, two splinter Orthodox movements collapsed in Leningrad. Leningrad had been an important center for the Renovationist (*Obnovlenchesky*) movement, also referred to as the Living Church. First appearing briefly in St. Petersburg in 1905 and then again in 1917, its proponents sought to liberalize the Church by democratizing its structure (most importantly by allowing married priests, not just celibate monks, to become bishops) and separating Church from state. Renovationists also advocated use of modern Russian in the liturgy instead of Old Church Slavonic. The movement reemerged during the famine at the end of the Civil War, when the communist leadership backed it in exchange for Renovationist support of state confiscation of Church valuables. The movement reached its peak in this period of fierce persecution of the mainstream Church when thousands of clergy and active lay people were shot, and especially following May 1922, when Patriarch Tikhon was imprisoned. For a while, the Renovationists controlled 70 percent of church parishes; however, fears of the movement's growing appeal prompted the Soviet leadership to reverse course and free Tikhon in June 1923 as the assault on the Church subsided. Thereafter, the Renovationist movement was in decline as it came to be viewed by most Orthodox believers as a pawn of the Communists and a traitor to the Church.[255] Nevertheless, the movement retained significant support in Leningrad. Of the ten functioning Orthodox churches trapped in the blockade in the fall of 1941, three were Renovationist. However, in the first two years of the war, as Leningrad's political leadership carved out a limited public role for the Church and the metropolitan ardently backed the war effort, the government had little use for the Renovationists. Their church at the Serafimskaia Cemetery closed for three months in January 1942 and then reopened under the metropolitan's jurisdiction. In September 1942, the Renovationists were deprived of their church near the train station at Lisy Nos, a town northwest of the city along the Finnish Gulf. The reinstitution of the patriarch marked the final demise of the schism. On 9 January 1944, the Renovationist clergy of Spaso-Preobrazhensky Cathedral repented and submitted to the patriarch.[256] The movement came to an end altogether in the USSR in 1946.

The other, smaller schism that ended in Leningrad during the war was the Josephite Movement (*Iosiflianstvo*). It originated in the fall of 1926 after Father Joseph, who had recently been named Leningrad metropolitan, was arrested and exiled for protesting the Church's recognition of the communist state, which had effectively put the Church under state control. The Josephites broke with the patriarch in 1927. In the early 1930s, the state suppressed the movement, leaving its devout adherents little recourse but to join the emerging underground "Catacomb Church." By 1934, the only Josephite church in the USSR that was still officially active was Sviataia Troitskaia in Leningrad's northern Lesnoy section. In the summer of 1941, the Josephites did not support the city's military leadership as fervently as did the rest of the Orthodox; however, through the blockade ordeal patriotic sentiment grew within the small congregation as did the desire for unity with the rest of the Church. On 24 November 1943, the parishioners of Sviataia Troitskaia officially submitted to Metropolitan Aleksy.[257] About a month later, Aleksy removed from office the last holdout Josephite cleric, Father Pavel Ligor. In a statement to the *gorispolkom*, Aleksy accused him of "perjury before God, betrayal of conscience, and trampling upon the sanctity of the holy service to God."[258]

State authorities made common cause with the Church against the Josephites, who, except for the parishioners of Sviataia Troitskaia, were characterized as belonging to an underground church and therefore treated as unrecognized "sectarians" subject to arrest and criminal prosecution. According to two reports written by Kubatkin on 1 October 1942, seven "church-sectarian" groups had been arrested during the war and charged with KR offenses. One of the groups consisted of eighteen underground Josephites in Leningrad's northern suburb of Kolomiagakh, who reportedly engaged in anti-Soviet activity.[259] According to Shkarovsky, many from this group were summarily shot.[260] There were specific regulations (articles 17 and 18 of the 1929 law "On Religious Associations") that banned unofficial religious practice; however, organizing an underground church could also easily be prosecuted as anti-Soviet agitation (article 58-10 of the Soviet criminal code), because a religious dissenter was apt at some point to "express dissatisfaction with measures of Soviet power" or "praise prerevolutionary . . . conditions."[261] In this case, the religious dissenter would be convicted under part two of article 58-10 and executed for "exploitation of the religious or national prejudices of the masses" during wartime.[262]

By the end of the war, the Russian Orthodox Church had a recognized patriarch, new capabilities to publish literature and train priests, and many times the number of active churches than had existed before the war, including church buildings confiscated from other Christian denominations in the western borderlands. Moreover, the Church had solidified as two schisms ended. Yet, Stalin did not keep the promise he made to the metropolitans in 1943 that "the Church can rely on the comprehensive support of the Government in all questions connected with strengthening and developing its organization."[263] Although Orthodox parishioners and clerics were for the most part willing to partner with the state to defend the *rodina* and were generous in their contributions, they did not receive the freedom of worship they desired. Outside the western territories, few churches were reopened during the war. For more than four decades after the war, the resuscitated Church basically functioned as a pliant tool of the state and was carefully controlled by the security organs, which screened appointments within the hierarchy. There were prominent dissident priests in the postwar Soviet era, but they were few in number, and church leaders dutifully and consistently gave their public support to Soviet foreign policies. Conditions for the Church worsened after the war. During Stalin's final years, about 7 percent of church parishes were deregistered. Then, under Khrushchev, close to six thousand churches (or about 44 percent of those functioning in 1958) and most seminaries and monasteries were closed in a new wave of repression which began in 1959. Children under the age of eighteen continued to be prevented from attending church services.[264] Until the Gorbachev era opened a new space for religion from 1988 onward, Leningrad's five million residents had fewer functioning houses of worship of any faith than did typical American small towns.

CHAPTER 3

Policies of Total War

Perhaps no other city in history experienced the phenomenon of total war to the extent that Leningrad's *blokadniki* did. City leaders sought to control the people's actions and shape their thoughts as completely as possible, especially during the first six months of the war, in order to keep the city from being erased from the face of the earth and to send weaponry and ammunition to other threatened fronts. The party, military, and NKVD went to extraordinary lengths to mobilize and propagandize the population and compel its strict obedience. Taken as a whole, their policies mobilized around two million people and were instrumental in defending Leningrad, which is not to say that all programs or decisions were enforceable, effective, or even appropriate.

Mass Mobilization in 1941

During the first few weeks of the war, several hundred thousand men from Leningrad were mobilized into the army and navy. Many of those not subject to the draft joined what became the largest improvised military formation of the war: the *opolchenie*.[1] On 27 June, the Leningrad *gorkom* decided to create one *opolchenie* division from each of the city's fifteen *raiony* for use mainly as reserves. By this time, approximately two hundred thousand people had volunteered for the Leningrad *opolchenie*. (Reasons why people did so are discussed below, pp. 333–34.) However, as the situation at the front deteriorated rapidly, party and military leaders decided on 4 July to abandon that plan in favor of immediate formation of three divisions for front-line duty. The first was assembled almost entirely from the workers at the Kirov factory and, hence, came to be called the Kirov Division. Workers from factories in the Moskovsky and Frunzensky *raiony* made up the second and third divisions. Approximately 60 percent of those selected for the *opolchenie* in the summer of 1941 (roughly sixty-seven thousand people) were factory workers, mainly from the defense plant giants, such as Kirov, Stalin, Bolshevik, Elektrosila, and Skorokhod. Workers from these war factories were selected because they had been exempt from the mobilization of military reserves and thus were practically the only sizable core of hale and hearty young men left in the city. Other *opolchentsy* were men who were too old for the military reserves. The *opolchenie* accepted volunteers up to the age of fifty.[2]

Another distinctive feature of the *opolchentsy* was their relatively high concentration of party personnel. Of approximately 135,000 *opolchentsy* who comprised ten divisions and many of the auxiliary battalions and detachments that were formed by the end of September, around 20,000 were party members and candidates, and another 18,000 belonged to the Komsomol. Nearly all high-ranking officers were affiliated with the party. The fact that the proportion of *opolchentsy* who belonged to the party (28 percent) was higher than the corresponding proportion among factory workers (which was also relatively high at slightly less than 20 percent) indicates that the selection committees sought to fill the *opolchenie* with as many party members as possible. The *opolchentsy* were thrust into near suicidal missions with only the most primitive means to defend themselves. The authorities wanted their ranks to consist of the most loyal people available.[3]

After Pskov fell on 8 July, Soviet troops retreated to the Luga River, the last defense before Leningrad. As the table below[4] indicates, the first three divisions departed for the Luga almost as soon as they were formed. They received virtually no training; many had never served in the armed forces or held a rifle.

Formation of the First Three *Opolchenie* Divisions

Division	Size	Date formed	Date dispatched to the front
First	11,589	4 July	10 July
Second	9,210	12 July	14 July
Third	10,094	15 July	15 July

Opolchentsy made up roughly half of all Soviet forces along the Luga Line. Their casualty rate was extremely high; their units were essentially destroyed.

The *opolchenie* campaign continued in the latter half of July as the Red

Army retreated toward the Luga. On 19 July, a fourth division was formed from the Dzerzhinsky and Kuibyshevsky *raiony* and hastily sent to the front. Formation of the first of the so-called guard divisions commenced the following day. The "guard" designation was meant to convey that these were elite units, which would prove more successful than their predecessors. To the volunteers themselves, who continued to come from the ranks of defense plant workers, the guard status implied that they would receive better training and equipment. The first three guard divisions, which comprised a total of 31,237 volunteers, in fact did train for three to four weeks before being dispatched to the Luga Line. A fourth guard division was formed on 13 August. It was larger than the others by about 2,000 troops and was intended to function as a reserve for them. It was not thrown into battle until after the start of the siege. The guard divisions, however, were no more successful than the earlier *opolchenie* units. Their weaponry was just as poor, and their officers just as lacking in experience. Voroshilov and Zhdanov admitted that the longer training period the guards received was of little benefit. Their casualty rate was around 50 percent.[5]

The final major wave of *opolchenie* formation consisted of the worker detachments and battalions described in chapter 2 that were to defend Leningrad itself with whatever means were left. These units made up two divisions. During the hectic days of the last week in August, *Leningradskaia pravda* encouraged all city residents who could carry a weapon to enlist in the *opolchenie*. Much of the training that volunteers received at this time was in the use of cold steel: knives, bayonets, and pikes. Propagandists bestowed a particular reverence on skillful use of the bayonet in keeping with its prominent role in Russian military history. On 15 August, *Leningradskaia pravda* ran an article, "The Bayonet—a Terrifying Weapon," which recounted the good use Russian soldiers had made of the bayonet in 1812 and, allegedly, in 1918. The population was also taught desperate tactics to be employed against enemy tanks. On 26 August, *Leningradskaia pravda* provided detailed instructions on how two or three people in slit trenches, armed with long poles, mines, grenades, and bottles of gasoline, could destroy tanks at a range of ten to fifteen feet (Figure 20).

Document 31 summarizes Leningrad's military mobilizations during the first three months of the war.

· Document 31 ·

Report by Antiufeev and the *gorkom*'s War Office Head Pavlov on mobilization for the Red Army and Red Baltic Fleet, October 1941, TsGAIPD f. 24, op. 2v, d. 4819, l. 45.

────────────

As of 1 October 1941, more than 431,000 men have been mobilized, including 54,078 Communists and 93,000 Komsomol members.

Mobilized by the City Military Commissariat [GVK]	−298,700
including senior officers	−47,000
junior officers	−39,000
rank and file	−161,000
for the navy	−20,000

Those mobilized by the GVK include 25,000 to 35,000 sent to the *Narodnoe Opolchenie* army.

Under the latest draft for the RKKA and RKKF	−21,000
Sent to military academies	−10,700

To the *Narodnoe Opolchenie* army, in fighter battalions and partisan brigades — 156,413

including: 10 divisions	−100,000
16 machine gun battalions	−16,800
7 partisan detachments	−6,600
66 partisan detachments	−2,013
in fighter battalions	−19,000
in reinforcement battalions	−12,000

Sent as political fighters in the party mobilization for political work — 9,786 men.

Sent as nurses and militiawomen, to the Red Army and KBF, and working in hospitals — 31,925 female Komsomol members.

Head of the War Office, GK VKP(b) Pavlov
Head of the Organizational-Instructional Office, GK VKP(b) Antiufeev

Among the different ways that Leningraders were mobilized for the war effort, the process of dramatically raising the output of munitions has received less attention from historians than it deserves.[6] At the start of the war, Leningrad was one of the world's largest military-industrial centers. It accelerated production of munitions in the summer of 1941 and continued to produce weaponry and ammunition throughout the war, even, to a limited extent, during the winter of 1941–42. To be sure, there was much disorganization in the city's military industries. The enemy's quick and unexpected success in severing all road and rail links with the rest of the nation by the end of August 1941 resulted in tremendous logistical confusion. Machinery and materials that were supposed to be evacuated were left exposed to the elements at various sites between Leningrad and Lake Ladoga for months and even years. The loss of electrical power toward the end of the year brought most industrial production to a halt. However, production levels rose again in the spring of 1942. Throughout 1942, the city manufactured 46 heavy KV tanks and repaired 108 others (as compared to 526 manufactured and 168 repaired between the start of the war and

15 December 1941). During 1942, city factories also produced tens of thousands of automatic rifles; millions of mines, mortar rounds, artillery shells, and aerial bombs; over a million hand grenades; and more than 120 million ignition capsules, detonators, and fuses.[7] Production totals increased the following year. In short, the weaponry and ammunition produced in the city were vital to its defense and its final liberation in 1944. The industrial transformation had several components. Many defense plant employees continued in their former jobs but were required to accelerate production and work longer hours. Others had to retool workshops to meet the demands of the military. Still other workers and engineers, such as those attached to the engine workshops of the Kirov plant, were evacuated to industrial centers in the Urals and farther east. Another segment of the industrial work force was relocated within the blockade zone to areas less prone to enemy bombardment.

General decisions regarding industrial production in Leningrad were made by the GKO in consultation with heads of industrial commissariats, and, to some extent, with Leningrad's political leaders. It was up to the *gorkom* to implement those decisions and toward that end to coordinate relations among the city's factories. Hence, *gorkom* secretaries remained in continual contact with the GKO and commissariats in Moscow as well as with Leningrad's factory directors. The GKO on occasion issued specific instructions for individual factories, especially concerning evacuation of machinery. On the eve of the war, the Leningrad *gorkom* was structured largely according to the industrial sectors, especially the military ones, of the city's economy. Six of the thirteen *gorkom* departments in 1940 (general industrial, defense industry, shipbuilding, machine construction, food processing and sale, and electric power stations and electronics) directly concerned industry.[8] This organization facilitated further rapid conversion to production of war matériel. On 3 July, the *gorkom* assigned individual secretaries responsibility for sectors of the wartime economy. Kapustin was put in overall command of heavy industry. Among those reporting to him were secretary for machine construction Moisei Dlugach, who supervised tank and flame-thrower production (and later became director of the Kirov factory), secretary Basov, who oversaw production of mortars, artillery, hand grenades, and ammunition, and secretary of local industry B. A. Serdobintsev, who was put in charge of assembling mines.[9]

In defense plants managers relied on speed-up campaigns developed in the first three Five Year Plans to boost output. The number of "shock workers," "Stakhanovites," and "operationists" proliferated. In early July, the *gorkom* ordered all Komsomol members to overfulfill their daily norms by at least 200 percent. Production incentives in the form of bonuses and public acclaim for plan overfulfillment and punishments for failure to meet the plan proliferated in factory workshops. By the middle of the month, most important defense plants were in operation around the clock, and cases of herculean work performance multiplied. The Krasnaia Zaria telephone factory, for example, increased daily production from 166 to 1,800 units. Also in July, some workers at the Stalin metal works achieved 800 percent of their work norms. On 13 July, *Leningradskaia pravda* praised one worker who labored for thirty-six hours straight. The party committee of the Kirov factory considered failure to meet production goals a "terrible state crime" (though it is unclear how such "criminals" were treated) and on 5 August, professional agitators at the factory introduced the slogan: "Work Twice and Three Times as Hard to Replace Your Friends Who Have Gone to the Front!"[10]

Leningrad's industries had retooled extensively for war production during the third Five Year Plan, yet they still managed to master production of eighty-four new kinds of equipment, arms, and ammunition in the summer of 1941 before the start of the blockade. Workers in established defense industries had to learn to use new machinery, while factories that had served the local economy became war plants. Some of the new weaponry included the 76-millimeter gun, the 45-millimeter antitank gun, the PPD automatic rifle, new types of tank turrets, and shells for captured German mortars. On 19 July, the GKO ordered the Leningrad *gorkom* to begin working on producing rocket-propelled artillery, the so-called Katiusha rocket and launcher. From 27 July, Secretary Kuznetsov headed up this project and chose the Skorokhod shoe factory to be the main production facility. Eventually, forty other plants manufactured parts for the Katiushas. The first Leningrad Katiusha was assembled on 27 August. By the fall of 1941, over three-quarters of the factories that had produced goods and services for the local economy prior to the German invasion were working on defense orders.[11]

The total amount of munitions produced increased sharply beginning in July, when 250 tanks and armored cars, 200 artillery guns, 185 tank guns, 300 mortars, and 710,000 antipersonnel mines were turned out. The Kirov factory remained the city's largest defense plant. It was in charge of manufacturing all heavy tanks and, from 12 July, heavy guns. Parts of the production process were outsourced to other plants. In early July, there were eleven subcontractors for tanks and four for artillery; by autumn the numbers would grow to about forty and sixty, respectively, as more factories converted to producing war matériel. Production of simpler weapons rose even more dramatically. On 10 July, the GKO ordered Leningrad's factories to assemble 100,000 grenades as soon as possible. By the end of July, grenade production increased fivefold over June, and thirteen and fifteen times in September and October. The GKO also ordered Leningrad on 10 July to start filling 9,000 bottles with flammable liquid per day. University and secondary school students were called upon to help in this task, and by the end of the month they had doubled the quota, filling more than a million bottles.

The table below[12] is a partial listing of factory conversions that were started or completed during the summer of 1941. The table shows that industries made logical changeovers. Most machine-construction plants that were not already engaged in defense production switched to manufacturing ammunition and parts of weaponry. Metalworking plants increased output of armored plating and artillery shells. Clothing and shoe factories went over to making uniforms, great coats, and army boots. Construction firms made materials for defense fortifications. Workers in beverage and perfume industries just started putting flammable liquid into their bottles. Some factories in light manufacturing and production of consumer goods — turning out such things as toys, musical instruments, and candy — joined the mass of civilians who began to assemble simple antitank mines (700,000 were made in July) and hand grenades, and fill Molotov cocktails.[13]

Leningrad Factory Conversions in 1941

Factory	Prewar Output	Wartime Assignments
Barrikada	construction materials	rails for tank barriers
Bolshevik	steel, armaments, tanks	mortars, artillery shells, tanks, Katiusha rockets
Burevestnik	X-ray machines for hospitals	artillery shells
Elektroapparat	electrical components	mines
Elektroinstrument	electrical instruments	mine casings
Elektrosila	electric machinery	electric machinery, tank parts, mines, 120-mm shells
Gorny Institute	mining research	artillery shells, explosives
Grim	perfume	mines, Molotov cocktails
Ilich	machine tools	explosives
Izhorsk (in Kolpino)	steel, machinery, ship-building, tank assembly, armor plate	tank armor, artillery shells, Katiusha rockets
K. Marx	textile machines	mortars, shell and mine casings
Kassovaia apparatura	cash registers	mines
Kirov Theater	stage props	wooden and papier-mâché decoys of guns, tanks, and airplanes
Kirov	tractors, turbines, aircraft engines, tanks, guns, equipment for Moscow-Volga Canal	KV tanks, heavy guns, ammunition

Factory	Prewar Output	Wartime Assignments
Kozitsky	radios	radio transceivers for partisans
Krasnaia Bavariia	beer, kvass, fruit juice, beer production equipment	Molotov cocktails, artillery shells
Krasnaia zaria	telephones	field telephones
Krasnoe znamia	knitwear, stockings	artillery shells
Krasnogvardeets	surgical instruments	surgical instruments, parts for KV tanks, military knives, hand grenades
Krasny instrumentalshchik	gears, other heavy machinery	mines
Krasny treugolnik	rubber shoes	covers for barrage balloons
Krasny Vyborzhets	light metalworking	explosives, detonators, parts for tanks and airplanes
Krupskaia	candy	Molotov cocktails
Lenfilm	motion pictures	mines
Lenigrushka	metal toys	hand grenades
Lenin	machine construction, steel pipes, boilers	aerial bombs
Leningradsky metallist	bicycles, saws, wash stands	artillery shells
Liker-vodochny	vodka, other liquors	Molotov cocktails
Linotip	typesetting machines	machine guns
Lunacharsky	musical instruments	grenades
Metallist-kooperator	metal dishes, bicycles	mines, grenades
Metalloigrushka	metal toys	mines, grenades
Mikoyan	candy	antitank mines
Muzykalnye dukhovye instrumenty	musical instruments	mines
Nevgvozd	nails	rails for tank barriers
Nevsky khimichesky	superphosphates	sinal (explosive)
Nevsky mylovarenny	soap	artillery shells
Okhtinsky	chemicals	electric motors, explosives
Optiko-mekhanichesky	cameras, movie projectors	artillery shells, hand grenades, detonators for antitank mines
Ordzhonikidze	shipbuilding	artillery shells, gun carriages, shipbuilding
Parfiumernaia	perfume	Molotov cocktails, camouflaged mine casings
Piatiletka	paper	mines
Pnevmatika	pneumatic machines	artillery shells, Katiusha rockets

Factory	Prewar Output	Wartime Assignments
Proletarskaia pobeda	shoes, boots	army boots
Russky dizel	diesel engines	tank motors, automatic rifles
Rybosportinventar	fishing equipment	camouflage nets
Sevkabel	communication and electric lines	field communication lines
Skorokhod	shoes, boots	army boots, belts, sacks, shell casings, Katiusha rockets, mines
Solodo-drozhzhevoy	yeast	mines
Stalin	steel production, steam turbines, heavy machinery	20 new types of arms and ammunition, parts for KV tanks, automatic rifles, armored trains
Stroitelny trest 189	construction materials	rails for tank barriers
Svetlana	light bulbs, vacuum tubes	mines, shell casings, bayonets
Tekstilny kombinat	textiles	camouflage nets
Telman	wool textiles	greatcoats
Uritsky	tobacco	mines
Volodarsky	men's outer garments	army uniforms, Katiusha rockets
Voskhod	footwear	military footwear
Voskov (in Sestroretsk)	industrial and military instruments	assembly and repair of rifles, machine guns, light artillery
Vpered	machine construction	mines
Yegorov	railroad cars	field kitchens, picks, axes
Zhdanov	shipbuilding	shipbuilding, heavy mortars

The massive conversion to war production occurred as the mobilization of military reserves and the *opolchenie* drive exacerbated the preexisting labor shortage. To compensate, productivity had to increase significantly, and factories had to recruit and train thousands of new workers. As early as 29 June, *Leningradskaia pravda* cited examples of workers who held four different factory jobs simultaneously. By the end of the summer of 1941, the concept of a prescribed work day ceased to exist at many plants. Employees simply had to work until emergency assignments were completed. The prime target of recruitment of new workers was women, mainly nonworking mothers. One of the most prominent official slogans at the start of the war was: "The Motherland Is in Danger. Men to the Front. Women to the Factories!" (After the blockade was lifted, women were called upon to play a major role in reconstruction work—Figures 65, 70.) On the third day of the war, *Leningradskaia pravda* described women who had replaced their husbands at the Elektrosila factory. Party agitators canvassed apartment buildings, especially those belonging to factories, and convinced nonemployed housewives to enter the work force. Many reported to their husbands' workshops. In the words of Anna Rybina, wife of a Krasnogvardeets worker: "I accompanied my husband to the army, and now I want to work in his workshop." The total number of women who entered Leningrad's work force is not known, but it wasn't nearly enough to make up the shortages. For example, about 500 workers' wives took jobs at the Kirov works during the first several months of the war, while the number of Kirov workers who joined the first *opolchenie* division was about 9,000. The main reason why more women did not enter the work force at this time was that most married women were already employed. Nevertheless, during 1942 women accounted for most of the city's new factory workers. Over 16,000 women went to work in twenty-seven machine construction factories that year. At the Kirov plant women accounted for 1,802 of 2,216 new workers in 1942. By spring 1943, women who had gone to work since the start of the war made up approximately 60 percent of Leningrad's factory workers.[14]

There were other sources of replacement workers. Pensioners returned to their former jobs, and employees from nonessential enterprises that were being closed down were transferred to factories working on defense orders (Figure 12). Another way to increase the size of the work force was to condense and accelerate courses for teenage students in industrial training schools in order to get them into full-time work as soon as possible. Boys and girls as young as fourteen became regular workers.

One sizable group that was generally banned from working in factories was the more than 100,000 refugees who poured into the Leningrad area prior to the start of the blockade. They were herded into reevacuation centers, generally just outside the city, from where they were to be sent farther eastward as quickly as possible. The authorities wanted to isolate the refugees, because they feared that large numbers of them might sow defeatist sentiment and panic among the population. They were also concerned that spies and provocateurs might slip into the city among the hordes of refugees (Figures 16 and 17).[15]

During the latter half of 1941, Leningrad's various mobilization campaigns competed for the same personnel, which spawned tension among the emergency programs. The goal of increasing production of munitions conflicted with the formation of the *opolchenie*. The Kirov Division provides the best example for assessing the profound impact of the *opolchenie* on workers and factory production, since most of the division came from one factory. When plant director Zaltsman returned from Cheliabinsk and Moscow with the ambitious order to commence mass production of

KV tanks, he was stunned and angry to learn that at least fifteen thousand of his draft-exempt employees, roughly half of the factory's entire labor force, had volunteered for the *opolchenie*. He called the mass enlistments "insane" and succeeded in reducing the size of the volunteer force by at least five thousand before they left for the Luga Line.[16] In September 1943, a later Kirov works director, N. D. Puzyrev, told correspondent Alexander Werth that "everyone without exception volunteered for the front." He added: "If we had wanted to, we could have sent 25,000 people; we let only 9,000 or 10,000 go."[17] Nevertheless, more than a quarter of the personnel of the city's most important defense plant departed for the front. *Leningradskaia pravda* boasted on 13 July that the Kirov factory had sent "the best of the best" to the *opolchenie* and portrayed the factory as a model for others to follow (Figure 14).

As noted above, the Kirov Division, like the others, was poorly equipped and trained. Sixty percent of its members had no previous military training, and only ten of its 1,824 officers had served as officers in the Red Army. Most members of the division never returned to the Kirov works. Tank assemblers armed with old rifles and gasoline bombs were no match for German tanks. With virtually no air cover, the volunteers were helpless victims of Stuka dive bombers and Messerschmitt fighters that attacked in waves of up to a hundred planes each. Far better use could have been made of the skilled workers from Kirov and other defense plants who joined the *opolchenie*. Even with fully staffed workshops, most factories would have been hard pressed to fulfill their demanding and urgent assignments. By dispatching metal cutters, smelters, fitters, welders, and assemblers to the front, Leningrad was depriving itself of a sizable and important component of its defense industry (Figures 11, 13, 18, and 19).

Despite the brief German testimonials mentioned in chapter 1, it has not been demonstrated that employing untrained *opolchenie* units in the front lines produced positive results. The deployment of the volunteer divisions did coincide with a slowing of the German advance, which was crucial to saving Leningrad. It took Army Group North from 10 July to 7 August to advance seventy-five miles from Pskov to the Luga Line. During that interval, disagreements within the German High Command over which city, Leningrad or Moscow, should be the primary objective consumed valuable time. Hitler maintained that he wanted to encircle Leningrad before turning full attention to Moscow; however, he did not divert substantial forces from Army Group Center to the north until 8 August, when he sent the Eighth Air Corps and large armored forces to Army Group North.[18] The terrain between Pskov and the Luga River favored the defenders as much of it was swampy with dense undergrowth. Roads in the area were primitive. To the Red Army's credit, the Eleventh Army launched a surprise counterattack west of Pskov that destroyed or damaged 70 of the 150 tanks of the Eighth Panzer Division.[19]

The defenders also used the time to fortify the Luga Line as quickly as possible. All ongoing construction in Leningrad was halted, and the workers were sent to the Luga,[20] together with those who had been conscripted to build pillboxes and bunkers, lay mines, dig tank traps, and place concrete and metal obstacles in the enemy's path. Workers who had performed early excavation work for the city metro used their digging and tunneling skills at the Luga Line.[21] German intelligence of the Eighteenth Army claimed that Soviet convict labor, excluding recidivists, political prisoners, and ethnic Germans, Finns, Balts, and Belorussians, had been mobilized for fortification work.[22] The hastily built defenses were more instrumental in slowing the enemy than was the military resistance put up by the *opolchenie* soldiers (Figure 21).

The drafting of civilians to build fortifications did not produce conflicts with industrial managers that were as sharp as those sparked by formation of *opolchenie* divisions, because the fortification builders were drawn largely from lesser-skilled workers who did not work in munitions plants. Textile, clothing, and food industries, which employed mainly women, sent a very high percentage of their workers to the construction sites (Figure 22). The Skorokhod footwear factory is a prime example. Before the war the plant's work force, which probably numbered around fifteen to twenty thousand, was predominantly female. The following table shows that far more Skorokhod employees served in construction crews in 1941 than in all other mobilization programs combined.

Mobilization of Skorokhod Employees in the Latter Half of 1941
1,000 to Red Army in the first week of the war
400 to second *opolchenie* division in the first half of July
750 to worker detachment in late July
120 to sanitary crew in late July
130 to *opolchenie* in late August
12,000 to fortification construction between July and December

For Skorokhod employees, the average time spent at the construction sites was eighteen days.[23]

As the enemy approached the outskirts of Leningrad, skilled defense workers assumed a larger role in fortification construction. The Special Defense Works Commission, which directed fortification construction between the Luga Line and Leningrad, was created in late July and headed by Kuznetsov. It included Kirov works director Zaltsman, which reflects the key role that defense plant workers in general, and Kirov workers in particular, played in building fortifications. Up through mid-September, the commission ordered the construction of six zones between the Luga and Leningrad. The last zones included villages along the southern edge of the city (Avtovo, Alekseevka, and others) as well as along the railroad that ran along the city's southern perimeter. The Kirov works, Elektrosila, Bolshevik, the Lenin works, and other important defense plants were located in this area. Starting in early September, workers from these plants had to fortify quickly their factories and surrounding territory. By the middle of September, they were also preparing to abandon and blow up their factories in the event that they were not successful in defending them (Figure 23).

During August and September additional workers were needed for fortification work. Accordingly, on 9 August, the *gorkom* extended the age category of those subject to the draft by five years to include men up to fifty-five and women up to fifty. By this time, it would appear that some factory managers were resisting sending their workers to build defenses out of concern that they were needed to fulfill production assignments, because the *gorkom* resolution also prohibited managers from firing workers who were sent to the construction sites.[24] As the enemy approached closer to the city, the need for fortification workers continued to grow, as did, presumably, conflicts between factory management and the organizers of the labor draft. On 29 August, the VSLF expanded the draft again, and the following day, 235,000 people were building defenses just outside the city. On 2 September, *Leningradskaia pravda* for the first time referred to fortification construction inside Leningrad. The next day, the VSLF ordered the mobilization of an additional 5,000 people per *raion*. Workers began turning shops into machine gun nests, erecting pillboxes (nicknamed "Voroshilov hotels"), barricades, and other defenses, and camouflaging factory buildings. Workers at the Stalin metal works, for example, put hundreds of tons of scrap metal shavings on the factory's roofs and sprayed them with green paint to make the industrial complex look like a large garden from the air.[25]

While workers were preparing to defend Leningrad street by street, much of the war matériel manufactured in their factories during the summer was sent out of the city to the GKO's strategic reserves. This policy continued after the blockade began and Hitler shifted his sights to Moscow. Maintaining high levels of production strained the city's limited capacity to generate electrical power. Prior to the war, most of Leningrad's electricity and fuel had come from outside the area that would become the blockade zone. Apparently no one had thought of laying either electrical transmission lines or a fuel pipeline under Lake Ladoga to its eastern shore as emergency backups in case the city would be militarily threatened as it had been by the White army of General Yudenich during the Civil War, perhaps because the official rhetoric of the 1930s emphasized that any invading foe would be quickly defeated. Leningrad lost two-thirds of its capacity for generating electricity when German troops occupied power plants outside the city. The city's power-generating system, Lenenergo, could not continue for long to supply current to factories that continued to run at or near full capacity. The high level of activity forced the city to consume supplies of coal, oil, and peat that it might have kept in reserve for the winter. Lenenergo had the futile task of trying to satisfy competing claims for electricity from factory directors who were under great pressure to fulfill production orders. Rationing of current on a daily basis began on 2 November, when *gorkom* secretary P. T. Taliush, who was in charge of electricity allocation, sent a notice to the directors of eleven ammunition factories ordering them to report to him each day by 11 A.M. how much ammunition they could produce and how much electricity they would need. The *gorkom* then gave Lenenergo orders on levels of electrical current to furnish to specific factories.[26] Transmission of electricity became increasingly intermittent in November and December. Factories lost power very often with no warning.

As soon as the cutbacks began, factory directors started petitioning the *gorkom* for special permission to receive more current. By early December the *gorkom* was inundated with such pleas.[27] Another approach taken by plant directors was to request a reduction in their work orders and to criticize Lenenergo for inconsistent supply of current. For example, on 10 December, director Bogoliubov of the Zhdanov shipyard (referred to in the documentation simply as factory No. 190) complained to Kapustin in a sharply worded letter that his plant had been experiencing periodic blackouts since 12 November and would lose power suddenly several times in a given day. He contended that Lenenergo continually changed the amount of current it promised to provide but then did not fulfill its promises. The erratic current flow subverted work schedules and worker morale suffered. He added that some workers who had been transferred to his plant from other factories that were closer to the front had walked ten kilometers to work only to find out that little could be accomplished because Lenenergo had cut off power without notice. Bogoliubov wrote: "From our point of view, Lenenergo either is deceiving the *gorkom*, exaggerating its capability, or it does not want to work out an orderly plan of supply of electricity to factories for a month, or even for half a month in advance . . ." He recommended that factories function only a few days each week, thereby requiring less electricity, and making it easier for Lenenergo to stick to a consistent supply schedule. A reduced workload would also allow workers to rest, which, he said, was "extremely needed in light of food shortages." Kapustin scrawled across the top of Bogoliubov's letter: "It is necessary to think through this question. Comrade Bogoliubov is right."[28]

Despite Kapustin's comment, the *gorkom* in general did not heed advice to slow output, because the GKO continued to insist that defense plants keep producing as much as possible. When production targets were not met, directors and chief engineers often were fired.[29] Forcing the pace of production in such an environment, however, resulted in considerable material waste. For instance, the percentage of ruined metal castings in November and December at the city's main metalworking plants varied between 25 and 90 percent.[30] The continued emphasis on defense production left Leningrad unprepared for the coming winter under siege. In October, only one railroad car of firewood was being chopped per day for the city. As late as 10 December, fewer than a thousand people were chopping firewood in the entire city.[31] To be sure, thousands would have starved to death whether or not fuel and materials had been conserved during the autumn, given the continuance of the blockade. Even so, the excessive burdens put on Leningrad's industry to produce for the front in the autumn of 1941 made the city's plight going into the winter that much more desperate.

Maintaining Public Order and Political Control

Policies of total war extended beyond the extraordinarily high degree of mobilization of people and materials. They also included an attempt to maintain strict obedience to the decisions Leningrad's political and military leaders made during the city's struggle for its very existence, which entailed among other things controlling as thoroughly as possible the behavior of the people, including how Leningraders expressed themselves. The control apparatus for the civilian population comprised the party and the NKVD, as well as the offices of the Military Procuracy and the Military Tribunal, which worked closely with the NKVD. The city police force (*militsiia*) was a separate unit within the NKVD and dealt with nonpolitical crimes.

The Communist Party had a much larger presence in Leningrad than did the NKVD. At the start of the war there were approximately six times as many full-time officials at all levels of party committees in the city as there were NKVD officials. There were about 1,600 operational staff members in the NKVD administration (UNKVD), the large majority of whom were under forty years old and had only an elementary or middle-level education. By comparison, there were roughly 10,000 party officials out of a total party membership, including candidates, of 153,531 on 1 July 1941 (Document 46).[32] Party officials were more numerous because they were intimately involved in all aspects of the war effort, and every organization—from factories to institutes of higher learning to concert halls—had its party committee (*partkom*). The factory workshop was the backbone and main recruiting ground of the LPO. At the start of 1941, while one Leningrader in approximately twenty was either a party member or a candidate,[33] the figure for factory workers was one in every five or six. To put it another way, 69 percent of party members were workers (*rabochie*), most of whom worked in factories. Party members were concentrated in largest numbers in massive machine construction plants; approximately 40 percent of the entire LPO worked in this branch of industry. The Kirov factory had the largest party organization of any enterprise in the city. The factory's fifty-seven party cells, or primary party organizations, located in forty-three workshops, included 3,454 members or 35–40 percent of all Communists in Leningrad's Kirovsky *raion*. Party committees in factories and elsewhere remained in close working contact with the city's fifteen *raion* party committees (*raikomy*), which employed a total of 528 officials at the start of the war. The *raikomy* reported directly to the *gorkom*. The locus of political power in Leningrad, the *gorkom*, comprised fifteen secretaries with a total staff of 170 in June 1941. The *gorkom* secretaries implemented their programs through a *biuro*, which in turn worked through a full-time staff, or *apparat*. The *apparat* enlisted hordes of part-time activists (*aktivisty*), who were charged with chores connected with molding political consciousness, such as writing propaganda essays and giving "agitation" talks. At the beginning of 1940, the city's *aktiv* employed some sixty thousand agitators.[34] In security matters, the role of the LPO was limited essentially to surveillance of the population, composing agitprop in support of the war effort, and oversight of the functioning of the NKVD. Almost all of the members of the UNKVD staff were party members and therefore subject to decisions of party committees. There was significant turnover during the first year of the war in all ranks of the LPO, including the *gorkom* and the *raikomy*, as more than half of all party members and candidates were sent to the front.[35]

During approximately two and a half years prior to the German invasion, the operating procedures of the NKVD had changed significantly. On 30 July 1937, Nikolai Yezhov, head of the NKVD, had presented to the Politburo Order No. 00447, "On Repression of Former Kulaks, Criminals, and Other Anti-Soviet Elements," which included priests, non-Orthodox Christians or "sectarians," White Guards, and members of political parties other than the Communist Party, among others. This order subsequently established quotas for the number of people to be arrested, confined in camps, exiled within the USSR, and executed. Close to 400,000 were condemned to death. At the same time, almost a quarter million others were killed in "national operations" against Poles, Germans, Finns, and several other ethnic groups.[36] Some sixteen months after he launched the Great Terror, however, Stalin began to rein it in. On 17 November 1938, a Politburo resolution, signed only by Molotov and Stalin, ended mass arrests and exilings without a court order or prosecutor's sanction and terminated the special judicial troikas, which had sentenced millions. Henceforth, only the courts (*narsudy*), the Military Tribunal (VT), or, in rare cases, the special board (*osoboe Soveshchanie*) of the USSR NKVD would hear cases. Moreover, convictions would have to be based on more than the confession of the accused. On 10 January 1939, Stalin forbade beatings to elicit confessions from all but "clear and still dangerous enemies." The Politburo resolution essentially asserted that the mass operations had become counterproductive, but Stalin did not admit that the hunt for enemies had been misguided. Rather, he decided to deflect the blame for the disruption that the terror had caused onto its executors: Yezhov and the NKVD. The resolution stated that "enemies of the people and spies employed by foreign intelligence agencies, having wormed their way into both the central and the local organs of the NKVD and continuing their subversive activities, sought in every way possible to hamper the work of investigators and agents. They sought to consciously pervert Soviet laws by carrying out mass, unjustified arrests while at the same time rescuing their confederates (especially those who had joined the NKVD) from destruction." The document went on to state that "officials of the NKVD had totally abandoned work with agents and informers in favor of the much simpler method of making mass arrests without concerning themselves with the completeness or with the high quality of the investigation . . . the investigator is satisfied with obtaining from the accused a confession of guilt and totally fails to concern himself with corroborating this confession with the necessary documents (testimonies of witnesses, the testimony of experts, material evidence, etc.)." The statement ended by warning "all officials of the NKVD and the procuracy that the slightest violation of Soviet laws and of the directives of the Party and the government by any officials of the NKVD and the procuracy, regardless of who the person is, shall be met with severe judicial penalties." In sum, the general message that was conveyed by the statement was that, in the words of historians Getty and Naumov, "enemies were still dangerous, but they were to be destroyed carefully and selectively," and violators of the new policy would be held strictly accountable.[37]

Just prior to the Politburo's resolution, there were several indications that Stalin had turned against Yezhov. His high-ranking protégés in the NKVD were disappearing, and in a highly visible and symbolic event, at the 7 November military parade and official demonstration, Yezhov was replaced by Beria atop the Lenin Mausoleum. His actual fall from power proceeded swiftly. Two days after the Politburo resolution was issued, in a nighttime grilling that lasted five hours before members of the Politburo in Stalin's Kremlin office, Yezhov was charged with failing to unmask conspirators among his own lieutenants. On 23 November, following another such session, Yezhov submitted his resignation as NKVD chief.[38]

In the months that followed, the USSR Supreme Court commenced to review and reverse the convictions of around 35,000 to 40,000 people sentenced for KR crimes. In addition, the NKVD conducted its own internal review of convictions handed down by the troikas and during 1939–40, which resulted in the release of, perhaps, a few thousand more. As Peter Solomon has concluded, "these instances of reversal and rehabilitation involved only a small proportion of the cases of unfair and unfounded repression."[39]

The new instructions for criminal prosecutions brought the Military Procuracy (*voennyi prokuror* or VP) into all phases of investigation of KR crimes. From November 1938 and through the war years, a KR case was to proceed along the following lines. If the UNKVD wanted to develop a case, it had to secure a sanction for arrest from the VP. Once the arrest was made, the matter was sent to the VP, which would either send the case on to the VT, return it to the UNKVD for further work if the original investigation seemed sloppy or inconclusive, or terminate it. If the case reached the VT, there were four options: conviction and sentencing, acquittal, return of the case to the UNKVD for further investigation, or termination (which occurred most often during the war when the accused died in prison).

From the start of the German invasion, the NKVD and NKGB were extremely active in Leningrad and functioned according to yet another set of guidelines that represented a partial reversion to the policies of Yezhov's mass operations of 1937–38. On the first day of the war, the Presidium of the Supreme Soviet issued a decree on emergency war measures, which included an open-ended statement on the right of the military authorities to exile or relocate (*vyselit'*) from areas near military fronts people who were deemed to be "socially dangerous." Following Stalin's 26 June telegram to Zhdanov and his national address of 3 July, the security organs had a mandate to clear large numbers of refugees from evacuation routes and to prosecute ruthlessly all military deserters, cowards, saboteurs, and anyone who spread "false rumors" that excited alarm. The Leningrad NKVD and NKGB formulated directives on these matters on 4 July that repeated the order to resettle "socially dangerous elements" from territories under martial law.[40] However, since Leningrad did not seem to be directly threatened in the first weeks of the war, these decrees were not fully applied until the latter part of August.

By the end of July refugees from the Baltics and the western RSFSR were pouring into the Leningrad *oblast'* (which at that time included Pskov and Novgorod) and Leningrad itself. The authorities were deeply concerned that they would foment panic and that enemy agents would be concealed in their midst. Earlier in July the NKGB reportedly apprehended one of the first spies who admitted being recruited by the Germans to gather intelligence. An added concern was that German aircraft were dropping propaganda leaflets in the *oblast'*. On 28 and 29 July, NKGB head Ogoltsov ordered the "careful filtration of all refugees from occupied regions who are detained by blocking detachments." Security personnel were ordered in particular to watch out for and arrest four types of fifth columnists (a phrase borrowed from the Spanish Civil War): [41] saboteurs, those attempting to signal enemy aircraft with lights or radios, distributors of anti-Soviet or pro-German leaflets, and, finally, the largest and most ill-defined category, disseminators of defeatist "anti-Soviet agitation."[42] Camps were set up to prevent saboteurs, spies, and panic-mongers from reaching the city. This period marks the beginning of the official policy, which was practiced throughout the USSR until nearly the end of its existence, of treating as politically suspect those who had spent any period of the war under enemy occupation. One's whereabouts during the war became a critical part of one's official résumé. In his 28 July order, Ogoltsov gave specific responsibilities to two departments within state security. He charged the Secret Political Department (*sekretno-politicheskii otdel* or SPO) with monitoring members of the academic and technical intelligentsia who were drafted for fortification work outside Leningrad and with discovering the authors of critical anonymous letters and KR leaflets. The Counterespionage Department (*kontrrazvednyi otdel* or KRO) was ordered to maintain security at defense plants to ensure uninterrupted production and to prevent fifth columnist counterrevolutionaries from disrupting transport, especially along the railroads.[43] Other responsibilities of the NKVD at the end of July and through August included hunting down deserters from the army, navy, and *opolchenie;* organizing partisan units that would slip behind enemy lines to gather intelligence and disrupt communications and supply; and forming fighter battalions composed mainly of factory workers who were to prepare to defend their workshops should the enemy attempt an invasion of the city.

On 24 August, Piotr Kubatkin, the chief of the Moscow *oblast'* NKVD since 1939, was sent to Leningrad to head up its UNKVD. A close associate of Beria, Kubatkin already had a reputation for zealously exposing and swiftly punishing alleged spies, saboteurs, wreckers, and those who expressed "anti-Soviet sentiment." From 1937 to 1939, he had worked in the central organs of the SPO, which played a major role in carrying out the great party purge of 1937–38.[44] Kubatkin's career, however, was also molded by the resolution of 17 November 1938 that aimed to curtail the mass NKVD operations. He tried to reconcile that reform with the central edicts issued at the start of the war that demanded a heightened state of vigilance and swift and harsh punitive action via military tribunals against broad and ill-defined categories of KR behavior, and the forced relocation of mass populations. Kubatkin served as Leningrad's NKVD chief throughout the blockade and was indefatigable in the pursuit of suspected spies and saboteurs, and all forms of KR expression. His definition of what constituted a KR crime was very broad. For him, anti-Soviet agitation included overheard comments that were critical of the authorities or the army's performance in the war as well as any form of "defeatist" sentiment. Party chief Zhdanov held a narrower view of what constituted anti-Soviet agitation, at least among military personnel. Zhdanov argued in a letter to the prosecutor of the USSR Viktor Bochkov that ordinary indiscipline and idle conversation among those in the armed services, even if directed against commanders, ought not to be considered KR. Kubatkin, whose jurisdiction did not extend to the military, applied his broader interpretation to the civilian population.[45] In wartime Leningrad unguarded comments critical of the Soviet system or its conduct of the war, or praise for the enemy could prompt the VP to issue an order for arrest on the charge of anti-Soviet agitation. The VP could refuse to issue the order if it determined that the case lacked merit or had not been based on the November 1938 guidelines; however, such refusals were rare.[46] Conviction of anti-Soviet agitation specifically during wartime (part 2 of article 58-10) could result in execution. From the available data, it would appear that the percentage of those convicted of anti-Soviet agitation in wartime Leningrad who were executed was as high as, perhaps higher, than the percentage of those executed for convictions of all other KR crimes (article 58) combined. According to a report from the VP for the month of May 1942, 110 people were convicted of anti-Soviet agitation, of whom 32 (29 percent) were executed. Seventy-five were sentenced to ten years in prison, while the remaining 3 received eight-year terms. Between 1 July 1941 and 1 July 1943, 20 percent of all those convicted on KR charges in Leningrad were shot.[47]

KR cases were hardly ever terminated after an arrest had been made, and it was unusual in wartime Leningrad for the VP to return the case of someone arrested for a KR offense to the NKVD for further investigation; although, in rare cases, the arrestee could eventually be freed. Between July and October of 1942, the UNKVD sent 290 cases of arrest for anti-Soviet agitation, with some involving more than one person, to the city VP and closed only eight cases. During that same period, the VP sent 365 people charged with this offense on to the VT, while closing one case and returning six others to the NKVD for further investigation.[48] Other data show that between 1 July 1941 and 1 August 1943, only 0.6 percent of all state security cases in Leningrad—not just KR ones, but theft of socialist property, burglary, cannibalism, and other crimes—were closed by the VP before reaching the VT. 93.6 percent of cases tried by the Leningrad

VT between 1 July 1941 and 1 July 1943 (14,443 of 15,426 cases), resulted in convictions, and close to half of the rest of the cases were closed because the accused died in custody.[49] Thus, in the overwhelming majority of cases in wartime Leningrad, an arrest on a KR charge led directly (and quickly) to conviction. The fact that the offices of Leningrad's VP and VT were not large—altogether employing only eighty to ninety officials[50]—is an indication that they were not intended to devote considerable attention to individual cases, despite the reforms of 1938 which were supposed to increase their involvement. According to another tabulation (which is partially inconsistent with other available statistical data), between 1 July 1941 and 1 July 1943, 3,799 Leningraders were convicted of all forms of KR offenses, which accounted for 25 percent of all VT convictions (15,193) for that period.[51] Of the KR convicts, 759 (20 percent) were shot, and the rest received long prison sentences.[52] During the first year of the war in particular, a prison term in Leningrad often amount amounted to a death sentence, because conditions in the jails were so poor.[53]

Document 42 provides arrest data for the critical period of 15 October to 1 December 1941, when enemy bombardment was intense and the first starvation deaths occurred. The data reveal that there were more than two and a half arrests for speculation and banditry for each arrest for KR activity, and that on average seventeen people were executed per day by the military tribunals.

In late August 1941, as Voroshilov, Zhdanov, and Popkov publicized Leningrad's dire predicament, the NKVD made its most concerted effort of the war to remove from the city several categories of people who were considered to be politically unreliable. The relocation eastward of some of the 15,500 inmates who on the eve of the war were held in prisons in Leningrad and the *oblast'* had already commenced in early July. The day after Kubatkin's arrival in Leningrad, and while the GKO team was inspecting the city to determine how best to defend it, Ogoltsov, Kubatkin's new assistant, compiled a list of the number of people to be arrested or exiled from among the city's "counterrevolutionary element" (Document 32). This operation was to be carried out at the same time that thousands were being detained on suspicion of desertion from the army and *opolchenie* or for not possessing residence permits.[54] Ogoltsov's list of people to be removed is very specific, indicating that they were already known to the authorities and probably under surveillance. They were fairly easily rounded up but not all were arrested or sent out of the city prior to the start of the blockade. The detailed operations of purging Leningrad of those suspected of being disloyal (as well as a massive relocation of ethnic Finns and Germans described below) shows that the security organs were more concerned with removing such people than with evacuating most Leningraders who were not vital to the war effort, including hundreds of thousands of children.

Ogoltsov's list reads as an anachronism. Beria and his deputies stubbornly continued to try to apprehend groups that had been blamed for conspiring against the Soviet state in the 1930s and even as early as the Civil War era. The Leningrad NKVD continued to pursue phantom conspirators, such as former noblemen, SRs, and Mensheviks, despite the clear and present danger posed by the enemy invasion. The fact that Trotskyites were placed first in the list shows that the official obsession with liquidating any remaining followers of the assassinated Trotsky endured. The Leningrad NKVD planned to arrest or exile at least one person for each designated category, even identifying a Zinovievite and a Kadet, which suggests that the UNKVD was consciously trying to cover every conceivable category of opponent to Soviet authority. The large majority of those slated for arrest and exile were in the broad and amorphous category of "anti-Soviet element," while the number of people identified as actually having participated in counterrevolutionary organizations was minuscule. Throughout the siege, the largest number of political arrests was for anti-Soviet agitation, based on overheard conversations. Ogoltsov's list shows that the UNKVD in fact planned to devote most of its resources to squelching words and deeds that it considered to be defeatist, anti-Soviet, or pro-German and would pay comparatively little attention to the designated political targets from the 1920s and 1930s.[55] Finally, it should be noted that only political transgressors, which included practicing Catholics and Protestant "sectarians," were slated for arrest. Thieves, burglars, brothel owners, and prostitutes were only to be exiled.

· Document 32 ·

Report by the Leningrad NKVD's Deputy Head Ogoltsov on the removal of the counterrevolutionary element from Leningrad, 25 August 1941, Arkhiv UFSB RF po SPb i LO f. 21/12, op. 2, p.n. 18, d. 11, ll. 13–14.

				Top secret
No.	TENDENCY [*Okraska*]	TO ARREST	TO EXILE	TOTAL:
1.	Trotskyites	16	8	24
2.	Zinovievites	1	–	1
3.	Right wingers	4	1	5
4.	SRs [Socialist Revolutionaries]	7	98	105

				Top secret
No.	*TENDENCY* *[Okraska]*	*TO* *ARREST*	*TO* *EXILE*	*TOTAL:*
5.	Mensheviks	4	41	45
6.	Anarchists	2	30	32
7.	Bundists	1	23	24
8.	Kadets [Constitutional Democrats]	—	1	1
9.	Expelled from VKP(b) for political reasons	6	171	177
10.	Churchmen, sectarians, Catholics, and clerics	27	38	65
11.	Nationalist k/r [counterrevolutionaries]	5	30	35
12.	Former noblemen	52	42	94
13.	Former officers in the White Army	3	27	30
14.	Former officers in the tsarist army	6	42	48
15.	White bandits	—	3	3
16.	Former prominent merchants	2	2	4
17.	Kulaks	40	10	50
18.	Suspected of espionage	30	41	71
19.	A/s [anti-Soviet] element	442	378	820
20.	Former participants in various k/r organizations	6	8	14
21.	Formerly incarcerated for espionage, sabotage, wrecking	3	4	7
22.	Deserters, Harbiners[a]	4	11	15
23.	Connection with foreign country	6	23	29
24.	Political emigrants	2	5	7
25.	Connection with consulate	13	—	13
26.	Wrecking, sabotage, and terror	21	8	29
27.	Thieves	—	305	305
28.	Burglars	—	35	35
29.	Brothel owners and prostitutes	—	160	160
		703	1545	2248

DEPUTY HEAD OF THE ADMINISTRATION of the NKVD LO and the City of Leningrad
Senior Major of State Security Ogoltsov

[a]"Harbiners" (*Kharbintsy*) were mostly former employees of the Chinese Eastern Railway, which had been built through Manchuria in the late tsarist period. When the USSR sold its share of the railroad to the Japanese occupying government in 1935, the "Harbiners" reemigrated from Manchuria (Manchukuo) to the USSR. During the purges, they were accused en masse of spying for Japan. Jansen and Petrov, *Stalin's Loyal Executioner*, 97.

According to a top secret report that Kubatkin later sent to the *gorkom* (Document 45), a total of 40,231 "socially alien" and 30,307 criminal "elements" had been exiled from the Leningrad area by 1 October 1942.

Document 33 is a report on KR arrests that Kubatkin sent to Moscow to the central SPO chief N. D. Gorlinsky in February 1942. In it Kubatkin responded precisely to the KR categories that Gorlinsky had identified in a request for information the day before. (Interestingly, Gorlinsky demanded information not only on the number of spies arrested who were German or from nationality groups allied with Germany, but also on the number of English spies caught. Soviet efforts to unmask English agents were not curtailed even after the alliance with Britain was formalized in the spring of 1942. Kubatkin responded that only German and Finnish spies had been arrested.)[56] Kubatkin's report shows that by February 1942 Moscow was no longer focusing primarily on the old KR categories. The emphasis had shifted to targeting political crimes directly connected with the defense of the nation at war. The largest number of arrests continued to be for anti-Soviet agitation, followed by treason. On 24 December 1941, the VP of the Leningrad Front had issued a set of instructions on how to investigate treason. Toward the end of the lengthy document, the VP attempted to differentiate treason, which according to the penal code was punishable by execution or by ten years of imprisonment and confiscation of property if there were mitigating circumstances,[57] from anti-Soviet agitation, which in besieged Leningrad resulted in execution about one-fifth of the time. A charge of treason had to be supported by some sort of practical attempt to carry out the intended act, beyond mere words.[58] The period covered by Kubatkin's report to Gorlinsky coincides with the time when starvation reached its peak. The average number of arrests for KR crimes per day during this time (about twenty-one) represented one of the highest rates for Leningrad during the war.[59]

· Document 33 ·

Report from Kubatkin to NKVD USSR Third Administration Chief Senior Major of State Security Gorlinsky detailing arrests of 958 people for counterrevolutionary crimes from 1 January to 15 February 1942, 19 February 1942, Arkhiv UFSB RF po SPb i LO f. 21/12, op. 2, p.n. 11, t. 1, d. 4, ll. 95–96.

Transmitted over "VCh" [high frequency radio]
In reply to your inquiry via VCh, I report:
    I. During the period from 1 January to 15 February 1942, the NKVD LO administration arrested 958 people for counterrevolutionary crimes, including:

    1) Spies — 18, including

a) German	17
b) Finnish	1
2) Betrayers of the Homeland [*Rodina*] and traitors	398
3) Saboteurs	2
4) Terrorists	21
5) Wreckers	32
6) For anti-Soviet agitation and spreading counterrevolutionary rumors	446
7) For other counterrevolutionary crimes	41

II. During the same period of time, 67 counterrevolutionary groups were liquidated, including:

1) Right-Trotskyites[60]	9; arrested — 22 people
2) SRs, TKPs,[61] Mensheviks	2; arrested — 5
3) Insurgents	7; — " — " 39
4) Nationalists	14; — " — " 39
5) Church-sectarians	1; — " — " 2
6) Among youth	5; — " — " 11
7) Among Intelligentsia	15; — " — " 41
8) Among White Cossacks and former White and Tsarist Army officers	2; — " — " 4
9) Other KR groups	12; — " — " 25

NKVD LO ADMINISTRATION CHIEF STATE SECURITY RANK COMMISSAR KUBATKIN

In late August 1941, ethnic Finns and Germans residing outside Leningrad were also considered to be a dangerous element, as likely allies to the approaching enemy, and therefore in need of immediate relocation to the country's deep interior. Finns had been victims of resettlement campaigns going back to 1935, when the NKVD had removed close to 7,000 of them who lived near the Estonian and Finnish borders. During the terror of 1937–38, Finns in the Leningrad *oblast'* had suffered disproportionately. As the storm clouds of war had gathered in Europe, Finns were considered by the authorities to be potentially disloyal. All Finnish-language newspapers, publishing houses, radio broadcasts, schools, and churches in the Leningrad *oblast'* were shut down.[62] Then, at the end of the Winter War in 1940, Finns were deported to Siberia from territory in the Karelian Isthmus that the USSR annexed.[63]

The enormous operations to relocate ethnic groups from Soviet borderlands between September 1939 and June 1941 — most notably the uprooting of roughly one million Poles and the systematic murder of close to 22,000 of them — were gross violations of the Politburo's decision of November 1938 that limited deportations from border areas to individual cases.[64] The Supreme Soviet decree of 22 June 1941 provided the missing official sanction for mass ethnic resettlement as it had for the mass arrest and deportation of the "socially dangerous" population. The decree specifically recommended the evacuation of ethnic Finns from the Leningrad *oblast'*;[65] however, their forced and rapid resettlement commenced in earnest only when Leningrad's defense was directly threatened and the authorities acknowledged the danger. On 26 August, the VSLF ordered the "mandatory evacuation of the German and Finnish population" from districts around Leningrad where they were heavily concentrated. An unspecified number of people were to be sent to the northeast to the Komi and Kot-las Archangel regions.[66] Two days later, Merkulov issued from Leningrad the specific instructions in Document 34. His plan ordered the removal of 95,400 Germans and Finns by train and barge from the Leningrad area. The quota was derived from the 1939 census, and the targeted population was mainly collective farm laborers, whose grain and livestock were to be confiscated. Merkulov changed their final destination to a series of regions in Siberia and northern Kazakhstan. Troops under NKVD command were dispatched to the villages to ensure compliance with the evacuation, which was supposed to be completed within ten days. On 30 August, Beria added a quota of another 36,000 Finns and Germans to be deported by barges to the city of Cherepovets and then on to Kazakhstan. The reason for the increase appears to have been the presumption that the Finnish and German population had grown considerably since 1939. (In early October, the command of the German Eighteenth Army besieging Leningrad estimated that 30,000 to 40,000 Germans lived within Leningrad, and like the NKVD assumed that most favored surrendering the city without a fight.)[67] The expulsion of Finns and Germans from the Leningrad area was among the first of many massive operations to resettle ethnic groups within the USSR during the Soviet-German War. Preparations to remove ethnic Germans from the Moscow area and elsewhere commenced in September, and by the end of 1941, a total of 799,459 Germans had been exiled to the east from several regions of the Russian Republic as well as from the Georgian, Armenian, and Azerbaiji Republics. Close to half of the total (371,164) were removed from the Volga German Autonomous Republic, which was abolished on 28 August.[68] During the course of the war, Kalmyks, Karachays, Chechens, Ingush, Balkars, Crimean Tatars, Crimean Greeks, Meskhetian Turks, Kurds, and Khemshils were subjected to a similar fate.[69]

· Document 34 ·

NKVD plan for the forced resettlement of 95,400 Finns and Germans from the Leningrad *oblast'*, 28 August 1941, Arkhiv UFSB RF po SPb i LO f. 21/12, op. 2, p.n. 18, d. 11, ll. 3–8.

TOP SECRET

PLAN OF ACTION

On implementation of the Leningrad Front Military Council resolution of 26 August 1941, No. 196/ss, "On the Mandatory Evacuation of the German and Finnish Population from Suburban *Raiony* of Leningrad *Oblast'*."

In accordance with the Front Military Council's resolution, the following are subject to expulsion from eight *raiony* of Leningrad *oblast'* (Oranienbaumsky, Krasnoselsky, Slutsky, Krasnogvardeisky, Tosnensky, Mginsky, Vsevolozhsky, and Pargolovsky):

Finns . . . . 88,700 people

Germans . . . . 6,700 people

[. . .] In order to ensure the evacuation of the indicated German and Finnish population, the following actions must be taken:

1. Assign the evacuation to the UNKVD LO, for which an operations troika must be created consisting of: UNKVD LO Head Com. KUBATKIN, SPO NKVD Deputy Head Com. DROZDETSKY, and UNKVD LO Deputy Head Com. MAKAROV.

2. Require the VKP(b) Leningrad *Obkom* (Com. NIKITIN) and *Lenoblispolkom* (Com. SEMIN) to render the NKVD organs every assistance in carrying out the evacuation.

3. Locally, in the *raiony*, create operations troikas to be assigned responsibility for carrying out the evacuation. Approve operations troikas made up of the following: [. . .]

4. Require the UNKVD *Oblast'* Operations Troika (Comrades KUBATKIN, DROZDETSKY, and MAKAROV):

a. To painstakingly instruct the chairman of the NKVD *raion* operations troikas on the procedure for carrying out the evacuation.

b. To ensure the evacuation, employ the NKVD *raion* apparatus, the militia apparatus, and, with the agreement of the secretaries of the RK and the Chair of the RIKs [*raion* executive committees], the local council of party apparatuses.

c. To assign 5 UNKVD LO operations workers and 2 militia operations workers to assist each NKVD RO [*raion* section]. Attach operations groups consisting of 7 men apiece (see supp. no. 3) to the locations where those being evacuated are loaded onto barges or RR cars.

d. To monitor the rapid movement of the RR trains and barges out of Leningrad *Oblast'*.

5. Require the NKVD *raion* Operations Troikas:

a. To compile lists of the kolkhozes and points of settlement subject to mandatory evacuation, indicating the name of the kolkhoz or point of settlement, the number of the population subject to evacuation, the individuals responsible for the evacuation from among the NKVD workers or militia attached to the Operations Troika.

To establish that the individual assigned responsibility for the evacuation is delivering the population to the place of embarkation for the barges or the train.

b. To appoint one of those being evacuated responsible for the evacuation (the kolkhoz chairman or someone else).

c. To explain to the population being evacuated that they have to take food along (up to 200 kg. per family), bedding, linens, shoes, winter clothing, and small household implements (dishes, buckets, knives, forks, and so forth),

d. small agricultural equipment (saw, ax, shovel, and so forth). Total baggage weight (including food) must not exceed 600 kg.

e. To assign to each echelon an echelon head to accompany the echelon to the appointed location and find housing for them in coordination with the authorized local organs.

f. In the event that resistance is offered by individuals subject to evacuation or of refusal to leave, to identify and arrest the instigators and perform the appropriate explanatory work simultaneously in conjunction with party and *sovet* organs.

g. At the embarkation locations, to set aside special buildings temporarily for those being evacuated, until the means of conveyance are provided, and to organize the sale of food, and provide hot water and medical services.

6. Require the *raion* offices of *Zagotskot* [Livestock Storage Office] and *Zagotzerno* [Grain Storage Office] to accept livestock as well as surplus grain from the population being evacuated and to provide a receipt.

7. Require the RIK chairmen:

a. To issue to the head of a family being evacuated an evacuation certificate indicating that the family is being evacuated from such-and-such an *oblast'* and listing the family members.

b. To register and provide security for all abandoned buildings.

c. To put at the disposal of the NKVD *raion* Operations Troikas a sufficient number of workers from the local *sovet* and party activists to ensure that the evacuation is carried out.

8. Require that the commander of the rear security guard, Major General STEPANOV, send the necessary number of soldiers and command staff under the UNKVD LO allotment, in order to maintain order in the *raiony* of the evacuation.

9. Send the population being evacuated to the following places in accordance with the instructions from the evacuation council:

to Krasnoiarsk *krai* . . . . 24,000 people
Novosibirsk *oblast'* . . . . 24,000 "
Altaisk *oblast'* . . . . 12,000 "
Omsk *oblast'* . . . . 21,000 "
Northern Kazakhstan *oblast'* . . . . 15,000 "

10. Require the Railway Administration Head (Com. KOLPAKOV) to provide properly equipped railroad cars (heated) on time and in the right quantity, in accordance with the requests of the UNKVD LO at the point of entrainment of the population being evacuated.

Require the River Transport Administration Head (Com. LOGACHEV) to provide properly equipped barges on time and in the right quantity in accordance with the requests of the UNKVD LO.

11. Require the Railway TO [Transport Section] Head for the UNKVD LO, BEZHANOV, to ensure the timely provision of train cars at the points of entrainment in accordance with the enclosed plan (see attachment), as well as to monitor the speedy movement of railroad trains and barges out of Leningrad *oblast'*.

12. Require the UNKVD LO *Oblast'* Operations Troika (Com. KUBATKIN) to report to the VKP(b) *Oblast'* Committee and USSR NKVD daily on the progress of the operation under way.

13. Complete the evacuation by 7 September 1941.

14. Assign Leningrad VKP(b) OK Secretary Com. NIKITIN and USSR Deputy People's Commissar of Internal Affairs Com. MERKULOV, respectively, to observe and monitor the progress implementing the present actions.

NIKITIN   MERKULOV

Stalin's role in the forced resettlement is not clear. The morning after Merkulov (and Nikitin) composed the plan of action, Molotov, Malenkov, Kosygin, and Zhdanov transmitted from Leningrad a message to Stalin, in which they informed him that they had decided to relocate the Finns and Germans. It would seem that they did not seek Stalin's permission to remove the ethnic minorities, because that type of operation had been authorized at the start of the war, although it is possible that Stalin ordered the operation verbally. The GKO members requested confirmation from Stalin only on the specific details of the proposed plan of distribution of the deportees in the regions of Siberia and northern Kazakhstan.[70]

The resettlement plan was far too ambitious, and the severing of the last rail link with the "Mainland" on 29 August crippled the effort right when it started. Some 11,000 Germans were deported before the start of the blockade.[71] German forces ended up occupying territory where a majority of the Finns resided, and Germany subsequently evacuated over 76,000 of them to Finland.[72] By 1 March 1942, a total of 22,900 Finns and Germans had been relocated to eastern parts of the USSR from Leningrad's suburban areas.[73] NKVD reports from late autumn 1941 noted alleged active support for the enemy among Finns who had not been relocated from Leningrad's suburbs. Among other things, they were accused of undermining the resettlement operation and hiding food reserves (Document 42).

On 7 March 1942, while many thousands continued to starve to death, Zhdanov issued a draft resolution under the auspices of the VSLF to resume the resettlement of Finns and Germans, together with a remaining "anti-Soviet element," on 15 March by sending them in trucks over the ice road. Unlike the expulsion order of 28 August, the new order included Finns and Germans located within the city of Leningrad.[74] On 29 March, Kubatkin notified Beria that 6,888 Finns and Germans were among the 9,785 people who had been sent out of Leningrad during 17–18 March. On 4 April, Kubatkin further informed Beria that during the latter half of March, 39,075 people, including 35,162 Finns and Germans, had been removed from Leningrad and the surrounding area. Those being resettled were generally given twenty-four hours to pack up their belongings. In some cases, they got only six to eight hours' notice. He observed that during the process there were "no incidents of anti-Soviet manifestations."[75]

The quotas established in August for expulsions of Finns and Germans were not attained. As Document 45 shows, a total of 58,210 Germans and Finns were removed from Leningrad and its surrounding area by 1 October 1942, which represents less than half of number targeted in August. Starvation killed many who were slated for resettlement. Documents 35 and 36, written in the latter part of March 1942 by secretaries of *raikom*s in the heart of the city, indicate that others selected for mandatory evacuation could not be located. The data reveal the acute difficulty of accounting for any segment of the civilian population during the winter of 1941–42. Neither the police nor the housing administration had a firm grasp on who lived where or whether people whose deaths had not been recorded were actually alive. The siege conditions, however, were not solely to blame for poor NKVD record keeping. Some unknown percentage had died or moved away from Leningrad between the 1939 census and the start of the blockade.

The two documents also provide revealing glimpses into the mistakes and confusion that accompanied the attempt to remove the "anti-Soviet element." Party officials and a nationally prominent surgeon ended up on resettlement lists. Popular novelist Vera Ketlinskaia, who inspired besieged Leningraders in radio addresses to persevere, was given notice to leave the city. At the time, she was writing a fictional account of the blockade. Perhaps her close friendship with the poet Olga Berggolts, who was under NKVD suspicion (see below, pp. 247–48), was the reason she was considered to be a political risk.[76] The documents further indicate that NKVD deportation orders could be reversed by party officials. *Raikom* secretaries believed that support from the *gorkom* could be decisive in securing a reversal, and the order to exile Ketlinskaia was annulled.[77] In the case of one Comrade Semenova in Smolninsky *raion*, it appears from the text that the *raikom* itself was able to prevail upon the NKVD to reverse her deportation order.

· Document 35 ·

Report from Smolninsky *raikom* secretary Stelmakhovich to *gorkom* secretary A. P. Smirnov on the forced resettlement of Finns and Germans from Leningrad's Smolninsky *raion*, 20 March 1942, TsGAIPD SPb f. 24, op. 2v, d. 5838, ll. 1–2.

Leningrad *obkom* and *gorkom* VKP (b) SPECIAL SECTOR
Secret

MEMORANDUM

At the instruction of the above organs, the evacuation commission of Smolninsky *raion*, together with the NKVD district office, has evacuated 276 Finns
and Germans.

According to reports from the NKVD *raion* office, there were 736 Finns and
Germans (heads of families) in the district,

of the 736 Finns and Germans (heads of families), previously
evacuated — 128
went into the RKKA[78] — 27
sick — 51
dead — 106
not ascertained — 73

There was not room in the evacuation for 275 people, although they were
ready to go.

Along with the evacuation of the Finns and Germans on the NKVD lines, it
has been proposed to evacuate individuals who had particulars that compromised them.

However, the RK VKP(b) could not know why it was suggested that some
citizens be evacuated, since the materials were in the NKVD *oblast'* administration. Among these citizens there were obvious mistakes with their evacuation. Thus, for example, it was proposed that Com. SEMENOVA, secretary of
the party office of Mashgiz printers, leave. Previously, Com. Semenova had
been married to Nikitin, but 5 years before his arrest she married someone else,
who is at the present time in political work in the Red Army.

The RK VKP(b) felt that there were no grounds for the evacuation of Com.
Semenova, however, and the cancellation of her evacuation was achieved after
long disputes with the NKVD organs. Second fact. The Dzerzhinsky *raion*
evacuation commission proposed evacuating Com. A. I. ZOTIK, who works
with us as head of the RK VKP(b) organizational-instructional office. It turns
out that in 1935 Com. Zotik was released from his job as secretary of the Push-
kinsky RK VKP(b), but he was subsequently rehabilitated and restored to the
party and all this was known in the party organization. It was proposed that
Com. N. N. PETROV, a corresponding member of the Academy of Sciences and
one of the country's best surgeons, be evacuated.

Such facts may take place in the future given existing conditions.

SECRETARY OF THE SMOLNINSKY RK VKP(b): STELMAKHOVICH
LENINGRAD.

· Document 36 ·

Report by the chairman of the Evacuation Commission for Dzerzhinsky *raion*, Vinogradov, on the forced resettlement of Finns and Germans from that *raion*, 26 March 1942, TsGAIPD SPb f. 24, op. 2v, d. 5812, ll. 10–11.

After receipt of the order from the City Commission on the mandatory evacuation from Leningrad of certain categories of citizens, contact was established with the NKVD *raion* office and on 12 March the first list of 209 people was received from them.

In notifying citizens to appear at the *raion* Commission regarding their evacuation, it immediately became clear that the *raion* Commission has been doing a lot of unnecessary work, since the notice could be delivered to only 81 of the 209 people. Of the remaining number, 38 had been evacuated previously, 26 had died, moreover some of them had died several years before, and 63 no longer resided at the indicated address.

Subsequent lists confirmed that a large number of the citizens were not in the district at all and their place of residence was unknown.

Altogether, the *raion* Commission summoned 1,267 people, and of them only 300 appeared, and 127 of them were sent off, including 63 Germans, 31 Finns, and 32 others.

Also speaking to the fact that the accounting for the given category of citizens is not being done at the proper level and that the NKVD knew little about these individuals is the fact that such prominent specialists as Professor Griboedov, a man with a world reputation, Doctor of Medicine and Professor Kholdin, Citizen Chibisova, who is the niece of the poet Nekrasov and who a few days before this had received a food package from Smolny, Academy of Sciences Presidium member and academic pensioner Belenky, the writer Vera Ketlinskaia, as well as two deaf and blind ninety-year-old women, were called in.

It is characteristic that the overwhelming majority of citizens called in did not want to leave Leningrad, and only after lengthy discussion did they agree to fill out the documents. After sending off the rest of the citizens, apart from the Germans and Finns, some citizens expressed dissatisfaction, since they had sold their things on an emergency basis and cheaply and now they were working persistently to obtain their departure.

Chairman of the Evacuation Commission for Dzerzhinsky *raion* Vinogradov

Secretary Ganichev of the Vasileostrovsky *raikom* sent the *gorkom* a similar complaint on 20 March. He questioned why the list of people to be resettled from his *raion* included: "Professors Navalatsky and Martynov; the family of the president of the Academy of Sciences, Karninsky; the head of the administrative-economic administration of the Leningrad Branch of the Academy of Sciences, Fedoseev; and a series of others."[79]

The *gorkom* official in charge of writing summary reports on the popular mood, L. M. Antiufeev, noted in March 1942 that a majority of the people were against the forced resettlements. One person was overheard saying: "Why are they sending all of them out, when among them there may be good people?"[80]

Another security task was to try to prevent the population from being exposed to enemy propaganda. Radio receivers were confiscated in the first days of the war (around the same time that all photography without official permission was banned),[81] and the public was strictly prohibited from reading enemy leaflets that were dropped on the city starting in September. Large quantities of leaflets were dropped on 29 October, 6 November, and 10 November.[82] Possession of enemy propaganda could be used in support of a charge of KR activity or of treason, especially since leaflets often included a printed pass to cross over to the German lines. The following two documents contain examples of German propaganda leaflets dropped over Leningrad in the fall of 1941, which the NKVD turned over to the *gorkom*'s chief of propaganda and agitation, N. D. Shumilov. The leaflets conflate a virulent anti-Semitism and anticommunism in the image of the Soviet political leadership and were intended to appeal to soldiers and workers as well as the mothers, wives, and daughters of military personnel. Soviet troops were actively encouraged to cross over to German lines; however, German officers had orders to prevent civilians from defecting by shooting any who might attempt to do so.

· Document 37 ·

German propaganda leaflets dropped on Leningrad on 29 October 1941,
TsGAIPD SPb f. 25, op. 10, d. 307a, ll. 28, 29, 33.

TOP SECRET.
USSR PEOPLE'S COMMISSARIAT OF INTERNAL AFFAIRS
NKVD ADMINISTRATION FOR LENINGRAD *OBLAST*
Department: Secretariat
1/11 1941, No. 9712
Leningrad, 4 Volodarsky Prospect
Telephone: switchboard NKVD
Brief content
STRICTLY PERSONAL
TO THE SECRETARY FOR PROPAGANDA AND AGITATION OF THE LENIN-
GRAD GORKOM VKP (b) Comrade SHUMILOV
Enclosed herewith are examples of fascist leaflets dropped from the enemy's planes on 29 October of this year above Petrogradsky, Dzerzhinsky, and Vyborgsky *raiony*.

ENCLOSURE: the above-mentioned 3 pages.
DEPUTY HEAD, NKVD LO ADMINISTRATION IVANOV

Proclamation

To All Men and Women Citizens of the Soviet Union,
and to the Honest Commanders and Soldiers of the Red Army.
THE HOUR OF LIBERATION HAS STRUCK for all the peoples of the multi-national USSR. The victorious German Army will cast off the chains of the yoke of the Communist and the Yid [*zhidovskogo iga*].
Help the German Command actively to create a new order.
YOUR HAPPINESS AND LIFE ARE IN YOUR HANDS.
Don't believe the lying words of Communist-Yid propaganda.
THE COMMUNIST PARTY AND ITS LEADERS, LENIN AND STALIN, MADE YOU EMPTY PROMISES OF A FREE AND HAPPY LIFE, AND THEY DIDN'T KEEP A SINGLE ONE OF THEIR PROMISES.
The peoples of the USSR have been turned into slaves. Do you really want to defend this slavery?
The dawn of a new cultural life and work is rising.
ABANDON YOUR DEFENSE AND TAKE UP ARMS AGAINST YOUR COMMU-NIST AND YID OPPRESSORS. Go over to the side of Germany. This way you will hasten your liberation and put an end to your people's pointless blood-shed. Harvest the crop. Don't let the economy be destroyed, as has already happened in some towns. Remember that it belongs to you, and you will keep the fruits of your labor.
The German and Russian peoples have never been enemies. Lying Commu-nist and democratic propaganda pushed you into this war, which neither of us needs.
THROUGHOUT ALL OF HISTORY, ENGLAND HAS ALWAYS BEEN RUSSIA'S TRUE ENEMY, forcing it to defend its own interests.
DOWN WITH STALIN, THE GANG OF YIDS AND COMMUNISTS!
DOWN WITH ENGLAND, THE WAR'S TRUE INSTIGATOR.
HERE'S TO A HAPPY NEW LIFE!
Long live freedom and peace!

Proclamation

TO THE COMMANDERS, RED ARMY SOLDIERS, AND MEN AND WOMEN CITI-ZENS OF LENINGRAD!
The German High Command calls upon all of you to stop the pointless war forced on you by the Communist Yids.
TURN YOUR BAYONETS AROUND ON YOUR OWN OPPRESSORS.
Abandon your defense. By doing this you will save your own life and will help destroy the Communist yoke, which is more terrible than serfdom.
DON'T LET THEM BLOW UP AND DESTROY THE FACTORIES, BUILDINGS, AND BRIDGES OF YOUR MARVELOUS CITY.[83]

Your commissars and political workers are already getting ready to flee. They're to blame for your situation, but they're going to abandon you to the tyranny of fate. The airplanes are ready for the traitors' flight.

ARREST YOUR COMMISSARS, NKVD HANGMEN, AND YID AGITATORS.

Having provoked a war against Germany, they're now laying the consequences of defeat entirely upon you. Your struggle is pointless.

Whose interests are the tormented and enslaved people fighting for?

The selfish interests of political scoundrels and Yids.

Each one of you has to ask yourselves why there are no Yids at the front or on the job digging trenches. Why have the Yids taken all of the senior places in the USSR administration? Because the Yids are parasites on all mankind.

WHY HAVE THE PEOPLE BEEN SUFFERING FOR MORE THAN 23 YEARS UNDER THE COMMUNISTS' YOKE AND TREMBLING FROM THE NKVD'S HORRIBLE RED TERROR?

The time has come to cast off this yoke with the help of victorious German arms.

SPEED AND DELIVERANCE DEPEND ON YOU ALONE.

Don't believe the lying words of the Communists and Yids, who are only trying to save their own skins.

Let's put a swift end to war, Stalin, and his henchmen and toadies.

LONG LIVE THE FREEDOM THE TROOPS OF GREAT GERMANY ARE BRINGING YOU!

· Document 38 ·

German propaganda leaflets dropped on Leningrad on 10 November 1941; the illustrations show portions of the originals. TsGAIPD SPb f. 25, op. 10, d. 307a, ll. 38–41.

———————

USSR PEOPLE'S COMMISSARIAT OF INTERNAL AFFAIRS
NKVD ADMINISTRATION FOR LENINGRAD *OBLAST'*
Secretariat

11 November 1941
Leningrad, 4 Volodarsky Prospect
Telephone: switchboard NKVD
TO THE SECRETARY OF THE LENINGRAD GORKOM VKP (b) Comrade SHU-MILOV.

Enclosed herewith are [. . .] examples of fascist leaflets dropped over Leningrad from enemy planes on 10 November of this year.

ENCLOSURE: as stated in text.

HEAD OF UNKVD LO SECRETARIAT TSYGANOV

Смоking
is allowed!

We are stopping
the pointless resistance, since we know
the German Army treats prisoners of war
WELL!

COMMANDERS AND FIGHTERS!

German troops are waiting outside Leningrad. They have already taken Kiev. Moscow is being evacuated. The Red Army's situation is hopeless. Soviet power will soon disappear!

Stop the senseless bloodshed! Think about your future. By destroying towns and villages, bridges, railroads, and warehouses as you retreat, you are destroying the means necessary to restore your homeland.

THE GERMAN ARMY

fights exclusively against the terror and tyranny of the Communists. The German Army promises you good treatment. Throw down your weapons and come over to our side!

**Kick out the commissars,
who have been restored to your ranks
in order to undermine the cause of peace!**
Long live peace and the prosperity of the free peoples of your homeland!

The next leaflet (p. 221) included a surrender pass printed in Russian and German.

Beat[84] the Yid political instructor!
His kisser's begging for a brick!
Commissars and political instructors make you resist pointlessly.
Drive out the commissars and come over to the Germans.
Come over to the Germans using either the slogan:
Beat the Yid political instructor!
His kisser's begging for a brick!
or else this pass:

> This pass is valid for an *unlimited number* of RKKA commanders and fighters coming over to the side of the German troops.
> ### PASS
> Show this pass if you're against the pointless bloodshed in the interests of the Yids and commissars, leave the vanquished Red Army, and come over to the side of the German Armed Forces. *German officers and soldiers will give whoever comes over a good welcome, feed him, and give him a job.*
> (See the adjacent translation into German)

Commanders and fighters
of the Red Army!

Your situation is hopeless.
The iron ring of German forces is closing tighter and tighter around you.

Бей жида - политрука, рожа просит кирпича!

Комисары и политруки принуждают вас к бессмысленному сопротивлению.

Гоните комисаров и переходите к немцам.

Переходите к немцам пользуясь либо лозунгом:

Бей жида-политрука, рожа просит кирпича!

либо пропуском:

You don't have enough ammunition, supplies, or food, your rulers and leaders are incapable of anything; they're running away and abandoning you to the arbitrariness of fate.

Many of you have been oppressed all this time by Communist rule and have lost all your rights, and now it is exploiting you in defense of its regime. **Your struggle is useless!**

Can you really let your leadership out of obstinacy keep driving you mercilessly to inevitable death?

No, your life is precious to you! Preserve it for a better future and for your families.

COME OVER TO THE GERMANS — YOU CAN EXPECT GOOD TREATMENT and nourishment, as well as a speedy return to your homeland.

Hurry!

In the regions they've occupied, the Germans have already begun to resolve the land question.

Red Army soldiers, don't be late, otherwise you'll be left landless!

They demand peace! They want to live! MOTHERS, WIVES, DAUGHTERS!

STALIN'S BLOODY RULE, which made you drink from a bottomless cup of grief and shed a sea of tears, is now committing its final crime against you: IT IS DRIVING YOUR FATHERS, SONS, AND HUSBANDS TO THE SLAUGHTER for interests alien to you. This war, which Stalin has already lost, suffering defeat after defeat, is being waged by him not to improve your life but to keep power in his own hands! So that his NKVD can continue to execute your near and dear and send them away to concentration camps! So that other peoples can suffer under Stalin's rule, too!

The German Army is fighting for your liberation from the heavy Stalinist yoke! We are bringing you peace and freedom, we are bringing confidence in the coming day!

No longer will you weep at night over the fate of your sons and husbands who are languishing innocently in Stalin's torture chambers.

Mothers and wives of Red Army soldiers!

Through base deceit, bloody terror, false promises, and the fear of punishment, BESOTTED BY VODKA, Stalin is driving your dear ones to certain death. DO NOT ALLOW THIS! Explain to your husbands and brothers that by fighting for Stalin they are fighting for the continuation of your torments and sufferings. Call on them to turn their bayonets against Stalin, the sole enemy of the people, the hangman who has lodged himself in the Kremlin. He is to blame for the fact that millions of human lives are now being sacrificed to interests alien to you.

Mothers and wives of RKKA commanders and soldiers!

You can rid your people of their endless torments if you demand an end to the senseless bloodshed. Hurry—death is standing on your doorstep now! Think of your children, your husbands, sons, and brothers!

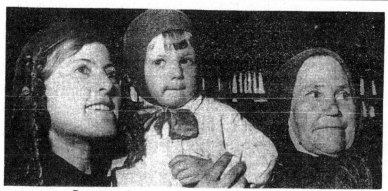

Они требуют мира! Они хотят жить!

МАТЕРИ, ЖЕНЫ, ДЕВУШКИ!

КРОВАВАЯ СТАЛИНСКАЯ ВЛАСТЬ, принудившая вас выпить бездонную чашу горя, заставившая пролить море слез, делает сейчас свое последнее преступление перед вами: за чуждые вам интересы ГОНИТ НА УБОЙ ВАШИХ ОТЦОВ, СЫНОВЕЙ и МУЖЕЙ. Эта война, которую Сталин

уже проиграл, терпя поражение за поражением, ведется им не за то, чтобы улучшить вашу жизнь, а за то чтобы удержать власть в своих руках! За то, чтобы его НКВД, как и раньше, мог расстреливать и ссылать в концлагеря ваших родных и близких! За то чтобы под сталинской властью страдали и другие народы!

Германская армия борется за ваше освобождение от тяжелого сталинского гнета!

Мы несем вам мир и свободу, несем уверенность в завтрашнем дне!

Вы не будете больше оплакивать по ночам судьбу ваших сыновей и мужей, без вины томящихся в сталинских застенках.

Матери и жены красноармейцев!

Подлым обманом, кровавым террором, лживыми обещаниями и страхом расправы с вами, ОДУРМАНИВАЯ ВОДКОЙ, Сталин гонит ваших близких на верную смерть. НЕ ДОПУСКАЙТЕ ЭТОГО! Об'ясните вашим мужьям и братьям, что борясь за Сталина, они борются за продолжение ваших мук и страданий. Зовите их повернуть штыки против единственного народного врага и палача, засевшего в Кремле Сталина. Он виноват в том, что миллионы человеческих жизней приносятся сейчас в жертву чуждым вам интересам.

Матери и жены командиров и бойцов РККА!

Вы можете избавить ваш народ от безконечных мучений, если вы потребуете прекращения бессмысленного кровопролития. Торопитесь — смерть стоит уже перед вашей дверью! Подумайте о ваших детях, о ваших мужьях, сыновьях и братьях! 175 BF

Party and NKVD informants noted an increase in anti-Semitic outbursts in July and especially in August, followed by a sharp rise in September in the circulation of leaflets that called for pogroms against Jews.[85] Anti-Semitic leaflets bore similarities to German propaganda and no doubt were influenced by it. City authorities monitored closely the rise in anti-Semitism and devoted considerable efforts to eliminating it in part because Leningrad had a large Jewish population.[86] There were about 200,000 Jews in the city on the eve of the German invasion, comprising over 6 percent of the population. Leningrad had the highest proportion of Jews of any city in the RSFSR, and there were almost as many Jews in Leningrad at that time as all other ethnic minorities combined. Almost a quarter of the RSFSR's urban Jews resided in Leningrad. Jews were well represented in several professions, including law, medicine, teaching, journalism, and retail trade.[87] Prior to the war, anti-Semitic activity had been prosecuted under article 59-7 of the criminal code, which forbade expression that was intended to incite national or religious enmity or discord. Sentences under article 59-7 during wartime (part 2) included execution; however, the death sentence was supposed to be applied only in "especially aggravated circumstances." By contrast, execution was listed as the first option for punishment for anti-Soviet agitation during wartime (58-10, part 2), but was actually applied in less than half of the cases in besieged Leningrad.[88] Following the German invasion, anti-Semitic hate speech was viewed as a type of anti-Soviet expression, because hatred of Jews was a core part of the ideology of Nazi Germany, which sought to depose Soviet power. A conflict arose within the ranks of the procuracy and the VT over the meaning of anti-Semitic outbursts, which were sharply increasing in number. On 1 October, city prosecutor Popov complained in a letter to Zhdanov that such speech was not being prosecuted, as it ought to be, as anti-Soviet agitation, but instead under article 59. Moreover, he alleged that the VP had reduced charges from article 58 to 59. He cited the example of one D. Ya. Rogulin, who allegedly said, "Beat the Yids, save Russia." Although Rogulin had originally been charged under article 58-10, Popov stated that the VP had reduced the charge to article 59-7. He was sentenced to seven years of hard labor plus five years of deprivation of rights. In another instance, A. T. Strunkin was heard saying in a beer hall, "Our information bureau screws everything up, we have to beat the Yids now." He repeated the phrase, "Beat the Yids." Popov claimed that the VT had convicted Strunkin under article 59 even though he had been charged under article 58. His sentence was five years of hard labor and three years of loss of rights.

A member of the VP named Erenburg responded by letter to Popov's allegations on 4 October. He stated that since the start of the war, the VP had considered 695 KR cases. In a "significant number" of them, the arrestee had made comments of "a pogrom character" in addition to other inflammatory remarks. Arrestees in such cases were charged with anti-Soviet agitation, and those convicted were either shot or given long prison terms. Erenburg added that "several workers of the VP and VT with the goal of establishing a more just juridical qualification decided when the accusation was solely anti-Semitic to charge the person with 59-7, part 2 and not 58-10, part 2." He admitted that this classification was a mistake as anti-Semitism is a "programmatic issue for fascism" but claimed that the mistake had occurred only in the second half of August. Erenburg blamed the VT for reclassifying cases and claimed that several members of the VP had protested the changes to both the VT and the city prosecutor.

In an attempt to turn the tables on the city prosecutor, Erenburg claimed that Popov himself had sent the VP cases of anti-Semitic speech charged under article 59-7. He cited two examples. On 11 August, one G. A. Bakhvalov said: "The Jews must be beaten, beat the Yids, crush the Yids, I will go to the front, I will beat the Jews." On 26 August, A. D. Mutovkin was heard saying: "There are no Yids at the front, the day after tomorrow we will beat the Yids . . . the Yids drank our blood,[89] and in three days we will get drunk on their blood." The day after Erenburg wrote his letter, a member of the VT named Marchuk sought to defend himself by stating that he was not to blame for lightening sentences.[90]

One point on which Popov and Erenburg seemed to agree was that there was a tendency beginning in the latter part of August to prosecute anti-Semitic hate speech under article 59 instead of under article 58, as had been done during the war up to that time. Why exactly the shift occurred is not explained; however, it would seem to have been linked with the increase in reported anti-Semitic conversations and, perhaps, with the concomitant growing anxiety throughout the city following the leadership's admission that Leningrad was imperiled. Officials in the VP and VT may have begun to fear that if the city fell to the enemy, reprisals would be taken against those who harshly punished anti-Semitic hate speech and writing.

Historian Sheila Fitzpatrick made the astute observation regarding the dilemma of those in charge of monitoring public opinion in the 1930s: "The Soviet regime was wary of allowing citizens to express uncensored opinions about matters of public import in public. At the same time, it was extremely anxious to know what people were thinking."[91] Surveying the city's popular mood (*nastroenie*) took on added significance during the siege. When Leningrad's very existence was at stake, the party and the NKVD tried extremely hard to measure and control political sentiments. Yet, taking the population's political pulse proved difficult because a general fear of being jailed or shot for anti-Soviet agitation made people guarded and cautious. The party and the NKVD relied on secret informants placed in apartment houses, factories, institutions of higher learning, hospitals, bread shops, and elsewhere to gauge public opinion and in that way to uncover and eliminate anti-Soviet expression. They also kept tabs on morale within their own ranks. The information networks of the party and the NKVD were large and separately maintained. The number of NKVD informants alone exceeded ten thousand in Leningrad in the autumn of 1941. Throughout the blockade, that number appears to have remained fairly stable, or perhaps even grown, as those who died, left the city, or became inactive for other reasons were generally replaced by new recruits. As many as 1,000 agents and informants (mainly the latter) were lost in the worst of the starvation months, while the number of replacement recruits reached as high as 1,500 per month. It would appear that the closest cooperation between the party and the NKVD in terms of surveillance occurred in apartment buildings. Security there was maintained by so-called "political organizers" (a separate group from NKVD and party informants) who were selected jointly by the heads of the *raiotdely* of the NKVD and the *raikom* secretaries but were subordinate solely to the NKVD. Responsibilities of the political organizers, who were armed, included checking residents' documents to make sure that they had the required residence permits. The political organizers also regularly canvassed custodians, night guards, and other "indicated people" for comments they had overheard or acts they had witnessed of an anti-Soviet or pro-German nature. The political organizers reported such information directly to the *raion* NKVD authorities. By September 1941, there were ten thousand political organizers in city apartment buildings.[92]

NKVD and party officials at the *raion* level wrote reports on the political content of overheard conversations. Their reports became the basis of city-wide summaries of the public mood produced separately by the NKVD and the party. Kubatkin wrote a myriad of reports during the siege. The longest were special reports (*spetssoobshcheniia*), which he produced at intervals of a month or six weeks (for example, Document 42). These comprehensive summaries of NKVD actions, which were sent to Zhdanov and Kuznetsov as well as to Beria and Merkulov and the Leningrad Front commander, included assessments of public opinion based on overheard conversations, descriptions of arrests and convictions for KR activity and of alleged conspiracies to overthrow Soviet power, as well as information on nonpolitical crimes, including theft of ration cards and food, the mortality rate, and cannibalism. In addition, Kubatkin wrote a summary *spetssoobshchenie* to Zhdanov or Kuznetsov with a copy to Beria or Merkulov once every week or two starting on 13 September.[93] Kubatkin also wrote numerous shorter reports each week on individual urgent matters (for example, Document 54). He briefed Beria and Merkulov on all aspects of the UNKVD's work, sometimes sending numerous *spetssoobshcheniia* daily to Moscow by telegraph or special post.[94] Within the LPO, the head of the *gorkom*'s Organizational-Instructional Office, L. M. Antiufeev, wrote "information summaries" (*informatsionnye svodki*) every few days that included descriptions of the public mood. Antiufeev also wrote special reports on the public's reaction to important events, such as changes in the food rations, a speech by Stalin, or a meeting of Soviet leaders and foreign dignitaries.

The following four documents, two each from Antiufeev (assisted by an office administrator named Klebanov), and Kubatkin, highlight the similarities and differences between party and NKVD reporting on popular mood. (Changes in the popular mood itself are covered in chapter five.) The reports were written between 22 November and 6 December 1941, which was a critical period. The city had endured almost three months of intensive aerial and artillery bombardment, and an early and very cold winter had set in. Supplies reaching Leningrad over Lake Ladoga were meager as the enemy held the vital transportation center of Tikhvin, and new roads had to be hacked through forests. As a result, bread rations had been cut on 13 and 20 November, which in turn resulted in the first deaths by starvation. The crisis facing Moscow at this time was nearly as alarming. German panzer divisions were closing in on the capital. Prior to the Soviet counteroffensive to save Moscow, which commenced on 6 December, some German units had reached within thirteen miles of its suburbs.[95]

Documents 39, 40, and 41 have the most in common as they trace changes in popular mood following the reduction in the bread ration on 20 November. Antiufeev's summary of 26 November (Document 40) focuses specifically on the lengthening bread lines and the critical sentiments articulated by those standing in them. Kubatkin's report of 6 December (Document 42) is of a different kind. It is a lengthy summary (the longest document included in this book) of all important UNKVD activities over the preceding six weeks, including assessment of public mood. Among other things, the report shows the level of detail that Kubatkin passed on to Moscow. It illustrates that Kubatkin kept NKVD headquarters regularly informed of KR arrests and of ongoing investigations even before arrests were made. By contrast, Antiufeev never sent copies of his reports on the public mood to Moscow. His summaries throughout the blockade consistently asserted that most people remained loyal to Soviet authority. Such an example is found in the first line of Document 39. His description of the public mood followed his usual formula, which proceeded from examples of pro-Soviet comments to criticism of specific policies to "unhealthy, defeatist statements." The latter category included several examples of pessimistic predictions for the city, but only the last example comprised an appeal to take action against the government. Kubatkin's surveys of the public mood, while including examples of those who "stoically endure food hardships," placed more emphasis on the "anti-Soviet and backward elements" and cited more examples of Leningraders who expressed the hope that the enemy would take the city. In the section on popular mood from the 6 December report, Kubatkin included only examples of "negative" mood—"hostile elements" that were "attempting to incite the backward portion of the population to organized counterrevolutionary actions." He included no overheard expressions of loyalty.

Antiufeev's reports give the impression of a more objective attempt to assess the aggregate mood during a critical time, although the fact that the *gorkom* was also keen to demonstrate broad support for the party introduces a bias in its assessment of public opinion that likely explains Antiufeev's repeated insistence that a "substantial mass"" (*osnovnaia massa*) of the population supported official policy. (Prior to November, he used the phrase "overwhelming majority" [*podavliaiushchee bol'shinstvo*] to convey a sense of greater support.) His summaries often do not include speakers' names, and even when individuals were identified by name, it is unclear what action was taken against them, as the party *svodki* generally do not contain information on subsequent arrests. Although the *gorkom* wanted to stamp out perceived anti-Soviet sentiment, it was not primarily interested in identifying individual critical voices as it attempted to assess public opinion. Kubatkin, on the other hand, was supremely interested in gathering information for arrests and convictions; hence, he was keen to identify those who denounced Soviet power or policies. He reported on cases as they developed. Kubatkin's report from 6 December 1941 shows clearly that during the first months of the siege as starvation became widespread, only a very small percentage of those heard expressing KR views were arrested. The low arrest rate was probably a function of limited NKVD resources and the inability of informants to identify those who spontaneously uttered anti-Soviet comments. The report states that during November 300–350 "anti-Soviet manifestations" were occurring daily; yet, the total number arrested for all kinds of KR offenses from 15 October to 1 December was 957, or about 20 per day.[96] Despite the fact that only a small percentage of observed "anti-Soviet manifestations" led to arrests, the reliability of evidence that security organs gathered in political investigations is called into question by the fact that they were under considerable pressure to uncover KR activity and make arrests. Security officials had to produce results. Leningrad NKGB chief Ogoltsov's order of 28 July 1941 (above, p. 202) outlined new priorities for ensuring state security.[97] The final two sentences of the order read: "I warn the entire operational and directing staff that the appearance of passivity, indecisiveness, and especially inactivity on the front of the struggle with counterrevolution will be considered as toleration of the enemy. From the heads of the departments I demand precise and flexible work of all sections under them in the operational apparatus, in a decisive way nipping in the bud the smallest indications of placidity, slackness, and disorganization in agent-operational work."[98] This message was passed along to agents and informants. The fact that the Leningrad NKVD severed relations with, and cut off privileges for, hundreds of informants each month for alleged "passivity"[99] (which presumably included physical inactivity resulting from starvation as well as failure to furnish incriminating evidence upon which cases could be built) provided incentive for informants to exaggerate anti-Soviet sentiment in their surveillance reports and even fabricate reports outright. Any subsequent investigation of KR crime based on doctored informant reports might expose the distortions or fabrications, which could result in harsh sentences for the informants; however, many informants may have been willing to run that risk to retain life-saving privileges provided by the NKVD.[100]

· Document 39 ·

Report from Antiufeev and office administrator Klebanov to Zhdanov, Kuznetsov, Kapustin, and Shumilov on public reactions to reductions in bread rations, 22 November 1941, TsGAIPD SPb f. 24, op. 2v, d. 4819, ll. 103–6.

Leningrad *obkom* and *gorkom* VKP(b) SPECIAL SECTOR
INFORMATION SUMMARY

The explanatory work done on the reasons for the repeated reduction of the bread allowance shows that a substantial mass of Leningrad's laborers regard these compulsory measures with understanding.

Here are a few characteristic speeches and statements:

"Everyone realizes that this is a temporary situation, since Leningrad is surrounded. Right now we need to take ourselves in hand, not moan, but through our work hasten victory." (Nikonov, driver for NKVD Main Administration for Material and Technical Supply).

"We understand why the bread allowance has gone down. For the time being, we have to put up with it . . ." (Khlobystov, caretaker at the Metrology Institute).

"This is a temporary difficulty caused by the blockade of Leningrad. Once our units break through the front, the food allowances will be increased." (Shelkovnikov, worker, 33rd Shop, Marti factory).

"We clearly understand the troubles that Leningrad is going through, but we have to be prepared for even harder trials." (Guranda, worker, 10th Shop, Sudomekh Plant).

A worker from Proletarian Victory Factory No. 1, Com. Putitsin (who has four sons at the front) said at a meeting: "We will get through the whole difficult time and certainly win." At meetings in Shop No. 1, Proletarian Victory Factory No. 2, old workers, Coms. Shilov and Yershova, spoke. They talked about the hard times they lived through during the Civil War years and made an appeal—to work better and in greater solidarity, in order to help the Red Army break the ring of encirclement.

Much attention has been paid at these meetings to issues of improving the work of food stores and public dining facilities. Thus, for example, at nearly all plants and institutions in Oktiabrsky *raion*, they indicated the need for eliminating lines and organizing uniform distribution of food to the various stores. At the Metrology Institute, in the course of a discussion, Com. Eller, a mechanic, spoke and stated:

"The policy of strict food allowances is the sole correct policy. We need to make clever use, in a public-spirited way, and distribute each gram of food there is in reserve until the Red Army breaks the ring of the blockade. I think we need to demand that food stores sell prepacked goods in advance."

At many meetings the question has been raised about setting up worker oversight over the activities of cafeterias and stores.

The leaders of several enterprises are showing valuable initiative in seeking out substitutes for foods. The director of the Poliustrovets Plant proposed the manufacture of tea rum, which is considered an important and nutritious beverage. In the cafeterias of the Voroshilov Sudomekh Plant and several other enterprises of the Oktiabrsky *raion,* vegetable waste is not thrown out, as it used to be, but rather processed, reground, and put into circulation again, as a supplemental food.

Many mothers have expressed alarm over their children's fate. At the Anisimov Factory, Red Banner Factory No. 29, the Rubber Footwear Plant, and others, during discussions, exclamations like these have been heard:

"It's nothing for us, we'll suffer through, but you see we have nothing to feed our children. . . ."

"We need to introduce strict oversight over food allowances in nurseries. . . ."

And worker Kolosova (sewing shop, Red Banner Factory), suggested:

"The question needs to be raised of reducing the work day, since working for 10 hours given this kind of nourishment—we aren't strong enough. After all, workers who have several children give their bread to their children and nourish themselves just with tea. . . ."

Workers in occupations involving heavy labor and workers doing intense intellectual labor complain especially about the shortage of bread.

A smith from the 4th Shop, Factory No. 5 (Primorsky *raion*), Com. Alekse[ev,] stated at a meeting:

"It's impossible to work in a smithy on that kind of bread ration."

A surgeon at the Lenin Hospital, Com. Katsnelson, in a private conversation, complained about his hunger:

"I have to work in five clinics, perform operations on the skull and nasopharynx, go up and down three or four flights several times a day. This is very hard. Believe me, a few days ago, during a complicated bandaging, my head spun so badly that I had to grab onto the wash-stand to keep from falling. . . . But how can you divide up 125 grams of bread for a full day when you have to be on duty? . . . I love my work and want to work, but I've been forced to ask them to release me from one job. . . ."

Along with this, there are unhealthy, defeatist statements:

Kopokhnovskaia, a worker in Shop No. 1 in the production combine of the Industrial Goods Administration, in response to an appeal to render assistance to the front by sewing quilted jackets, stated:

"We are simply starving to death, and the idea that victory will be ours—that's nothing more than a fairy tale."

At the same enterprise, worker Smirnova said:

"We'll die, we won't last until a victory. We started trying to break through the encirclement too late. . . ."

At workers' meetings at the Anisimov Factory, there were individual shouts:

"Pretty soon we won't be able to put one foot in front of the other. . . . In a week they're going to cut it again. . . . They used to say there were reserves for 10 years, but where are they now?"

Savinykh, a worker at Hosiery Shop No. 2 of the Red Banner Factory, broke out in curses against the government and the soldiers, who "are spilling their blood in vain," and concluded:

"Let's pounce on the bread and loot it, let them know. . . ."

Head of the Organizational-Instructional Office, City Committee VKP(b) Antiufeev

Office Adminstrator Ia. Klebanov

6 copies

· Document 40 ·

Report from Antiufeev to *gorkom* secretaries Zhdanov, Kuznetsov, Kapustin, and Shumilov on the attitudes of people standing in bread lines, 26 November 1941, TsGAIPD SPb f. 24, op. 2v, d. 4819, ll. 108–10.

Leningrad *obkom* and *gorkom* VKP(b)

SPECIAL SECTOR

[Handwritten note] To Kuznetsov and Popkov. Shouldn't Popkov publish a discussion on these issues

Zhdanov [illegible]

INFORMATION SUMMARY.

A rumor has spread in the city that as of 1 December the adult population of Leningrad will be issued oilcake instead of bread, and children biscuits. Rumors have also been exaggerated about the breakthrough of the enemy's blockade ring being delayed and the food reserves in the city running out. In connection with this, in recent days, huge lines have formed at food stores and bread bakeries. People are beginning to gather at three or four o'clock in the morning, and they stand there all day in anticipation of some kind of food.

On 24 November, for example, a line formed beginning at four o'clock in the morning[101] at Store No. 48 (corner of Gaz Ave. and Ogorodnikov Ave.). During the day, no food was brought here, but the people did not disperse and by seven o'clock at night there was still a line here of a little over 200 people. The store's director, Com. Poshibailov, warned the people more than once that no food was expected today, but the line continued to wait.

The same day, a huge line (400–500 people) formed at Store No. 57, Leninsky *raion*. Someone had said they would be giving out sausage and vermicelli here. When the director started trying to talk the crowd into dispersing, since there wasn't going to be any sausage at all and there was only enough vermicelli for 70 people, a great furor rose. Cries were heard:

"Look at the kissers on you, you've been stuffing 'em at our expense. . . ."

"I haven't eaten anything all day, and I've been standing here since four o'clock in the morning. . . ."

"I can't go home, I have hungry children there. . . ." etc.

At seven o'clock in the evening, the director was forced to shut the store's doors in order to stop the excessive crowding and jostling, but the women started banging on the door and crying and wailing for him to open it.

On 25 November, at Dairy Store No. 2, Smolninsky *raion*, there was a line all day in anticipation of "something." In spite of a disturbance, which lasted several hours, people would not disperse.

At the Vasileostrovsky department store, on 25 November, a line began forming at three-thirty in the morning and got as big as about 2,000 people. They came here from various districts of the city, since someone had said that they would be giving out butter here. But it wasn't brought in. The women started cursing the director. One told him:

"You have it easy, there are airplanes all set for you to get out of Leningrad in case of trouble, while we kick the bucket here. . . ."

Another woman shouted that they were hiding from the workers when and which products were going to be brought in, while under the table "they themselves" (presumably, "management") were giving out foods to their acquaintances and friends.

In the stores a few days ago, excerpts were hung from a decision of the Leningrad City Council's Executive Committee on issuing fats, chocolate, etc. instead of bread. Citing this resolution, the people are demanding that the directors issue these foods.

Trade workers and many laborers are suggesting organizing the assignment of the population to stores and at some defense enterprises opening stalls for distributing foods to workers who do not have the opportunity to spend time standing in line.

Speculators and secondhand dealers are operating unpunished in Leningrad's markets. For bread, oilcake, cigarettes, and wine, they acquire valuable things: outerwear, shoes, watches, etc. At the Maltsevsky, Senny, Sytny, and other markets, people are bringing out all their fur coats, wool coats, boots, watches, firewood, small stoves, etc. But no one is selling anything for money. For a man's jacket with a fur collar they were asking a loaf of bread; a winter fur cap was sold for 200 grams of bread and 15 rubles in cash; for 400 grams of bread one man bought leather gloves; for deep rubber galoshes for felt boots they were asking a kilogram of bread or two kilograms of oilcake; and for two bundles of firewood they were asking 300 grams of bread, etc. Many have become victims of swindlers. Thus, a few days ago one woman gave up two bottles of champagne for two kilograms of semolina. But subsequently it turned out that instead of semolina they had slipped her a mixture used to make glue.

It is almost impossible right now to get a pair of boots repaired for money by a private cobbler, to hire sawyers to saw up firewood, or to hire a carpenter to carry out any kind of minor repair in an apartment. They're asking for bread, sugar, semolina, or vodka for everything.

Head of the Organizational-Instructional Office of the City Committee VKP(b) Antiufeev

Office Adminstrator Ia. Klebanov

6 copies

· Document 41 ·

Report from Kubatkin to Zhdanov, Kuznetsov, and Khozin, commander of the Fifty-fourth Army, on the public mood and on food-related crime, 25 November 1941, Arkhiv UFSB RF po SPb i LO f. 21/12, op. 2, p.n. 19, d. 12, ll. 16–21.

TOP SECRET

NKVD USSR Administration for Leningrad *Oblast'* and the City of Leningrad

SPECIAL REPORT

The city's workers have expressed their readiness to stoically endure food hardships and to help the front even more in order to break the blockade and ensure victory over the enemy.

PERFIRYOV, chief of the planning office at the "PLASTMASS" factory, says:

". . . We can expect them to issue even less bread. But that shouldn't stop us. Leningrad must be Soviet, even if that means going to 50 grams of bread. . . ."

ANDREICHIK, bookkeeper, Leningrad Railway:

". . . It's all right, we'll get through this. Let them reduce my bread even more and give it to the workers engaged in the important, heavy sectors of the defense plants."

YEGOROVA, student, Textile Institute:

". . . This measure of the Leningrad Front command is correct. We'll get through this hardship, too. Just so the fascists are beaten."

DMITRICHENKO, blacksmith, LENIN factory:

". . . I agree to enduring any deprivation, just so we drive this scum out of Leningrad."

Letters that have passed through the military censor attest to the readiness of Leningrad's population to endure food hardships caused by the city's blockade:

". . . They cut our bread. Our situation's very hard, but everyone who truly loves his Homeland will endure these hardships calmly. We'll never surrender to the enemy. I'll go beat the vipers—the Germans—but I won't surrender to them alive."

"... Life is very hard, there's nothing at all to eat. This is what the cursed German has done to us, but he's going to catch it bad, and soon, he'll find his grave outside our Leningrad."

"... Victory over the enemy requires sacrifices, so we have to endure everything. The time will come when the Germans will answer for all their devastations to our land. We'll make them all rise up. The beast Hitler will be destroyed."

Anti-Soviet and backward elements, exploiting the food hardships, are attempting to sow panic among the population, intensifying their defeatist and fascist propaganda.

PORETSKY, department head, Electrotechnical Institute of Communications:

"... Now in Leningrad we have famine. The solution to the current food situation is to surrender Leningrad to the Germans."

POMORSKY, doctor of physics and mathematics:

"... If the army lets the Germans get a cannon shot away from Leningrad when it was still fresh, tough, and well fed, then how can it defend Leningrad and break the encirclement now, when it's ragged and half-starving?"

MIKULIN, worker, Leningrad Station, Oktiabrskaia Railroad:

"... If the German came here, we'd be full, but if Soviet power stays, then we're all going to starve to death."

IVANOV, engineer, Oktiabrskaia Railroad:

"... The city is running out of food. It's all the government's fault; it didn't get food to Leningrad. We're never going to break through the ring around the city."

VOLKH, engineer, Scientific Research Institute of Communications:

"... Leningrad's going to surrender to the Germans. The city is in a more serious situation than before, and our troops are too weak to break through the German blockade. Leningraders face a question, whether to starve to death or to surrender the city to the Germans."

POSPELOVA, associate, Food Trade Administration:

"... Why all these pointless torments? After all, Leningrad can't hold out anyway. Better we surrender to the Germans. They're a cultured, decent people. Everything they say about the Germans on the radio is lies."

Speculating on the food hardships, anti-Soviet elements are refusing to work and attempting to call for organized actions and to try to get an increased bread ration.

KHRUSTALEV, inspector, Factory No. 371:[102]

"... We're putting up with the hunger because lots of Communists settled here. They have nowhere else to go and they won't surrender.

"We need to organize down to the last man and demand either that they surrender the city or that they supply us properly. The Germans will come and show us how to work and how to feed the people."

SHAZLINSKAIA, a worker in the same factory:

". . . We need to be organized about quitting work. They can't shoot everyone. We have to take everything they're saying about Hitler in the opposite way."

VOLKOV, worker, "Skorokhod" factory:

". . . People aren't going to put up with this kind of life for long. There's going to be a coup inside the country soon."

TERENTEV, welder, to the administration's suggestion that he stay and work overtime, replied:

". . . First you have to feed me, then you can try to make me work."

IAKOVLEV, a blacksmith at the same factory, refused to work overtime, declaring:

". . . After meals like this I'm not going to work anymore, I don't care if you put me on trial."

KUZNETSOV, BURTSEV, and VOROPAEV, workers at the MARTI factory, after working eight hours apiece, left, saying that they were hungry and couldn't work anymore.

On 20 November, an hour before the usual time, BAZULITSKY, LIVSHITS, PALATKIN, and others, workers at Factory No. 190,[103] quit work and left the factory.

Worker LATINTSEV struck BARANOV, a janitor who tried to prevent their departure.

On 22 November, 13 workers from the weaving shop at "Lenkooptekstil'," FOMINA, ANDREEVA, and EFIMOVA, quit work and went home three hours before the usual time.

An investigation has established that workers FOMINA and ANDREEVA incited workers to a collective work stoppage. Among the workers, FOMINA said:

". . . We all have to leave together, then they can't do anything. We can't work hungry, let's each leave our station. . . ."

Worker ANDREEVA, supporting FOMINA, also called for an organized departure from work. FOMINA and ANDREEVA were arrested.

After the daily bread ration was reduced, hostile elements sent counterrevolutionary letters to the leaders of the party and the government threatening strikes and demonstrations and demanding an increase in the bread ration and an end to the war. For example:

". . . We workers are asking for more bread, we're sick of working hungry for 12 hours at a stretch and without days off. If you don't add some, we're going on strike. We need bread, we need freedom, down with the war!"

". . . Give us bread. This note is being written by hundreds of workers, so that you'll give us bread, otherwise we'll strike, we'll all rise up, and then you'll find out how you're wearing the workers out."

Criminal elements, exploiting the food hardships, have unleashed their activities, stealing food and engaging in speculation.

In November, 98 people were arrested for food speculation. Confiscated from them was:

flour and bread	5,452 kg
cereals and macaroni	559 "
Meat	162 "
sugar and candies	462 "
Oils	110 "

The investigation into the cases of the 63 arrestees is complete, the criminals have been handed over to trial, and 10 people have already been shot.

In November, 20 people were arrested for forging food ration cards. The investigation is complete, and the cases have been sent for review to the Military Tribunal.

HEAD OF THE NKVD ADMINISTRATION FOR LENINGRAD *OBLAST'*
AND THE CITY OF LENINGRAD, STATE SECURITY
COMMISSAR 3RD RANK
(KUBATKIN)

Distributed to: Com. ZHDANOV, Com. KHOZIN, Com. KUZNETSOV

· Document 42 ·

Report from Kubatkin to Beria and members of the VSLF on counterrevolutionary activity between 15 October and 1 December 1941. 6 December 1941, Arkhiv UFSB RF po SPb i LO f. 21/12, op. 2, p.n. 11, t. 1, d. 4, ll. 52–69.

Top Secret
USSR NKVD Administration for Leningrad *Oblast'* and the City of Leningrad
No. 10019

Sent to:
Com. BERIA
Com. ZHDANOV
Com. KUZNETSOV
Com. KHOZIN
Com. MERKULOV

SPECIAL REPORT

The LO NKVD Administration, during the period from October to 1 December 1941, uncovered and eliminated 51 counterrevolutionary groups.

Agent and investigation materials on these groups show that hostile elements set as their main task the rendering of aid to the Germans in the seizure of Leningrad and conducted subversive work along the following lines:

a) Establishing contact with German intelligence and conducting hostile work on their assignment.

The counterrevolutionary group of LAURSEN, ZASTROVA, et al., on assignment from German intelligence, selected technical and scientific personnel from hostile circles to organize cultural and economic life in the city after its occupation.

The group drew up lists of Communists and Soviet workers in order to turn them over to the Germans.

b) Preparing candidates taken from their own circles to form a new "government."

A counterrevolutionary fascist organization of scientific workers led by Professor IGNATOVSKY intended, by utilizing their connections in German circles, to secure the offer of two ministerial portfolios in the future "government."

The organization's participants carried on defeatist propaganda among the intelligentsia, trying to prove that Leningrad should be surrendered to the Germans.

A counterrevolutionary organization, "RUSSIAN PARTY," composed of the physicians MARKIN, VUDNOV, FEDOROV, et al., set as their task the overthrow of Soviet power and the restoration of capitalism in the USSR.

The organization intended, in the event of the city's capture by the Germans, to establish ties with them and to take part in the creation of organs of local self-government.

c) Training for acts of terror against Communists, antifascists, and Soviet worker activists and compiling lists for turning them over to the Germans

—Participants in the counterrevolutionary group—BLIUM, MURAVIEV, SKVORTSOV, et al., gathered information on Communists and Soviet workers in order to be able to hand them over to the Germans in the event of Leningrad's occupation. They intended to take part personally in the murders of Communists and Young Communists.

An anti-Soviet group of former people [*byvshie liudi*—connected with the tsarist and capitalist order]— ANDREEV, PUSHKOVA, et al.—was preparing lists of Communists and Soviet activist workers known to them for handing over to the Germans.

d) Distributing counterrevolutionary leaflets and anonymous letters in which they called the population to rebellion, strikes, pogroms, etc.

An espionage group led by KOLONITSKY composed a counterrevolutionary appeal, "TO THE PEOPLE AND THE RED ARMY," in which they called for taking action against the Soviet government and for rendering assistance to German troops.

e) Involving in counterrevolutionary activity the anti-Soviet-inclined segment of the intelligentsia, on whom the Germans might rely after the city's occupation.

Preparations were made for organizing the city's economic life on capitalist principles (opening private enterprises, banks, and so forth).

A counterrevolutionary group of former people and merchants— ZHUKOV, MARKOVA, et al.—was preparing to take active part in trading and financial activity under the Germans, and the former banker SHAPIRO was intending to open a private bank.

f) Exploitation of food difficulties for carrying on defeatist propaganda. They were trying to convince people of the necessity of surrendering the city to the Germans.

An anti-Soviet group made up of former nobles—SOKOLOV, KAMENEV, BOCHAGOVA, et al.—systematically waged defeatist-profascist propaganda in their circles, in an attempt to prove the inevitability of the USSR's defeat.

Agent and investigation information has established that German and Finnish intelligence are sending into Leningrad from the occupied regions spies, diversionists, and provocateurs, as they attempt to bring about a weakening of the Red Army's rear and the demoralization of the population.

GERMAN INTELLIGENCE.

Practicing massive recruitment, especially among adolescents and women, the Germans are sending them across the front line into Leningrad with the following assignment:

a) Collect espionage information on the distribution of Red Army units, arms, and the location of weapon emplacements.

Clarify the results of bombings. Reveal the plants working for defense and during aerial raids signal their location.

Adolescents recruited by the Germans in Krasnoselsky *raion*—ANDREEV, LAPTEV, VOROBEV et al. —were equipped with rockets and sent to Leningrad with an assignment: during an air raid alarm, to release the rockets from the grounds of defense plants and from places where military units were located.

MAKSIMOV, who was recruited by the Germans in Slutsk *raion,* crossed the front line several times and carried out assignments for German intelligence, collecting espionage information on the numbers and arms of Red Army units.

b) Carry out diversionary actions to put out of action defense sites, depots, and bridges.

K. KOROBENKO, who was arrested for espionage, was sent over by the Germans into the Kolpino area in order to scout out ammunition depots and destroy them. For this purpose, KOROBENKO was equipped with grenades.

The spy A. S. IVANOV had an assignment from German intelligence: to destroy rail lines and set fire to depots in the suburbs of Leningrad.

c) In public places and lines, to distribute counterrevolutionary leaflets. To carry on fascist propaganda and try to prove to the population that the inhabitants of territory seized by the Germans live well and are not being subjected to any kind of harassment on the part of the Germans.

The spy YURCHENKOVA was given an assignment to go along the food lines and conduct fascist propaganda among housewives, to try to prove that the population in the occupied territory lives well and is not being subjected to harassment.

FINNISH INTELLIGENCE

In Vsevolozhsky and Pargolovsky *raiony*, counterrevolutionary groups of Finns have been exposed who, for the purpose of rendering aid to German-Finnish troops, have conducted subversive work on the kolkhozes.

a) They undermined efforts by Soviet and military organs to evacuate the population and to hand over food surpluses to the Red Army.

In the village of Lepsari, a group of Finns headed up by the kolkhoz chairman, KHANIKAINEN, began carrying on propaganda among the kolkhoz workers to refuse evacuation and to hide food surpluses from the local authorities.

As a result, most of the kolkhoz workers hid in the forest, and food surpluses were not handed over.

b) In anticipation of the German-Finnish troops, they carried on propaganda for disbanding the kolkhozes and spread provocative and panic-raising rumors.

A counterrevolutionary group—BARAIUN, KHAIPONEN, MUSKALEVA, et al.—carried on propaganda for disbanding the kolkhoz.

At the initiative of the group's participants, kolkhoz workers dismantled nearly the entire kolkhoz farm. Some of the property was turned over to individual peasant farmers.

c) They prepared armed actions in the Red Army's rear and terrorist acts against local workers.

In the unoccupied part of Novgorod *raion,* a group of Finns led by kolkhoz chairman KHIANKIAINEN stole grenades and pistols from one of the Red Army's military units.

The group prepared terrorist acts against the *raion*'s activist collective. Simultaneously, it intended, under the guise of organizing a partisan brigade, to draw into the group anti-Soviet-inclined Finns for an attack on small units of the Red Army.

Lately, as a result of the shortage of food in Leningrad and the reduction of the bread allowance connected with this, negative moods have intensified among the population.

Defeatist-profascist propaganda has intensified especially.

While in early October the intelligence service of the Operations Offices and *raion* Offices noted 200–250 anti-Soviet manifestations daily, then in November this number rose to 300–350.

Anti-Soviet moods come down mostly to the following:

a) The Red Army cannot break Leningrad's encirclement and the city's population is going to starve to death.

b) The population is in no condition to endure further food difficulties, and in order to ease the food situation, Leningrad must be surrendered to the Germans.

c) In German-occupied territory the population is not experiencing famine, since upon capturing points of settlement, the Germans immediately resolve the food issue positively.

The writer SOROKIN states:

". . . We haven't been able to bring about a rupture in the ring of the German blockade. The Germans will starve us to death.

"Regardless of the war's outcome, Soviet power will exist, but it will be somewhat different.

"There will not be kolkhozes on such a broad scale. We need to restore small peasant farms, cottage industry, and small-scale private trade. The policy of Soviet power will change, England is going to insist on that."

"ENERGOREMTREST" technician MERZHVINSKY:

". . . I regret that the Germans are not going to enter Leningrad for a long time. With their arrival in the city we will not suffer.

"In Kiev, Kharkov, and other cities, people have a full, joyous, and cheerful life.

"Our newspapers write a great deal about the fact that the Germans are fiends, that the population of the occupied countries has been turned into slaves. All this is untrue. In other countries workers organize strikes, present their demands, and these demands are met, but just try in our country to strike or demand anything and they'll wipe off the face of the earth not only the guilty parties but thousands of innocent people into the bargain."

German-language teacher STRUVE:

". . . The Germans are certainly going to capture Moscow and Leningrad. Hitler has managed to establish a blockade of Leningrad and has disrupted supplies to the city, and therefore famine and the various disruptions possible in connection with this will hasten Leningrad's surrender."

SHABASH, head of the fire-duty guard for the Promkombinat Mechanical Plant, Kirovsky *raion*:

"The population of Kiev, before its surrender to the Germans, could not walk due to hunger. People revived when the Germans came and appointed their commandant. Immediately all foodstuffs went on sale. A kilogram of bread there costs 40 kop[eks].

"Here in Leningrad it would be the same situation."

MASLOVSKAIA, a worker at the "ELEKTROSILA" plant:

". . . In order not to starve to death, we're going to have to storm the storehouses, stores, and bakeries. There's nothing else left to do."

Economic manager PASHKOVSKY said:

". . . Our government has decided to starve us to death. Soon the bread allowance will be reduced to 50 grams a day. It's reached the point that there's nothing to feed the Red Army.

"I wish the Germans would come soon. They'll open up private trade and then we'll have everything. If Soviet power wins, then the Jews are going to smother us again."

Testifying, too, to the strengthening of negative and anti-Soviet moods on the grounds of food difficulties is information from the military censors.

While the number of documents not allowed through by the military censors at the beginning of the war (June–July) was 1.2 percent, then by late November the percentage of documents not allowed through reached 3.5–4 percent.

A particularly large number of negative moods provoked by the tense food situation has been noted among women.

Authors of certain correspondence have expressed complaints about the shortage of food, and appealing to the soldiers, they have called on them to throw down their weapons and end Leningrad's defense.

". . . They give us 125 grams of bread a day. We're very hungry. There are no rations. We eat bread and water. People have started swelling up from starvation. Our feet no longer walk. We feel like we're all going to have to die.

"Fools, we believed the chatter that there was enough grain for 10 years. Now we don't believe it anymore, since we're sitting here starving."

". . . They give us 125 grams of bread a day. There's such starvation here that we're hardly going to survive. We're eating the cats and dogs."

". . . Our government is full, and they don't care about us. Our husbands are suffering at the front, and we're here starving to death.

"Put down your arms and end the fighting, we're going to die anyway."

". . . We in the city are starving, while you on the front are spilling your blood."

". . . They give us 125 grams of bread a day. I've decided to write the whole truth, even though you're upright [*pravdy*] and don't like that. Everything they're broadcasting over the radio about other countries is really about us."

". . . All the workers are dissatisfied. There's enough of a spark to set a flame burning. Evidently, that's just what our people want.

"And what of it? They want it and they'll get it, because hunger knows no bounds."

The activization of anti-Soviet elements has increased, too, along the lines of spreading anonymous letters and counterrevolutionary leaflets.

While in the first month of the patriotic war instances of spreading anonymous documents were isolated, then of late their number has increased to 15 pieces per day.

Anonymous letters are being sent out, primarily, to the leaders of the party and government. The authors of the anonymous letters are supposedly acting in the name of existing counterrevolutionary organizations, collectives, housewives, factory workers, etc.

An anonymous document of counterrevolutionary content sent in November to the radio center supposedly comes from the housewives of Smolninsky *raion*. The document's author, citing food difficulties, demands a halt to the battle for Leningrad and its surrender to the Germans.

An anonymous letter sent in November to the radio committee supposedly comes from an underground organization that counts as many as 900 people in its ranks.[104] The anonymous letter expresses terrorist intentions with respect to the leaders of the Party and the Soviet government.

Two anonymous documents, supposedly coming from Leningraders, are addressed to the Red Banner Baltic Fleet.

The documents' authors, in the name of the mothers, wives, and children, suggest to the sailors that they end the battle for Leningrad and carry out reprisals against Communists and Jews.

In a document to the Military Council of the Leningrad Front, they write:

"You cannot hold the city, merely because our children are fighting and they know how we are living. We will exact harsh vengeance on you unless you surrender the city."

In late November, in the Oktiabrsky and Frunzensky *raiony,* incidents were noted of the distribution of anti-Soviet leaflets coming from the "People's Committee of the City."

At one of the buildings on Sennaia Square, an anti-Soviet leaflet, handwritten, was discovered:

"Housewives, if you want bread and peace, organize mutinies in the lines, smash the stores and cafeterias, and beat up Jews, store heads, cafeteria heads, and trust directors."

"PEOPLE'S COMMITTEE OF THE CITY"

Anonymous letters with reports of the death of relatives on the Finnish front have started being received by individual citizens residing in Leningrad. In the anonymous letters, besides reporting the death of a soldier relative, the authors demand an end to the war and slander the leaders of the party and government.

"... The Finnish and German armies are fighting not against the Russian people but against the Bolshevik gang. By their victories they are bringing the Russian people a peaceful, free life, without the terror of the NKVD, without forced labor at pauper's pay, without kolkhozes, without a hungry existence, without endless lines. Down with Bolshevism, down with the war."

As a result of the measures taken, some of the authors of anonymous anti-Soviet documents have been uncovered and arrested:

1. *V. I. KACHALIN.* Former scientific associate, systematically sent anonymous letters of a defeatist nature to leaders of the party and government. Arrested, confessed.

2. *A. E. GARINA.* Telephone operator for Plant No. 189.[105] In the name of the wives of Red Army soldiers of Vasileostrovsky and Sverdlovsky *raiony,* sent anonymous letters to leaders of the Party and government.

GARINA, in the anonymous letters sent, demanded an increase in the bread allowance and an end to the war with Germany.

Condemned to VMN.

3. *A. I. KOLOSOVSKY.* Design engineer, sent anonymous letters to government organs in which he expressed defeatist moods and terrorist intentions with respect to leaders of the party and government.

Condemned to VMN.

4. *A. A. KUZNETSOV*. Pensioner. In anonymous letters, demanded an end to the war, citing the impossibility of further repelling the German-fascist forces. Arrested, confessed.

Hostile elements, exploiting the food difficulties in the city, are attempting to incite the backward portion of the population to organized counterrevolutionary actions.

BETTSIKH, a bookkeeper for the Copyright Protection Administration, said:

"... Our higher-ups have never considered us before and they never will. They're going to do whatever they want because we don't know how to act in an organized way, as a whole plant or factory, but express our dissatisfaction either one-on-one or in small clusters."

STREGLO, an engineer for the Leningrad office of "GLAVINSTRUMENT":

"... Many Party members agree that an uprising is the only solution to the current situation, but for now everyone is waiting for the plants to act.

"Sooner or later, the city's population, under the influence of famine, will rise up. It is essential to give this movement leadership and then, in the name of the masses, we can talk with the Germans."

ANOKHINA, worker at the K. Marx Plant:

"... At one of the plants, the workers organized an uprising and after that they started getting fed better, but you, you fools, you don't say anything, don't protest that they're feeding you badly. You need to act the same way those workers did."

BURMISTROV, plumber for the Leningrad Commercial Port:

"... They surrendered Odessa after the bread allowance for the population was reduced to 50 grams a day.

"The same thing is going to happen in Leningrad, too, though here many are starving to death already, cursing the government for bringing them to such a pass. Just what are our workers waiting for? I hope they have their uprising soon."

SHISHEININA, cafeteria guard at the Anisimov factory, said, among the cafeteria workers:

"... We don't get enough bread. We need to organize a revolt. The women should gather in small groups and storm one bakery after another. There's no point waiting. When we storm the bakeries, then we'll find out who's to blame for the fact that we don't get enough bread."

Not limiting themselves to appeals for strikes and pogroms, counterrevolutionary elements are agitating for armed actions against Soviet power. "[illegible]POGROM MAKERS."

At Plant No. 522, a fascist-insurgent group made up of A. D. DOMENEN-KOV, N. S. TROSHANOV, et al. has been exposed.

At their gatherings, the group's participants, praising the "invincibility" of the German army, cultivate pogrom and insurgent moods.

At one of the anti-Soviet gatherings, DOMENENKOV stated:

". . . We need to turn our arms against those who created the kolkhozes, Communism, and the famine situation in the country."
[illegible]

According to agent information, an anti-Soviet group made up of A. N. TIKHOMIROV, B. I. ROMANOV, and LARIONOV is attempting to train personnel for an active struggle against Soviet power.

Among confederates, they say there will be a speedy change of government. The new government supposedly will be made up of "representatives of the true Russian people," under the slogan, "RUSSIA FOR RUSSIANS."

A counterrevolutionary group made up of V. V. KUZNETSOV, K. F. POSADKOV, and M. S. TSIVIAN is attempting to prepare an armed uprising.

For this purpose, the participants in the counterrevolutionary group, workers in the food industry, have been assigned to slow down bread baking so as to create dissatisfaction among the population on those grounds.

Simultaneously with this they are spreading provocative rumors and are striving to evoke mistrust for the leaders of the party and the Soviet government.

In November there were instances of rioting and looting of food stores.

On the territory of the Irinovsky peat bog (Vsevolozhsky *raion*), a group of workers numbering 23 men carried out an attack on the peat bog's store wagon.

The group beat up three loaders and the dispatcher and took 184 kilograms of bread.

Participants in the attack have been arrested and handed over to the court of the Military Tribunal.

Two Red Army deserters, A. LAPKIN and V. LAPKIN, sawed off the rifle in their possession and carried out an attack on the bread and bakery store in Vasileostrovsky *raion*.

Brandishing their weapon, they took bread, confectioneries, and bread coupons and tried to make their getaway.

When about to be captured, they opened fire.

The LAPKINS were arrested and handed over to the court of the Military Tribunal.

Exploiting the food difficulties, speculators and marauders have directed their criminal activity at the theft of foodstuffs.

During this period, 160 criminal groups were uncovered, from which 487 people have been arrested.

In searches of the rooms of arrested speculators and thieves, about 180 metric tons of food products have been confiscated and handed over to City Trade Office.

A predatory group in the Krasnogvardeisky cafeteria trust has been systematically stealing regulated foods issued for the nourishment of students of the trade school.

The group's participants have been sentenced to various terms of imprisonment, and three of them have been shot.

A predatory group made up of workers from the bread factories and stores of the Vyborg office of Khlebtorg [Bread Trade Office] has been systematically stealing bread and bakery goods.

The group's participants have been sentenced, and six of them have been shot.

Workers from the bread and bakery store of the Smolninsky *raion* Bread Office, AKKONEN and SREDNEVA, were systematically stealing bread products and selling them at speculative prices.

AKKONEN and SREDNEVA have been shot.

At the Volodarsky print shop, a group has been discovered and exposed that was systematically stealing in large quantities food coupons issued for the population.

In stealing the food coupons, the print shop workers entered into a criminal liaison with workers from the bread stores through which they received foods.

Upon the arrest of the group's participants, 570 food coupons were confiscated. In November alone, the group had stolen about 1,000 kilograms of various foods.

The guilty parties have been handed over to the court of the Military Tribunal.

By intensifying its agent-operational work, conducting the deliberate recruitment of agents from hostile circles, and infiltrating those agents into existing anti-Soviet groups and organizations, the LO NKVD Administration, in the last month and a half, has uncovered several counterrevolutionary groups.

It has uncovered and eliminated 51 counterrevolutionary groups with a total of 148 participants.

Altogether during this period the NKVD Administration and militia organs arrested 3,480 people, including:

for counterrevolutionary activity — 957 people

for speculation, banditry, and theft of public property — 2,523 people

During this period, 790 people have been shot in accordance with the sentences of the Military Tribunals.

LO NKVD ADMINISTRATION HEAD
State Security Commissar 3rd rank
KUBATKIN

Sent to:
Com. BERIA
Com. MERKULOV

During the first year of the war, the party and the NKVD had to recruit thousands of secret informants and agents to replace those who were mobilized or evacuated, or who perished in the hungry winter or by enemy fire. Relatively little is known about how the party or the NKVD recruited informants and agents or the instructions they received. Undoubtedly, many volunteered their services out of patriotic or ideological conviction or in hopes of furthering their careers. The NKVD could also rely on methods honed in the 1930s to coerce people into service. It could threaten someone who had previously come under investigation to turn informant or face arrest, or it could offer lenient treatment to arrestees or convicts in return for their relatives becoming informants. Furthermore, Leningraders who had served time in labor camps or had been exiled often desired to return home after their release. The NKVD offered some of them residence permits in exchange for agreement to inform. The security organs could also offer inducements such as relocation to a better apartment or assistance in getting relatives evacuated from the city.

An important incentive that the NKVD could *not* offer in significant measure to prospective informants and agents during the siege was extra food. The NKVD was able to secure supplemental allotments for its operational staff members, but even so seventy-three of them starved to death in the first blockade winter. However, the NKVD could easily recruit informants in enterprises and institutions where food was relatively plentiful under threat of reassigning the recruits elsewhere if they refused to cooperate. Hospitals, for example, had relatively good food supply during the starvation winter (see below, p. 299), and the NKVD had many informants among their employees. The NKVD actively recruited informants in military hospitals in particular. The entire medical staff of one of the city's largest military hospitals, No. 268, reportedly was required to eavesdrop on patients, as the NKVD went to great lengths to keep wounded soldiers from complaining to starving civilian relatives and vice versa. The fact that nurses and orderlies in this hospital received 400 grams of bread per day during the late autumn when most of the city subsisted on 125 grams and that they received special clothing, worked in heated rooms (while much of the rest of the city froze), and were exempt from the compulsory labor draft made them receptive to NKVD demands to become informants.

The NKVD and the party were also deeply concerned about the political mood among factory workers and people queuing in bread lines. At all costs, the authorities wanted to prevent bread riots and industrial strikes, the likes of which had engulfed Petrograd in 1917 and toppled Nicholas II and the Provisional Government in quick succession. The NKVD also had obvious security concerns in plants that manufactured munitions for the city's defense and its eventual liberation from the blockade. As it turned out, the industrial strikes and attacks on food shops that did occur in the critical years of 1941 and 1942 were relatively small and isolated. Comments by factory workers and those in line at bread shops feature prominently in party and NKVD reports on the popular mood, which reflect the large number of informants located there. The larger *rabochii* food rations and the opportunity to "acquire" extra food in the shops, as well as in cafeterias, were powerful inducements that the party and the NKVD could use to recruit informants. At the same time, those employed in the processing and distribution of food who were caught stealing were severely punished.[106]

A primary method of recruiting NKVD agents was to force them into service by threatening to exploit compromising information from their past. A high percentage of agents in SPO were intellectuals who were former nobles, tsarist officers, Mensheviks, or who allegedly had connections to Trotsky or other prominent "enemies of the people."[107] SPO used such people to pursue phantom networks of the kinds of counterrevolutionaries that the security organs had tried to unmask in the 1920s and 1930s.

The case of Olga Berggolts, the renowned patriot and poet of the siege, who wrote many poems about the blockade and broadcast them to the city's inhabitants and beyond the borders of the USSR over Radio Leningrad, shows that SPO also wanted to recruit as informants acquaintances of intellectuals who had been connected to purported counterrevolutionaries in the 1930s. Berggolts's memorable words, "No one is forgotten and nothing is forgotten," are carved on the monument to the deceased *blokadniki* at the Piskayovskoe Cemetery. Her poetry exemplified the sense of pride that many Leningraders, especially intellectuals, felt toward their city, and their desire to defend it. Berggolts also described an ironic feeling of inner liberation during the siege in the poem that includes the line above:

> In mud, in darkness, hunger, and sorrow,
> where death, like a shadow, trod on our heels,
> we were so happy at times,
> breathed such turbulent freedom,
> that our grandchildren would envy us.[108]

Her idea was that the omnipresence and acceptance of death stripped fragile life to its most essential traits that transcended all other mundane concerns, thus freeing the individual's spirit. One felt strangely unencumbered when one had little to lose but life itself and that life was profoundly threatened. This sense of inner freedom was accompanied by a relaxation in censorship that allowed for and even encouraged public veneration of prerevolutionary institutions and famous people so long as the main intent was to support the war effort. However, if *Leningradskaia pravda* occasionally referred to Leningrad as *Piter* and if calls to defend the *rodina* increased while communist slogans appeared in print less frequently, the control apparatus endeavored to step up efforts to uncover and eliminate any expression that might serve to weaken the war effort. Berggolts emerged as the blockade's bard of inner liberation; yet, she herself was carefully monitored by the NKVD. She had been caught up in the Great Terror, arrested on 13 December 1938, shortly after the arrest of her former husband, the poet Boris Kornilov. He was executed. Berggolts, who was then pregnant, was released on 3 July 1939, but only after she was savagely and repeatedly kicked in the abdomen. She miscarried and could no longer bear children.[109] During the war, the NKVD endeavored to monitor the actions of everyone who had previously been arrested for a political offense and remained in Leningrad. The NKVD tried to recruit Berggolts's father, who was a doctor in a factory, to inform on her and her circle of colleagues and acquaintances. When he refused to cooperate, he was exiled to the town of Minusinsk, located along the Yenisei River south of Krasnoiarsk in Siberia.[110] Berggolts was in Moscow from 1 March to 20 April 1942, during which time she received desperate messages from her father as he was being sent to Siberia. She pleaded in vain with NKVD officials in the capital for his release. (He returned to Leningrad in 1947 and died the following year.)[111] Berggolts reflected bitterly on the NKVD's refusal in her diary: "I'm fighting so that their disgusting, degenerate institution, which attacks our own people, can be removed from the face of the Soviet earth. I'm fighting for the freedom of the Russian word—we would have worked so much more and much better if we had enjoyed complete trust. . . . I'm fighting so that good Soviet people can be allowed to live peacefully without the fear of exile or prison. I'm fighting for free and independent art."[112] In April 1943, SPO succeeded in infiltrating Berggolts's circle by recruiting a thirty-four-year-old doctoral candidate in literature and editor of *Goslitizdat* (the State Literary Press), who was identified as "P. Borisov" in a SPO report. He described Berggolts and about nineteen others as politically unreliable. The denunciation made them vulnerable to NKVD manipulation. They were kept under surveillance, and cases were assembled against them. According to the file, Borisov also claimed an acquaintance with the well-known authority on Russian literary history Boris Eikhenbaum and several of his colleagues. Borisov characterized the political views of this latter group as reactionary and anti-Soviet. They were evacuated from Leningrad but not before cases were prepared against them.[113]

In addition to closely monitoring conversations, the NKVD paid very careful attention to the written word. As Kubatkin's 6 December report (Document 42) indicates, the NKVD opened letters, especially those sent from the city to soldiers at the front. During the first year of the war, Kubatkin meticulously tabulated and reported the percentage of letters that were not delivered because they expressed "negative mood," which included descriptions of starvation, criticism of the authorities for not providing more food, and appeals to soldiers to cease fighting in order to allow the enemy to take Leningrad. On occasion, Kubatkin reported daily totals on confiscated mail. Toward the end of January 1942, the percentage of letters that Leningrad's approximately three hundred NKVD censors intercepted reached its highest level—20 percent—which coincided with the peak period of starvation.[114] Content from private correspondence, as well as from personal diaries, was used as evidence to support prosecution for KR offenses; however, in almost all cases the writers of the confiscated letters were not arrested. Thousands of letters went undelivered each day due to "negative" content, whereas the number of people arrested for KR offenses peaked at twenty-six per day during the worst period of the starvation.[115] One who was arrested was Nadezhda Lapenkovnaia, a girl of seventeen or eighteen who worked as a knitter in an *artel* of invalids. She was arrested for some ten letters that she had sent in January to her sister in Krasnoiarsk *krai*. She was charged with disseminating letters containing KR content. In one letter she wrote: "Our leaders sit in the Kremlin, have banquets there, while we expire here from hunger. The working class doesn't care whom it works for—Germans or Jews. When spring arrives Hitler will reach the Urals. Then I will laugh."[116]

The NKVD was careful to isolate and insulate from the civilian population soldiers and *opolchenie* fighters who had been wounded at the front and were being treated in city military hospitals. A Red Army lieutenant colonel, who wound up in the West after the war, described measures the NKVD took to isolate the wounded servicemen so that they could not spread defeatist sentiment within the city. In an article published in the mid-1950s in the émigré publication *Novyi Zhurnal*, V. Yershov depicted conditions at military hospital No. 268, which specialized in hand wounds.[117] During the siege it treated upward of two thousand patients at any given time. Yershov claimed that all employees at the hospital, including doctors and nurses, were prohibited under threat of execution from mailing letters from patients to any relatives they had in Leningrad (a large percentage of servicemen on the Leningrad Front were from the city) or from conveying any information by any means to soldiers' relatives regarding their presence in the hospital. Letters to relatives that servicemen placed in the hospital mailbox were never delivered; instead, security personnel perused them for evidence of KR sentiment. Doctors were instructed to be on the lookout for wounds that appeared to be self-inflicted and for those who might be faking an illness. Doctors who uncovered the largest number of such acts of deception were given awards. Patients convicted of wounding or mutilating themselves to avoid service were sentenced to be shot. The medical staff was also charged with eavesdropping on patients and reporting any subversive comments overheard. Those who made defeatist, anti-Soviet remarks were confronted and pressed to sign protocols confessing their guilt. Following release from the hospital—and, according to Yershov, there was a quota of 7 percent to be released per day—they were sent directly to penal companies, where they would be used to clear minefields or perform other very dangerous work. There were instances of soldiers with clean records who upon their release from the hospital immediately deserted for a couple of hours to visit with their families with the knowledge that upon their return they would be sent to penal battalions. Yershov stated that they simply wanted to see their relatives before dying at the front. He also asserted that there were many instances of wounded soldiers who tried to escape. Upon being caught, they were apt to be severely beaten. Suicides following such beatings were not uncommon.[118]

The forms of written expression that the NKVD was most anxious to eliminate were opposition leaflets and anonymous letters sent to city leaders. (See examples in Document 42.) It was the responsibility of SPO to investigate all cases involving anti-Soviet leaflets and letters, collect all known copies, and uncover and prosecute those who produced the anti-Soviet propaganda. Often, those convicted of writing or posting such literature were shot. The authorities feared that anti-Soviet leaflets and handbills posted in public places were evidence of major conspiratorial activity and could quickly spread a contagion of defeatism. City leaders seemed to take very seriously and personally anonymous hostile letters sent to them and to consider it a victory for security and a point of pride to identify and apprehend their authors. In the autumn of 1941 and during the early part of winter, SPO tried to identify and arrest the author of several hostile letters to Soviet leaders, who always signed his name as "Academician Tupolev." One of his letters is included below:

· Document 43 ·

Scathing letter from "Academician Tupolev" to Stalin, 30 October 1941,
Arkhiv UFSB RF po SPb i LO f. 12, op. 2, p.n. 5.

"Moscow, the Kremlin: To the Chairman of the Committee of Defense of the country"
Stalin, Stalin!!
The people curse you[119] together with your talentless gang of dim-witted and dull fools. There has never been in history nor will there ever be in one government such talentless leaders. . . . What have you done for the people and the country during the 24 years you have been in power? . . . How could one permit the losses of the war and not be prepared for the war? . . . Bragging about beating the enemy on his own territory, and with little blood spilt to boot, oh

you bandits and curs. . . . Good-for-nothing people and actions are exposed by facts, and the facts are at hand. An immediate reorganization of the structure is demanded and a complete sorting out of people. . . .
30 October 1941 Academician Tupolev

Kubatkin took a particular interest in this case. He wrote in the margins of another hostile anonymous letter from mid-December: "Did Tupolev write this?" By early January SPO investigators found what they considered to be a handwriting match and arrested a certain Riabkov, charging him with writing the "Tupolev" letters.

The following document is from late in the siege period. It reveals the extraordinary lengths to which SPO went to unmask a sole leaflet and letter writer. In this investigation, which lasted almost two years, handwriting on more than 100,000 documents was checked.[120] One historian recently exaggerated the threat posed by this individual, asserting that he "was dangerous to physical security, morale, and political stability. He had to be caught."[121] There is no evidence that the handwritten leaflets that the anonymous writer copied with carbon paper during the winter of 1941–42 attracted any kind of following, and the anti-Soviet letters he sent directly to Zhdanov and other leaders at Smolny in late 1942 and 1943 were not made public. The obsession with catching the anonymous "insurgent" was extremely costly and appears to have become an intensely personal matter for those on the receiving end of his missives. Catching the culprit probably gave them and the SPO investigators a certain measure of satisfaction.

· **Document 44** ·

Report from Kubatkin to Kuznetsov on the case of "The Insurgent," an anonymous author of anti-Soviet leaflets and letters, 12 December 1943, Arkhiv UFSB RF po SPb i LO f. 21, op. 12, p.n. 56, d. 1, ll. 28–29, in Lomagin, ed., *Neizvestnaia blokada*, vol. 2, 57–60.

TOP SECRET
NKVD Administration for Leningrad *Oblast'* and the City of Leningrad
To the Secretary of the Leningrad GK VKP(b), Leningrad Front Military Council member
Lieutenant General A. A. Kuznetsov
SPECIAL REPORT
Between 1941 and 1943, in the city of Leningrad, anti-Soviet leaflets and anonymous letters were distributed whose author was known by the pseudonym "The Insurgent."

On 24 December 1941, anti-Soviet leaflets whose content called for pogroms and mutinies were discovered on a footpath near the Moscow train station.

The leaflets were written by hand using carbon paper. In all, 70 leaflets were collected.

The same kind of anti-Soviet leaflets, 80 copies, were discovered a second time on the morning of 9 January 1942, on a platform of the Moscow train station.

We cite the text of a few leaflets:

"Citizens! Down with the state, which is starving us to death!"

"Citizens, storm the warehouses and shops, the scoundrels are robbing us blind, starving us to death. Down with famine, we're still living people, be decisive."

"Citizens, go to the district party committees, demand bread. Down with the leaders."

"Citizens! Why are they deceiving us and not giving us food? Down with the district party committees. Open the front and let everyone leave the city!"

"Citizens! They're taking the troops out of the city and starving us to death. Down with our leaders!"

The following measures were taken to expose the distributor of the counter-revolutionary leaflets:

a) in the morning hours, the Moscow train station was covered with outside surveillance using operatives, the militia force was instructed, outside posts were reinforced, and patrols were organized in the station and on its territory;

b) transportation organ agents were instructed and sent to search actively for the author and distributor of the counterrevolutionary leaflets;

c) the operations force checked the handwriting of the approximately 18,000 personal files of laborers and office workers of the October RR.

However, these measures yielded no result.

During the course of the agent investigations, a need arose to examine the handwriting of all the employees of the Kartontol plant and the Konnaia Tiaga [Horsepower] workshop, a total of 227 people, but this yielded no positive results.

On 30 September 1942, the military censor seized an anonymous anti-Soviet document that had been addressed to Comrade Zhdanov. As it turned out, as a result of a handwriting comparison, this document had also been written by "The Insurgent."

On 6 November 1942, a new provocative document arrived addressed to Comrade Zhdanov, done in different handwriting, but placed in an envelope of the "little secrets" kind used by "The Insurgent."

Expert analysis by the Administration's chemical laboratory established a correspondence between the paper used to make envelopes of this type used by "The Insurgent" and this unknown author.

It was established that envelopes of the "little secrets" kind were sold only in the Smolninsky and Volodarsky *raiony* of the city. In connection with this, filtration of the civilian postal correspondence by the military censor was set up to find and identify the sender of the correspondence sealed in the pink envelopes of the "little secrets" kind. In all, 1,023 senders of correspondence and their relatives were checked in this way.

On 30 January 1943, the military censor seized 3 anonymous anti-Soviet documents that had arrived addressed to Comrade Zhdanov, Leningrad *Sovet* Chairman Com. Popkov, and Leningrad *sovet* Deputy Chairman Com. Andreenko.

In one of the documents, "The Insurgent" expressed his dissatisfaction about criminal prosecution for violating labor discipline. In view of these circumstances, individuals against whom criminal charges had been brought for absenteeism in the people's courts of Smolninsky and Volodarsky *raiony* were identified. All of them, a total of 753 people, as well as their relatives, a total of 2,100, were subjected to verification through a handwriting comparison.

At the same time, the district councils of workers' deputies of Smolninsky and Volodarsky *raiony* examined more than 13,000 statements by citizens in an effort to uncover matching handwriting.

Militia departments compared the handwriting of 27,860 citizens from documents filled out while registering for military cards.

Simultaneously, a general check was made of the handwriting of all individuals with secondary technical training for the enterprises of Smolninsky and Volodarsky *raiony*. 5,732 such individuals were checked.

At 16 major enterprises, 64,770 applications and personal files of laborers and office workers were studied.

All these measures yielded no results.

On 27 September 1943, "The Insurgent" sent to Smolny, addressed to Comrades Zhdanov and Popkov, three anti-Soviet documents. In one of the documents he revealed himself to be a worker in the foundry shop of a plant and expressed his dissatisfaction with the distribution of supplemental food coupons. Since these kinds of shops are only in plants in the Volodarsky *raion*, all measures were concentrated in this *raion*.

Upon checking the personal files of workers in the Bolshevik plant's foundry shops, a steel founder in Shop No. 42 attracted attention and aroused suspicion.

Sergei Vasilievich Luzhkov, born 1893, native of Opochka, Kalinin *oblast'*, peasant background, Russian, not a party member, twice convicted for stealing firearms and for fraud. Has relatives in Poland.

Handwriting analysis showed a perfect match between Luzhkov's handwriting and the handwriting of "The Insurgent," in connection with which Luzhkov was arrested.

In questioning, Luzhkov wholly admitted that he was guilty of authoring and distributing counterrevolutionary leaflets and letters [. . .]

Luzhkov testified that he had written and distributed all the counterrevolutionary leaflets and anti-Soviet letters himself personally, admitting and involving no one else in this matter.

The investigation is over. The case has been sent for review by the Military Tribunal.

HEAD OF THE NKVD LO ADMINISTRATION
State Security Commissar 3rd Rank
KUBATKIN

[Kuznetsov wrote a note on the document to *raikom* secretary Yegorenkov: "How did Luzhkov get enrolled in the shop and what did the party organization know about him? Please check into this and report to me orally. 21 December 1943."]

Sentences for disseminating anti-Soviet agitprop were either a long prison term or execution. The authorities could be far more lenient, however, in dealing with children. In December 1942, two eleven-year-old boys, Dmitry Sarosek and Leonid Korolev, were accused of writing four copies of an anti-Soviet leaflet and distributing them in their school in the Kuibyshevsky *raion*. They were simply given a stern lecture as a warning.[122]

Aside from dealing with KR activity and expelling potential fifth columnists, the NKVD, including the *militsiia*, performed numerous other functions. Some of these tasks were ones they had carried out before the war; most, however, were new. In addition to confiscating radios (early in the summer) and telephones (not long before the start of the siege), they demanded that the city's general population hand over firearms to the *militsiia*. Between 22 July and 30 August, the *militsiia* seized over 11,000 small-caliber rifles and hunting guns, close to a quarter-million rifle cartridges, 2,000 kilograms of gunpowder, and almost 2,800 kilograms of buckshot. This cache was so large that the military departments of the *raikomy* initially objected to having to store the arms and ammunition.[123] In time much of the confiscated weaponry was distributed to the *opolchenie,* worker detachments and battalions, and fighter battalions. These auxiliary formations were controlled by the NKVD with some assistance from the party, as were the 6,344 partisans from Leningrad who were sent behind enemy lines between August and October of 1941.[124] The NKVD also supervised the mining of important installations in the city and the Baltic Fleet, when it appeared that German division might try to seize Leningrad. City fire fighters and antiaircraft defense workers, both of which came under the jurisdiction of the NKVD, had to deal with the effects of the more than 100,000 incendiary bombs that the Luftwaffe dropped on Leningrad during the siege. During the starvation winter, the NKVD combated cannibalism and assumed responsibility for placing orphaned children in homes. In late 1942, the NKVD began to provide material assistance to families of service personnel, after the *raionnye sovety* and the military registration and enlistment offices proved unable to handle the task.[125]

When the starvation became widespread, the *militsiia* and the NKVD had to contend with related escalating crimes of individual and group theft, violent attacks by armed gangs on food stores, murder, and cannibalism.[126] Theft became the most pervasive crime, and although the *militsiia* on occasion simply released some thieves,[127] punishments meted out were generally very harsh. The thieves typically were among those who had received the lowest food rations. Those arrested for *spekuliatsiia* (selling goods at a profit) were often employees who sold state property, mainly foodstuffs, on the black market. The NKVD also attempted to guard against other forms of corruption among officials (while the NKVD itself benefited from access to special, though limited, supplies of food), such as bribery. In April 1942 and later, it discovered officials in several *raion* recruitment centers who took bribes in return for providing exemptions from the military draft.[128] The most common bribes were bread and vodka.[129] In Document 45, Kubatkin provides summary arrest totals through the end of September 1942 as well as arrest figures for specific crimes. He also provides a figure for the total number of executions.

· Document 45 ·

Report from Kubatkin to the *gorkom* on the number of people arrested, convicted, and exiled during the war, 1 October 1942, TsGAIPD SPb, f. 24, op. 2b, d. 1323, ll. 83–85, in Dzeniskevich, *Leningrad v osade,* 441–43.

---

1 October 1942
Top secret
During the Patriotic War, the Administration of the NKVD LO has arrested 9,574 people, including 1,246 spies and saboteurs planted by the enemy.

625 counterrevolutionary groups and formations have been uncovered and eliminated, including:

spy-traitor	169
terrorist	31
insurgent	34
nationalist	26
church-sectarian	7

Those arrested included:

Former kulaks, merchants, landowners, noblemen, and officials	1,238
Lumpen element	1,243
Workers	2,070
Office workers	2,100
Intelligentsia	559

Collective farmers	1,061
Individual farmers	258
Others	1,045

In accordance with a decision by the Military Council and the Administration of the NKVD, during this time the following were exiled from Leningrad and adjacent districts of the *oblast'*:

a) Finns and Germans	58,210
b) socially alien element	40,231
c) criminal element	30,307
Total:	128,748

During this period, organs of the militia arrested and handed over for trial 22,166 people, including:

for banditry and brigandage	940
for burglary	1,885
for domestic homicide	206
for theft	11,378
for stealing socialist property	1,553
for speculation	1,598
Groups eliminated:	
bandits and brigands	66
robbers	147
thieves	256
speculators	183

Those arrested include:

individuals without definite employment	8,684
workers	10,081
office workers	3,295

10,288 deserters and servicemen without their documents were arrested and handed over to the prosecutor's office and commandant's office.

In all, 31,740 people were arrested and handed over for trial by the organs of the NKVD and militia.

On the basis of sentences from military tribunals and courts, 5,360 people were shot.

The principal contingent of those arrested for speculation and theft of socialist property comprises office workers in trade and supply organizations (the trade network, warehouses, bases, and dining halls).

The main object of theft and speculation is food items and other scarce rationed goods.

Valuables and goods worth more than 150 million rubles were confiscated from the thieves and speculators arrested.

Included in what was confiscated:

cash	9,656,000 rubles
gold coins	41,215 rubles
state bonds	2,556,000 rubles

gold bullion and wares ..... 69 kg
silver .... 563 kg
diamonds .... 1,537 items
gold watches .... 1,295 items
food items .... 483 metric tons

as well as a large quantity of industrial goods, including 36,000 meters of dry goods.

Of late, the predominant type of criminal activity has been theft, mainly from the apartments of citizens who have been evacuated and inducted into the Red Army.

The individuals arrested for crimes belong primarily to the following groups: individuals without definite employment, housewives and adolescents, and domestic workers.

The number of recidivist thieves has dropped to nil, in connection with the systematic purging of the city of the criminal element.

Confiscated from the criminal element, deserters, and individuals without the appropriate documents:

Military rifles 1,113
Machine guns 3
Submachine guns 10
Hand grenades 820
Revolvers and pistols 631
Rifle and revolver bullets 69,000

Head of the NKVD LO Administration
State Security Commissar 3rd rank
P. Kubatkin

This chapter has tried to highlight different ways in which the party and the NKVD implemented and enforced policies of total war. Top *gorkom* officials were members of the VSLF and as such played a key role in planning Leningrad's defense. In addition, the party directed the mobilization of human resources and materials with the aim of maintaining the highest levels of production at the city's war plants through the end of 1941. Party leaders also made the crucial decisions regarding food distribution and evacuation from Leningrad of people and machinery. The NKVD's job was to maintain public order and eliminate all forms of speech and writing that criticized the Soviet system, its institutions, and leaders or that praised the enemy, as well as to gather intelligence on the enemy and conduct counter-intelligence operations. The party's role in controlling popular expression was limited mainly to producing its own written and spoken agitprop and listening in on the public voice through an informant network. It was in this last area, eavesdropping, that party and NKVD functions most closely overlapped.

The LPO carried out its tasks for the first two years of the war while its membership declined sharply. By contrast, the Leningrad NKVD does not appear to have experienced a similar reduction. On 16 July 1941, the Politburo authorized the dispatching of political commissars to the front to supervise decisions of commanders. Ever since the Red Army had been established by Trotsky in 1918, tension had existed between officers who had received their professional training under the tsars, and revolutionaries, such as Voroshilov, who had had to learn the art of warfare on the job during the Civil War. What was at stake was whether officers could be trusted to make decisions on their own or whether their actions should be overseen by party officials. The political watchdogs had been employed when the party was most concerned about controlling the military. Hence, they had been introduced in the Civil War. Military officers attained unity of command in the mid-1920s but commissars were again introduced to monitor the actions of military officers during the purges in 1937, when Voroshilov was defense commissar. However, after Stalin sacked Voroshilov in the spring of 1940 for his mishandling of the Finnish campaign, his successor as defense commissar, Semen Timoshenko, reinstituted unitary command in August.[130] The pendulum shifted again in favor of dual command after the German invasion. In July 1941, *partkom* secretaries were sent to the front to serve as commissars. As Document 46 shows, 58,000 communists left Leningrad by March 1942. Party functions were curtailed and numerous PPOs disappeared. The exodus of party members from Leningrad represented an exaggerated version of what was happening nationwide. During the first six months of the war about a million party members in the USSR, mainly from urban areas, went to the military. As this was a time of terrible defeats for the Red Army, national party membership dropped by about the same number from approximately 4 million to 3,064,000 by the end of 1941. The membership of the LPO was cut almost exactly in half during this period and reduced by two-thirds by July 1942. The number of candidate members—that is, new recruits into the LPO—declined even more precipitously by the end of 1941 from 30,682 to 12,386, a reduction of 60 percent. The city's Komsomol lost 90 percent of its members.[131] There is no evidence that the introduction of political commissars at the military fronts improved the performance of the Red Army. In fact, the opposite would seem to have been the case, as the army enjoyed its greatest success after unity of command was restored in October 1942.

At the same time that the party was shrinking during the crisis of the first months of the blockade, there was tremendous turnover within its ranks. There were 170 officials in the *gorkom* at the start of the war. During the first year, 102 left for work elsewhere. By 1 July 1942, as a result of advancement up from the *raikom* level, the *gorkom* employed 104. A similar situation prevailed in the *raikomy,* where 528 worked at the start of the war. Within a year, 485 had departed.[132] Within the LPO as a whole, by the beginning of 1942 party members and candidates were older and slightly less educated than their counterparts from the start of the war. A higher percentage were female (up from 25 percent to 36 percent), although the total number of women in the LPO had declined.

As is clear from the aggregate figures on party membership, new admissions to the party and Komsomol could compensate for only a fraction of those who left, despite the fact that the *gorkom* continually exhorted local party organizations to recruit new members. As German forces advanced toward Leningrad in August and by mid-September seemed poised for an assault to seize it, new admissions into the party declined and reached their lowest level for the war. The next document shows that even during February 1942, when as many as ten thousand may have starved to death each day and thousands of others were evacuated over frozen Lake Ladoga, more Leningraders joined the LPO as members and candidates than in September.[133] During that pivotal and precarious month of September and on through the darkest days of the starvation winter, the LPO was approaching a crisis of existence as it continued to shrink, which hampered its ability to mobilize people and resources for the war effort and protect Leningraders from the effects of enemy bombardment and the cold and hunger of the winter. The LPO would grow in size and expand its functions only from the latter half of 1943.

· Document 46 ·

Report from Antiufeev to Zhdanov on the size of the LPO and the number of new enrollments by month, March 1942, TsGAIPD SPb f. 24, op. 2v, d. 5447, ll. 12–13.

Top Secret

REPORT
*on the available Communist staff in the Leningrad city
party organization and the number accepted into the party.*

	VKP(b) members	Candidates	Total	Total women
Staff of city party organization as of 1 July 1941	122,849	30,682	153,531	38,312
Available staff in city party organization as of 1 January 1942	61,842	12,386	74,228	26,809
The same as of 1 March 1942	57,400	11,930	69,330	25,380

Number accepted into the party.

	As VKP(b) candidates	As VKP(b) members	Total
22 June–1 July 1941	57	134	191
July	441	633	1,074
August	389	628	1,017
September	286	280	566
October	385	426	811
November	445	383	828
December	563	407	970
January 1942	462	333	795
February	385	230	615
Accepted during the war (22 June 1941–1 March 1942)	3,413	3,454	6,867

NOTE: The party organization diminished primarily because many Communists left to join the Red Army and VMF (58,000), or were evacuated along with workers and enterprise and institution employees (25,000), or for other reasons.

In January and February 1942 alone, 7,812 people were taken off the party rolls, including 2,407 evacuated, 3,140 dead, and 720 who joined the Red Army.
Head of the Organizational-Instructional Office, Gorkom VKP(b) Antiufeev

Another dimension of the crisis faced by the party was that as its ranks were diminishing in the autumn of 1941, it had to prepare for the eventuality that the city might fall. Just as plans were made for the destruction of the Baltic Fleet and large defense plants in Leningrad in the event of the city's capture, the party prepared for underground activity in an occupied Leningrad. On 25 October 1941, the *biuro* of the *gorkom* ordered the creation of the "illegal" party organization (*nelegal'naia Leningradskaia organizatsiia VKP(b)*, or NLO). (The NKVD had created an underground section consisting of ninety members in August.)[134] Its mission was to prepare to conduct secret agitprop work among the population in order to demonstrate a continued party presence in the occupied city.[135] The underground party organization would also carry out acts of sabotage and terror against occupation forces, supervise partisan activities, erode the enemy's morale, and gather intelligence. By the end of November, it consisted of 260 members. By August 1942, its membership had dropped to 163. The decline resulted from the death by starvation of some members and the evacuation of others, but also from the fact that thirty-seven were expelled for gross violation of party secrecy rules and another eighteen were removed for cowardice or for abuse of their positions (*rvachestvo*). The NLO, though small, continued to exist through the end of the blockade, which indicates that the party leadership never felt entirely safe from the threat of enemy capture until German forces were driven out of artillery range. By 1 June 1943, the NLO had been built back up to its size during the autumn of 1941 and had slightly more women (137) than men (122). Many of the men were physically impaired. The NLO had stopped recruiting able-bodied men under the assumption that they would be eliminated by enemy occupiers. By this time the weaponry of the NLO consisted almost exclusively of pistols. They also possessed some twelve hundred doses of strychnine and arsenic. The underground party was largely dismantled in October 1943. When it was disbanded altogether in February 1944, it had only thirty-nine members.[136]

In general, the policies of total war achieved mixed results in Leningrad, especially during the critical first year of the war. They did not halt the enemy's advance up to the southern edge of the city, nor prevent the massive bombardment and historically unprecedented starvation that resulted from siege warfare. At the same time, Leningrad continued to furnish the armed forces with men and women and to manufacture and repair remarkably large quantities of war matériel. Food-related crime, including theft by pickpockets, transport workers, and cafeteria administrators, as well violent crimes such as murder and cannibalism, was only partly checked. But in the final analysis neither crime bred from the extreme deprivations, nor the sense of deep resentment toward the authorities and their policies harbored by some unknown proportion of the populace, nor the shrinking size of the LPO seriously threatened to break the overall control that the *gorkom* and the UNKVD exerted over the city's inhabitants.

CHAPTER 4

The Struggle to Survive:
The Dying City

On 24 June 1941, a workshop cafeteria in the Kirov factory delayed serving lunch for over an hour because its shipment of bread had not arrived. An informant for the Kirovsky *raikom* overheard one worker say to another: "It's only the second day of the war and already there is no bread. If we fight for a year, we'll die of hunger."[1] The off-hand comment would become an eerie prophesy for many in half that time.

Leningrad had experienced food shortages prior to the German invasion, and food and livestock had been diverted from the city in the war's first months. As a result, Leningrad had only seventeen days of bread and grain on hand when the blockade began (Document 4). Germany targeted Leningrad's food supply. A recorded 700 incendiary bombs hit the Badaev food warehouses on 8 and 10 September at the beginning of the air blitz. The same month enemy aircraft sank several food-laden barges bound for Leningrad. However, in October divers were able to save 2,800 metric tons of sprouted grain, which were dried out, remilled, and mixed with good flour. The salvage effort was important, because, overall, little food arrived in the city by ship across Lake Ladoga before it froze over in November.[2] Stalin refused to authorize a massive airlift of food to the beleaguered city in the autumn, although between 14 and 28 November, during the month that Germany held Tikhvin, he improved the situation somewhat by authorizing thirty to fifty cargo planes per day to fly in a total of 1,200 metric tons of high calorie food. Nevertheless, the city was left in a desperate state by the start of winter.[3] The food shortage was compounded by similarly diminishing levels of coal and oil, which limited the use of machinery and generation of electrical power inside the blockade zone.

Daily bread rations were cut five times between 2 September and 20 November (see Appendix A). By the time of the last reduction, the *rabochii* ration had dropped from 800 to 250 grams, with office workers, dependents, and children receiving only 125 grams. Rations for bread and other foods (Appendix C) should have been reduced in August to save food in anticipation of later shortages. Another mistake was that food was sold in unrestricted quantities in as many as fifteen commercial restaurants until 11 November; those resources should have instead been directed into the rationing system.[4] The experience of food shortages during the Winter War should have made Leningrad's leaders more concerned during the summer of 1941 over the impending crisis and better trained to deal with it.

According to the distribution system, in addition to the daily bread ration, the population was supposed to receive monthly allotments of meat, cereals and macaroni, fish, sugar and candy, and fat. (Appendix B.) In reality, however, during the winter people rarely received anything except bread until the middle of February 1942. With few exceptions, meat was unavailable between the latter part of October and 14 February.[5] In late November informants reported that people stood on line for many hours for food products such as sausage, butter, and vermicelli that never arrived (Document 40). According to an NKVD report: "Beginning with the last ten days of December 1941, food ration cards are not issued. Aside from bread . . . the population receives no other products."[6] And, the bread that was available was in very short supply. From the start of the blockade, the city was scoured for untapped grain sources and for edible substitutes. In early September about 5,000 tons of oats used to feed army horses were remilled for bread. Around the same time some 8,000 tons of malt were removed from breweries that were shut down and given to the flour mills, which ground it up for bread filler. (At the Stenka Razin brewery, aside from malt, 100 tons of grain, almost five tons of sugar and molasses, and six tons of rusks were discovered by the NKVD between 28 November and 8 December.) The malt gave the bread a distinctly unpleasant taste. By early November barley flour was exhausted and the malt additive was running low. Workers at the city harbor suggested using cottonseed oilcake, which was used for ship fuel. It had never been used as food as it was believed to contain a poisonous substance, gossypol. However, baking the oilcake eliminated that problem. After being milled, the oilcake became a major additive.[7] Leningrad's rumor mill quickly seized hold of and circulated the secret information on oilcake, as revealed by party informants in Document 40.

By mid-November, the VSLF had to confront the grim reality of the dire food shortage. On 13 November, it cut bread rations for the first time since 1 October, and then had to reduce them again exactly one week later. On

19 November, the VSLF under the signatures of Zhdanov, Kuznetsov, and Khozin ordered city bakers to use "edible cellulose as an admixture for baking bread" to replace diminishing grain reserves.[8] *Gorkom* secretary P. G. Lazutin coordinated a group of scientists who endeavored to use a hydrolysis process to make the cellulose from wood and cotton edible.[9] In short order, they claimed to have conquered the task.[10] The processed cellulose added to the volume and weight of the bread; it helped fill people's stomachs, and was therefore deemed "edible." The filler, however, had no nutritional value and was not digestible. After triggering the sensation of having eaten something, the cellulose passed through the digestive tract, producing some abdominal discomfort, before being eliminated from the body. By the end of 1941, 6,059 tons of malt, 4,511 tons of oil cake, and 490 tons of "edible" cellulose from wood and cotton were among the substitute ingredients baked into the bread. During the second half of November and the first half of December 1941, the city's bread consisted of 60 percent rye, oat, and barley flour and 40 percent of the various additives. At this time, oilcake made up 15 percent of the bread and cellulose 5 percent.[11] Yelena Kochina, a mother in her mid-thirties who managed to survive the hungry winter with her husband and infant daughter, wrote in her diary on 20 November: "The bread contains all kinds of junk and only a little flour."[12]

Never before in history had so many people in one city depended so heavily on one source of food. Yet, Leningrad had many people who had previously survived starvation during the Revolution and Civil War era (19,516 died of hunger in Petrograd between 1917 and 1923),[13] in the widespread famine of 1932–34, the smaller famines of the winters of 1936–37 and 1940–41,[14] or in any of a number of forced-labor camps. The more experienced and savvy among the populace divided their meager rations into small parts and ate them slowly, turning the bread around in their mouths for a long time before swallowing it. In this way, they took nourishment, as minuscule as it was, at even intervals and created the illusion of eating larger portions.

Starving people imagined the foods they would like to eat. Valia Chepko wrote down her food fantasy:

· Document 47 ·

The fantasy menu of one starving Leningrader, Valia Chepko,
during the winter of 1941–42, GMMOBL op. 1, d. 7.

———————

My dream. If I don't die, but live to a good life: I will never alter this menu, because I have learned of starvation by bitter experience. Menu after starvation, if I remain alive.

First course.
> Soups. Potato with mushrooms
> Oat
> Pearl barley
> Fermented cabbage soup with meat

Second course.
> Kasha: Oats and butter
> Millet
> Pearl barley
> Buckwheat
> Rice
> Semolina

Meat dishes: Cutlets with purée
> Sausages with purée or with kasha

I don't even dream about this, because I won't survive to it!

Chepko died in February. Bread itself became the object of fantasy and extreme endearment as the starving referred to it in diminutive form. Kochina wrote in her diary on 2 January:

> Bread!
> We almost never talk about it, but we think about it constantly.
> Bread!
> Soft, fragrant, with a crunchy crust. The thought of it drives us crazy.
> It tastes better than chocolate, it tastes better than cakes, it tastes better than sweet rolls.
> We don't want anything the way we want bread.
> If only we could eat our fill of it!
> If only we could just once more plunge our teeth into its redolent warmth, its fragrant body, and tear it, chomp it, eat it without stopping, feel it move down the gullet, distend the stomach, and fill the body with a blissful satiation.
> Bread!
> We dream about it passionately, we dream night and day, we dream with every cell of our bodies.
> Why don't I have a cow's stomach? I could chew the same crust all day—belch, chew, and belch again. That would be wonderful!
> Bread!
> The Russian's strength is contained in it. No, even more—life itself is contained in it! The Russian peasant understood this. That is why he called it *khlebushka*.[15]
> We have only now realized the full meaning of *khlebushka*.
> It sounds like music to us now.[16]

For some, consuming the ration took on the religious significance of the "daily bread" in the Lord's Prayer, and eating small portions of the daily ration with a cup of weak tea or plain water became a kind of secular sacrament.

Leningraders' obsession with bread increased as a result of standing in long bread lines in subzero temperatures. The winter of 1941–42 was unusually cold. Temperatures remained below freezing for most of December. The average January temperature in Leningrad during the preceding fifty years had been nineteen degrees Fahrenheit, but in 1942 it was minus two. The temperature continued to dip below zero through the beginning of March, and only on 25 March did it climb above freezing. The coldest day of the blockade was 24 January when the temperature plunged to minus forty. The following day warmed slightly to minus twenty-two. The amount of electricity generated in the city that day reached its lowest level since 1917, and only Smolny and bread bakeries received current. Radio Leningrad temporarily ceased broadcasting on the twenty-fifth, and *Leningradskaia pravda* failed to appear for the only time during the blockade on that day. Without current, the pumps of the city waterworks stopped running for a day and a half, which caused water mains to freeze, and many burst. Bakeries were left with no running water. Bucket brigades were formed to carry water by hand from the Neva River or canals to bakeries, and ships of the Baltic Fleet anchored in the river pumped water for bakeries. Despite these arduous efforts, little bread was baked in Leningrad between the twenty-fifth and the twenty-seventh, even though bread rations were officially raised on 24 January. Some bakeries simply distributed the uncooked flour with its raw ersatz ingredients. On 25 January, bread lines began to form at around 4 A.M.[17] Yelena Skriabina, a mother of two, noted in her diary that she stood in line for twelve hours that day before receiving her family's bread rations.[18] The Kuibyshevsky and Dzerzhinsky *raiony* in the center of the city received less than one-third of their bread allotments on 26 January. The following day, people began to stand in line at 3 A.M.; by 9 A.M. eighteen bread stores in these *raiony* had no bread left.[19] When people did manage to obtain their larger bread rations in late January, extreme frustration could turn to elation. In the words of Dr. Stern, the head of Military Hospital No. 902: "A lot of people didn't know about the ration increase until they actually came to the stores for their bread. Some of them went wild with joy, kissing the bread, fondling it as if it were the most precious thing in the world—which, in a way of course, it is."[20]

Most homes lost their running water during the winter. Fetching water from the Neva, a canal, or an open hatch or pipe was dangerous and difficult, particularly since there was little daylight during the winter (Figure

35). Spilled water froze almost immediately. As a result, mounds of ice formed near water sources. Corpses were occasionally frozen into the mounds, which could reach several feet in height.[21]

Doctors in Leningrad's hospitals saw their first cases of hunger disease, which they termed "alimentary dystrophy," as early as September among refugee children from the city's suburbs,[22] and the first deaths from starvation were recorded in early November. However, *golod* (hunger or starvation) was not mentioned in the Leningrad press until 1943. Twenty-three-year-old Aleksei Yevdokimov wrote in his diary on 15 November: "Besides the daily bombardment and artillery fire, a fierce hunger has begun in the city. How sorrowful it is to look at the unfortunate children swollen from hunger."[23] The city's Perovsky hospital recorded its first death by starvation in the first half of the month.[24] Thus, city authorities knew that starvation had set in before they lowered the bread ration to its lowest level on 20 November.[25] In the latter half of the month another nineteen had perished from hunger-related illnesses at that hospital. People began to faint at work and on city streets at the end of November, during the period when the bread ration was at its lowest level. Yevdokimov wrote in his diary on 30 November: "O, you, hunger, hunger, hunger! How on earth to survive you. Whoever will live will never forget these days and will always know the price of life. Almost the entire population is swollen from hunger. Horses, cats, and dogs are disappearing from the streets. The children especially are dying."[26] A young boy named Valery Sukhov laconically noted in his diary on 3 December how his family consumed their pet cat: "Yesterday we caught and killed the cat. Today we ate it grilled. Very tasty."[27] The disappearance of cats resulted in a dramatic increase in the city's rat population. Rats ate corpses and made their way into food storage areas. According to one eye witness: "I saw a swarming, living army of rats before me. They crossed the road as one solid mass." Eventually, cats were brought to Leningrad from the Urals to help protect the food supply.[28] Sukhov's diary continues:

· Document 48 ·

The diary entry of a young boy, Valery Sukhov, for 23 December 1941,
GMMOBL op. 1, d. 388.

---

23 December: Papa barely walks. Mama staggers. We're hoping for January. In the evening I sat down to draw. I forgot about everything. A week ago I began to study German. We cooked soup from carpenter's glue and ate all of the starch. [. . .] Papa is prepared to eat the corpses of those killed in the bom-

bardment. Mama refuses. It's already been a whole month since we had solid food in our stomachs, besides the daily portion of bread of 125 grams, there's been nothing [. . .]
28 December: We got flour and meat [. . .]

His only entry for January was: "28 January: Papa died."

The NKVD tried to monitor the unfolding tragedy by tabulating every five or ten days throughout the winter the number of deaths recorded by the fifteen *raion* registry offices (*otdel zapisi aktov grazhdanskogo sostoianiia,* or ZAGS) within city limits.[29] But ZAGS became overwhelmed in January and February. Although each *raion* had an official collection post for bodies,[30] many deaths went unreported as corpses were stacked like firewood at cemeteries, factories, apartment houses, and other places. During the spring of 1941, between 3,300 and 3,900 people had died each month in Leningrad. In October 1941, when the city's civilian population had dropped from about 3.2 million before the war to approximately 2.5 million, 6,199 deaths were reported to ZAGS. Enemy bombardment accounted for 808 of those deaths (plus another 3,230 wounded). Most of the remaining excess mortality in October over the prewar average was likely due to army and *opolchenie* personnel who died in Leningrad hospitals, and the first starvation deaths likely occurred near the end of the month. The city's death toll in November was 9,183, which represented an increase of 2,984 over the October level. The enemy bombardment killed 922 more Leningraders in November than October (with the number of wounded rising by 1,667). Hence, there was an increase in the number of deaths not attributable to enemy fire of 2,067 in November over October. Starvation deaths made up part of that number.

In December, the official number of deaths increased sharply to 52,612, while the number killed from the bombardment (probably not including those who died from wounds inflicted earlier) dropped by 1,087 from the November tally to 643. The NKVD was particularly concerned about the effect on popular mood of people dropping dead from starvation on the streets and for December kept track of the numbers on a daily basis. The acceleration in starvation is evident:

Deaths from Hunger on Leningrad Streets

7 December	34 people
8 December	112
9 December	122
10 December	159
11 December	171[31]

The next document, a survey of conditions in city morgues from mid-December, indicates that it was precisely at this time that the death rate began to exceed the city's ability to bury corpses.

· Document 49 ·

Report from Senior *Militsiia* Major E. Grushko to Chairman of the *Lengorispolkom* Popkov on the state of the city's morgues, 12 December 1941, TsGA SPb f. 7384, op. 3, d. 5, ll. 85–86.

---

top secret
personal
An audit of the state of work at the morgues on 11 December 1941 has established the following:
1. MORGUE AT THE "VESELYI POSELOK" CEMETERY, VOLODARSKY RAION.
In the morgue there are 35 unburied corpses, of which 32 corpses are unidentified. All 35 corpses have been lying on racks in the morgue for 6–7 days.
Burial has been delayed due to a lack of manpower: there are no gravediggers. The *Raisovet* is refusing manpower.
Present at a burial are: a representative of the *militsiia*, *Raifo* [District Financial Office], and a doctor. Valuables are transferred to *Raifo,* according to a statement, and passports to the *militsiia* station.
2. MORGUE AT BOGOSLOVSKOE CEMETERY, KRASNOGVARDEISKY RAION.
In the morgue there are 12 corpses, and in the snow of the cemetery lie 5 corpses left by relatives. In all, 17 corpses have been lying there unburied for 5–6 days.
3. MORGUE AT SMOLENSKOE CEMETERY, SVERDLOVSKY RAION.
In the morgue there are 115 corpses, of which 15 corpses have been unburied since 5 December 1941, and the remaining corpses came in after 5 December 1941. All the corpses in the morgue are lying on racks and have been registered in accordance with instructions.
Present at a burial are: a representative of the *militsiia*, *Raifo,* and a doctor. Valuables and property, according to statements, in the presence of relatives, are transferred to the latter, and in the absence of such, surrendered to *Raifo*.
There has been a delay in the burial of corpses due to the lack of manpower and the inability to make identifications and as a result of the untimely appearance of the *Raifo* representative and doctor. On 8 December 1941, the doctor did not appear, and on 10 December 1941, the *Raifo* representative and the doctor did not appear.
4. MORGUE AT SERAFIMOVSKOE CEMETERY, PRIMORSKY RAION.
In the morgue there are 7 corpses, which came in on 6 December 1941, and 70 corpses left by relatives have been lying in coffins at the cemetery since 1 December 1941, 77 corpses altogether.

Burial has been delayed due to a shortage of gravediggers, of whom there are only 4.

Burial instructions are being observed. In the original statements, clothing was not listed in full. There are no tags.

In the morgue at B. Okhtenskoe Cemetery and Volkovo Cemetery there are no corpses. The mound of earth over the buried corpses at B. Okhtenskoe Cemetery does not exceed 20 centimeters.

The Funeral Trust is not providing for the timely removal of corpses from apartments or for the supply of coffins, which is creating censure among the public.

Informing you of the aforesaid, I request instructions for the Funeral Trust.

LENINGRAD *MILITSIIA* ADMINISTRATION HEAD SENIOR *MILITSIIA* MAJOR
E. GRUSHKO

Mass graves were dug for the first time in mid-December as the death toll continued to rise. According to NKVD documents, in January 96,751 deaths were reported in Leningrad. The death toll declined slightly in February to 96,015 and in March to 81,507. The data show that the mortality rate peaked in Leningrad during the first ten days of February, when 37,296 deaths were confirmed. By that time, however, with so many perishing, not all deaths were discovered immediately; hence, it can be assumed that the death rate actually peaked a little earlier, probably in late January when the temperature plunged and the output of bread was temporarily interrupted.[32]

Russian historians have debated for decades the total number of Leningraders who died in the war, primarily as a result of the starvation of the winter of 1941–42. Although declassification of party and NKVD materials from the siege period has revealed some new data on mortality, it has not uncovered entire collections of information that resolve the controversy. The ZAGS-based NKVD mortality figures are not comprehensive. Hundreds of thousands of bodies were hastily buried in several mass graves in and around the city and in numerous smaller plots, which made precise tallies impossible. Moreover, people had an incentive to conceal deaths, as they could generally get away with using the ration cards of the deceased until the beginning of the following month when registration in person was required to receive new ration cards.[33] (In 1941, 11,100 Leningraders were discovered to be in possession of ration cards for "dead souls" through special verification checks.)[34] The most thorough attempt to count the dead was commenced in the summer of 1943 by the "Extraordinary Commission for Investigation of the Crimes of the Fascists," which eventually drew upon the services of 31,000 party and government officials and others, including ZAGS, in all of the city's *raiony*.[35] In the various editions of his book *Leningrad v blokade,* Dmitry Pavlov, who was the GKO's representative in charge of food supply for Leningrad from early September 1941 through the end of January 1942, contended that precisely 632,253 civilians in Leningrad starved to death and that when figures for Kronstadt and Kolpino are added, the number of starvation deaths among civilians becomes 641,803.[36] Pavlov's figures were based on the commission's research. When deaths from enemy artillery and aircraft are factored in, the civilian death toll from all war-related causes becomes exactly 649,000 for Leningrad proper and 671,635 for the larger blockaded area. These figures were cited by Soviet officials in 1946 at the Nuremburg trials.[37]

In 1965, two historians, V. M. Kovalchuk and G. L. Sobolev contended that no fewer than 800,000 Leningraders had died of hunger.[38] They did not try to count documented deaths but calculated their figure from other data. They noted that Leningrad's civilian population dropped by 1.9 million between the start of the blockade and the end of 1943 (when a census was conducted), of whom about 1 million had been evacuated and another 100,000 mobilized into the armed forces. The remainder, they deduced, represented those who perished. This estimate became widely, but not universally, accepted among Leningrad's scholars. The fifth volume of *Ocherki istorii Leningrada,* published in 1967 with Kovalchuk as editor in chief, represented the official history of the blockade from the Leningrad branch of the Academy of Sciences for the Brezhnev years. It repeated the figure of 800,000 and added (on page 692) that about one million died in Leningrad and its suburbs during the war. Marshal Zhukov accepted the estimate in his memoirs, which were published in 1974, the year he died. On 19 November 1975, Pavlov, who continued to revise his memoirs after having served as Soviet Minister of Trade and as a deputy in the Supreme Soviet, sought to end the historical dispute in his favor once and for all by administrative means rather than persuasive scholarship. He wrote a letter to Mikhail Suslov, the ideology and mass media chief in the Politburo pointing out that for the last eleven months of the blockade, Leningrad was connected to the rest of the nation by rail and that no one knew how many people had departed from the city by train, thereby implying that Kovalchuk and Sobolev might have counted among the dead those who left Leningrad by rail. Pavlov concluded his letter as follows:

> I, as a participant in the defense of the city, who had available all of the data, am convinced that the figure on the death toll for the time of the blockade, which was enunciated by our government representative at the Nuremburg process, is factual.
>
> To change the figure known to the entire world—642 thousand, for another—800 thousand, after 30 years will offer nothing useful, and will

only undermine the stability of official statements of our government. Whom does that benefit?

I ask you not to allow publication of the other figure.

Suslov sent copies of the letter to G. V. Romanov, first secretary of the Leningrad *obkom* and candidate member of the Politburo, and G. L. Smirnov, the deputy head of Propaganda Department of the Central Committee, for their views. Romanov replied that 800,000 deaths was "not proven in documentation." Smirnov noted that various figures, including "even a million," had been published on blockade deaths and ended his letter evasively with the general admonition to "leaders of the means of mass information to direct their attention to the need for a more strict approach to the publication of data" on the matter.[39] Pavlov's request was not granted, and both figures continued to be cited by historians.

In a recent article, Nadezhda Cherepenina, a senior archivist in St. Petersburg's State Historical Archive with excellent access to all extant documentation on wartime mortality, calculated that for the first eleven months of the blockade, approximately 653,000 Leningrad civilians died within the city. Based on this figure, among those Leningrad civilians who were not evacuated over the ice road,[40] approximately 37 percent perished as a result of the hunger and cold of the war's first winter. Of the number who resided in Leningrad in November 1941, 27–28 percent died there as a result of the winter.[41] What remains unknown are the number of people who died in the Leningrad *oblast'* within the blockaded territory, including refugees who fled into the area at the beginning of the war, and the large number of starving Leningraders who died as refugees.[42] Emergency facilities at Kobona and Lavrova on the eastern shore of Lake Ladoga were overwhelmed with starving refugees. According to a report from NKVD head Kubatkin, 2,394 refugees died between the Finland Station in Leningrad and the rail stations on the eastern shore of Lake Ladoga from 22 January to 15 April 1942,[43] but this figure is probably low, given the large number of people who were evacuated in emaciated condition. Corpses of those who died on the long train rides after crossing the lake were often simply discarded along the tracks and likely were not counted (Figure 47). Trains loaded with evacuees lacked fuel and a sufficient number of locomotives. As a result, they traveled very slowly, often covering less than sixty miles per day. When trains got stuck in deep snow, local inhabitants had to be rounded up to dig them out. Some trains remained stuck for up to six days with few provisions.[44] According to one calculation, at least 15,000 Leningrad evacuees perished in the Vologda and Yaroslavl *oblasti* through December 1942. (Between 26 January and 15 April 1942, a recorded 554,186 Leningrad evacuees traveled through Vologda.)[45] Vologda could not cope with disposing of so many corpses. According to a commissar from the city's No. 1 Evacuation Hospital: "What distressed me most was a big cart in the courtyard, with two decks . . . filled to bursting with frozen corpses that you had no way to get rid of . . . we lacked the courage and the strength to hack them apart with an axe. What's more, there were no graves ready; anyway . . . it was decided to leave them until spring, until it thawed."[46] But, how many died before reaching those areas, after passing through them while still in transit, or from the effects of starvation and related diseases after reaching their final destination is not known. If the mortality rate among the ice road evacuees was half that of those who remained in the city, then the number of Leningrad civilians who perished as a result of the winter of 1941–42 either in the city or as refugees was approximately 762,000.[47] This estimate does not include the unknown number of starvation deaths among residents of blockaded parts of the *oblast'*, where 343,000, including tens of thousands of desperately poor refugees, had lived at the start of the blockade.[48] If the mortality rate among them was comparable to that in the city, the number of deaths from the hunger and cold for the entire besieged territory was probably close to 900,000.

This estimated total figure on mortality does not include those who survived the siege but whose deaths several months or even years later can be linked at least in part to the siege's adverse effects. Hypertensive disease, which was often called "Leningrad hypertension" and was largely caused by prolonged starvation, became a leading cause of death in Leningrad between the end of the starvation winter of 1941-42 and the lifting of the siege in 1944.[49] Evidence also shows that those who survived the siege in their youth died on average between 1.3 and 1.8 years earlier than others of their age who had not gone through the siege.[50]

While the combination of lack of food and extreme cold was by far the leading cause of death during the blockade, another 16,747 Leningrad civilians were listed as having died from the 107,158 bombs and more than 150,000 artillery shells that reportedly hit the city. Another 33,782 were wounded in the air attacks.[51]

It should be noted that a lengthy report from April 1943 submitted by the burial section of the city's communal services administration states that between 1 July 1941 and 1 July 1942, 1,093,695 bodies were buried in city cemeteries. (This figure would appear to include the ashes of 117,300 corpses that were cremated at the No. 1 brick factory.) However, the report cautioned that the number of burials was far from precise, and might be too high, which would in fact seem to be the case. The raw data on which the composite figure was based have not been located.[52]

Demographic patterns among starvation victims can be identified from the data. Women survived the effects of starvation longer than did men for several reasons. Women generally are smaller and thus require less food, have a greater percentage of body fat, and require fewer calories per pound of body weight. In addition, women have stronger cardiovascular systems (Figure 44). The month in which the largest number of males perished was January 1942; for females it was March. Even though there were more women than men in the civilian population, 71–73 percent of starvation deaths in December and January were of males. In February, when the sex ratio was skewed even more in favor of females, males still accounted for 60 percent of starvation deaths. In the middle of March for the first time more females died than males, although the percentage of males who died was higher than that of females.[53]

The most vulnerable segments of the general population, which succumbed to starvation first, were elderly men and nursing infants. During the first ten days of December, 47 percent of those who died of starvation (4,417 people) were fifty years of age and older. Most were men. At the other end of the age spectrum, during the same period, one in seven who died (1,326 people) was under one year old. For the entire month of December, infants accounted for 5,671 of the 53,843 recorded deaths in Leningrad, Kronstadt, and Kolpino. For all of 1942, 24,365 infants died in those three locations. During the first year of the war in the blockade zone, the large majority of newborns perished.[54] The sense of extreme frustration felt by starving mothers who lost the ability to nurse their children because they could no longer lactate was aptly expressed by Kochina in her diary entry for 9 October 1941: "My milk has dried up. At night I drink a whole pot of water, but this doesn't help. Lena screams and tears at my breast like a small wild animal (poor thing!). Now we give her all the butter and sugar we get with our ration cards."[55]

In a typical family, the father was off at the front, or if he remained in the city was more vulnerable to death by starvation than was the mother. By the middle of the winter, many families consisted of a mother and one or two children, with mothers making every sacrifice imaginable to keep the children alive. However, during the latter part of the winter, the mothers were perishing in great numbers. Tens of thousands of Leningrad's children, the city's most precious treasure, were therefore left without either parent to care for them. The orphans were mainly older than infants and toddlers but younger than teenagers. In general, during the fall of 1941, Leningrad's leaders made few preparations to protect the city's civilian population for the coming winter. Initial efforts during the winter to locate and protect waifs were woefully inadequate. In December food ration cards were printed for approximately 440,000 children up to the age of twelve. Roughly 90,000 of them would starve to death.[56] It is not known how many children remained in Leningrad when the ice road shut down in late April, but the number was likely around 180,000 to 200,000. (According to NKVD figures, at the beginning of August 1942, there were still

144,927 children in the city out of a total population of 807,288.)[57] As many as 70,000 to 80,000 children may have been left without either parent for some part of the starvation winter. The city's preexisting network of children's homes was too small to care for so many. In December 1941, the *Lengorispolkom* took the very modest step of deciding to add two new children's homes to the approximately seventeen that already existed. By the beginning of 1942, city leaders were aware of the growing problem. On 4 January, the *gorkom*'s instructional-informational section sent a report to Zhdanov, Kuznetsov, and other top party leaders that opened with the words: "The number of orphans in the city has recently increased. The educational organs and social organizations have not shown sufficient concern for these children, who are in a very difficult situation."[58] That month another twenty-three homes were opened. As the number of orphaned and unsupervised children grew rapidly, the NKVD in February intervened to place children in homes in each city district. The lead article in the 19 February issue of *Leningradskaia pravda* focused on childcare needs. The Komsomol joined the search for unsupervised children only on 16 March. According to a July 1943 report from the Leningrad *gorispolkom* to Aleksei Kosygin, who by that time was deputy chairman of the *Sovnarkom* of the USSR, the number of children in the homes reached 14,300 in March 1942. All told, between January and May, eighty-five homes were opened, which took in about 30,000 waifs.[59] Hence, perhaps half of the children in the city who lacked parents were cared for by the state, and most of them received services only late in the winter or in early spring. The remaining neglected children during this period were taken in by relatives, friends, or even strangers, or they remained alone in dark, freezing communal flats.

A ten-year-old boy, Nikolai Vasiliev, kept a brief and sporadic diary of the events between January and April that turned him into one of Leningrad's legion of waifs. One of the youngest known diarists of the blockade, he made his entries on the pages of a calendar. His style was laconic and unemotional, revealing how he had become accustomed to the horrors of the blockade. In this respect, his diary is similar to the one written by eleven-year-old Tania Savicheva, which has been described in many histories of the siege.[60] However, young Vasiliev wrote beyond his years. It seems that he was trying to write as an adult to record the tragic events for posterity and at the same time to fit his own experience into a larger context and somehow make sense of it all. At the end of each entry he signed his name "N. Vasiliev" and underlined it as if authenticating the document. He barely survived the starvation winter and was an orphan by the beginning of April 1942. After the war Vasiliev studied in the drama department of the Lunacharsky State Institute of Theatrical Art and in the mid-1950s joined an acting group in Arzamas-16, the secret research and development center for Soviet nuclear weapons.

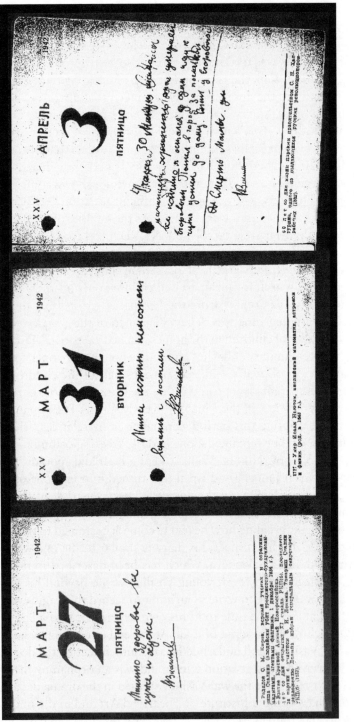

In his diary, Nikolai Vasiliev tersely described his mother's decline and death.

· Document 50 ·

Diary entries of ten-year-old Nikolai Vasiliev from 2 January to 4 April 1942,
GMMOBL op. 1, d. 329. The illustration shows the entries for
27 March, 31 March, and 3 April.

———————

Friday, 2 January 1942: I have lived in Leningrad where at the time there
was starvation. I passed the new year starving in Leningrad.

Saturday, 10 January: The first misfortune struck father. They stole his
bread ration card from him and that's why he died.

Tuesday, 27 January: I went to the city for bread because they are not baking
any bread in Lesnoy.[61] There was no firewood or running water. I went to the
Vyborgsky Side. While returning, I fell several times and slowly made it to
the market. I met Alka and his friend, and he helped me get up and took me
to the "Svetlana" factory.[62] I warmed up in a small hut[63] and set out again for
home. I fell in a ditch and nearly froze, but Mama came by and carried me
home. And on this very day at 10:00 Papa died, sitting on the bed.

Wednesday, 28 January: The mother of Sergei and Tonya Gusev died and
the father of their neighbor Kolya died. In the month of March Tonka went to
a children's home.[64] Sergei remained at home.

Thursday, 29 January: Lesha (my brother) sixteen years old (already seventeen) died at 5:30 in the morning. Too much work and not enough food each
day in the end wore him out, and having weakened, he died.

Friday, 30 January: In December my friend Tolia Sysoev died. Tolia, Vania
and Katia Fillipov and also Shura Kulashkin remain among the living.

Saturday, 31 January: I live in Leningrad and have survived a lot (I live with
Mama). They give 250 grams of bread and nothing else. People are dying.
Corpses lie all over the streets. We're being bombed and shelled. Few pay attention to this. All think about one thing—about eating. January has been the
hardest month for the population of Leningrad. Many have died.

Sunday, 1 February: Leningrad is an old city. The city is beautiful and big.
But what has become of it. Destruction at every step. There's nowhere to put
the dead.

Monday, 2 February: Leningrad is the city of the Great October Revolution, city of glory. But what has become of it? Life has died out. It's as if the
city were empty. Gloomy houses are glazed in an icy horror that gives one
the creeps. Sometimes a German artillery shell whistles by and then it's quiet
again. People do not peek out of their houses. Only sometimes does a rare
pedestrian flash by and disappear around the corner. It's as if everything has
died out.

Sunday, 8 February: They buried Lesha (burned him in the oven)

Tuesday, 3 March: What's happened to Leningrad? Nobody knows. There's
no light, no water. It's as though the city were extinct. Damn Hitler is guilty of
all of this. Death to the Germans.

Tuesday, 17 March: Shura Kulashkin died of hunger. [Illegible] was healthy and good, but hunger has killed everyone. 22 people in our house have died of hunger.

Sunday, 22 March: A pilot came on foot for us, but didn't take us.

Wednesday, 25 March: We're waiting for the pilot.

Friday, 27 March: Mama's health is getting worse and worse.

Tuesday, 31 March: Mama is lying down. She can't get up from the bed.

Friday, 3 April: 4:30 in the morning. Mama is beginning to wheeze. She is dying. It's all over. I'm left alone. I am going to the Yegorovs. I went to the city on an errand, just returned home. I slept at the Yegorovs. Death of Mama.

Saturday, 4 April: Nata (my sister)[65] flew in from Moscow for me and Mama. She didn't find Mama alive. I went to the children's home. They came for me. In the evening I left for the port for the steamship "Viacheslav Molotov." There is a sanatorium there. They fed me. I went to the shower and bath. I washed up.

Boys a few years older than Nikolai Vasiliev were another group that was particularly at risk. The rate of starvation for teenagers was not especially high in late autumn but climbed rapidly during the winter. Next to men between the ages of fifty and fifty-four, the five-year age bracket with the highest number of starvation deaths in 1942 was boys between fifteen and nineteen.[66] The food rationing scheme placed teenagers in the "dependent" category with the smallest rations, even though their growing bodies demanded a high calorie diet. Boys were far more vulnerable than girls. Many of the city's teens were enrolled in trade schools (*remeslennye uchilishcha*) and factory apprenticeship schools (*shkoly fabrichno-zavodskogo obucheniia*), where they worked up to eleven hours per day. Teens who were discovered to lack parental care were generally placed in these schools. The schools' cafeterias distributed little food, and what little they provided was of very poor quality. According to one account, the large majority of those who attended these schools starved to death.[67] In the late autumn, the NKVD conducted an investigation of sixty-four trade schools and found widespread deviant behavior, including theft, "hooliganism," gambling, and labor code infractions. Dormitories were unheated and dirty. Worse still from the point of view of the NKVD, many students were trying to defect to the enemy.[68] (German policy was not to allow civilians to defect to their lines; however, there are only a few recorded instances in which German troops actually fired on fleeing Leningrad civilians. It would appear that relatively few Leningraders attempted such flight.)[69] The party and Komsomol were accused of doing little to attempt to remedy the problems.[70] Conditions deteriorated through the winter. Kosygin, who had replaced Pavlov as GKO plenipotentiary to Leningrad in late January, was troubled over the plight of teenagers in the trade schools. Between January and April he helped arrange for 92,419 of them to be evacuated over the ice road and given supplemental rations.[71] On 16 February, Kosygin visited Trade School No. 33 and the following day described in a letter to Zhdanov what he had observed. All of the students were lice-ridden and slept two and three to a bunk. Their dorms were filthy, and sick students were not separated from the rest. Their food was of very poor quality and served in portions smaller than prescribed in the rations. Moreover, the school's food supply was vulnerable to theft. As a result of Kosygin's visit, the cafeteria's director was sentenced to one year of corrective labor and the cook to two years in prison.[72]

In addition to segments of the general population that had high mortality rates (infants, teenagers, and old men), two particular groups succumbed quickly to starvation. They were refugees who entered Leningrad in the first months of the war, either from the north fleeing the Finnish advance or from the southwest in advance of the Germans, and prison inmates. Up to the start of the blockade, approximately 147,500 refugees passed through Leningrad on their way eastward. Others remained trapped within the blockaded territory. Those who were officially registered by the passport service as refugees were supposed to receive the same food rations as the rest of the civilian population, but that was not always the case. Unregistered refugees received no rations. NKVD head Kubatkin wrote a top secret report to Kuznetsov on 28 November 1941, describing the plight of the refugees. He stated that 64,552 refugees, including 23,246 children, resided in Leningrad and in the Vsevolozhsky and Pargolovsky *raiony* to the east and north of the city, respectively. He depicted their living conditions as "extremely unsatisfactory" and noted that most living quarters were unheated, filthy, and lacked running water. The refugees had virtually no medical care. Many were not receiving food rations and were therefore starving. They ate cats and dogs.[73] How many of the refugees starved to death is unknown, but the rate must have been very high as reflected in the fact that most people arrested for cannibalism in Leningrad were from outside the city.

The mortality rate (not counting executions) among inmates in Leningrad's prisons was frightfully high. In January of 1941, a total of thirty-one prisoners, all of whom were male, died in all city jails. Between February and June of that year, another fourteen perished, including two females. Prison deaths increased steadily from the very start of the war. Ten died in July, forty-five in August, and fifty-five in September. The first starvation deaths may have occurred as early as late October, because that month the death toll more than doubled to 117. The number nearly doubled again in November, when 201 died in prison. Prison deaths then escalated sharply:

	Male deaths	Female deaths	Total
December 1941	1,166	6	1,172
January 1942	3,567	172	3,739
February	2,602	339	2,941
March	1,412	641	2,053
April	1,495	770	2,265
May	1,335	989	2,324
June	758	571	1,329

For the ten-month period from November 1941 through August 1942, 18,546 inmates died in Leningrad jails, of whom 4,637 were females. Incarceration in Leningrad during the first winter and spring of the siege was often a death sentence. Many starved to death awaiting trial. Among the civilian population generally, about thirty times as many people died in January and February of 1942 as in any given month before the German invasion. However, among the prison population the increase was considerably greater. Forty-five inmates died in the city's jails in the first six months of 1941. During the same period in 1942, 14,651 died. The difference in survival rates between incarcerated males and females reflects the pattern among the civilian population as a whole. The largest number of males died in January, while female mortality peaked in May. The death rate dropped during the last four months of 1942 to a total of 540 in December; however, starvation during the second siege winter raised the death toll in January 1943 to 815. Throughout the rest of 1943, more inmates died each month than had died in October 1941. From September 1941 through December 1942, a total of 26,123 inmates, including 7,388 females, perished.[74]

According to one account, by the spring of 1942, there were thousands of corpses at the infamous Kresty Prison, which before the war according to one rough estimate may have housed 30,000 inmates.[75] Many of the dead were political prisoners. During the winter a number of inmates committed suicide by jumping from the prison's cupola. By the beginning of July 1942, there were only some 800 inmates who could stand without assistance. They were sent by barge over Lake Ladoga to Vologda, where they were fed meat, kasha, and bread. Nevertheless, 150 of them died there. The survivors were sent on to Solikamsk, along the Kama River north of Perm. The approximately 200 who reached Solikamsk were distributed to nearby labor camps.[76]

The city could not cope with the corpses that accumulated at the jails, training schools, factories, in courtyards, along streets, and elsewhere. There was no effective way to gather and deliver them quickly to city cemeteries, where four thousand workers, not counting those who operated the earth-moving machinery, buried them.[77] Many thousands of people dragged the bodies of their relatives to cemeteries on small sleds (Figures 45 and 46). Yelena Averianova-Fyororova wrote in her diary in late January:

> We took my grandmother to the cemetery on a sledge, pulling it in turn—myself, Mother, Tania and Shura. We could barely drag our own feet along. With such food, I don't know how we're still alive. . . . And now we were behind someone else—in an endless chain of dead people, mostly without coffins. But that's not the only thing. It's all right if people are taking their own relatives, but what's much worse is that whole lorries are going past laden with bodies, undressed, unshod bodies, all lying anyhow and in different bits of clothes. . . . While we were there six lorries and three horse-drawn carts full of bodies arrived. It was horrible to see! And how many more there were that had been brought there earlier but hadn't yet been buried! The workers who had been sent from factories (because not all factories are operating) can't keep up with the digging and burying.[78]

The city's largest mass grave was the Piskaryovskoe Cemetery, which was located along the city's northeastern edge. Its long and wide trenches were filled with more than 400,000 bodies. Bodies lay throughout the city for a long time, even in prominent public places. Vera Kostrovitskaia, a prominent ballet dancer and teacher, wrote in her diary in April:

> And, there, across from the entrance to the Philharmonic, by the square, there is a large lamppost.
>
> With his back to the post, a man sits on the snow, tall, wrapped in rags, over his shoulders a knapsack. He is all huddled up against the post. Apparently he was on his way to the Finland Station, got tired, and sat down. For two weeks . . . he "sat"
> 1. without his knapsack
> 2. without his rags
> 3. in his underwear
> 4. naked
> 5. a skeleton with ripped-out entrails
> They took him away in May.[79]

During the winter, city authorities were concerned over the prospect that mass epidemics could break out as a result of malnutrition and through infection from corpses and fecal material. Scurvy became widespread; however, a process for extracting vitamin C from pine needles, developed by a Professor A. D. Bezzubov, helped counteract that disease. Over sixteen million doses of the extract were produced in the city in 1942.[80] Health workers inoculated about half a million people against the infectious diseases of typhus, typhoid fever, and plague by mid-March. The fact that there were only localized outbreaks of typhus and typhoid and no plague epidemic was also partly the result of the massive clean-up campaign in March and April. To expedite the removal of corpses, a brick factory was converted to serve as a massive crematorium. Document 51 consists of instructions for setting up the crematorium. The eighty-four workers who would cremate corpses were to receive the largest civilian food rations and a supplement of 100 grams of vodka. During the siege period, allotments of vodka were a special reward for performing the most dangerous or repellent tasks. Cemetery workers received the same vodka supplement, and those who transported corpses to cemeteries received 50 grams of vodka or 100 grams of wine, plus 100 grams of bread for each delivery completed beyond the first one in a given day. In the absence of effective safeguards, the incentive induced some drivers to falsify the number of deliveries they made.[81] One source asserts that executioners were entitled to 600 grams of vodka for each person shot.[82] (Others sought access to state supplies of alcohol. Requests by factory directors for large quantities of grain alcohol purportedly for servicing machinery increased sharply from November.)[83] According to a report from the city's construction-materials industry from 9 December 1942, 117,300 corpses were cremated between 7 March and 1 December 1942.[84] Thus, it would appear that the instructions below were issued on the day that the brick factory began to function as a crematorium, which coincided with the start of the major effort to clean up the city. It would appear that city authorities anticipated finding many corpses during the removal of ice, snow, and debris.

· Document 51 ·

Decision of the *Lengorispolkom* to convert the 1st Brick and Pumice Factory to a crematorium, 7 March 1942, TsGA SPb f. 7384, op. 38, d. 72, l. 59–590b.

Secret

DECISION NO. 157C OF THE REDUCED SESSION OF THE EXECUTIVE
COMMITTEE
OF THE LENINGRAD CITY COUNCIL OF WORKERS' DEPUTIES

On the Issue:

On the organization of the cremation of corpses at the "Lengorpromstrom" [Leningrad City Building Materials Industry Administration] 1st Brick Factory.

1. Require the head of the Building Materials Administration of the Executive Committee of the Lengorsovet [Leningrad City Council of Worker Deputies], Com. Vasiliev, to organize the cremation of corpses at the 1st Brick and Pumice Factory after putting into operation one of the factory's tunnel fur-

naces by 10 March 1942, and a second by 20 March 1942, with the appropriate modifications to the trolleys.

2. Release to the "Gorpromstrom" Administration, for work on reequipping furnaces, 160,000 rubles out of the funds allocated by the government for the local budget for the first quarter to carry out antiepidemic and public health measures for the city of Leningrad. [. . .]

3. Propose that the chairman of the Executive Committee of the Moskovsky *raion* Council of Worker Deputies, Com. Tikhonov, supply the 1st Brick Factory with fuel based on a calculation of 50 cubic meters of firewood per day from wooden structures in the district, assigning 30 workers daily to prepare said fuel.

4. Ask the Food Commission of the Leningrad Front's Military Council to put the workers engaged in cremating corpses, who number 84, on an equal footing for food rationing with the factory workers in hot shops, issuing them an additional 100 grams of vodka daily.

5. Propose that the head of the Supply Administration of the Lengorsovet Executive Committee, Com. Bialy, release to the 1st Brick Factory 60 pairs of rubber boots, 150 pairs of overalls, 300 pairs of canvas mitts, and 50 waterproof aprons for the workers employed in cremating corpses.

6. Require the head of the Motor Transport Administration of the Lengorsovet Executive Committee, Com. Klimenko, to assign to the 1st Brick Factory one three-ton truck for hauling building materials until the work on equipping the furnaces for cremating corpses is completed.

7. The deputy chairman of the Lengorsovet Executive Committee, Com. RESHKIN, shall assign two tons of gasoline for the month of March of this year for the motor transport of the factory and the blocking station.

8. Require the Communal Services Enterprises Administration of the Lengorsovet Executive Committee (Com. Karpushenko) and "Gorpromstrom" within five days to work out with the state health inspectors provisional rules for the use of all the buildings involved in the process of cremating corpses.

9. For the continuous assurance of public health requirements, propose that the "Gorpromstrom" Admin. bring onto the factory's staff one public health doctor, with his wages coming out of the funds indicated in point 2 of the present decision.

10. Responsibility for the precise implementation of the present decision is placed on the head of "Gorpromstrom," Com. Vasiliev.

CHAIRMAN OF THE LENGORSOVET EXECUTIVE COMMITTEE S.Z.
[REDUCED SESSION] POPKOV
SECRETARY OF THE LENGORSOVET EXECUTIVE COMMITTEE
S.Z. MOSOLOV

This was not the only crematorium that operated in the blockade zone. Another in Kolpino, south of Leningrad, cremated five thousand corpses.

Keys to Survival

For most Leningraders, the food rations were insufficient to keep them alive.[85] An expert on medical effects of Leningrad's starvation, P. F. Gladkikh, estimated the population's daily caloric intake during the winter of 1942:

	January	February	March
Workers, engineers, and technicians (ITR)	707	962	1,009
Office workers	473	755	823
Children under 12	423	580	650
Adult dependents	403	570	618[86]

During this period, Leningraders burned far more calories than they consumed. According to one study, the average twenty-five-year-old man of 150 pounds who works eight hours, involved in strenuous labor only occasionally, expends approximately 3,200 calories per day. A woman of the same age, weighing 120 pounds and performing the same work, burns about 2,300 calories. The average six-year-old child requires 1,700 calories and a twelve-year-old 2,400 calories. A well-known research project from the Second World War measured the precise effects of prolonged malnutrition. On the campus of the University of Minnesota in 1944–45, thirty-two healthy men between the ages of twenty and thirty (all of whom were conscientious objectors) subsisted on a diet of 1,570 calories, which consisted of whole-wheat bread, potatoes, cereals, turnips, and cabbage. Each man worked fifteen hours per week, had free time during the evening, and spent most of the remaining time attending college classes. After twenty-four weeks, the average weight loss (factoring out the accumulation of excess water in the body) was fifty pounds, or one-third of body weight. Participants also suffered deterioration of heart muscle tissue.[87]

The authorities' collectivist response to the siege crisis included the essentially egalitarian food-rationing system, the massive clean-up campaign in the spring of 1942, antiaircraft defense, fire prevention, and other emergency measures. However, these state initiatives were insufficient. The population had to devise ways to find extra food and access to places that were heated. In some cases people deliberately pursued what might be called "survival strategies," in other cases they were the beneficiaries of fortunate circumstances. In the keys to survival described below, individual initiative, both legal and illegal, emerges as the single most common characteristic. Spontaneous cooperative activity (that is, not organized by the authorities), including self-sacrificing generosity, is also featured prominently.[88]

Evacuation

An obvious way for Leningraders to increase their chance of surviving the first winter of the war was to leave the blockade zone prior to becoming emaciated. Yet, during the first two months of the war, there was little reason to suspect that mass starvation was likely to occur. As previously noted, before 21 August, most Leningraders did not even know that their city was directly imperiled, and relatively few nonworking people had been forced to evacuate. Most people probably had felt no great urgency to leave. Moreover, after trainloads of evacuated children had come under enemy fire, major efforts were made to bring evacuated children back to the city. Of 395,091 children evacuated from Leningrad by 27 August, 175,400 had returned to the city by the start of the blockade.[89] The number of Leningraders who wanted to leave increased after the announcement of 21 August and accelerated rapidly after Germany started bombarding the city and starvation set in two months later. However, after the last rail line out of Leningrad was severed on 29 August, most Leningraders had no chance of evacuating until Stalin devoted more resources to the ice road in late January 1942. Families often did not cross the frozen lake together. Employees had to secure permission from their employers before they could legally leave. Thus, parents often departed after they had made arrangements for their children to leave.[90]

By the time the ice road became fully operational, many who traveled it were barely alive. According to official figures, 554,186 people were evacuated over the frozen lake (which brought the total of evacuees from Leningrad since the start of the war to 1,295,100, of whom 324,382 were people who had fled into Leningrad at the start of the war, people from the Leningrad *oblast'*, and wounded military personnel).[91] Awareness of the mass starvation in Leningrad spread throughout the USSR via the emaciated refugees.

Some members of the city's political and industrial elite, as well as those with connections to them, used their influence (*blat*) to leave Leningrad, or arranged for their families to leave. *Gorkom* secretaries and top *sovet* officials were among the very first to have their families evacuated. Wives and children of at least sixteen of Leningrad's most prominent individuals, including *gorkom* secretaries Kuznetsov and Kapustin, chairman of the *gorispolkom* N. V. Solovev, and *oblispolkom* secretaries T. F. Shtykov and M. N. Nikitin, were evacuated to Cheliabinsk prior to 10 July.[92] Those lacking permission to leave naturally resented the early flight of the elite. For example, in August the city prosecutor's office requested that the party investigate a situation at the Voskov munitions plant in Sestroretsk, just northwest of Leningrad along the Finnish Gulf, where the director's wife and several women having no affiliation with the factory had been allowed to evacuate, while many workers who were mothers with husbands at the front had to stay at the plant, which was not far from the Finnish lines. The prosecutor's report indicated that there were serious morale problems at the factory and among the rest of the population of Sestroretsk.[93]

Party archives also include several accounts of factory directors and others who looted state funds and secured transportation in order to leave the city during the first summer of the war. For example, shortly after the start of the blockade, the director of the Red Chemist factory, one Rovinsky, ordered his bookkeeper to fetch him fifty thousand rubles. He then requisitioned a car and might have made good his escape if the bookkeeper had not alerted authorities, who arrested Rovinsky.[94]

Many Leningraders used any means available to get on the trucks crossing the lake during the starvation winter. Kochina described how she encountered by chance a former colleague, who generously arranged for Kochina, her husband, and her infant daughter to evacuate with members of the colleague's institute. On 30 March, the four of them arrived by train at the western shore of Lake Ladoga but soon discovered that the trains were bringing far more people than could fit into the trucks that crossed the lake. "People had been sitting on their things under the open sky for several days. Those who hadn't survived were stacked in a pile." They managed to secure places on a truck by slipping approximately one liter of vodka to the driver.[95] (In another account, a driver who accepted a bribe for driving someone over the lake was arrested and given a nine-year sentence.)[96] The most dangerous means of flight, attempted by an unknown number of desperate people, was walking across the frozen lake with the hope of avoiding military checkpoints and finding a sympathetic truck driver.

The other way to escape the siege, which entailed considerable risk, was to desert to the enemy. As noted in chapter 2, over fifteen hundred army personnel defected in the fall of 1941. Among civilians, those who were most likely to attempt to flee to enemy lines were the teenage students in the trade schools and factory apprenticeship schools. These growing youths studied and worked up to eleven hours each day; yet, they received only the "dependent" category of food rations. An NKVD report from late November claimed that at least (and probably far more than) 270 students from twelve schools had attempted either successfully or unsuccessfully to reach German lines in October and November. Perhaps these reports were part of the reason Kosygin took a direct interest in the plight of trade school students during the winter. Some teenagers who were employed full-time in factories and received the higher *rabochii* rations also attempted to escape to the enemy in the autumn.[97]

Hoarding Food

Before the Bolshevik Revolution roughly one harvest in three in Russia was insufficient, and the most fundamental deficiency of the Soviet economy before and after the Second World War was its recurrent inability to feed the population. The massive famines of the 1920s and 1930s, which were largely manmade, had impressed upon the survivors the importance of hoarding food in times of crisis. Leningraders had stored away food during the war with Finland. As soon as Molotov announced the start of the German invasion, long lines formed at Leningrad's banks and shops.[98] For the next twenty-six days, there were no legal restrictions on the amount of food that could be purchased. Hoarding was rampant during this interval, which produced an uneven distribution of food throughout the city. In an environment of scarcity, the hoarders could survive longer at the expense of the others.

Leningrad traditionally depended heavily on collective farms to the north and south of the city for potatoes, cabbage, carrots, beets, and other vegetables. The siege commenced right when the harvest was ripe. Some of the farmland was lost to the enemy. On 4 September, the day that enemy artillery fire first hit the city, the VSLF ordered that the part of the harvest that could be salvaged was to be transported to Leningrad by the city's *raisovety*. Twelve days later, however, the head of the Commissariat of Procurement for the Leningrad *oblast'*, E. Furdman, notified the *obkom* and *oblispolkom* that only a small portion of the available harvest had been delivered. He complained that transportation was inadequate and disorganized. In several *raiony* not even one truck was being used to transport crops to Leningrad. Part of the harvest was just lying in the fields. He noted that of 1,300 tons of potatoes and vegetables that had been harvested in the outlying districts, only 500 tons had been delivered to Leningrad. A significant portion of the harvest, he claimed, had been looted or transferred by local *raisovety* to military units: "It is completely inadmissible that a situation has been created in almost all harvest areas that people take as many potatoes and vegetables as they can carry, and no one tries to stop this. One can observe on the highways and on the suburban trams hundreds of people carrying the harvest from the fields in sacks and baskets, which is a direct violation of the resolution of the Military *Sovet*, which established that the personal share of the harvest is determined in the district food trading organizations. Failure to take urgent measures to stop this anarchy will lead to squandering the entire harvest away into private hands."[99] The sacks and baskets of vegetables helped many Leningrad families make it through the winter. Through late autumn city party organizations continued to enlist large numbers of Leningraders, including 80,000 schoolchildren, to help bring in the harvest from the suburban areas and other parts of the *oblast'* farther from the city. All told, according to official data, 32,000 tons of potatoes, 33,000 tons of vegetables, 6,700 tons of grain, and 1,700 tons of cabbage leaves were harvested, although it is not clear how much was turned over to the authorities and how much was kept by those who gathered the crops. Security personnel were supposed to monitor food brought into the city, but much slipped through. Some of the scavengers labored almost literally under the noses of the enemy and were subjected to enemy aircraft and artillery fire.[100]

There was another burden on the food resources of the suburban areas. Some of the settlements, such as Dachnoe and Kupchino, which were located south of Leningrad's southern industrial districts, were inhabited mainly by workers at the defense plant giants the Kirov works, Elektrosila, and others. Many of them had migrated from the countryside in the 1930s, and they continued to cultivate gardens and raise chickens, goats, sheep, and other animals to supplement their diet. Leningrad's experience coincided with the general Soviet trend in the 1930s of extensive gardening along the outskirts of major cities. During the fall of 1941 and beginning of the winter, masses of starving refugees who had poured into the suburban areas over the summer tried to steal the livestock, which brought them into conflict with their owners. There were too few police to keep order.[101]

Working with Food

Place of employment played a critical role in determining who survived the hungry winter. The most coveted jobs were in bakeries, candy factories, other food-processing plants, retail food shops, cafeterias, buffets, and hospitals. There was fierce competition to get on their payrolls, and they attracted crowds of starving beggars. In a statement dictated in October 1942, Maria Fedorova, the secretary of the *partbiuro* of Bakery No. 14, recalled:

> I particularly remember the most difficult time—the months of December and January, when they distributed to the population of Leningrad 125 grams of bread with various admixtures. Dozens of starving women and children gathered at the bakery. They sat on the steps and begged for pieces of bread. It was impossible to walk by when I saw the children with their little hands outstretched to me begging for bread. And here the feeling of humanity asserted that it was necessary to help, to feed, and to save them, but the feeling of duty said that it was impossible to feed them all, that right now in Leningrad each gram of bread was accounted for and the entire population received the established minimum ration. These two feelings always battled within me and it was very difficult to endure all of this.[102]

But each gram was not in fact accounted for. Employees in food industries inevitably ate some of the food to which they had continual access, despite the fact that starting in November 1941, theft of food was punishable by execution.[103] Facilities that processed or handled food became excellent havens for their employees; starvation rates there were very low. In fact, at several food plants no one perished from hunger during the winter. Food workers could rationalize their pilfering with the argument that they had to continue to live in order to provide food for others and save their families. Of the 713 people employed at the start of the winter at the Krupskaia candy factory, none starved to death.[104] Likewise, no one succumbed to starvation at the city's Bakery No. 4 (Figure 42).[105] At the Baltika bakery, 276 people, mainly women, were employed on the eve of the war. By the beginning of winter the work force had grown to 334. Twenty-seven Baltika employees (8 percent), all men, starved to death.[106] At the city's only margarine factory, there were large quantities of linseed, sunflower seeds, and even coconuts during the winter. On the eve of the war, this plant had obtained two thousand tons of coconuts from the Philippines. Employees there lived off the oil-bearing crops, and not one starved to death.[107] In the following account, a foreman who worked in the second sausage factory states that in his section only men who would not or could not eat raw meat starved to death.

· Document 52 ·

Portion of the memoir of Nikolai Sergeev, head of the raw materials section of the Sausage Factory, during the winter of 1941-42, 3 February 1943, TsGAIPD SPb f. 4000, op. 10, d. 628, ll. 1-2.

SHORTHAND REPORT

Leningrad Meat Combine

Citizen Nikolai Sergeevich Sergeev, head of the raw materials section of the Sausage Factory, born 1883. Has worked in the meat industry since 1899, in the meat combine since 1935.
. . . During the hard months of the winter of 1942, there was a lot of work in the section, the section was fully loaded with work. The staff had already been renewed, we had students in the section, too, but here it worked out that the students came to us starving badly, they had little interest in work, they kept looking for someplace to get something to eat, and there were even cases of theft, of people getting caught with meat, and they were fired. So of the 45 students that came at different times, right now only 15 are working.

True, people got their dinner with us, they got soup and a second course on their ration cards, but each of them had a family, they wanted to take something home, and so a man was tempted by a piece of pork or meat, got caught, it was taken away from him, and people were put on trial.

In our section, five of the new workers died of starvation. This happened because the old workers are used to eating raw meat, but the new ones couldn't, and they starved and died. A few of the old workers died, too, it's true. These were those who didn't have any teeth to deal with the raw meat. It was men exclusively dying; our women didn't die, not a one.

By spring, the people were beginning to starve, there was less and less meat. Here many had already been evacuated, by May 1942 we had only about 60 people working. By this time there was very little raw material, and the program got smaller. . . .

It must be said that the period of famine affected my family, too. Of my family, I buried five people. I buried my young son-in-law, who was 28, my nephew, a daughter, and a granddaughter—all this happened during December and January. True, my daughter didn't die of dystrophy. The doctor diagnosed a heart defect. She worked at the Mikoyan Factory.

In the winter I wasn't home very much, I was always at work, it was hard to walk.

My family—my wife and a daughter—were evacuated in the month of March. One daughter left with her small child, then my wife left with our daughter who was a student at the medical institute and was being evacuated with the institute. I had five daughters altogether, and now only one is left, she works here at the second sausage factory.

Since spring, working has gotten easier, I had a garden, I planted vegetables, I tended them, I picked the cabbage, now I'm eating my own cabbage and I can even help others, I have a reserve of cabbage, since I pickled about 50 poods[108] in the fall. I support my daughter and I eat it myself and I have given it to my nephew. [. . .]

During the starvation winter some food workers were robust and well fed, even overweight (Figures 40, 41, and 42). The famous artist and book illustrator Anna Ostroumova-Lebedeva noted in her diary on 22 May 1942, that a friend "had recently been to the public baths and was completely astounded by the large number of well-fed Rubenesque young women with radiant bodies and glowing physiognomies. They are all workers in bakeries, cooperatives, soup kitchens, and children's centers."[109] Olga Berggolts described a similar bathhouse scene, in which the women had "dark bodies with raw skin," shrunken breasts, and caved-in bellies. But, then a healthy woman entered:

> Firm, round, pert breasts with cheeky pink nipples . . . a milky skin. . . .
> Oh, how ghastly she is with her normal, blooming health and eternally
> feminine flesh. . . . Yes, how dare she come like that into this terrible build-

ing where the monstrous humiliation and horrors of the war were displayed, how dare she, the bitch, how dare she insult all that with her lovely,
healthy body?

—She must have been sleeping with the manager of a restaurant!

—She has been robbing us and our children!

—Hey, beautiful, stay away from here, otherwise we'll eat you up!

Everybody avoided her, recoiled from her. . . . She gave a scream, started
to cry, threw down her washbasin and fled.[110]

Although none of the starving women knew who the mysteriously healthy
woman was, they naturally suspected that she was connected with some
sort of institution that distributed or processed food.

Women whose husbands had been sent to the front often sought employment in places that handled food. In late October around 7 A.M. each day
lines of about three hundred women and their children formed at the social
security services of the Primorsky *raion*. Most of the women sought work
in cafeterias, buffets, and military hospitals. On one occasion, a woman
threw her baby onto the floor and cried, "They took his father away to the
front, they don't give me work, the children are hungry, there's nothing.
Let them trample him, I'm not sorry." Some refused physically demanding
work. When one Petrova, the wife of an enlisted man, was offered a job in
peat extraction, she replied, "You must be crazy to think that I would take
such work." Another woman named Kuznetsova, whose husband was a
factory worker who had been mobilized, demanded work in either a cafeteria or hospital. When her request was denied, she said, "We will write our
husbands at the front about how you help us, how you want us to starve to
death."[111]

A number of factories not involved in food production possessed large
quantities of raw materials that included some edible ingredients, such as
lubricating oil (which contained vegetable oil), oilcake, leather drive belts,
industrial alcohol, industrial casein, dextrin, and albumen. Workers often
had the permission of their administrations to attempt to extract nourishment from such materials. They were not prosecuted for food theft as these
raw materials were not legally considered to be food. At the Kozitsky radio
factory seven tons of glue, which often contained dextrin, and reserves of
industrial alcohol were consumed during the winter. Horses were slaughtered and eaten at some factories.[112]

The Factory Enclave

Employment provided advantages beyond the prospect of gaining access to
edible materials and products. Tens of thousands of Leningraders sought
work in factories to get the larger and better food rations they offered.

By 20 November 1941, the daily bread ration for office workers, dependents, and children had dropped to 125 grams, but *rabochie* and ITR received twice as much bread, and metalworkers and other workers in "hot"
workshops got three times as much. When bread rations were raised on
25 December, allotments for *rabochie* and ITR and workers in the "hot"
workshops rose by 100 and 125 grams, respectively, while the bread ration
for the rest of the population increased by only 75 grams. Factory workers
also often received special servings of food in their cafeterias. Many received meager, but hot, meals by exchanging their ration cards for cafeteria
coupons. Cafeteria offerings became a major attraction of factory employment as reflected in the words of Mikhail Pelevin, a fifteen-year-old machine operator at the Kulakov factory: "It is no secret that . . . boys tried
every means possible to get into the factory, because at the factory cafeteria
you could receive immediately three bowls of hot yeast soup and a bottle
of soya milk in exchange for a ration coupon for 12½ grams of groats."[113]
Moreover, on 5 November the *Lengorispolkom* decided that over a hundred
defense plants could serve food to *rabochie* and ITR outside the ration system, that is, without requiring them to use up ration coupons.[114] Those at
the Kirov factory, for example, received three meals each day during most
of the winter. The servings, however, usually consisted only of bread; a
weak soup made from water, ersatz flour, vegetable oil, and soy; and small
flat cakes made partly from sawdust. The purpose of serving food at usual
mealtimes was as much psychological as it was nutritional. In the words
of the Kirov works director Puzyrev: "We tried to keep people going by
making a sort of yeast soup, with a little soya added. It wasn't much better,
really, than drinking hot water, but it gave people the illusion of having
'eaten' something."[115]

Factories received their above-ration food allotments in several ways.
Hospitals and factory cafeterias were the main recipients of the potatoes
and vegetables that were harvested outside the city during the autumn and
handed over to the authorities, and factories received much of the meat
that arrived over the ice road. In addition, the VSLF permitted several
major defense plants to send their own trucks across Ladoga to pick up
food parcels, which probably resulted in better and more consistent supply,
as there was considerable corruption within the military and the city food
distribution systems.[116] In addition, on 21 December, the VSLF decided to
transfer from strategic naval reserves stored on Kronstadt Island some three
hundred tons of concentrated food reserves, which included soy, powdered
milk, albumen yeast, casein gum, fruit syrup, seaweed, and acorn coffee.
Defense plants received a large portion of these reserves. Finally, workers
obtained extra food through barter exchanges with soldiers, who received

higher rations, when they went to the front either in repair crews or as part of "goodwill" delegations.[117]

Factories provided other benefits which, combined with the extra food they received, had the effect of transforming some of them into largely autonomous enclaves. When the last of the major defense plants lost their electrical power by mid-December and could no longer work on major production orders for the front, workers turned their workshops into mutual support centers. By the third week in December, trams ceased to function and most homes, shops, and industries lost their electrical power. Leningraders became increasingly isolated during the darkest and coldest months. At this time, the factory workshop became a source of much-needed companionship. Industrial party organizations that continued to function maintained "Red corners" (a communist overlay of the Orthodox tradition of keeping icons in a corner of the home) where workers could warm up next to a stove, converse with co-workers, and read the abbreviated two-page version of *Leningradskaia pravda* as well as their own factory newspaper, if they were employed at one of thirty-seven plants that continued publishing a newspaper during the winter. Factories were more likely than other places to have enough light for reading, and some generated their own electrical power. It is estimated that over a third of all industrial work space was illuminated. Having access to a heated and lighted area had considerable psychological, as well as physical, value.[118] According to the chief mechanic of the Stalin metal works, Georgy Kulagin, who kept a diary during 1942: "I remember how I wanted very much to . . . return to the factory more quickly, to enter the power station room, which was flooded in light, to flop down on my bed, assured that not the entire world consisted of cold and darkness."[119] Party agitators read propaganda lectures that often focused on military heroes from Russia's past. Party and trade union officials encouraged workers to read between work shifts, and a few of the largest factories kept open small lending libraries. Works that focused on Russian patriotism, including nineteenth-century classics of fiction, such as Tolstoy's *War and Peace,* and Soviet-era historical studies, such as Tarle's *Napoleon,* were popular throughout the war.[120]

Some employees stole industrial materials for use at home. In December and January, a total of 228 people at the Kirov factory were detained for trying to take home kerosene, oil, soap, electric cables, and various instruments, among other things. Sheds and warehouses were dismantled for their lumber. The information officer of the plant's *partkom* claimed that security was lax as no one was paying much attention to this theft.[121]

Workers formed "service brigades" (*bytovye brigady*) to carry out everyday chores, although the first one was formed only on 14 February in the

Primorsky *raion*. The brigades consisted mainly of female workers from the Komsomol. On 28 February, city Komsomol leaders ordered all *raiony* to emulate the Primorsky brigade, so that an effort that may have started out as a spontaneous initiative became an official program. By the end of the winter the brigades comprised around 10,000 members. They cleaned up factory barracks; repaired shoes; mended clothes; fixed up laundries, baths, and showers; and set up warming stations. Their work extended beyond factory grounds. They brought food to workers who were too weak to go to the factory and routinely cleaned about 30,000 apartments. They also maintained some 900 hot water stations, laundries, and public baths; provided basic medical assistance to over 8,000 people; and helped thousands of others gain permission to evacuate over the ice road.[122]

The Kirov works had perhaps the city's most active brigade. It formed a cleaning crew, shoe repair shop, and a sewing group, set up several warming stations in the factory, and distributed passes to one of the few public baths still open in the city. During the winter the brigade attended to more than 800 homes and delivered meals and firewood to between 500 and 600 worker families. From the flats of dead or evacuated workers the Kirov brigade collected items for other needy families. It also cleaned apartments and courtyards, moved elderly people into apartments on lower floors, advised evacuation commissions on which people should be sent out of the city immediately, and opened a children's home. Starting from the first week in January, the brigade also helped bury the bodies of about 1,000 employees in a mass grave on factory grounds.

Authorities at the Kirov plant also tried to use the brigade for surveillance purposes, to verify that workers who did not report to work for more than three consecutive days were indeed ill. However, the brigade did not fulfill this role well, because at least 1,000 Kirov employees went missing during the winter. Most likely, the majority of them perished.[123]

Factories performed several important functions that benefited not only their employees, but the city at large. The shifting of the *gorkom*'s priorities away from production for the front in favor of addressing the city's immediate problems was reflected in *Leningradskaia pravda*'s banner headline of 13 February: "The important task of industrial cooperatives is to serve the needs of the population." The *gorkom* ordered many factories to provide services and products to 151 military hospital branches in the city. Workers repaired plumbing and supplied hospitals with stoves, towels, soap, lamps, buckets, utensils, oil cloths, sheets, and pillow cases. Factories in the Oktiabrsky *raion* made about 300 *burzhuiki* stoves for twelve hospitals. Hospitals were not the only beneficiaries of this new emphasis in production. In December 1941, the *ispolkom* ordered factories to assemble 28,000 *burzhuiki* for a variety of institutions. Factories also manufactured buckets, rakes, shovels, and other implements for the spring gardening campaign (Figure 50).[124]

The improvised *burzhuiki* generated heat very well, but they were also to blame for many house fires. Between 1 January and 10 March, 1,578 fires were reported in the city that did not result from German artillery fire. With most houses lacking running water, people often resorted to trying to extinguish fires with snow. The threat of house fires was so great that *Leningradskaia pravda* devoted its entire issue of 24 January to fire prevention.[125]

After trams quit running in the third week in December, many employees moved closer to their workplaces to avoid long commutes on foot and take advantage of the amenities that the factory enclaves provided. They occupied rooms or parts of rooms that had become vacant through the death or evacuation of former tenants. (Only a few categories of people, including army officers and members of the Academy of Sciences, were entitled to retain possession of their flats after leaving the city.) As the winter progressed, factories increasingly took control of houses in their vicinity, enabling their workers to live close by. Some workers did not leave factory premises for weeks at a time. There were, however, three disadvantages to living on or very near factory grounds. The first was that the city's defense plant giants, including the Kirov works, the Stalin metal works, and the Ordzhonikidze shipyard, were prime targets for German artillery. The fact that the Germans fired an estimated 21,000 shells at these and other targets in the first three months of 1942, causing just under 2,000 casualties, likely dissuaded many defense plant workers from choosing to live in factory barracks. The heavily industrialized Kirovsky *raion* was the one shelled most frequently. German intelligence developed detailed knowledge of the layout of factories through air reconnaissance during the latter half of 1942 in order to pinpoint their attacks (Figure 9). The second disadvantage was that those who lived at the work site were expected to show up for work regularly, whereas those who walked a great distance reported less frequently. When starvation rates were high, workers at the Kirov factory who were not on sick leave and did not live on factory grounds were expected to show up for work only twice a week.[126] This was in sharp contrast to conditions prevailing the preceding autumn when an unauthorized absence from a defense plant was a very serious matter, especially if the factory was near the front lines. Marshal Zhukov's Order 0064 from September stated that anyone who abandoned his post without written permission would be shot immediately. Although Zhukov's order pertained to the military, factories located along the southern periphery of the city, which had been turned into defensive bastions, were considered part of the front, and their workers might be included in Zhukov's order. A shop foreman named Khlusov at the Kirov plant left work for four days in September to move his family from the village of Alekseevka, which was near the factory and like the factory was threatened by the German advance, to the safer confines of the Petrogradskaia Storona *raion*. He was fired and "made accountable" (*privlechen k otvetstvennosti*) for his actions, which was a euphemism that in wartime indicated some form of extreme punishment. The fact that he was also heard to complain that "the leadership is in hiding while it sends us to the slaughter" might have figured in his punishment.[127] During the winter, however, when most people were genuinely very ill, many doctors stopped issuing certificates of illness, and, hence, factory administrators could not force ill workers to present them upon returning to work. As absenteeism rose sharply, many factories simply put all those who did not report for work on sick lists until the end of the month, at which time the workers would have to report to work to receive new ration cards. Without private telephone service, which the NKVD had terminated early in the war, or public transportation, managers generally did not bother to check up on absent workers. Valentina Bushueva, who was in her late teens and worked in a factory during the winter of 1941–42, recounted in 1995 that she received a sick leave certificate from a doctor when she began to swell up from hunger. Throughout March and April 1942, she remained in bed but was able to continue receiving the *rabochii* rations. In May she was laid off from work due to her absences and then was almost immediately drafted to dig peat outside the city to boost the city's fuel reserves.[128]

Party leaders suspected that many workers taking sick leave were not actually ill. On 27 February, *Leningradskaia pravda* reminded factory managers that sick workers were required to show certificates of illness when they returned to work. The party also admonished medical personnel to exercise better judgment in granting certificates. On 26 March, an article in *Leningradskaia pravda* stated that inspectors had discovered that over half of the employees on sick lists at several factories were not ill; however, with starvation so widespread that assessment seems doubtful. In either case, absenteeism remained high during the spring. In April 1942, only 51 percent of workers (101,002 of 197,466) at 436 factories surveyed were reporting to work.[129]

Other factors contributed to the replacement of strict labor discipline with more lenient and flexible practices. For one, the growing labor shortage gave workers greater job security. Managers were not likely to punish workers for minor infractions if the workers' labor was indispensable for fulfilling urgent work assignments or might be needed in the coming months when factory production revived. Furthermore, during the winter most factories that continued in operation did not keep individual performance records. In fact, many did not even compile aggregate records on percentage of plan fulfillment. The lack of record-keeping afforded workers and managers more flexibility in arranging work schedules.[130] Even if one was unfortunate enough to be arrested for labor truancy and convicted, the punishment was a fine and not imprisonment, at least through September 1942.[131]

Those workers who moved into factory barracks, on the other hand, had access to better health and medical care. Starting in late December, many factory administrations set up rudimentary clinics (*statsionary*). The Stalin metal works established the city's first factory clinic, and by spring a total of 109 clinics were reportedly aiding 63,740 Leningraders, primarily workers. The clinics typically consisted of rows of beds and a few *burzhuiki* for warmth. They offered hot soup or kasha and perhaps hot wine, glucose injections, or even antibiotics.[132] Although the provisions were meager, a single glucose injection applied at the critical moment when someone hovered between life and death could save that person's life. That was precisely what happened to Dr. Svetlana Magaeva, who is now a senior research fellow at the Institute of Pathology and Pathophysiology of the Russian Academy of Medical Sciences, when she was a young girl in the siege. Whether one lived or died often depended on seemingly unimportant actions. According to Magaeva: "I have never ceased to be amazed how very little sufficed to support a life on the point of extinction."[133]

The benefits of factory employment, especially the higher food rations, attracted many Leningraders. On the eve of the war, there had been about 750,000 industrial and nonindustrial *rabochie* in Leningrad.[134] By 6 October 1941, after successive waves of army mobilization and *opolchenie* volunteering and the industrial evacuation had removed at least 200,000 *rabochie* from the city, the number of Leningraders officially receiving *rabochii* food rations was 831,400.[135] Hence, at least 281,400 people acquired *rabochii* and ITR status during the first three and a half months of the war. Not all of them were employed in factories, and some in fact were not workers, engineers, or technicians. Several groups successfully petitioned city authorities for *rabochii* or ITR status for rationing purposes. For example, doctoral candidates were put into the ITR category from 9 February.[136]

The number of Leningraders receiving *rabochii* rations did not decline significantly during the winter, despite the fact that *rabochie* were supposed to drop down to the "dependent" category once their factories were shut down. In December approximately 837,000 people received *rabochii* rations; in January that figure dropped only to 800,000.[137] It is inconceivable that during the winter, when the *gorkom* closed 270 factories and only 18 of 68 leading industries maintained any semblance of activity,[138] anywhere near a majority of factory workers were actually working. Many

were probably in a situation similar to that in which Skriabina found herself on 15 January: "Friends found me a position in a sewing shop. This
puts me in the first category as far as rationing goes. True, the workshop
does very little; there is no light or fuel, but they give out the rations just the
same. In this way I get a little more bread, and now every crumb is vital."[139]
In most cases it was not until at least the spring of 1942 that the *gorkom*
redistributed workers from closed plants to working ones. In a zero-sum
environment where the amount of food available was fixed, the fact that so
many people managed to obtain the higher *rabochii* ration added pressure
to cut rations further.

Of all the means of survival considered in this study, the one for which
there is the most data for assessing effectiveness is factory employment.
While there is no composite mortality figure for industrial employees,
available information from individual factories reveals that mortality
varied considerably. As noted above, the enterprises that afforded the best
protection were those that processed or handled edible materials. In a second category were factories that did not have extraordinary access to food
or edible materials but did not demand much work from their workers
who, nevertheless, continued to receive *rabochii* rations. Mortality at such
plants was lower than the city average. City power plants fit into this group.
Only one plant generated electricity throughout the siege period; yet, the
industry as a whole in December 1941 employed more workers than it did
in 1940. The starvation rate among workers at power plants was 20–25 percent of the number that was employed on the eve of the war.[140]

The situation at the city's largest defense plants was mixed. Some afforded relatively good protection. For example, of the nearly 12,000 who
were employed at the Bolshevik arms plant at the beginning of 1942 and
were not subsequently evacuated over the ice road, "only" approximately
22 percent died in the winter.[141] However, mortality rates at other major
defense plants were higher. Kulagin estimated that approximately 35 percent starved to death at the Stalin metal works. According to documentation on the Kirov factory, 25–34 percent of its work force starved to death
during the winter.[142] In 1942, 3,063 Kirov employees died.[143] At the smaller
Nevgvozd plant, which had switched from manufacturing nails to rails
for tank traps, 102 of 250 employees (42 percent) died in the first half of
1942.[144]

Data on large defense plants reveal a paradox. With their enhanced food
supply, Komsomol brigades, and *statsionary*, one would expect their mortality rates to be significantly lower that the city average. However, three
special conditions at major defense plants combined to increase mortality.
First, as noted above, they were special targets for German aircraft and
artillery, especially those such as the Kirov works that were located in the
city's southern districts. Secondly, on a per capita basis, more men than

women starved to death, and of all types of industry, major defense plants had the highest proportion of male workers. Large concentrations of men had continued to work in defense plants because jobs there often required a high skill level, which men were more likely to possess, and skilled defense plant workers were granted exemptions from military service. Thirdly, in early March 1942, the GKO ordered a number of Leningrad's large defense plants to resume limited operations. The effort required to carry out the March orders probably finished off many emaciated workers. At the Kirov plant over half of all cases of death by starvation reportedly occurred in March and April. Records from the Bolshevik factory show that three-fourths of the deaths of the winter and spring occurred in April.[145] The effect of the survival benefits at large defense plants, therefore, was partly offset by these other factors. Had defense plant workers not had special privileges, it can be assumed that their mortality rates would have far surpassed the city average.

The fragmentary information that is available on mortality among various other professions highlights the striking differences that existed in the city and provides a comparative context for assessing survivability at factories. Among medical doctors, only 61 of 3,000 (2 percent) starved to death. Doctors such as Katsnelson (Document 39) worked hard and long shifts in several clinics and received only the *sluzhashchie* food rations; however, doctors received the best medical care and had access to extra food sources. Kyra Petrovskaya, a young actress who became a nurse in Military Hospital No. 902, described the favorable conditions there. She not only was able to care for an orphaned boy but also kept a dog, at a time when most pets were killed for food: "I didn't need to have worried about supporting the dog on our rations. Snezhinka was the fattest, the best fed member of our entire medical establishment. Everyone shared his food with her, and the little glutton had to be watched not to overeat."[146] The survival rate among military personnel of the Leningrad Front was comparable to that of healthcare professionals. Of the roughly 500,000 troops in the blockade zone, 12,416 (2.5 percent) died of hunger. The chances of survival for registered artists were closer to the city's average rate: 83 of 225 (37 percent) perished. Among the 560 employees of the Hermitage Museum who remained in the city, 130 (23 percent) died as a result of the winter. Of 289 employees at the city library who were not evacuated, 89 (30.1 percent) died.[147]

Exploiting Privilege

As the USSR "built socialism" in the mid-1930s, it also constructed official hierarchies of privilege. From the time of the second Five Year Plan (1933–37), the revolutionary ethos of egalitarianism gave way to an increasing social stratification. There were distinct layers of power and privilege in Leningrad during the siege years. It has already been observed that privilege and personal connections played a role in determining who was able to leave Leningrad. Privilege was also commonly used to secure special access to food. The food rationing scheme, which resembled the system employed during the early 1930s, was egalitarian to a point (see Appendixes A and B). According to the system, all people within a ration category received the same amount of food, and the only major difference between civilian categories was the preference given to *rabochie,* especially those in "hot" workshops, and ITR. At the same time, there existed important legal, but generally unpublicized, privileges for various elites. For instance, in factories there were often "closed" cafeterias and a "directors'" cafeteria, which provided marginally better food and larger portions to engineers, managers, and directors.[148] In addition, a wide range of various groups, from blood donors to pregnant women, doctors, university administrators, and musical composers, among others, would be singled out for special food allotments. On 26 December in anticipation of the New Year and the celebration that it traditionally occasioned, academicians and corresponding members of the Academy of Sciences were allowed to purchase outside the rationing system small quantities (typically, half a kilogram each) of cooking oil, canned meat or fish, sugar, chocolate, and cookies, in addition to thirty eggs, three kilograms of wheat flour, and two bottles of wine. On 18 January, a special food store was opened for the twenty-two fellows of the Academy of Sciences and a few others selected by the deputy chairman of the *ispolkom,* I. A. Andreenko. They could purchase a small amount of extra food on a monthly basis.[149]

The Communist Party as a whole constituted an elite group that benefited from privilege. Party personnel had a much better chance of surviving the starvation winter than did the general civilian population. During the first year of the war, 12,419 members and candidates of the LPO died. Of that number, 11,193 died in the first six months of 1942, which represented 15.1 percent of the 74,228 who were listed as party members or candidates on 1 January 1942. Of those in the LPO on 1 January who did not leave the city (57,753), 19.4 percent died by the end of June 1942.[150] Comparing this information with Cherepenina's data cited above, it becomes clear that mortality among party members and candidates was roughly half that of the general civilian population. Within the LPO, the upper echelons—officials in the *gorkom* and *raikomy*—fared considerably better than rank-and-file members and candidates.[151]

Document 19 shows how party and NKVD officials in one *raion* had access to a special cafeteria and that the *raikom* secretary illegally requisitioned additional food. Some party officials spent considerable time in close proximity to food during the starvation winter. Fedorova, the secretary of the *partbiuro* of bakery No. 14, recollected later in 1942 that during the winter "the directors of the *raion* party organization were at the bakery almost all the time." But she implies that the main reason for their presence was to make "every effort to bake bread all the time."[152]

The operational staff of the NKVD (that is, members of the UNKVD, not its informant network) had a high survival rate, despite the fact that most were classified as *sluzhashchie*. There were approximately 1,290 UNKVD staff members in the city at the start of the winter. Seventy-three (5.6 percent) of them died of hunger.[153] The *militsiia* was part of the massive NKVD structure, but it had a much lower survival rate. It would appear that the average policeman had little or no comparative advantage. In the summer of 1941, 1,200 police had patrolled the city's streets, in addition to those employed in the traffic police and in stationhouses. In January 166 police died of starvation, and another 212 perished in February. Some died on the job.[154]

Party headquarters at Smolny—the peak of power and privilege in the city—had a wide range of food in abundant supply. According to one account, Smolny's Cafeteria No. 12 provided bread, sugar, cutlets, kasha, and small pies on a regular basis at least into November. Employees were strictly forbidden to take bread out of this cafeteria.[155] A *gorkom* official, who was new to his job, reported that on every single day of March 1942 he saw in a special cafeteria (perhaps the same No. 12) "meat, mutton, chicken, goose, turkey, sausage (all kinds), fish, caviar, cheese, pies, chocolate, coffee, tea, 300 grams of white bread and sometimes brown bread a day, 30 grams of butter, and 50 grams of drink at lunch and dinner. . . ."[156] As observed in chapter 2, Zhdanov reportedly received regular shipments of fresh food by airplane throughout the siege period. Figure 43 shows a rather porcine Zhdanov in 1942.[157] Vasily Yershov, a deputy commander of food supply for an army division, claimed in an unpublished and unverified account that he was sent to the airport in the fall of 1941 to collect foodstuffs that had been left over from a huge shipment flown to family members and assistants of *gorkom* secretaries who had been evacuated earlier. He claimed that he organized dozens of trucks to retrieve ten tons of rice, about fifteen tons of white flour, over two tons of caviar, approximately five tons of butter, more than two hundred smoked hams, and large quantities of many other products. Some of these foodstuffs were delivered to Smolny.[158]

Private Trade

Prior to the war, private trade occurred primarily through the city's several collective farm markets (*rynki*), but they were closed at the start of the blockade in an attempt to stifle the growing black market and keep food within the rationing system. Nevertheless, as hunger set in, private trade increased exponentially and occurred mainly at the *rynki,* although some Leningraders slipped out to the countryside to buy food from villagers. During the early autumn, Leningraders bought food at inflated black-market prices. This form of trade was illegal (*spekuliatsiia*) but widely practiced, and as the food rations shrank in size prices on the black market rose. Party and NKVD informants monitored the *rynki* and noted black-market prices in their reports. The table shows the growth of inflation:

	October	November	December
1 small piece of candy	1 ruble	3	25
1 small lump of sugar	0.8	1.2	20
200 grams of bread	8	20	120
100 grams of butter	12	60	150–170
100 grams of chocolate	N/A	80	120–140[159]

As the ruble depreciated significantly in value, black-market food transactions were increasingly conducted as barter exchanges, which were also illegal. As early as late November, party informants flatly asserted (Document 40) that black-market purchases of food were no longer being made with rubles (in contradiction to the chart above, which shows that rubles were being exchanged for food in December). As winter progressed, vodka increasingly became a valuable currency. Barter transactions were ubiquitous; most memoirs mention them. Leningraders walked to the *rynki* to stand with a pair of galoshes or a coat in the hope of trading them for a little food. (Throngs of sellers trudging to the *rynki* with personal possessions were not unlike the bazaars that spontaneously formed around *rynki* in the early 1990s when ruinous inflation turned pensioners and even many employed people into paupers.) On 26 November, following cuts in the bread ration on 13 and 20 November, the acting director of the City's Market Administration, one Kirillov, suggested to the *gorispolkom* that it consider legalizing the barter markets (*tolkuchki*). He contended that neither *rynok* officials nor the police had been able to halt barter trade and that more than one thousand people each day engaged in the practice at each of five city *rynki.* Because their actions were illegal, barter sellers tried to conceal their activity from the authorities or moved to adjoining streets to evade them. Kirillov proposed legalizing private barter trade and introducing a modest fee for permission to engage in it. The state would receive revenue of more than 100,000 rubles a month, and the quality of food and the fairness of transactions could be supervised.[160] Party leaders rejected Kirillov's idea; however, throughout the winter the police essentially condoned barter trade if the items being exchanged had been obtained legally.

During January and February 1942, black-market prices for food, whether in rubles or exchanged goods, reached their peak; however, they varied to such an extent throughout the city that it is questionable whether a defined underground "market" actually existed. According to party informants, in January, each of the following items could purchase one kilogram of bread: one fur jacket, one Western suit of clothes, three pairs of felt boots (*valenki*), one gold watch, one gold picture frame, fifteen packs of cigarettes, and one liter of vodka. According to one account, during the winter a gold watch bought three to four turnips, an ordinary fur coat a half kilo of bread, and a large Persian rug two chocolate bars.[161] Another states that a personal library containing rare books was exchanged for a frozen horse leg.[162] Obviously, those with valuable items to sell could benefit more from barter exchanges. Not all transactions were conducted at the *rynki*. Some people posted notes of the items they wanted to sell. For example, on 6 February 1942, the following notice was posted on a city street (Figure 36):

I will trade for food:
1. Gold cufflinks
2. Material for a skirt (dark blue wool)
3. Men's boots: yellow. N40 and patent leather N41
4. Kettle. coal-fired samovar type
5. "FED" camera[163] with enlarger
6. Hand drill
A fine-stitch Singer sewing machine, model 72, a barometer, and a rocking chair are for sale right now.
Apply at the address:
Dzerzhinsky St. house 17, apartment 91. Gladkova
from 11 A.M. to 4 P.M.

Reading between the lines of this detailed note, which was very neatly written, we can surmise that Gladkova was a meticulous and well-organized woman. The items she wanted to trade for food suggest a measure of pre-revolutionary affluence, and because she was at home during the day, she may have been retired or too ill to work. Her husband or some other man (the owner of the boots) seems to have left or perhaps died.

It would appear that a thriving market in works of art existed during the worst of the starvation. Sellers met around the city's five or six art shops and exchanged paintings and other forms of art for food. The sellers of art objects naturally tried to retain their cherished and valuable possessions as long as they could and traded them only as a last resort. Some buyers who had access to special sources of food acquired considerable art collections during the mass starvation. In one case, a woman with the ironic surname of Golod (hunger) purchased a small Fabergé piece for three loaves of bread. Her husband was a news correspondent who flew into and out of

Leningrad. Golod's technique for buying artwork was simple. She would offer one loaf more than other buyers were willing to trade.[164]

The authorities focused their efforts on arresting those who had stolen state property, especially food, and then tried to sell it at the markets. However, once the worst of the starvation period had passed, during the first eighteen days of April, the police tried to crack down on all forms of private trade by conducting sixteen raids on the markets. A total of 20,452 summonses were issued. The large majority consisted of small fines of about fifty rubles for breaking market rules. Most of these fines were probably for conducting simple barter trade. Only 336 of the lawbreakers were arrested for criminal activity, including 53 charged with theft and a somewhat larger number for *spekulatsiia*.[165]

Barter transactions were common between civilians and military personnel. Soldiers often lacked warm clothing and other personal items but, as the table below indicates, received a higher bread ration than most civilians. From 13 November, the bread ration for troops in rear units was greater than the *rabochii* allotment but less than what *rabochie* in "hot" workshops received; however, the troops were better off than the metal-workers, because they generally did not have to work as hard. Soldiers were also more likely to receive meat from slaughtered horses. Although there was starvation within the military, some troops were willing to trade a portion of their food for the civilians' possessions. Soldiers on occasion walked right into starving people's communal flats and offered food for their belongings. As early as late October, soldiers would regularly meet with women and teenagers at a rail junction where bread from the Badaev bakery was sent to military units to trade cigarettes, wine, and beer for military bread. The bakery's security staff tried to halt the trade, but the military personnel refused, claiming that the bread was theirs and the matter was none of the bakery's business. City party leaders, including Zhdanov, were informed that a policeman was unable to stop the barter trade.[166]

Comparison of Daily Bread Rations in 1941

	Front-line soldiers	Soldiers in rear units	Rabochie in "hot" workshops	Other rabochie	All other people
1 Oct.	800 grams	600	600	400	200
13 Nov.	600	400	450	300	150
20 Nov.					
25 Dec.	500	300	375	250	25[167]

Two particular functions brought soldiers and civilians together and thereby provided a venue for barter exchange. Defense plant workers formed crews to travel to the front to make repairs on the weapons that they manufactured. For example, the Kirov factory, located only two and a half miles from the front lines, sent three-person teams by night to repair tanks and artillery guns. During the fall of 1941, seventy-four "field workshops" combined to form a "factory on wheels," which repaired a wide range of weaponry and transport vehicles.[168] Few repair crews returned to their plants empty-handed. In addition, various organizations sent goodwill delegations to the front to present gifts they had collected or made or to perform for the troops, and generally to help boost morale. Visitors to the front usually received food in exchange. Ksenia Matus, an oboist and student of the Conservatory who was one of the last surviving musicians who played in the famous performance of Shostakovich's Seventh (Leningrad) Symphony on 9 August 1942, which was broadcast around the world via Leningrad radio, stated in an interview in 1996 that she performed at Avtovo, near the front, with other conservatory students for the 7 November 1941 celebrations. After the concert, the soldiers invited the musicians to a bountiful supper of meat cutlets, small pies, bread, and vodka. Tamara Nekliudova, who was either an actress or musician, was sent to entertain front-line troops. The menu of the food she received on 12 December 1941, listed below, is exhibited at the Museum of the Defense of Leningrad:

Breakfast: First course: soup with macaroni
Second course: coffee, bread with vegetable oil and fat
Lunch: First course: soup with macaroni
Second course: boiled pearl barley with fat (not eaten, saved for Leningrad)
Dinner: Banquet to decorate 140 Heroes of the Patriotic War (by invitational coupon)
Portion per person: 100 grams of grain alcohol, 2 glasses of beer, 300 grams of bread, sunflower seeds, 50 grams of salted pork fat, 1 white roll, 2 cutlets with gravy and buckwheat from concentrate, 1 glass of cocoa with milk, 1 pack of Belomor cigarettes, 1 box of matches.

Nekliudova added that "beer in bottles and a kilo of candy was brought for the women. We . . . took about 400 grams to Leningrad."[169] Many groups of factory workers made official goodwill visits to the front. According to one estimate, approximately a hundred such visits occurred in November and December.[170] Kulagin from the Stalin metal works observed in his memoir that he sought to visit the front as often as possible: "There I could eat until full and occasionally pick up a loaf of soldiers' bread. . . . Without this, I would not have survived."[171]

Gardens and Factory Subsidiary Farms

During the winter, Leningraders became obsessed with the hope of planting vegetable gardens in the coming spring. Preparations began as early as
January for what would become a massive growing campaign that city authorities and the people enthusiastically supported. As previously noted,
Leningraders were well acquainted with gardening. During the famines of
the 1930s, many had planted gardens, and thousands of peasant farmers
had sought refuge in the city. The first plans for the garden campaign of
1942 were published on 11 January in *Leningradskaia pravda*. Two professors from the Agricultural Institute claimed that home-grown vegetables
and potatoes could feed half a million Leningraders. Five days later the
newspaper announced that several factories had been ordered to manufacture various gardening and farm tools (even though most workers were in
no condition to resume work). From January through the spring the city
sovet conducted a campaign to teach people about gardening, which included thirty radio discussions, twenty-five different brochures, and twenty
articles in *Leningradskaia pravda*. The gardening campaign is a prime example of the authorities attempting to organize and mobilize the masses to
become more self-reliant, to take initiative independent from collectivized
state control. Aleksei Yevdokimov noted in his diary on 10 June: "They
are conferring on gardening the especially important character of a political campaign."[172] As early as February, some 5,700 people were attending
gardening classes organized by *ispolkomy* at the *raion* level.[173] The intent
of the publicity through about the end of March appears to have been as
much psychological as practical in that the authorities wanted to bolster
public morale by keeping the prospect of mass cultivation of vegetables
and potatoes alive.

On 19 March, the city *sovet* announced procedures for registering and
obtaining seedlings for private gardens. Families received 0.15 hectare plots
(about 130 feet square) from the city's agricultural department. Altogether,
the *sovet* set aside over five square miles of parks, squares, and other open
areas for gardens. Despite early publicity and planning, the *gorkom* was
dissatisfied with the development of the gardening campaign. As was true
for every program designed to protect the civilian population during the
winter and spring of 1941–42, few preparations were made far in advance.
People were to purchase seedlings from the "Green Construction Trust"
of the city *sovet* through work or from housing administrations, but seedlings often were not available until late in the spring. An added problem
was that many inhabitants were still too weak to obtain a plot and lay out
a garden. On 11 May, the *biuro gorkoma* discussed agricultural deficiencies
and ordered each *raion* party organization to appoint a secretary to take

charge of gardening and farming.[174] In the meantime, as seedlings were being grown and distributed, the emaciated populace devoured the first edible wild vegetation to appear in and around the city—over a hundred types of grasses and herbs. The Botanical Garden of the Institute of the Academy of Sciences held Sunday lectures on identification and preparation of edible plants.[175]

The home-grown garden vegetables ripened later in the summer when rations for bread and other foods had risen above starvation levels. Altogether, an estimated 276,000 Leningraders planted over seven square miles of private gardens, which grew cabbages, lettuce, beets, tomatoes, cucumbers, green beans, rutabagas, carrots, radishes, and onions in practically every patch of available soil. These crops filled a very important supplemental role in the diet, but for the most part they were consumed by people who had already begun to recuperate from the starvation winter (Figures 49 and 57).[176]

At the same time, factories and other enterprises organized 633 so-called "subsidiary farms" (*podsobnye khoziaistva*), the produce from which went to the enterprises' cafeterias, to the city's general food supply, and to the workers themselves who labored on the farms. Such farms had existed before the war to supplement workers' diet; in 1942 they came to include the sites of some fifty-four abandoned state and collective farms. Most of the subsidiary farms, which had an average size of ninety-six acres, were located in suburban areas, especially the northern Pargolovsky and Vsevolozhsky *raiony;* about a quarter of them were within city limits. Almost all of the work was done by hand, although the farms managed to scare up a total of 54 tractors and 197 horses.[177]

The vegetable-growing campaign provides an interesting comparison of the effectiveness of a state-run collectivized program with that of individual effort during a time of extreme deprivation. Although the subsidiary farms were given higher priority in obtaining seeds, tools, and machinery, most Leningraders preferred working on their own gardens, because everything they grew on their own plots was theirs. All previous rent payments for gardens and taxes on their produce were abolished. The private garden campaign proved so successful throughout the USSR that the Supreme Soviet on 4 November 1942 decided to let people keep their plots under the same conditions for five to seven more years.[178] For Leningraders, the gardening campaign, despite its shortcomings, may have been the most popular program that the city's Communist leadership ever organized.

By contrast, those who labored on the subsidiary farms did not have as direct an interest in the outcome of their work. They had to turn over part of the produce to industrial cafeterias and to the city's general food reserve. Another disincentive was that they had to leave their homes for several weeks at a time to work on the farms; yet, even so, those who planted the seedlings and potato seed tubers often were not the same people as those who gathered the harvest. When the planting was finished, many factory directors ordered workers back to their workshops to fulfill industrial assignments. The growing crops were then neglected; they suffered from a lack of irrigation and fell prey to weeds. When they ripened, many workers were occupied with other tasks, such as chopping firewood for the coming winter or building defense fortifications in anticipation of further attempts by the enemy to take the city. Army units and thousands of civilian labor draftees were needed to help finish gathering the harvest. To make matters worse, part of the harvest was squandered due to shortages of crates, storage sheds, and transport vehicles. The overall plan for the subsidiary farms was reportedly fulfilled at 86 percent, and the city *sovet* expressed its disappointment. It should be noted that area state farms (*sovkhozy*) that existed before the blockade and continued to function in 1942 outperformed the subsidiary farms. The state farms had a conscripted workforce including many schoolchildren. They overfulfilled their plan for 1942 at 136 percent.[179]

Between the planting and harvest seasons, there were only thirteen to seventeen thousand people working on the subsidiary farms. Early on, party leaders recognized people's preference for their own gardens and vainly tried to encourage more to work on the subsidiary farms.[180] By the end of the harvest season, the individual gardens, the subsidiary farms, and the *sovkhozy* each reportedly yielded nearly the same weight of crops for a total of around seventy-five tons. The gardens, however, were cultivated far more intensively: their calculated yield was almost three times as great per hectare as the subsidiary farms.[181]

Not surprisingly, theft of produce appears to have been fairly common. Some factories provided guards for their farms. Petrovskaya described the park by the Admiralty on 21 May: "Along the paths, where grass once grew . . . there were even rows of tiny vegetable plots. . . . The plantings were just sprouting. . . . On the benches along the paths sat motionless figures of watchmen. People didn't trust one another, and they stayed in the park until curfew, guarding their seedlings from one another."[182] On 30 May, Popkov introduced jail sentences of five years for stealing vegetables or seedlings. "Particularly blatant" offenders were subject to execution; however, it is not known to what extent the punishments were enforced. On 4 September, *Leningradskaia pravda* stated that theft was increasing as plants grew, especially in the Taurida Gardens. The newspaper commented that many people thought that the police were too lenient in assessing fines of only ten to twenty-five rubles for garden theft.[183]

Criminal Schemes

While some Leningraders engaged in activities that were technically illegal but widely condoned, such as trading personal items on the black market, others resorted to actions to survive the hungry winter that were criminal by any standard. Information that has come to light recently, especially from NKVD files, shows that food theft was far more common than previously thought. The documents reveal the number of arrests for various crimes and list the vast amount of food, money, and merchandise that was recovered. For example, as Document 45 indicates, 483 metric tons of stolen foodstuffs were recovered by the authorities throughout the city by 1 October 1942. The extent of food-related crime that went undetected, however, can only be imagined. The entire "food chain," from the transport network that brought food to the city (and took out starving refugees) to those who dispensed rations in shops and cafeterias, was riddled with embezzlers and thieves. The starving populace devised ingenious ways to steal food from shops and locked storerooms. The police and the NKVD naturally endeavored to eradicate criminal activity, but they knew they could only contain the problem. Theft was too pervasive for the police, who were themselves starving to death, to eliminate. The NKVD staff was too small, and moreover, it was partly diverted to hunting down phantom political criminals.

Right from the start of the war, thieves were active among those who handled food. On 24 June 1941, a cafeteria cook was arrested in possession of nearly a half-ton of various foodstuffs and goods worth 300,000 rubles. Not long after the first cases of cannibalism were recorded, the NKVD inserted agents into the food distribution network. Around this time, the director of a food wholesale enterprise, B. P. Baranov, and his assistant were arrested for illegal sales of several thousand kilograms of wheat and soy flour, and the director of a food store in the northern part of the city together with his assistant and the store's warehouse manager were arrested for stealing 700 kilograms of food. In another example, employees at the Badaev bakery reportedly stole flour on at least ninety-eight occasions during the winter and spring.[184] In November a crime ring in the Krasnogvardeisky *raion* consisting of the head cook of a cafeteria, the manager of a cafeteria storehouse, a senior accountant of a group of cafeterias, and a factory trade school administrator, among others, managed to steal two metric tons of bread, 1,230 kilograms of meat, and 150 kilograms of sugar before being caught. The food was intended for trade school students. At least three members of the crime ring were executed.[185] The same month, three metric tons of unregistered flour and other foodstuffs were found in the warehouses belonging to Osoaviakhim, the Society for Air and Chemical Defense, which performed civil defense functions and served as a flying club, and to Osoaviakhim's auto club. It was also determined that Osoaviakhim was siphoning off some of the aviation and auto fuel it was supposed to deliver to the front. The chairman of Osoaviakhim's Leningrad *sovet,* one Khropov, his assistant, a Colonel Kucherenko, as well as the group's supply chief, Raevsky, and the auto club's head, Ivanov, were fired. Raevsky tried to flee to the army but was apprehended. The case was turned over to the Military Procuracy in mid-December.[186] Also in November, employees in the Volodarsky print shop systematically stole large quantities of food coupons and conspired with bread store employees to steal about one metric ton of various foods. (See Documents 41 and 42 for further details on food theft by administrative personnel.) As these examples indicate, the motive for some theft was not simply self-preservation but the desire to become wealthy at the expense of starving people. A party summary of the public mood from July 1942 (Document 59) contended that among those who refused to evacuate were "marauders who have taken advantage of this difficult moment . . . to enrich themselves." Upon seeing boys selling hot water for fifty rubles a glass among the throngs of frozen and starved refugees on the eastern shore of Lake Ladoga, Kochina wrote bitterly in her diary: "No doubt there'll be enterprising people even in hell!"[187]

If truck drivers were heroes for braving enemy fire and a melting ice road to make an extra food run into the city or to take an additional truckload of starving people out, an unknown number were motivated at least in part by greed, because bribery and theft were common. As noted above, Kochina had to bribe a truck driver with vodka to secure passage over the lake in early spring 1942. The army controlled the ice road, but right from its beginning the Twenty-third Division of the NKVD was in charge of security.[188] Nikolai Zinoviev, who worked as a transport commissar on the ice road, stated in January 1944 that some drivers accepted bribes and stole food but added that punishments were severe for those caught. He claimed that one driver who accepted a bribe of a watch and two thousand rubles received a sentence of ten years of solitary confinement. He stated that if a driver was charged with food theft, a military tribunal was summoned immediately. If found guilty, the thief was shot in the presence of assembled drivers of the battalion. He cited one specific example in which the convicted thief was made to kneel in the snow as ten executioners fired on him.[189]

Kyra Petrovskaya worked as a nurse on the ice road during the last three weeks of December. In her memoirs she described a scene from the final days of her stint, which suggests that food theft was not uncommon:

Our friend from the field kitchen, Sergeant Kukushkina, brought us a whole ham as a parting gift.

"Where did you get it?" we queried. She only laughed, showing her neat, white teeth.

"Never mind! Just eat it and enjoy it."

"She stole it," said her helper. "We came upon a bombed-out food supply truck. The soldiers were reloading it, so there was plenty of stuff laying [*sic*] around."

"So I grabbed the ham and ran," laughed Kukushkina. "The guys yelled at us, but we just stepped on the gas."

"Don't you want it for yourselves?" asked Zina.

"We have another one!" laughed the helper. "Kukushkina grabbed two hams."

"Might as well. The punishment for stealing would be the same for one as for two," she explained cheerfully.

"What's the punishment?" Zina was curious.

"A firing squad," said Kukushkina simply.

Concerning food theft, Kukushkina added, "We don't do it often."[190]

A secret report written on 24 March 1942, by the chief of police of the Leningrad *oblast'* Nazarov to the *Lenoblispolkom* summarized the known dimensions of theft on the ice road. He noted that altogether 818 people had been detained for food theft, of whom 586 were military personnel. The overwhelming majority of thefts were committed by army drivers. More than thirty-three metric tons of food had been confiscated from those detained. Toward the end of the winter, the police were proving more successful in finding hiding places for stolen food. During the first fifteen days of March, more than half a ton of food was discovered hidden in the snow. Kazarov's report also gave examples of large bribes demanded by drivers. One driver received 14,875 rubles from a group of evacuees.[191]

From the beginning of the blockade, the punishment for food theft was typically eight years in prison; however, starting in November, when the bread ration was cut twice to starvation levels, through the end of the winter, it became a capital offense. In Leningrad during the first two years of the war, 25 percent (508 of 2,005) of those convicted of theft of socialist property and 45.5 percent (425 of 934) of those convicted of burglary (*ograblenie*) were executed.[192] City authorities did not disclose all convictions for theft among food workers; but *Leningradskaia pravda* did occasionally publish exposés on crime. For instance, on 30 October 1941, the newspaper ran an article by the city's police chief Grushko that included description of cafeteria workers who stole food by short-changing people on their food rations. On 6 December, city prosecutor N. Popov published a detailed account of the cafeteria theft in Krasnogvardeisky *raion* noted above. Popov stated that two of the thieves had been shot (the NKVD document cited three executions) and the rest given long prison sentences. The main reason for publicizing punishment for food theft was to deter further crime. Whether that purpose was achieved cannot be measured; however, disclosure of theft among food workers almost assuredly reinforced the widespread perception that the city's network of food production and distribution was riddled with corruption.

Food theft by the general public took many forms. Memoirs include numerous examples of starving teenage pickpockets, including students in industrial trade schools, who snatched rations and ration cards from the unwary around food stores.[193] With shops poorly illuminated and packed with people wearing long loose-hanging coats, it was not very difficult to steal loaves of bread. Kochina described how on 20 December her husband Dima sharpened the end of his walking cane to spear a loaf. ("I found a bread store," he said, "where it's very easy to steal bread. It's as black as pitch there.") The next day as he tried to steal another loaf, a customer saw him. On the street she demanded half of the purloined loaf as her price for not turning him in to the police.[194] Theft of even small amounts of food by the starving populace could result in the death penalty. Secretary Kuznetsov stated in the spring of 1942: "I will tell you plainly that we shot people for stealing a loaf of bread."[195] But, this did not always happen. Kochina's husband in broad daylight walked up to sleds that were used to transport bread to the shops and took a loaf. He was immediately arrested but was subsequently released when he told his police interrogator, who was himself starving, that he was an engineer.[196]

Criminal schemes involved stealing ration cards and coupons, counterfeiting them, and using cards of those who had died. Some people also managed to obtain food in cafeterias without surrendering rationing coupons. To counteract such fraudulent activity, in mid-October 1941, all Leningraders holding ration cards were required to verify their identities in person. After the verification, the number of ration cards issued for bread dropped by 88,000, and for meat by 97,000.[197] This process, however, did not solve the problem. Dark and crowded shops also provided a convenient setting for using counterfeit ration cards. Twenty people were arrested for forging ration cards in November (Document 41). Also in November workers at a print shop stole ration coupons, which they used to obtain about one metric ton of various foods. Occasionally, armed gangs, which included young men who avoided military service and army deserters, attacked shops (Document 42). The NKVD recorded eighty-nine cases of planned robberies of food transports or stores from November 1941 to March 1942.[198] In addition to stealing food, some people resorted to looting possessions from the flats of the deceased, of servicemen at the front, and of those who had been evacuated.

Kochina's recording of her husband's thefts in her diary is exceptional. The natural tendency to omit details that portray oneself, family members, or close friends as less than honorable was accentuated in the Stalinist context, because information from diaries was used as evidence in criminal trials in about a dozen cases. According to the editors of a recent collection of blockade diaries, who have read through many of the approximately two hundred diaries from that period that exist in the libraries and archives in St. Petersburg: "Practically in all of the diaries of the war era an element of severe self-censorship was present."[199] Kochina, however, made a moral distinction between stealing from another starving individual and filching loaves from the city's food supply network. She considered theft from an individual abhorrent, and according to her account, Dima never stole another's food ration or any personal possessions. Yet, they viewed bread shops as fair game, because they were convinced that the sales staff was short-changing them. The bread Dima stole from a shop might well have been stolen by the clerks if he did not take it first. Kochina was confirmed in her suspicion when on 23 November she received a bread ration that was light by a hundred grams. She returned to the shop and demanded the remaining portion from the same saleswoman, who gave it to her without saying a word.[200] Her entry for 23 December reads: "Dima brought a loaf of [stolen] bread again. Well, after all, the salespeople really are robbing us blind. In return for bread they have everything they want. Almost all of them, without any shame at all, wear gold and expensive furs. Some of them work behind the counter in luxurious sable and sealskin coats.[201] On 18 January in order to preserve his own life and save his wife and infant daughter, Dima broke into a factory storeroom that he had been casing and stole some twenty pounds of buckwheat and a bar of coconut butter. The diary indicates that by 23 January, Dima had a new potential problem: "Dima is gaining weight quickly. But he goes without shaving and washing as before, so that the neighbors won't notice this: after all, they could guess that we have provisions and steal them. And perhaps even kill us, who knows!"[202] The buckwheat sustained the family for twenty days through the very worst weeks of the winter.

Document 45 provides a statistical summary of arrests for food-related crimes from the start of the war through September 1942. Of the total of 31,740 people arrested for all crimes by the NKVD and police in that period, over 17,000 were arrested by the police for crimes involving some sort of theft (including speculation, theft of socialist property, and so forth). During the winter, police recovered a total of 455 metric tons of stolen bread, grain, groats, and sugar. For the entire blockade period, the following were confiscated from criminals: 23,317,736 rubles in cash, 4,081,600 rubles in bonds, 73,420 gold rubles, 6,428 carats of diamonds, 1,687 pounds of silver, and 40,846 dollars. In addition, 1,369 gold watches, 11,739 winter coats, 21,989 suits, 10,790 summer coats, and 81,976 women's dresses were confiscated from thieves and black-marketeers.[203]

Cannibalism

The combination of pervasive starvation and the presence on any given day of thousands of corpses, which were well preserved in the cold winter, made the phenomenon of cannibalism a fact of life in the dying city.[204] The thought of consuming human flesh has caused most people throughout recorded history to recoil instinctively in horror. Anthropophagy exists as one of the most fundamental taboos within the human psyche and is generally relegated to the realm of the macabre, something practiced by only the extremely depraved or insane, even when it happens under threat of death from starvation. Perhaps the best-known example of cannibalism in North American history is connected with the ill-fated Donner Party, which became trapped in twenty-foot snow drifts while trying to cross the Sierra Nevada Mountains on their way to California in the winter of 1846–47. Forty-one of the journeying American immigrants died. Many of the survivors endured by feeding on the corpses of their fellow travelers. However, only one of the survivors subsequently spoke openly of eating human flesh, and "he was reviled as a man-eater and ghoul."[205]

Cannibalism had occurred in Soviet history during the great famines of the 1920s and 1930s and in some of the labor camps. Yet, it remained a taboo subject for Soviet historians; scholars of the Leningrad siege were not permitted access to archival documents on cannibalism and were barred from discussing it in their publications. Those prohibitions, like so many others, ended with the Soviet Union. Materials that have become available since 1991 show that cannibalism took several forms. It is likely that thousands of starving Leningraders ate human flesh without knowing it by purchasing meat of unknown origin in black-market exchanges at the city markets, particularly the old Haymarket, which was the busiest place in Leningrad.[206] Many may have suspected that meat they had bought was from a cat or dog or even a human corpse, but they had no way to know for certain.

Another category of cannibals were starving Leningraders, including parents of starving children, who cut flesh from corpses that they came across. On the eve of the war, horses were still used for transportation, and their butchered carcasses could be seen on the street (Figure 37). By

November severed human remains were being discovered, and the first four arrests for consumption of human flesh occurred that month. As starvation spread and corpses accumulated in public places, more of them showed signs of dismemberment. Aleksei Vinokurov, a geography teacher, wrote in his diary on 14 March 1942: "On Pokrovsky [now Turgenev] Square I saw a crowd of people looking quietly at the cut-up corpse of a young, stout woman. Who did this and why? Isn't this confirmation of the persistent rumors of cannibalism?"[207]

Cannibalism occurred where there were large numbers of corpses. Cemetery workers saw evidence of cannibalism as did those who worked at the brick factory that was converted to a massive crematorium.[208] One eyewitness reported seeing fifteen to twenty prisoners in the city's Shpalerny Prison eating corpses in broad daylight during the winter.[209] Yershov, the army food supply officer, described a cannibal ring of some twenty medical workers, including doctors, who he claimed ate corpses, particularly amputated legs. He alleged that all of them were shot by order of the VLSF.[210] In October 1944, Aleksandra Bobina, a prosecutor for Petrogradskaia Storona *raion,* described the case of a hospital worker who ate corpses. "Yukhnevich" pulled gold fillings from cadavers and stole the bodies of small children, which he dismembered. At home he and his young daughter ate the body parts. He was apprehended and shot. It could not be shown that the daughter knew she had consumed human flesh, and it appears that she was released.[211] Another source contends that a student and four research assistants from the anatomy department of a Leningrad pediatric clinic ate cadavers.[212]

NKVD records show how arrests for *liudoedstvo* ("people eating") increased through the winter before declining in the spring:

December 1941	43
January 1942	366
February	612
March	399
April	300
May	326

The NKVD, which created a special group for investigating cannibalism, tabulated the arrests in ten-day intervals. The interval when the most arrests (311) were made was 1–10 February.[213]

A top secret report from Leningrad's military procurator, A. Panfilenko, to Kuznetsov on 21 February (Document 53) provides a demographic profile of those arrested for cannibalism. Although the report deals with *liudoedstvo* generally and does not specify the various forms it took (murder and cannibalism, dismembering a corpse for food, and so forth), it can be concluded that the main motive for consuming human flesh was self-preservation and protection of one's children. Almost two-thirds of those prosecuted for cannibalism were women; 85 percent were refugees from other areas; over half were either unemployed or "without definite employment"; and only 2 percent had any prior conviction. In other words, a substantial proportion of those prosecuted for cannibalism were ordinary women with little or no means of subsistence who had sought refuge within Leningrad but had not managed to be evacuated before the start of the blockade. Probably many of them did not have ration cards. They were desperate for nourishment and to feed their children any way they could. These people had few, if any, alternatives. They were not "ghouls."[214] Most were probably ordinary people caught in circumstances of extraordinary deprivation. As Dmitry Likhachev, the renowned authority on Old Russian literature who survived the blockade, stated in his memoirs: "When your child is dying and you know that only meat will save it—you'll cut some off a corpse."[215]

Panfilenko wrote his report while a special conference of eight top medical experts was meeting between 20 and 23 February. The conference was chaired by Lieutenant Colonel Dr. David Verkhovsky, head of the Military-Sanitary Administration of the Leningrad Front, and included at least two prominent psychiatrists. The purpose of the conference was to provide advice to prosecutors and military tribunals on how to adjudicate cases of cannibalism. Presumably, the medical experts received a copy of Panfilenko's report. If so, it helped them assess the state of mind of the accused cannibals. The authorities wanted advice on whether people who ate flesh from corpses could be considered "mentally [*dushevno*] healthy people," and therefore responsible for their actions, and whether such people would be "socially dangerous" in the future. The experts concluded that psychiatrists and psychologists must consider very carefully each instance of cannibalism. In cases involving teenagers, pediatric psychiatrists should be consulted. They also advised that most cases of corpse eating were committed by people who were essentially sound mentally but who were somewhat degraded. Finally, they concurred that all manifestations of cannibalism presented an indisputable danger to the social order and had to be isolated, but that each case should be decided individually.

Historian Dzeniskevich states that "the recommendations of the conference henceforth were used in the work of the prosecutor's office and by the military tribunals."[216] It would appear that the medical conference influenced military tribunals to treat convicted cannibals more leniently. Up to the time of the conference, according to a report that Kubatkin sent to Beria on 23 February, of 554 people who had been charged with cannibalism or murder-cannibalism and whose cases had been sent to the tribunals,

329 were executed (59.4 percent). Between 23 February and 2 June 1942, according to Kubatkin, the cases of an additional 1,359 people charged with the same offenses were sent to the tribunals, resulting in 257 executions (18.9 percent).[217]

· Document 53 ·

Memorandum from Military Procurator A. I. Panfilenko to Kuznetsov on cannibalism (*liudoedstvo*), 21 February 1942, TsGAIPD SPb, f. 24, op. 2b, d. 1319, ll. 38–46, in Dzeniskevich, *Leningrad v osade*, 421–22.

Top secret

In the conditions of Leningrad's special situation, created by the war with fascist Germany, a new type of crime has arisen. [. . .]

All murders for the purpose of eating dead people's flesh, due to their special danger, have been classified as banditry (Art. 59-3, UK RSFSR [Criminal Code of the Russian Union of Federated Soviet Republics]).

Bearing in mind at the same time that the overwhelming majority of the above-mentioned type of crimes concerned the eating of corpse flesh, the Leningrad City Prosecutor's Office, guided by the fact that by their very nature these crimes pose a special danger to orderly administration, has classified them, by analogy, with banditry (under Art. 16-59-3 UK).[218]

Ever since this type of crime arose in Leningrad, i.e., from early December[219] 1941 through 15 February 1942, the investigative organs have brought to criminal account for commission of these crimes the following: in December 1941, 26 people;[220] in January 1942, 366 people; and in the first 15 days of February 1942, 494 people.

Entire groups of individuals have participated in a number of murders for the purpose of eating human flesh as well as in the crimes of eating corpse flesh.

In individual instances, the individuals who have committed crimes like this have not only eaten corpse flesh themselves but have sold it to other citizens. . . .

The social makeup of the individuals handed over for trial for committing the above-mentioned types of crimes is characterized by the following data:

   1. By sex:
       men — 322 (36.5%) and
       women — 564 (63.5%).
   2. By age:
       16–20 — 192 (21.6%)
       20–30 — 204 (23.0%)
       30–40 — 235 (26.4%)
       over 40 — 255 (29.0%)
   3. By party membership:
       VKP(b) members and candidates members   — 11 (1.24%)

| VLKSM [Komsomol] members | −4 (0.4%) |
| non–party members | −871 (98.51%) |

4. By type of employment, those brought to criminal account are distributed in the following manner:

workers	−363 (41.0%)
office workers	−40 (4.5%)
peasants	−6 (0.7%)
unemployed	−202 (22.4%)
individuals without definite employment	−275 (31.4%)

Those brought to criminal account for commission of the above-mentioned crimes include specialists with a higher education. [. . .]

Of the total number of those brought to criminal account for the indicated category of cases, 131 (14.7%) were born in Leningrad (natives). The remaining 755 (85.3%) arrived in Leningrad at various times. Moreover, they include 169 natives of Leningrad *Oblast'*, 163 from Kalinin *Oblast'*, 38 from Yaroslavl *Oblast'*, and 516 from other *oblasti*.

Of the 886 people brought to criminal account, only 18 (2%) had a criminal record.

As of 20 February 1942, 311 people had been convicted by the Military Tribunal of the above-mentioned crimes.[221]

Leningrad City Military Procurator Brigade Military Counsel A. Panfilenko

As the report indicates, motives for cutting flesh off human corpses extended beyond simple survival. Some sought to make a profit by selling the meat they obtained, and the hospital worker "Yukhnevich" described above probably sold the gold he extracted from corpses' teeth. There were others who were not content with cannibalizing a corpse they happened to find but committed murder as a means to obtain human flesh. (560 murders were reportedly committed in 1942, although not all were connected with cannibalism.)[222] Murderer-cannibals might themselves consume the flesh of their victims and/or prepare it for sale. Document 54 is the first known account of acts of cannibalism and murder-cannibalism that was sent to Moscow. Kubatkin kept Beria well informed of the grotesque effects of starvation in Leningrad.[223]

· Document 54 ·

Report from Kubatkin to Beria and his deputy Merkulov detailing nine
cases of cannibalism, most of which involved murder, 13 December 1941,
Arkhiv UFSB RF po SPb i LO f. 21/12, op. 2, p.n. 19, d. 12, ll. 91–92.

SENT TO: Moscow, USSR NKVD, Com. BERIA
Kuibyshev, USSR NKVD, Com. MERKULOV

In connection with the food difficulties in Leningrad, nine instances of cannibalism have occurred recently.

1. K.—born 1912, Red Army soldier's wife, suffocated her younger daughter, aged a year and a half. Used the corpse to prepare food for herself and her three children.

2. K.—previously treated at the Psychiatric Hospital, on 27 November killed his two daughters, aged seven years and one year. K. ate some of the corpse of the older daughter.

3. On 30 November, temporary unemployed V., who previously had worked as a master in a tire factory, killed Z., born 1923, a worker at the same factory who had been living with him. V. testified that he had committed the murder in connection with the fact that he was starving and intended to eat the corpse of Z.

4. On 2 December, A., a worker at the K. Marx Factory, and his son Anatoly, born 1925, a metalworker at the same factory, killed two women who were living in their apartment, P. and M. U. They ate some parts of P.'s corpse.

5. On 6 December, in a tramcar, a bag was discovered containing the bones of a man and a charred human head. Expert analysis established that the bones had been cooked, stripped of flesh, and partially picked clean.

6. On 6 December, B., a former plumber at a packing plant, killed his wife. He cooked and ate parts of it and fed it to his son, a metalworker at the Kirov plant, and his two nephews, workers at the Proletarian Victory plant, and told his son and nephews that he was feeding them meat from a killed dog he had bought.

7. On 11 December, B., born 1911, a rate-setter at the SVERDLOV factory, in his wife's absence, killed their two sons, ages four years and 10 months, with an ax. He used the corpse of the younger son for food.

8. On 8 December, S., born 1904, a shipbuilding engineer, unemployed for the last three months, showed up at the morgue of the Bogoslovskoe Cemetery. S. stated that he supposedly was a resident of a workers' dormitory and identified a woman who had gone missing from the dormitory. After taking receipt of the unknown woman's corpse, supposedly for the purpose of burying it, S. took it to his apartment, cut it into pieces, took out the liver and heart, cooked them, and ate them.

9. On 12 December, at the Bolshevik factory, in the locker of milling machine operator K., a man's leg wrapped in a cloth was discovered. Based on the direction of K. himself, two more human legs were found behind the factory fence, wrapped up in a sack. K. testified that on 12 December he had chopped these three legs off unburied corpses at the Serafimovskoe Cemetery for the purpose of using them as food.

All the criminals have been arrested and handed over for trial to the Military Tribunal. The Military Tribunal has heard the case of K.[the first case mentioned], and K. has been sentenced to VMN [execution].

HEAD OF THE NKVD LO ADMINISTRATION
State Security Commissar 3rd rank
KUBATKIN
Correct: HEAD OF THE UNKVD LO SECRETARIAT
State Security First Lieutenant
TSYGANOV

Kubatkin filed another report of a similar nature after the starvation rate had begun to recede in the spring. The report was sent only to VSLF leaders, but a copy of it may have been included later in correspondence to Beria. A difference in the profile of the alleged perpetrators is that all but one of those identified in the December document were male; whereas all six convicted murderer-cannibals in the May document were women of child-bearing age. This difference is consistent with the fact that women endured the effects of starvation longer than did men. The place of arrest in the second document is probably significant. The Pargolovsky *raion*, located north of Leningrad proper, contained thousands of inhabitants of the Karelian Isthmus who had fled south before the Finnish advance. The latter three arrestees, who were "without definite employment," were likely refugees.[224]

· Document 55 ·

Report from Kubatkin to Zhdanov, Kuznetsov, and Khozin on a band of murderer-cannibals in the northern suburban Pargolovsky *raion*, 2 May 1942, Arkhiv UFSB RF po SPb i LO f. 21/12, op. 2, p.n. 19, d. 12, ll. 264–65.

Top Secret

In Razliv village, Pargolovsky *raion*, a band of murderer-cannibals has been arrested:

V.—born 1921, b/p [not a party member], lineman, Finliandskaia Line, Oktiabrskaia Railroad;

Sh.—born 1913, b/p, lineman, Finliandskaia Line, Oktiabrskaia Railroad;

K.—born 1909, b/p, guard, Finliandskaia Line, Oktiabrskaia Railroad;

Sh.—born 1917,

G.—born 1917,

K.—born 1910,

all three b/p, without definite employment.

During the months January–March of this year, this band committed murders of citizens residing in Razliv village and in the town of Sestroretsk and used the corpses of the murdered people for food.

The band's participants would visit bread and food stores, mark their victim, and lured her to G.'s apartment, supposedly to exchange items for food.

During conversation in G.'s apartment, V., a female band participant, would commit the murder with a blow of an ax to the back of the head. Band members dismembered the corpses of the dead women and used them for food. They shared the clothing, money, and food cards among themselves.

During the months January–March, band members murdered 13 people. In addition, they stole 2 corpses from a cemetery and used them for food.

The Military Tribunal sentenced all 6 participants to death by firing squad. The sentence has been carried out.

> HEAD OF THE NKVD LO ADMINISTRATION
> STATE SECURITY COMMISSAR 3RD RANK
> KUBATKIN

Sent to:
Com. ZHDANOV
Com. KHOZIN
Com. KUZNETSOV

Examples of medical personnel who ate cadavers have already been cited. There may also have been instances of murder-cannibalism in or near hospitals, as Kochina's diary entry from 12 January suggests: "I took Lena to the clinic. Waiting for the doctor, I put her on the table. 'Don't leave the child unattended,' a nurse whispered, coming up to me. 'We've had cases of children being kidnapped.'"[225]

Yershov claimed that murder to consume flesh also occurred in the army. He alleged that in January twenty food couriers from his division, which was stationed south of Leningrad near Kolpino, were ambushed and killed, and their bodies eaten by isolated pockets of Red Army troops.[226]

Official data on the number of people arrested and convicted for cannibalism and the sentences they received are not consistent. An appendix to a report by the city's military procurator, Kuzmin, from the latter half of 1943 states that from 1 July 1941 through 1 July 1943, military tribunals convicted 1,700 people under the "special category" of article 16-59-3 of the criminal code, which was the designation for cannibalism. Of that number, 364 were executed, and the remaining 1,336 were imprisoned.[227] However, a report from Kubatkin to leaders of the VSLF from 2 June 1942, states that up to that time 1,965 people had been arrested for "using human flesh as food." Investigation into the cases of 1,913 of the arrestees had been completed. The Military Tribunal had sentenced 586 to be executed and 668 to prison terms of varying lengths.[228] The inconsistency in the number executed cannot be easily reconciled. The first set of data derives from a report on "Judicial Repression by Military Tribunals for Cases Considered from 1 July 1941 to 1 July 1943." Dzeniskevich commented that the figure of 2,093 executions determined by the tribunals for all capital offenses contained in that report is lower than cited elsewhere.[229] Kuzmin's report may contain important omissions.

The two sets of data might, however, be reconciled various ways. Some cannibals were shot immediately upon being apprehended.[230] It may be that the higher figure for executions includes those who were summarily shot, while the lower figure represents only those whose cases were actually considered by the tribunals. It is also possible that some of those sentenced to be shot died in prison before they could be executed. Kubatkin's report noted that 586 *had been sentenced to* execution, while Kuzmin's report referred to *measures of punishment,* with the implication that the sentences had actually been carried out. Another report by Kubatkin from 10 February 1942 states that a total of 724 people had been arrested for cannibalism, of whom forty-five had died in prison.[231] It is also possible, though unlikely, that the sentences of some of those who were condemned to be shot were commuted to prison terms.

The data raise other important points. Although historians have contended that all apprehended cannibals were shot, the data show that regardless of how many were actually executed, the number represented only a fraction of those arrested for consuming human flesh.[232] In Kuzmin's report, 21.4 percent of the arrestees were executed; according to Kubatkin's data from early June 1942, 30.6 percent of completed cases resulted in a death sentence. The alternative punishment was generally a ten-year prison term,[233] which, it is safe to guess, few inmates managed to survive. What the determining factors were in sentencing cannibals is not known; however, it would seem likely that those who had only consumed human flesh were treated less harshly than those who also committed murder or sold meat from corpses.

There is also the matter that Kubatkin's data do not account for the fate of 659 people, the investigation of whose cases had been completed, but who had been neither executed nor sentenced to prison. Undoubtedly, some of them perished in prison while their cases were being considered. Hundreds of others, however, must have been sentenced after Kubatkin submitted his report on 2 June 1942. Kubatkin noted that 668 cannibals had been sentenced to prison, but more that a year later, Kuzmin stated that 1,336 received prison terms. The increase in the number of convicts was not caused by many further arrests for cannibalism. Those arrests dropped off sharply from the summer of 1942. In July, only fifteen people were arrested for cannibalism; in August, four. Arrests may have risen somewhat during the second siege winter; however, only two people were arrested for committing acts of murder and cannibalism in December 1942.[234] An important part of the reason why 659 cases had not been adjudicated by early June 1942 was that the military tribunals in general devoted considerable attention to cases of alleged cannibalism, at least from the end of February. Assembling expert medical testimony for individual cases and evaluating it took time.

Altogether, according to NKVD reports, around 2,000 people in Leningrad were arrested for cannibalism. The fact that the large majority were convicted and sentenced to prison, including even the tragic cases of destitute mothers who cut meat from corpses simply to feed themselves and their starving children, is confirmation that the official view that "by their very nature these crimes pose a special danger to orderly administration" (Document 53) was enforced. No matter how understandable the motive, cannibalism was fought aggressively by the NKVD. As noted above, according to Kuzmin, 1,700 people were convicted under the "special category" of banditism. If Kubatkin's data are consistent with Kuzmin's report, there were about 300 arrestees who were not convicted. It is likely that many died before their cases were tried; others may have been released from custody following a period of counseling. The panel of medical experts recommended that the length of time that people who ate from corpses should be "isolated" from society ought to depend on the specific circumstances involved and the background of the accused.[235] The advice did not rule out the possibility of release.

Generosity of Others

The keys to survival discussed thus far consist of conscious decisions that people made to protect themselves. Of course, there is no way to determine what percentage of Leningrad's population made self-preservation its top priority. As in any massive human catastrophe, in the siege of Leningrad one can find examples of very selfish activity as well as striking examples of selflessness. Untold thousands of Leningraders survived through the generosity of others. Such actions, which sought no reward or even recognition in return, are difficult for the historian to uncover and impossible to quantify. The hungry winter was a time when the most seemingly minor acts of generosity or selfishness produced great consequences. Lev Pevzner, who worked in a prosecutor's office during the blockade and later became a Soviet defense attorney of some notoriety before emigrating to the United States, often spoke with students at Indiana University of the starvation winter. He recalled that one day as he was slowly trudging across the city in an exhausted and emaciated state, he decided to rest for a while against a metal grill in a snow bank. A sense of resigned contentment came over him, and he may have begun to drift into unconsciousness. A woman, who apparently saw him sink down, approached and yelled sharply at him to get up. He did, and she helped him home. Pevzner reckoned that she likely saved his life, that in a few moments he might have quietly slipped away as many thousands did.[236] Adamovich and Granin stated in their collection of accounts by siege survivors that "each had a savior,"[237] such as parents who saved meager meals they received at work for their starving children

or truck drivers who made extra trips across Lake Ladoga to bring food
into the city and take starving refugees out at the risk of crashing through
melting ice and/or being targeted by enemy aircraft. Siege survivor Svetlana Pronberg was thirteen years old during the starvation winter. In an
interview in 2003, she recalled that before the war two elderly spinsters
were neighbors of her family. They had a dog of which they were especially
fond: "At the peak of the hungriest blockade winter of 1941 to 1942, my
sister and I were almost dying from hunger. Then the two ladies brought
us their dog. They said they could not eat the dog themselves, but they
gave it to us so that we would survive."[238] Siege survivor Liudmila Bokshitskaia remembered: "Our neighbor Nadezhda Kupriyanova came into
our room. She decided that we were dead, since in our apartment, where
a lot of people had been living, there seemed to be no one left alive. . . .
Seeing that we had already 'taken to our beds,' that we were indifferent to
our own condition, she went out, saying that she was not going to let the
family . . . die. She soon came back, bringing some firewood. She lit the
stove and fetched some water. Then, saying that she had been given a rabbit
at the military hospital where she worked, she put it in a pot on the stove.
While the soup was cooking, she washed us. . . . She didn't tell us it was a
cat . . . until we had eaten it. That dinner and our neighbor's care kept us
going until the 10th of January 1942."[239] Such acts of kindness became defining moments in people's lives and shaped personal relationships from
that time onward.

Generosity, of course, was not limited to one-time deeds. One of the
most widely practiced forms of self-sacrifice, which was also one of the
most profound, was the care that mothers provided for their children.
While often simultaneously caring for a starving husband or other relatives, mothers endured extraordinary hardship in trying to keep their children alive. Routine care became extremely arduous. Kochina wrote in her
diary on 11 January: "Lena is even worse. She is constantly throwing up a
foul-smelling green slime. I have to change her diapers and shirts often. In
order to prevent her from catching a cold in the process, I throw a quilted
blanket over her and crawl under it. The result is something like playing
in the dark. I crawl out red, disheveled, and smeared with excrement. I
wash the diapers in ice water. My hands have deep cracks in the skin from
this—the flesh is visible. When I plunge them into the icy water, I wail from
the unbearable pain. But that's only for the first few seconds. Then it gets
better."[240] In this entry Kochina did not describe the even greater ordeal of
fetching the water to change the diapers.

The efforts of Kochina and other parents were remarkable; yet, one ex-
pects parents to make major sacrifices for their children. Another form of
ongoing generosity was extraordinary: strangers caring for some of the

many thousands of orphaned, unattended, and/or homeless children who were not placed in city-run children's homes. Kyra Petrovskaya, whose mother had been killed while digging trenches outside Leningrad, took in a homeless youngster named Shurik Nikanorov. She found him digging under the rubble of his bombed apartment home searching for his mother. Shurik's father was a sergeant in a tank battalion at the front. Petrovskaya nursed Shurik back to health and cared for him through the hungry winter until he was evacuated the following June to the Urals with a convalescing soldier who adopted him.[241] Petrovskaya survived the war but never saw Shurik again.

Stress Management and a Reason to Live

Survival did not depend entirely on the external factors of food, warmth, shelter, and the generosity of others. Survival also depended in part on one's state of mind. Dr. Magaeva, who nearly starved to death in the blockade as a child, has explored the effects of emotional stress on survival in the siege. Her starting point is the simple and valid observation that "some extremely emaciated people survived when less emaciated ones died," and she recalled from her own experience in a children's home during the siege that two girls, who were not starving, suddenly died following an air raid in which they were not injured. Their death, she asserts, "must have been connected with fear of death." She also claims that a psychosomatic connection exists between anxiety and death by starvation. She states that "those who acutely felt alarm and fear" were physically weakened to the extent that "nutritional dystrophy could take a more severe course."[242] Prolonged apprehension could also lead to an overwhelming sense of impending doom and a desire to be liberated at any cost from bombardment, hunger, and cold, which in turn often induced a state of profound psychological resignation (like that described by Lev Pevzner). Siege accounts are full of examples of Leningraders who drifted into a state of listlessness and apathy in which they became flaccid, losing muscle tone right before they lost consciousness and died. Typically they took to their beds ("to lie down and wait" was a phrase often used) and became increasingly uncommunicative, finally giving the impression "of being barely alive, scarcely reacting to external stimuli." This last stage of starvation could last between a few days and several weeks.[243]

While stress could literally kill, Magaeva contends that successfully controlling it could sustain life by means of unlocking what she calls "latent reserves." She cites a Professor M. V. Chernorutsky, a retired therapist who survived the siege, who attested to the power of mind over body: "We saw quite a few cases in which, when other conditions were equal, a weakening of the will to live, depression and giving up the routine of ordinary living considerably hastened the course of the disease and led to a sharp deterioration in the general condition of the patients, and brought forward an unfavourable outcome. Conversely, a firm and purposeful will to live, cheerfulness, continual optimism and an invariable pattern of organized life and work, seemingly gave it new strength."[244] As the winter progressed, Leningraders became adept at detecting these signs of "giving up," and the authorities understood the importance of maintaining a sense of dignity and self-worth. Propagandists encouraged the populace to preserve a positive attitude in many ways, including by maintaining a clean, neat, and groomed appearance.

One important key to diminishing the fear of death and thereby relieving the stress produced by blockade conditions was to impute special significance to one's own survival by viewing it as the necessary means of achieving the greater goal of saving others. In Magaeva's words, "I am convinced that holding on to a reason for living may help in overcoming nutritional dystrophy. . . . There is . . . every reason to assume that the greatest humanity of spirit may be manifested under extreme conditions and may be the key to maintaining psychosomatic interrelationships within limits that preclude the development of irreversible disorders."[245] That is to say, the beneficiaries of generous acts were not only those on the receiving end but also to some extent those who gave of themselves. As noted above, among civilians within the blockade zone probably no group was more inclined to display that nurturing, selfless "humanity of spirit" than mothers of young children. Another group whose actions were characterized by repeated acts of self-sacrifice was doctors—both practicing physicians and medical researchers—although, as has been observed, they could afford to be relatively generous as they often had access to extra food, heated work places, and, of course, the best supply of medicine. Their devotion to their patients and to their research often constituted their will to survive. Professor Vladimir Garshin was a pathologist, who attempted to improve the procedures for caring for starvation sufferers: "all I had left was my will, and that was what compelled me to work. . . . I saw the same thing in others."[246]

A critically minded student of the blockade might be skeptical of Magaeva's thesis that "latent reserves" exist that are triggered in the most adverse circumstances and make one stronger. She does not definitively explain what the reserves are or how, if they exist, they are activated. Moreover, her emphasis on "humanity of spirit" as a source of resiliency coincides closely with the prescribed emphasis in Soviet historiography on the "heroic" sacrifices of ordinary blockade survivors. Yet, the scripted Soviet theme contained some truth. There are too many examples from diaries and memoirs and Soviet archives of Leningraders fiercely devoting themselves to the survival of others, and thereby increasing in their own eyes the importance of their own survival. Furthermore, it is certainly true that those who became resigned to their own demise were more likely, all else being equal, to perish.

To what extent having a reason to live increased one's chances of survival in the siege cannot be measured or even roughly approximated. And, whatever benefits Magaeva's "latent reserves" provided were diminished by the costs of self-sacrifice. The mother who gave her factory rations to her child was deliberately starving herself.

Conclusion: Survival and the State

Official policy on food distribution was largely egalitarian. The state provided practically the same food rations for everyone trapped within the blockade zone, except for military personnel, workers, engineers, and technicians, who received more food, and unregistered refugees who received no rations. It is no surprise that the military received top priority in food distribution, and soldiers and sailors who did not engage in combat survived at a much higher rate than civilians. Workers, engineers, and technicians—and there were vastly more workers than engineers and technicians—were favored for at least two reasons. Their work was deemed critical for the war effort, and they, especially workers, were expected to work harder than office workers or nonemployed people. A possible third reason was that they were considered to be the most politically reliable element in the civilian population, since most party members came from their ranks. Yet, despite the preferential treatment, workers as a whole did not have significantly higher survival rates than lower-priority groups, and workers at major defense plants had at best only a marginally greater chance of surviving.

The food rations by themselves were insufficient to sustain most civilians. In addition, the state could not provide sufficient access to clean water or enough heated living or work space during the first blockade winter. The official policy that proved most effective in saving lives was the massive evacuation across the Ladoga ice road. It did provide an exodus for over half a million civilians; however, its effectiveness was limited by the fact that it became fully operational only toward the end of January, when the starvation was at its peak. An undetermined number of those who traveled the ice road died en route or at their evacuation destinations. In addition, the process was only partly successful in evacuating targeted groups. Those who succeeded in reaching the eastern shore of the lake were often those who were the most persistent, patient, and resourceful.

To a great extent, Leningraders were left on their own to contend with the hunger and cold. Survival depended largely on spontaneous, individual initiative, which included legal means, such as hoarding food, seeking out and securing a job that provided warmth and extra food without much extra work, and planting a garden in the spring; quasi-legal means, such as bartering for food; as well as theft and other criminal activity. Circumstances or luck was also a factor. Assistance from a generous friend or even a stranger or having the good fortune to work with edible products prior to the start of the siege saved many. Finally, biological characteristics (sex, age, general state of health on the eve of the starvation period) and one's psychological and moral character were important contributing factors in determining who survived the hungry winter. As a result, during the first winter of the war there was considerable variation in survival rates among different groups of the population.

Figure 1. Andrei Zhdanov, leader of
the Leningrad Party Organization
during the blockade. Courtesy of
Nikita Lomagin.

Figure 2. Aleksei Kuznetsov, second
secretary of the Leningrad Party
Organization during the blockade.
Courtesy of Nikita Lomagin.

Figure 3. Pyotr Kubatkin, head of the Leningrad section of the NKVD during
the blockade. Pictures show him before and after his arrest in 1949 as part
of the Leningrad Affair. Courtesy of Nikita Lomagin.

Figure 4. Kliment Voroshilov, commander of the Leningrad Front during the summer of 1941. He returned to coordinate Operation Iskra in the winter of 1942–43. Courtesy of Nikita Lomagin.

Figure 5. Georgy Zhukov, commander of the Leningrad Front during the critical month of September 1941. He also took over running Operation Iskra from Voroshilov in January 1943. Courtesy of Nikita Lomagin.

Figure 6. Leonid Govorov, commander of the Leningrad Front from 1942 to 1945. Courtesy of Nikita Lomagin.

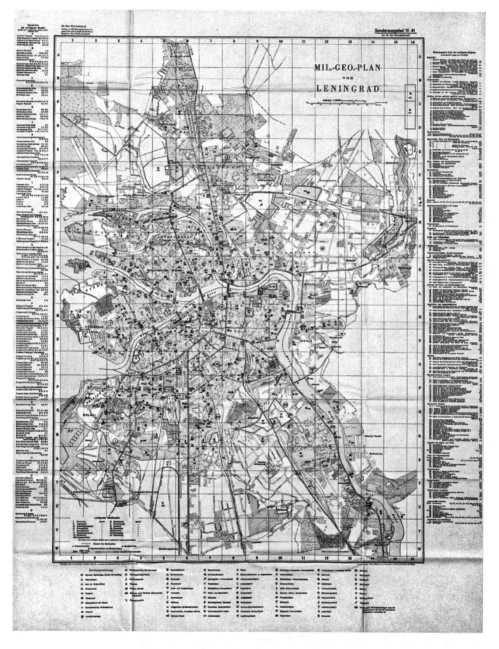

Figure 7. Detailed German map of Leningrad from April 1941 showing key military-industrial installations. It was superimposed on a 1936 Soviet map of Leningrad that was published in 10,000 copies. Germany, Bundesarchiv, Militärarchiv H29/ID2.20.

Figure 8. German aerial reconnaissance photo of Leningrad focusing on the city's southern industrial districts, taken at 6:26 A.M. on 30 May 1943. U.S. National Archives 373, GX3211–1119 Sk, exp. 17.

Figure 9. German aerial reconnaissance photo of the Kirov factory, taken at 10:35 A.M. on 15 September 1942. At least twenty-two other factories had been similarly photographed and analyzed in June 1942. U.S. National Archives 373, DT-TM5–6462.

Figure 10. Workers at a mass meeting at the Stalin metal works on 23 June 1941 receive information about the German invasion. TsGAKFFD, Ar 99384 (Box 300).

Figure 11. Milling machine operator Vladimir Goncharov leaves the Sverdlov machine construction factory on the second day of the war to volunteer for what will become the *opolchenie*. He shakes hands with his Stakhanovite foreman, V. I. Kuznetsov, who had fought in the Civil War. Admiring co-workers look on. TsGAKFFD, Ar28162 (Box 300).

Figure 12. Timofei Semenov worked at the Skorokhod ("Fleetfoot") shoe factory for fifty years before retiring in April 1941. He returned to the plant shortly after the start of the war. His daughter worked at the factory and so had his son, who, when this picture was taken on 9 July 1941, had become a decorated pilot. TsGAKFFD, Ar34395 (Box 300).

Figure 13. Two third-year students of the Philological Department of Leningrad State University, V. V. Geidina and P. I. Pavlenko, are shown during the first week of the war. They have volunteered as army nurses. TsGAKFFD, Ar24484 (Box 294).

Figure 14. D. M. Gagarina and her husband A. N. Gagarin, a Kirov worker, serve in the *opolchenie*, 8 July 1942. TsGAKFFD, Ar7525 (Box 294).

Figure 15. Evacuation of children in the summer of 1941. TsGAKFFD, Vr31952 (Box 295).

Figure 16. Women and children refugees near Lake Ladoga, July 1941. TsGAKFFD, Ar16835 (Box 295).

Figure 17. An unidentified Russian boy in German-controlled territory near Leningrad. U.S. National Archives 242-GAP-266-A-11.

Figure 18. Aleksandra Ivanovna Solovieva says farewell to her son on 10 July 1941, before he leaves with an *opolchenie* unit for the front. TsGAKFFD, Vr17440 (Box 294).

Figure 19. *Opolchenie* soldiers heading for the front during the summer of 1941. TsGAKFFD, Ar66412 (Box 294).

Figure 20. After completing their work shift on 8 August 1941, two men in a slit trench learn how to try to disable a tank at close range with hand grenades. Their fellow workers look on. TsGAKFFD, Ar24407 (Box 294).

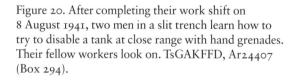

Figure 21. A Soviet fortified firing point outside Leningrad. U.S. National Archives 242-GAP-232-E-22.

Figure 22. Workers of the Petrogradskaia Storona *raion* digging communication trenches on 23 November 1941. TsGAKFFD, Ar10058 (Miscellaneous collection).

Figure 23. An armed detachment of Kirov workers in front of their factory in September 1941. TsGAKFFD, Gr21669 (Box 294).

Figure 24. Obligatory military training in front of the Kazan Cathedral, adorned with pictures of Stalin and Zhdanov and other posters on 23 October 1941. TsGAKFFD, Ar45799 (Box 294).

Figure 25. P. Kolosov, a trade school student in Frunzensky *raion*, prepares to defend Leningrad in October 1941. TsGAKFFD, Ar24440 (Box 294).

(left) Figure 26. Stakhanovite lathe operator S. K. Kozlov at the Maks Gelts factory is shown fulfilling his work quota at 200 percent on 5 October 1941. The fact that he had three sons at the front likely accounts for his grim expression. TsGAKFFD, Ar22754 (Box 300).

(below) Figure 27. Foreman S. V. Pivovarov inspects machine guns at the Voskov Works in Sestroretsk along the Finnish Gulf north of Leningrad near the Finnish front on 8 October 1941. TsGAKFFD, Ar10106 (Box 300).

Figure 28. A BT-5 light tank is driven through Leningrad to the front on 7 November 1941. TsGAKFFD, Ar28224 (Box 294).

Figure 29. Bomb damage, September 1941. TsGAKFFD, Ar17086 (Box 305).

Figure 30. Two women sit among the ruins of their apartment, which was hit by enemy fire in 1942. TsGAKFFD, Ar99428 (Box 305).

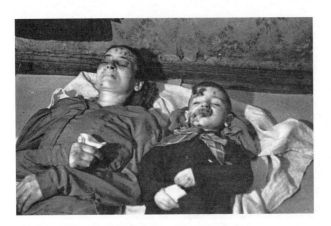

Figure 31. The bodies of a woman named Ivanova and her four-year-old son. They and others were killed by a bomb that hit their home at 16 Saperny Lane on the night of 13–14 November 1941. TsGAKFFD, Ar10397 (Box 306).

Figure 32. An elephant in the city zoo was killed in an air raid on 10 September 1941. TsGAKFFD, Gr82347 (Box 300).

Figure 33. A starving man has just received his bread ration on 7 April 1942. TsGAKFFD, Ar10247 (Box 246).

Figure 34. Trams and trolleybuses, including this one on
Nevsky Prospect, shut down during the winter of 1941–42
due to shortage of electricity. TsGAKFFD, Ar99177
(Box 306).

Figure 35. Fetching water from an underground pipe on Nevsky
Prospect in early 1942. TsGAKFFD, Ar99414 (Box 306).

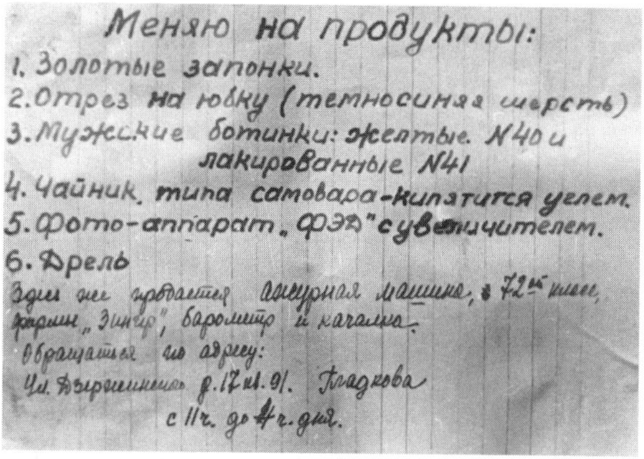

Меняю на продукты:
1. Золотые запонки.
2. Отрез на юбку (темносиняя шерсть)
3. Мужские ботинки: желтые. №40 и
     лакированные №41
4. Чайник, типа самовара-кипятится углем.
5. Фото-аппарат „ФЭД" с увеличителем.
6. Дрель

Figure 36. A handwritten note in downtown Leningrad on 6 February 1942 offering to trade various items for food. See above, p. 303, for translation. TsGAKFFD, Ar26840 (Box 306).

Figure 37. Two women cut meat from a dead horse on a street in early 1942. A human corpse lies nearby. TsGAKFFD, Ar99412 (Box 306).

Figure 38. Vehicles on the Ladoga ice road in 1942. The sign points toward Kobona on the lake's eastern shore. (Note that the signpost in Russian is misspelled.) TsGAKFFD, Ar8533 (Box 295).

Figure 39. Truck crossing the melting Ladoga ice road in the spring of 1942. TsGAKFFD, Ar77824 (Box 295).

Figure 40. On 12 December 1941, when food rations were at their lowest level and mass starvation had set in, a robust senior shift foreman, V. A. Abakumov, inspects products at the Mikoyan candy factory. TsGAKFFD, Ar26641 (Box 300).

Figure 42. A well-fed baker in starving Kolpino, south of Leningrad right near the front, shows off her work during the starvation month of February 1942. TsGAKFFD, Ar27057 (Box 300).

Figure 41. Workshop head Ia. N. Reingold of Vkusprom ("Taste Works") and the plant's corpulent chief of technical control I. V. Brun sample sour cream from a large vat on 23 April 1942. TsGAKFFD, Ar22407 (Box 300).

Figure 43. Aleksei Kuznetsov and a rotund Andrei Zhdanov in 1942. TsGAKFFD, Ar145152 (Box Zh).

Figure 44. A woman pulls a weakened man on a child's sled on 7 April 1942. TsGAKFFD, Ar10246 (Box 306).

Figure 45. A woman pushes a shrouded corpse on a cart along October 25th Prospect (Nevsky Prospect) on 12 April 1942. TsGAKFFD, Ar26839 (Box 306).

Figure 46. Transporting a corpse for burial in May 1942. TsGAKFFD, Ar20901.

Figure 47. Corpses piled at Kobona Station along the eastern shore of Lake Ladoga on 12 April 1942. TsGAKFFD, Ar10253 (Box 306).

Figure 48. Leningraders take part in a massive effort
to clear the city of ice and other debris on Volodarsky
Prospect on Sunday, 8 March 1942, which happened to
be International Women's Day. TsGAKFFD, Ar14899
(Box 300).

Figure 49. Factory workers from the city's northern
Vyborgsky *raion* turn over the soil on 16 May 1942,
to plant carrots. TsGAKFFD, Ar25811 (Box 303).

Figure 50. D. M. Beskorovainaia and G. V. Oreshina
manufacture watering cans on 1 June 1942 for the
city's gardening campaign. Their *artel*, "Kooperator,"
produced three thousand cans in May. TsGAKFFD,
Ar27340 (Box 300).

Figure 51. Women undergo mandatory military training in Dzerzhinsky *raion* in April 1942. TsGAKFFD, Ar9186 (Box 234).

Figure 52. On 28 May 1942, women engage in compulsory military drill on Tchaikovsky Street. TsGAKFFD, Ar9199 (Box 294).

Figure 53. On 12 June 1942, party organizer V. I. Smolovik reads an announcement to an assembly of workers at the Stalin metal works of increased cooperation with the Western Allies, including the "promise" of a second front in 1942. TsGAKFFD, Ar19837 (Box 300).

Figure 54. Children from Kindergarten No. 38 in Kuibyshevsky *raion* are loaded onto a bus to be taken to a train station for evacuation in July 1942. TsGAKFFD, Ar45908 (Box 295).

Figure 55–56. Two panoramic photos taken in quick succession: Two girls with pencil-thin legs shake their fists at German POWs as they are paraded through the city in August 1942. TsGAKFFD, Ar8855 (Box 290).

Figure 57. Nikita Baimakov from the Petrogradskaia Storona *raion* beams with pride on 30 September 1942, as he shows off the enormous cabbage that he grew in his garden. TsGAKFFD, Ar34634 (Box 303).

Figure 58. In an unidentified munitions plant, workshop foreman N. N. Vasiliev (right) poses with two lathe operators, I. I. Grigoriev and V. E. Tsirsh, on 2 November 1942. The workers had completed 700 percent and 415 percent, respectively, of their allotted production quotas. TsGAKFFD, Ar2965a (Box 300).

Figure 59. Metropolitan Aleksy, with the Nikolsky Cathedral in the background, shows his medal "For the Defense of Leningrad," awarded on 15 October 1943. In 1945, Aleksy was named patriarch of the Russian Orthodox Church and served until his death in 1970. TsGAKFFD, Ar415 (Box 1453).

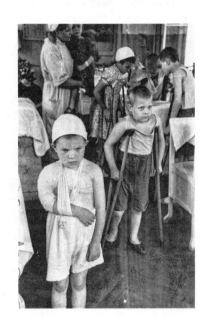

Figure 60. Children at the Leningrad State Pediatric Institute wounded by artillery fire, July 1943. TsGAKFFD, Ar45862 (Box 306).

Figure 61. In an undated photo, Tatiana Serova turns out artillery shells at the Karl Marx factory. TsGAKFFD, Ar100500 (Box 300).

Figure 62. Lathe operator and Komsomol member Sasha Zinoviev fulfills his work norm at 300 percent at Trade School No. 12 in July 1943. An anti-Hitler poster and map of the USSR are in the background. TsGAKFFD, Ar5648 (Box 306).

Figure 63. A fireworks display with one of the Rostral Columns in the foreground on 27 January 1944, celebrating the end of the blockade. TsGAKFFD, Ar99470 (Box 306).

Figure 64. Women in the Field of Mars park watching the fireworks on 27 January 1944. TsGAKFFD, Ar18032 (Box 306).

Figure 65. Two young women repair the roof of Gostiny Dvor on Nevsky Prospect in the summer of 1944. TsGAKFFD, Ar99069 (Miscellaneous collection).

Figure 66. Piotr Popkov (far left), Andrei Zhdanov, Aleksei Kuznetsov, Yakov Kapustin (right foreground), and others on a reviewing stand beneath Stalin's name on Uritsky (Palace) Square, 1 May 1945. TsGAKFFD, Dr6150 (Box 37).

Propaganda Posters from Wartime Leningrad

Figure 67. "Our Cause Is Just. Victory Will Be Ours" (1941). © "Aurora" Leningrad, 1983.

Figure 68. "We Will Avenge!" Leningrad's Admiralty spire is shown in the background. TsGAKFFD, Grp III (Box 242).

Figure 69. "We Will Finish Off the Vermin!" Published in January 1944, the month the blockade ended, the poster shows a bestial German soldier being bayoneted by the Leningrad and Volkhov Fronts. © "Aurora" Leningrad, 1983.

Figure 70. "We Defended Leningrad. We Will Rebuild It!" (1944). © "Aurora" Leningrad, 1983.

CHAPTER 5

The Popular Mood

This chapter describes the public's response to the enemy's siege tactics and to the official policies of total war examined in chapter 3.[1] The siege of Leningrad was a pivotal period in Soviet history. The city's defense was precarious and strategically important. It is hard to imagine that the vast majority of Leningraders did not realize that the siege had ushered in a defining, existential moment for their city and perhaps for their nation. Staunch defenders of Soviet ideology and power were put to the supreme test, while those who had never internalized communist ideology and Soviet policies had their best chance since 1919 to overthrow the system. Those in the middle—who identified to varying degrees with the ideas and practices of the state—would see their political views shaped largely by specific circumstances wrought by the siege. For many, the failure of the state to keep its promises, at the most basic level to protect their lives, turned them into angry critics of Soviet policy and in some cases outright opponents of communism. Practically everyone, however, understood that a massive revolutionary upheaval could lead to only one result: enemy seizure of the city, if not immediately, then after some period of siege. There was no viable alternative, liberal or otherwise, to Soviet rule or eventual enemy occupation. The historian is compelled to attempt to reconstruct the mindset of ordinary Leningraders at this crucial time. How did they interpret the unfolding momentous events? When their actions really mattered, when communist rule was most vulnerable, where did their political loyalties lie?

Assessing the mood (*nastroenie*) of Leningrad's civilian population, identifying political allegiances, the strength of those bonds, and the underlying reasons for them, are very difficult undertakings for several reasons. Leningraders' views of the war, the enemy, and their own political system and leaders were nuanced and complicated, even contradictory, and continually in flux as circumstances changed, especially during acute crises. In addition, there are source limitations for measuring public opinion. Although many groups attempted to gauge the popular mood—party and NKVD public opinion analysts, siege survivors who detailed their experiences beyond the confines of severe Soviet censorship (either in emigration or in post-Soviet Russia), and German wartime army intelligence officers who tried to monitor public opinion from outside the blockade zone—none did so systematically. The armies of party and NKVD informants produced thousands of individual reports on the popular mood; however, the aggregate of overheard comments was not broken down into quantifiable categories. The reports do not indicate, for example, what percentage of all comments overheard praised official policy and what percentage was critical or "defeatist."[2] The summaries of popular mood consist of a massive accumulation of anecdotal evidence.

How the party and NKVD determined what exactly constituted KR activity or "anti-Soviet" agitation—anti-Soviet agitation was considered a type of KR activity—is another problematic issue. The Soviet leadership modified its self-image right from the start of the war by increasingly emphasizing Russian patriotism at the expense of international Marxism; however, the definition of "anti-Soviet" expression did not change accordingly. Party and NKVD informants continued to be on the lookout for critics of the basic Marxist doctrine of the need to foment working-class revolution in the leading industrialized nations when in fact official propaganda dropped that rhetoric.

Reporting on anti-Soviet moods is complicated further by the different missions of the party and the NKVD. While Leningrad's party leadership wanted to prove that it was doing its job by demonstrating that the large majority of people remained politically loyal, the NKVD desired to catch criminals. Not surprisingly, therefore, NKVD informants managed to come up with more examples of anti-Soviet agitation than did their counterparts in the party.

One has to scrutinize carefully official characterizations of anti-Soviet agitprop for another reason. To put it mildly, the party and especially the NKVD were sensitive to criticism during the war. They tended to view pointed criticism of a specific policy failure as constituting a fundamental refutation of Soviet power and as aiding the enemy. However, much of the reported criticism represented frustration over the fact that state and party promises to protect public welfare were not kept during the war. Such criticism could mean that the critic basically internalized Soviet ideology and simply wanted the authorities to live up to their rhetoric. (Of course, it might also mean that the critic was clever enough to cloak his basic rejection of the system in the language of official policies.) What is very difficult to determine is the point where wartime hardships became so severe that "loyal" or politically passive criticism of specific shortcomings developed into a fundamental rejection of the existence of the Soviet state and its foundational ideology. It should also be noted that the opposite phenomenon existed. Some Leningraders who were indeed "anti-Soviet" kept their views to themselves, either because they feared that any expression of dissent could lead to their arrest[3] or because they considered enemy occupation of Leningrad to be a worse alternative. One final caveat concerning reliability of official informant reports is that individual informants may have falsified examples of KR activity as a way of settling personal grudges, despite the fact that proven false denunciations were severely punished.

The popular mood of wartime Leningrad, nevertheless, can be meaningfully described, although analysis is necessarily impressionistic rather than comprehensive. The problem of bias is reduced by cross-checking sources. If party and NKVD reports, private individuals' diaries and memoirs, and even German intelligence reports agree on some matter, chances are that the common account is reasonably accurate. This chapter analyzes popular attitudes on important topics during several critical periods in the first year of the war as well as, to a lesser extent, during the remainder of the blockade period.

The First Days of the Great Patriotic War

Leningraders' initial reactions to the German invasion are significant because they had not yet been conditioned by knowledge of German atrocities on Soviet soil. To be sure, the invasion was mainly viewed from the outset as an unprovoked and heinous act, but the genocidal practices of the German military against the Soviet people were yet to come. Thus, popular attitudes at the start of the war were more of a reflection of views toward Soviet officialdom than were attitudes later in the war.

Many Leningraders reacted to Molotov's announcement of the German invasion by hurrying to banks to withdraw their savings and then lining up at shops to hoard all manner of foods and consumer goods.[4] The invasion, however, did not induce widespread panic in the streets or large public displays of anti-Soviet sentiment. In fact, a prominent reaction to the first days of the war was "a sharp rise in patriotism," of expressions of devotion to the attacked homeland.[5] Nevertheless, informants also overheard criticism of the Soviet system and its leaders. A party informant reported that on 22 June several people in the central Dzerzhinsky *raion* had condemned the Soviet government for its naiveté in trusting the Germans: the Russians had been feeding the Germans, but the Germans had double-crossed them. Anti-Soviet criticism was mixed with anti-Semitic comments. It was not "Russian minds" that governed the country, some claimed, but Jewish ones, and "therefore, this is what has happened." A report from the same district on 8 July documented further anti-Semitic sentiment and noted that while most people were responding in a patriotic manner, several had refused the mobilization order to build defense fortifications. One P. A. Raevskaia was overheard saying: "Well, when Hitler arrives, the Jews will get theirs. . . . Russian fools all the time are called upon to work, while the Jews shirk work."[6]

The fact that Stalin did not address the nation until 3 July made people question the resiliency and stability of the central government. Lack of precise and timely news from the front during the war's first days, a trend that would continue while the USSR was in retreat until the battle for Stalingrad, also instilled a sense of unease among the public, as the following anonymous letter addressed to Zhdanov indicates.

· Document 56 ·

Anonymous letter to Zhdanov asking why Stalin has not addressed the nation on the war, 27 June 1941, TsGAIPD SPb f. 24, op. 2g, d. 326, l. 14.

———————

Com. Zhdanov!

I must say outright that an announcement that we are at war is a serious situation, and the loudspeakers are shouting not to turn off the radio, but it makes us sick to our stomachs, people are dying somewhere, while we have the music roaring, and in the stores it's a nightmare, the population is collecting reserves, if they have money, of course. Instead of music it would be better to give encouragement to people not to sow panic. I believe that the *militsiia* must plain and simply disperse the lines, or else we will have total panic. In the lines you can hear all kinds of provocations, they're already gossiping that Russia has been sold out, that Stalin is already in hiding. It would be good to hear Stalin on the radio. He is the chairman of the Council of People's Commissars and should address the people about our food situation, etc., and instead we have the masses in a panic, the government is silent, and the music is roaring as if it were some kind of celebration. I believe it is essential to broadcast the situation at the fronts more often over the radio, since all the people are interested in this, and, most importantly, we are waiting for a speech from Com. Stalin. Where is he? We have never seen him on the podium in Leningrad. What, is he afraid of his own people? Let him go up to the loudspeaker so that the people hear the voice of the one about whom so much is sung.

The most important mass expression of spontaneous enthusiasm for defending the nation at the start of the war that occurred in Leningrad, or anywhere in the USSR for that matter, was volunteering for military service among those not mobilized. During the afternoon of 22 June, for example, a total of 2,475 volunteered at the Ordzhonikidze and Zhdanov shipyards. Similarly high numbers were recorded at other large factories. On 23 June, F. F. Rastorguev, the head of the Military Department of the *ispolkom*, informed *gorkom* secretary Kuznetsov that altogether 100,000 Leningraders had volunteered for military service. Their only knowledge of the war was Molotov's brief description of air attacks on western Soviet cities and the start of the ground invasion. Another 112,000 Leningraders would volunteer over the next six days.[7] Male workers in defense plants, who generally were exempt from the draft, accounted for a large percentage of the early volunteers; the first three volunteer divisions were formed almost exclusively from workers in the city's southern industrial districts. But they were not the only ones who enlisted: teachers, writers, artists, scientists, and others signed up. Teenagers and pensioners volunteered, too. A typical example was Stepan Chudin, who was sixty-four years old when the war started and was employed at the Red Dawn telephone factory. After seeing his four sons go off to the Red Army, he volunteered for military service. Women signed up, and even though they were generally not accepted until late August, they came to comprise about a quarter of all who served in the volunteer units. Whole families offered themselves for military service. For example, one E. E. Emelianov, his son Viktor, and his daughter Antonina, who were all employed at the Kirov factory, volunteered. Even purged military officers' children, who were not subject to the draft, signed up.[8]

It is unclear, however, what the volunteers thought they were volunteering for. Because the fighting was far from Leningrad during the war's first few weeks, during which time little was divulged in the media about the enemy's rapid advance, and because Soviet propaganda in the years preceding 1941 had confidently stated that any invader would be quickly repulsed, there is no reason to assume that they thought they would end up fighting on front lines with extremely poor equipment and weapons and with virtually no training in some cases within days of volunteering. Many or most probably thought they had enlisted in reserve units. In other words, although most of the volunteers suffered a tragic fate, their volunteering may not have been as bold an action as it appears in hindsight.

It would be incorrect to presume that all of the enlistees were true volunteers. In general, pressure from higher-ups to enlist increased over time, especially for males of working age. The 100,000 who volunteered in the first twenty-four hours or so of the war were subject to the least compulsion. However, the factory workers among them may have been urged to volunteer at the mass meetings that many factory administrations held during the afternoon and evening of 22 June (Figure 10). The rate of volunteering subsided for three days after 23 June. Then, on 27 June, Zhdanov requested permission from the main command of the Red Army to form seven volunteer divisions. Permission was granted on the twenty-ninth, and the process of assembling units commenced on the thirtieth. Hence, between 27 and 30 June, mass volunteering changed from being a largely spontaneous movement to one that was encouraged and organized by the city's party leadership. Many of the volunteers enlisted only when the movement became "official." The number of volunteers at the Kirov factory, which supplied most of the members of the first volunteer division, rose quickly at this time. Up to 26 June, some 900 of the plant's employees, from a total of over 30,000, had volunteered. By the end of the month, however, 15,000 had volunteered.[9] In September 1943, Kirov director N. D. Puzyrev told correspondent Alexander Werth that "everyone without exception volunteered for the front." He added, "If we had wanted to, we could have sent 25,000 people."[10]

Pressure to enlist increased further on 3 July when Stalin spoke to the nation over the radio for the first time since the invasion and ordered the formation of *narodnye opolcheniia* in all cities threatened by enemy attack. He thereby lent the movement his personal imprimatur and made enlistment nearly obligatory for many. Stalin's endorsement of the *opolchenie* made it easier for *partkom* secretaries, trade union chairmen, and other recruiters to compel people to enlist. One eyewitness stated that a recruiter assigned especially to him said that it was necessary to volunteer "to show political face." The recruiter tried to convince him to join the *opolchenie*, "which is organized," the recruiter emphasized, "by the directive of Comrade Stalin."[11] Stalin's speech was a clear signal for party personnel to enlist. In fact, refusal to enlist could lead to expulsion from the party. Party members responded accordingly. For example, all remaining party members in one workshop of the Ordzhonikidze shipyard and every Komsomol member at the Vulkan machine construction plant joined the *opolchenie* right after Stalin's speech. Few employees at Vulkan had enlisted previously. The Komsomol contingent of the city's Primorsky *raion* volunteered en masse only after the radio address. It is clear that before Stalin's speech there had been some reluctance among party personnel to volunteer.[12]

Enemy at the Gates!

Leningrad was most vulnerable to a ground attack between 20 August, when German forces reached the suburban city of Krasnogvardeisk, and 2 October, when Germany launched the northern part of Operation Typhoon, the offensive for Moscow. The turn toward Moscow demonstrated that Hitler would not attempt to seize Leningrad immediately but instead try to subdue it through blockade and intense bombardment.

The populace was surprised by the enemy's rapid advance toward Leningrad. Nothing in Soviet prewar propaganda or in the press coverage during the first two months of the war had prepared them for that eventuality. In the popular mind the main culprits for the alarming state of affairs included the double-crossing German "fascists" and the nations allied with them, the "naïve" Soviet leadership which had fed the German war machine since 1939, and incompetent and/or cowardly Red Army commanders.

Informant reports also reveal that some Leningraders looked to their Christian faith for solace and deliverance. A League of Militant Godless (SVB) report from August noted that churches were becoming more active following the start of the invasion. Many were beginning to hold daily services. Attendance was on the rise, and more children were being baptized. The numbers praying for saintly intercession and taking communion were increasing. At least five churches were administering communion to several groups simultaneously.[13] With the Church giving its full support to defending the homeland, identification with Russian Orthodoxy for many Leningraders became part of their patriotic response to the enemy's invasion. The fusion of Orthodox Christianity with patriotism is reflected in an example included in a report filed in December by an official named Galko, who was in charge of monitoring opinion for the *partkom* of the Kirov factory: "It was characteristic that worker Makarova, hearing the news of the Moscow battle, out of joy started crossing herself and saying 'Lord, help our soldiers to beat the Germans more.'"[14]

The SVB cited several examples of religious believers who asserted that the war represented divine punishment. Prior to the start of the blockade, a priest at the Voskresenskaia Church reportedly said in a sermon that "the war is punishment of sins" and then seemed to imply that God's wrath could be assuaged when he stated that people should go to church more often, repent of their sins, believe, and christen their children. In November an elderly woman named Fedotkina expressed a more fatalistic variation on this theme when she reportedly told a group of housewives: "God is punishing us because we allowed the churches to be destroyed. Hitler is God's punishment, which you will accept as you should. Opposition is pointless. I have two sons at war, but they and our Red Army will be slaughtered." During the autumn "nuns, holy fools (*iurodivye*), and hysterics (*klikushki*)" outside of churches, in cemeteries, especially the Nikolsky Cemetery of the closed Aleksandr Nevsky Monastery, and in homes were heard to say that the spreading hunger was God's punishment for those who were not being punished by death and suffering at the front.[15]

Some believers proselytized through religious chain letters. Between 20 and 30 September, the SPO learned of an appeal to "read the Lord's Prayer and be saved." The handwritten document asked each recipient to make nine copies and circulate them among acquaintances.[16] In his public opinion summary of 7 October, *gorkom* secretary Antiufeev described this phenomenon in detail. He stated that for a long time a letter had circulated in all of the city's *raiony* that contained the following: "In the city of Jerusalem there was heard the voice of the savior. He said, 'Pray, read the Lord's Prayer and be saved. Receive this note; write it nine times and distribute them to believers and in two days you will receive joy. Don't distribute them and you will die.'" Antiufeev added that copies of the letters were found in mailboxes, in pockets of people's outer garments, and at factory workshops. No one knew who was circulating them. (Zhdanov underlined this statement in his copy of the report.)[17] Also in October the *partkom* of the Kirov factory noted that a cleaning woman named Aleksandra Ivanova had brought to work a packet of sectarian prayers and recommended to a female co-worker, who was a party member (and probably informed on her), to read a prayer, make copies, and distribute them to others. The report indicates that Ivanova's words constituted counterrevolutionary speech.[18]

There can be no doubt that a large majority of Leningraders was not deterred by the start of the blockade and bombardment and steadfastly desired to defend their city. The defenders of Leningrad included ardent communists, nationalists, and patriots who cared little about ideology, and those who simply wanted to protect themselves, their families, and friends. Yet, some degree of war-weariness was setting in. At the same time that combat detachments and battalions were being formed and armed at factories in mid-September, and some workers were logging twenty-hour shifts on 17 September at the Kirov factory within a few miles of the front,[19] isolated instances of insubordination were occurring more frequently, although such disobedience was probably not motivated by a desire to aid the enemy. On 15 September, thirty-five female workers at the Engels factory refused to work more than eight hours on the night shift. The plant director gave in to their demand and let them leave. A similar situation occurred in another part of that factory three days later. A month later, on 19 October when food supplies were running short, twelve workers in the mechanized foundry left work two hours early, claiming that "one bowl of soup did not give them enough strength for twelve hours of work."[20] In addition, there were accusations of cowardice. On 17 September, a *partkom* secretary at the Kirov works complained that of the seven hundred workers in his workshop, two hundred were loafers or in hiding. Representatives from the factory were dispatched to workers' homes to force them to work. The "cowards" were reprimanded.[21] On 20 September, Aleksandr Volkov, the director of the Vpered factory, was fired and expelled from the party for repeatedly refusing an order to go to the front.[22]

Despite the forced evacuation in late August of those who were considered to be politically unreliable, a "defeatist" sentiment began to emerge. The assertion by Alexander Werth that "there was no one, except a few anti-communists, who even considered surrender [of Leningrad] to the Germans" understates the amount of such sentiment.[23] Some people did not care who controlled Leningrad "if only there was some sort of end to all this," as one put it.[24] Stridently anti-Soviet and pro-German viewpoints were also encountered more often, as were threats of retribution against the Communists once the city fell to the enemy. During the first days of October, a construction worker at the Kirov plant named Yershov reportedly said that "Hitler will come and feed us bread." His comments were repeated by others.[25] Shortly before 15 September, around the time that arms were being distributed to the worker battalions, one F. I. Piletsky was heard to say, "If they gave me a gun, I wouldn't shoot the fascists, but you, the police. . . . Today, you take us, but tomorrow Hitler will arrive and we will shoot you."[26] On or about 17 September, a Kirov worker named Stashkevich was arrested for predicting that the Germans would soon conduct a massacre of all communists.[27] German documents contain a report of a wife of a party member who was threatened by an old woman: "When the Germans come, we will denounce you." An émigré's memoir states that one worker threatened: "Well, we'll be going through the apartments soon to take care of people who need it."[28] In early October a woman named Smirnova was reported to the authorities for wandering around apartments along Stachek Prospect near the Kirov factory and writing down names of party and Komsomol members who lived in one building.[29] The security forces were not immune to anti-Soviet views. Sergei Logunov, a *militsiia* junior lieutenant, was arrested for anti-Soviet agitation on 18 August for saying that Hitler would take Leningrad. In the presence of an NKVD senior inspector, he allegedly praised Hitler and stated that he did not believe Soviet accounts of the war.[30] Several employees of the UNKVD were accused of displaying a defeatist attitude; their cases were reviewed at meetings of the *biuro* of the Dzerzhinsky *raikom*.[31]

Anti-Soviet and pro-German writings also appeared and circulated more frequently as the military situation deteriorated in late summer. Hand-drawn swastikas were occasionally noticed as early as July.[32] Prior to the German invasion, security organs had recorded on average 30 to 40 anti-Soviet anonymous letters and leaflets per month. In June 1941, SPO identified 42 examples, and 135 in July. The following month the number reached a peak of 286 but declined in September to 140 before increasing again later in the fall.[33] The writings included appeals to surrender Leningrad, that is, make it an "open" city. Those who made that plea, however, had no way of knowing that Hitler had ruled out an attempt to occupy the city in the fall of 1941. Below is an example of one such handwritten leaflet.

· Document 57 ·

Report from Antiufeev and Klebanov to Zhdanov, Kuznetsov, Kapustin, and Shumilov on a handwritten note found in a bomb shelter, signed by the "Nationality of the Russian People," calling for the surrender of the city, 11 October 1941, TsGAIPD SPb f. 24, op. 2v, d. 4819, l. 25.

A Communist from the Petrogradsky RONO [District People's Education Office], Com. Piatnitskaia, brought to the VKP(b) *raikom* a handwritten note found in the bomb shelter at 33a Karl Liebknecht Prospect, with the following content:

"Citizens! Our 'rulers,' if you will, have abandoned us utterly to the tyranny of fate, to the dung heap, you could say, and are giving the Germans the chance to bomb our residences. For over 20 years, our side has not been preparing for war, and we, fighting, have for 3 months had to hide in damp, dirty cellars—and this is our shelter. Well, isn't this a disgrace? The city is surrounded. There is no delivery of foods. What is going to happen next? Added in the near future to the misfortune in which we now find ourselves will be the most terrible thing of all—famine and disease.

"Thanks to our good rulers, the evacuation has fallen apart. There are many children, women, old people, and sick here. What awaits them? If our rulers, led by the worst convict among them—the Georgian Jew, or Tatar, or Gypsy—said, 'Not one step back, we'll blow the city up, but we won't surrender it,' so you yourselves understand what's going to happen to the children, women, old people, and sick. The Tatar convict is going to live, while we all perish.

"All against Stalin!!! The city should be made open, like Paris!

"Their government is going to fall soon anyway, so why should we perish?

"Down with the convict! Bread and peace! After our 20-year tribulation, we have no strength left to endure.

"Let us unite in a council of liberation for the Russian people from the convict's yoke, but know that only Voroshilov and Budenny are with us, and down with all the rest.

"Everyone into the street! Everyone for the battle against bolshevism!"

"Nationality of the Russian People"

The leaflet has been handed over to the district department of the NKVD, which is investigating the case.

Head of the Organizational-Instructional Office, City Committee VKP(b) Antiufeev

Office Administrator Klebanov

Similarly, in early October a nurse at the Botkin Hospital, Ekaterina Tiunina, was arrested for writing an anonymous letter to Marshal Voroshilov which called for a coup to rid the government of non-Russians. Under interrogation, Tiunina admitted to urging people standing in lines to stage anti-Soviet demonstrations and overthrow the Soviet government.[34]

This letter and the leaflet printed above demonstrate that one manifestation of anti-Soviet expression was Russian chauvinism, which disparaged all non-Russians, especially Jews. As Sarah Davies has shown, a strong undercurrent of anti-Semitism existed in Leningrad's popular opinion during the 1920s and 1930s and was the "most common form of expression of ethnic hostility in Leningrad." Anti-Semitism, which had notoriously deep roots in Imperial Russian history, developed during the early Soviet decades in part because Jews, the largest ethnic minority in the city, "were constantly identified with a ruling elite, which included party members, state servants, and the 'Soviet intelligentsia'" while "few Jews worked in factories, and even fewer in agriculture."[35] In the mindset of Leningrad's masses of factory workers and transplanted peasants, criticism of those in power could lead rather easily to expressions of virulent hatred of Jews.

Party informants detected a sharp rise in anti-Semitic speech in July and August 1941, and in mid-September SPO observed a marked increase in leaflets that called for pogroms against Jews;[36] however, arrests for these crimes cannot be quantified because anti-Semitic utterances were lumped together with other forms of anti-Soviet agitation.[37] Jews were sometimes castigated as a privileged and cowardly elite. One Iakov Vlasov was arrested for uttering the following while arguing against the evacuation of children from the city: "Where can they go? There's nowhere to go. The Jews can go, they give them separate rail cars, but Russians have to sit wherever they can find a seat and go wherever. The Jews have been beaten, but only a little. They've got to be beaten more."[38]

Anecdotal evidence suggests that anti-Semitic sentiment was more prevalent in the city's southern industrialized Kirovsky *raion*. In July a port worker in the district was heard saying: "Nowhere do the Jews live as well as in Russia, therefore they ought to have been more willing to defend the homeland than others, but they use every possibility to leave Leningrad." Another person in the same district at that time stated that she heard her neighbor say that all the Jews were fleeing Leningrad. A *raikom* report of 29 August states that anti-Semitic remarks and conversations had been heard at the Kirov plant and at least five other factories in the district, in queues, on public transport, and especially in communal housing.[39]

Anti-Semitic attitudes were not restricted to the working class. Anna Ostroumova-Lebedeva was an artist, printmaker, and book illustrator who kept a diary during the war. Despite her own warm relations with various

Jewish intellectuals, her contempt for the city's Jews surfaced repeatedly. In her entry for 6 July, she described a visit to the Russian Museum: "In the drawing and watercolor department, the professional staff was filled with indignation at the behavior of the Jews working in the Museum. When there was an appeal at a meeting for volunteers, they spoke very fervently and patriotically, but in practice they all managed to find warm and safe places for themselves, all of them without exception. Some of them even took advantage of staff reductions to secure better positions for themselves than they had had before. In a word, my friends said that all of this was insultingly vile and mean." Two days later, she wrote: "In the evening Olga Anatolevna visited. She is surrounded by panic-stricken co-workers, because they're all Jews. In that institution there is a 5 percent quota for Russian workers.[40] Everyone is running around looking for a way to leave. And all this is done on the sly with exceptional cunning and pushiness." Her entry for 2 August includes the statement: "They evacuate especially hastily those institutions that are headed up by Jews."[41]

Anti-Semitism was also detected within the party. On 7 October, NKVD head Kubatkin denounced the agitprop head of the Volodarsky *raion*, Dertin, to *gorkom* secretary Kuznetsov, stating that Dertin was "systematically drunk" and when in a drunken state among nonparty people "trumpets" secret details about the situation at the front and makes such anti-Soviet remarks as that "the Jews are traitors and one can only despise them." Early in the morning on 3 October, Dertin, armed with a rifle and a grenade, was arrested for making defeatist comments to civil defense workers.[42]

It is unsurprising that the German Eighteenth Army outside Leningrad concluded from prisoner interrogations and its agents' reports that by 2 October "a large part" of Leningrad's prewar Jewish population had already fled.[43]

Any assessment of how Leningrad's Jews regarded the evacuation question would be based on the premise that Jews had a separate self-identity, and it is not clear that such a premise is valid. Few Leningraders of Jewish descent attended the city's lone functioning synagogue.[44] Jews spoke Russian and intermingled with Russians and other nationalities in many different professions. However, the nearness of Germany's genocidal racism must have forced those of Jewish lineage in Leningrad increasingly to think of themselves in terms of the Nazi definition of who was a Jew, that is, someone having at least one Jewish grandparent, and it is likely that those who held anti-Semitic views identified "Jewishness" in approximately the same way. There is no way to measure whether Leningrad's Jews generally had a greater desire to leave the city or whether they evacuated in proportionately greater numbers. It may be that since the city's Jews were well represented in skilled professions they were ordered to evacuate in disproportionately large numbers, because they were employed in institutes and factories that were relocated to the east. Recent research would suggest that Jews were as determined to defend Leningrad and the country as the rest of the city's population.[45] Jews indeed had a powerful incentive to try to protect the city at all costs, and if they concluded that it could not be defended and the Germans took over, to avoid being identified as Jews.

The general population obtained from the Soviet media only occasional glimpses of Germany's genocidal anti-Semitism. Atrocities committed by Germany were featured prominently in Soviet press coverage but generally without mention of a targeted ethnic group. The official myth was that all ethnic groups of the one Soviet family were being more or less equally brutalized by the invading enemy. This tendency to conceal the Holocaust, especially as it was carried out on Soviet soil, grew stronger as the war progressed, even though Stalin was well informed about the extermination of Jews and other groups. It has been suggested that the reason for minimizing reporting on the Holocaust was that the Soviet government did not want to signal to the populace that the Red Army had been tasked with saving Jews. Ascribing such an obligation to the army might inflame anti-Semitism and thus encourage support for the enemy. Nevertheless, there were exceptions to this tendency, particularly during the first year of the war. On 26 July 1941, *Leningradskaia pravda* described ghettos and murders of Jews by Germans in Poland and took a definite stand against anti-Semitism. Exactly one month later, the newspaper published the founding appeal of the Jewish Antifascist Committee to "Jewish Brothers in the Whole World." On 27 September, *Izvestia* printed an article by one N. Petrov, apparently a pseudonym for the Soviet head of state, Mikhail Kalinin, entitled "Hatred of a People." The article stated that according to fascist ideology, the Jews "must be destroyed."[46] On 2 October, *Leningradskaia pravda* carried a lengthy feature article on German atrocities against Jews. It condemned the torture and killing of Jews and noted that Jews were leaders in many walks of life in the USSR. In mentioning the receipt of the title Hero of Socialist Labor by Isaak Zaltsman, the director of the Kirov factory (one of 188 Kirov employees who had been given special awards at that critical time), *Leningradskaia pravda* described him on 21 September as a Soviet Jew who was making vital contributions to the war effort.[47] Citing Zaltsman's efforts may have been an attempt to combat the circulating rumors that Jews were cowards. Hence, by the time of the start of the blockade, Leningraders understood that German occupation of their city would most likely mean the mass elimination of Jews, in addition to party personnel. German propaganda and accounts from refugees who reached the Leningrad area reinforced this understanding. Not everyone was repelled by the prospect of mass murder of the city's Jews.

As one Kirov worker reportedly said in November: "The Germans will not shoot everyone, but sift them through a sieve."[48] The same month a metal worker named Grigoriev at the "Bolshevik" arms plant was more explicit when he was overheard saying: "It makes no difference, the Germans will come and give out sausages and potatoes, and they will kill only Jews and communists."[49]

The party and the NKVD went to great lengths to repress anti-Semitic expressions but do not appear to have examined carefully why that sentiment was becoming more common. Leaving aside the perception in some quarters that Jews were anxious to flee, one likely reason for the upsurge in anti-Semitism was that some Leningraders internalized German propaganda that equated the Bolshevik with the Jew, which served to increase anti-Semitic attitudes that predated the war.[50] In this way, Jews became a scapegoat: the Bolshevik-Jew was the source of the people's misery, and if it weren't for him, Germany would not have invaded. In addition, the emphasis that Soviet propaganda placed on Russian patriotism may have inadvertently stimulated anti-Semitism by implicitly placing Jews outside the bounds of "Russianness." The idea that Jews were non-Russians who had come to dominate Russians through communism was reportedly articulated during the war by a Leningrad State University lecturer (*dotsent*): "It is indeed terrible—Russia quit being a national Russian (*russkoe*) government. The Soviets are not a government and are not Russia. The policy of internationalism is nonsense, which has led Russia to ruin. Russians (*Russkie*) have become drunk on the illusions that they are the masters of the country. They do not see the actual situation of things, that all the basic government posts are occupied by Jews and other nationalities. . . ." In early February 1942, SPO reported on a professor of the Military Electro-Technical Academy who had expressed a similar view and in the process made the plight of Jews in Nazi Germany appear tolerable: "The question of the nation is an important question. Germany is for Germany. Russia for Russia. We, the true Russian (*russkie*) people, desire good above all for Russia, but the communists fight for the idea of world communism and want to create it at our expense—out of the Russian people. Take Germany—it is above all for Germans, and Jews as an alien nation are partially limited in their rights. Here Jews have all rights—they are the ruling class, but we Russians are kept down and occupy a secondary place." Another professor transformed the invader into a liberator: "The people cannot understand that the Germans came to liberate Russia from the Jews and communists and from Soviet Russia to create the real Russia."[51]

Morale within the Communist Party weakened subtly but noticeably when the city was most imperiled. There are several indications that members' sense of loyalty to the party was diminishing to some extent. Many candidates and full party members chose to dissociate themselves from the party without taking the reckless step of severing ties altogether. One memoirist wrote that for part of September some uniformed party personnel stopped wearing their uniforms.[52] There was much political fence-sitting during the critical moment when the blockade commenced. Party members had strong motivation to defend Leningrad, because they knew that the Germans were killing Communists whom they captured. (In this sense, their predicament was similar to that of Jews.) For the same reason, they would have incentive to conceal any party affiliation the moment that the enemy gained control. Many in the party seemed to be quietly preparing themselves for this eventuality. Candidate members in overwhelming numbers did not attain full membership within the defined candidacy period, which was generally one year. In the heavily industrialized Moskovsky *raion*, not far from the front in the southern part of the city, at the end of October, 966 of 1,072 candidate members (90 percent) had failed to apply on time. In the Krasnogvardeisky *raion*, 1,067 of 1,168 candidate members (91 percent) were delinquent.[53] No doubt in some cases candidates were simply unable to advance because the local party cell had collapsed when members had been sent to the front or been evacuated, or because the cell was too preoccupied to accept candidates into full membership. However, such high percentages of delinquency would suggest that some were deliberately not applying for full membership.

Candidate and full party members also often refrained from paying their dues, which was another way to distance oneself from the party, although nonpayment probably also resulted from other factors connected with the demands of the war. The *partkom* of the Kirov factory acknowledged in late December 1941 that many members had not paid dues since the start of the war.[54] At the Engels factory, where 64 of 160 party members had not paid their dues during the late summer of 1941, an employee named Danilov was asked why he had not paid. He replied, "Why pay? Soon the Germans will come and it won't matter."[55] His motive appears not to have been fear of retribution per se but a sense that the party had no future.

Another concern of the party was the increase in lost membership cards. During the first year of the war, 784 candidate and full members lost their cards, for which some members were expelled. Although the total number of lost documents represented a very low percentage, the month of September was one of two months when losses were the highest, and the Kolpino *raion*, located south of Leningrad adjacent to the front, had the highest percentage of lost cards.[56] Since burning a party card was an easy but irrevocable act, it is logical to presume that most of those who contemplated severing all links to the party would wait until the moment before the enemy arrived to do so.

It is impossible to know how many of the recorded lost cards were hidden or secretly destroyed. Party officials claimed to have uncovered several cases. Not long after the start of the siege, eighteen party members from the Vyborgsky *raion* were accused of hiding their documents in an attic. An employee of the Kalinin tram park named Povaliaev allegedly burned his party card together with his copy of Stalin's *Short Course of the History of Communist Party.*[57] There were also cases of Communists openly renouncing their membership, as obviously dangerous as that was. For example, in August two long-term members in their mid-forties from the Kirovsky *raion,* Matvei Adamiants and Maria Buzanova, officially requested to be excluded from the party.[58] An employee of the Okhtensky chemical factory named Kondratenko told his local party secretary around early October: "Please do not write my name in the membership list, for then it would be easy to find out that I am a Communist." In another case, a worker at the Bolshevik arms plant, who had joined the party in 1918 and been a model member, engaged in what appears to have been viewed as an act of deception when he went to his local *partkom* right at the start of the war and said: "Hitler will arrive. I will conceal myself to work underground, so I give you this literature to save my life, because it must not be shown in my home that I was a Communist."[59]

In their relations with the rest of the civilian population, party workers shrank back from denouncing defeatist sentiment as the enemy approached Leningrad. At the same time that the NKVD was carrying out the purge of suspected counterrevolutionaries, professional agitators and other visible agents of party authority often refrained from chastising hecklers or responding to threats of reprisal, likely out of fear that scores would be settled if the city fell. On 2 September, *gorkom* secretary Antiufeev wrote in a report to Zhdanov and other top leaders: "At many factories Communists do not unify or lead the nonparty masses, nor give a rebuff to disorganizers, panickers, and anti-Soviet elements, but frequently lag behind in a backward state of mind. Several Communists show themselves to be cowards and panickers, refusing to take part in party mobilizations to the army and armed detachments, and have quit fulfilling their own basic obligation—to pay party membership dues."[60] On 24 September, *Leningradskaia pravda* echoed his words: "In these ominous days when life tests the steadfastness of the Bolshevik ranks, there are some party members and candidates who show insufficient courage, show faintheartedness. The party of Lenin and Stalin will not tolerate them for a single day in its ranks."[61]

At the same time, noncommunists displayed an increased reluctance to join the party. As shown in Document 46, up to the beginning of March 1942, the month of weakest party recruitment was September. Admonitions from party higher-ups to recruit new members and the readmission of some members who had been previously expelled from the party[62] made little difference. During the first three months of the war, *partkomy* at each of ten prominent city factories admitted no more than three people to candidate membership.[63] Of course, part of the reason why few joined the party during this period is that they were too busy with far more pressing demands. In addition, party records were disorganized as reams of materials were destroyed or sent out of the city during the summer. The general confusion of war, however, is not the only explanation. Many probably chose not to join the party out of fear that the Germans would take the city and hunt down and kill party members.

All for the Front! (on 125 to 250 Grams of Bread Per Day)

During the latter half of the autumn of 1941, Leningrad was faced with a new deadly dilemma. As the enemy artillery and aerial bombardment continued, bread rations were cut twice in November to starvation levels, in large part because the Germans had seized the important rail center of Tikhvin on 8 November, which greatly complicated Soviet efforts to send food across Lake Ladoga. Yet, between that time and late December, when the last of city's factories lost electrical power and had to cease large-scale production, Leningrad's defense plant workers had to continue working eleven-hour shifts to supply the front.[64] The enormous effort summoned by the ubiquitous propaganda slogan "All for the Front!" exhausted hundreds of thousands of workers as the first cases of death by starvation appeared. The remaining two-thirds of the civilian population who were not *rabochie,* and who received smaller rations, were also suffering the effects of acute hunger and prolonged stress by the start of the winter.

Between early November and late December, Leningraders were becoming more pessimistic, angry, and critical of the authorities' inability to protect them. The number of instances of anti-Soviet activity or speech, as defined and recorded by the NKVD, rose from 150–170 per day at the end of September to 250 in mid-October to 300–350 in November. All letters mailed in the city were opened, and the percentage of letters written by Leningraders that were not delivered because they contained "negative" sentiment rose from 1.2 percent in June and July to 1.5–1.7 percent in August to 2.0–2.5 percent in October to 3.5–4.0 percent in November. In December the percentage of seized correspondence rose from 2.3 percent at the beginning of the month to 7.0 percent at the end.[65] German intelligence claimed that by 24 November about half of the workers in many factories were openly calling for the surrender of the city. This exaggerated figure likely derived from a combination of information obtained from prisoners and defectors who wanted to ingratiate themselves with German authorities and wishful thinking on the part of the intelligence analysts and their bosses.[66]

Arrests for KR activity show a somewhat different pattern. They had risen sharply starting in late August (Document 32) largely due to the NKVD operation to rid the city of suspected counterrevolutionaries.[67] It would appear that the rate of KR arrests in August and early September was the highest for the war years, probably over 30 per day.[68] Document 42 shows that 957 people were arrested for KR activity between 15 October and 1 December (a rate of 20 per day). KR arrests declined in December to 344 (11 per day).[69] Hence, the KR arrest rate actually declined during the late autumn, the reasons for which are not clear.

Documents 39–42 were written between 22 November and 6 December and include party and NKVD summaries of the popular mood. These documents depict in detail how the populace became angrier as rations were cut. As noted in chapter 3, Kubatkin's two reports contain more examples of hostile comments directed toward Soviet authorities than Antiufeev's two reports. Antiufeev's report of 26 November (Document 40) reveals that the *gorkom* was especially concerned about popular frustration over lengthening bread lines. Kubatkin reported on 25 November (Document 41) that "anti-Soviet elements are refusing to work and attempting to call for organized actions and to try to get an increased bread ration." Starving industrial workers resorted to all three means noted by Kubatkin. In the 22 November report, Antiufeev included comments from a woman who reportedly claimed that workers could not work for ten hours on the food they received, especially when they saved their bread for their children. Many workers tried to shorten their working day on their own in ways they hoped would not be noticed, such as by spending prolonged periods in the factory cafeteria, leaving work early, or not showing up for work at all. In some factories enforcement of labor regulations had weakened significantly by November. The practice that was recorded in September and October of workers refusing to work overtime continued into November. A group of eighteen workers walked off the job at an unidentified factory in Sverdlovsky *raion* on 16 November, announcing that "they feed us poorly, we have no strength for more work, we worked as much as we could." When told that their salaries would be docked by 15–20 percent, one responded: "I could give up more. I don't need more as there is nothing to buy." What is as noteworthy as the insubordination itself is the fact that no one tried to prevent these workers from leaving, even though their actions might be construed as desertion in a war zone.[70] During the blockade the NKVD recorded seventeen work stoppages in the city.[71] In October and November hundreds of hungry teenagers working in factories and trade schools attempted to defect across enemy lines, where they believed they would find food and a better life.[72] In other cases, labor discipline was more strictly enforced. A foundry worker named Tushina was fired and arrested for stating during the night shift of 25–26 October: "We don't need land mines. They make us work 18 hours without a break and they give us a dish of water to eat."[73]

Most of the critical or "negative" opinions presented in Documents 39–42 fit into a range of categories, which are listed below in ascending order of severity of the criticism:

1. Constructive suggestions and complaints, such as appeals for better worker oversight in cafeterias, more food, and a shorter work shift
2. Pessimistic assessment that the Red Army would not be able to break the blockade and the city's inhabitants would starve
3. Blaming the government for the lack of food
4. Appeals for specific direct action intended to gain access to more food: work stoppages and attacks on bread shops
5. Calls for surrendering the city to keep people from starving to death
6. Assertions that life would be better under the Germans

Kubatkin classified all six categories as "anti-Soviet," whereas Antiufeev more accurately characterized all but the first as "unhealthy, defeatist" but did not indicate that they represented a rejection of Soviet power. Kubatkin classified the comment, "First you have to feed me, then you can try to make me work" as anti-Soviet; however, Antiufeev portrayed a similar comment—"It's impossible to work in a smithy on that kind of bread ration"—simply as a complaint, but did not assign it to the "unhealthy, defeatist" category.

In fact, the only sentiments that were unambiguously motivated by an anti-Soviet view were those in category 6. Comments in category 5 might have been anti-Soviet. While it is true that the surrender of Leningrad in late 1941 would have been a major victory for Germany (if Germany would accept the surrender), someone who advocated that course of action might have seen things differently. Such a person might not have desired German victory in the war, just a temporary, but necessary, forfeiture of Leningrad until the Soviet Union could retake it later on. The other types of "negative" sentiment (categories 2, 3, and 4) were not necessarily prompted by the hope of enemy victory. Someone who predicted that the Red Army would not be able to break the siege probably in fact hoped that it could. Blaming the government for not providing enough food presupposed that the government could have and should have done a better job. Even calls for strikes or attacks on bread stores were likely more often motivated solely by hunger than by a desire to overthrow the Soviet system and welcome the enemy into the city.

Although the overall level of popular dissatisfaction had increased by early December, it is not clear that there were more expressions of pro-German sentiment than there had been three months earlier. Those who had hoped for enemy occupation just prior to the start of the siege were probably less likely to articulate such a view as winter set in. They would be more inclined to keep their sympathies to themselves as the prospect of a German attempt to seize Leningrad receded. Moreover, following three months of blockade and bombardment, the vast majority of Leningraders could hardly view the enemy as "a cultured, decent people" (as reportedly characterized by one person in Document 41) and had no basis to expect humane policies from an occupation regime.

Other forms of anti-Soviet sentiment included favorable references to the tsarist policies and hopes for a future devoid of both Communists and fascists. In November metal worker Vladimir Yermakov was denounced to the secretary of his workshop's party committee at the Kirov factory for praising Stolypin and his reforms. A colleague of his said on 19 November, in response to news of the Allied conference in Moscow at which Lord Beaverbrook and Averell Harriman promised to furnish additional arms and loan money to the USSR: "Even if the USSR with help from England and the US defeats Germany, a transformation to a bourgeois democratic republic is nevertheless inevitable."[74]

Despite the fact that public opinion became more critical during the autumn, expressions of protest remained the exception rather than the rule. Leningraders' capacity for enduring deprivation and terror was remarkable. During the late fall of 1941 and on into the winter, most appear to have believed that their city could be liberated in the near future. The successful counteroffensive before Moscow and the recapture by the Red Army of Tikhvin in early December kept those hopes alive. Defense plant workers were motivated to work long shifts as food disappeared in part because they believed that the extra work effort was needed to produce enough munitions to enable the Red Army to break through the siege and end the bombardment. The siege ring, however, would not be pierced until February 1943 and not eradicated entirely for almost a year after that. In the meantime, the greater work effort made Leningraders more vulnerable to death by starvation and cold in the coming winter.

The Hungry Winter

By the middle of December, Leningrad was shutting down. Trams quit running, homes and most enterprises lost electricity as only one city power plant barely continued functioning, and heating pipes froze and burst. The mortality rate soared as Leningrad entered into an apocalypse of cold and starvation unprecedented in history. Not surprisingly, indicators of popular mood reveal that the public vented its anger toward, and contempt of, the authorities more frequently, and became more pessimistic ("defeatist") as the death rate increased. Critical mood (as reflected, albeit imperfectly, in arrest totals for KR activity) and the mortality rate peaked at precisely the same time. Arrests for KR activity, having declined to 11 per day in December, rose to 19 between 1 and 10 January and reached a peak for the winter of 26 between 16 and 20 January (but the arrest rate was lower than in late August and early September of 1941). The daily KR arrest rate then dropped to 24 between 1 and 10 February and for the first half of March declined further to 16.[75] One would expect, however, that the arrest rate would have been much higher during the worst period of starvation when perhaps as many as 10,000 Leningraders perished on individual days, especially given the NKVD's broad definition of what constituted anti-Soviet expression and its vigilance in trying to extirpate that sentiment.

Data from mail censorship show a somewhat different pattern. The period when the highest percentage of letters was not delivered because they contained "negative" sentiments was in late January, when the death toll peaked; however, the percentage of seized correspondence rose far more steeply than the KR arrest rate. If 2.3 percent of letters were not delivered at the beginning of December, the rate rose in early January to 6–9 percent and then peaked at 20 percent in the last week of January. By mid-February it had dropped to 18 percent.[76] The difference in the rate of increase in KR arrests as compared to seized correspondence resulted from several factors. It was partly due to the NKVD's diminished resources for building criminal cases during the worst of the winter, even though the number of employed informants and agents appears to have remained more or less stable and may even have grown. It also would appear that during the winter the NKVD tolerated more criticism of the authorities' failures to better protect the population. Moreover, the high rate of confiscation of mailed letters reflected the authorities' determination to prevent deterioration of morale at the front by preventing knowledge of starvation in Leningrad from reaching the troops. But the difference between the KR arrest rate and the rate of seized mail also suggests that there existed a split between public and private attitudes at this time. The basis of most KR arrests was overheard conversations involving several people at least one of whom was an informant. A letter, however, was private communication between two people. Many seized letters were farewell messages to soldiers from starving wives or other family members. People poured out their inner feelings in the letters (though some must have assumed that the mail was being monitored), but they exhibited far more restraint while standing in line or at work. If one letter in five contained content that the

NKVD found objectionable, the ratio for overheard speech was nowhere near as high. As a worker named Kotonov at the Red Dawn factory reportedly said in early February, "People in the city are dying like flies, but the people are quiet."[77] The letters often blamed the authorities for the city's plight; however, some letters and conversations were nonpolitical, merely describing the extent of the starvation and the city's desperate situation. One letter that was not delivered read in part: "Leningrad has become a morgue, the streets have become avenues of the dead. The dead are stored in the basement of each house. Along the streets are rows of corpses. In hospitals stacks of them. Everyone has died at the factory. A city of dead, there is no light, no water, the trams don't run."[78]

The fact that the KR arrest rate at the height of the starvation was only a little higher than it had been in November and lower than in August–September is explained by other factors as well. During the winter Leningraders devoted their ebbing physical and mental faculties to searching for the life-sustaining essentials of water, food, and warmth. In general, most other considerations, including political ones, were of far less importance. It is worth noting that this phenomenon of massive starvation diminishing political protest was not new in Soviet history. Far more instances of outright protest of, and opposition to, forced collectivization occurred throughout the USSR in early 1930, when the campaign began, than during the devastating famine of 1932–33.

Moreover, during the coldest weeks of winter, people were physically more isolated. They bundled themselves up in their apartments and ventured out only as needed. When around others, emaciated and exhausted, they tended to speak less to conserve energy and thus were less likely to be reported for subversive comments. Yelena Kochina noted her diary on 9 January: "In our room we live as if we were on an ark, seeing nothing and meeting no one. We don't even know what's going on at the front. Only by chance do we learn something while standing in line."[79] Lidia Ginzburg, another siege survivor, wrote in her memoirs: "During the days of the great hunger, people mostly kept quiet."[80]

The enemy's actions and policies also played a major role in shaping political attitudes and served to limit the growth of anti-Soviet expression. During the winter, the Wehrmacht's retreat all along the front reduced further the prospect of a German occupation of Leningrad and discouraged German sympathizers in Leningrad from expressing their views openly. More important, however, was the fact that Germany's tactic of trying to subdue Leningrad by starvation and continued artillery bombardment had come to be viewed as monstrously barbaric. Popular hatred and contempt for the enemy had emerged from the first days of Operation Barbarossa and increased when the blockade began. During the last week in

September, a Kirov factory employee had written in a statement: "The fascist swine is puking on our city in full force. As a result of the artillery fire, shells are hitting our factory. Let the fascist vermin know that we will not abandon our duty. We will produce as many artillery shells as it takes to destroy the fascists outside Leningrad."[81]

During the winter, official rhetoric and popular mood coincided to a large extent. In newspaper articles, published cartoons, and propaganda posters, as well as in monitored conversations, Germany's leaders were increasingly portrayed as despicable beasts, rodents, and vermin, as subhuman and demonic, for the suffering they imposed. The growing hatred engendered a widespread desire for retribution (Figures 68 and 69.) The summaries of popular mood from the Kirov factory *partkom* files provide many examples. On 17 December, following the liberation of the city of Kalinin, Tekia Petrova told 180 of her fellow foundry workers: "I am full of sorrow. My husband is dead. The fascist bandits who have attacked our Soviet land are guilty of his premature death. However, not dwelling on grief, I today rejoice with you, together with all people. I, like all of us, rejoice in the great victory of the Red Army. From the depths of my soul and heart I want to cry out so that my voice could be heard by the heroic troops, our defenders: 'Kill the fascist reptiles to the very last one, don't let up, kill the fascist reptile who has brought us such grief and deprivations.' I am certain that the fate that befell the German robber-army before Moscow awaits them before Leningrad. But for this we are obliged to work better, to give the front more ammunition."[82] Starting in the autumn of 1941, factory workers had been encouraged by trade unions to sign a "vengeance score" (*schet mesti*), which was a pledge to overfulfill the work norm by an amount equal to the norm of a co-worker who had been killed or incapacitated by enemy fire or the spreading hunger.[83] This practice was similar to pledges made by front-line troops to avenge a fallen comrade by killing an enemy soldier. In early January *partkom* members of the Kirov works made a group pledge, which reveals the depth of their hatred for the enemy, in response to a report by Molotov that described German atrocities. The pledge read in part:

> We will neither forget nor forgive the unheard-of, monstrous evil crimes of Hitler's plundering army. . . .
> The horde of aggressors, robbers, and murderers bestially devastates and ravages our cities and villages. . . .
> We demand retribution.
> Retribution, let the most ruthless retribution rain down on the heads of the bestial fascist predators. . . .
> This retribution will be carried out by what we produce, which we with abundant energy will give to the fighters of the Red Army.
> This retribution will destroy and wipe from the face of the earth the

entire pack of fascist beasts, whose real face has been exposed by their wild barbarian evil acts.

Neither Hitler nor his accomplices will escape this retribution. . . .[84]

Soldiers often visited the Kirov factory, which was located about three miles from the front. On 23 February, Red Army Day, workers met with members of the 14th Red Banner Rifle Regiment. When one or two of the soldiers claimed to have killed about eighty enemy troops, the workers burst into applause. On another occasion, a partisan named Yevdokia Ivanova told a group of Kirov workers that Germans had killed her father and mother and beat her younger sister half to death. They had then proceeded to plunder her house and burn it to the ground. She managed to escape and join a band of partisans. "We . . . burn with hatred toward the vile invader," she said. During her talk, German guns fired at the factory, but no one left the meeting.[85] During the third week in March, a medic's assistant named Orlova told a group of workers that all of her closest relatives had gone to the front, and many had died. She claimed to have saved the lives of, or led to safety, over a hundred combatants. She saw her mortally wounded husband on the battlefield. At the end of her talk, she told her audience: "As long as I live, as long as blood courses through my veins, I will calmly take part in the battles to save the lives of wounded soldiers, commanders, and political workers. And I call on you, comrade Kirov workers, to put all your effort into giving the front more ammunition and arms."[86]

Anfisa Kharitonova, a sixty-year-old woman who worked in a candy factory, provides a similar example. She knitted a wool scarf and took it with her when she visited the front with a delegation of workers. At an airstrip, she asked the commander to point out the pilot who had "annihilated the largest number of Germans." He introduced her to one who had downed sixteen enemy fighters. Kharitonova hugged and kissed the pilot and pulled from her breast the scarf, which she lovingly wrapped around his neck. She told him: "My dear son, this is for you, for your bravery, for your love for the homeland and for Leningrad." The pilot was overcome with emotion, tears welled up in his eyes, and he hugged and kissed the elderly woman. Later, at an assembly of workers, Kharitonova said: "No words can express all the boiling hatred for the damned fascist curs. When I hear of all the evil deeds they have committed against our brothers and sisters and against our little children, my heart bleeds. . . . I cry with hatred for the enemy of my Motherland. We know that the wilderness has lions, tigers, and jackals. These innocent creatures, transformed by the swastika, have ransacked the wilderness and seized our flourishing land. If I were younger, I would grab a gun and mercilessly kill those beasts."[87] A group of German POWs was met with jeers when they were paraded through Leningrad in August 1942 (Figures 55 and 56).

Germany's declaration of war on the United States on 11 December, four days after Japan's attack at Pearl Harbor, was covered in Leningrad's press, but appears to have had little immediate effect on morale in the city. Mention of America's entry into the war rarely shows up in diaries, memoirs, or informant reports, although workers at a group meeting at the Kirov plant on 12 December asked whether help could be expected from the United States or England following the U.S. entry into the war.[88] No doubt, Leningraders welcomed the news, but likely figured that their city's fate would be decided before any American operations could benefit Leningrad directly or indirectly. As is discussed below, Leningraders became interested in Allied policy in June 1942, when the U.S. government practically promised that a second front in Europe would be opened later that year.

All the while, political attitudes continued to fluctuate in reaction to changes in food rations. The bread ration, which accounted for most of the food consumed during the worst of the starvation period, was raised four times in the winter. Following the last increase, on 22 March, most workers received 600 grams of bread daily; dependents and children got 400. If cuts in rations during the fall sparked protest, the first increase in the bread ration on 25 December produced temporary jubilation. People naturally welcomed larger rations, but many also interpreted the increase to mean that the city's liberation must be at hand. The authorities, they felt, must be so confident that the siege would end in the very near future that they could risk depleting scarce food reserves. (On the other hand, many interpreted the mass exodus across the Ladoga ice road as a preliminary step to surrendering the city.) In early January Antiufeev reported that the bread ration was widely viewed as a barometer of victory or defeat at the front.[89] Many also guessed correctly that another reason rations could be raised during the winter was that there were far fewer mouths to feed as a result of the starvation.

In November party informants had overheard people criticizing Stalin when rations were lowered. For instance, a female worker named Shemiakina at Lenenergo at the end of a work shift had reacted to Stalin's address commemorating the Bolshevik Revolution with the following words: "If Stalin received 300 grams of bread a day, we would see how much he would work. It's too bad that the army doesn't desert the front. I've had enough of the blabber from the radio. These Communists are responsible for all of it."[90] Yet, following the first increase in the bread ration, praise for Stalin was noted. For example, Kirov workers said that the increase was proof that Stalin cared for them.[91] This sense of relief, optimism, and gratitude, however, proved fleeting when the siege did not quickly come to an end. Antiufeev wrote on 9 January: "If in the first days after the increase in the bread ration the hopes of the city's population were raised, then in the last few days, those hopes have fallen into despondency for a large part of the population." A German intelligence report of Task Force (*Einsatz-gruppe*) A[92] from 12 January stated that Stalin's name was used surprisingly little in propaganda appeals in Leningrad.[93] A week or so later, just as Moscow was about to enlarge operations on the Ladoga ice road, one person was heard by a party informant to say sardonically, "Soon they will evacuate us to the Volkov cemetery."[94] Cafeteria workers and bread shop clerks were frequent targets of verbal abuse. Between 10 and 12 January, a group of female Kirov workers yelled at the staff of one of the factory's cafeterias after they had received only bread for about the last twenty days: "Swine, parasites, you clip ration coupons for groats and butter, but give a little bit of water in return. You're stuffed and fat yourselves, and you feed the workers water." The information officer of the workshop's *partkom*, one Cherniadiev, tried to intervene to explain that the entire city was short of food, but the workers responded: "You all go to hell."[95]

The bread ration was increased on 24 January, but within three days, when the temperature had dropped to about minus forty degrees Fahrenheit and many stores received less than a third of their usual bread supply, the popular mood turned ugly. The city's leaders were excoriated by those standing for several hours in lines of seven or eight hundred people in the pitch dark early on 26 and 27 January. A common refrain was that city leaders lived a privileged existence and lacked for nothing, while the population starved: "I myself saw them bringing the bread to Smolny. They're probably sitting there stuffed. . . . Our rulers, of course, are full. They get not only bread, but also lunch and dinner. So, they don't care about us, about starving people." On or about the same day, an employee named Silin at Bakery No. 8 said to a member of the Sverdlovsk *raikom* named Makanov: "Aha, the bureaucrats from the *raikom* ran away when they saw the lines at the bread stores. The bureaucrats sit in warmth and light and stuff themselves and don't see how the people are suffering and dying. And when they see food lines, they flee and start looking for the guilty little people. The little people aren't guilty, but you bureaucrats from the *raikom* and the *raisovet* are. Zhdanov sits there and who knows what he thinks." At this time, the bookkeeper of the Comedy Theater, one Lishina, was heard to say: "The people are starving, but they bring Zhdanov cocoa in bed." (Zhdanov underlined these two references to himself.)[96]

Recovery and Endurance

The evacuation over Ladoga was suspended for a month following the breakup of the ice road. By the last week in May, the ice had melted sufficiently to allow ships to resume crossing the lake. Throughout the rest of

1942, as the city's population was pared down to those who were essential for its defense, and as the number of starvation deaths declined significantly, Leningrad achieved a measure of stability. Defenses were strengthened, gardens planted, energy and fuel lines were laid under Ladoga, and firewood was stockpiled in preparation for a second winter under siege.

Although the enemy remained encamped just outside the city and Soviet troops were reeling in retreat in the summer of 1942, Leningraders could pause for the first time to reflect upon the unprecedented ordeal to which the city had been subjected in the first year of the war. The occasion for the beginning of this reflection process was the production of a documentary film on the blockade. At the same time that the evacuation over the ice road came to a halt in April, the film *The Defense of Leningrad* was completed. However, city leaders including Zhdanov, Kuznetsov, and Popkov roundly denounced the film when they privately screened it on 17 April. They criticized the film for showing lines in front of bread shops, frozen cars stalled on the ice road, and snowed-in trolley cars. In the words of Popkov, the film displayed "our complete disorder." They demanded the replacement of images that portrayed a suffering population with scenes showing enthusiastic workers, successful production, and tanks rolling straight from the factory to the front. They also ordered that the opening shot of the equestrian statue of Peter the Great that traditionally symbolized his city be replaced with a Lenin monument.[97]

As Document 58 shows, the reworked film was released under the title *Leningrad in Battle*. It ran for one and a half to two hours and premiered on 9 July in Leningrad, in Moscow (where fifty thousand people viewed it that day), and perhaps elsewhere. It included scenes from the front, defense plants, fortification construction sites, antiaircraft defense, the ice road, and the massive city clean-up. Front commander Govorov, who was among the first to see the film, was quoted in *Leningradskaia pravda* as saying: "The grand epic of the defense of the city is shown correctly, without embellishment."[98] However, as the document reveals, not all Leningraders agreed with Govorov's official assessment. Many correctly perceived and complained that the film represented a sanitized and distorted view of reality. This document is an excellent example of the origin of the distinct parting of the ways between the official rendition of the blockade and popular memory.[99] The film articulated themes that endured through the rest of the Soviet era: heroism, steadfast defense by soldiers and civilians, and unity of front and rear. Although these themes contained a great deal of truth, as the critical comments in the document show, images of blockade life that revealed the failures and shortcomings of the military and political leadership were absent. The mass starvation and lack of transportation and electrical power during the winter were only obliquely suggested or ignored altogether, and how Leningrad came to be blockaded was not explained.

· Document 58 ·

Report from Antiufeev and Office Administrator Bulgakov to *gorkom* secretaries Zhdanov, Kuznetsov, Kapustin, and A. I. Makhanov on public reaction to the documentary film *Leningrad in Battle*, 22 July 1942, TsGAIPD SPb f. 24, op. 2v, d. 5761, ll. 137–40.

LENINGRAD OBKOM AND GORKOM OSOBYI SEKTOR
INFORMATION SUMMARY

On 9 July, a new documentary film, *Leningrad in Battle*, began showing on the city's screens. The film first played on five screens, and later on nine of the twenty-eight[100] operating in the city.

In eleven days, the film was viewed by 115,300 people. The overwhelming majority of the population in such *raiony* as Kirovsky, Moskovsky, Volodarsky, and Dzerzhinsky have still not seen this picture.

Leningraders are giving the film high marks; they approve of its honesty and express satisfaction with the cameramen's work. Here are characteristic statements:

"*Leningrad in Battle* is one of the best films I have ever had occasion to see. It tells the story simply and honestly about the difficult days our city has lived through. Each frame restores to memory familiar, difficult scenes and gives rise to anger and ill will toward the enemy." (Com. Eferiev, party organization secretary at the Leningrad River Port).

"This film has great power and its power is in its truth. When you see it, you feel like working even more and helping the front even better." (Com. Novikov, director of Plant No. 154).

"A fine and honest film. Our Kirovsky *raion* is shown very well." (Com. Ivanova, worker at the Red Confectioner factory).

Com. Byrdina, party office secretary at the Zheliabov factory, says:

"Among the Leningraders building the fortifications around the city, I see workers from my factory, too. A girl on a tower is looking at the sky, searching it for enemy predators. She looks so much like Golikova, the factory worker, a brave girl who in the days of the heaviest bombing never left the factory tower. The picture was shot honestly. We should give the cameramen our enormous thanks."

Com. Smirnova, an instructor in the agitation and propaganda office of the VKP(b) Petrogradsky *raikom*, said:

"Disturbing pages—the road of ice. An unforgettable moment when the last vehicles are going over the water. I saw my apartment building with its little tower in the film. I've been through more than 300 air raids on that tower and I was a witness to everything that happened."

Viewers greet with applause the appearance on the screen of Comrade Stalin and Comrade Zhdanov, and they admire the partisans' military actions. At the sight of the pathetic, cowardly figures of the captive Hitlerites, approving remarks and ridicule are heard in the halls. Some frames, especially the first ones, where they show the blooming city in peacetime, make many people cry.

They emphasize that the film does a good job of reflecting the work of the defense factories during aerial bombardments and mortar attack, as well as the steadfastness and courage of the workers fulfilling defense orders during the harsh winter days. Everyone is delighted by the heroic work on Lake Ladoga's road of ice.

Of course, in some viewers' opinions, the film still doesn't show well enough the real life in the besieged city: the people black from soot and dirt, people with dystrophy, people dying on planks, corpses lying in the streets, etc. Some citizens state that the frame with composer Asafiev is not convincing enough. They want to see sooty apartments with temporary stoves and dying people, people wrapped up in quilts lining up from two in the morning at the stores.

Also expressed were wishes like these:

"In one of the frames we see 125 grams of bread being given out to the public. Why not demonstrate, right away, what this led to. After all, those episodes with transporting the dead on sleighs that they show can be explained only by the absence of public transport in the city."

People also feel that the frames about cleaning the city don't give a complete notion of the tremendous effort expended on this work. They say this:

"In the film, cleaning the city is reduced to just cleaning the sidewalks and the thoroughfares of snow and ice. Where is the work cleaning the courtyards and staircases of trash and filth?"

Some would have liked to see a procession of sleighs with the boxes of trash and filth heading toward the Neva, the Fontanka, and the Bypass Canal, and the condition of the city after the cleaning.

They also comment that the movie does not show the selfless work of the factory collectives and the women and children extinguishing incendiary bombs and the resulting fires, the heavy freight trains with food for Leningrad, the work on universal military training, the tending for the injured Red Army soldiers and commanders, the caring for children, the moments of rescuing people buried in rubble.

The main bookkeeper of the Red Guard factory, Com. Bruk, draws this conclusion:

"When you see the film, you wonder how a hero city that had put up such a powerful defense could have ended up in such a grave position. An explanation for this fact should have been given in the movie."

In the opinion of individual viewers, the film has a few distortions and mistakes:

"In the attics we first poured sand on the bombs and then used as much water as was needed. The film shows incendiary bombs being put out with water." (Com. Vasilieva, worker at the Marti factory).

"The store buildings weren't as clean and bright as they look in the film. In most stores, even during the daytime, they worked with oil lamps."

"The people getting bread in the store look fat and healthy. At that time it was very rare to encounter people like that."

"The labors to clean the city are shown unsuccessfully. They shot the moments when people were doing more standing than working. Any impression is lost."

Some comrades believe that as a result of all these shortcomings, the film doesn't give a full notion of the situation in Leningrad to the people who were not in the city at that moment. People are also saying:

"The film is honest but not vivid enough. It seems to me that for those who did not see Leningrad in those days, the film doesn't give a full sense of the hardships we were suffering." (Com. Fedorova, party organization secretary, 14th Bread Factory).

"The daily life of Leningraders is shown very poorly. In my opinion, the film will be understood in full measure only by those who lived through it all themselves. It won't be sufficiently understandable to anyone who wasn't in the city." (Com. Kudriavtsev, *partkom* secretary, 2nd Five Year Plan Factory).

Based on viewers' responses, the quotations from Comrades Lenin and Stalin were not cited successfully at the very end of the film. At that point the light was often going on in the halls and people were leaving.

Head of the Organizational-Instructional Office of the *gorkom* VKP(b) Antiufeev

Office Administrator Bulgakov

While Leningrad became better fortified and provisioned in the summer of 1942, its remaining inhabitants grew uneasy over Germany's military offensive in the south, because collapse of the Soviet war effort there might lead to a renewed German effort to seize Leningrad. By mid-July, German armies had taken Kerch on the eastern end of the Crimean peninsula, Voronezh on the upper Don, and Sevastopol. The fall of the Black Sea naval base at Sevastopol on 4 July, which was reported almost immediately in the Leningrad press, particularly affected Leningraders because of its similarity to their own predicament. Sevastopol, like Leningrad, was a key coastal military objective that had withstood a prolonged siege. Antiufeev acknowledged in the first week of July that the level of pessimism had increased. One person was quoted as saying, "Last year's history is being repeated. After Kerch, Kupiansk,[101] after Kupiansk, Sevastopol, and now it's Leningrad's turn." Antiufeev also noted that the desire to evacuate from Leningrad increased after Sevastopol fell.[102] As Germany's successes mounted in the south, lingering pro-German sentiment in Leningrad was rekindled as the next document shows.

· Document 59 ·

Report from Antiufeev and Bulgakov to Zhdanov, Kuznetsov, Kapustin,
and Makhanov on anti-Soviet public sentiment, 13 July 1942,
TsGAIPD SPb f. 24, op. 2v, d. 5761, ll. 117–20.

SUMMARY REPORT

Recently, certain anti-Soviet elements that had been lying low in the city have become active.[103] Taking advantage of the Hitlerites' partial temporary successes along certain sectors of the front and of measures taken to evacuate some the city's population, they are attempting to shake Leningraders' moral stability and high political consciousness.

On 11 July, at one of the workshops of the Liquor and Vodka Factory, a fascist leaflet was discovered pasted to a door ("An Appeal to the Women of Leningrad"). A check conducted after this in parts of the factory uncovered three more such hostile leaflets lying around in different places. The matter has been handed over to the NKVD organs. A certain *Lenskaia*, who works as a nurse in Clinic No. 22 and resides at 61/1 Mezhdunarodny Prospect[104] handed over to building manager Com. Mytareva a scrap of paper on which was written by hand:

"Down with the Stalinist regime. Too much blood has been shed. 3 1/2 million people are perishing and there is no end in sight.[105] The time has come to help the Hitlerite army. Down with Stalin's reign. It can only lead to the people's ruin."

At the bottom it said that whoever received the leaflet should make five copies of it and drop them in apartment house mailboxes. The case of this sortie by enemy agents is being investigated by organs of the NKVD.

Enemy elements are attempting to sow panic, trying to defile the Red Army, and extolling the Hitlerite aggressors. Shubin, who works in the Financial Office of Vasileostrovsky *raion*, has these thoughts:

"I have little faith in the Red Army's victory over fascism. The only reason the Germans aren't bombing is because they're hoping to take Leningrad without having to do that."

Semenova, who works as a yard-keeper in housekeeping at 11/10 Nakhimson Prospect, to a remark by political organizer Morozov about her poor work, replied with irony and a threat:

"Just wait, just you wait. There's going to be a holiday on our street, too."

Orlovskaia, a worker in the scrap shop of the Skorokhod factory, while working on defense installations, said:

"Carrying ties and frames—that's not women's work. The foremen themselves don't work. They pay too little for our work. The Germans don't make you work like that."

Not long ago, two workers, Vorobieva and Dedova, went up to Com. Kalinin, foreman of shop 41 at the Bolshevik factory, and worker Com. Timofeev and asked: "Why are they making gun mountings in our shop?" After

Com. Timofeev gave the appropriate explanation, Vorobieva and Dedova, in the presence of other women workers, made the following anti-Soviet speech:

"Here you say that the Germans are mocking the Soviet Union's citizens. Ours are mocking our citizens, too. In the village of Rybatskoe, our army lieutenants killed citizens Karavaeva and Rybyshkina. They killed seven families altogether and burned down their houses and no measures of any kind were taken against the guilty parties."

The case has been handed over to the factory's NKVD officer.

Instances have been noted of enemy agents attempting to play on the feelings of individual citizens subject to evacuation and trying to defile and undermine evacuation measures. A certain Eidelman, who resides at 20 Goncharova Street, was agitating against the evacuation, trying to convince building residents not to go, frightening them with the hardships of the move and life in a new place, characterizing the Hitlerites as "people who have done nothing to disturb the peaceful population." Eidelman was arrested on 11 July. Com. Bobrovsky, instructor at the Smolninsky RK VKP(b), held special discussions with the residents of this building and explained to them the reasons for the evacuation.

Among individuals who are persistently refusing to leave Leningrad, there are marauders who have taken advantage of this difficult moment for Leningraders to enrich themselves and to arrange for their own personal prosperity. Housewife Komissarova, who resides on [address blocked out] Prospect, shouted at a political organizer:

"Swine. You want to evacuate us, so why aren't you going yourself? I'd rather strangle my child and hang myself. How would you like that for an evacuation?"

It turns out that Komissarova's husband, who was somehow released from being drafted into the Red Army, got himself a job as a cook in one of the cafeterias, bought up and traded lots of valuable things, and exchanged their room for a separate apartment.

Recently, people have been turning up at evacuation points and picking out the elderly and most helpless citizens. They offer them "services" of some kind and then engage in extortion.

Many people are raising a question about strengthening our readiness and taking more decisive measures to fight marauding. They believe we have to improve security for enterprises and especially for lines defending property on territory located near where military units are stationed (tractors, barrels of fuel, and so on). They point out that it is unacceptable for people to be walking about freely along the defense lines carrying sacks and gathering herbs without anyone checking their documents. Accounts from the Kuybyshevski RK VKP(b) report on the arrest along one of these routes of a certain Vorobiev, who had worked in an advertising graphics studio of the Film Making Administration and been brought here to work. Vorobiev was making sketches of the installations including the [serial] numbers.

In connection with the impending elimination of some of the city's enter-

prises and institutions, the question arises <u>of preventing any possible theft of their property and valuables.</u>
Head of the Organizational-Instructional Office, gorkom VKP(b) Antiufeev
Office Administrator Bulgakov

For the same reasons that Leningraders followed closely news from the USSR's other fronts, they continually expressed a deep interest in the wider war. For example, among the questions that usually surfaced at assemblies of workers in large defense plants was the Soviet Union's relations with Japan, which revealed the ongoing anxiety over the prospects of having to fight a two-front war. Leningraders were also interested in relations with the Allies. In the spring of 1942, Molotov traveled to Britain and the United States. On 26 May, he signed a twenty-year treaty of alliance with the British, and on 11 June, while he was in Washington, the U.S. government released a public statement that included the sentence: "In the course of the conversations full understanding was reached with regard to the urgent task of creating a second front in Europe in 1942." The same day, a wider Lend Lease agreement between the United States and the USSR was also concluded. The Soviet government chose to interpret the statement on the second front to be a firm guarantee that it would be opened in 1942 and reported it immediately as such to the Soviet public; however, a close reading of the sentence above shows that it was a little less than that, and in fact Army Chief of Staff George Marshall reportedly opposed any mention of 1942 in the communiqué.[106]

In his report of 12 June on Leningrad's popular mood, Antiufeev observed that workers applauded the "promise" to open a second front in 1942, that they were inspired to boost output to bring the day of victory closer (Figure 53). A brigade leader named Aladin at the Marti shipyards was heard to say: "In order to finish off fascism more quickly, we have to increase the output of ammunition and arms. This is our sacred duty." A female worker at the Ekonomaizer plant named Moshnova said: "It's good that they've concluded a treaty and agreement. It's obvious that Hitler's demise will come soon and that means an end to the war." Workers at the Bolshevichka factory asked whether the accords dealt specifically with breaking the blockade. Antiufeev added that a small percentage of the public suspected that the United States and Britain might betray the USSR as Hitler had done in 1941.[107]

Ogoltsov, Kubatkin's assistant, wrote at least four reports between 13 and 20 June that summarized popular reactions to the Allied accords. While acknowledging that "the overwhelming majority of the population approves" of the agreements, the NKVD reports characteristically devoted more attention to "negative" opinions than did Antiufeev's summary. People were heard to say that the English could not be trusted, that the "English and Americans are only playing with us," that the Western Allies just wanted to use the Soviet Union against Germany to weaken both adversaries, and that the USSR could expect war with Japan as a result of the pact with England. Karl Eliasberg, director of the Leningrad Radio Committee Symphony, who famously conducted Shostakovich's Seventh Symphony in August 1942, was under surveillance by the NKVD. He was heard saying that England was responsible for ruining the alliance between the Soviet Union and Germany in 1941 but that at present the only viable course of action was a close union with England, though such an alliance would be more beneficial to England.[108]

As news of successive defeats in the south reached Leningrad, people became more impatient for the second front and began to link Leningrad's fate with the awaited offensive. In late June Antiufeev observed that some Leningraders believed that another front was needed to draw enemy troops away from Leningrad. One worker was quoted as saying, "What are England and America waiting for? Why don't they open a second front? Hitler can concentrate more forces on the Leningrad Front and then it will become very difficult here."[109]

Document 60 shows that Churchill's arrival in Moscow on 12 August significantly boosted hopes that the second front would be opened in the very near future, which is ironic since one of Churchill's reasons for traveling to Moscow at that time was to inform Stalin that Britain and the United States had opted instead to invade North Africa that year. At the same time, the number who doubted that the Western Allies would invade Europe had risen since the plan for a second front had been announced in June. An NKVD report of 19 August cited someone who said that the situation was very poor due to defeats in the south, "and help from the Allies will only be in words." Another commented that the Allies wanted to delay opening the second front in order to allow Germany to bleed the USSR white.[110] The document below shows that Churchill's visit also sparked wild rumors about a secret agreement to give control of Leningrad to the Western Allies as the price for wartime aid. The NKVD had picked up similar rumors back in late April 1942.[111]

· Document 60 ·

Report from Antiufeev and Klebanov to Zhdanov, Kuznetsov, Kapustin, and Makhanov on public reaction to Churchill's visit to Moscow, 18 August 1942, TsGAIPD SPb f. 24, op. 2v, d. 5761, ll. 182–182ob.

LENINGRAD OBKOM AND GORKOM OSOBYI SEKTOR
INFORMATION SUMMARY

The Anglo-Soviet communiqué published today on the talks between Churchill and Com. Stalin has been the cause of great excitement among the laborers and intelligentsia of Leningrad. The arrival in Moscow of Great Britain's prime minister and the U.S. president's representative is considered to be a fact of exceptional importance for joint actions by the countries allied against fascist Germany.

Leningraders are expressing their opinion in various ways, but most are expressing confidence in the imminent opening of a second front in Europe. The following statements are characteristic:

"It looks like a second front's going to be opened soon."

"Churchill didn't come to Moscow for nothing. You have to think it wasn't just a visit but that they were setting deadlines for opening a second front."

"In the next few days we should expect decisive events."

In a personal conversation with engineer Vishniakov, Com. Filatov, dean of the Blood Transfusion Institute, stated:

"This is such an unexpected announcement. After all, no one guessed that Churchill was in Moscow. They were probably talking about pinning down the specifics of the agreement. After this we should be expecting the imminent opening of a second front."

Com. Vainshtein, head of the planning office at the Transport Bureau of the Breadbaking Trust, said with satisfaction:

"Up until now, I thought the press and the public were more concerned than the governments with opening a second front in England and America. Now I'm convinced I was wrong. After Churchill's visit to Moscow, I and a lot of others have no more doubts that England and America are preparing to open a second front and in the near future a second front will be opened." The overwhelming majority of statements boiled down to this.

"It's nice to read Churchill's statement about how no matter what the difficulties England is going to fight arm in arm with us, like comrades and brothers, until we've put an end to the Hitlerite regime." (Com. Plakunova, political organizer of the 6th precinct, Leninsky *raion*).

"When I heard over the radio that Churchill had been in Moscow and talking with Com. Stalin about the further conduct of the war, I immediately thought, Well, now we don't need to worry about a second front, there's going be one, there has to be." (Com. Anashkina, worker, Bolshevichka factory).

"If I'd learned about this a day earlier, I wouldn't have evacuated my family. Now we can be certain that our allies will shift from words to actions, and this will quickly create a drastic turnabout on our front." (Com. Viktorov, engineer, Elektroapparat factory).

"The people had begun to doubt our allies' sincerity. But Churchill's arrival and his talks with Com. Stalin give us hopes that in a week or two our allies will open a second front." (Com. Shneider, party organization secretary, model shoe factory, Frunzensky *raion*).

Many are asking perplexedly:

"Why cover the meetings in England and America in the newspapers so broadly if right at that time Churchill was in Moscow and discussing opening a second front with Com. Stalin?"

Some are still skeptical toward the Anglo-Soviet communiqué. Kachanov, a worker in the 19th Fire Crew (Kirovsky *raion*), says:

"Look at them coming and lulling us with their talk, but there's no point counting on their real help. They've promised a lot, but there hasn't been anything yet. We have to win victory by ourselves."

At the payroll office of the Pneumatics factory, the following conversation took place between employees Petrova and Ivanova:

"All this is nothing but talk."

"Yes, they've been yapping about a second front for how many months? But things are right where they started. Is there ever going to be an end to this jawing? The workers are demanding a new front, not discussions about it."

At the newspaper displays you can hear conversations like this:

"More chatter. . . . If they did as much as they talked, the Germans would have been beaten a long time ago."

All kinds of rumors have started to spread. People are saying, for instance, that in England they've published Churchill's statement about how the agreement with the Soviet Union is being carried out precisely, that a second front will be opened in August.

The Communist Gusakova, a worker at a Vasileostrovsky confection shop, told Com. Samokhvalova, the party organization secretary at the machine factory of the Sverdlovsky industrial combine:

"They've agreed to sell Leningrad to the Americans, things are going badly for us, soon they're going to be introducing American passports for us, and Communists are going to be in trouble. . . ."

It should be pointed out that party organizations are being slow and clumsy about explaining the significance of this event. They cite the shortage of newspapers and the absence of any instructions from above, etc.

Head of the Organizational-Instructional Office of the *gorkom* VKP(b) Antiufeev

Office Administrator Klebanov

When the second front failed to materialize by the end of the year, confidence in the Allies deteriorated further as concern about the coming winter increased. In the words of a lathe operator named Storonkin at the Karl Marx factory in mid-October: "Soon winter will come. It will be worse than the last one. Again people will begin to die from hunger. All hopes for opening a second front are lost. We have allies that equally hate Germany and the Soviet Union."[112]

Morale in Leningrad, as elsewhere in the USSR, rose considerably after the victory at Stalingrad in February 1943, which turned the tide in the Soviet-German War, and more so after the massive tank battle in the Kursk salient six months later, which made a German retreat from Soviet territory nearly inevitable. In late June 1943, on the eve of the Allies' campaign in Italy, Leningraders continued to complain about the lack of a second front in Europe. As one person said, "our allies stand like outside spectators."[113] (At the same time, the Soviet government concealed from its people the extent of Lend Lease supply in 1943 and 1944, which played a considerable role in the Soviet victory.)

On 25 May 1943, party and NKVD reports described public reaction to the disbanding of the Comintern, which had been announced in *Leningradskaia pravda* on 23 May. A number of people were overheard approving the decision on the grounds that dismantling the Comintern would strengthen the wartime alliance by undercutting German propaganda that portrayed the USSR as a threat to nations by fomenting worldwide worker revolution. Some lamented the decision as a concession to the Allies, that religious circles in the West had forced the change, and that hopes for world revolution were buried forever.[114] What is most noteworthy is what was almost entirely absent from both reports, especially the NKVD one. Always on the lookout for anti-Soviet sentiment, though pursuing it less aggressively in 1943 than in 1941,[115] the NKVD heard few voices that contended that the end of the Comintern would lead to a fundamental restructuring of communist ideology or a weakening of its authority within the Soviet Union as a whole or in Leningrad. One store employee reportedly stated that under pressure from the Allies, "we should expect extensive changes in government structure in the USSR." Likewise, the head of the chemical laboratory of the Radishchev leather factory was heard to say that "after the war we should have a workers' government, but adjusted a little—the bourgeois will not be criticized severely."[116] Toward the end of the blockade period and on into 1944, the populace seems to have hoped and expected the party to relax some of its control. The party and the NKVD, for example, detected signs of renewed interest in Christianity in 1944. Leningraders expected that new freedoms granted to the Orthodox Church in 1943 would give the Church a more prominent voice in society, that communism and Christianity could co-exist.[117] Yet, Leningraders by and large appear to have assumed and basically accepted, reluctantly or willingly, that the party would control political life.

In 1943, the Communist Party of the Soviet Union, including the LPO, was reviving and rebuilding. In the latter half of 1943, 366 primary party organizations in Leningrad, representing a quarter of the city's party members, held elections for the first time since 1941. Propaganda articles began to feature more prominently themes on communist ideology and to extol the party's wartime exploits.[118] The resurgence of the LPO in 1943 stands in sharp contrast to its predicament in September 1941, when it was shrinking rapidly because it was able to replace only a small fraction of its members who had gone to the front, and when many of the members who remained in Leningrad were secretly dissociating themselves from the party. The lack of widespread, fundamental criticism of the existence of communism in 1943 was not a function of a lack of things to complain about. The frustrations and deprivations of living in a besieged city, not to mention physical danger from increased artillery shelling in the latter half of 1943, continued. For example, in August 1943, Antiufeev wrote a separate report on servicemen and their wives and mothers, who complained about rude, callous, slothful, and bureaucratic officials who would take up to several months to resolve such matters as safeguarding housing and storing personal belongings for those who were away from their homes for long periods, receiving food ration cards and pensions, and sending parcels to the front.[119]

An exception to the pattern of declining pro-German and profoundly anti-Soviet sentiment emerged in a most surprising place in the summer of 1943: Leningrad's NKGB headquarters. On 30 July, a handwritten leaflet was discovered on the sixth floor. It read:

> Charwomen, doormen, workers, and custodians, don't listen to the agitators, they all lie.
> The German is not insulted and is not freezing from hunger. It's only the Russians, all of us are insulted and freezing from hunger, and they don't want to feed you. . . . Go over to the Germans—it will be better there. I was there and know well that things are good with the Germans. Russians are very satisfied there and there are no kolkhozes.
> Damn these kolkhozes and the authorities. They sit and stuff themselves. But the workers' and peasants' blood flows for reasons they don't understand.
> Down with Communists, down with commissars. . . . Down with the authorities.

Through handwriting analysis, it was determined that the forty-one-year-old charwoman of the sixth floor, M. I. Kuznetsova, had written the leaflet.[120]

In the last year of the blockade popular hatred of the enemy, of Germany more than Finland, increased. Fear of a new German attempt to seize Leningrad virtually disappeared as Germany continued its retreat in the south, and so did any lingering pro-German sympathy. As anticipation of a victorious end to the war grew, attention turned toward prosecution of

Germany for war crimes. On 17 July, Antiufeev reported on popular reaction to readings throughout the city of materials pertaining to crimes committed by Germany and its allies during their occupation of the Krasnodar area. He noted that the populace "expresses indignation, anger, and hatred toward the German people and their auxiliaries—traitors to the homeland." The unanimous opinion in the report was to vanquish as thoroughly and quickly as possible the vile invader, who was portrayed as inhumane and inhuman. Below are a few examples he cited from various industrial employees, all of whom were women:

> "We will never forget the bloody evil deeds and murders of the hated enemy. . . . The Hitlerite marauders will pay dearly for all torment and torture inflicted on our children, wives, and old people."
> "I want more quickly to wipe these vermin from the face of the earth. . . ."
> "My heart bleeds and hatred becomes strong like armor plating. Nothing will atone for their guilt. . . ."[121]

A month earlier Antiufeev had quoted an old metal worker who said: "I will work around the clock. My son was killed at the front defending the city of Lenin. My daughter took his place in the Red Army. I'm an old man, but if necessary I'll go to the front."[122]

Leningraders became more outraged at the enemy when artillery shelling of the city increased in July. While bombing raids practically ceased in the second half of 1943, shells hit the city every day in August. Artillery fire reached its peak intensity for the blockade period in September when a reported 11,394 rounds were fired at the city. Forty-six percent of the enemy's artillery fire on Leningrad occurred in 1943.[123] The bombardment infuriated Leningraders who rightfully understood that it was militarily pointless, conducted out of frustration and spite, since Germany had practically no chance of taking the city by that time. On 24 December 1943, Antiufeev quoted a factory worker named Nechaeva: "The fascist beast doesn't have any large hopes of victory. He senses that he is living his last days before Leningrad, and that's why he's shelling the city." In the same report, a worker with forty years of experience who had two sons at the front reportedly said: "In recent days the fascists, like exhausted beasts, are thrashing about in a cage. They launch their beastly missiles at a peaceful population. This increases our hatred toward the enemy. To all of the attacks of the German bandits, we will respond with Stakhanovite work, by raising the productivity of labor."[124] One month later in late January, many workers in Leningrad's southern districts climbed to their rooftops to watch the spectacle of some half a million artillery shells screaming overhead toward German positions as the Red Army launched the offensive that finally liberated Leningrad.

CHAPTER 6

The Question of Organized Opposition

The existence of fluctuating degrees of pro-German and anti-Soviet sentiment in wartime Leningrad naturally raises the question to what extent those attitudes coalesced into active organized opposition to Soviet power through instigation either by enemy agents or by Leningraders themselves. That, in turn, raises another question: How reliable are NKVD assessments of KR activity?

In Document 45 Kubatkin stated that from 22 June 1941, through the end of September 1942, the NKVD arrested a total of "1,246 spies and saboteurs planted by the enemy," though it is unclear from this information how many were arrested in the city rather than in outlying areas closer to enemy lines and what the precise reasons were for the arrests. Many, and probably a majority, of the enemy agents described in any detail in NKVD documents were apprehended in the *oblast'*. One has to wonder how many of those arrested anywhere in the blockaded territory were falsely charged with collaborating with the enemy by overzealous NKVD officials, because not one major act of sabotage has been definitively shown to have been carried out by enemy agents within Leningrad during the blockade.[1] German documents examined for this study are not illuminating in this matter. Documents from the German Eighteenth Army Command and Task Force A refer to agent reports from within Leningrad but do not indicate how many Germans or collaborating Soviet residents were sent into any part of the blockade zone.

There is practically no evidence that any conspiracy, whether connected to enemy agents or not, targeted Leningrad's leaders, despite testimony to the contrary contained in Kubatkin's report of 15 March 1942 (Document

65). There is one sensational account of a possible attempt to poison Voroshilov and Zhdanov in 1943, even though Zhdanov reportedly had a total of ninety-five bodyguards. On 11 June 1943, one Fedor Shcherba, a custodian in the commandant's office in Smolny, committed suicide allegedly in connection with his refusal to take part in a conspiracy with two cafeteria workers and a recidivist thief to kill the two leaders. The three accused conspirators confessed that they had planned to poison the leaders, and if that failed, to kill them either with a grenade or a revolver or to bomb one of their homes. They were executed and security was subsequently tightened at Smolny.[2]

Among Leningrad's population at large, there were few public demonstrations of defiance of official policies during the war. In addition to the small groups of factory workers who occasionally refused to work overtime without receiving extra food, an unpublished memoir deposited at Columbia University describes an extraordinary anti-Soviet protest of the siege period. The presumed author, Vasily Yershov, claimed to have been a lieutenant colonel in charge of food supply for an army division stationed in Leningrad.[3] He later emigrated to the United States. Yershov states that on 7 November several hundred people, mainly children between the ages of ten and fourteen, organized a demonstration along Stachek Prospect not far from the Kirov factory to appeal for "opening" Leningrad so that starving women and children could leave. Many carried printed leaflets with words approximating the following: "Dear fathers and brothers, your children, wives, and mothers are dying of hunger. The authorities decided to destroy us by a most terrible death. You were able to destroy tsarist power 24 years ago, you are able as well to destroy the hated Kremlin and Smolny executioners as long as you have guns!" According to this account, a divisional army commissar named Kuplivatsky ordered security guards to open fire on the crowd. The guards, however, refused, at which point Kuplivatsky himself shot into the assembled children. A German artillery attack commenced at this moment, and the crowd scattered. Shortly thereafter, a Major Kalugin and three others were arrested for not carrying out the initial order to open fire, and eventually hundreds of men, women, and children were arrested for participating in the demonstration. Who organized the demonstration and printed the leaflets could not be determined. Yershov states that some sixty soldiers and officers were shot for allegedly belonging to an underground organization connected with the demonstration.

If this account seemed plausible before Soviet archival materials became available (some of its general, minor details are accurate), it is now highly unlikely that the event it describes took place.[4] Neither NKVD nor Kirovsky *raikom* documents describe anything resembling the incident. Two

German reports do describe events that bear some similarities. A Task Force A intelligence report from 10 December without citing sources relates a disturbance that ended violently at the Kirov plant. The report states that in mid-October workers refused to work and demanded an end to the war after learning that several thousand of their fellow workers who had been sent to the Finnish Front had been taken prisoner. An NKVD unit purportedly fired on the striking workers and killed many. The remaining ringleaders were arrested. Another Task Force A intelligence report, from 2 January 1942, briefly mentions rumors of disturbances at two Leningrad defense plants in early November. The report also describes a riot that allegedly occurred on 7 November at the Haymarket (located about three miles from Stachek Prospect and the Kirov works) in which starving masses called for political revolution. The police fired into the crowd killing several and wounding many. Since these accounts also are not mentioned in party or NKVD summary reports, it is practically certain that they, like Yershov's description, are fabrications or were based on false rumors.[5] Kubatkin would have had no reason to conceal these events, particularly in his lengthy report of December 6 (Document 42). Perhaps the German accounts, which probably came from prisoners or collaborators, and Yershov's are related in origin.

Exaggerated fears among the population at large that the city was infested with enemy agents and sympathizers, particularly during the summer and fall of 1941, are another reason to suspect that some unknown percentage of those arrested for espionage, sabotage, and KR activity was innocent. Salisbury noted that "spy mania seized the city" in the war's first days, and that people who looked somehow foreign were often accosted by passersby or seized by security patrols.[6] When the most intense aerial bombardment of the blockade period commenced in September, there was widespread fear that enemy agents were identifying targets from the ground by means of light signals and flares or small rockets. Those supposedly setting off the incendiary charges were called "rocketmen" (*raketchiki*).[7] Catching signalers and rocketmen was given a high priority. On the night of 13 September, some 4,450 party, NKVD, and police personnel were mobilized to detect signaling activity and apprehend those responsible. The following night 10,000 observers reportedly took part. They must have been fairly well trained and restrained in their work, because they identified only twenty-five sites where rockets had been fired (in some cases spotters claimed that up to ten rockets had been fired from one location) and nine cases of signaling German planes with lights, which led to eleven people being detained as suspects. During the nights of 19 and 20 September, the observers reported rockets fired from twenty-one locations.[8] The number of sightings for these four nights is small, but German air raids continued sporadically into 1943. Given the heightened concern about a fifth column signaling the enemy, some of the sightings and arrests that resulted during the blockade period were probably false. In early December 1941, Kubatkin noted that two youths had been arrested who had been recruited outside Leningrad by German officials to signal locations of industrial and military installations within the city to bombers during air raids (see Document 42); however, there is no evidence from German official sources that there were such signalers within the city.[9] Whether or not this was the case, pro-German Leningraders may have taken it upon themselves to try to signal German aircraft.

In his summary report of 1 October 1942 (Document 45), Kubatkin stated that since the start of the war, "625 KR groups and formations" had been "uncovered and eliminated." NKVD records are indispensable for analyzing opposition sentiment and activity, because they contain the most abundant and detailed data on crime; however, NKVD investigators were often less than objective in analyzing political crimes, because their mission was to arrest such criminals. They were especially vigilant and probably rather jittery under siege conditions when security was given utmost priority. Kubatkin's attitude during the war echoed the sentiment uttered by Yezhov in October 1937: "Better too far than not far enough,"[10] because an undetected conspiracy might seriously impair further the city's security. (At the same time, with the exception of the forced exiling of ethnic Germans and Finns during the war, the Leningrad NKVD did not establish in advance quotas for arrests in mass operations as occurred in the 1930s.) Conviction rates in cases brought before the VT were extremely high during the siege (see above, pp. 203–04); verdicts basically reflected the prosecutor's view. The accused had practically no means for mounting a defense before the VT. This is not to say that Kubatkin readily believed every allegation of KR conspiracy. He could display a skeptical side. In his report of 6 December 1941 (Document 42), he noted: "An anonymous letter . . . *supposedly* comes from an underground organization that counts as many as 900 people" (emphasis added).

A major case of alleged treason shows the NKVD making arrests based on ambiguous evidence. During the first half of February 1942, at a secret factory cited in the NKVD documentation only by the number 363 (but identifiable as the Ust-Izhora shipyard),[11] the deputy director N. V. Smirnov, chief technologist V. I. Konenkov, as well as the chief engineer and the head of the supply section were arrested for preparing an armed insurrection that would lead to Leningrad's surrender. In reports from 16 February and 9 March, Kubatkin alleged that they had illegally stockpiled weapons.[12] The four plant leaders had reportedly conspired to conceal 430 rifles, one machine gun, one mortar, 520 grenades, and 992 bottles filled with flammable liquid. It seems equally plausible, however, that the weapons were gathered to defend the plant in case of an enemy attack as many factories did in the late summer and fall of 1941. The backgrounds of the accused may have sealed their fate. Smirnov was the son of a former Moscow bank manager, and Konenkov had served under General Kornilov. By 9 March, three of them had been sentenced to be shot, the other given an eight-year prison term.

The next two documents reveal that a procedure did exist, though it was very rarely employed, whereby the party committee of the NKVD could review quickly and overturn arrests for KR offenses before the cases were sent to the VP. This example identifies an overzealous NKVD investigative team that either unintentionally exaggerated or deliberately distorted the extent of KR sentiment among those it was targeting. The investigative team was punished as a result.

Document 61, an excerpt from a report by Kubatkin of mid-February 1942, describes a case, code-named the "Activists," of several professors accused of conspiring "to organize a meeting of the starving scholars of Leningrad" and encouraging their colleagues to join the National Socialist Party if the Germans took the city. Kubatkin sent the report, as he usually did in cases of arrests of major spy rings, directly to Beria and Merkulov. Throughout the entire existence of the USSR, the security organs closely monitored the intelligentsia. During the war, party and NKVD surveys of the city's popular mood regularly included overheard comments from individual professors and other prominent intellectuals (see, for example, Document 41). The report on the "Activists" identified Professor (A. I.) Nikiforov as the group's leader, and he was the only one listed as having been arrested.

The investigation was handled by SPO, which was the largest subdivision within the Leningrad NKVD and was charged with monitoring the city's intellectuals. By late 1941, SPO's membership included a larger percentage who had served under Yezhov than was the case in other branches of the NKVD. As a result, during the summer and autumn of 1941, the Leningrad SPO was hunting for the same types of enemies that it had in 1937–38, including former Trotskyites, Zinovievites, and so forth (Document 32). For example, during the first ten days of October, SPO claimed to have exposed 252 former Trotskyites. By early December, however, the Leningrad SPO had redirected its sights. In the first ten days of the month, only three of its new cases centered on the old targets of "former" people. SPO turned its attention to "spontaneous" cases of anti-Soviet activity. As winter progressed, SPO also became far more active. SPO's efforts culminated in 123 arrests between 1 and 20 September 1941, but it produced 405 arrests between 20 January and 10 February 1942, even though there were fewer overall arrests for KR activity during this latter period. SPO's efforts increased during midwinter because the NKVD feared that the mass star-vation could spark mass demonstrations calling for surrendering the city.[13]

A unit within the Leningrad SPO, led by SPO's deputy head, Senior Lieutenant V. I. Minichev, was responsible for eliminating KR agitprop and organized opposition among artists and scholars. This special SPO unit was designated as "n/SPO" with the prefix "n" standing for "secret" or "silent" (*neglasnyi*). The unit was created on 15 November 1941, and like the "illegal" branch of the party organization, was formed for the pos-sibility that the city might fall to the enemy: it would continue function-ing underground in occupied territory. In the autumn of 1941, n/SPO had twenty-eight members; by April 1942, its ranks had grown to fifty city-wide.[14]

The second document on the "Activists" case was found in the papers of the *partkom* of the city's Dzerzhinsky *raion,* where NKVD headquar-ters were located. This document reveals that in addition to Nikiforov, his colleague at the Pokrovsky Institute Professor Gul was also arrested dur-ing the winter. In April of 1942, the Leningrad SPO sent another report directly to Beria, apparently bypassing Kubatkin,[15] on the investigations conducted by Minichev's group. On 12 May, however, the *partkom* of the Leningrad NKVD met for about two hours to hear the results of a special investigation that it had conducted with the NKVD administration into the case against Nikiforov and Gul as well as individuals in five other cases who had been investigated by Minichev's team and arrested for anti-Soviet agitprop and for taking part in organized activities directed against the state. The session produced a transcript of over a hundred pages, excerpts from which comprise Document 62.

It is unclear when this inquiry began or exactly what prompted it, but it does reveal an interesting case of the NKVD's *partkom* exposing faulty NKVD investigative work and forcing the release of arrestees in an im-portant political case. NKVD *partkom* member Bolotov indicates at the beginning of the document that the "*Partkom* has received signals from several Communists" of irregularities in the investigations. The case's files had been sent to Smolny for verification, apparently by Beria. The inquiry showed that although Nikiforov had "various anti-Soviet waverings," there was no hard evidence that either he or Gul had any connection with an anti-Soviet fascist organization or that Nikiforov was actually organizing the alleged meeting of the starving scholars. The two were released from custody. (The document does not reveal the fate of the other "Activists" mentioned in Kubatkin's February report. Since they were not arrested at that time, and Nikiforov, the group's alleged organizer, was released, perhaps they too were cleared.) Charges against professors and cultural figures in the other five cases were dropped, while Minichev and his investigative team were cited for violating the Stalin-Molotov resolution of 17 November 1938 reining in the secret police, and were told that they would bear "party and administrative responsibility."[16] According to the record, at least one of the NKVD secret agents who supplied false information in one of the cases was arrested and convicted.

An intriguing and murky dimension of the case is the assertion in the NKVD party committee report that Professors Nikiforov and Gul had been arrested by the USSR NKVD, not the Leningrad NKVD, based on "inaccurate information" provided by Beria. The available documentation suggests that the case against the two started in the Leningrad NKVD, because Kubatkin described the unfolding KR investigation to Beria prior to their arrest.[17] It appears that Beria then took control of the case directly.

This case weakens the view that there existed an active political opposition in Leningrad, because the charges of conspiracy ultimately could not be substantiated. On the face of it, the case would also seem to give some measure of credibility to NKVD assessment of KR offenses, because those unjustly arrested were subsequently exonerated and a slipshod secret agent punished, even though that action required the intervention of the NKVD's *partkom* and, it appears, the Dzerzhinsky *raikom* and the *gorkom*. However, the case may have been more than, or perhaps something other than, a matter of overturning an unjust verdict. If Minichev had indeed gone over Kubatkin's head in reporting directly to Beria, Kubatkin (and Zhdanov) could support the reversal of the verdict and not be discredited by it. Moreover, through the exoneration of Nikiforov and Gul, Kubatkin could punish his underling Minichev for bypassing him and at the same time send a signal to Beria not to intrude into investigations in Leningrad.

· Document 61 ·

Excerpts from a report from Kubatkin to Beria and Merkulov on the "Activists" case involving professors accused of preparing to organize a National Socialist Party in the event that Germany captured Leningrad, 16 February 1942, Arkhiv UFSB RF po SPb i LO f. 21/12, op. 2, p.n. 11, t. 1, d. 4, ll. 88–89.

SPECIAL REPORT

[. . .]

In the agent case "ACTIVISTS" it was earlier reported that a group of professors—PLATONOV,[18] NIKIFOROV, GUL and others intended to organize a meeting of "hungry scholars of Leningrad." The initiator of the organization of the meeting NIKIFOROV was arrested.

According to newly received agent reports, the participants of the group are preparing cadres for joining the National Socialist Party in the event of the capture of the city by the Germans. A participant of the organization USTIU-GOV declares:

"... A group of Russians is affiliated with the National-Socialist Party. We ought to be connected with this group, join it and carry out its instructions."

Other known participants of this group are professors: MOISEEV, KARGIN, TOKOV.

We will send by post a detailed report of this case.

[. . .]

HEAD OF THE ADMINISTRATION OF THE NKVD LO
Commissar of State Security of the Third Rank
KUBATKIN

· Document 62 ·

Excerpts from the report of the meeting of the *partkom* of the Leningrad NKVD that condemned as unwarranted the arrests of Professors Nikiforov and Gul in the "Activists" case, 12 May 1942, TsGAIPD SPb f. 408, op. 2, d. 184.

Top secret

Minutes No. 18
(shorthand report)
Meeting of the UNKVD LO *Partkom*
12 May 1942
Partkom members in attendance: Comrades Bolotov, Kubatkin, Baskakov, Skladchikov, Palchikov, Efimov, Voronkov, Sakharovsky, and Belov.
From the VKP(b) City Party Committee: Com. Zalnov.
Department heads: Comrades Kozhevnikov, Zakharov, Bezhanov, Medvedsky, Poliakov, Poliansky, Podchasov, Falin, Tsvetkov, Basov.
Party organization secretaries: Comrades Zharov, Sviatokum, Leonov, Labukin, Gagarin.

Agenda

I. On the violation of the SNK and TsK VKP(b) Resolution of 17 November 1938 by the SPO UNKVD LO.

Com. Bolotov: The *partkom* has received indications from several Communists that in its espionage work the secret SPO has committed a provocation that has led to unfounded arrests among Leningrad's scientific workers. To verify these indications, the *partkom* and Administration leadership have created a commission whose chairman, Com. Basov, will now report to us on the results of the verification.

Com. Basov: For your information, I will report that the commission consisted of Comrade Basov from the Administration leadership, Comrade Baskakov, *partkom* deputy secretary, Comrade Tsvetkov, 1st Special Section head, and

Com. Sviatokum, SPO department head. The commission was assigned to examine several cases in which the TsK VKP(b) and Sovnarkom Resolution of 17 November 1938 was violated.

So as not to go on too long, I will simply read the reports on these cases and the commission's conclusion.

Conclusion

Composition of the commission: NKVD LO Administration Deputy Head State Security Major Com. Basov, *partkom* Deputy Secretary State Security Lieutenant Com. Baskakov, UNKVD LO 1st Special Section Head State Security Captain Com. Tsvetkov, and UNKVD LO SPO Department Head State Security Lieutenant Com. Sviatokum, having examined the agent and investigation materials against the individuals arrested by the n/SPO and released from arrest,

rule as follows:

it is clear from the examined cases listed below that individual associates of the n/SPO and agents in contact with them, in the process of their espionage work, permitted provocative methods aimed at triggering counterrevolutionary activities by the subjects under investigation. As a result, unwarranted arrests were made of several individuals and the nature of the counterrevolutionary activities of certain subjects of the investigations were incorrectly characterized. [. . .]

II. The case of Professors Nikiforov and Gul of the Pokrovsky Institute (the "Activists" case)

Nikiforov and Gul were arrested by the USSR NKVD as a result of inaccurate information from People's Commissar Com. Beria about the essence of the agent materials against Nikiforov and Gul as some of the main participants in a fascist organization in existence among Leningrad scholars. Com. Beria's special report said:

". . . In-depth agent work on the case has allowed us to establish that the intention of organizing a provocative demonstration of scholars was just one of the forms of the subversive activity of the participants in the fascist organization in existence in Leningrad."

Based on the materials from the "Activists" file, there were not sufficient grounds for talking about the presence of any National Socialist fascist organization as was stated in the plan of operations on the "Activists" case dated 26 April 1942:

". . . Those under investigation represent a group of anti-Soviet-inclined scholars who have manifested a desire to unite for organized struggle against Soviet power."

Based on an examination of agent materials, and as was later established by the investigation, there was no organizational tie between Nikiforov and Gul and the other individuals involved in the case (other than contact in the cafeteria at the House of Scholars). The special report says that the participants in this organization "propagandized intensively for the organization of protests by hungry old women." There are not enough materials about this in the file; in the two summaries by agent "Istomina" there are just the following statements by Ustiugov:

". . . Only the Germans can give Russia back its former status, I look with indignation and rage at this beaten people stripped of their rights, *where even the old women can't protest*" (Summary dated 28 January 1942).

There are no grounds for writing, on the basis of this, that the participants in this organization "propagandized intensively for the organization of protests by hungry old women."

The materials in the case do not make it obvious that an appeal to the fascist command was being prepared laying out a program for collaboration with the Germans, as was indicated in the report. The arrested professors Gul and Nikiforov have at present been released from arrest, since:

". . . An inquiry into the present case has not established Nikiforov's membership in an a[nti]/Soviet fascist organization. Nor did the inquiry obtain any information about A. I. Nikiforov preparing 'a demonstration of starving Leningrad scholars,' and based on its content, the letter attached to the present file, addressed to the leader of the party and government, cannot be defined as an a[nti]/Soviet letter containing any provocative intentions, etc." (From the resolution on the release of Nikiforov)

[. . .]

The commission also considers it essential to point out that in the cases against [. . .] Nikiforov, Gul, [. . .] the arrest warrants were not written in line with the materials on the basis of which the arrests were made.

Based on everything stated above, the commission believes that Comrades Minichev, Pinchuk, Zviagin, Sorokovik, and Balashev, in their work, violated the TsK and SNK Resolution of 17 November 1938 and for this must bear party and administrative responsibility.

NKVD LO Administration Deputy Head
State Security Major Basov
UNKVD LO *partkom* Deputy Secretary
State Security Lieutenant Baskakov
Commission
UNKVD LO 1st Special Section Head
State Security Captain Tsvetkov
UNKVD LO SPO Department Head
State Security Lieutenant Sviatokum

[. . .]

[In an act of self-criticism, Minichev explained the mistakes made by n/SPO]

Second case, case of Nikiforov and Gul.

In this case, essentially the same mistakes were made, and they were expressed in an uncritical attitude toward agent materials. A number of materials were not analyzed and verified. In particular, the fact that a demonstration was called was not verified. The materials on the demonstration were mainly contributed by a single agent, "Mal," and in part by operations associate Gusev. However, as is clear from the results of the case, "Mal" did not report the information he had about this demonstration accurately.

Nikiforov experienced various anti-Soviet waverings. First he intended to organize an anti-Soviet demonstration and address it with an appeal to foreign scholars, then he intended to send a letter to the leaders of the party and government—Comrades [*sic*] Zhdanov and Comrade Stalin, then he wanted to go to the command of the British navy, which was supposedly at Murmansk, and so on.

There was nothing to be insisted upon firmly. Therefore it is clear that all these materials should have been handled very differently and the issue of arresting Nikiforov and Gul raised only when all these materials had been thoroughly verified. If we had firmly established that such a demonstration was truly being organized and that it truly had a counterrevolutionary intent, then we should have reported this case and raised the question of calling to account and arresting Nikiforov and Gul.

[. . .]

The report that was read out loud here was written incorrectly, of course. Much in this report was overblown, to put it mildly, and incorrect conclusions were drawn from the operations materials that led the higher leadership of the NKVD organs astray. [. . .]

The treatment of Nikiforov and Gul was an anomaly, because almost all arrests for political offenses turned quickly into convictions, and very few were overturned during the course of the blockade. Historians can only guess how many of those arrested for KR activity, such as the members of the so-called "Russian Party" and others identified by Kubatkin in Document 42, and then convicted and sentenced by military tribunals, were actually guilty, according to Soviet definitions of crime. Another target of a Minichev investigation who was not as fortunate as Nikiforov and Gul was Mikhail Platonov, a prominent chemist, who was arrested during the night of 13–14 February 1942.[19] Platonov's colleague and close friend, H. F. Krivoshlykov, had been detained a week earlier, and the testimony forced from him under interrogation by Minichev's unit was used to arrest Platonov. The head of the Department of Analytical Chemistry at the Chemical-Technological Institute and the author of some fifty scholarly works over a twenty-year career, Platonov was the son of the famous historian Sergei Platonov, whose career spanned the 1917 revolutionary divide. The fame of the elder Platonov, a scholar of the "Time of Troubles" at the end of the sixteenth and beginning of the seventeenth centuries, protected him from arrest through the 1920s, but he was purged in 1930 and died three years later in exile in Samara. As the son of a "former person" and not one to conceal his antipathy toward Communist policies, such as restrictions placed on the scientific community, Mikhail Platonov had been under surveillance since the inception of the Cheka. When he was arrested in 1942, he was charged with anti-Soviet agitation, membership in a KR organization, and treason. The latter two charges were based on the fact that on 2 January he had applied to the Commissariat of the Rubber Industry to be sent from Leningrad to Erevan with other chemists to continue research on acetone synthesis. Although the commissariat had approved the request, Minichev's overzealous n/SPO team interpreted the application to be part of a ruse to attempt to flee across the border to Turkey, and labeled his supposed conspiracy the "Escape" case.

Platonov stated during interrogation that he "was raised in a rich noble family" and that he "regarded the October Revolution with hostility." He noted that he confided among his friends his "thoughts of vengeance toward Soviet power for the death of his father." He did not agree with the purges of higher education, "which eliminated talented people." Regarding science, he stated that "it loves freedom, but such conditions don't exist in the USSR." He even went so far as to say: "I acknowledge that I am guilty as charged under article 58-10, part 2" (anti-Soviet agitation in wartime). However, he flatly denied that he had intended to flee the USSR. He pointed out that in 1924 he had rejected his father's advice to arrange a research trip abroad as a way to emigrate and added that he and other researchers had had an opportunity to leave Leningrad in July 1941 but that he had chosen to remain with his "valuable library and laboratory." Regarding his application in January 1942 to be evacuated from Leningrad, Platonov told the investigator: "I wanted to leave Leningrad and agreed to go wherever was convenient, not necessarily to Erevan."

On 20 March 1942, Platonov was convicted and sentenced by the VT to be executed for treason with confiscation of all of his property. He was shot on 27 March with the approval of VSLF member Kuznetsov. Platonov left behind a wife, a disabled thirteen-year-old son, and a twelve-year-old daughter. He was not officially exonerated until 1958 during Khrushchev's campaign to rehabilitate innocent victims of Stalinist repression.

Documents 63–66 describe a case that grew over the course of several months from various subcases, like streams merging to form a river. The case was a complicated one which the Party Control Commission of the Central Committee reopened fifteen years after the Leningrad Military Tribunal had sentenced those convicted. The inquiry revealed that during the original criminal investigations the arrestees had been forced into making fictitious confessions and falsely implicating other innocent people in KR crimes. The victims, as in the Platonov case, were exonerated in 1958.[20]

Like those arrested by Minichev's SPO team, the target group in this case was intellectuals. The investigation was conducted by the Counterintelligence Department (KRO) of the Leningrad NKVD. At least thirty-five scholars were eventually arrested, including distinguished professors and academicians from a variety of fields. Not all of the arrestees were named, but of those identified, none had been a target of the SPO investigation. Most of those in the KRO case had received their education prior to the Bolshevik Revolution, and many had been members of the nobility in Imperial Russia's capital and had forged close ties with foreign universities and enterprises, especially German ones. It is hardly surprising that such a profile would draw the attention of the NKVD during the siege. The first three documents presented here, which were written by Kubatkin between October 1941 and March 1942, lay out a mounting campaign against the scholars who were charged with conspiring together to overthrow Soviet power, collaborate with the Germans, and restore capitalism. Kubatkin filed each report within a couple of weeks after arrests were made and before the cases were tried by the military tribunals.

The document trail of this investigation begins with description imbedded in a sixteen-page summary of KR activity in Leningrad written by Kubatkin in October 1941 and excerpted below. The conspirators, who were dubbed the "Academicians," were distinguished specialists who had previously worked for German firms and were charged with among other things "giving practical aid to the Germans in seizing Leningrad." Kubatkin implied that the group's ringleader was Professor and Academician Ignatovsky, an ethnic German (despite his Russian surname) who was a physicist and expert in optics. Ignatovsky allegedly had been associated with the "notorious traitor" Marshal Tukhachevsky (who in fact had been arrested on falsified charges of treasonous collaboration with Germany and Japan and summarily executed in June 1937). Kubatkin also stated that his agents had learned that the "Academicians" had selected candidates for a new government that would work with Germany once the USSR was defeated. Two of the four conspirators were listed as candidates.

· Document 63 ·

Excerpts from a report from Kubatkin to Beria, Merkulov, Zhdanov, and Kuznetsov on the "Academicians" case involving distinguished specialists who had previously worked for German firms and were accused of selecting candidates for a government that would work with Germany once the USSR was defeated, 18 October 1941, Arkhiv UFSB RF po SPb i LO f. 21/12, op. 2, p.n. 11, t. 1, d. 4, ll. 6–21.

SPECIAL REPORT

[. . .] According to agent reports, anti-Soviet elements are strengthening agitation among workers for the organization of uprisings, elimination of Communists, and the rendering of practical aid to the Germans.

This is supported by agent case materials, which were acquired in October of this year [. . .]

2. Agent case "ACADEMICIANS"

A counterrevolutionary fascist group of academicians and professors in Leningrad was secretly uncovered. The group consists of:

V. S. IGNATOVSKY—corresponding member of the Academy of Sciences, German

N. N. KACHALOV—honored scientist, professor

L. G. TITOV—professor–optics specialist

G. A. SHAKH-BAZOV—assistant director of the Institute of Mechanics and Mathematics, and a series of other distinguished specialists, who worked at various times in German firms.

It is established that IGNATOVSKY, being before the Revolution connected with the German firm "Tseiss" [Zeiss],[21] from the first years of the existence of Soviet power up to 1936–37 conducted widespread espionage-sabotage work in the optics industry, where he occupied a leading role.

In the following years IGNATOVSKY, having established a connection with the TUKHACHEVSKY group and taking up a more active struggle with Soviet power, began to establish counterrevolutionary cadres for overthrowing the established order and restoring capitalism in the USSR.

At the beginning of military operations against Germany, members of the group, who refused to be evacuated from Leningrad, set before themselves a task—to give practical aid to the Germans in seizing Leningrad. Toward this end they unleashed defeatist and anti-Semitic agitation, arguing that the city's surrender to the Germans was inevitable. They worked out a program of restructuring the political order in the USSR with the help of the Germans and nominated a series of candidates from the number of scholars to staff a new government. According to agent reports, Professor KACHALOV, Professor TITOV, Academicians ROZHDESTVENSKY, TARLE, UKHTOMSKY, and others were nominated to the new government.

We are speeding up the agent work [. . .]

HEAD OF THE ADMINISTRATION OF THE NKVD FOR THE LENINGRAD RE-GION AND CITY OF LENINGRAD, Commissar of state security of the third rank (KUBATKIN)

A subsequent report by Kubatkin from 25 October 1941 stated specifically that Professor Kachalov had been nominated by the group as the future premier and the prominent historian E. V. Tarle as minister of foreign affairs. Professor Chanishev, a former colonel in the tsarist army, would become the war minister, and an engineer named Dukhon was the choice to head up the finance ministry.[22] This group showed up again briefly in Kubatkin's lengthy report of 6 December (Document 42). In two sentences he described "a counterrevolutionary fascist organization of scientific workers led by Professor Ignatovsky."

The association of Evgeny Tarle, who was a Jew, with the case against accused profascist counterrevolutionaries is one of its strangest aspects. Among the most prolific of Russia's historians during the twentieth century, he had started his teaching career at St. Petersburg University in 1903 at the age of twenty-eight. In 1917, he served on a special commission of the Provisional Government that investigated the fall of Tsar Nicholas II. Ten years later he was elected to the Soviet Academy of Sciences but was arrested in 1930 as a primary figure in a purge of intellectuals known as the "Academician Case." According to this OGPU (forerunner of the NKVD) fabrication, the group aimed to overthrow Soviet power. OGPU analysts had assigned Tarle the role of future minister of foreign affairs in the plot.[23] Tarle spent a year in prison in Leningrad and then was exiled to Kazakhstan. It is widely believed, however, that Stalin personally intervened to rehabilitate Tarle,[24] who returned to his positions at Leningrad State University and the Academy in late 1934 and, according to an NKVD report, resumed contact with a KR group.[25] His reinstatement coincided with an official turn in Soviet historiography toward emphasizing patriotism, nationalism, and the important role of individuals in affecting change. His epic biography, *Napoleon,* was published in 1936, and within a year or so, he turned out a separate work, *Napoleon's Invasion of Russia.* Like Tolstoy's *War and Peace,* Tarle's books were published in several editions during the war, and it appears that they were widely read. (Stalin's secretary Poskrebyshev had included *Napoleon's Invasion of Russia* as suggested reading for his chief not long after the start of the German invasion.) On the third day of the German invasion, Tarle predicted that Hitler's Reich would end up like Napoleon's empire, and the following month 110,000 copies of his brochure on Napoleon's defeat in Russia in 1812 were published in Leningrad. During the winter of 1941–42, the first volume of his *Crimean War* was printed in the starving city. It was awarded a Stalin Prize for History in mid-February. The NKVD documents presented here do not identify Tarle as one of the conspirators, and another NKVD report states that he had no contact with them.[26] There is no evidence that the popular historian of patriotic themes, who had not joined the party, was arrested, although as Document 66 shows, Tarle was among a total of 128 academics who were connected to a fabricated KR conspiracy by those arrested during their interrogations.[27] Thirty-two were convicted of KR offenses in 1942; the identity of most of the rest and their subsequent fate are unknown. Tarle's appointment in 1942 to the state commission that recorded German atrocities on Soviet territory during the war, as well as to a commission on questions concerning peace negotiations and postwar reconstruction that was chaired by Maxim Litvinov in 1943, are evidence of his continued good standing, as was the fact that he won the history prize in 1942 and received the award again in 1943.[28] Nevertheless, simply by having been allegedly nominated to serve in a pro-German successor government by accused counterrevolutionaries placed him in jeopardy. One of the other alleged nominees from Kubatkin's 25 October report ended up being executed, and another died in prison.

In other reports from the starvation winter, Kubatkin described a related investigation, which bore the code name "Emissary." In an undated report from December, he claimed that an inspector named Streglo from the Main Machine Instrument Bureau was taking advantage of the "food difficulties" to try to persuade factory workers to prepare to overthrow Soviet power. Kubatkin also charged that Streglo was trying to establish contact with the German military command and was selecting candidates for a "Committee for Public Salvation" that would serve as a transition administration after the Red Army abandoned Leningrad and prior to the formation of a German government.[29] Similar information on Streglo was included in Kubatkin's report of 6 December to Beria and Merkulov (Document 42). On 5 January 1942, Kubatkin reported that Streglo's group, which included a Finnish engineer named Ekgolm who was to be the go-between with German military leaders, had been liquidated.[30]

In mid-February near the peak period of the starvation, additional intellectuals were arrested and charged with belonging to the "Committee for Public Salvation." Kubatkin noted in the same 16 February report that described the "Activists" case (Document 61) that the liquidated committee included eight scholars who had endeavored to carry out terrorist acts against party, *sovet*, and military leaders (Document 64). Two of the four members named, N. S. Koshliakov and N. V. Roze, were professors at the university. Koshliakov was also a corresponding member of the Academy of Sciences and winner of a Stalin Prize.

· Document 64 ·

Excerpt from a report from Kubatkin to Beria and Merkulov on an alleged "Committee for Public Salvation" consisting of scholars who were preparing to serve as a transitional administration after the Red Army abandoned Leningrad and prior to the formation of a German government, 16 February 1942, Arkhiv UFSB RF po SPb i LO, f. 21/12, op. 2, p.n. 11, t. 1, d, 4, l. 88.

SPECIAL REPORT

Over a ten-day period in February, 241 people were arrested for counterrevolutionary activity. The militia arrested 719 people, 209 of them for banditry and 268 for speculation and theft of socialist property.

17 counterrevolutionary groups have been eliminated.

138 have been executed under sentences of Military Tribunals.

In connection with the case of the liquidated insurgent organization, "Committee for Public Salvation," which was made up of engineering-technical and scientific workers, the following have been arrested: KOSHLIAKOV, SUPERANSKY, ROZE, VERZHBITSKY — 8 people total.

Agent reports and testimony from arrestees establish that the organization, using the food difficulties, is making active preparations for an uprising and operating under the name, "Committee for Public Salvation."

With this purpose in mind, the organization's participants are recruiting rebellious cadres from the hostile intelligentsia and preparing to distribute leaflets calling for an uprising and to commit acts of sabotage in the city's housing services. The organization has set acts of terror as its objective.

Arrestee SUPERANSKY testified:

". . . The immediate objectives the Committee for Public Salvation set for itself . . . to prepare and commit terrorist acts against the leaders of the party organization, the Leningrad *sovet*, and the command of the Leningrad Front."

We are sending a detailed report by post [. . .]

On 15 March, Kubatkin sent a thirteen-page report (parts of which make up Document 65) to Zhdanov and Kuznetsov on the continuing investigation into the "Committee for Public Salvation." The number of scholars arrested in the conspiracy had reached thirty-five, and Kubatkin promised to make further arrests. The four identified ringleaders, who included Streglo and Roze, were each from a different institution, which seemed to signal a widespread conspiracy. Kubatkin boasted that his investigation had uncovered an "underground center for KR organization" intended to coordinate all anti-Soviet activity. This center was bent on overthrowing Soviet power through armed insurrection in order to create a new government subservient to Germany that would restore a market economy and abolish collective farms. Among the committee's specific tasks were the distribution of anti-Soviet leaflets calling for an uprising of the starving, attacks on food stores, and the organization of demonstrations. The report also claimed that the group had received grenades and bombs from its members in the Red Army. Members also claimed (in part of the text not included in Document 65) that the organization's structure was sufficiently flexible and decentralized to be able to survive "a break in a link." At the same time, and somewhat paradoxically, the quoted fragments of confessions highlighted collaboration among the members; the accused did not appear reluctant to name their fellow conspirators.

· Document 65 ·

Report from Kubatkin to Zhdanov and Kuznetsov on the alleged "Committee for Public Salvation," which is described as "an underground center of counterrevolutionary organization that directs all the hostile work of anti-Soviet groups," 15 March 1942, Arkhiv UFSB RF po SPb i LO, f. 21/12, op. 2, p.n. 11, t. 1, d, 4, ll. 101–13.

TOP SECRET

SPECIAL REPORT

Concerning the case of the uncovered counterrevolutionary organization "Committee for Public Salvation."

In January 1942, the Administration of the Leningrad *Oblast'* NKVD received agent reports on anti-Soviet moods among the professorial and teaching staff of institutions of higher education and the engineering and technical intelligentsia.

Further agent work established that anti-Soviet groups were active at the University, the Institute of Precision Mechanics, the Polytechnic Institute, the Forest Technology Academy, and other institutions of higher education in Leningrad.

In spite of the apparent dissociation of the groups, a characteristic quality for them was their use of identical forms and methods of subversive work.

The groups' participants, who were in favor of the USSR's defeat in the war against Germany, conducted defeatist propaganda among the intelligentsia, prepared to meet the Germans and render them practical assistance, and produced leaflets calling for hunger strikes and organized demonstrations against Soviet power.

Analysis of all the agent materials gathered on the activities of the indicated groups has led to the conclusion that there is in Leningrad an underground center of counterrevolutionary organization that directs all the hostile work of anti-Soviet groups.

Agent reports have indicated that one of the center's leading participants is Professor STRAKHOVICH of the University, who was arrested in December 1941 in another case.

In order to reverify the agent reports and quickly expose the counterrevolutionary organization, the arrested STRAKHOVICH was interrogated. STRAKHOVICH confirmed the existence of a counterrevolutionary organization that is making preparations for an uprising and named several of its participants.

On the basis of STRAKHOVICH's statements and agent materials, the leading participants in the anti-Soviet groups were arrested:

at the University	—Professor ROZE;
at the Refrigeration Institute	—Senior Lecturer SUPERANSKY;
at the Glavsbyt (Main Sales Administration) of the People's Commissariat of Machine-Tool Construction	—Senior Inspector STREGLO;
at the Agricultural Institute	—Senior Lecturer GORBOVSKY.

Arrestees ROZE, SUPERANSKY, STREGLO, and GORBOVSKY fully confirmed the agent reports in our possession. Immediately after this, arrests were made of other participants in the organization:

N. P. VINOGRADOV	—professor, Polytechnic Institute, former nobleman;
L. V. KLIMENKO	—professor, Polytechnic Institute, former nobleman;
N. S. KOSHLIAKOV	—corresponding member, Academy of Sciences, professor, Leningrad State University, former nobleman;
A. [?] FEDOROV	—senior lecturer, Engineering and Economics Institute;
A. M. ZHURAVSKY	—professor, Mining Institute, former nobleman;
V. G. STROGANOV	—senior lecturer, Electrotechnical Institute, lifetime honorary citizen;
B. I. IZVEKOV	—professor, Leningrad State University, doctor of physics and mathematics of the main observatory;
A. [?] POPKOV	—professor and deputy director, Institute of Water Supply;
S. S. RUZOV	—senior lecturer, Herzen Pedagogical Institute;
V. N. CHURILOVSKY	—professor, Institute of Precision Mechanics and Optics;
A. A. SOLO [?]	—professor, Institute of Precision Mechanics and Optics, former nobleman;

and others, 35 people total.

The confessions of these arrestees—VINOGRADOV, FEDOROV, ROZE, SUPERANSKY, GORBOVSKY—have established that there is a widespread counterrevolutionary organization operating actively in Leningrad named the "COMMITTEE FOR PUBLIC SALVATION."

As the inquiry has established, the counterrevolutionary organization dates back to 1939, from anti-Soviet groupings of the reactionary segment of Leningrad's scientific and technical intelligentsia; it unleashed its active subversive work with the start of Germany's war against the USSR.

Arrestee GORBOVSKY testified on 23 February of this year:

". . . With the start of the war against Germany, in our opinion, quite a favorable situation had taken shape for the appearance of our organization, whose activism had been mounting as the German troops advanced toward Leningrad, having achieved its high point at the moment of the Germans' imminent approach to the city."

The political platform of the counterrevolutionary organization came down to the overthrow of Soviet power by means of an armed uprising, the restoration of the capitalist system in the USSR, and the formation of a "new Russian government" acting under the control of Germany.

Arrestee FEDOROV testifies:

". . . Our organization envisaged the restoration of capitalism, which was supposed to serve as a social base for a new regime in Russia. The right to exist was officially recognized for industry, trade, and the banking business, along with private-capitalist enterprises and state and cooperative ones. Virtually all the prerequisites were being created for the prosperous development of the former to the detriment of the latter. Broad credit assistance was planned for capitalist enterprises, and tax privileges were also envisioned for them.

"In agriculture the emphasis was placed on eliminating the kolkhozes and setting up fairly prosperous midsize farms."
And further:

". . . All legislative and executive power was collected in the hands of Russian self-government, acting in close contact and under the control of the German occupation authorities. The domestic policy of the organs of self-government stemmed from the essence of the political regime, which was a military dictatorship of the fascist type, turned against the workers.

"Regarding the ethnic issue, the emphasis was placed on inflaming the Russian population's chauvinistic feelings and disparaging the ethnic minorities.

"The organs of the Communist Party were subject to rout, and their leaders, workers in the Soviet punitive organs, as well as all those suspected of complicity in the Soviet order, to physical annihilation, at best to imprisonment in a concentration camp and condemnation to a slow death."
Analogous testimony was given by arrestee ROZE:

". . . The goals of our counterrevolutionary organization were defined in the following form:

"1. The struggle to change the political order existing in the USSR by means of the violent overthrow of Soviet power;

"2. The formation of a 'new Russian government,' the elimination of the Socialist economic system in the USSR, and the restoration of private property.

"The organization set as its objectives:

"a) — Recruitment of cadres for an armed uprising for the purpose of overthrowing Soviet power and rendering aid to the Germans in capturing the city.

"b) — Commission of terrorist acts against the leaders of Leningrad's party and Soviet organs and military command.

"c) — Carrying out acts of diversion and wrecking in the defense industry and at Leningrad's most important enterprises.

"d) — Dissemination among the population of anti-Soviet leaflets calling for hunger strikes, the storming of bakeries and food stores, and organized demonstrations.

"e) — Establishment of contact with the German command for engaging in mutinous activities and receiving instructions and arms."
Arrestee SUPERANSKY, on 13 February of this year, testified:

". . . Beginning in the fall of 1941, when our counterrevolutionary organization began preparing for an uprising in Leningrad, I received from an active member of the organization, Professor KROTOV of the Polytechnic Institute, several specific assignments which came down to informing the participants in my counterrevolutionary group about the preparations for an uprising, as well as about the main objective of our organization for this period of time, and sending them out to propagandize the idea of an armed uprising among the population [. . .]

". . . The main forms and methods of our counterrevolutionary activities during the first period of the war consisted of helping the German-fascist troops in their military actions against the USSR, by means of conducting counterrevolutionary defeatist propaganda and spreading provocational fabrications aimed at the disintegration and demoralization of the Soviet rear. During this period, we were expecting the Germans in Leningrad and believed that they would be able to capture the city as a result of a direct strike, without any substantial help on our part.

"During the second period of our subversive activities, our organization assumed that the Germans would not be able to capture Leningrad without our support from the inside. In connection with this, taking advantage of the food difficulties, we unleashed broad activity to organize counterrevolutionary forces and prepare for an armed uprising."

In their preparation for the uprising, the emphasis was placed on an armed demonstration simultaneously in the city and in the Red Army. With this goal in mind, the organization's participants, who had counterrevolutionary connections among the servicemen, attempted to detect and draw into mutinous activity anti-Soviet-inclined soldiers in the Red Army and studied the opportunity to obtain arms through servicemen [. . .]

Arrestee GORBOVSKY, at a 23 February interrogation, stated:

". . . On 30 January of this year, I paid FEDOROV a visit. In a conversation with me that time he expressed the need to distribute in the queues these short but pointed leaflets with a call to sack the stores, come out actively against Soviet power, and demand the city's surrender to the Germans.

"FEDOROV indicated that he knew from organization member MEIER about the existence at the Industrial Institute of a group of individuals who had the ability to duplicate those kinds of leaflets."

Lately, the counterrevolutionary organization has set about preparing diversionary acts in the defense industry, public transportation, and housing, by which they mean to commit arson against buildings, workshops, warehouses, etc.

FEDOROV gives evidence on the organization's diversionary activities:

". . . In conversations with GORBOVSKY, during the Soviet-German war, in September 1941, if I'm not mistaken, I pointed out the logic of destroying the foundries of the major Leningrad plants — the Kirov and Izhorsk works, 'BOLSHEVIK' — which should have brought work in the defense industry to a halt."

GORBOVSKY testifies to the same:

". . . I felt it was essential to activate the struggle against Soviet power, having suggested to FEDOROV that acts of sabotage be carried out in the form of blowing up RR bridges and viaducts. I offered myself as the person to carry out this kind of sabotage act."

In its practical activities, the organization also scheduled the commission of terrorist acts against the leaders of Leningrad's Soviet and party organs [. . .]

[Gorbovsky testified]:

". . . FEDOROV was counting on obtaining grenades and bombs from military units through participants in our organization who were serving in the Red Army, in particular, through AKKERMAN."

The terrorist acts at the same time were supposed to act as a signal for the uprising.

I. M. SUPERANSKY says:

". . . The commission of terrorist acts against the leaders of the Leningrad party organization of the Leningrad Soviet and the Leningrad Front command was supposed to serve as the immediate signal for the uprising."

While preparing for the uprising and seizure of power, the organization's participants discussed the issue of creating a "new Russian government."

It has been established that in its practical work the organization was connected to the German command.

The connection was made through an active participant in the organization, Professor KROTOV of the Polytechnic Institute. In January 1942, upon a repeat attempt to make his way through to the Germans to obtain practical instructions on counterrevolutionary work, the latter perished in a train wreck.

We are forging ahead with the investigation. We are arresting the organization participants brought to light during the investigation.

HEAD OF THE NKVD LO ADMINISTRATION
State Security Commissar 3rd Rank
KUBATKIN

Sent to:
Com. ZHDANOV,
Com. KUZNETSOV

A report to the Party Control Committee (KPK) of the Central Committee of the Communist Party of the Soviet Union from 3 February 1958 (Document 66) portrays the entire case of the "Committee for Public Salvation" as a fabrication by KRO officials, who were all too ready to believe questionable and unsubstantiated reports from their secret informants (which included a "Viktorov" and a "Garold") in order, it would appear, to crack open a sensational case of subversion and treason. The KPK report on the KRO investigation describes abuses similar to those detailed by the special commission in its inquiry into SPO practices.[31] The report states that an "agent-provocateur" Merkulov[32] admitted that at the end of 1941 he had passed along "slanderous materials against several Leningrad professors" who were then arrested, and that later in the war he had fabricated an underground "Union of the Old Intelligentsia" in order to better "milk the organs" so that he might finagle receipt of a doctorate degree without completing a dissertation. Those KRO officials involved in the case were hauled before the KPK eleven days after the report was written and expelled from the party.

The KPK report states that the case originated with an investigation of Professor E. G. Krotov of the Polytechnical Institute, who allegedly belonged to a KR fascist group. KRO deputy head Altshuller used unconfirmed informant reports of dubious quality to incriminate Krotov. One report referred to a meeting with Krotov, which supposedly took place several days after Krotov had in fact died. Krotov became one cornerstone upon which the case was built as other accused scholars were connected to him. The circle of arrests widened as KRO officials beat confessions from the accused and promised to review and revise the sentences of those condemned to execution in exchange for incriminating testimony against other academics. All thirty-two of the scholars who were convicted of belonging to the committee were originally sentenced to death. Five were in fact shot, but the others had their sentences commuted to ten years of incarceration by the Supreme Soviet of the USSR within about a month of their conviction.[33]

There are no significant discrepancies between Kubatkin's reports and the KPK document in terms of factual details, such as names and dates of events. The party investigation of the 1950s, however, contended that the wartime confessions were falsified, and it provided new details to support that conclusion. The NKVD special report of 15 March 1942 noted that thirty-five scholars had been arrested and charged with being members of the Committee for Public Salvation; the KPK report stated that thirty-two were convicted and originally sentenced to be shot. Kubatkin's report of 18 October identified Academician Ignatovsky as a main recruiter in the "Academics" case. The KPK document places his arrest in November and states that only under torture did he implicate others, including university professor K. I. Strakhovich. This linking of Ignatovsky with Strakhovich connects the "Academics" with the "Committee for Public Salvation." According to Kubatkin's 15 March report, evidence provided by Strakhovich was in turn instrumental in the arrest of several leading members of the committee, including a senior lecturer at the Refrigeration Institute named Superansky. The KPK report claims that Strakhovich testified in 1956 that Altshuller offered to commute his death sentence if he confirmed that several others, including Krotov, Superansky, and even his own brother were members of the committee. Strakhovich complied.

Kubatkin's short statement from 16 February had identified Superansky as one of eight members of the committee who had recently been arrested. Kubatkin included a fragment from Superansky's confession indicating that the committee had endeavored to prepare and carry out terrorist acts against the city's leaders. Kubatkin unmasked three other committee members in this document: university mathematics professors N. S. Koshliakov and N. V. Roze, and a senior lecturer in mathematics from the Military-Mechanical Institute, B. D. Verzhbitsky.[34] The KPK investigation revealed that during the first half of February, Superansky underwent three grueling nights of interrogation during which he "confessed" that the committee planned armed insurrection. He connected seven others, including his wife, to the committee's treasonous activity. Both Superanskys subsequently perished in labor camps. They would be among twelve of the thirty-two convicted scholars in the case who died either in prison or in the camps, in addition to five others who were shot.[35]

Verzhbitsky and Roze died in prison on 7 March and 12 April, respectively. Whether they perished from the pervasive hunger and cold or from torture during interrogation, or a combination of the two, is unclear.[36] The KPK report did state that through "prohibited methods" senior investigator of the Leningrad NKVD KRO N. F. Kruzhkov elicited a fictitious confession from Roze that he was the leader of the KR group at the university.[37] Roze also gave information that led to the arrest of seven others. In part of Kubatkin's 15 March report that has not been included in Document 65, Roze named Strakhovich and Koshliakov, together with himself, as leaders of the group.

A closer investigation of the backgrounds of some of the accused and their tormentors reveals a curious common denominator. At least fifteen (thirteen convicts and two secret police officials) were connected to the study of mathematics at Leningrad State University. Koshliakov was a former nobleman who was teaching higher mathematics at the university at the start of the Soviet-German War. Roze had been in the reserves of the White Army in Archangel from 1918 to 1920 and served as dean of the mathematical-mechanics department at LGU in 1941. Verzhbitsky had taught math at a naval school on Kronstadt Island and had been wounded during the anti-Bolshevik mutiny of 1921. In 1930, he completed doctoral candidacy work in physics and mathematics at LGU and worked as a senior lecturer in the university's mechanics department. The brutal NKVD investigator Kruzhkov had completed a degree in mechanics at LGU. Most intriguing is the background of Beria's deputy, Merkulov, who received Kubatkin's reports. He was a military officer's son, who had studied in the physics and mathematics department at St. Petersburg University but had not completed his degree prior to being drafted into the army in 1916. He never returned to his studies; instead, he accepted employment with the Cheka in September of 1921. It appears likely, therefore, that Kruzhkov and Merkulov had been acquainted many years earlier with Koshliakov, Roze, and Verzhbitsky, which in turn raises the possibility that Kruzhkov, with Merkulov's support, may have chosen to target these successful and distinguished scholars as a way of settling some old personal score.[38]

As in the SPO investigation of 1942, in the case of the "Committee for Public Salvation" documents do not reveal precisely when or why doubts first arose regarding the convictions. They may have surfaced even before the convictions were obtained. One of the investigators named Shevelev refused to sign several interrogation protocols when he saw they had been "corrected" by his boss, who appears to have been senior investigator Kruzhkov. Shevelev was subsequently removed from the case.[39] The KPK report states that on 6 April 1942, Kubatkin's deputy, S. I. Ogoltsov,[40] approved an order to halt the case against one of the accused, Churilovsky, due to lack of evidence, but there is no indication that Ogoltsov or Kubatkin doubted the merits of cases against the other arrestees. Nevertheless, the Supreme Soviet in Moscow, which certainly acted on orders from a higher authority, had some reason for reducing the sentences from execution to ten years in labor camps. An NKVD report from the autumn of 1942 that summarizes NKVD operations for that year mentions abuses by KRO investigators that led to arrests of innocent people.[41] At least one of those convicted in the case, Koshliakov, and probably others, was officially pardoned by the Presidium of the Supreme Soviet on 27 September 1942, though he continued to languish in a labor camp.[42] There is also the rather cryptic comment on the interrogation of "agent-provocateur" Merkulov during which he admitted presenting false materials on several Leningrad professors, but why he was interrogated on this topic in 1945 is not disclosed in the KPK report. In the late 1990s, it was revealed that Kubatkin signed an order on 7 February 1946, firing several heads of investigative departments for "illegal methods of investigation," including "application of measures of physical pressure," after their subordinates testified against them in a party conference. Kubatkin sent the dossiers on the offending department heads to a special inspection unit within the NKVD for criminal prosecution.[43]

The KPK report is significant for another reason. The plot fabricated by the KRO investigators was elaborate and the false testimony they demanded of those arrested was very detailed. NKVD officials had fertile imaginations when it came to inventing KR schemes. Given their access to actual security information, they could inject realistic details into their fabrications. For example, Senior Lecturer Fedorov was coerced into confessing that "in September 1941, I pointed out the logic of destroying the foundries of the major Leningrad plants the Kirov and Izhorsk works, 'BOLSHEVIK.' . . ." In September the NKVD in fact mined these factories with explosives, which were to be detonated if the Germans were on the verge of seizing the plants. The historian Jan Gross has hypothesized that during the postwar Communist takeover of Poland, the natural allies of the Communist Party were those who had most actively assisted the German occupiers and were therefore the most compromised and vulnerable when the Red Army drove the Germans out. Joining another repressive bureaucracy was preferable to going to jail, or worse. "People devoid of all principles," Gross suggests, would quickly switch one totalitarianism for another.[44] One wonders whether a version of such thinking existed among officials in the Leningrad NKVD or the party in the late summer and early fall of 1941. It is reasonable to assume that in late August and September, a large portion of Leningrad's population expected the city to fall. Although the Soviet media gave scant coverage to the 1939–40 war with Finland, Leningraders had ample evidence in their city—from increases in munitions production to power blackouts to casualties from the front—to convince them that Finland had put up fierce resistance. In 1941, Finland had a most powerful ally in Germany, which had rolled over France in six weeks and which no European power had managed to defeat. By September, with Finns and Germans shelling Leningrad from close range, the city's capitulation must have appeared imminent to many. NKVD officials realized that, like party members and Jews, they would be eliminated if the city were taken. They also understood, however, that they possessed information valuable to the enemy, which they might be able to trade for their lives and even employment. Hence, with proof from Document 66 that NKVD officials *could* concoct elaborate KR schemes, it is logical to presume that some actually *did so*, or, since engaging in such activity was extraordinarily dangerous, made secret plans to approach the enemy should Leningrad capitulate. There is no confirming evidence, however, from available documentation that any such plots existed within the party or NKVD. To the contrary, according to one account, among Leningrad's NKVD personnel, there was not even one instance of treason or flight to enemy lines during the Soviet-German War.[45]

· Document 66 ·

Report of a meeting of the Party Control Committee of the TsK KPSS exonerating those arrested in the "Committee for Public Salvation" case, 14 February 1958, *Istochnik: Dokumenty russkoi istorii* 1996, No. 6, 72–78.

Between November 1941 and March 1942, 32 Leningrad scientific workers, including USSR Academy of Sciences corresponding members V. S. Ignatovsky and N. S. Koshliakov, Professor A. M. Zhuravsky, and others, were brought up on criminal charges by the NKVD Administration for Leningrad *Oblast'*, and then sentenced to the highest measure of punishment by the Military Tribunal of the forces of the Leningrad Front and the Leningrad *Okrug* NKVD. The execution sentence was carried out against Ignatovsky, Ignatovskaia, Artemiev, Chanyshev, and Liubov, but the highest measure of punishment was subsequently commuted to long prison terms for all the others.

Those arrested were accused of forming an anti-Soviet organization called the Committee for Public Salvation, whose goal was to change the existing political order and restore capitalism in the USSR with the help of the German aggressors.

It has now been established that the scholars were coerced into fabricating testimony against themselves, as a result of the application of prohibited interrogation methods and measures of physical and moral suasion and the use of agents provocateurs.

Professor K. I. Strakhovich, who survived from this group, informed the party organs that investigators Kruzhkov and Artemov obtained confessions of participation in the counterrevolutionary organization from him by means of lengthy nighttime interrogations and threats of retribution against his relatives.

In 1954, Professor Koshliakov informed the prosecutor's office of the Leningrad Military District about how statements were obtained from the arrested scholars:

"At the very beginning of the investigation Kruzhkov and the others warned me that if I didn't admit I was guilty of the stated charges, they would force me to admit I'd committed the crime, since they had many means at their disposal for doing this. And when I attempted to refuse to sign the document composed by Kruzhkov, he beat me severely. After that, I no longer resisted. . . . I was in a state of utter exhaustion and possessed no will whatsoever" (vol. 10, p. 250).[46]

Professor Yushkov, against whom criminal charges had been brought, informed the prosecutor's office that he "was called in to see one of the officials, whose last name he doesn't remember. He gave me tea and candies, treated me kindly, and promised not to send me on to the next investigator if I realized what he needed from me. What he actually said was, 'They won't beat you now, but if it turns out you were leading the investigator around by the nose and confrontations expose you, we'll break all your ribs.'"

In a complaint dated 17 June 1954 and addressed to USSR Supreme Soviet deputy Com. M. D. Kovriginaia, Senior Lecturer Postoeva wrote:

"During the investigation . . . illegal methods of interrogation were used, as a result of which, as well as due to my dystrophy, I was compelled to falsely accuse myself of serious counterrevolutionary crimes. . . .

"In the trial, I confirmed the statements given at the preliminary inquiry because the investigator threatened to use a weapon, having said to me before my case was examined in the military tribunal, 'Just try to say something different in court'" (vol. 10, p. 273).

Analogous statements were made to the party organs by Professors Vinogradov and Timofeev.

The first of the group of Leningrad scholars to be arrested in November 1941 was Professor V. S. Ignatovsky, who was accused, on the basis of unverified agent denunciations, of belonging to a counterrevolutionary organization that allegedly existed among Leningrad's scientific-technical workers.

Merkulov, an agent provocateur questioned in 1945, stated that in late 1941 he submitted slanderous materials against several Leningrad professors who were subsequently arrested on the basis of these materials. He further testified:

"My slander reached its high point in the years 1944–1945, when I made up the fictitious Union of the Old Intelligentsia. In creating the fictitious Union of the Russian Intelligentsia, I was hoping . . . to interest the organs in a widely dispersed alleged organization so that I would become a necessary and important official of the organs and thereby gain the opportunity to 'milk the organs' better and win support in the organs to award me an academic degree as a doctor of technical sciences without having to defend a dissertation" (vol. 8, pp. 194–195).

I. A. Kozhemiakin, former head of the 1st division of the KRO of the Leningrad *Oblast'* UNKVD, and his deputy K. V. Suslov (who died in 1944) did not try to verify the agent's dubious reports, and working from them, depicted Ignatovsky as a participant in a fascist organization already established in Leningrad and connected with German circles.

The order for Ignatovsky's arrest, which was signed by Coms. Suslov and Kozhemiakin and former KRO chief Com. Zanin and approved by Ogoltsov, made the unfounded accusation that Ignatovsky belonged to a fascist organization that knew the German command's plan for Leningrad's occupation by the Germans.

After measures of physical persuasion prohibited by law were applied, Ignatovsky confessed that he was a participant in the fascist organization that allegedly existed among the professorial and teaching staff at Leningrad State University.

In an interrogation on 24 November 1941, in the office of former KRO chief Altshuller and a senior investigator from the same department, Kruzhkov (subsequently condemned to 20 years' imprisonment for falsifying investigation materials), Ignatovsky confessed that he was guilty of espionage and gave testimony about his recruitment of Professor L. G. Titov of the Institute of Optical Mechanics in 1925 for espionage against the USSR.

On the basis of the statements by Ignatovsky and his wife, Professors S. M. Chanyshev, V. I. Milinsky, K. I. Strakhovich, N. A. Artemiev, and K. I. Liubov, a senior engineer from the Institute of Precision Mechanics, were arrested.

Orders for the arrest of the professors were processed by Suslov, Kozhemiakin, Zanin, Podchasov, and Artemov and confirmed by Ogoltsov.

Just like Ignatovsky, the scholars also slandered themselves and other individuals concerning the commission of serious crimes against the state after illegal methods of interrogation were used on them.

On the basis of falsified materials, Ignatovsky and the five other professors arrested on 13 January were sentenced to VMN and, with the exception of

Strakhovich, executed. Strakhovich was used as a "witness" in cases against a group of Leningrad scholars unjustly accused of belonging to a counterrevolutionary fascist organization called the Committee for Public Salvation.

As has now been established, there was in reality no such organization among Leningrad scholars; it was invented by workers in the former administration of the Leningrad *Oblast'* NKVD themselves. Moreover, the principle for its creation was laid down by Altshuller, who was working up Professor E. G. Krotov of the Polytechnic Institute as a spy. Altshuller obtained several denunciations from agents "Viktorov" and "Garold" about Professor Krotov declaring anti-Soviet and defeatist moods.

In one of the denunciations, "Viktorov" charged that Krotov "makes a point of striking up conversations with servicemen in the street, trying to assess the likelihood of an uprising. He and a Red Army man from the aviation unit stationed at Galernaia Harbor allegedly had the following discussion. The Red Army soldier complained to Krotov that they were offended at the population for not starting an uprising, which the Red Army soldiers would have joined. Krotov . . . tries to convince the Red Army soldier that the Red Army should start the uprising."

This denunciation was so fictitious and inauthentic that Ogoltsov was forced to write on the denunciation: "It's very doubtful that Krotov, being a professor, took this route in his counterrev. work. Ogoltsov 23 November." However, Altshuller did not take measures to verify "Viktorov's" denunciation. Moreover, in his account of agent operations, citing the denunciations of agents "Viktorov" and "Garold," Altshuller declares Krotov, his wife, Professor Tur, and the artist Charushin to be participants in a counterrevolutionary fascist group.

In another denunciation, "Viktorov," reporting on a meeting with Prof. Krotov that allegedly took place on 6 January 1942, said that Krotov had expressed his anti-Soviet views to him. Despite this obviously fabricated denunciation by the agent about a meeting with Prof. Krotov that could not have taken place on 6 January 1942, since Krotov died on 3 January 1942, Altshuller still continued to use his agent materials in working up Krotov. Moreover, Altshuller started distorting the essence of the agent materials he did have in order to provide a foundation for his accusation against Prof. Krotov as "the leader of a fascist group seeking means to illegally send their messenger across the front line in order to establish practical contact with the German command." Altshuller himself was forced to admit his guilt, that in compiling summary documents, he and other workers from the administration erred in the direction of exaggerating the criminal activities of those being worked up (vol. 1, p. 194).

In January 1942, Altshuller received several denunciations from agent "Viktorov" on the anti-Soviet and defeatist moods of Refrigeration Institute Senior Lecturer Superansky and his wife, as well as about the Superanskys' contacts with Prof. Krotov. However, since there was no proof in these denunciations of anti-Soviet activity by those being worked up, the investigation decided to obtain compromising material against them from Prof. Strakhovich, who had already been sentenced to VMN but had not yet been shot.

Exploiting Strakhovich's desperate position, in exchange for a promise to review his VMN sentence, Altshuller, Podchasov, and Kruzhkov obtained testimony from Strakhovich against a large group of Leningrad scholars who had allegedly conducted organized anti-Soviet activity. Among the anti-Soviet scholars named by Strakhovich was Superansky.

In a face-to-face confrontation with Altshuller on 11 June 1956, Prof. Strakhovich reported:

"Altshuller told me that I might be saved from execution and even freed if I agreed to cooperate with the NKVD organs and give testimony about the counterrevolutionary activities of Leningrad scholars. When I stated that I didn't know anything about this, Altshuller cited several scholars' names for me, including Krotov, Superansky, and my brother S. I. Strakhovich, and Podchasov or Kruzhkov, who were also present, added the name of N. P. Vinogradov, and Altshuller immediately confirmed, 'and Vinogradov.'

"It was emphasized to me that my fate—i.e., whether I lived or they shot me—depended on whether or not I wrote that the individuals named were engaged in anti-Soviet activity.

"At the demand of Altshuller and Kruzhkov and Podchasov, who were also present, I signed a knowingly false statement, slandering scholars who were guilty of nothing, naming about 20 names" (vol. 1, pp. 297–298).

Superansky, placed in a difficult position by Artemov after three nights of interrogation, admitted that he belonged to a counterrevolutionary group from the Refrigeration Institute and was its leader. Among the participants in the counterrevolutionary group, Superansky in turn named another seven people, who were subsequently arrested, including Senior Lecturer Smirnov and the main bookkeeper at the Refrigeration Institute, F. A. Zeits. In an interrogation on 9 February 1942, Superansky testified that the counterrevolutionary group he led was preparing an armed uprising and that the Committee for Public Salvation would be in the vanguard of this uprising. Superansky was interrogated twice by Ogoltsov and Zanin. At an interrogation on 13 March 1942, they obtained statements from Superansky on the counterrevolutionary connection between his group and the German command, which was established in particular through Superansky's wife. Ogoltsov was forced to admit the "inquiry's gross inadequacy" (vol. 10, p. 27).

The falsification of the case against the Leningrad scholars is especially evident from the materials of the investigation referring to Prof. Vinogradov, from whom they obtained through investigator Artemov fabricated statements about the existence in Leningrad of a "Committee for Public Salvation."

On 27 February 1942, Vinogradov was interrogated again by Ogoltsov and Artemov, who compiled his statements in a report 65 pages long. In spite of the obvious dubiousness of Vinogradov's statements about the activities of the "Committee for Public Salvation," which had allegedly taken under its influence about 20 institutions of higher education, about regular contact between the "Committee" and the German command, and about the readying of terrorist acts against Leningrad *sovet* and party leaders, Ogoltsov never undertook any measures to verify them. On the contrary, on the basis of these statements, on 10–11 March 1942, Senior Lecturer N. D. Boginsky and Professors Timofeev and G. T. Tretiak were arrested. A few days after these individuals' arrests, in interrogations on 17 and 23 March, Vinogradov retracted his statements against Timofeev, Tretiak, Popkov, and other scientific workers, stating that he had testified incorrectly about these individuals' participation in a counterrevolutionary organization. In spite of the fact that Vinogradov himself declared his slander of 11 people, that is, half of the Leningrad scholars he had named previously, Ogoltsov and Zanin twice (on 29 March and 2 April 1942), in interrogating Vinogradov, made no attempt even to clarify the reason for his slander of all these other individuals. Nor were any decisions taken with respect to the arrested Timofeev and Tretiak (vol. 10, pp. 28–30).

On the basis of testimonies by Prof. Strakhovich, Professor N. V. Roze was arrested. In the order for Roze's arrest, Suslov, Kozhemiakin, and Altshuller indicated that Roze was a member of V. S. Ignatovsky's insurgent fascist organization and that he had been exposed in criminal activity by the testimony of the arrested Strakhovich.

After conducting an inquiry into this case, Kruzhkov obtained fabricated testimony from Roze about him being the leader of a counterrevolutionary organization at Leningrad State University. On the basis of the statements obtained from Roze, another 7 people were arrested, the order for whose arrest was signed by Altshuller. In interrogations, confessional statements were obtained from all the arrestees through the use of prohibited interrogation methods.

On 3 February 1942, on the basis of an order falsified by Suslov, Kozhemiakin, and Zanin, Professor V. N. Churilovsky of the Institute of Precision Mechanics and Optics was arrested as a participant in the fascist and espionage organization allegedly created by Ignatovsky. The arrest order indicated that V. N. Churilovsky had been exposed by the statements of the arrested Titov, Chanyshev, and Ignatovsky. Meanwhile, the indicated arrested men had not given such testimony in the preliminary investigation; nonetheless, on 20 February 1942 Churilovsky was accused of committing serious state crimes. This order was affirmed by Podchasov. However, in spite of exhaustive questioning and coercion, Churilovsky did not give statements about his own anti-Soviet activity.

Instead, in order to put an immediate halt to the case to free Churilovsky from jail, as wrongly arrested, measures were taken to gather compromising materials against him and condemn him by any and all means. With this goal in mind, from 6 February to 31 March 1942, four of Churilovsky's co-workers were interrogated; however, they did not give any statements about Churilovsky's anti-Soviet activity. Then M. I. Ignatovskaia, who by that time had been condemned to VMN, was questioned as a "witness." Ignatovskaia testified to the defeatist statements Churilovsky had allegedly made at a chance meeting with her on the street. Churilovsky denied these statements both in questioning and in a face-to-face confrontation with Ignatovskaia conducted by investigator Suslov on 6 March 1942.

Having failed to obtain a confessional statement from Churilovsky and not having other proof of his membership in the anti-Soviet organization of Roze, Koshliakov, and others, on 31 March 1942 Altshuller was forced to confirm the order drawn up by Suslov on putting the materials against Churilovsky into separate proceedings, and on 6 April 1942 Ogoltsov approved the order to halt the criminal prosecution.

S. I. Ogoltsov, who was questioned over the falsification of this case, stated that from his point of view there had been no indications of the case's falsification and he had been deceived by Suslov, Kozhemiakin, and Zanin, who had referred in the arrest order for Churilovsky to statements that did not exist (vol. 10, p. 32).

The present verification has established that there was a widespread criminal practice in the KRO UNKVD for Leningrad *Oblast'* of interrogating prisoners after they had been condemned to VMN. In these interrogations, the compromising statements needed against other individuals were extorted by means of promises to save the lives of those condemned to execution. Those condemned to VMN—Strakhovich, Ignatovskaia, Ignatovsky, and Timofeev—were interrogated. Moreover, all of them, except Strakhovich, were executed after the interrogations.

During the investigation into the cases against the Leningrad scholars, slanderous statements were obtained from several of those arrested against Academicians Tarle, Rozhdestvensky, and Baikov, corresponding members of the USSR Academy of Sciences Kravets and Kachalov, and many others (128 scholars).

In 1954 and 1955, by a determination of the Military Collegium of the USSR Supreme Court and the Military Tribunal of the Leningrad Military District, the sentences against the condemned were rescinded, and the cases against them were closed for failure to constitute a crime.

For this very crude violation of socialist legality, I believe it is essential to call S. I. Ogoltsov, S. F. Zanin, I. K. Altshuller, I. V. Podchasov, and I. A. Kozhemiakin to strict party accountability [. . .]

For their work in the organs of state security, Ogoltsov, Zanin, Altshuller, Podchasov, and Kozhemiakin received orders and medals. As has been clarified at the present time, their activities in the organs were defective and antiparty.

TsK KPSS KPK Office Administrator   V. Ganin
3 February 1958

List of the dead

1. V. S. IGNATOVSKY   —corresponding member, USSR Academy of
                             Sciences, professor—shot.
2. S. M. CHANYSHEV   —professor—shot.

3. E. M. SUPERANSKAIA	—professor—died in camp.
4. L. V. KLIMENKO	—professor—died in camp.
5. F. I. MALYSHEV	—professor—died in camp.
6. N. V. ROZE	—professor—died in prison.
7. L. G. TITOV	—professor—died in prison.
8. G. T. TRETIAK	—professor—died in camp.
9. V. I. MILINSKY	—candidate of sciences, died in prison in preliminary investigation.
10. K. A. LIUBOV	—senior lecturer—shot.
11. N. A. ARTEMIEV	—candidate of sciences—shot.
12. M. I. IGNATOVSKAIA	—professor's wife—shot.
13. I. M. SUPERANSKY	—candidate of sciences—died in camp.
14. V. I. KROTOVA	—candidate of sciences—died in camp.
15. B. D. VERZHBITSKY	—candidate of sciences—died in prison.

An unsubstantiated account from a surprising source has proposed a radically different interpretation of the "Committee for Public Salvation" case, which suggests a possible explanation of why it was reopened. Lavrenty Beria's son, Sergo, stated that after the war he studied mathematics for two years with Professor Koshliakov, who had been arrested during the war allegedly for "attempting to form a government that would collaborate with the Germans."[47] According to Beria, Koshliakov claimed that although he was a prisoner, he was allowed to work at his specialty. Beria included an extended direct quote from Koshliakov describing his arrest:

> It was at the beginning of the war. Leningrad was under siege and the Germans might enter the city at any moment. One fine day Zhdanov summoned me, along with a dozen other scholars and scientists working in various fields. He assembled us and said that the Party's regional committee had decided, with approval from higher authority, to get ready a group of people who would constitute the Russians' representatives in the administration that the Germans would set up. They would be responsible for contacting the Germans if they took over Leningrad. Most of us were far from enthusiastic. Politics held no attraction for us. But nobody asked us for our opinions, and documents were manufactured for us which were to show that, even under Soviet rule, we had been carrying out underground activity aimed at seizing power. These preparations came to nothing because the Germans did not take Leningrad, and eventually Zhdanov ordered the arrest of our whole group. We were accused of being counter-revolutionaries in cahoots with the Germans! It was no good our reminding the authorities that we had acted on their instigation, with the NKVD's full knowledge. They locked us up and we signed our confessions. The oddest thing was that Zhdanov, at an audience he gave me, denied that he had fostered this collaborationist government.[48]

Sergo Beria added that he asked his father to grant amnesty to Koshliakov, but that the elder Beria had replied: "The only way I can do that is to release him along with some others. If I release him on his own, that may come back on me. Appoint him director of a research project, even if he doesn't take much part in it, and I'll see what I can do." Beria claimed that he followed his father's advice, and Koshliakov was freed.[49]

There are strong reasons to doubt this account, which has not been corroborated elsewhere.[50] Koshliakov may have lied to gain the sympathies of both Berias. Such a lie would have been difficult to expose, because by the early 1950s, the main Leningrad leaders who might contradict Koshliakov—Zhdanov, Kuznetsov, and Kubatkin—were dead. More likely, Sergo Beria may have falsified Koshliakov's story to vilify his father's rival, Zhdanov. In the original Russian version of his memoir, Sergo Beria stated directly that Zhdanov wanted Koshliakov and his colleagues shot.[51] Or, Beria may have simply wanted to rehabilitate his father's image and burnish his own by claiming that together they had rehabilitated the unjustly convicted Leningrad academics. Beria's account does not explain why Zhdanov would want to select a government that would work with the Germans, although he suggests that the reason was linked to the desire to "save the historical and cultural treasures of the city."[52] Other possible explanations, however, would be that Zhdanov hoped to subvert German control in Leningrad through a collaborationist regime that really remained loyal to the Communists or, just the opposite, that he was attempting to create a mechanism to collaborate indirectly with a victorious enemy.

If Sergo Beria's account is accurate, both the original NKVD case and the KPK report were seriously flawed, because any in-depth investigation would have revealed the accusation that Leningrad's leaders had launched the "Committee for Public Salvation." Although it is unlikely, that may have been what happened. If Zhdanov created the "Committee for Public Salvation," he might not have informed Kubatkin about it—despite Sergo Beria's claim that the NKVD was part of the conspiracy—in which case the course of the aggressive and coercive NKVD investigation is more understandable (which is not to say correct or just). In this scenario, Kubatkin and his investigators may have really thought that they had cracked a major spy case and brushed aside protestations to the contrary from those arrested. If the members of the KPK in the mid-1950s uncovered the Koshliakov-Beria version (as they likely would have if it was true), they may have secretly decided to blame the Leningrad KRO NKVD anyway for the debacle. Following the execution of Lavrenty Beria and his deputies, the security organs were an easy target. Similarly, it is conceivable that the KPK may have wanted to protect the reputations of Leningrad's other party leaders and Kubatkin, who had become victims of the Leningrad Affair, from embarrassing accusations of indirect collaboration with the enemy during the war. The major figures from the Leningrad Affair had been officially rehabilitated in April 1954,[53] and Khrushchev had declared in the "secret speech" at the Twentieth Party Congress in February 1956 that the Leningrad party officials had been innocent victims of Beria's murderous machinations.

Certain details of Koshliakov's life, which have come to light in recent years, are consistent with Sergo Beria's story. He was imprisoned in the Solikamsk labor camp from 1942 to 1945. He may have worked on war-related problems in that camp. In 1945, he was sent to work in a special research institute prison (a so-called *sharashka*) outside Moscow and was freed from that institution in October 1951 after a petition was submitted (by exactly whom is unclear) that pointed out the Supreme Soviet's pardon from the fall of 1942. His convictions were finally expunged by the Presidium of the Supreme Soviet on 5 February 1953.[54] He was officially rehabilitated on 20 December 1954. Superansky and Professors N. P. Vinogradov and L. V. Klimenko were not rehabilitated until 9 February 1955.[55]

It should also be noted that the Koshliakov-Beria version does not contradict the hypothesis that the NKVD selected members for the "Committee for Public Salvation" based on a previous acquaintance with some of the city's prominent intellectuals. It is possible that the NKVD and the party leadership selected the committee members not because of an old, unrelated grudge but, on the contrary, because they considered them to be respectable scholars, whom the Germans might trust because of their ties to Germany before the Revolution. If the enemy were to occupy Leningrad, a handpicked collaborationist government could provide obvious advantages to the city's former party and NKVD leaders. However, when the Leningrad Front stabilized, the committee's existence would have become worse than an embarrassment—it could be construed by Moscow as a treasonous plot to surrender the city. City leaders who had fomented the plot would feel compelled to deny it and imprison or eliminate all who might know of it. If the whole affair had been concocted by Zhdanov, the commutation of sentences to ten-year prison terms might have been a life-saving gesture several months later to the convicts who were still alive, in return for their cooperation.

In sum, from the documents that are available, the Koshliakov-Beria account can be neither proven nor refuted. What is virtually beyond doubt is that the members of the alleged "Committee for Public Salvation" were not spies or saboteurs as Kubatkin's arrest reports contended. Their considerable talents could have been far better utilized for the war effort.

The outcome of the SPO cases demonstrates that the NKVD, or at least its *partkom*, was able to some extent to assess critically KR activity, because at least two of the accused were released about three months after their arrest following an official inquiry (although their release may have resulted from overriding political considerations). However, using the KRO case to gauge credibility of NKVD verdicts yields a more complicated and disturbing conclusion. On the one hand, the record shows that there were substantial doubts within the Leningrad NKVD administration right from the spring of 1942 over whether the accused were actually guilty of their crimes. Five were executed, but the rest who were condemned to death had their sentences mysteriously commuted. A few months later, at least one of the convicts was pardoned. These actions are strong indications that authorities inside and outside the Leningrad NKVD believed that the convicts were either innocent of their alleged crimes or did not deserve the punishments they received. Nevertheless, the convictions were overturned only sixteen years after they were imposed, after many of those convicted had died.[56]

Finally, the cases of unsubstantiated arrests and convictions for belonging to KR organizations depicted in this chapter raise doubts regarding the "625 KR groups and formations" that had been "uncovered and eliminated" in the blockade zone through the end of September 1942. How many other convictions were based on unfounded fears of NKVD investigators or on their unbridled and cynical ambition will probably never be known. Although some small anti-Soviet conspiracies may have gone undetected, it would appear from the cases discussed above that the number of "groups and formations" that actually conspired to subvert Soviet policies was probably substantially fewer than 625. What is certain is that regardless of how many such groups existed, whether supported by enemy agents or not, their number was extremely small in comparison to the number of people who were overheard at some point expressing defeatist, anti-Soviet, and pro-German sympathies. If the enemy had taken Leningrad, he would have found many willing helpers among the city's residents. Informant reports and some private recollections strongly suggest that an indeterminate, though not insignificant, portion of the population either had not learned to speak or think fluently "in Bolshevik" before the war or reached their moment of disillusion with communism during the blockade. Beneath the surface, there was much suppressed anger against communist rule and much identification with alternative ideologies and forms of political and social order. Yet, notions of resistance to Soviet power hardly ever translated into organized activity in wartime Leningrad. No single, large anti-Soviet conspiracy within the blockaded city has been substantiated, and the overall effect of organized anti-Soviet opposition was negligible.

Conclusions

Access to Soviet-era archives in Russia and to other unpublished and published primary source materials, such as diaries and memoirs, and periodicals printed in the blockaded territory, affords a sharper and deeper understanding of a range of critical historical issues regarding the siege. It is now known with certainty that despite Leningrad's isolation during the ordeal, the Kremlin was well briefed on a regular basis on major developments within the blockade zone. Even though Stalin taunted Zhdanov on 1 December 1941 that he contacted Moscow so infrequently that it seemed as if he and Leningrad were in the Pacific Ocean, communication at the highest levels between the two cities suffered few interruptions. The most active and stable channel appears to have been the one between Kubatkin and Beria.

Stalin's transmissions to Smolny were full of ridicule and threats, and Leningrad's leaders in response were willing to disagree with Stalin up to a point; however, there is no evidence to support the suspicion that Stalin may have deliberately imperiled Leningrad's defenses in support of intrigue by Malenkov and Molotov against Zhdanov.[1] Although Stalin expressed serious doubts around the time of the start of the blockade regarding whether the city could be defended, his top priority was to safeguard the army and weaponry that might have to be evacuated. In the fall of 1941, he wanted the Leningrad Front to break through the siege ring and establish contact with the Volkhov Front in part to provide an avenue of escape for the military in the event that Leningrad could not be held. In a dispatch to Fediuninsky, Zhdanov, and Kuznetsov on 23 October 1941, Stalin stated that whether or not Leningrad could be defended, "for us the army is more important." Of secondary importance were warships and defense industries and their skilled employees. Stalin ordered the mining of ships, war plants, and other important objectives, which were to be blown up if the city's fall appeared to be imminent. The fate of the rest of the city's population—housewives, children, pensioners, and those employed in nondefense jobs—seemed of relatively little concern to him. Beria was informed of Leningrad's first cases of cannibalism on 13 December 1941; yet, it was not until 22 January that Stalin agreed to allot enough resources to the Ladoga ice road to permit a massive evacuation of starving civilians.

Probably no other people in history were so thoroughly mobilized for war as were Leningraders. Those who were not drafted into the armed forces or evacuated to the interior of the country served in the *opolchenie,* built defense fortifications outside and inside the city, trained for combat, dug air raid trenches, watched for enemy aircraft, put out fires during air raids and repaired damage afterwards, relocated to safer parts of the city after the start of the artillery bombardment, unbolted machinery and packed it up for evacuation, went to work in defense plants, retooled factories to produce munitions, and logged work shifts of eleven and even fourteen hours while starving to death to produce matériel, much of which was sent out to other fronts. Even though bread rations and allotments of other foods were cut twice in September, once more at the beginning of October, and twice again in November to a level that could not sustain the average person, workers in defense plants were forced to continue to work overtime until the city's capacity to supply factories with electricity was depleted. One of the last major defense plants to cease large-scale production was the Kirov factory. It lost electrical power on 20 December.[2]

The people of Leningrad would have fared better if more attention had been devoted during the autumn to preparing for a siege winter and less attention paid to manufacturing weapons and ammunition that were transported to other parts of the country. Extended work shifts were exhausting, and hardly any precautions were taken to prepare communal housing and work space for loss of electrical power and heat. It is also likely that even if the tempo of production had not been eased, Leningrad's security, and the security of the country as a whole, would have been enhanced if more of the produced munitions had been sent to the Leningrad Front with the aim of trying to pierce the siege ring along Lake Ladoga's southern shore. From the viewpoint of the Soviet leadership, however, the situation during the winter of 1941–42 was not entirely bleak. There was some reason for hope, as the German blitzkrieg had been halted. Although the

Red Army had sustained staggering losses in the first six months of the war, Moscow had been saved, and the Leningrad Front, the Baltic Fleet, and Leningrad's defense industries were essentially intact. Germany and Finland had failed to implement a complete blockade of Leningrad. The Ladoga lifeline was tenuous but vitally important. If it had not existed, almost everyone in Leningrad would have perished in the war's first winter. Kiev had been overrun, but unless Hitler suddenly turned into a champion of Ukrainian independence, its loss was of less consequence than the loss of either Moscow or Leningrad. As dismantled Soviet factories rolled east to be rebuilt and brought back on line in 1942, and with Hitler's declaration of war on the United States, the Soviet leadership realized that time was on its side. Yet, if Stalin's strategy had been more clever and sophisticated, he might either have prevented the Leningrad blockade in the first place, if Leningrad had been allowed to keep more of its produced weaponry in the summer of 1941, or pierced the blockade ring during the massive Soviet counteroffensive of December 1941, as in fact would occur in early 1943. Instead, the Red Army attacked in depth along a very lengthy front with overly ambitious goals. Stalin hoped to encircle Army Group Center, retake the Ukrainian industrial heartland, and end Leningrad's siege all at the same time. Close to half a million Soviet soldiers were killed in this general offensive.[3] A limited and more focused thrust by the Leningrad and Volkhov Fronts, which were only about ten miles apart, toward each other along the coast of Lake Ladoga might have succeeded at this time. The siege would not have ended, but Leningrad could have been supplied by rail. And, even if such an operation had failed, it might have weakened German defensive positions enough just south of Ladoga to allow a subsequent attack in 1942 to be successful. As it was, the Red Army launched several offensives to break the blockade, but the Kremlin could have given a higher priority to trying to lift the siege in late 1941.

Within Leningrad's leadership structure, there were three powerful entities: the party, the military, and the NKVD/NKGB. *Gorkom* leaders Zhdanov and Kuznetsov together with the commander of the Leningrad Front made military decisions designed to implement military policies established by Stalin, the GKO, and the *Stavka*. Decisions regarding Leningrad's civilians and the city's productive resources were made by the *gorkom* in compliance with Moscow's broader goals. The security organs tried to enforce military and political policies and decisions, combat crime, and eliminate any political opposition or dissent. Both the party and the NKVD had large secret informant networks. Generally speaking, in practice none of these three groups was supreme in Leningrad, as each exerted checks over the others. While Zhdanov worked closely with whoever was Leningrad Front military commander, he kept his distance from Kubatkin, as he did from Kubatkin's superior, Beria, who had been Zhdanov's rival before the war. During the starvation winter, the party decided how food was distributed, but as the Kharitonov case shows (Document 19), the NKVD monitored the process at the *raikom* level. The NKGB conducted secret surveillance within the *gorkom*, as evidenced by the Bakshis affair (Document 18). The NKVD also kept watch over high-ranking military officers. An NKVD official assisted the *Stavka*'s representative in the VSLF in June 1942 in his denunciation of the personal life of Front Commander Khozin—at least according to Khozin. The attempt to portray Khozin as a lecherous alcoholic was almost assuredly part of an effort to blame him for the loss of Vlasov's Second Shock Army. Khozin's deferential plea to Zhdanov in which he defended his personal behavior (Document 17) demonstrates his acknowledgment of Zhdanov's authority. The investigation that the Leningrad NKVD's *partkom* and administration conducted in May 1942 into the so-called "Activists" case may represent an example of the party's check over the NKVD.[4] This investigation revealed that the KR charges against prominent intellectuals were based on faulty evidence worked up by NKVD investigators (Document 62). In addition, the party and the NKVD checked each other through their vast eavesdropping networks, which employed different standards for identifying anti-Soviet agitation. An NKVD employee could show up in a party report and vice versa.

There was a brief period when Leningrad had a recognized and undisputed boss within the city. When Zhukov replaced Voroshilov as front commander during the crisis month of September 1941 and organized Leningrad's defenses for about three weeks, no one dared challenge his authority. Party chief Zhdanov's position at that time was precarious. He probably feared that like Voroshilov he might be recalled to Moscow for his failure to prevent Leningrad from being surrounded. Zhukov's dismissive attitude toward Kubatkin is demonstrated in a terse response that he sent the NKVD head on 24 September (Document 14). During this time, Zhukov even nullified Stalin's order to mine warships of the Baltic Fleet.

The Leningrad Party Organization experienced a crisis during the first six months of the war. As a result of mass mobilization to the front, party membership in Leningrad was cut in half, and despite attempts to recruit members, the number of new candidates plummeted when it appeared that Germany was about to invade Leningrad in September 1941. At the same time, candidate members were not advancing to full membership. The LPO did not revive until the latter half of 1943. The NKVD, which had far fewer employees than the party had members, does not appear to have experienced a proportional drop in its ranks, although it lost considerable personnel through the evacuation over the ice road.[5] Its operations were uninterrupted during the summer and fall of 1941. The extreme difficulties with which the party had to cope during the first year of the war produced severe tension among *gorkom* secretaries, as evidenced by Lysenko's suicide (Documents 20 and 21).

Among the civilian population as a whole, survival rates varied considerably and did not correlate strongly with one's ration category. Because the basic rations that were distributed between mid-November 1941 and late January 1942, which consisted primarily of bread, were generally insufficient to sustain life, survival depended to a large extent on one's ability to acquire extra food. Of secondary importance were conserving one's strength by avoiding strenuous activity, finding warm places to work and live, and maintaining a will to live. One's sex also played a role, as women can endure longer periods of malnourishment than men can. Employees in food-processing plants, who were primarily women and in the low *sluzhashchie* ration category, had among the highest documented survival rates, comparable to soldiers away from the front, whose rations were considerably larger than those of civilians, and to medical doctors, who had better access to food, warmth, and medicines. *Rabochie* in idle factories were more likely to survive than those who toiled hard in a large defense plant such as the Kirov works, which was kept in operation as long as possible, even though the workers there received extra food. Nonworking dependents, especially fast-growing teenagers, were very likely to starve to death. The most defenseless were the very young and the elderly. The operational staff of the NKVD had a higher rate of survival than party members as a whole, who in turn were about twice as likely to survive as the average civilian. The authorities had no option but essentially to condone pervasive and unregulated barter transactions during the hungry winter, and theft of food by administrators in charge of distributing it was massive and widespread, though such thieves were punished swiftly by execution if caught.

Party propaganda portrayed the war more often as a struggle to protect the *rodina*, including *rodnoi Piter,* and its culture, as well as to support troops at the front, than it cast the war as a defense of the party and its ideology. Yet, after the war and throughout the Soviet Union's final decades, the state used the defense of Leningrad and Soviet victory in the war to try to legitimize its existence and its one-party system. Victory in the war became an integral part of the state's foundational ideology. The wartime propaganda's emphasis on traditional institutions and values apparently matched the predominant popular mood, as *blokadniki* seemed more ready to fight for their homeland, heritage, family, and friends, as well as their faith than for the political system. The Russian Orthodox Church was accorded a more active role in society, and more people attended church services. Atheistic propaganda ended in Leningrad at the beginning of the war, and few Russian Orthodox priests were persecuted in the city during the war, although the state continued to use church buildings for any purpose it desired. In July 1941, Leningrad's metropolitan publicly called for the "defeat [of] the cunning and malicious foe" and defense of the homeland, and the Church was allowed to collect funds for the army and Red Cross.

All available sources (with the exception of some German intelligence reports and recollections of individual emigrants) indicate that a large majority of Leningraders wanted to defend their city throughout the siege period. Pro-German sentiment was most noticeable when Leningrad's defense was most in doubt—during several weeks before the start of the siege and several thereafter. The available evidence, which is admittedly fragmentary, strongly suggests that at this time large segments of the population were secretly preparing themselves for the possibility or likelihood of adapting to life under enemy occupation, which is not to say that they welcomed that eventuality. However, as long as the leadership conveyed a determination to defend Leningrad and maintained a strong security presence, the essential "social contract" of obedience in return for protection prevailed. By contrast, the announcement in Moscow on 16 October that German forces had broken through defenses near the capital and the nearly simultaneous commencement of a massive and visible evacuation of central government offices sparked widespread panic and looting. Order was restored in the capital three days later when martial law was declared, which signaled that the city would indeed be defended.

When it became clear by midautumn that Germany had postponed or abandoned plans for an offensive into Leningrad, and as the enemy's intensive aerial bombardment continued when hunger set in, praise for Germany within the city was detected less frequently. In its place there arose an ardent desire for vengeance, as Leningraders became the first large population in unoccupied Soviet territory to experience first-hand for an extended period of time the effects of the enemy's brutal policies. A growing hatred of the enemy mixed with bitter criticism of Soviet failure to afford better protection and expressions of pessimism and defeatism as the death toll reached its peak in late January. The arrest rate for KR activity (at best, a partial reflection of anti-Soviet sentiment) rose in January, and by the end of the month almost attained the level of August, when there had been a large round-up of suspected subversives. The percentage of mailed letters that were confiscated by NKVD censors because, among other things, they purportedly contained defeatist comments that could ruin morale at the front reached a maximum of 20 percent during the last week of January.

The crescendo of criticism presents a paradox, because at the same time, it would appear that the large majority of Leningraders ardently welcomed the city government's basic shift, albeit a late one, toward giving top priority to the local economy. When large defense plants lost electrical power and could no longer produce for the front, they devoted their meager resources to manufacturing, often by hand, water buckets, wood-burning stoves, and other items that residents sorely needed. Workers were encouraged by factory managers to use their initiative to help the city survive. Moreover, Leningraders obviously welcomed the additional resources allotted in January to the Ladoga ice road to facilitate the mass exodus. The party and the people shared the essential goal of survival. Perhaps at this basic level they had never been so unified in purpose during the Soviet era. What people often complained about was that too few resources had been devoted too late to the city's survival and that mistakes and corruption at high levels were all too common.

Pro-German or anti-Soviet sentiment rarely developed into organized activity designed to undermine Soviet power. Even when the prospect of enemy occupation appeared greatest in the last weeks of summer, there were few blatant and public acts of defiance of the authorities. The opening of Soviet archives has not confirmed the existence of even one major conspiratorial plot or large antiwar or anti-Soviet demonstration. The most visible group acts of public disobedience were the handful of small, spontaneous strikes that occurred mainly in the fall of 1941, when factory workers refused to complete long shifts without getting extra food. It can be shown today that some of the arrests and convictions for anti-Soviet conspiratorial activity were groundless or built on coerced confessions, which casts doubt generally on NKVD definitions of KR activity and raises the question of how many of those arrested for KR (article 58) offenses actually engaged in the activity of which they were accused. It would seem that a combination of three factors explains why critical or "negative" sentiment did not lead to more and greater anti-Soviet organized activity. Many of the overheard comments merely criticized specific failures of government, party, or the military and did not constitute a fundamental rejection of Soviet ideology and power. Those expressing such complaints may simply have wanted those in charge to do a better job. Secondly, the Soviet system, with all its shortcomings, was generally viewed as preferable to enemy occupation, which was the only alternative. Finally, fear of Soviet security forces likely deterred some would-be counterrevolutionaries from engaging in conspiratorial activity.

Despite the fact that so many died during the siege, *blokadniki,* most of whom were women, demonstrated remarkable courage, resilience, resourcefulness, and shrewdness in responding to extraordinary dangers and challenges. Their will to survive was balanced and complemented by heroic self-sacrifice for children, other relatives, and close friends. They coped with the direct effects of the enemy's siege—continual bombardment and lack of food, heat, and running water—by moving to parts of buildings which were not in the line of artillery fire, sneaking out near enemy lines to dig up peat for fuel and potatoes, planting gardens in empty patches of soil throughout the city, and trudging long distances to scoop water from the river, a canal, or a broken pipe. *Blokadniki* also had to cope with the extraordinary demands of their own leaders, especially during the first six months of the war; misguided policies, such as sending food out of the city at the beginning of the war, concentrating too much food in the Badaev warehouses, and not preparing the city for the first siege winter; and Stalin's refusal to commit fully to development of the ice road until late January. Many Leningraders walked a fine line between trying to satisfy the authorities and surviving. Their complaints were often carefully expressed in the language of, and in response to, official promises and policies. Their acts of defiance were measured and constrained, and they took advantage of relaxed work discipline in 1942 to tend to their own needs.

Russians throughout their history had faced similar types of hardships, and many *blokadniki* had lived through war, famine, forced labor, and terror prior to the Second World War. Knowledge gained through prior experiences probably helped many survive the blockade. Near the end of the war, an engineer named V. A. Inostrantsev at the Lenriprogaza plant was overheard by an NKVD informant saying:

> The Russian people are patient and hardy. They survived 300 years of the Tatar yoke, 300 years of Romanov oppression, all of the Five Year Plans, and the difficulties of the present war.[6]

The blockade was arguably their biggest challenge.

APPENDIX A

Daily Bread Rations

	Workers, engineers, technicians	Workers in "hot" workshops	Office workers	Adult dependents	Children under 12 yrs.
From					
18 July 1941	800 grams	1,000	600	400	400
2 Sept.	600	800	400	300	300
12 Sept.	500	700	300	250	250
1 Oct.	400	600	200	200	200
13 Nov.	300	450	150	150	150
20 Nov.	250	375	125	125	125
25 Dec.	350	500	200	200	200
24 Jan. 1942	400	575	300	250	250
11 Feb.	500	700	400	300	300
22 March	600[a]	700	500	400	400

Source: Amosov, "Rabochie Leningrada," 211–13.
[a] Starting on 22 February 1943, workers, engineers, and technicians in defense industries received 700 grams of bread per day.

APPENDIX B

Official Monthly Rations for Food Other than Bread

		Workers, engineers, technicians[a]	Office workers	Adult dependents	Children under 12 yrs.
Groats					
	From 18 July 1941	2,000 grams	1,500	1,000	1,200
	September	1,500	1,000	600	1,200
	February 1942	2,000	1,500	1,000	1,200
Meat					
	From 18 July 1941	2,200	1,200	600	600
	September	1,500	800	400	400
	January 1942	400	350	300	400
	February	1,350	750	375	375
	March	1,500	800	400	400
	April	1,800	1,000	600	600
	May	1,800	1,000	500	500
Fat					
	From 18 July 1941	800	400	200	400
	September	950	500	300	500
	November	1,235	500	300	600
	December	600	250	200	500
	January 1942	250	200	150	225
	February	150	100	100	100
	March	800	400	200	400

		Workers, engineers, technicians[a]	Office workers	Adult dependents	Children under 12 yrs.
Sugar and candy					
	From 18 July 1941	1,500	1,200	1,000	1,200
	September	2,000	1,700	1,500	1,700
	November	1,500	1,000	800	1,200
	January 1942	550	450	400	650
	February	600	500	400	500
	April	900	500	400	500
Fish[b]					
	From 18 July 1941	1,000	800	500	500
	September	600	400	300	300
	October	400	200	200	200
	November	100	100	100	100
	April 1942	500	400	250	250

Source: Amosov, "Rabochie Leningrada," 211–13.

[a] No distinction was made between workers in "hot" workshops and other workers.

[b] Rations for fish were not published from December 1941 through March 1942. Fish was often included as part of the meat ration starting in December and extending through the rest of the siege period.

APPENDIX C

Rations Actually Distributed Other than Bread, 1 January–31 March 1942, According to *Leningradskaia Pravda*

		Workers, engineers, technicians	Office workers	Adult dependents	Children under 12 yrs.
19 January	Groats	400 grams	200	100	300
	Fat	0	0	0	75
	Sugar, candy	100	100	100	250
20 January	Meat & by-products	100	100	100	100
6 February	Butter	200	150	100	150
12 February	Groats	500	375	250	300
13 February	Sugar	300	250	200	250
14 February	Meat & by-products	450	250	125	125
20 February	Dried vegetables	150	150	150	150
21 February	Meat & by-products	450	250	125	125
24 February	Cocoa, chocolate	25 (choc.)	25 (cocoa)	25 (cocoa)	25 (cocoa)
	Kerosene	0.25 liter	0.25 liter	0.25 liter	0.25 liter
26 February	Meat & by-products	450 grams	250	125	125
	Groats	500	375	250	300
27 February	Sugar, candy	300	250	200	250
	Cranberries	150	150	150	150
5 March	Meat & by-products	300	200	100	100
	"Special mixture"	0	0	0	150
	Matches	2 boxes	2 boxes	1 box	1 box

		Workers, engineers, technicians	Office workers	Adult dependents	Children under 12 yrs.
6 March	Sugar, candy	300 grams	250	200	250
	Dried fruit	100	100	100	100
7 March	Macaroni, groats	300	200	200	200
11 March	Meat & by-products	300	150	100	100
12 March	Macaroni, groats	300	200	200	200
16 March	Groats	300	200	200	200
	Sugar	300	0	0	0
18 March	Meat & by-products	300	150	100	100
19 March	Butter	200	100	0	100
22 March	Sugar, candy	300	250	200	250
25 March	Groats	300	300	300	300
	Vegetable oil	200	100	100	100[a]
26 March	Meat & by-products	300	150	100	100
28 March	Groats	400	300	200	200
29 March	Butter	200	100	0	100
	Meat & by-products	300	150	0	0
30 March	Groats	400	300	0	200

[a]Children received butter instead of vegetable oil.

Notes

INTRODUCTION

1. Warsaw's death toll, including Jews sent to Treblinka, was almost as high and represented a higher percentage of that city's population.

2. Glantz, *The Siege of Leningrad*, 180. For Soviet military losses on different fronts during the war, see Krivosheev, *Grif sekretnosti sniat*, 128–393.

3. See below, pp. 270–73.

4. There is no entirely adequate or generally agreed-upon name for the war that Germany and its allies waged against the Soviet Union between 1941 and 1945. "World War II on the Eastern Front" implies a Western perspective. The Soviet and contemporary Russian usage of "Great Patriotic War" has an even more pronounced slant.

5. See, for example, Amir Weiner's ground-breaking study of the Ukrainian region of Vinnytsia, *Making Sense of War*; Jeffrey Jones's work on the war's impact on Rostov on the Don, *Everyday Life*; and Karl Qualls's *From Ruins to Reconstruction*.

6. Kochina, *Blockade Diary*, 30.

7. This is one of the important themes of Weiner's *Making Sense of War*.

8. See Blair Ruble's "The Leningrad Affair and the Provincialization of Leningrad."

9. The most detailed street guide of Leningrad ever made was produced by the CIA in 1977 for embassy and consular staff and visiting scholars. It was 175 pages long and included street numbers for every building.

10. The most exhaustive bibliography of Soviet books on the war is Parrish, *The U.S.S.R. in World War II*. It provides information on 7,521 books, with an addendum for works published between 1975 and 1980.

11. See Lisa Kirschenbaum's excellent analysis of the contrast between official and unofficial interpretations of the siege, *The Legacy of the Siege of Leningrad*.

12. Salisbury, *The 900 Days*, 514.

13. Kirschenbaum, "Innocent Victims and Heroic Defenders," 283.

14. In the introduction to Parrish, *The U.S.S.R. in World War II* (p. xvii), John Erickson states that Soviet authors produced fifteen thousand books on the war up to 1980.

15. Important exceptions include Dzeniskevich, *Voennaia piatiletka*, the first and only Soviet-era study of Leningrad's large wartime industrial work force, and V. M. Koval'chuk's *Leningrad i Bol'shaia zemlia*, which described the functioning of the Ladoga ice road.

16. Magaeva, "Physiological and Psychosomatic Prerequisites for Survival and Recovery," 142.

17. Putin, *First Person*, 5–9.

18. Such as Tokarev et al., *Deviat'sot geroicheskikh dnei*.

19. This was the methodology I used to write my dissertation, "Workers at War," in 1987. I published a summary of its themes as a short monograph under the same title.

20. Demidov and Kutuzov, *"Leningradskoe delo,"* and Volkogonov, *Triumf i tragediia*.

21. Dzeniskevich, "The Social and Political Situation," 73–74.

22. Dzeniskevich, *Rabochie Leningrada*.

23. For example, in 1999 I was denied access to documents in the Central State Archive of Historical-Political Documents in St. Petersburg (TsGAIPD SPb) that I had read in 1993.

24. Examples include: Lomagin, *Neizvestnaia blokada*, vol. 2; Volkovskii, *Blokada Leningrada;* and Shkarovskii, "V ogne voiny." See also Gladkikh's collection of documents and commentary, *Zdravookhranenie i voennaia meditsina*.

25. Loskutova, ed., *Pamiat' o blokade*.

26. Lomagin, *Neizvestnaia blokada*, vol. 1 and *Leningrad v blokade;* Dzeniskevich, *Front u zavodskikh sten* and *Na grani zhizni i smerti*.

27. Filippov, *Noveishaia istoriia Rossii*.

28. See Figes, "Putin vs. the Truth."

29. Werth, *Leningrad*. He later included most of this book as a chapter in *Russia at War*.

30. Goure, *The Siege of Leningrad*, 301.

31. Ibid., 307–8.

32. *The 900 Days* is not richly documented, however, as Salisbury included brief chapter summaries of sources but not specific citations.

33. Salisbury, *The 900 Days*, 266–68.

34. See note 19 above.

35. Glantz, *The Battle for Leningrad*.

36. Jones, *Leningrad: State of Siege*. See Bidlack's "Lifting the Blockade on the Blockade," for a review of several recent publications on the blockade.

37. Anna Reid, *Leningrad: The Epic Siege of World War II, 1941-1944 (New York, Walker & Company, 2011)*. This book was published just as the present study was going into press. Reid has relied extensively for information on Lomagin's previous publications and to a lesser extent on Bidlack's works, as well as on many other published and unpublished materials.

38. Boterbloem, *The Life and Times of Andrei Zhdanov*.

39. *Life and Death in Besieged Leningrad*.

40. Simmons and Perlina, *Writing the Siege of Leningrad*, 17.

41. See, for example, the published dissertation by the German-American scholar Aileen Rambow, *Überleben mit Worten.* Her article "The Siege of Leningrad" contains the main ideas from the book.

42. Lomagin et al., *Leningradskaia epopeia,* and Lomagin, *Bitva za Leningrad,* respectively.

43. Lomagin, *Neizvestnaia blokada.*

44. Kotkin, *Magnetic Mountain.* On the theme of resistance, see several studies by Lynne Viola including *Peasant Rebels Under Stalin;* and Rossman, *Worker Resistance Under Stalin.* The inaugural issue of the journal *Kritika* (winter 2000) included six articles in a forum on "Resistance to Authority in Russian and the Soviet Union." In contrast to the situation in the 1930s, opponents of Soviet authority during the Leningrad blockade could not realistically hope for any political alternative to communist rule other than surrendering their city to Nazi control.

45. See Solzhenitsyn's interview in *Der Spiegel,* 23 July 2007. Solzhenitsyn cited the figure of 100,000 files.

46. See Bernev, Chernov, et al., *Blokadnye dnevniki i dokumenty;* Bernev and Lomagin, *Plan "D";* Eroshin, *Organy gosudarstvennoi bezopasnosti SSSR v Velikoi Otechestvennoi voine,* vol. 2; Lomagin et al., *Mezhdunarodnoe polozhenie glazami leningradtsev;* and Lomagin, *Neizvestnaia blokada,* vol. 2.

47. Hosking, *Rumors and Victims,* 191, 438.

CHAPTER 1. LENINGRAD DURING THE SECOND WORLD WAR AND ITS AFTERMATH

1. TsGAIPD SPb f. 24, op. 2v, d. 5115, ll. 21–22, 27, 30; Bubis and Ruble, "The Impact of World War II on Leningrad," 190; Amosov, "Rabochie Leningrada," 97; Tiul'panov, *Industrializatsiia Severo-Zapadnogo raiona v gody vtoroi i tret'ei piatiletok,* 218; Filonov, *Leningrad za 50 let,* p. 9; Dzeniskevich, *Voennaia piatiletka,* 8; Dzeniskevich, *Rabochie Leningrada,* 7, 30, 205; Kuznetsova, *Leningradskaia partiinaia organizatsiia,* 82; Skomorovsky and Morris, *The Siege of Leningrad,* 17; and Korol'chuk, *Istoriia . . . obuvnoi fabriki "Skorokhod,"* 413. Some of the employment figures may be low as official data may have concealed the number of employees at secret defense installations and NKVD slave laborers.

2. For example, between 1929 and 1931, the Ford Motor Company completely re-equipped Krasny Putilovets (whose name was changed to Kirovsky [the Kirov works] after the murder of Sergei Kirov) to produce a Russian version of the Fordson tractor. German firms helped enlarge the city's port facilities, which by 1941 handled approximately one-quarter of the USSR's exports and up to half of its imports, and modernized several factories including Bolshevik, which was one of the nation's largest tank assembly plants. See Zaloga and Grandsen, *Soviet Tanks and Combat Vehicles,* 18–21, 35, 36, 43; and Sutton, *Western Technology and Soviet Economic Development,* 1:141.

3. Filonov, *Leningrad za 50 let,* 9; Dzeniskevich, *Voennaia piatiletka,* 8; Dzeniskevich, *Rabochie Leningrada,* 7, 205; Kuznetsova, *Leningradskaia partiinaia organizatsiia,* 82; Skomorovsky and Morris, *The Siege of Leningrad,* 17; and Korol'chuk, *Istoriia . . . obuvnoi fabriki "Skorokhod,"* 413.

4. Amosov, "Rabochie Leningrada," 121; Dzeniskevich, *Rabochie Leningrada,* 206–8; Kuznetsova, *Leningradskaia partiinaia organizatsiia,* 83, 103, 105, 107, 110, 208; and Salisbury, *The 900 Days,* 144.

5. In August 2002, members of the human rights group Memorial discovered a grave site in a one-square-mile forest near an artillery range outside Toksovo about eighteen miles north of St. Petersburg. Scores of skulls were excavated, and each had a bullet hole in the back. Memorial believes that the site may contain up to thirty thousand bodies. To date, the FSB denies that the Toksovo site was an NKVD burial ground, and has refused Memorial access to files that might shed light on the matter. In the late 1990s, another site, the Levashovo Cemetery, located just west of Toksovo, was officially designated a memorial cemetery. It contains remains of about forty-five thousand victims of political terror, including some twenty-four thousand who were shot in 1937–38. Online version of *St. Petersburg Times,* 12 August 2003 (http://www.sptimesrussia.com/archive/times/892/top/t_10052.htm) and *Christian Science Monitor,* 10 October 2002, 1, 8.

6. Volkogonov, *Stalin,* 554, and Zalesskii, *Imperiia Stalina,* 165, 210.

7. Kozlov, *Velikaia Otechestvennaia voina,* 372, 750; Dzeniskevich, *Rabochie Leningrada,* 128–29; and Zalesskii, *Imperiia Stalin,* 93–94, 239, 455.

8. Kuznetsov, "Osazhdennyi Leningrad i Baltiiskii Flot," 108.

9. U.S. National Archives, RG 373, File DT, Misc., 175 and File DT-RL 189.

10. Boterbloem, *The Life and Times of Andrei Zhdanov,* 199; and Fischer, "The Katyn Controversy," 69 n. 6.

11. Boterbloem, *The Life and Times of Andrei Zhdanov,* 201–2.

12. Krivosheev, *Grif sekretnosti sniat,* 103. Finnish historians have estimated Soviet war dead at approximately 200,000.

13. N. N. Shpanov's short novel *Pervyi Udar,* published in the USSR in 1939, posited such a short and victorious war scenario.

14. Salisbury, *The 900 Days,* 42–43, 222 and Glantz, *The Battle for Leningrad,* 14, 17–21.

15. For example, see Samsonov et al., *Kratkaia istoriia SSSR,* vol. 2, chaps. 6 and 7; Kolesnik, *RSFSR v gody Velikoi Otechestvennoi voiny,* chaps. 1 and 2; Zinich, *Trudovoi podvig rabochego klassa,* chap 1; and Bychkov et al., *Stal' dlia pobedy,* chaps. 1 and 2.

16. TsGAIPD SPb, *klassifikator* for *fond* 24, *opis'* 2b.

17. TsGAIPD SPb f. 24, op. 2b, d. 5676, ll. 54, 66.

18. Zaloga and Grandsen, *Soviet Tanks and Combat Vehicles,* 120; Vannikov, "Iz zapisok narkoma vooruzheniia," 81; Kostiuchenko et al., *Istoriia Kirovskogo zavoda,* 611; Zalesskii, *Imperiia Stalina,* 81; and Volkogonov, *Stalin,* 373.

19. TsGAIPD SPb f. 25, op. 13a, d. 1, ll. 95, 239, cited in Dzeniskevich, "Front u zavodskikh sten"; TsGAIPD SPb f. 4000, op. 10, d. 834, ll. 1–5; f. 24, op. 2v, d. 5676, ll. 4–5, 8–9, 34–43, 69–77. The authors are grateful to Dzeniskevich for sharing his unpublished manuscript.

20. TsGAIPD SPb f. 24, op. 2b, d. 983, ll. 106, 120–21.

21. Knight, *Beria,* 110 and Overy, *Russia's War,* 76.

22. Dzeniskevich, *Iz raionov oblasti soobshchaiut,* 28.

23. TsGAIPD SPb f. 24, op. 2v, d. 5115, ll. 21–22, 27, 40 and Dzeniskevich, *Rabochie Leningrada,* 26–28.

24. Kuznetsova, *Leningradskaia partiinaia organizatsiia,* 129, 140 and Dzeniskevich, *Rabochie Leningrada,* 12, 14, 149–52.

25. TsGAIPD SPb f. 24, op. 2v, d. 5115, l. 6.

26. Davies, *Popular Opinion in Stalin's Russia,* 44, 68.

27. TsGAIPD SPb f. 24, op. 2v, d. 5115, ll. 17, 27, 91.

28. Dzeniskevich, *Rabochie Leningrada,* 66, 69. Running water was far more common by the end of the thirties.

29. Davies, *Popular Opinion in Stalin's Russia*, 99.

30. TsGAIPD SPb f. 24, op. 2v, d. 5115, l. 27.

31. TsGA SPb f. 7384, op. 3, d. 7, l. 158.

32. Werth, *Russia at War*, 97–100.

33. Dzeniskevich, *Rabochie Leningrada*, 55.

34. TsGAIPD SPb f. 4000, op. 10, d. 298, l. 3.

35. TsGA SPb f. 7384, op. 17, d. 226, ll. 65–66.

36. Dzeniskevich, *Rabochie Leningrada*, 48–49. The rationing scheme and gardening activity of the 1930s, in turn, resembled measures that had been adopted in Petrograd during the Civil War years.

37. Kuznetsova, *Leningradskaia partiinaia organizatsiia*, 87–88, 100, 112 and Dzeniskevich, *Rabochie Leningrada*, p. 118.

38. TsGAIPD SPb f. 24, op. 2v, d. 5069, l. 5.

39. TsGAIPD SPb f. 24, op. 2v, d. 5676, l. 54, 65, 78.

40. Davies was one of the first scholars to make use of the summaries (*svodki*) of popular mood, produced at the *gorkom* level. See her *Popular Opinion in Stalin's Russia*, esp. 100–101.

41. Ibid., 47, 185.

42. Ibid., chap. 8.

43. Dzeniskevich, *Rabochie Leningrada*, 38 and Davies, *Popular Opinion in Stalin's Russia*, 27–28, 74,129, 134.

44. TsGAIPD SPb f. 24, op. 2v, d. 5279, ll. 6–8.

45. TsGAIPD SPb f. 24, op. 2g, d. 156, ll. 2–31, 41; d. 296, ll. 16–18.

46. TsGAIPD SPb f. 24, op. 2b, d. 983, ll. 27–55, 84–85.

47. See Murphy, *What Stalin Knew*.

48. Glantz, *The Battle for Leningrad*, 37, 471–72 and Salisbury, *The 900 Days*, 93–94.

49. See Glantz, *The Battle for Leningrad*, 51–69.

50. Belozerov, "Protivopravnye deistviia," 245 and Dzeniskevich, *Leningrad v osade*, 364.

51. See articles from 27, 29 July, and 5 August. The statement of 21 August was also broadcast over the radio and posted along city streets.

52. Mannerheim, *Memoirs*, 405–23.

53. Ganzenmüller, *Das belagerte Leningrad*, 28–29.

54. Goure, *The Siege of Leningrad*, 17; Glantz, *The Battle for Leningrad*, 69, 95–86; Ganzenmüller, *Das belagerte Leningrad*, 1941-1944, 40, 49–50.

55. Ganzenmüller, *Das belagerte Leningrad*, 24.

56. Dzeniskevich, *Leningrad v osade*, 374.

57. Kriukovskikh et al., *V gody surovykh ispytanii*, 125, 128. Air raids were heaviest from 6 to 27 September. During the remainder of 1941, they diminished to a rate of about three per day. Air bombardment dropped sharply in January and ceased in May. It intensified in October 1942 but diminished for the rest of 1942. German air raids in 1943 targeted mainly the rail line that pierced the blockade (Glantz, *The Battle for Leningrad*, 128, 247–48).

58. Dale, "Rats and Resentment," 120.

59. Werth, *Russia at War*, 159.

60. Kriukovskikh et al., *V gody surovykh ispytanii*, 89; Bidlack, "Workers at War" (1987), 48, 55; and Volkovskii, ed., *Blokada Leningrada*, 660–61.

61. Korol'chuk, *Istoriia . . . obuvnoi fabriki "Skorokhod,"* 418.

62. U.S. National Archives, RG 338, FMS, T-17, BI 4-g, 30; BI 4-c, 6.

63. Volkovskii, *Blokada Leningrada,* 649–50.

64. Pavlov, *Leningrad 1941,* 6; Koval'chuk, ed., *Ocherki istorii Leningrada,* 79; Karasev, *Leningradtsy v gody blokady,* 70–71; and Bidlack, *Workers at War* (1991), 11.

65. U.S. National Archives, RG 338, FMS, T-22, p. 11. Interviews were conducted by U.S. officials in Germany in late 1947 and 1948. The principal officer questioned in collection T-22 was General Gerhard Raus, who commanded in succession a panzer division, a corps, an army, and an army group.

66. U.S. National Archives, RG 338, FMS, T-17, BI 4-f, p. 42.

67. See U.S. National Archives, RG 373, D/T TM5.

68. Goure, *The Siege of Leningrad,* 38; Glantz, *The Battle for Leningrad, 1941–1944,* 128.

69. Karasev, *Leningradtsy v gody blokady,* 47–48; Dzeniskevich, *Voennaia piatiletka,* 20; and Sirota, "Voenno-organizatorskaia rabota Leningradskoi organizatsii VKP (b)," 27.

70. Dzeniskevich, *Iz raionov oblasti soobshchaiut,* 40, 570; Dzeniskevich, *Leningrad v osade,* 301; Karasev, *Leningradtsy v gody blokady,* 90; Adamovich and Granin, *Blokadnaia kniga,* 223–26; Koval'chuk, *Ocherki istorii Leningrada,* 102–3; and Burov, *Blokada den' za dnem,* 27.

71. Shvetsov, "Deiatel'nost' Smol'ninskoi raionnoi partiinoi organizatsii," 69; Karasev, *Leningradtsy v gody blokady,* 78.

72. Burov, *Blokada den' za dnem,* 36–37 and Karasev, *Leningradtsy v gody blokady,* 137.

73. Kiev's fall on 27 September was ignored by *Pravda* (Brooks, "*Pravda* Goes to War," 13).

74. Dzeniskevich, *Leningrad v osade,* 442.

75. Before the war, the USSR purchased a license to manufacture the Douglas DC-3. The Soviet version was called the PS-84 up to December 1941. Thereafter, it was designated as the Li-2.

76. Arapova, "Trudovaia deiatel'nost' leningradtsev," 280.

77. Lomagin, *Neizvestnaia blokada,* vol. 2, 282.

78. Another report gives a lower figure of 6,000 to 7,000 corpses (Dzeniskevich, *Leningrad v osade,* 331, 340).

79. Karasev, *Leningradtsy v gody blokady,* 199; Koval'chuk, *Leningrad i Bol'shaia zemlia,* 163; and Dzeniskevich, *Leningrad v osade,* 302.

80. Koval'chuk, *Leningrad i Bol'shaia zemlia,* 200.

81. TsGAIPD SPb f. 4000, op. 10, d. 246, l. 7.

82. Koval'chuk, *Leningrad i Bol'shaia zemlia,* 170, 185, 305.

83. Likhachev, *Reflections on the Russian Soul,* 238.

84. The quote from Adamovich and Granin is the title of chap. 11 of their *Blokadnaia kniga.*

85. Bakhmeteff Archive, general manuscript collection, L. S. Rubanov file, 12–14, 19.

86. *Leningradtsy v dni blokady,* 60.

87. As quoted in Broekmeyer, *Stalin, the Russians, and Their War,* 82.

88. Salisbury, *The 900 Days,* 284, 496 and Broekmeyer, *Stalin, the Russians, and Their War,* 82.

89. Bidlack, "Survival Strategies in Leningrad," 98, citing Piterkin, "Leningradskie pozharnye komandy."

90. Werth, *Russia at War*, 326.

91. Lomagin, *Neizvestnaia blokada*, vol. 2, 323. Article 59-3 covered "banditry," which included murder. Article 16 referred to actions that were deemed "socially dangerous" but were not specifically banned under other laws. (See the Criminal Code of the RSFSR [*http://www.cyberussr.com/rus/uk-rsfsr.html*]).There was no law against eating human flesh, but it was considered to be socially dangerous and similar to banditry (Article 59-3). Hence, someone accused of murder with intent to consume human flesh was charged with banditry, 59-3. Someone accused only of eating from a corpse was charged with 16-59-3. Someone accused of murder and cannibalism was charged under 59-3 and 16-59-3.

92. Dzeniskevich, *Leningrad v osade*, 421–22.

93. Tucker, *Stalin in Power*, 325. See chaps. 2–6 in David Brandenberger's *National Bolshevism* for a detailed analysis of the development of Russocentric patriotism in the USSR during the latter half of the 1930s.

94. Werth, *Russia at War, 1941-1945*, 159.

95. This depiction of the war contrasts with that recently put forward by Amir Weiner in *Making Sense of War*: "The Revolution, as experienced by contemporaries, members of the political elite, and ordinary citizens alike, was a constantly unfolding enterprise with the imposition of a linear evolution toward the ultimate goal of communism . . . the war was universally perceived as the Armageddon of the Revolution, the ultimate clash dreaded yet expected by the first generation to live in a socialist society . . . (p. 17). Our study, however, would largely concur with Weiner's thesis regarding the profound impact that the Soviet-German War had on Soviet society.

96. Evan Mawdsley made this observation in *The Stalin Years*, 132.

97. Brandenberger, *National Bolshevism*, 119.

98. Brooks, "Pravda Goes to War," 22; Brandenberger traces the historiographical controversy in chap. 7 of *National Bolshevism*.

99. *Propaganda i agitatsiia*, 1941, Nos. 21–22; 1942, No. 10 (p. 31), No. 12 (p. 29), No. 13 (p. 47), No. 14 (p. 24); 1943, No. 2 (p. 39).

100. Amosov, "Rabochie Leningrada," 275–78, 281–82.

101. Boterbloem, *The Life and Times of Andrei Zhdanov*, 236 and Kirschenbaum, *The Legacy of the Siege of Leningrad*, 37–38.

102. Brooks, "Pravda Goes to War," 24.

103. Between the start of the war and 1 October 1942, a total of 5,360 civilians were executed in the city for all capital offenses (Dzeniskevich, *Leningrad v osade*, 442, 461).

104. Bidlack, "The Political Mood in Leningrad," 102.

105. For example, see Moskoff, *The Bread of Affliction*, and Stites, *Culture and Entertainment in Wartime Russia*.

106. Burov, *Blokada den' za dnem*, 153.

107. Dzeniskevich, *Leningrad v osade*, 316–17. Volkovskii, *Blokada Leningrada*, 687, includes different, but essentially similar, figures on infectious disease.

108. Koval'chuk, *Ocherki istorii Leningrada*, 298–99; Amosov, *Rabochie Leningrada*, 118; and Burov, *Blokada den za dnem*, 176, 190.

109. Volkovskii, *Blokada Leningrada*, 288–89.

110. Bidlack, *Workers at War* (1991), 31.

111. A VSLF resolution of 5 July called for 11,000–14,000 peat workers and between 3,650 and 7,000 to cut firewood. Manakov, "Ekonomika Leningrada v gody blokady," 27; Kriukovskikh et al., *V gody surovykh ispytanii*, 284–85; Shvetsov, "Deia-

tel'nost' Smol'ninskoi raionnoi partiinoi organizatsii," 232; Zakharov et al., *Ocherki istorii Leningradskoi organizatsii KPSS*, 518; and Koval'chuk, *Ocherki istorii Leningrada*, 327.

112. See chap. 7 of Glantz's *The Battle for Leningrad* for a complete description of these events and pages 207–8 for the casualty figures cited here. Vlasov was captured by the Red Army at the end of the war and hanged on 1 August 1946.

113. Glantz, *The Battle for Leningrad*, 228.

114. Bellamy, *Absolute War*, 386.

115. Karasev, *Leningradtsy v gody blokady*, 265–68. The bombs dropped in 1942 killed more people than the artillery fire.

116. *Leningradskaia pravda*, 3 June and 18 July, 1942 and Koval'chuk, *Ocherki istorii Leningrada*, 291.

117. Glantz, *The Battle for Leningrad*, 235.

118. Karasev, *Leningradtsy v gody blokady*, 251; Komar, *Arsenal energovooruzheniia*, 67; and Kriukovskikh et al., *V gody surovykh ispytanii*, 107.

119. Dzeniskevich, *Voennaia piatiletka*, 101–2.

120. Volkovskii, *Blokada Leningrada*, 127, 129–30.

121. See Glantz, *The Battle for Leningrad*, 273–87.

122. Ziemke, "Siege of Leningrad," 686; Koval'chuk, *Doroga pobedy osazhdennogo Leningrada*, 178; Tokarev et al., *Deviat'sot geroicheskikh dnei*, 215–16; Zakharov et al., *Ocherki istorii Leningradskoi organizatsii KPSS*, 415–17; Burov, *Blokada den' za dnem*, 310; and Dzeniskevich, *Voennaia piatiletka*, 133–36.

123. GMMOBL rukopisno-dokumental'nyi fond, op. 1, d. 30, ll. 114, 121.

124. Arkhiv UFSB RF po SPb i LO f. 21/12, op. 2, p.n. 19, d. 12, ll. 340, 366, 374.

125. Kriukovskikh et al., *V gody surovykh ispytanii*, 273; Dzeniskevich, *Voennaia piatiletka*, 82–83; Amosov, "Rabochie Leningrada," 227–28; and *Biulleten' Leningradskogo soveta deputatov trudiashchikhsia*, 1943, Nos. 7–8, p. 9. Calculations of the total weight of produce from several tens of thousands of private gardens were rough estimates at best. It is likely that part of the reason for the registered increase in output from gardens and farms in 1943 was that more thorough records were kept than in 1942.

126. Amosov, "Rabochie Leningrada," 232, 246; Kriukovskikh et al., *V gody surovykh ispytanii*, 273–74; and Manakov, "Ekonomika Leningrada v gody blokady," 29.

127. Ganzenmüller errs in contending that Bidlack construes a conflict between Smolny and the Kremlin over the resumption of sending materials to other fronts. Bidlack did note that in October 1943, Zhdanov reported to the GKO that unless the evacuation of machines from Leningrad was halted, the city could not meet production targets. (Ganzenmüller, *Das belagerte Leningrad*, 198; Bidlack, "Workers at War" [1987], 252).

128. Kniazev et al., *Na zashchite Nevskoi tverdyni*, 492 and Zakharov et al., *Ocherki istorii Leningradskoi organizatsii KPSS*, 422.

129. For example, see *Propaganda i agitatsiia*, 1943, No. 10.

130. Karasev, *Leningradtsy v gody blokady, 1941–1943*, 296–97 and Volkovskii, *Blokada Leningrada*, 149.

131. Karasev, *Leningradtsy v gody blokady*, 304.

132. Manakov, "Ekonomika Leningrada v gody blokady," 29; Karasev, *Leningradtsy v gody blokady*, 304, 309; Ziemke, "Siege of Leningrad," 686; and Burov, *Blokada den' za dnem*, 458.

133. Glantz, *The Battle for Leningrad*, 469.

134. Volkov, *St. Petersburg: A Cultural History*, 449–50.

135. Brandenberger, "Stalin, the Leningrad Affair, and the Limits of Postwar Russocentrism," 245.

136. In October 1944, Zhdanov went to Helsinki as chairman of the Allied Control Commission that was charged with implementing the agreement that ended the Soviet-Finnish War (Rieber, *Zhdanov in Finland*, 4, 14).

137. Boterbloem, "The Death of Andrei Zhdanov," 276.

138. The day before Zhdanov died his X-ray specialist, Dr. Lydia Timashuk, informed Zhdanov's bodyguard that the regimen of moderate exercise that his other doctors had prescribed for him could be lethal given his condition; however, an autopsy concluded that he was in such bad shape that his death could not have been prevented (ibid., 270–71).

Those arrested in the later Doctors' Plot affair were charged with murdering Zhdanov. In an interview in the summer of 2003, Russian historian Iakov Etinger described how he had been arrested with his father, who was one of the accused physicians. The younger Etinger claimed that in late 1951, he had shared a cell at Lefortovo prison in Moscow with Ivan Dmitriev, who at the time of his arrest in connection with the Leningrad Affair had been Kharitonov's successor as head of the *Lenoblispolkom*. He stated that Dmitriev told him that Leningrad NKVD head Kubatkin had confided that he had information that Beria's agents had killed Zhdanov. There is no confirmation of this rumor. (Online version of the *Moscow News*, 2003, No. 26—http://www.mn.ru/English/issue.php?2003-26-11).

139. The first victims, N. A. Voznesensky, Kuznetsov, Rodionov, Popkov, Kapustin, and Lazutin, were shot in Leningrad at 2 A.M. on 1 October 1950 (*Izvestiia TsK KPSS* 1989, No. 2, 132). Voznesensky's brother Aleksandr, rector of Leningrad State University, and his sister Maria, first secretary of Leningrad's Kuibyshevsky *raion*, were also shot.

140. These data are from a report that Sergei Kruglov, minister of internal affairs, and his deputy Ivan Serov sent to Central Committee first secretary Nikita Khrushchev on 10 December 1953 (GARF f. 8131, op. 32, d. 3289, l. 63).

141. *Izvestiia TsK KPSS* 1989, No. 2, 126, 131. David Brandenberger quotes Leningrad's party secretary Frol Kozlov as stating in 1957 that "tens of thousands of innocent people were deported from Leningrad into exile, many of whom were imprisoned or executed, and many others of whom perished" ("Stalin, the Leningrad Affair, and the Limits of Postwar Russocentrism," 245).

142. *Izvestiia TsK KPSS* 1989, No. 2, 124–37.

143. In 2001, Aleksandr Iakovlev's Mezhdunarodnyi fond "Demokratiia" published three documents on its website (http://www.idf.ru). For other revelations, see Zubkova, "Kadrovaia politika i chistki v KPSS"; Pyzhikov, "Leningradskaia gruppa"; Gorlizki and Khlevniuk, *Cold Peace*, 79–89; and Brandenberger, "Stalin, the Leningrad Affair, and the Limits of Postwar Russocentrism."

144. Gorlizki and Khlevniuk, *Cold Peace*, 32 and Boterbloem, "The Death of Andrei Zhdanov," 274, 277–78.

145. Knight, *Beria*, 140–41.

146. Salisbury, *The 900 Days*, 574–75 and Volkov, *St. Petersburg: A Cultural History*, 448.

147. TsAMO RF f. 217, op. 1217, d. 165, l. 214.

148. For example, Arkhiv UFSB RF po SPb i LO f. 21/12, tom 1, op. 2, p.n. 38, d. 10, l. 126.

149. Arkhiv UFSB RF po SPb i LO 21/12, op. 2, p.n. 56, d. 1, ll. 18–22.

150. Ruble, *Leningrad,* 59–60.

151. Lomagin, *Neizvestnaia blokada,* vol. 1, 325–29.

152. Demidov and Kutuzov, *"Leningradskoe delo,"* 38–39. Benjamin Tromly cites this speech in support of his portrayal of Kuznetsov as a proud Leningrader ("The Leningrad Affair and Soviet Patronage Politics," 715–16).

153. Salisbury, *The 900 Days,* 576.

154. Mikoian, *Tak bylo,* 565. However, they were married after Kuznetsov's fall from power.

155. One wonders whether Kuznetsov or anyone else in late 1948 or early 1949 voiced ironic comparisons between the German siege of Leningrad and the Soviet blockade of Berlin, despite their obvious and major differences. Also, the contrast in how the respective besieged cities were supplied must have made an impression on Leningraders. The Western Allies conducted over a quarter of a million flights into West Berlin (on average a plane landing every two to three minutes over the entire duration of the airlift) to feed and provision the capital of their former enemy. Stalin permitted only around thirty planes to make flights into starving Leningrad in the late fall of 1941 (see below, pp. 103–04).

156. The Kharitonov and Bakshis cases and other matters concerning the relationship between Leningrad's leaders and the Kremlin during the war are explored below, pp. 151–58.

157. Montefiore, *Stalin,* 593 and Volkogonov, *Stalin,* 521.

158. *Izvestiia TsK KPSS* 1989, No. 2, 127–28.

159. Gorlizki and Khlevniuk, *Cold Peace,* 81.

160. *Izvestiia TsK KPSS* 1989, No. 2, 128.

161. Medvedev and Medvedev, *The Unknown Stalin,* 56.

162. *Izvestiia TsK KPSS* 1989, No. 2, 128–29.

163. As cited in Tromly, "The Leningrad Affair and Soviet Patronage Politics," 726 n. 58.

164. Gorlizki and Khlevniuk have made this observation (*Cold Peace,* 81–82).

165. Mikoian, *Tak bylo,* 390–91. Boterbloem ("The Death of Andrei Zhdanov," 280) was among the first scholars to draw attention to Mikoyan's recollection.

166. *Izvestiia TsK KPSS* 1989, No. 2, 129–30.

167. Dedijer, *Tito,* 312. See pp. 308–14 on Djilas's trip to the USSR.

168. Hahn, *Postwar Soviet Politics,* 123–24.

169. See Brandenberger, "Stalin, the Leningrad Affair, and the Limits of Postwar Russocentrism," and our exchange of views on interpreting the Leningrad Affair, Bidlack and Brandenberger, "Contributors' Exchange: The Leningrad Affair Interpreted."

170. GARF f. 8131, op. 32, d. 3289, l. 63.

171. We are grateful to Steve Maddox for this information.

172. See chap. 50, "The Leningrad Affair" (571–84) in Salisbury's *The 900 Days;* Demidov, and Kutuzov, *"Leningradskoe delo",* 352–62; and Kirschenbaum, "Innocent Victims and Heroic Defenders," 284.

CHAPTER 2. WHO RULED LENINGRAD?

1. This chapter does not examine the role played by the city *sovet* since it essentially carried out instructions from the *gorkom.*

2. *Izvestiia TsK KPSS* 1990, No. 6, 217.

3. Boterbloem, *The Life and Times of Andrei Zhdanov*, 226–27. In an earlier work ("The Political Mood in Leningrad," 100), Bidlack erroneously stated that Zhdanov did not return to Leningrad until 27 June.

4. Salisbury, *The 900 Days*, 144–45 and *Izvestiia TsK KPSS*, 1990, No. 6, 217. Like many others who wrote on these events prior to the release of Stalin's appointment ledger in 1990, Salisbury mistakenly believed that Stalin was essentially incapacitated at the start of Operation Barbarossa and met with virtually no one until his radio address to the nation on 3 July. It is now known that he went into seclusion only during 29–30 June.

5. Details on defense industries were tightly held secrets during the Soviet era. The top secret Politburo decision of 27 June listed only the identification numbers of the factories. Defense plants often did not appear on published Soviet maps, and when a factory was mentioned in *Leningradskaia pravda* during the war, it was often simply called "Factory X" (*N-skii zavod*). The names of the four Leningrad factories and basic information about them were obtained from the online database, *The Factories, Research and Design Establishments of the Soviet Defence Industry* maintained by Keith Dexter and Ivan Rodionov.

6. Koval'chuk, *Ocherki istorii Leningrada*, 120.

7. Ibid., 102–3.

8. TsGAIPD SPb f. 24, op. 2v, *chast'* 5, d. 4808, ll. 1–3. Some of the first files burned pertained to a city party conference in May 1937 during which members of the *gorkom* were elected; others concerned foreign relations between 1932 and 1934.

9. Eroshin, *Organy gosudarstvennoi bezopasnosti SSSR v Velikoi Otechestvennoi voine*, vol. 2, 183–84.

10. Lomagin, "Upravlenie NKVD," 323 and TsGA SPb f. 1253, op. 3, d. 127, l. 106.

11. TsGAIPD SPb f. 24, op. 2a, d. 188, l. 4. The typed document identified Tiumen as the destination, but that city was crossed out and Cheliabinsk was written in by hand. The personnel files of the *osobyi sektor* of the *gorkom* and *obkom* alone occupied 186 boxes.

12. TsGAIPD SPb f. 24, op. 2v, d. 5069, l. 58.

13. Werth, *Russia at War*, 163.

14. TsGAIPD SPb f. 4000, op. 10, d. 820, l. 5.

15. Conquest, *The Great Terror*, 742, 745.

16. TsGAIPD SPb f. 24, op. 2v, d. 5126, ll. 47–55.

17. Overy, *Russia's War*, 78.

18. Later in the war, A. I. Mikoyan, L. M. Kaganovich, N. A. Voznesensky, and N. A. Bulganin were added to the GKO.

19. Tskulin, *Istoriia gosudarstvennykh uchrezhdenii SSSR*, 35–36 and Sinitsyn, "Chrezvychainye organy Sovetskogo gosudarstva," 34, as cited in Lieberman, "Crisis Management in the USSR," 60.

20. Lieberman, "Crisis Management in the USSR," p. 60.

21. Pavlov, *Leningrad 1941*, 11.

22. Glantz, *The Battle for Leningrad*, 47.

23. Ibid., 37, 53, 59–60 and Burov, *Blokada den' za dnem*, 42.

24. Burov, *Blokada den' za dnem*, 22; Dzeniskevich, *Voennaia piatiletka*, 59; Dzeniskevich, *Leningrad v osade*, 301.

25. See Boterbloem, *The Life and Times of Andrei Zhdanov*, 251.

26. Amosov, "Rabochie Leningrada," 100.

27. Karasev, *Leningradtsy v gody blokady,* 79; Stremilov, "Leningradskaia partiinaia organizatsiia," 107; and Burov, *Blokada den' za dnem,* 42.

28. Burov, *Blokada den' za dnem,* 42.

29. TsGAIPD SPb f. 24, op. 2b, d. 986, l. 13.

30. The first paragraph of the Kremlin's first message indicates that it had previously expressed its displeasure over the formation of the Leningrad Military Defense Council.

31. See, for example, Goure, *The Siege of Leningrad,* 112–13, Salisbury, *The 900 Days,* 217–20, and more recently Boterbloem, *The Life and Times of Andrei Zhdanov,* 231.

32. The authors are grateful to Evgeny Kogan for bringing this document to our attention in the early 1990s. The transcript was made from the tape of a *Baudot* telegraph machine (Boterbloem, *The Life and Times of Andrei Zhdanov,* 450).

33. Pavlov kept revising his book. The sixth edition from 1985 added a sentence describing Stalin's concerns that the public might interpret the absence of Voroshilov and Zhdanov from the Council's membership as an indication that the two leaders did not believe the city could be defended (*Leningrad v blokade,* 21).

34. Voroshilov and Zhdanov issued a resolution on 25 August that described the 150 planned units as *opolchenie* battalions, which shows that by this time there was no real distinction among the auxiliary civilian formations (Volkovskii, *Blokada Leningrada,* 660; Karasev, *Leningradtsy v gody blokady,* 105).

35. Kriukovskikh et al., *V gody surovykh ispytanii,* 107 and Amosov, "Rabochie Leningrada," 100.

36. Dzeniskevich, *Leningrad v osade,* 54–55.

37. Komar, *Arsenal energovooruzheniia,* 60 and Kalugin, *Dnevnik i pamiat',* 30.

38. Sirota, "Voenno-organizatorskaia rabota Leningradskoi organizatsii VKP(b)," 25.

39. The word that appears in the typed transcript is *beznachal'nyi,* which means "without beginning." It would appear that *beznachalie* was intended.

40. TsGAIPD SPb f. 24, op. 2v, d. 4766, l. 14.

41. Koval'chuk, *Ocherki istorii Leningrada,* 578.

42. *Izvestiia TsK KPSS,* 1990, No. 9, p. 209.

43. Berezhkov, *Piterskie prokuratory,* 212. Not long after he arrived in Leningrad, Kubatkin went to the front lines with secretary Kuznetsov and commanders Popov and Kulik. They had a close brush with a German patrol and had to flee in their Mercedes staff car (Afanas'ev, "Pobeditel'," 388–408).

44. *Voenno-istoricheskii zhurnal,* 1992, No. 6–7, 16.

45. Burov, *Blokada den' za dnem,* p. 48 and *Izvestiia TsK KPSS,* 1990, No. 9, 214.

46. Koval'chuk, *Ocherki istorii Leningrada,* 103–4.

47. Dzeniskevich, *Leningrad v osade,* 301; Karasev, *Leningradtsy v gody blokady,* 92, 94; and Koval'chuk, *Ocherki istorii Leningrada,* 105–6.

48. Nikolai Shvernik was chairman of the Evacuation Council of the USSR.

49. Bidlack, "Workers at War" (1987), 122–23. The Senichev quote is from Koval'chuk, *Ocherki istorii Leningrada,* 121.

50. TsGAIPD SPb f. 4000, op. 10, d. 298, ll. 1–5.

51. Mikoian, "V dni blokady," 45–54. Some of the material from this 1977 article is repeated in pages 426–36 of Mikoyan's memoir, *Tak bylo,* published posthumously in 1999.

52. Tokarev et al., *Deviat'sot geroicheskikh dnei,* 38–40.

53. TsGAIPD SPb f. 24, op. 2v, d. 5069, l. 78.

54. *Izvestiia TsK KPSS*, 1990, No. 8, 220–21.

55. Dzeniskevich, *Iz raionov oblasti soobshchaiut*, 55–56, 70.

56. *Biulleten' Leningradskogo soveta deputatov trudiashchikhsia*, 1941, No. 28–29, 23.

57. Salisbury, *The 900 Days*, 292.

58. Anastas Mikoyan was chairman of the Committee for Unloading Transit Cargo, and Lazar Kaganovich was Commissar of Communications.

59. Glantz, *The Battle for Leningrad*, 67.

60. Salisbury, *The 900 Days*, 279–80 and Volkovskii, *Blokada Leningrada*, 29–31.

61. Marshal Voronov, and perhaps others in the GKO mission, remained in Leningrad until 31 August (Voronov, "V trudnye vremena," 76).

62. Kriukovskikh et al., *V gody surovykh ispytanii*, 40.

63. Mikoian, *Tak bylo*, 429.

64. Pavlov, *Leningrad 1941*, 52.

65. Dzeniskevich, *Leningrad v osade*, 188, 267.

66. Belozerov, "Protivopravnye deistviia," 246–48.

67. RGASPI, f. 644, op. 1, d. 10, ll. 1–2.

68. Volkovskii, *Blokada Leningrada*, 66–67.

69. RGASPI f. 644, op. 1, d. 14, l. 3.

70. Mikoian, *Tak bylo*, 427–28 and Volkovskii, *Blokada Leningrada*, 67–70.

71. TsGAIPD SPb f. 24, op. 2v, d. 5180, ll. 46–49.

72. Kovalev, *Transport v Velikoi Otechestvennoi voiny*, 227; Kriukovskikh et al., *V gody surovykh ispytanii*, 194; and Mikhel'son and Ialygin, *Vozdushnyi most*, 4–5.

73. Mikoian, *Tak bylo*, 427–31 and Volkovskii, *Blokada Leningrada*, 663–64, 670.

74. Kniazev et al., *Na zashchite Nevskoi tverdyni*, 126; Salisbury, *The 900 Days*, 263; and Glantz, *The Battle for Leningrad*, 64.

75. Volkovskii, *Blokada Leningrada*, 178–79.

76. Glantz, *The Battle for Leningrad*, 75.

77. Werth, *Russia at War*, 307.

78. In his memoirs, Zhukov stated that he flew to Leningrad on 10 September, but a chronicle of his military career that was published later claims that he arrived in Leningrad late on the ninth (Zhukov, *Marshal of the Soviet Union G. Zhukov*, 415 and Glantz, *The Battle for Leningrad*, 559 n. 57).

79. Chaney, *Zhukov*, 146.

80. Glantz, *The Battle for Leningrad*, 75 and Boterbloem, *The Life and Times of Andrei Zhdanov*, 454 n. 116.

81. Volkovskii, *Blokada Leningrada*, 195–96.

82. Chaney, *Zhukov*, 147.

83. Salisbury, *The 900 Days*, 282; Parrish, *The Lesser Terror*, 187.

84. Volkovskii, *Blokada Leningrada*, 46, 51 and Glantz, *The Battle for Leningrad*, 83, 323.

85. Michael Jones also makes this assertion in *Leningrad: State of Siege*, 125.

86. Chaney, *Zhukov*, 145.

87. Zalesskii, *Imperiia Stalina*, 349, 498 and Chaney, *Zhukov*, 41.

88. TsGAIPD SPb f. 1012, op. 3, d. 53, l. 48.

89. Glantz, *The Battle for Leningrad*, 83 and Parrish, *The Lesser Terror*, 188–90. Zalesskii, *Imperiia Stalina*, 99, 259. Kulik was executed in August 1950 in a purge of allegedly treasonous army generals.

90. Beria, *Beria, My Father*, 75.

91. Malenkov, *O moem ottse Georgii Malenkove*, 44–45.

92. Chaney, *Zhukov*, 145.

93. Kuznetsov, "Osazhdennyi Leningrad i Baltiiskii Flot," 115.

94. Ibid.

95. Dzeniskevich, *Blokada i politika*, 98.

96. The document's first attachment, which is not included here, lists the ships, submarines, docks, cranes, and other items in the identified areas that were subject to destruction.

97. For an analysis of the size of Soviet forces within the blockade zone in September 1941, see Dzeniskevich, *Blokada i politika*, 125–34.

98. A fragment of the original plan was copied by hand from TsAMO RF f. 132, op. 2642, d. 225, ll. 83–85 and published in *Voenno-istoricheskii zhurnal*, 1992, No. 6–7, 17. The copy reproduced here is from the telegram received and preserved by Admiral Kuznetsov, located in Tsentral'nyi voenno-morskoi arkhiv f. 2, op. 1, d. 546, ll. 1–4 and published on pages 140–45 of Knyshevskii et al., *Skrytaia pravda voiny*. Stalin's note from seven days later was published in the *Voenno-istoricheskii zhurnal* version. Kuznetsov also contends that around the autumn of 1942, the NKVD informed Stalin that Baltic Fleet commander Vladimir Tributs was being accused of having panicked in ordering the premature mining of his fleet. "I happened to have a copy of the report. I had to bring up urgently what actually happened and refute the allegations made against the leadership of the fleet." (Kuznetsov, "Osazhdennyi Leningrad i Baltiiskii Flot," 115).

99. Volkogonov, *Triumf i tragediia*, 329–30.

100. Churchill, *The Second World War*, vol. 3, 390–92 and Churchill Archive Centre, 20/87, 150.

101. Afanas'ev, "Pobeditel'," 401–2.

102. Dzeniskevich, *Leningrad v osade*, 583 n. 24.

103. Afanas'ev, "Pobeditel'," 401.

104. Valery Kuznetsov was interviewed for a documentary program by historian John Barber on the Siege of Leningrad and the Leningrad Affair that was broadcast on the History Channel on 14 September 2003.

105. A curious message from Merkulov to A. A. Kuznetsov would seem to indicate that the decision to plan for "special measures," which at this time was the official euphemism for demolition, was made earlier, even before Leningrad was subjected to artillery fire. In a one-page statement dated "3 September," and classified "Top Secret. Personal," Merkulov complained that preparations were proceeding slowly in all of the city's *raiony* and called for them to be completed as soon as possible. Merkulov elaborated on the shortcomings of the operation in a seven-page attachment. His message implies that mining operations had been ongoing for at least several days. It seems almost certain, however, that the document was dated incorrectly, even though Soviet officials were generally very careful about such details. The day of the month of NKVD documents was generally handwritten, and on the original of this particular correspondence the "3" was written in red pencil. However, the document's number (69) indicates that it was written later. NKVD documents were numbered consecutively, and another one written by Merkulov from the Plan "D" collection (identified in text below), No. 31, was written on 17 September. Information in the "3 September" document would also point to its having been composed later. Explosives were not delivered to factories until the third week of September. Moreover, Merkulov prefaced his first sentence with the phrase: "in connection with a lull at the front and several of our successes." The days prior to 3 September were filled with alarming Soviet defeats. The

most likely explanation is that the statement was written on 3 October and Merkulov mistakenly used a letter blank from September. Front line positions outside Leningrad stabilized at the end of September.

Most of the one-page statement and some of the details from the attachment were published in the article Bernev, "Plan 'D'," which accepted the document's date at face value. However, when the document was included two years later in the book Bernev and Lomagin, *Plan "D"* (p. 182), after Bidlack noted the discrepancy, the book's editors stated that the document should have been dated 3 October.

106. RGASPI f. GOKO.564, d. 8, l. 9.

107. RGASPI f. GOKO.573, d. 8, l. 19.

108. See Bernev and Lomagin, "Plan 'D.'"

109. Bernev, "Plan 'D.'"

110. Dzeniskevich, *Blokada i politika*, 100–108; Dzeniskevich, *Leningrad v osade*, 61, 383–85; and Lomagin, *Neizvestnaia blokada*, vol. 2, 113, 118.

111. Bernev, "Plan 'D.'" On 19 February 1944, all documents pertaining to Plan "D" were sent to sent to Leningrad's NKVD archive. See the individual documents published in Bernev and Lomagin, *Plan "D"*.

112. Zhukov, *Vospominaniia i razmyshleniia*, 169.

113. Chaney, *Zhukov*, 147.

114. Volkogonov, *Stalin*, 466.

115. Jones opines that "Zhukov had bequeathed Leningrad a poisoned chalice. . . . Too many lives were . . . thrown away in wholly unnecessary counter-attacks." (*Leningrad: State of Siege*, 124–25).

116. At 10:45 P.M. on 16 September, the first secretary of the Moskovsky *raikom* summoned the *raion's* factory directors to tell them to expect an attack at any moment (Karasev, *Leningradtsy v gody blokady*, 159–60).

117. Ibid., 105–6, 108, 162; Koval'chuk, *Ocherki istorii Leningrada*, 60–79, 162–63; Dzeniskevich, *Voennaia piatiletka*, 31–35; Salisbury, *The 900 Days*, 262, 356; Chaney, *Zhukov*, 155.

118. Vazhentsev, *Vo glave geroicheskogo kollektiva*, 83–90; Burov, *Blokada den' za dnem*, 55, 58, 59, 67; Kostiuchenko et al., *Istoriia Kirovskogo zavoda*, 624–26; Verkhovtsev, *Gvardiia tyla*, 178; and the Museum of the History of Leningrad.

119. Lomagin, "Nastroeniia zashchitnikov," 213, 241–43 and Arkhiv UFSB RF po SPb i LO f. 21/12, op. 2, p.n. 18, d. 11, ll. 26–27.

120. Dzeniskevich, *Leningrad v osade*, 57–58.

121. U.S. National Archives, Command of the 18th Army, Section 1s, T-312, reel 1579, 954–55 cited in Lomagin, *Neizvestnaia blokada*, vol. 2, 117. The translation in the German intercept of Stalin's phone message is not entirely accurate, but quite close, which suggests that it is highly probable that the German text of the response from the leaders in Leningrad is essentially reliable.

122. TsAMO RF f. 217, op. 1217, d. 32, ll. 279–80, 529 and d. 13, ll. 374–78 cited in Lomagin, "Nastroeniia zashchitnikov," 243–47.

123. Ganzenmüller, *Das belagerte Leningrad*, 118.

124. Chaney, *Zhukov*, 55.

125. Dzeniskevich, *Leningrad v osade*, 57–58.

126. Arkhiv UFSB RF po SPb i LO f. 21/12, op. 2, p.n. 43, d. 2, ll. 63–630b.

127. Glantz, *The Battle for Leningrad*, 67–70.

128. RGASPI f. 77, op. 3, d. 126, ll. 191–95. The authors are grateful to Evgeny Kogan for sharing this document with us.

129. Glantz, *The Battle for Leningrad*, 94.

130. Volkogonov, *Triumf i tragediia*, 237.

131. RGASPI f. 77, op. 3, d. 126, ll. 30-41.

132. Volkovskii, *Blokada Leningrada*, 73-74.

133. Glantz, *The Battle for Leningrad*, 114-15.

134. Ibid., 60.

135. RGASPI f. 77, op. 3, d. 126, ll. 86-95.

136. RGASPI f. 77, op. 3, d. 130, ll. 1-3.

137. John Barber offered this estimate in the television documentary on the History Channel on 14 September 2003. See casualty totals for specific fronts during particular periods in Krivosheev, *Grif sekretnosti sniat*, chap. 3.

138. Glantz, *The Battle for Leningrad*, 116.

139. Voronov, "V trudnye vremena," *Voenno-istoricheskii zhurnal*, 1961, No. 9, 67-72, 76.

140. Afanas'ev, "Pobeditel'," 403.

141. RGASPI f. 644, op. 1, d. 14, l. 134.

142. Karasev, *Leningradtsy v gody blokady*, 133; Kniazev et al., *Na zashchite Nevskoi tverdyni*, 241; and Dzeniskevich, *Leningrad v osade*, 63.

143. Arapova, "Trudovaia deiatel'nost' leningradtsev," 280.

144. Ziemke, "Battle for Moscow," 762.

145. Bidlack began to develop this argument in *Workers at War* (1991), 16-20. It is opposed to Ganzenmüller's view that Stalin could not have afforded to devote significantly more resources to Leningrad in the autumn of 1941 given the threat to Moscow (*Das belagerte Leningrad*, 167-70). The success of the Red Army's offensive in the winter of 1941-42 along a very long front would argue that there were sufficient reserves of munitions to better supply Leningrad.

146. Kozlov, *Velikaia Otechestvennaia voina*, 802.

147. Koval'chuk, *Ocherki istorii Leningrada*, 224.

148. Burov, *Blokada den' za dnem*, 91, 93, 94 and Salisbury, *The 900 Days*, 412.

149. Cherepenina, "Golod i smert' v blokirovannom gorode," 48.

150. Mikoian, *Tak bylo*, 432.

151. Kriukovskikh et al., *V gody surovykh ispytanii*, 91.

152. Volkovskii, *Blokada Leningrada*, 233-35.

153. In his diary Nikolai Gorshkov kept a daily record of the temperature (Bernev, Chernov et al., *Blokadnye dnevniki i dokumenty*, 44-54).

154. Cherepenina, "Golod i smert' v blokirovannom gorode," 69.

155. Karasev, *Leningradtsy v gody blokady*, 199.

156. Kriukovskikh et al., *V gody surovykh ispytanii*, 47 and Salisbury, *The 900 Days*, 493.

157. Jones, *Leningrad: State of Siege*, 224.

158. Montefiore, *Stalin*, 388, 710 n. 14.

159. Kozlov, *Velikaia Otechestvennaia voina*, 351, 372; Adamovich and Granin, *Blokadnaia kniga*, 325; Karasev, *Leningradtsy v gody blokady*, 199-201; Boldyrev, "Doroga na bol'shuiu zemliu," 305-6; Kovalev, *Transport v Velikoi Otechestvennoi voine*, 222-23; Goure, *The Siege of Leningrad*, 208.

160. Salisbury, *The 900 Days*, 416-17.

161. Diakin, *Istoriia rabochikh Leningrada*, 310 and Dzeniskevich, *Voennaia piatiletka*, 116.

162. Burov, *Blokada den' za dnem*, 149, 153, 154, 156-57; Volkovskii, *Blokada Lenin-*

grada, 98–100; Salisbury, *The 900 Days*, 511, Malkin, "Agitatsionno-propagandistskaia rabota Leningradskoi organizatsii KPSS," 25; Stremilov, "Leningradsiaka partiinaia organizatsiia," 109, 111; Karasev, *Leningradtsy v gody blokady*, 215; Kulagin, *Dnevnik i pamiat'*, 124; Kostiuchenko et al., *Istoriia Kirovskogo zavoda*, 637; Vazhentsev, *Vo glave geroicheskogo kollektiva*, 169; and Kats, "Oktiabr'skaia raionnaia partiinaia organizatsiia," 123.

163. Zalesskii, *Imperiia Stalina*, 455. Ustinov had a meteoric career during the Great Terror. He rose from the position of engineer to director of Leningrad's Bolshevik munitions plant between 1937 and 1941. Two weeks before the German invasion, at the age of thirty-two, he was named Commissar of Weaponry.

164. The authors are grateful to Evgeny Kogan for providing a copy of this document.

165. The 26 December decree stated that all employees of defense industries were "tied to the enterprises employing them" for the rest of the war. Unauthorized leaving of employment was punishable by five to eight years in prison (Barber and Harrison, *The Soviet Home Front*, 62).

166. Dzeniskevich, *Voennaia piatiletka*, 90, 183–85, 187.

167. Manakov, "Ekonomika Leningrada v gody blokady," 28–29; Zakharov et al., *Ocherki istorii Leningradskoi organizatsii KPSS*, 519; Kriukovskikh et al., *V gody surovykh ispytanii*, 213; Kostiuchenko et al., *Istoriia Kirovskogo zavoda*, 672; Arapova, "Trudovaia deiatel'nost' leningradtsev," 142; and Amosov, "Rabochie Leningrada," 18, 128.

168. Dzeniskevich, *Leningrad v osade*, 177–78.

169. Kriukovskikh et al., *V gody surovykh ispytanii*, 210.

170. Glantz, *The Battle for Leningrad*, 178, 182–83.

171. Zaporozhets was *Stavka* representative and commissar of the Military *Sovet* of the Leningrad and Volkhov Groups of the Leningrad Front. Tiurkin was a commissar of the Military *Sovet* of the Volkhov Group (Burov, *Blokada den' za dnem*, 174 and Kozlov, *Velikaia Otechestvennaia voina*, 280).

172. Dzeniskevich, *Leningrad v osade*, 82–84.

173. Vlasov, who had been the deputy commander of the Volkhov Front, was appointed commander of the Second Shock Army on 20 April 1942, the same day that the *Stavka* announced the merging of the Leningrad and Volkhov Fronts (Volkovskii, *Blokada Leningrada*, 103).

174. Ibid., 100.

175. Glantz, *The Battle for Leningrad*, 175, 202, 203, 208 and Volkovskii, *Blokada Leningrada*, 281.

176. Dzeniskevich, *Leningrad v osade*, 84.

177. Tucker, *Stalin in Power*, 272.

178. Sudoplatov was one of the most notable secret police officials in Soviet history. His deputy Leonid Eitingon had organized Trotsky's murder in 1940, and after the war, Sudoplatov headed the *Spetsburo,* which carried out assassinations and other operations in eastern Europe. He also supervised Soviet atomic espionage and claimed in his memoirs that the USSR had a valued source inside the Manhattan Project in the latter half of 1942, who has not been identified. That source may have been George Koval, who in November 2007 was revealed by Russian President Putin to have been "the only Soviet intelligence officer" to infiltrate the Manhattan Project's secret plants (Zalesskii, *Imperiia Stalina*, 432–33; Andrew and Gordievsky, *KGB: The Inside Story*, 309; Haynes and Klehr, *Venona*, 320–21; and *New York Times*, 12 November 2007).

179. Kokurin and Petrov, *Lubianka*, 32–33.

180. In early 1942, Kuprin had been transferred to Moscow, where he was soon promoted to head of the Third Directorate of the NKVD. He was killed on 11 November 1942, en route to Leningrad when his airplane was shot down by German fighters over Lake Ladoga. Berezhkov, *Piterskie prokuratory*, 209 and Chernov, *Bol'shoi Dom*, 69.

181. Glantz, *The Battle for Leningrad*, 201.

182. Volkovskii, *Blokada Leningrada*, 490.

183. Kozlov, *Velikaia Otechestvennaia voina*, 773 and Glantz, *The Battle for Leningrad*, 203–4, 208–10.

184. Volkovskii, *Blokada Leningrada*, 545–46 and Zalesskii, *Imperiia Stalina*, 176–77.

185. Volkovskii, *Blokada Leningrada*, 111–12 and Glantz, *The Battle for Leningrad*, 203.

186. Glantz, *The Battle for Leningrad*, 207–8.

187. The NKGB had first been separated from the NKVD on 3 February 1941, then reintegrated into the NKVD on 20 July. On 14 April 1943, it was again spun off to concentrate on counterintelligence, espionage, and internal political security. In 1946, the people's commissariats were renamed ministries. On 5 March 1953, the day Stalin died, the ministries of State Security (MGB) and Internal Affairs (MVD) were merged into a unified MVD (Knight, *Beria*, 106, 124 and Zalesskii, *Imperiia Stalina*, 591, 601).

188. One such inquiry is described below, pp. 373–77.

189. Dzeniskevich, *Leningrad v osade*, 448–49 and Lomagin, "Upravlenie NKVD," 359.

190. TsGAIPD SPb f. 24, op. 2b, d. 1324, l. 73.

191. TsGAIPD SPb f. 24, op. 2b, d. 1325, l.1.

192. TsGAIPD SPb f. 24, op. 2b, d. 988, l. 4.

193. TsGAIPD SPb f. 24, op. 2b, d. 1324, ll. 21–22.

194. Berezhkov, *Piterskie prokuratory*, 220 and Dzeniskevich, *Leningrad v osade*, 447–49.

195. TsGAIPD SPb f. 24, op. 2v, d. 5761, ll. 144–45.

196. Zalesskii, *Imperiia Stalina*, 210; and Demidov and Kutuzov, *"Leningradskoe delo,"* 131–34. Kapustin was officially charged with being a British agent, which was tied to his experience in 1935–36 in Manchester, England, where he had been sent to learn about large steam turbines, though his case was lumped together with those of the other Leningrad defendants.

197. The authors are grateful to Nadezhda Iurevna Cherepenina, head of the publication division and reader service at TsGA SPb, for biographical information on Kharitonov. His name surfaced in testimony provided by V. P. Volkov, another victim of the Leningrad Affair who worked in one of Leningrad's *raikomy* during the war, who claimed that Kharitonov in 1944 had spread a rumor that Leningrad was to become the capital of the RSFSR. (Brandenberger, "Stalin, the Leningrad Affair, and the Limits of Postwar Russocentrism," p. 243) Such testimony may have been important in linking Kharitonov with the alleged conspirators of the Leningrad Affair; however, since high-ranking officials in Leningrad's party and *sovet* administrations were the main target group of the purge, his fate may have been determined by his position alone.

198. Ivanov filed a copy of his report in the NKVD archive: Arkhiv UFSB RF po SPb i LO f. 21/12, op. 2, p.n. 43, d. 2, l. 97.

199. Zalesskii, *Imperiia Stalina*, 165–66, 251–52.

200. Arkhiv UFSB RF po SPb i LO f. 21/12, op. 2, p.n. 19, d. 1, l. 210.

201. Beria, *Beria, My Father,* 36.

202. Kriukovskikh et al., *V gody surovykh ispytanii,* 79; Zakharov et al., *Ocherki istorii Leningradskoi organizatsii KPSS,* 369; Grodzinskii, *Trudovoe zakonodatel'stvo voennogo vremeni,* 21; Karasev, *Leningradtsy v gody blokady,* 47; Kozlov, *Velikaia Otechestvennai voina,* 310.

203. *Ogonek,* No. 40, (1985), 14 and Boterbloem, *The Life and Times of Andrei Zhdanov,* 239. Anatoly Sobchak, who was elected chairman of the Leningrad city *sovet* in 1990 and later became the city's mayor, asserted that peaches were flown in for Zhdanov during the hungry winter. (Volkov, *St. Petersburg: A Cultural History,* 538).

204. Boterbloem, *The Life and Times of Andrei Zhdanov,* 233, 239–41, 244 and Adamovich and Granin, *Blokadnaia kniga,* 332.

205. Arkhiv UFSB RF po SPb i LO f. 21/12, op. 2, p.n. 19, d. 1, l. 206.

206. Boterbloem, *The Life and Times of Andrei Zhdanov,* 245.

207. Arkhiv UFSB RF po SPb i LO f. 21/12, op. 2, p.n. 19, d. 1, l. 210.

208. Afanas'ev, "Pobeditel'," 388–403.

209. TsGAIPD SPb f. 24, op. 2v, d. 5760, ll. 2–3, 8–9, 12, 34–43 and Burov, *Blokada den' za dnem,* 131–32.

210. Dzeniskevich, *Leningrad v osade,* 426, 429.

211. Salisbury, *The 900 Days,* 420–21.

212. Dymshits, *Podvig Leningrada,* 288.

213. TsGAIPD SPb f. 24, op. 2b, d. 1324, ll. 3–4.

214. TsGAIPD SPb f. 24, op. 2v, d. 5889, ll. 80–84.

215. Fitzpatrick, *Everyday Stalinism,* 172–75.

216. In 1999 the administration of TsGAIPD SPb refused to allow the authors access to Lysenko's party file, except for his picture. An archivist did read aloud to us a few fragments from the file. In late 2003, we were refused all access to Lysenko's file.

217. Volkovskii, *Blokada Leningrada,* 677–78.

218. TsAMO RF f. 217, op. 1258, d. 166, ll. 5–6.

219. Salisbury, *The 900 Days,* 421.

220. Konarev, *Zheleznodorozhniki v Velikoi Otechestvennoi voine,* 188, 193. The authors are grateful to archivist Nadezhda Iurevna Cherepenina at TsGA SPb for biographical information on Kolpakov.

221. This section covers church-state relations. Popular views on religious faith are discussed in chapter 5.

222. Freeze, "Russian Orthodox Church," 1321 and Davis, *A Long Walk to Church,* 12–13.

223. Davis, *A Long Walk to Church,* 11.

224. See *inter alia* Husband, *Godless Communists;* Peris, *Storming the Heavens;* and Coleman, *Russian Baptists and Spiritual Revolution, 1905–1929.*

225. The only recent book-length study in English on Church-state relations in the wartime USSR is Miner, *Stalin's Holy War.* Mikhail Shkarovsky, an archivist at TsGA SPb, has pioneered research on the Orthodox Church during the Leningrad siege. (See entries in bibliography.)

226. Fitzpatrick, *Stalin's Peasants,* 204; Miner, *Stalin's Holy War,* 33; Davies, *Popular Opinion in Stalin's Russia,* 73–82.

227. Davis, *A Long Walk to Church,* 16.

228. Cherepenina and Shkarovskii, *Spravochnik po istorii pravoslavnykh monastyrei i soborov g. Sankt-Peterburga,* 4–6 and Ilic, "The Great Terror in Leningrad," 1529.

229. Davies, *Popular Opinion in Stalin's Russia,* 74–81; Shkarovskii, "Religioznaia

zhizn' Leningrada v gody voiny," 262–63; Shkarovksii, "V ogne voiny," 264; Davis, *A Long Walk to Church,* 12; information conveyed to the authors by Catriona Kelly.

230. Cherepenina and Shkarovskii, *Spravochnik po istorii pravoslavnykh monastyrei i soborov g. Sankt-Peterburga,* 6.

231. TsGAIPD SPb f. 25, op. 10, d. 279, ll. 1–14. A young woman named Elizaveta Lezhaeva attended Easter service at the church by the Volkov Cemetery. She reported thirty minutes late to work at a carburetor factory on Easter morning. Her excuse that she and everyone else in her apartment had overslept because they had attended the service was not accepted. She was sentenced to four months of forced labor.

232. Shkarovskii, "V ogne voiny," 260.

233. Shkarovskii, "Religioznaia zhizn' Leningrada v gody voiny," 263. The statement was not published until 1943.

234. Dzeniskevich mistakenly gives the date of the appeal as 26 June.

235. Rothstein, "Homeland, Home Town, and Battlefield," 79.

236. Cherepenina and Shkarovskii, *Sankt-Peterburgskaia Eparkhiia v dvadtsatom veke,* 208, 237.

237. TsGAIPD SPb f.25, op. 10, d. 279, ll. 18–20; Shkarovksii, "V ogne voiny," 260–61 and "Religioznaia zhizn' Leningrada v gody voiny," 264, 269; and Davis, *A Long Walk to Church,* 17–18. Govorov also personally thanked a priest who convinced his own son to leave work in a defense plant to enlist in the army.

238. Peris, *Storming the Heavens,* 201, 221–22. The SVB was officially disbanded in 1947 and replaced by the All-Union Society for the Dissemination of Political and Scientific Knowledge.

239. TsGAIPD SPb f. 25, op. 10, d. 279, l. 28.

240. TsGAIPD SPb f. 25, op. 10, d. 279, l. 21–23.

241. Arkhiv UFSB RF po SPb i LO f. 12, op. 2, p.n. 5, ll. 466–731 and Lomagin, "Upravlenie NKVD," 336, 357.

242. Shkarovskii, "V ogne voiny," 262.

243. The *dvadtsatka* is the registered congregation of the church. The congregation had to include at least twenty members to be officially recognized.

244. Shkarovskii, "V ogne voiny," 262 and Dzeniskevich, *Leningrad v osade,* 336.

245. This would appear to be the "Chairman Belous" mentioned in Document 19.

246. Shkarovskii, "V ogne voiny," 277–78.

247. Miner, *Stalin's Holy War,* 76. The "defense fund" did not exist as a single, distinct fund-raising campaign but as a collective title for various drives. The funds collected by the Nikolsky Cathedral for the Red Cross seem to have been included in the defense fund in Document 26. The only working synagogue also made regular contributions to the defense fund. (Shkarovskii, "Religioznaia zhizh' Leningrada v gody voiny," 236).

248. The Nikolsky Cathedral's contributions to the Red Cross in Document 25 appear to have been channeled to the defense fund, as shown in Document 26.

249. Shkarovskii, "Religioznaia zhizn' Leningrada v gody voiny," 264, 269–70. This church was Renovationist at the time. The Renovationist schism is discussed below.

250. The monastery bearing his name was constructed during the reign of Peter the Great on the precise location, according to legend, of his victory.

251. Miner, *Stalin's Holy War,* 76.

252. This is a reference to the Living Church described below.

253. Miner, *Stalin's Holy War,* 124–30, 136–37, 264–70; Davis, *A Long Walk to Church,* 18–25; Werth, *Russia at War,* 435–38; and Volkogonov, *Stalin,* 487.

254. Miner, *Stalin's Holy War*, 138 and Shkarovksii, "V ogne voiny," 269–70.
255. Roslof, "Living Church Movement," 866–67. Also see Roslof, *Red Priests*, 2002.
256. Shkarovskii, "V ogne voiny," 263, 272.
257. Ibid., 263–64, 272–73. Shkarovskii, *Iosiflianstvo* was the first book-length study of the Josephites.
258. Ligor, who was forced to revert to his original name of Petr, returned to Church service in Leningrad in 1951 in the lesser role of psalm reader (ibid., 273, 284).
259. Dzeniskevich, *Leningrad v osade*, 441, 446–47.
260. Shkarovskii, "Religioznaia zhizn' Leningrada v gody voiny," 283.
261. Dzeniskevich, *Leningrad v osade*, 447.
262. Conquest, *The Great Terror*, 742, 745.
263. As reported in Miner, *Stalin's Holy War*, 126.
264. Davis, *A Long Walk to Church*, 28, 42. These figures cover a period that extends to January 1966, some fourteen months into the Brezhnev years.

CHAPTER 3. POLICIES OF TOTAL WAR

1. We do not consider the better-organized partisan units to be improvised formations. There were about 1 million Soviet partisans in the war compared to around 400,000 *opolchentsy*, plus another 300,000 in the combat (*istrebitel'nye*) battalions (Kozlov, *Velikaia Otechestvennaia voina*, 478, 530).
2. Bidlack, "Workers at War" (1987), 52–55.
3. Ibid., 21, 55.
4. Ibid., 56.
5. Ibid., 97–99.
6. The most prominent of the small group of Russian historians who have published works on the city's wartime industries and workforce is A. R. Dzeniskevich. See entries in the bibliography. The only works in English on the topic are Bidlack's dissertation, "Workers at War," (1987) and his paper with the same title (1991). Ganzenmüller's *Das belagerte Leningrad* contains two chapters on industrial production.
7. Volkovskii, *Blokada Leningrada*, 706–7 and Dzeniskevich, *Front u zavodskikh sten*, 193.
8. *Leningrad 1940*, 37–38.
9. Kriukovskikh et al., *V gody surovykh ispytanii*, 179–80.
10. Bidlack, "Workers at War" (1987), 68–69, 109–110.
11. Ibid., 111.
12. Ibid., 70, 75, 112.
13. Ibid., 38–43.
14. Ibid., 222–223.
15. Ibid., 75–77, 115–16 and Goure, *The Siege of Leningrad*, 59. The Rybina quote is from Burov, *Blokada den' za dnem*, 13.
16. Kniazev et al., *Na zashchite Nevskoi tverdyni*, 34–35 and Kostiuchenko et al., *Istoriia Kirovskogo zavoda*, 595.
17. Werth, *Russia at War*, 344.
18. Goure, *The Siege of Leningrad*, 17–18 and Glantz, *The Battle for Leningrad*, 37–39, 51–53.
19. Glantz, *The Battle for Leningrad*, 41–45.
20. Ibid., 39.

21. Zakharov et al., *Ocherki istorii Leningradskoi organizatsii KPSS,* 363.

22. Lomagin, *Neizvestnaia blokada,* vol. 2, 121.

23. Korol'chuk, *Istoriia . . . obuvnoi fabriki "Skorokhod,"* 420–23.

24. Goure, *The Siege of Leningrad,* 24–25 and Koval'chuk, *Ocherki istorii Leningrada,* 159–62.

25. Bibikov and Moskalev, *Profsoiuzy Leningrada,* 112; Karasev, *Leningradtsy v gody blokady,* 124; Kulagin, *Dnevnik i pamiat',* 29.

26. TsGAIPD SPb f. 24, op. 2b, d. 5678, l. 73.

27. TsGAIPD SPb f. 24, op. 2b, d. 4850a, l. 20; d. 5386, l. 56.

28. TsGAIPD SPb f. 24, op. 2b, d. 5369, ll. 101–3. The identity of the shipyard was determined from the online database of Dexter and Rodionov, *The Factories, Research and Design Establishments of the Soviet Defence Industry.*

29. TsGAIPD SPb f. 25, op. 2, d. 3834, l. 1.

30. TsGAIPD SPb f. 24, op. 2b, d. 5368, l. 164; f. 417, op. 3, d. 74, ll. 149, 165–67; f. 1012, op. 3, d. 53, l. 17.

31. Tokarev et al., *Deviat'sot geroicheskikh dnei,* 292; *Leningradskaia pravda,* 11 December 1941.

32. Dzeniskevich, *Leningrad v osade,* 444–49 and Kutuzov and Stepanov, "Organy gosbezopasnosti," 222. The Military Procuracy and the Military Tribunal together comprised another eighty to ninety officials (Lomagin, "Spetsifika politecheskogo kontrolia," 306).

33. If the party's youth division, the *Komsomol,* is included, about one in seven of all Leningraders was affiliated with the party (Goure, *The Siege of Leningrad,* 4).

34. Bidlack, "Workers at War" (1987); TsGAIPD f. 24, op. 2v, d. 5889, l. 170; Dzeniskevich, *Rabochie Leningrada,* 103.

35. For specific data, see TsGAIPD SPb f. 24, op. 2v, d. 5889, l. 170.

36. Jansen and Petrov, *Stalin's Loyal Executioner,* 87, 205.

37. Getty and Naumov, *The Road to Terror,* 531, 535–37.

38. Solomon, *Soviet Criminal Justice under Stalin,* 256–58; Jansen and Petrov, *Stalin's Loyal Executioner,* 159–64; and Getty and Naumov, *The Road to Terror,* 537.

39. Solomon, *Soviet Criminal Justice under Stalin,* 259.

40. Kutuzov and Stepanov, "Organy gosbezopasnosti," 222.

41. While advancing on Madrid in four columns in 1936, Franco's general Emilio Mola boasted that he had a secret "fifth column" of Nationalist supporters who would join the attack on the Republicans from within the city.

42. See below, pp. 202, 238, 370–71, for examples of those arrested for purportedly attempting to signal enemy aircraft. Anti-Soviet agitation was covered under article 58-10 of the criminal code.

43. Arkhiv UFSB RF po SPb i LO f. 8, op. 25, p.n. 18, d. 257, ll. 217–21; Lomagin, "Upravlenie NKVD," 326.

44. Berezhkov, *Piterskie prokuratory,* 216 and Zalesskii, *Imperiia Stalina,* 261.

45. Dzeniskevich, *Leningrad v osade,* 151–56, 446–47 and Berezhkov, *Piterskie prokuratory,* 316.

46. A report from the VP of the Northern Front from 3 August 1941 describes a refusal to grant an arrest order because the senior investigator's case was assembled "hastily, carelessly, and, chiefly, not in line with the materials of the case" (Arkhiv UFSB RF po SPb i LO f. 21/12, op. 2, p.n. 44, d. 3, l. 1).

47. TsGAIPD SPb f. 24, op. 2v, d. 5889, l. 21 and Dzeniskevich, *Leningrad v osade,* 461.

48. Lomagin, *Neizvestnaia blokada,* vol. 2, 73.

49. Dzeniskevich, *Leningrad v osade,* 456–57.

50. Lomagin, "Upravlenie NKVD," 363.

51. This report states that 2,093 people were sentenced to death by the VT between 1 July 1941 and 1 July 1943; however, a report from Kubatkin to Zhdanov from 2 April 1942 claims that 3,727 had been shot by the VT up to that point in the war. No explanation for the discrepancy has come to light. In Document 45, Kubatkin reported that 5,360 had been shot according to sentences handed down by the VT and the courts (*narsudy*) up to 1 October 1942. It should also be noted that the number of VT convictions in the two reports cited do not match (Dzeniskevich, *Leningrad v osade,* 17, 433, 442, 461).

52. Dzeniskevich, *Leningrad v osade,* 461.

53. See data on mortality in the city's jails below, pp. 278–81.

54. Lomagin, *Neizvestnaia blokada,* vol. 2, 12; ibid., vol. 1, 228; Lomagin, "Upravlenie NKVD," 324.

55. See the below, p. 347, for discussion of the complexities involved in defining "anti-Soviet" words and deeds. There were gaps in the dragnet to round up the "KR element." One remarkable survivor of the early decades of Soviet power was a Baroness von Manteuffel, who was born in St. Petersburg at the turn of the century. She concealed her class origins through marriage and thereby managed to survive the Red Terror of the Civil War years and the purges of the 1930s. A factory worker during the war, she was evacuated from Leningrad during the last weeks of the ice road in 1942, following her children who had been sent eastward a few weeks earlier. She returned to Leningrad with her children after the war and remained there until her death in 1990. The historian Viktor Georgievich Bortnevsky was her grandson.

56. Arkhiv UFSB RF po SPb i LO f. 21/12, op. 2, t. 1, d. 4, l. 91.

57. www.cyberussr.com/rus/uk58-e.html#58-14.

58. See Lomagin, *Neizvestnaia blokada,* vol. 2, 41–51.

59. See below, pp. 346–53, for analysis of changes in KR arrest rates over time.

60. At the February–March 1937 Central Committee plenum, Yezhov had accused Bukharin, Rykov, and other Rightists of having formed an alliance with Trotskyites in order to seize power (Jansen and Petrov, *Stalin's Loyal Executioner,* 59).

61. The Trudovaia Krestianskaia Partiia (Peasant Labor Party) was an imagined political opposition from the early 1930s.

62. Pohl, *Ethnic Cleansing in the USSR,* 23 and Ilic, "The Great Terror in Leningrad," 1521.

63. For an example, see Toivo Kurikka's account of his exile, *Put' iz Finliandii v Sibir'.*

64. Getty and Naumov, *The Road to Terror,* 535.

65. Pohl, *Ethnic Cleansing in the USSR,* 24.

66. Dzeniskevich, *Iz raionov oblasti soobshchaiut,* 63.

67. Ganzenmüller, *Das belagerte Leningrad,* 282; Bellamy, *Absolute War,* 358; Lomagin, *Neizvestnaia blokada,* vol. 2, 119.

68. Bugai, *Iosif Stalin—Lavrentiiu Berii,* 63–64, 75–76. By 1945, a total of 1,209,430 Germans were resettled in the East.

69. See Pohl's *Ethnic Cleansing in the USSR,* 5, for a chart that summarizes the major deportations.

70. *Izvestiia TsK KPSS* 1990, no. 9, 212–13.

71. Boterbloem, *The Life and Times of Andrei Zhdanov,* 233. J. Otto Pohl erred

when he claimed that the NKVD deported 89,000 Finns from the Leningrad *oblast'* to Kazakhstan by 7 September 1941 (*Ethnic Cleansing in the USSR*, 24).

72. Ganzenmüller, *Das belagerte Leningrad*, 283.

73. This information is from a report sent by Kubatkin to Merkulov on 9 March 1942.

74. TsAMO RF f. 217, op. 1258, d. 166, ll. 5–6. The text of the draft resolution, which includes Zhdanov's handwritten revisions, does not mention expulsion of the "anti-Soviet element"; however, the instructions he wrote at the top of the document ordered a commission, which included Kubatkin, to review the plans to "remove Finns, Germans *and* [underlined in the document] A/S E." It is not clear whether the additional 36,000 Finns and Germans whom Beria ordered relocated on 30 August included residents of Leningrad.

75. Lomagin, *Neizvestnaia blokada*, vol. 2, 35–37 and Dzeniskevich, *Iz raionov oblasti soobshchaiut*, 162.

76. Salisbury, *The 900 Days*, 373, 466–67.

77. She attended a writers' conference on 30 May 1942 (Burov, *Blokada den' za dnem*, 193).

78. *Raboche-Krest'ianskaia Krasnaia Armiia* (Workers' and Peasants' Red Army).

79. TsGAIPD SPb f. 24, op. 2v, d. 5803, ll. 1–2.

80. TsGAIPD SPb f. 24, op. 2v, d. 5760, l. 93.

81. Goure, *The Siege of Leningrad*, 64–65 and Volkovskii, *Blokada Leningrada*, 646.

82. TsGAIPD SPb f. 25, op. 10, d. 307a, ll. 27, 33, 38.

83. This statement indicates that German intelligence had learned some details of the secret plan to mine important objectives in the city.

84. The Russian verb employed here, *bit'*, can mean to beat or kill. The implication is a severe beating that can result in death.

85. Lomagin, "Upravlenie NKVD," 329–30.

86. Anti-Semitic attitudes themselves and reasons for their emergence are discussed below, pp. 332, 339–42.

87. See Beizer, "The Jewish Minority in Leningrad," 8, 10 cited in Davies, *Popular Opinion in Stalin's Russia*, 83–85.

88. www.cyberussr.com/rus/uk59-e.html#59-7and uk58-e.html#58-10.

89. This would appear to be a reference to the blood libel against Jews.

90. TsGAIPD SPb f. 24, op. 2b, d. 970, ll. 11–18.

91. Fitzpatrick, *Everyday Stalinism*, 164.

92. Lomagin, *V tiskakh goloda*, 13, "Spetsifika politicheskogo kontrolia," 297–99, 301, and "Upravlenie NKVD," 334–35.

93. Cherepenina, "Golod i smert' v blokirovannom gorode," 66.

94. Lomagin, "Upravlenie NKVD," 360.

95. Ziemke, "Battle for Moscow," 760.

96. In addition, as shown below, only a very tiny percentage of the thousands of pieces of mailed correspondence that were confiscated each day because they were deemed to contain "negative sentiments" led to criminal prosecution.

97. The order was issued a few days before the NKGB was subsumed into the NKVD.

98. Arkhiv UFSB RF no SPb i LO f. 8, op. 25, p.n. 18, d. 257, l. 221.

99. Lomagin, "Spetsifika politicheskogo kontrolia," 303–4.

100. Two fabricated KR cases are explored in chapter 6.

101. The underlining by hand appears in Zhdanov's copy of the report.

102. This munitions factory was generally referred to only by its number in war-era documents and in Soviet publications. Its name was the Leningrad metal factory named for Stalin. In this study it is identified as the Stalin metal works. We have used Dexter and Rodionov, *The Factories, Research and Design Establishments of the Soviet Defence Industry* to identify numbered factories.

103. This factory is the Zhdanov shipyards.

104. There is no evidence that any opposition group of this size in fact existed.

105. This is the Ordzhonikidze Baltic shipyards.

106. Ershov, "Rabota NKVD v gospitaliakh vo vremia voiny," 286; Lomagin, "Spetsifika politicheskogo kontrolia," 301–3; Lomagin, "Upravlenie NKVD," 343–47.

107. Lomagin, "Upravlenie NKVD," 339–40.

108. Volkov, *St. Petersburg: A Cultural History*, 438. The poem was translated by Volkov.

109. Ibid., 522 and Lomagin, "Upravlenie NKVD," 342.

110. Nina Koyzova, who worked in a factory during the siege, described a similar experience in her diary. She wrote that she was arrested and sentenced to forced labor after she rejected a request from the NKVD to serve as an informant. See Hass, "Making the Memory of War," 39.

111. Lomagin, "Upravlenie NKVD," 342 and Hodgson, *Voicing the Soviet Experience*, 24.

112. Hodgson, *Voicing the Soviet Experience*, 24. Hodgson translated the diary fragment.

113. Arkhiv UFSB RF po SPb i LO f. 12, op. 2, p.n. 5, ll. 798–798ob and Lomagin, "Upravlenie NKVD," 342. Eikhenbaum later returned to Leningrad; however, in 1949, during the *Zhdanovshchina* anti-Western cultural purge, Eikhenbaum was fired from his post as chair of the Russian literature department and not allowed to publish (Volkov, *St. Petersburg: A Cultural History*, 452–53).

114. Dzeniskevich, *Leningrad v osade*, 449 and Lomagin, *Neizvestnaia blokada*, vol. 2, 280. Robert Dale notes that Leningrad's military censor employed approximately 840 people between 1941 and 1945 ("Rats and Resentment," 124). The changing rate of intercepted mail is examined below, pp. 345–46, 349–50.

115. See below, pp. 346, 349, for description of how arrest totals for KR crimes changed over time. About twelve diaries were used as prosecutorial evidence during the blockade.

116. Arkhiv UFSB RF po SPb i LO f. 12, op. 2, p.n. 5, ll. 401–2.

117. Ershov, "Rabota NKVD v gospitaliakh vo vremia voiny," 2842–89. He would appear to be the "Vasily Yershov" mentioned below, pp. 301, 315, 321, 369–70. The name was likely a pseudonym.

118. Yershov claimed (p. 287) that from January to October 1943, more than forty were sentenced to be executed and over 150 were sent to penal companies.

119. Using the familiar form of address, *tebia*.

120. See Documents 56 and 57 in chapter 5 for other examples of an anonymous letter and a leaflet. For an example of a similar search for a lone letter writer from the early 1970s that lasted almost three years, see Andrew and Mitrokhin, *The Sword and the Shield*, 547.

121. Bellamy, *Absolute War*, 408.

122. Arkhiv UFSB RF po SPb i LO f. 12, op. 2, p.n. 5, l. 744.

123. TsGAIPD SPb f. 24, op. 2b, d. 995, ll. 1–2.

124. Kutuzov and Stepanov, "Organy gosbezopasnosti," 216.

125. Lomagin, "Upravlenie NKVD," 368–69.

126. These crimes are explored below, pp. 309–23.

127. For instance, see Elena Kochina's description of how her husband was released after openly stealing a loaf of bread from a delivery sled. The fact that he was a starving engineer who did not try to hide his theft was probably the deciding factor that spared him imprisonment or execution (*Blockade Diary*, 63).

128. Lomagin, "Upravlenie NKVD," 366–67.

129. See below, p. 286, for examples of bribes given to secure passage over the Ladoga ice road.

130. Overy, *Russia's War*, 57–58.

131. Bidlack, "The Political Mood in Leningrad," 102–3.

132. TsGAIPD SPb f. 24, op. 2v, d. 5766, l. 170.

133. Bidlack, "The Political Mood in Leningrad," 102 and TsGAIPD SPb 24, op. 2v, d. 5761, 144. Popular attitudes toward the Party at the start of the siege are explored below, pp. 334–45.

134. Kutuzov and Stepanov, "Organy gosbezopasnosti," 215. On 15 November, a "secret" SPO (*neglasnyi SPO,* or nSPO) was created for use as an underground unit (Lomagin, "Upravlenie NKVD," 335–36).

135. Foreign communist parties also maintained "illegal" sections which were to carry on party work clandestinely in the event that the legal party organization was disbanded. See Andrew and Mitrokhin, *The Sword and the Shield* on the "illegal" branch of the Communist Party USA.

136. Dzeniskevich, *Leningrad v osade*, 105, 113–16, 120, 125, 130–31.

CHAPTER 4. THE STRUGGLE TO SURVIVE

1. Dzeniskevich, *Leningrad v osade*, 469.

2. Pavlov, *Leningrad v blokade*, 98.

3. Glantz, *The Battle for Leningrad*, 133.

4. Dzeniskevich, *Leningrad v osade*, 267.

5. Appendix C and Bidlack, "Workers at War" (1987), 195 n. 1.

6. Cherepenina, "Golod i smert' v blokirovannom gorode," 53.

7. Pavlov, *Leningrad 1941*, 58–61 and TsGAIPD SPb f. 24, op. 2b, d. 992, ll. 12–14.

8. Dzeniskevich, *Leningrad v osade*, 195–96.

9. Cellulose is a complex carbohydrate that makes up the walls of plant cells. Unlike wood, cotton is almost entirely composed of cellulose.

10. Pavlov, *Leningrad 1941*, 62.

11. Dzeniskevich, *Leningrad v osade*, 212, 217.

12. Kochina, *Blockade Diary*, 46.

13. Cherepenina, "Golod i smert' v blokirovannom gorode," 49.

14. See Davies, *Popular Opinion in Stalin's Russia*, 55–56, for reactions among inhabitants of the Leningrad *oblast'* to the famine of 1940–41.

15. A diminutive of endearment for *khleb*, the Russian word for bread.

16. Kochina, *Blockade Diary*, 67–68.

17. Cherepenina, "Golod i smert' v blokirovannom gorode," 52; Amosov, "Rabochie Leningrada," 252; and Burov, *Blokada den' za dnem*, 131–32, 159.

18. Skrjabina, *Siege and Survival*, 59.

19. TsGAIPD SPb f. 24, op. 2v, d. 5760, l. 34.

20. Petrovskaya Wayne, *Shurik*, 114.

21. Adamovich and Granin, *Blokadnaia kniga,* 63.

22. Kirschenbaum, *The Legacy of the Siege of Leningrad,* 57.

23. GMMOBL op. 1, d. 30, l. 72.

24. Cherepenina, "Golod i smert' v blokirovannom gorode," 47 and Kirschenbaum, "Innocent Victims and Heroic Defenders," 288 n. 7.

25. Boterbloem made this observation in *The Life and Times of Andrei Zhdanov,* 236–37.

26. GMMOBL op. 1, d. 30, l. 73.

27. GMMOBL op. 1, d. 388.

28. Broekmeyer, *Stalin, the Russians, and Their War,* 75–76.

29. Cherepenina, "Golod i smert' v blokirovannom gorode," 40, 47.

30. Broekmeyer, *Stalin, the Russians, and Their War,* 75.

31. Arkhiv UFSB RF po SPb i LO fl. 21/12, op. 2, p.n. 19, d. 12, in Lomagin, *Neizvestnaia blokada,* vol. 2, 254 and Dzeniskevich, *Leningrad v osade,* 374. Of the 1,302 killed in the bombardment in September, 556 died from high explosive and incendiary bombs. German bombers were most active in September, when 675 planes dropped a recorded 987 high explosive bombs and 15,100 incendiaries on Leningrad. There were no bombing runs over the city from January to March of 1942. German planes returned in April to drop 611 high explosive bombs; thereafter, the highest monthly total was 174 (Volkovskii, *Blokada Leningrada,* 721).

32. Arkhiv UFSB RF po SPb i LO fl. 21/12, op. 2, p.n. 19, d. 12, in Lomagin, *Neizvestnaia blokada,* vol. 2, 253, 281, 300, 308.

33. Salisbury, *The 900 Days,* 479.

34. Lomagin, "Spetsifika politicheskogo kontrolia," 268. See description below of the process undertaken in mid-October for verifying the identity of ration card holders.

35. Salisbury, *The 900 Days,* 514.

36. Kronstadt and Kolpino, together with two towns that the Germans occupied, Peterhof and Pushkin, were subordinated to the *Lengorispolkom* in 1936. (Cherepenina, "Golod i smert' v blokirovannom gorode," 36).

37. Pavlov, *Leningrad v blokade,* 165 and Salisbury, *The 900 Days,* 514.

38. Koval'chuk and Sobolev, "Leningradskii 'rekvium'," 191–94.

39. Rubtsov, and Lur'e, "Blokada Leningrada: Vse li zhertvy uchteny?" 30–32.

40. According to official data, 590,304 were evacuated over the ice road in 1941–42 (Dzeniskevich, *Leningrad v osade,* 302).

41. A recorded 821 Leningraders were killed by enemy artillery and aerial bombardment from December 1941 through February 1942 (Dzeniskevich, *Leningrad v osade,* 374).

42. Cherepenina, "Golod i smert' v blokirovannom gorode," 79–80.

43. Dzeniskevich, *Leningrad v osade,* 303.

44. Broekmeyer, *Stalin, the Russians, and Their War,* 71–72.

45. Frolov, "Zabolevaemost' i smertnost' evakuiruemykh po puti ot Leningrada do Kostromy," 85, 96 and Broekmeyer, *Stalin, the Russians, and Their War,* 72.

46. Broekmeyer, *Stalin, the Russians, and Their War,* 72.

47. Given the fact that the ice road did not become fully operational until Leningrad's mortality rate was at its highest level, the death toll among the evacuees must have been high.

48. Pavlov, *Leningrad v blokade,* 82.

49. Magaeva, "Physiological and Psychosomatic Prerequisites for Survival and Recovery," 142–45.

50. Khoroshinina, "Long-Term Effects of Lengthy Starvation," 208.

51. Volkovskii, *Blokada Leningrada,* 736.

52. Dzeniskevich, *Leningrad v osade,* 316, 339, 593-94 n. 77.

53. Arkhiv UFSB RF po SPb i LO f. 21/12, op. 2, p.n. 19, d. 12, in Lomagin, *Neizvestnaia blokada,* vol. 2, 266, 305, 308.

54. Arkhiv UFSB RF po SPb i LO f. 21/12, op. 2, p.n. 19, d. 12, ll. 101-2, in Lomagin, *Neizvestvnaia blokada,* vol. 2, 266-67 and Cherepenina, "Golod i smert' v blokirovannom gorode," 51, 75.

55. Kochina, *Blockade Diary,* 44. Mother and daughter survived the blockade.

56. Pavlov, *Leningrad v blokade,* 114 and Cherepenina, "Golod i smert' v blokirovannom gorode," 75, 78.

57. Arkhiv UFSB RF po SPb i LO f. 21/12, op. 2, p.n. 19, d. 12, l. 307.

58. Dzeniskevich, *Leningrad v osade,* 414.

59. *Sbornik ukazov, postanovlenii, reshenii, rasporiazhenii i prikazov voennogo vremeni, 1941-1942,* 269; Koval'chuk, *Ocherki istorii Leningrada,* 209; Tokarev et al., *Deviat'sot geroicheskikh dnei,* 258-59, 373, 376; and Dzeniskevich, *Leningrad v osade,* 302, 345. 12,639 children from the homes were evacuated over the ice road in 1942.

60. Tania was evacuated but died subsequently of malnutrition (Kirschenbaum, "Innocent Victims and Heroic Defenders," 284-85).

61. Lesnoy was located in the northern outskirts of Leningrad, just north of the Bolshaia Nevka branch of the Neva River.

62. Svetlana, which manufactured light bulbs and vacuum tubes before the war, converted to producing mines, shell casings, and bayonets.

63. This is probably a reference to a security station at the factory's entrance.

64. This entry is obviously confusing. It would appear that Nikolai wrote it or the last two sentences of it at a later date, probably in March. Tonka is a diminutive form of Tonya.

65. *Sestra* could mean sister or female cousin.

66. Cherepenina, "Golod i smert' v blokirovannom gorode," 75.

67. This was noted in the documentary film *Blokada,* which was produced in 1994 by Fauna Films of St. Petersburg.

68. For more on this topic, see below, p. 286.

69. Ganzenmüller, *Das belagerte Leningrad,* 69-72.

70. TsGAIPD SPb f. 24, op. 2b/ d. 992, ll. 1-11.

71. Dzeniskevich, *Leningrad v osade,* 288-89, 302.

72. Ibid., 228, 588 n. 51.

73. Ibid., 274-75, 301.

74. Ibid., 349.

75. The estimate of the size of the inmate population is from Gustaw Herling, who passed through Leningrad in November 1940 on his Gulag odyssey (*A World Apart,* 9).

76. This account is from an article by S. Voloshin, a member of the human rights group Memorial, in the commemorative newspaper *Kresty,* which was published in the fall of 1993 on the hundredth anniversary of the prison's founding.

77. Dzeniskevich, *Leningrad v osade,* 331.

78. Adamovich and Granin, *A Book of the Blockade,* 146-47.

79. Simmons and Perlina, *Writing the Siege of Leningrad,* 50-51. For a similar example of a corpse that was gradually stripped and cannibalized over several days, see Magayeva and Pleysier, *Surviving the Blockade of Leningrad,* p. 110.

80. Salisbury, *The 900 Days,* 507.

81. Dzeniskevich, *Leningrad v osade*, 306, 330–31.

82. Vasily Yershov, a deputy commander in charge of food supply for an army division, claimed that executioners had their choice of 300 grams of grain alcohol (*spirt*) or 600 grams of vodka. If there was a group of executioners, each received either 200 grams of alcohol or 400 grams of vodka. ("Soviet War Preparation in 1941," 40–41).

83. A chief engineer named Rabkin of a section of the State Mechanical Factory No. 77, together with one of the plant's section bosses named Makarov, on 15 November requested 840 liters of grain alcohol for the remainder of the month. They claimed to need 4 grams of alcohol for each 122-millimeter shell and two grams for each 76-millimeter shell. They wrote that they realized the difficulty of granting such a request and claimed to have tried using gasoline or turpentine, but that those substances had not proved effective. Similar requests came from the Sverdlov and Nevsky machine construction factories (TsGAIPD SPb f. 24, op. 2b, d. 5368, 178; d. 5369, ll. 55–58, 241).

84. Dzeniskevich, *Leningrad v osade,* 316. The report from the city's communal-services administration from April 1943 cited above claims that the crematorium commenced work on 16 March, and by the end of 1942 had cremated 109,925 bodies (*Leningrad v osade,* 333).

85. An earlier version of portions of this section appeared in Bidlack, "Survival Strategies in Leningrad."

86. Gladkikh, *Zdravookhranenie blokirovannogo Leningrada,* 10.

87. Hensley, *Basic Concepts of World Nutrition,* 122.

88. In his book *The Bread of Affliction,* Bill Moskoff demonstrated that the Soviet state had to decentralize food production to try to feed the civilian population, especially during the early part of the war, which meant condoning private and quasi-private initiatives. Jeff Hass characterizes the reliance on individual initiative during Leningrad's starvation as a violation of socialist collective mentality in his unpublished manuscript, "Making the Memory of War."

89. Dzeniskevich, *Leningrad v osade,* 301.

90. Siege survivor and personal friend Marianna Viktorovna Korchinskaia told Bidlack that she and her cousins set out over the ice road for Central Asia weeks before her mother got permission to leave her job in Leningrad. The mother (who was born a baroness and had survived purges of the former nobility) was alarmed when she arrived at the designated final destination several weeks before her children. The family returned to Leningrad after the war.

91. Dzeniskevich, *Leningrad v osade,* 302.

92. TsGAIPD SPb f. 24, op. 2v, d. 5670.

93. TsGAIPD SPb f. 24, op. 2b, d. 970, l. 6.

94. TsGAIPD SPb f. 24, op. 2v, d. 4819, l. 38 in Bidlack, "Survival Strategies," 89. For similar examples, see TsGAIPD SPb f. 24, op. 2v, d. 5279, l. 44 and d. 5366, ll. 116, 181–84.

95. Kochina, *Blockade Diary,* 94–104.

96. TsGAIPD SPb f. 4000, op. 10, d. 246, ll. 8–9.

97. TsGAIPD SPb f. 24, op. 2b, d. 992, ll. 1–16; op. 2v, d. 5211, ll. 5–8; op. 2v, d. 4819, ll. 111–12; op. 2v, d. 5151, l. 139.

98. Salisbury, *The 900 Days,* 120.

99. Dzeniskevich, *Leningrad v osade,* 189–90 and Belozerov, "Protivopravnye deistviia," 249.

100. Kriukovskikh et al., *V gody surovykh ispytanii,* 259 and Goure, *The Siege of Leningrad,* 131–32.

101. Belozerov, "Protivopravnye deistviia," 249.

102. TsGAIPD SPb f. 4000, op. 10, d. 297, ll. 7–8.

103. Belozerov, "Protivopravnye deistviia," 254.

104. Frolov, "Istoriia konditerskoi im. N. K. Krupskoi," 35 and comments made by Frolov to Bidlack in January 1994.

105. TsGAIPD SPb f. 4000, op. 10, d. 592, l. 5.

106. TsGAIPD SPb f. 417, op. 3, d. 444, ll. 47–48.

107. Adamovich and Granin, *Blokadnaia kniga,* 249–52.

108. A pood, a traditional Russian weight measure, is equal to about thirty-six pounds.

109. Simmons and Perlina, *Writing the Siege of Leningrad,* 32.

110. As quoted in Broekmeyer, *Stalin, the Russians, and Their War,* 78–79.

111. TsGAIPD SPb f. 24, op. 2v, d. 4819, l. 58.

112. Dzeniskevich, *Nakanune i v dni ispytanii,* 103 and Belozerov, "Protivopravnye deistviia," 250.

113. Adamovich and Granin, *Blokadnaia kniga,* 82–83.

114. Cherepenina, "Golod i smert' v blokirovannom gorode," 63.

115. Bidlack, "Workers at War" (1987), 164 and Werth, *Leningrad,* 347.

116. See section below on criminal schemes.

117. Bidlack, "Workers at War" (1987), 136. See section below on private trade.

118. Ibid., 171–79.

119. Kulagin, *Dnevnik i pamiat',* 121.

120. Bidlack, "Workers at War" (1987), 177–78 and Brandenberger, *National Bolshevism,* 145–46.

121. TsGAIPD SPb f. 1012, op. 3, d. 138, l. 82.

122. The selfless dedication of the young women inspired Daniil Granin, co-author of *Blokadnaia kniga,* to help found in 1988 one of the first private charity groups in the USSR (*Christian Science Monitor,* 21 July 1988).

123. Bidlack, "Workers at War" (1987), 175–77.

124. Ibid., 179–80.

125. Karasev, *Leningradtsy v gody blokady,* 212.

126. Bidlack, "Workers at War" (1987), 172, 174–75.

127. TsGAIPD SPb, f. 1012, op. 3, d. 53, l. 14.

128. Simmons and Perlina, *Writing the Siege of Leningrad,* 133–36.

129. Dzeniskevich, "Novye dannye o vesne blokadnogo 1942 goda," 4–5.

130. Bidlack, "Workers at War" (1987), 172, 174–75, 179–80, 188–89.

131. TsGAIPD SPb f. 24, op. 2v, d. 5889, l. 47.

132. Bidlack, *Workers at War* (1991), 22.

133. Magaeva, "Physiological and Psychosomatic Prerequisites for Survival and Recovery," 150–51.

134. Amosov, "Rabochie Leningrada v gody Velikoi Otechestvennoi voiny," 119.

135. Karasev, *Leningradtsy v gody blokady,* 120.

136. Ibid., 216.

137. Pavlov, *Leningrad v blokade,* 114 and Kniazev et al., *Na zashchite Nevskoi tverdyni,* 284.

138. Koval'chuk, *Ocherki istorii Leningrada,* 215–16.

139. Skrjabina, *Siege and Survival,* 54.

140. Dzeniskevich, *Voennaia piatiletka,* 106.

141. TsGAIPD SPb f. 25, op. 13a, d. 46, l. 103.

142. Kulagin, *Dnevnik i pamiat'*, 221 and Tokarev et al., *Deviat'sot geroicheskikh dnei*, 175–76.

143. Salisbury, *The 900 Days*, 507.

144. TsGAIPD SPb f. 4000, op. 10, d. 499, l. 6.

145. Salisbury, *The 900 Days*, 507 and TsGAIPD SPb f. 25, op. 13a, d. 46, l. 103. It is likely, however, that some of those who were reported to have died in March or April actually perished earlier but were not counted until that time.

146. Petrovskaya Wayne, *Shurik*, 150.

147. Tokarev et al., *Deviat'sot geroicheskikh dnei*, 340 and Salisbury, *The 900 Days*, 294, 495, 516; TsGAIPD SPb f. 24, op. 2v, d. 5762, l. 90.

148. Kulagin noted, however, that the "directors'" cafeteria at the Stalin metal works gradually opened its doors to nonmanagerial personnel. (Kulagin, *Dnevnik i pamiat'*, 152).

149. Dzeniskevich, *Leningrad v osade*, 10, 209, 588 n. 49.

150. TsGAIPD SPb f. 24, op. 2v, d. 5761, ll. 144–45.

151. In comparing mortality rates between party and nonparty personnel, two demographic traits of party membership were particularly important and may have partly offset each other in terms of their effect on mortality. At the start of the war, 75 percent of the LPO were men, and men had higher mortality rates than women (and maybe higher rates than the civilian population as a whole). On the other hand, the party had practically no one under the age of twenty and few very elderly members; starvation rates among the young and very old were extremely high.

152. TsGAIPD SPb f. 4000, op. 10, d. 297, ll. 5–6.

153. Dzeniskevich, *Leningrad v osade*, 447–49 and Berezhkov, *Piterskie prokuratory*, 220. Somewhat more than one hundred NKVD officers went to the front with the *opolchenie* and partisans units.

154. Salisbury, *The 900 Days*, 449.

155. Adamovich and Granin, *Blokadnaia kniga*, 332.

156. As quoted in Broekmeyer, *Stalin, the Russians, and Their War*, 84.

157. Salisbury's portrayal of Zhdanov was generally sympathetic and positive. Without citing a direct source, Salisbury gave an exaggerated view of Zhdanov's diet when he asserted that the party chief and other leaders "ate a little better than the general population," receiving only "a military ration: a pound or more of bread a day plus a bowl of meat or fish soup and possibly a little cereal or kasha" (*The 900 Days*, 402–3). Montefiore repeats Salisbury's text almost verbatim (*Stalin*, 389).

158. Yershov, "Soviet War Preparation in 1941," 71–72.

159. As reported in Arapova, "Trudovaia deiatel'nost' leningradtsev," 383–84.

160. Dzeniskevich, *Leningrad v osade*, 196–97.

161. Columbia University, Bakhmeteff Archive, general manuscript collection, L. S. Rubanov file, 12–14, 19.

162. Belozerov, "Protivopravnye deistviia," 255. Polina Barskova is researching the fate of private book collections during the blockade.

163. This was a Soviet version of a German Leica camera that bore the initials of the founder of the Cheka, Feliks Edmundovich Dzerzhinsky.

164. Lomagin, "The Black Market in Besieged Leningrad." Lomagin and sociologist Jeffrey Hass have recently begun researching barter trade during the blockade.

165. TsGA SPb f. 7384, op. 4, d. 67, ll. 59–87.

166. TsGAIPD SPb f. 24, op. 2v, d. 4819, l. 52.

167. See Appendix A and Pavlov, *Leningrad 1941*, 79, 86, 88.

168. Karasev, *Leningradtsy v gody blokady*, 123 and Kostiuchenko et al., *Istoriia Kirovskogo zavoda*, 636–37.

169. Simmons and Perlina, *Writing the Siege of Leningrad*, 62–63, 147–54.

170. Amosov, "Rabochie Leningrada v gody Velikoi Otechestvennoi voiny," 269.

171. Kulagin, *Dnevnik i pamiat'*, 39.

172. GMMOBL op. 1, d. 30, l. 101.

173. Karasev, *Leningradtsy v gody blokady*, 241.

174. Burov, *Blokada den' za dnem*, 185.

175. Shvetsov, "Deiatel'nost' Smol'ninskoi raionnoi partiinoi organizatsii," 220; Adamovich and Granin, *Blokadnaia kniga*, 118; and Burov, *Blokada den' za dnem*, 193.

176. Bibikov and Moskalev, *Profsoiuzy Leningrada*, 122; *Propaganda i agitatsiia*, 1942, No. 9, 18; and *Leningradskaia pravda*, 15 May 1942.

177. Meyerovich and Okulov, *Meropriiatiia Leningradskoi partiinoi organizatsii*, 16; Karasev, *Leningradtsy v gody blokady*, 240, 243; and *Leningradskaia pravda*, 8, 12 May 1942.

178. Grodzinskii, *Trudovoe zakonodatel'stvo voennogo vremeni*, 76.

179. *Leningradskaia pravda*, 12 May, 9 and 11 June, 1 July, 13 September 1942; Karasev, *Leningradtsy v gody blokady*, 244–46; and Dzeniskevich, *Leningrad v osade*, 252, 254. On 31 October 1942, the *Biulleten' Leningradskogo soveta deputatov trudiashchikhsia* described the harvest from the subsidiary farms as worse than expected.

180. For example, see *Leningradskaia pravda*, 4 April 1942.

181. Dzeniskevich, *Leningrad v osade*, 251–54.

182. Petrovskaya Wayne, *Shurik*, 186.

183. *Leningradskaia pravda*, 31 May and 4 September 1942.

184. TsGAIPD SPb f. 24, op. 2b, d. 5168, ll. 17–19, 24 and Shvetsov, "Deiatel'nost' Smol'ninskoi raionnoi partiinoi organizatsii," 173.

185. Document 42; *Leningradskaia pravda*, 6 December 1941; and Belozerov, "Protivopravnye deistviia," 252.

186. TsGAIPD SPb f. 24, op. 2v, d. 4841, l. 46; op. 2b, d. 994, l. 28.

187. Kochina, *Blockade Diary*, 105.

188. Belozerov, "Protivopravnye deistviia," 262.

189. TsGAIPD SPb f. 4000, op. 10, d. 246, ll. 6–10. According to Zinoviev, there were eleven to twelve commissars for the four to five hundred vehicles in each transport battalion.

190. Petrovskaya Wayne, *Shurik*, 91–92.

191. Dzeniskevich, *Leningrad v osade*, 425–27, 429.

192. Ibid., 461.

193. For example, see Kochina, *Blockade Diary*, 55–56.

194. Ibid., 60–61.

195. Salisbury, *The 900 Days*, 450.

196. Kochina, *Blockade Diary*, 63.

197. Pavlov, *Leningrad 1941: The Blockade*, 72.

198. Belozerov, "Protivopravnye deistviia," 258 and Ganzenmüller, *Das belagerte Leningrad*, 267.

199. Bernev, Chernov, et al., *Blokadnye dnevniki i dokumenty*, 6–8.

200. Kochina, *Blockade Diary*, 46–47.

201. Ibid., 66.

202. Ibid., 78–83.

203. Belozerov, "Protivopravnye deistviia," 260; Bilenko, *Na bessmennom postu*, 31;

and Skriabin and Savchenko, *Neprimirimost'*, 171. The latter two references are cited in Piterkin, "Leningradskie pozharnye komandy."

204. The authors use "cannibalism" to mean the eating of human flesh, which is synonymous with the Russian *liudoedstvo* (people eating) and *trupoedstvo* (corpse eating). Russians tend to use *kannibalizm* to mean the crime of murder and consumption of the victim's flesh.

205. From "The Donner Party" broadcast on the PBS television series "American Experience" on 21 July 2003. Recent research, however, suggests that it was not members of the Donner family who consumed human flesh. See Sonner, "Scientists: Donner Family Not Cannibals."

206. See chap. 43 ("The Leningrad Apocalypse") of Salisbury's *The 900 Days*. The "Senny" market referred to in Document 40 is the Haymarket.

207. Vinokurov was executed in March 1943 for treason, based on the contention that he intended to defect to enemy lines, and counterrevolutionary agitation. His diary was seized during the search of his flat. The fact that the entry cited here was underlined by an NKVD investigator suggests that it was used to substantiate the charges against him. He was rehabilitated in 1999, when the charges against him were reviewed and deemed to be unsubstantiated (Bernev, Chernov, et al., *Blokadnye dnevniki i dokumenty*, 236–37, 253).

208. Salisbury, *The 900 Days*, 479 and Arkhiv UFSB RF po SPb i LO f. 21/12, op. 2, p.n. 19, d. 12, l. 299.

209. S. Voloshin recorded this event in the issue of the commemorative newspaper *Kresty* described above.

210. Yershov, "Soviet War Preparation in 1941," 40.

211. TsGAIPD SPb f. 4000, op. 10, d. 820, l. 8.

212. TsGAIPD SPb f. 4000, op. 10, d. 903, ll. 41–41a.

213. Arkhiv UFSB RF po SPb i LO f. 21/12, op. 2, p.n. 19, d. 12, in Lomagin, *Neizvestnaia blokada*, vol. 2, 282, 301, 322 and Belozerov, "Protivopravnye deistviia," 259.

214. A more recent example of cannibalism as a calculated, rational choice began to unfold on 12 October 1972, when an airplane carrying forty-five Uruguayans, including a team of Catholic rugby players, crashed in the Andes Mountains. Sixteen of the passengers survived for seventy-two days, primarily through eating the corpses of those killed in the crash. One survivor likened their ordeal to the Christian act of communion—the sacrifice of one to save many others.

215. Likhachev, *Reflections on the Russian Soul*, 234.

216. Dzeniskevich, *Na grani zhizni i smerti*, 104–7.

217. Lomagin, *Neizvestnaia blokada*, vol. 2, 297, 323; Reid, *Leningrad*, 291.

218. See above, chapter 1, note 91.

219. As noted above, the first arrests for cannibalism actually occurred in November.

220. The reason for the discrepancy between this figure and the figure cited above of 43 arrests for cannibalism in December, when the corresponding figures in the two reports for January are identical, is unclear.

221. The reason for the discrepancy in data between this report and Kubatkin's report of 23 February noted above is not clear. Kubatkin's data may include cases from blockaded territory outside Leningrad.

222. Piterkin, "Leningradskie pozharnye komandy," 140.

223. The authors of this study decided that due to the gruesome nature of the crimes described in documents 54 and 55, they would identify the arrestees, convicts, and victims only by the first letter of their surnames.

224. Those three had Russian surnames.

225. Kochina, *Blockade Diary,* 72.

226. Yershov, "Soviet War Preparation in 1941," 66-67.

227. Dzeniskevich, *Leningrad v osade,* 461.

228. Arkhiv UFSB RF po SPb i LO f. 21/12, op. 2, p.n. 19, d. 12, l. 291, in Lomagin, *Neizvestnaia blokada,* vol. 2, 323.

229. Dzeniskevich, *Leningrad v osade,* 17, 433.

230. For an example, see Salisbury, *The 900 Days,* 480.

231. Arkhiv UFSB RF po SPb i LO f. 21/12, op. 2, p.n. 19, d. 12, l. 175, in Lomagin, *V tiskakh goloda,* 199-200.

232. Based on Russian published accounts, Boterbloem (*The Life and Times of Andrei Zhdanov,* 237) and Broekmeyer (*Stalin, the Russians, and Their War,* 77) assert that all cannibals who were caught were executed.

233. Lomagin, *V tiskakh goloda,* 194, 206, 216.

234. Lomagin, *Neizvestnaia blokada,* vol. 2, 329, 335, 347.

235. Dzeniskevich, *Na grani zhizni i smerti,* 106.

236. See Katherine Currie's notes on a lecture that Pevzner gave at Indiana University on 8 October 1996 (www.crees.ku.edu/teachers/documents/SectionIII.pdf).

237. This is the title of chap. 11 of their book, *Blokadnaia kniga.*

238. Titova, "Smiles and Sorrow."

239. Adamovich and Granin, *A Book of the Blockade,* 419-20.

240. Kochina, *Blockade Diary,* 71-72.

241. See Petrovskaya Wayne's memoir, *Shurik.*

242. Magaeva, "Physiological and Psychosomatic Prerequisites for Survival and Recovery," 127.

243. Ibid., 132, 141.

244. Ibid., 138, 139, 148, 149.

245. Ibid., 140, 142.

246. Ibid., 140, 141.

CHAPTER 5. THE POPULAR MOOD

1. Some of the ideas and a number of examples in this chapter were explored in Bidlack, "The Political Mood in Leningrad."

2. The NKVD, however, did keep track of the percentage of letters sent through the mail that were not delivered because they purportedly contained "defeatist" sentiment.

3. Goure, *The Siege of Leningrad,* 80-81.

4. TsGAIPD SPb f. 408, op. 1, d. 1115, ll. 29, 32; Salisbury, *The 900 Days,* 120; Goure, *The Siege of Leningrad,* 22.

5. See Dzeniskevich, "The Social and Political Situation in Leningrad," 71.

6. TsGAIPD SPb f. 408, op. 1, d. 1115, ll. 11, 32. See discussion below on the upsurge in anti-Semitism around the start of the blockade.

7. Bidlack, *Workers at War* (1987), 50.

8. Bidlack, "The Political Mood in Leningrad," 99; TsGAIPD SPb f. 25, op. 10, d. 261, l. 37; Kriukovskikh et al., *V gody surovykh ispytanii,* 100.

9. Bidlack, "The Political Mood in Leningrad," 100.

10. Werth, *Russia at War,* 344.

11. Kripton, *Osada Leningrada,* 85-86, cited in Bidlack, "The Political Mood in Leningrad," 99-100.

12. Bidlack, "The Political Mood in Leningrad," 100 and "Workers at War" (1987), 52. John Barber's description of popular reactions in Moscow to the start of the war reveals a similar combination of enthusiastic willingness and reluctance to join the *opolchenie*, which was formed starting on 2 July (Barber, "Popular Reactions in Moscow," 3, 5 and Kozlov, *Velikaia Otechestvennaia voina*, 478–79).

13. TsGAIPD SPb f. 25, op. 10, d. 279, ll. 18–20.

14. TsGAIPD SPb f. 1012, op. 3, d. 53, l. 231.

15. TsGAIPD SPb f. 25, op. 10, d. 279, ll. 18–20.

16. Arkhiv UFSB RF po SPb i LO f. 12, op. 2, p.n. 5, l. 19.

17. TsGAIPD SPb f. 24, op. 2v, d. 4819, l. 23.

18. TsGAIPD f. 1012, op. 3, d. 53, l. 114. Ivanova's fate was not disclosed in the report.

19. TsGAIPD SPb f. 1012, op. 3, d. 53, ll. 6–9.

20. TsGAIPD SPb f. 24, op. 2v, d. 4819, ll. 1–4, 48.

21. TsGAIPD SPb f. 1012, op. 3, d. 53, ll. 6–7.

22. TsGAIPD SPb f. 24, op. 2v, d. 4882, ll. 1–2.

23. Werth, *Russia at War*, 356.

24. Goure, *The Siege of Leningrad*, 135.

25. TsGAIPD SPb f. 1012, op. 3, d. 53, l. 40.

26. TsGAIPD SPb f. 24, op. 2b, d. 970, ll. 15–16. At first, he was charged only with hooliganism, but that was later changed to anti-Soviet agitation.

27. TsGAIPD SPb f. 1012, op. 3, d. 53, l. 10.

28. Goure, *The Siege of Leningrad*, 80.

29. TsGAIPD SPb f. 1012, op. 3, d. 53, l. 48.

30. TsGAIPD SPb f. 408, op. 2, d. 44, ll. 20–21.

31. Lomagin, *Neizvestnaia blokada*, vol. 1, 225.

32. TsGAIPD SPb f. 408, op. 1, d. 1115, ll. 4, 8.

33. Arkhiv UFSB RF po SPb i LO f. 12, op. 2, p.n. 5, l. 11.

34. Arkhiv UFSB RF po SPb i LO, f. 12, op. 2, p.n. 5, l. 28.

35. Davies, *Popular Opinion in Stalin's Russia*, 85.

36. Lomagin, "Upravlenie NKVD," 329–30.

37. For the controversy over official classification of anti-Semitic speech, see above, pp. 223–25.

38. TsGAIPD SPb f. 24, op. 2b, d. 970, l. 30.

39. TsGAIPD SPb f. 417, op. 3, d. 85, l. 50; d. 34, ll. 2–3.

40. A sardonic insinuation that official quotas for Jews from the late Imperial period now applied to Russians.

41. Simmons and Perlina, *Writing the Siege of Leningrad*, 25–29.

42. TsGAIPD SPb f. 24, op. 2b, d. 991, ll. 1–3.

43. Lomagin, *Neizvestnaia blokada*, vol. 2, 121.

44. According to the YIVO Institute, in the national censuses of 1937, only 17.4 percent of Soviet Jews admitted to being believers. On the night of 11–12 April 1941, Passover Eve, about six hundred men went to the synagogue, which SVB observers estimated was 65–70 percent full (TsGAIPD SPb f. 4000, op. 10, d. 279, ll. 1–2).

45. See the collection of first-hand accounts contained in Aizenshtat, *Kniga zhivykh*.

46. Rambow, "The Siege of Leningrad," 166–67, 170. The most recent study of Soviet reporting on the Holocaust is Berkhoff's excellent article "'Total Annihilation of the Jewish Population.'" The quote from "Petrov" is found on page 72.

47. Bidlack, "Workers at War" (1987), 157.

48. TsGAIPD SPb f. 1012, op. 3, d. 53, l. 173.

49. TsGAIPD SPb f. 24, op. 2v, d. 4819, l. 68. In November a Soviet radio broadcast, heard in Leningrad, reportedly stated that fifty-two thousand Jews had been executed in Kiev (l. 97).

50. German leaflets circulated in Leningrad, albeit in small numbers, as early as late September 1941 (Lomagin, *Neizvestnaia blokada,* vol. 2, 110).

51. Lomagin, "Upravlenie NKVD," 330-31.

52. Goure, *The Siege of Leningrad,* 126.

53. TsGAIPD SPb f. 24, op. 2v, d. 4819, l. 72.

54. TsGAIPD SPb f. 1012, op. 3, d. 53, l. 159.

55. TsGAIPD SPb f. 24, op. 2v, d. 4819, l. 3.

56. 4.3 percent of party documents were lost in Kolpino in the first year of the war. (TsGAIPD SPb f. 24, op. 2v, d. 5761, l. 149).

57. TsGAIPD SPb f. 24, op. 2v, d. 4819, l. 36.

58. TsGAIPD SPb f. 417, op. 3, d. 34, ll. 8-9.

59. TsGAIPD SPb f. 24, op. 2v, d. 4819, l. 38. The report on the "Bolshevik" worker did not claim that his act was deceptive; however, the fact that his comment was included in the report strongly suggests that he was not believed.

60. TsGAIPD SPb f. 24, op. 2v, d. 4819, l. 3.

61. Goure, *The Siege of Leningrad,* 125.

62. TsGAIPD SPb f. 417, op. 3, d. 34, ll. 9-11.

63. TsGAIPD SPb f. 24, op. 2v, d. 4819, ll. 39-40.

64. One of the factories that received electricity the longest was the Kirov plant. It continued major operations until 20 December (Bidlack, "Workers at War" [1987], 146-47).

65. Lomagin, *Neizvestnaia blokada,* 2d ed., vol. 1, 322-23 and vol. 2, 251.

66. Lomagin, *Neizvestnaia blokada,* vol. 2, 170.

67. By contrast, another report claims that only 85 people arrested for anti-Soviet agitation were sent to the Military Tribunal between 23 June and 20 July (TsGAIPD SPb f. 24, op. 2v, d. 5125, l. 47).

68. From the start of the war through 25 October 1941, on average there were twenty-seven KR arrests per day (Lomagin, *Neizvestnaia blokada,* vol. 1, 323).

69. Arkhiv UFSB RF po SPb i LO f. 21/12, op. 2, p.n. 11, t. 1, d. 4, l. 82.

70. TsGAIPD SPb f. 24, op. 2v, d. 4921, l. 2.

71. According to Lomagin in a roundtable session on "Assessing the Popular Mood in Stalin's Russia," at the 2005 annual convention of the American Association for the Advancement of Slavic Studies.

72. Bidlack, "The Political Mood in Leningrad," 105-6. Starving teenage industrial students and workers are discussed above, pp. 278, 286.

73. TsGAIPD SPb f. 1012, op. 3, d. 53, l. 89.

74. TsGAIPD SPb f. 1012, op. 3, d. 53, ll. 146-50.

75. Lomagin, *Neizvestnaia blokada,* vol. 1, 281 and Arkhiv UFSB RF po SPb i LO f. 21/12, op. 2, p.n. 11, t. 1, d. 4, ll. 88, 97.

76. Lomagin, *Neizvestnaia blokada,* vol. 2, 280, 294.

77. Ibid., 286.

78. Ibid., 281.

79. Kochina, *Blockade Diary,* 70.

80. Ginzburg, *Blockade Diary,* 48.

81. TsGAIPD SPb f. 1012, op. 3, d. 53, l. 29.

82. TsGAIPD SPb f. 1012, op. 3, d. 53, ll. 267–68.

83. Bidlack, "Workers at War" (1987), 151–52.

84. TsGAIPD SPb f. 1012, op. 3, d. 138, l. 16.

85. TsGAIPD SPb f. 1012, op. 3, d. 143, ll. 2–3, 75a–76.

86. TsGAIPD SPb f. 1012, op. 3, d. 138, l. 54.

87. TsGAIPD SPb f. 24, op. 2v, d. 5771, ll. 5–6.

88. TsGAIPD SPb f. 1012, op. 3, d. 53, l. 236.

89. TsGAIPD SPb f. 24, op. 2v, d. 5760, l. 8.

90. TsGAIPD SPb f. 24, op. 2v, d. 4819, l. 92.

91. TsGAIPD SPb f. 1012, op. 3, d. 53, l. 270.

92. The main task of the four *Einsatzgruppen* was to eliminate Jews, Gypsies, and commissars, among others, in the USSR. The largest contingent in *Einsatzgruppe* A were members of the Waffen-SS (Edeiken, "An Introduction to the Einsatzgruppen").

93. Lomagin, *Neizvestnaia blokada*, vol. 2, 189. As was generally the case with German intelligence reports on besieged Leningrad, specific sources of information were not cited.

94. TsGAIPD SPb f. 24, op. 2v, d. 5760, ll. 8, 14.

95. TsGAIPD SPb f. 1012, op. 3, d. 138, ll. 24–25.

96. TsGAIPD SPb f. 24, op. 2v, d. 5760, ll. 35, 37.

97. Ganzenmüller, *Das belagerte Leningrad,* 320–21.

98. Burov, *Blokada den' za dnem,* 212.

99. See Lisa Kirschenbaum's detailed study, *The Legacy of the Siege of Leningrad.*

100. The underlining is in Zhdanov's copy of the report.

101. Located east of Kharkov.

102. TsGAIPD SPb f. 24, op. 2v, d. 5761, ll. 109–10.

103. The underlining is in Zhdanov's copy of the report.

104. Later renamed Moskovsky Prospect.

105. This is presumably a reference to Leningrad's prewar population.

106. Werth, *Russia at War,* 377–82.

107. TsGAIPD SPb f. 24, op. 2v, d. 5761, ll. 65, 68.

108. Lomagin et al., *Mezhdunarodnoe polozhenie glazami leningradtsev,* 48–60.

109. TsGAIPD SPb f. 24, op. 2v, d. 5761, ll. 104–5.

110. Lomagin, *Neizvestnaia blokada,* vol. 2, 379.

111. Lomagin et al., *Mezhdunarodnoe polozhenie glazami leningradtsev,* 44.

112. Lomagin, *Neizvestnaia blokada,* vol. 2, 388.

113. Dzeniskevich, *Leningrad v osade,* 485.

114. Ibid., 479–81, 602 and Lomagin, *Neizvestnaia blokada,* vol. 2, 395–97.

115. Lomagin, *Neizvestnaia blokada,* 2d ed., vol. 1, 402.

116. Lomagin, *Neizvestnaia blokada,* vol. 2, 397.

117. Lomagin, *Neizvestnaia blokada,* 2d ed., vol. 1, 409–13.

118. Bidlack, "Workers at War" (1987); *Propaganda i agitatsiia,* 1943, No. 10.

119. TsGAIPD SPb f. 24, op. 2v, d. 6259, ll. 67–70.

120. Arkhiv UFSB f. 12, op. 2, p.n. 31, d. 5, l. 62.

121. TsGAIPD SPb f. 24, op. 2v, d. 6259, ll. 22–24.

122. Dzeniskevich, *Leningrad v osade,* 482.

123. Ibid., 602.

124. TsGAIPD SPb f. 24, op. 2v, d. 6260, l. 159.

CHAPTER 6. THE QUESTION OF ORGANIZED OPPOSITION

1. Lomagin, "Upravlenie NKVD," 370.

2. Arkhiv UFSB f. 12, op. 2, p.n. 31, d. 5, ll. 70–71.

3. The manuscript, typed in Russian with an English title, "Soviet War Preparation in 1941," is part of the "Research Program on the USSR" collection of the Bakhmeteff Archive. The scene described is from pages 76 to 79. The title and name "Vasily Yershov" were written in English in pencil on the first page of the manuscript. This is the same person who described NKVD control in Military Hospital No. 268 and the relative abundance of food at Smolny; see above, pp. 249–50, 301.

4. Bidlack first reported on this alleged incident in "Survival Strategies in Leningrad," 100–101.

5. See Lomagin, *V tiskakh goloda*, 105, 109, 289.

6. Salisbury, *The 900 Days*, 170.

7. Goure, *The Siege of Leningrad*, 116–17.

8. Arkhiv UFSB RF po SPb i LO f. 12, op. 58, p.n. 19, t. 2, l. 49.

9. Goure, *The Siege of Leningrad*, 117.

10. Jansen and Petrov, *Stalin's Loyal Executioner*, ix.

11. It was located southwest of Leningrad right next to the front but seems to have been at least partly relocated in September 1941. See Dexter and Rodionov, *The Factories, Research and Design Establishments of the Soviet Defence Industry*.

12. Arkhiv UFSB RF po SPb i LO f. 21/12, op. 2, p.n. 11, t. 1, d. 4, ll. 88–89.

13. Lomagin, "Upravlenie NKVD," 348–52.

14. Ibid., 335–36.

15. Ibid., 360.

16. Each of the other five cases reviewed by the NKVD special commission consisted of no more than three people. In the "Geography" case, the special commission decided that LGU senior lecturer Sedychenkov, who had been arrested for organized KR activity (article 58-11), could not be considered a participant in a KR organization, because he had been induced to agree to take part in an NKVD provocation to engage in KR activity by the promise of extra food.

17. In a report to Beria, Merkulov, Zhdanov, Kuznetsov, and Leningrad Front commander Khozin from 5 January 1942, Kubatkin stated that "Activist" Gul was agitating among intellectuals for the formation of an autonomous Ukraine as a German protectorate. This report does not mention Nikiforov (Arkhiv UFSB RF po SPb i LO f. 21/12, op. 2, p.n. 11, t. 1, d. 4, l.77). Document 61, dating from 16 February 1942, alludes to an earlier report to Beria on both Nikiforov and Gul.

18. It is not clear whether this is a reference to the chemist Mikhail Platonov, whose case is discussed below.

19. The description of the Platonov case is based on Bernev and Lomagin, "Delo professora M. S. PLATONOVA." See also the description of Platonov's arrest in Arkhiv UFSB RF po SPb i LO f. 21/12, op. 2, p.n. 11, t. 1, d. 4, l. 89.

20. However, as shown below, at least one was mysteriously pardoned in September 1942 but continued to be confined in a labor camp.

21. The Zeiss company had an assembly shop in St. Petersburg before World War I. Ignatovsky had worked as an engineer in Germany from 1908 to 1914 (Ganzenmüller, *Das Belagerte Leningrad*, 307–8).

22. Arkhiv UFSB RF po SPb i LO f. 21/12, op. 2, p.n. 11, t. 1, d. 4, l. 31. An informant's report on Dukhon made its way into a survey of popular mood compiled by Ku-

batkin on 12 January 1942. Dukhon is quoted as stating that Leningrad's leaders did not care that thousands were perishing daily. He reportedly added that a small group could carry out a successful revolt (Lomagin, *Neizvestnaia blokada,* vol. 2, 272–73).

23. Grakina, *Uchenye Rossii v gody Velikoi Otechestvennoi voiny,* 63.

24. Brandenberger, *National Bolshevism,* 318 n. 61.

25. TsGAIPD SPb f. 24, op. 2b, d. 1324, ll. 7–11.

26. TsGAIPD SPb f. 24, op. 2b, d. 1324, ll. 7–11. Thirteen recent recipients of Stalin prizes were acclaimed academics who had previous convictions for KR or similar crimes.

27. Those arrested in the SPO investigation described above may have been included in this tally.

28. Rollins, "Tarle, Evgenii Viktorovich," 179–80; Brandenberger, *National Bolshevism,* 83, 170, 299; Margolis et al., *Leningradskii universitet v Velikoi Otechestvennoi voine,* 189, 192, 253–54; Kaganovich, *Evgenii Viktorovich Tarle,* 74–75; *Leningradskaia pravda,* 18 July 1941; and Kozlov, *Velikaia Otechestvennaia voina,* 707–8.

29. Arkhiv UFSB RF po SPb i LO, f. 21/12, op. 2, p.n. 11, t. 1, d. 4, l. 46.

30. Ibid., l. 74.

31. Only one Leningrad NKVD official, I. V. Podchasov, participated in both inquiries. He was an observing NKVD department head in the May 1942 investigation of the SPO and one of the KRO officers expelled from the party by the KPK in 1958.

32. This Merkulov is not to be confused with Beria's first deputy, V. N. Merkulov, who became *narkom* of the NKGB when it split off from the NKVD in 1943; however, it is possible that they were related. Although V. N. Merkulov was replaced in May 1946 by V. S. Abakumov, he subsequently held several nationally prominent posts until his arrest on 18 September 1953. Merkulov was executed along with Beria and Abakumov after Stalin's death.

33. Dzeniskevich, *Leningrad v osade,* 599 and Reznikova, "Repressii v period blokady Leningrada," 104–9. One account claims that both Ignatovskys were executed on 8 January; however, Document 66 shows that M. I. Ignatovskaia was still being interrogated after that date (Grakina, *Uchenye Rossii v gody Velikoi Otechestvennoi voiny,* 118). Several of the accused were sentenced to death between 23 and 25 April and had those sentences reduced on 28 May.

34. When Koshliakov was arrested in January 1942, he "confessed" to being one of the initiators of the Committee and of recruiting another eleven scholars to it. Koshliakov also admitted to preparing for a meeting with German occupiers of Leningrad and to conducting defeatist agitation. (Berezhkov, *Piterskie prokuratory,* 218).

35. In addition to the list of those who died provided at the end of Document 66, Senior Lecturer Stroganov and Professor Izvekov died in 1942 while under arrest (Berezhkov, *Piterskie prokuratory,* 218).

36. Reznikova, "Repressii v period blokady Leningrada," 104, 109.

37. After the war, Kruzhkov became head of the Ministry of Internal Affairs (MVD) in Novgorod but was sentenced to twenty years imprisonment on 28 October 1955 for falsifying evidence. He was released early in 1962 and worked in a radio factory in Novgorod until his death in 1966 (ibid., 106–7).

38. Zaleskii, *Imperiia Stalina,* 310–11; Reznikova, "Repressii v period blokady Leningrada," 104–9, and Lorentz, "Mathematics and Politics in the Soviet Union from 1928 to 1953," 36. Lorentz was one of Koshliakov's students prior to the start of the siege. He later taught mathematics at the University of Texas at Austin.

39. Kutuzov and Stepanov, "Organy gosbezopasnosti," 225.

40. Like the members of the Leningrad NKVD KRO, Ogoltsov was expelled from the Communist Party in 1958. He was lucky to have lived that long. He had escaped Kubatkin's fate in the "Leningrad Affair" and the execution of top security personnel following Stalin's death. Shortly after Stalin's death, Ogoltsov was sacked from the post of first deputy in the MGB, and on 3 April 1953, he was charged with the murder of Jewish theater director and actor Solomon Mikhoels, who had served as the head of the Jewish Anti-Fascist Committee during the war. However, on 6 August, following the arrest of Beria, Ogoltsov was fully rehabilitated and freed. On 14 February 1958, the PKP expelled him from the party for his role in the unlawful purge of the Leningrad intellectuals. The following year he was stripped of military rank and government awards. He died in 1976.

41. TsGAIPD SPb f. 24, op. 2b, d. 1324, ll. 65–69.

42. Reznikova, "Repressii v period blokady Leningrada," 106.

43. Quoted text is from Kubatkin's order as reported by Berezhkov in *Piterskie prokuratory*, 217.

44. Gross, *Neighbors*, 164–65.

45. Berezhkov, *Piterskie prokuratory*, 220.

46. The source for the quoted testimony in this document is unclear as the citations are incomplete.

47. Beria attributed the quoted words to Koshliakov (Beria, *Beria, My Father*, 74).

48. Ibid., 74.

49. Ibid.

50. Probably the most provocative assertion that Sergo Beria made, which most historians do not believe to be true, is that Robert Oppenheimer visited the Beria family in the USSR for two weeks at the end of 1939 to propose that the USSR undertake a project to build an atomic bomb (Beriia, *Moi otets—Lavrentii Beriia*, 288–89).

51. Ibid., 91–92.

52. Ibid.

53. Though cleared of their crimes at that time, they were officially reinstated into the party only in 1987–88.

54. Reznikova, "Repressii v period blokady Leningrada," p. 106 and Lorentz, "Mathematics and Politics in the Soviet Union, 1928 to 1953," 36.

55. Dzeniskevich, *Leningrad v osade*, 599.

56. The refusal to clear people of charges that were known to be unsubstantiated is reflected in another wartime case. In the summer of 1941, Aleksandr Maltsev of the All-Union Academy of Agricultural Sciences and Nikolai Kovalev, a doctoral candidate in the same field, were arrested and charged with participating in an anti-Soviet organization for allegedly supporting Nikolai Vavilov, a world-renowned geneticist, who had criticized Trofim Lysenko's officially approved, but scientifically unsupported, theories in genetics. (Vavilov had been arrested in August 1940 and perished in the Kolyma camps.) Maltsev and Kovalev were exiled to Cheliabinsk *oblast'* and their cases were sent by the VP to the Special Board of the USSR NKVD in Moscow. On 25 March 1942, however, due to lack of evidence against them, their dossiers were handed over to the Cheliabinsk NKVD. Nevertheless, in April 1945, the two scholars were exiled once again, this time to northern Kazakhstan for five years. In 1956, the Leningrad city court cleared them of all charges. (Berezhkov, *Piterskie prokuratory*, 208, and Zalesskii, *Imperiia Stalina*, 80).

CONCLUSIONS

1. Salisbury stated that Leningrad's fall would benefit Malenkov and Molotov in their rivalry with Zhdanov and that Stalin was under pressure to abandon the city, possibly from Malenkov and Molotov (*The 900 Days,* 266, 268).

2. Dzeniskevich, *Voennaia piatiletka,* 115.

3. Overy, *Russia's War,* 122.

4. Kubatkin may have wanted to use the *partkom* to punish the head of the SPO investigative unit for going over his head and communicating directly with Beria.

5. As a result, the NKVD was forced to recruit factory workers for sentry duty in some munitions factories (Ganzenmüller, *Das belagerte Leningrad,* 156).

6. Lomagin, *Neizvestnaia blokada,* vol. 2, 427.

Bibliography of Sources Cited

Primary Sources

RUSSIAN ARCHIVES AND LIBRARIES

St. Petersburg

TsGAIPD SPb—Central State Archive of Historical-Political Documents, St. Petersburg

    f. 24: Leningrad *obkom*

    f. 25: Leningrad *gorkom*

    f. 408: Dzerzhinskii *raikom*

    f. 417: Kirovskii *raikom*

    f. 1012: Kirov factory

    f. 1728: Communist Party personnel files, 1917–50

    f. 4000: Institute of the History of the Party of the Leningrad *obkom,* branch of the Institute of Marxism-Leninism of the Central Committee of the Communist Party of the Soviet Union

Arkhiv UFSB RF po SPb i LO—Archive of the Directorate of the Federal Security Service of the Russian Federation for St. Petersburg and the Leningrad *Oblast'*

    f. 8: Correspondence of the Leningrad Regional Directorate of the NKVD (UNKVD LO) with NKVD headquarters in Moscow on operational work

    f. 12: Correspondence of the UNKVD LO with the Military Council of the Leningrad Front, the Military Prosecutor's Office, and the Military Tribunal

    f. 21/12: Special reports of the UNKVD LO to NKVD headquarters in Moscow

TsGA SPb—Central State Archive, St. Petersburg

    f. 7384: Executive Committee of the Leningrad City Council (*Lengorispolkom*)

TsGAKFFD SPb—Central State Archive of Film, Photographic, and Phonographic Documents, St. Petersburg

BAN—Russian Academy of Sciences Library

RNB—Russian National Library

Moscow

RGASPI—Russian State Archive of Social and Political History
    f. 77: Personnel file of Andrei Zhdanov
    f. 644: State Defense Committee
GARF—State Archive of the Russian Federation
    f. 8131: Office of the Public Prosecutor of the USSR, 1924-1991
RGB—Russian State Library

Podolsk

TsAMO RF—Central Archive of the Ministry of Defense of the Russian Federation
    f. 217: Northern and Leningrad Fronts

OTHER ARCHIVES

U.S. National Archives
Bakhmeteff Archive, Columbia University
Churchill Archives Centre

MUSEUMS IN ST. PETERSBURG

GMMOBL—State Memorial Museum of the Defense and Blockade of Leningrad
GMISPb—State Museum of the History of St. Petersburg

PUBLISHED DOCUMENT COLLECTIONS

Afanas'ev, Iu. N. et al., eds., *Istoriia stalinskogo GULAGa: Konets 1920kh-pervaia polo-vina 1950kh godov. Sobranie dokumentov.* 7 volumes (Moscow: Rosspen, 2004-5).

Bernev, S. K., S. V. Chernov et al., eds., *Blokadnye dnevniki i dokumenty* (St. Petersburg: Evropeiskii dom, 2004).

Bernev, S. K. and N. A. Lomagin, eds., *Plan "D": Plan spetsial'nykh meropriiatii, provo-dimykh vo vremia Otechestvennoi voiny po obshchegorodskim ob"ektam gor. Leningrada* (St. Petersburg: Evropeiskii dom, 2005).

Bugai, N. F., ed., *Iosif Stalin—Lavrentiiu Berii: "Ikh nado deportirovat'": Dokumenty, fakty, kommentarii* (Moscow: Druzhba narodov, 1992).

Cherepenina, N. Iu. and M. V. Shkarovskii, eds., *Sankt-Peterburgskaia eparkhiia v dvad-tsatom veke v svete arkhivnykh materialov, 1917-1941: Sbornik dokumentov* (St. Petersburg: Liki Rossii, 2000).

Dymshits, A. et al., eds., *Podvig Leningrada: Dokumental'no-khudozhestvennyi sbornik* (Moscow: Voennoe izdatel'stvo Ministerstva Oborony Soiuza SSR, 1960).

Dzeniskevich, A. R., ed., *Iz raionov oblasti soobshchaiut . . . : Svobodnye ot okkupatsii raiony Leningradskoi oblasti v gody Velikoi Otechestvennoi voiny, 1941-1945: Sbornik dokumentov* (St. Petersburg: "Dmitrii Bulanin," 2006).

———, ed., *Leningrad v osade: Sbornik dokumentov o geroicheskoi oborone Leningrada v gody Velikoi Otechestvennoi voiny, 1941-1944* (St. Petersburg: Liki Rossii, 1995).

Eroshin, V. P., ed., *Organy gosudarstvennoi bezopasnosti SSSR v Velikoi Otechestvennoi voine: Sbornik dokumentov,* vol. 2, bk. 1: *Nachalo: 22 iiunia-31 avgusta 1941 goda,* and vol. 2, bk. 2: *Nachalo: 1 sentiabria-31 dekabria 1941 goda* (Moscow: "Izdatel'stvo 'Rus'," 2000).

Filonov, M. D., ed., *Leningrad za 50 let* (Leningrad: Lenizdat, 1967).

Grodzinskii, M. M., ed., *Trudovoe zakonodatel'stvo voennogo vremeni: Sbornik* (Moscow: VTSSPS Profizdat, 1943).

Knyshevskii, P. N. et al., eds., *Skrytaia pravda voiny: 1941 god. Neizvestnye dokumenty* (Moscow: Russkaia kniga, 1992).

Krivosheev, G. F., *Grif sekretnosti sniat: Poteri vooruzhennykh sil SSSR v voinakh, boevykh deistviiakh i voennykh konfliktakh* (Moscow: Voennoe izdatel'stvo, 1993).

Lomagin, Nikita Andreevich, ed., *Neizvestnaia blokada (Dokumenty, prilozheniia)*, vol. 2 (St. Petersburg and Moscow: Dom "Neva" and "OLMA-PRESS," 2002). This work reprints the documents from *V tiskakh goloda*. A second edition, published in 2004, is identical to the original edition.

———, ed., *V tiskakh goloda: Blokada Leningrada v dokumentakh germanskikh spets-sluzhb i NKVD* (St. Petersburg: Evropeiskii dom, 2000).

Lomagin, N. A. et al., eds., *Mezhdunarodnoe polozhenie glazami leningradtsev, 1941–1945 (Iz Arkhiva Upravleniia Federal'noi Sluzhby Bezopasnosti po g. Sankt-Peterburgu i Leningradskoi oblasti)* (St. Petersburg: Evropeiskii dom, 1996).

Sbornik ukazov, postanovlenii, reshenii, rasporiazhenii i prikazov voennogo vremeni, 1941–1942 (Leningrad: Lenizdat, 1942).

Shkarovskii, M. V., ed., "V ogne voiny: Russkaia pravoslavnaia tserkov' v 1941–1945 gg. (po materialam Leningradskoi eparkhii)," in *Russkoe proshloe*, vol. 5 (1994), 259–316.

Tokarev, Iu. S. et al., eds., *Deviat'sot geroicheskikh dnei* (Moscow: Nauka, 1967).

Volkovskii, N. L., ed., *Blokada Leningrada v dokumentakh rassekrechennykh arkhivov* (Moscow and St. Petersburg: Poligon, 2004).

REFERENCE WORKS

Leningrad 1940: Adresno-spravochnaia kniga (Leningrad: Lenizdat, 1940).

WARTIME PERIODICALS

Biulleten' Leningradskogo soveta deputatov trudiashchikhsia
Leningradskaia pravda
Propaganda i agitatsiia (Leningrad)

DIARIES AND MEMOIRS

Adamovich, Ales' and Daniil Granin, *Blokadnaia kniga* (Moscow: Sovetskii pisatel', 1982). An earlier edition was published in 1979.

———, *A Book of the Blockade*, translated by Hilda Perham (Moscow: Raduga, 1983).

Aizenshtat, L. A. et al., eds., *Kniga zhivykh: Vospominaniia evreev-frontovikov, uznikov getto i kontslagerei, boitsov partizanskikh otriadov, zhitelei blokadnogo Leningrada* (St. Petersburg: Akropol', 1995).

Beria, Sergo, *Beria, My Father: Inside Stalin's Kremlin*, edited by Françoise Thom, translated by Brian Pearce (London: Duckworth, 2001).

———, *Moi otets - Lavrentii Beriia* (Moscow: Sovremennik, 1994).

Boldyrev, A. S., "Doroga na Bol'shuiu zemliu," in P. L. Bogdanov, ed., *Na Doroge zhizni: Vospominaniia o frontovoi Ladoge* (Moscow, 1980).

Churchill, Winston S., *The Second World War*, vol. 3: *The Grand Alliance* (New York: Bantam Books, 1962).

Dedijer, Vladimir, *Tito* (New York: Simon and Schuster, 1953).

Ershov, V., "Rabota NKVD v gospitaliakh vo vremia voiny," in *Novyi Zhurnal* (New York) 37 (1954), 284–89. This is the same person as "Yershov," below.

Ginzburg, Lidiya, *Blockade Diary*, translated by Alan Myers (London: Harvill, 1995).

Herling, Gustaw, *A World Apart*, translated by Andrzej Ciolkosz (New York: Penguin, 1996).

Kochina, Elena, *Blockade Diary*, translated by Samuel C. Ramer (Ann Arbor: Ardis, 1990).

Kulagin, Georgii, *Dnevnik i pamiat': O perezhitom v gody voiny* (Leningrad: Lenizdat, 1978).

Kurikka, Toiva, *Put' iz Finliandii v Sibir'* (St. Petersburg: "Niva," 2003).

Kuznetsov, N. G., "Osazhdennyi Leningrad i Baltiiskii Flot," in *Voprosy istorii*, 40, no. 8 (August 1965), 108–20.

Likhachev, Dmitry, *Reflections on the Russian Soul: A Memoir* (Budapest: Central European University Press, 2000).

Loskutova, Marina, *Pamiat' o blokade: Svidetel'stva ochevidtsev i istoricheskoe soznanie obshchestva. Materialy i issledovaniia* (Moscow: Novoe izdatel'stvo, 2006).

Magayeva, Svetlana and Albert Pleysier, *Surviving the Blockade of Leningrad*, translated and edited by Alexey Vinogradov (Lanham: University Press of America, 2006).

Malenkov, A. G., *O moem ottse Georgii Malenkove* (Moscow: NTTs "Tekhnoekos," 1992).

Mannerheim, Carl Gustaf Emil, *The Memoirs of Marshal Mannerheim* (New York: Dutton, 1954).

Mikoian, Anastas Ivanovich, *Tak bylo: Razmyshleniia o minuvshem* (Moscow: Vagrius, 1999).

———, "V dni blokady," in *Voenno-istorichicheskii zhurnal*, no. 2 (1977), 45–54.

Petrovskaya Wayne, Kyra, *Shurik: A WWII Saga of the Siege of Leningrad* (New York: Lyons, 2000).

Skomorovsky, Boris and E. G. Morris, *The Siege of Leningrad* (New York: Dutton, 1944).

Skrjabina, Elena, *Siege and Survival: The Odyssey of a Leningrader*, translated by Norman Luxemburg (Carbondale: Southern Illinois University Press, 1971).

Vannikov, Boris, "Iz zapisok narkoma vooruzheniia," *Voenno-istoricheskii zhurnal*, no. 2 (1962), 78–88.

Voronov, N. N., "V trudnye vremena," *Voenno-istoricheskii zhurnal*, no. 9 (1961), 67–72.

Werth, Alexander, *Leningrad* (New York: Knopf, 1944).

Yershov, Vasily, "Soviet War Preparation in 1941," Research Program on the USSR, Bakhmeteff Archive, Columbia University, 125 pp. The author of this manuscript, the text of which is in Russian, is the same as "Ershov" above.

Zhukov, G. K., *Marshal of the Soviet Union G. Zhukov: Reminiscences and Reflections*, translated from the 2d edition by Vic Schneierson (Moscow: Progress Publishers, 1985).

———, *Vospominaniia i razmyshleniia*, 11th ed., vol. 2 (Moscow, 1992).

FICTION

Shpanov, N. N., *Pervyi udar* (Moscow: Sovetskii pisatel', 1939).

Secondary Acounts

REFERENCE WORKS

Burov, A. V., *Blokada den' za dnem* (Leningrad: Lenizdat, 1979).

Dear, I. C. B. and M. R. D. Foot, eds., *The Oxford Companion to World War II* (Oxford: Oxford University Press, 1995).

Cherepenina, N. Iu. and M. V. Shkarovskii, eds., *Spravochnik po istorii pravoslavnykh monastyrei i soborov g. Sankt-Peterburga 1917-1945 gg. (po dokumentam TsGA SPb)* (St. Petersburg: DEAN+ADIA-M, 1996).

Kokurin, A. I. and N. V. Petrov, eds., *Lubianka: VChK-OGPU-NKVD-NKGB-MGB-MVD-KGB, 1917-1960. Spravochnik* (Moscow: Materik, 1997).

Kozlov, M. M., ed., *Velikaia Otechestvennaia voina, 1941-1945: Entsiklopediia* (Moscow: "Sovetskaia entsiklopediia," 1985).

Parrish, Michael, *The U.S.S.R. in World War II: An Annotated Bibliography of Books Published in the Soviet Union, 1945-1975* (New York: Garland, 1981).

Petrov, N. V. and K. V. Skorkin, *Kto rukovodil NKVD, 1934-1941: Spravochnik* (Moscow: Zven'ia, 1999).

Zalesskii, K. A., *Imperiia Stalina: Biograficheskii entsiklopedicheskii slovar'* (Moscow: Veche, 2000).

Zaloga, Steven and James Grandsen, *Soviet Tanks and Combat Vehicles of World War II* (London: Arms and Armour Press, 1984).

UNPUBLISHED WORKS

Amosov, "Rabochie Leningrada v gody Velikoi Otechestvennoi voiny" (doctoral candidate dissertation [kand. diss.], Leningrad, 1968).

Arapova, L., "Trudovaia deiatel'nost' leningradtsev v period blokady (1941-1943 gg.)" (kand. diss., Moscow, 1965).

Beizer, M., "The Jewish Minority in Leningrad, 1917-1939," paper presented to the BASEES conference, Cambridge, England, March 1995.

Bernev, S. K. and N. A. Lomagin, "Delo professora M. S. Platonova: Istoriia fal'sifikatsii." (unpublished manuscript).

Bidlack, Richard, "Workers at War: Factory Workers and Labor Policy in the Siege of Leningrad" (Ph.D. dissertation, Indiana University, 1987).

Dzeniskevich, A. R., "'Front u zavodskikh sten': Trudiashchiesia leningradskoi promyshlennosti na zashchite goroda, 1941-1944" (unpublished manuscript, 1992).

———, "Novye dannye o vesne blokadnogo 1942 goda" (unpublished manuscript).

Frolov, M. I., "Istoriia konditerskoi im. N. K. Krupskoi" (part I) (unpublished manuscript).

Hass, Jeffrey K., "Making the Memory of War: Interpretations of War and the Construction of Normality. Lessons from the Siege of Leningrad," conference on "The Known and Unknown about the Siege of Leningrad," St. Petersburg, 2007.

Kats, Ia. F., "Oktiabr'skaia raionnaia partiinaia organizatsiia goroda Leningrada v gody Velikoi Otechestvennoi voiny Sovetskogo Soiuza" (kand. diss., Leningrad, 1958).

Lomagin, Nikita, "The Black Market in Besieged Leningrad: The Soviet Self and Soviet Power in the Context of War," paper presented at the 2009 annual convention of the American Association for the Advancement of Slavic Studies.

———, "Upravlenie NKVD po Leningradskoi oblasti v politicheskom kontrole v period bitvy za Leningrad," 323-72 (unpublished manuscript, was subsequently incorporated into Lomagin, *Leningrad v blokade*).

Piterkin, I. V., "Leningradskie pozharnye komandy" (kand. diss., Leningrad, 1989).

Shvetsov, L. A., "Deiatel'nost' Smol'ninskoi raionnoi partiinoi organizatsii v period blokady goroda Leningrada" (kand. diss., Leningrad, 1966).

BOOKS AND ARTICLES

Afanas'ev, A. V., "Pobeditel'," in *Oni ne molchali*, ed. A. V. Afanas'ev (Moscow: Politizdat, 1991), 388–408.

Andrew, Christopher and Oleg Gordievsky, *KGB: The Inside Story* (New York: Harper-Collins, 1990).

Andrew, Christopher and Vasili Mitrokhin, *The Sword and the Shield: The Mitrokhin Archive and the Secret History of the KGB* (New York: Basic Books, 1999).

Barber, John, "Popular Reactions in Moscow to the German Invasion of June 22, 1941," in *Operation Barbarossa: The German Attack on the Soviet Union, June 22, 1941*, ed. Joseph L. Wieczynski (Salt Lake City: Charles Schlacks Jr., 1993).

Barber, John and Andrei Dzeniskevich, eds., *Life and Death in Besieged Leningrad, 1941–44* (Basingstoke: Palgrave Macmillan, 2005).

Barber, John and Mark Harrison, *The Soviet Home Front, 1941–1945: A Social and Economic History of the USSR in World War II* (London: Longman, 1991).

Bellamy, Chris, *Absolute War: Soviet Russia in the Second World War* (New York: Knopf, 2007).

Belozerov, B. P., "Protivopravnye deistviia i prestupnost' v usloviiakh goloda," in *Zhizn' i smert' v blokirovannom Leningrade: Istoriko-meditsinskii aspekt*, ed. J. D. Barber and A. R. Dzeniskevich (St. Petersburg, 2001), 245–64.

Berezhkov, V. I., *Piterskie prokuratory: Rukovoditeli VChK-MGB, 1918–1954* (St. Petersburg: Russko-Baltiiskii informatsionnyi tsentr BLITS,1998).

Berkhoff, Karel C., "'Total Annihilation of the Jewish Population': The Holocaust in the Soviet Media, 1941–1945," *Kritika: Explorations in Russian and Eurasian History* 10, no. 1 (Winter 2009), 61–105.

Bernev, Stanislav, "Plan 'D,'" *Izvestiia—Sankt-Peterburg*, 8 May 2003.

Bibikov, Iu. and S. Moskalev, *Profsoiuzy Leningrada v gody sovetskoi vlasti, 1917–1959* (Moscow: Profizda, 1960).

Bidlack, Richard, "Lifting the Blockade on the Blockade: New Research on the Siege of Leningrad," *Kritika: Explorations in Russian and Eurasian History* 10, no. 2 (Spring 2009), 333–51.

———, "The Political Mood in Leningrad During the First Year of the Soviet-German War," *Russian Review* 59 (January 2000), 96–113.

———, "Survival Strategies in Leningrad," in *The People's War: Responses to World War II in the Soviet Union*, ed. Robert W. Thurston and Bernd Bonwetsch (Urbana: University of Illinois Press, 2000), pp. 84–107.

———, *Workers at War: Factory Workers and Labor Policy in the Siege of Leningrad*, The Carl Beck Papers in Russian and East European Studies, no. 902 (Pittsburgh: University of Pittsburgh Center for Russian and East European Studies, 1991).

Bidlack, Richard and David Brandenberger, "Contributors' Exchange: The Leningrad Affair Interpreted," *Russian Review* 64, no. 1 (January 2005), 90–97.

Bilenko, S. V., *Na bessmennom postu* (Moscow, 1969).

Boterbloem, Kees, *The Life and Times of Andrei Zhdanov, 1896–1948* (Montreal: McGill-Queens's University Press, 2004).

———, "The Death of Andrei Zhdanov," *Slavic and East European Review* 80, nos. 2–3 (April 2002), 267–87.

Brandenberger, David, "Stalin, the Leningrad Affair, and the Limits of Postwar Russocentrism," *Russian Review* 63 (April 2004), 241–55.

———, *National Bolshevism: Stalinist Mass Culture and the Formation of Modern Russian National Identity, 1931-1956* (Cambridge, Mass.: Harvard University Press, 2002).

Broekmeyer, Marius, *Stalin, the Russians, and Their War,* translated by Rosalind Buck (Madison: University of Wisconsin Press, 2004).

Brooks, Jeffrey, "*Pravda* Goes to War," in *Culture and Entertainment in Wartime Russia,* ed. Richard Stites (Bloomington: Indiana University Press, 1995), 9–27.

Bubis, Edward and Blair A. Ruble, "The Impact of World War II on Leningrad," in *The Impact of World War II on the Soviet Union,* ed. Susan J. Linz (Totowa: Rowman & Allanheld, 1985).

Bychkov, V. C. et al., *Stal' dlia pobedy* (Moscow: Mysl', 1983).

Chaney, Otto, *Zhukov,* rev. ed. (Norman: University of Oklahoma Press, 1996).

Cherepenina, N. Iu., "Golod i smert' v blokirovannom gorode," in *Zhizn' i smert' v blokirovannom Leningrade: Istoriko-meditsinskii aspekt,* ed. J. D. Barber and A. R. Dzeniskevich (St. Petersburg, 2001), 35–80.

Chernov, S. V., *Bol'shoi Dom bez grifa "sekretno"* (St. Petersburg: Izdatel'stvo Rus', 2002).

Coleman, Heather J., *Russian Baptists and Spiritual Revolution, 1905-1929* (Bloomington: Indiana University Press, 2005).

Conquest, Robert, *The Great Terror: Stalin's Purge of the Thirties,* rev. ed. (New York: Collier Books, 1973).

Dale, Robert, "Rats and Resentment: The Demobilization of the Red Army in Postwar Leningrad, 1945-50," *Journal of Contemporary History* 45, no. 1 (2010), 113–33.

Davies, Sarah, *Popular Opinion in Stalin's Russia: Terror, Propaganda, and Dissent, 1934-1941* (Cambridge: Cambridge University Press, 1997).

Davis, Nathaniel, *A Long Walk to Church: A Contemporary History of Russian Orthodoxy* (Boulder: Westview, 1995).

Demidov, V. I. and V. A. Kutuzov, eds., *"Leningradskoe delo"* (Leningrad: Lenizdat, 1990).

Diakin, V. S., ed., *Istoriia rabochikh Leningrada, 1703-1965,* vol. 2 (Leningrad: Nauka, 1972).

Dzeniskevich, A. R., *Na grani zhizni i smerti: Rabota medikov-issledovatelei v osazhdennom Leningrade* (St. Petersburg: Nestor, 2002).

———, "The Social and Political Situation in Leningrad in the First Months of the German Invasion: The Social Psychology of the Workers," translated by Robert W. Thurston, in *The People's War: Responses to World War II in the Soviet Union,* ed. Robert W. Thurston and Bernd Bonwetsch (Urbana: University of Illinois Press, 2000), 71–83.

———, *Blokada i politika: Oborona Leningrada v politicheskoi kon"iunkture* (St. Petersburg: Nestor, 1998).

———, *Front u zavodskikh sten: Maloizuchennye problemy oborony Leningrada, 1941-1944* (St. Petersburg: Nestor, 1998).

———, *Nakanune i v dni ispytanii: Leningradskie rabochie v 1938-1945 gg.* (Leningrad: Nauka, 1990).

———, *Rabochie Leningrada nakanune Velikoi Otechestvennoi voiny, 1938—iiun' 1941 g.* (Leningrad: Nauka, 1983).

———, *Voennaia piatiletka rabochikh Leningrada, 1941-1945* (Leningrad: Lenizdat, 1972).

Figes, Orlando, "Putin vs. the Truth," *New York Review of Books* 56, no. 7 (30 April 2009), accessed online (www.nybooks.com/articles/22642#fn12) 15 July 2009.

Filippov, Aleksandr, *Noveishaia istoriia Rossii, 1945-2006: Kniga dlia uchitelia* (Moscow: Prosveshchie, 2007).

Fischer, Benjamin B., "The Katyn Controversy: Stalin's Killing Field," *Studies in Intelligence* (Winter 1999-2000), 61-70.

Fitzpatrick, Sheila, *Everyday Stalinism: Ordinary Life in Extraordinary Times. Soviet Russia in the 1930s* (New York: Oxford University Press, 1999).

———, *Stalin's Peasants: Resistance and Survival in the Russian Village after Collectivization* (New York: Oxford University Press, 1994).

Freeze, Gregory, "Russian Orthodox Church," in *Encyclopedia of Russian History*, ed. James R. Millar, vol. 3 (New York: Macmillan Reference USA, 2004), 1319-21.

Frolov, M. I., "Zabolevaemost' i smertnost' evakuiruemykh po puti ot Leningrada do Kostromy" in *Zhizn' i smert' v blokirovannom Leningrade: Istoriko-meditsinskii aspekt*, ed. J. D. Barber and A. R. Dzeniskevich (St. Petersburg, 2001), 81-97.

Ganzenmüller, Jörg, *Das belagerte Leningrad, 1941-1944: Die Stadt in den Strategien von Angreifern und Verteidigern* (Paderborn: Ferdinand Schöningh, 2005).

Getty, J. Arch and Oleg V. Naumov, *The Road to Terror: Stalin and the Self-Destruction of the Bolsheviks, 1932-1939* (New Haven: Yale University Press, 1999).

Gladkikh, P. F., *Zdravookhranenie i voennaia meditsina v bitve za Leningrada glazami istorika i ochevidtsev, 1941-1944 gg.: Ocherki istorii otechestvennoi voennoi meditsiny* (St. Petersburg: "Dmitrii Bulanin," 2006).

———, *Zdravookhranenie blokirovannogo Leningrada* (Leningrad, 1980).

Glantz, David, *The Battle for Leningrad, 1941-1944* (Lawrence: University of Kansas Press, 2002).

———, *The Siege of Leningrad, 1941-1944: 900 Days of Terror* (Osceola: MBI, 2001).

Gorlizki, Yoram and Oleg Khlevniuk, *Cold Peace: Stalin and the Soviet Ruling Circle, 1945-1953* (Oxford: Oxford University Press, 2004).

Goure, Leon, *The Siege of Leningrad* (Stanford: Stanford University Press, 1962).

Grakina, E. I., *Uchenye Rossii v gody Velikoi Otechestvennoi voiny, 1941-1945* (Moscow: Institut Rossiiskoi istorii RAN, 2000).

Gross, Jan, *Neighbors: The Destruction of the Jewish Community in Jedwabne, Poland* (Princeton: Princeton University Press, 2001).

Hahn, Werner G., *Postwar Soviet Politics: The Fall of Zhdanov and the Defeat of Moderation, 1946-53* (Ithaca: Cornell University Press, 1982).

Haynes, John Earl and Harvey Klehr, *Venona: Decoding Soviet Espionage in America* (New Haven: Yale University Press, 1999).

Hensley, Elizabeth Selke, *Basic Concepts of World Nutrition* (Springfield: Charles C. Thomas, 1981).

Hodgson, Katharine, *Voicing the Soviet Experience: The Poetry of Ol'ga Berggol'ts* (Oxford: Oxford University Press, 2003).

Hosking, Geoffrey, *Rulers and Victims: The Russians in the Soviet Union* (Cambridge, Mass.: Harvard University Press, 2006).

Husband, William, *Godless Communists: Atheism and Society in Soviet Russia, 1917-1932* (DeKalb: Northern Illinois University Press, 2000).

Ilic, Melanie, "The Great Terror in Leningrad: A Quantitative Analysis," *Europe-Asia Studies* 52, no. 8 (2000), 1515-34.

Jansen, Marc and Nikita Petrov, *Stalin's Loyal Executioner: People's Commissar Nikolai Ezhov, 1895-1940* (Stanford: Hoover Institution Press, 2002).

Jones, Jeffrey W., *Everyday Life and the "Reconstruction" of Soviet Russia During and After the Great Patriotic War, 1943-1948* (Bloomington: Slavica, 2008).

Jones, Michael, *Leningrad: State of Siege* (New York: Basic Books, 2008) (Advance uncorrected proof).

Kaganovich, V. S., *Evgenii Viktorovich Tarle i Peterburgskaia shkola istorikov* (St. Petersburg: Izdatel'stvo "Dmitrii Bulanin," 1995).

Karasev, A. V., *Leningradtsy v gody blokady, 1941-1943* (Moscow: Nauka, 1959).

Khoroshinina, Lidiya, "Long-Term Effects of Lengthy Starvation," in *Life and Death in Besieged Leningrad, 1941-44,* ed. John Barber and Andrei Dzeniskevich (Basingstoke: Palgrave Macmillan, 2005).

Kirschenbaum, Lisa, *The Legacy of the Siege of Leningrad, 1941-1995: Myth, Memories, and Monuments* (Cambridge: Cambridge University Press, 2006).

———, "Innocent Victims and Heroic Defenders: Children and the Siege of Leningrad," in *Children and War: A Historical Anthology,* ed. James Marten (New York: New York University Press, 2002), 279-90.

Kniazev, S. P. et al., *Na zashchite Nevskoi tverdyni: Leningradskaia partiinaia organizatsiia v gody Velikoi Otechestvennoi voiny* (Leningrad: Lenizdat, 1965).

Knight, Amy, *Beria: Stalin's First Lieutenant* (Princeton: Princeton University Press, 1993).

Kolesnik, A. D., *RSFSR v gody Velikoi Otechestvennoi voiny* (Moscow: Nauka, 1982).

Komar, E. G., *Arsenal energovooruzheniia* (Leningrad: Gospolitizdat, 1945).

Korol'chuk, E. A., *Istoriia Leningradskoi gosudarstvennoi ordena Lenina i ordena Trudovogo Krasnogo Znameni obuvnoi fabriki "Skorokhod" im. Ia. Kalinina* (Leningrad: Lenizdat, 1969).

Kostiuchenko, S. et al., *Istoriia Kirovskogo zavoda* (Moscow: Izdatel'stvo sotsial'no-ekonomicheskoi literatury, 1966).

Kotkin, Stephen, *Magnetic Mountain: Stalinism as a Civilization* (Berkeley: University of California Press, 1995).

Koval'chuk, V. M., *Doroga pobedy osazhdennogo Leningrada* (Leningrad: Nauka, 1984).

———, *Leningrad i Bol'shaia zemlia* (Leningrad: Nauka, 1975).

———, ed., *Ocherki istorii Leningrada: Period Velikoi Otechestvennoi voiny Sovetskogo Soiuza, 1941-1945 gg.,* vol. 5 (Leningrad: Nauka, 1967).

Koval'chuk, V. M. and G. L. Sobolev, "Leningradskii 'rekvium' o zhertvakh naseleniia v Leningrade v gody voiny i blokady," *Voprosy istorii,* no. 12 (1965), 191-94.

Kovalev, I. V., *Transport v Velikoi Otechestvennoi voiny (1941-1945)* (Moscow: Nauka, 1981).

Kriukovskikh, A. P. et al., *V gody surovykh ispytanii: Leningradskaia partiinaia organizatsiia v Velikoi Otechestvennoi voine* (Leningrad: Lenizdat, 1985).

Kutuzov, V. A. and O. N. Stepanov, "Organy gosbezopasnosti na zashchite Leningrada" in *Narod i voina: 50 let Velikoi Pobedy,* ed. V. A. Ezhov et al. (St. Petersburg: Petropolis, 1995).

Kuznetsova, L. S., *Leningradskaia partiinaia organizatsiia v predvoennye gody* (Leningrad: Lenizdat, 1974).

Leningradtsy v dni blokady: Sbornik (Leningrad: Leningradskoe gazetno-zhurnal'noe i knizhnoe izdatel'stvo, 1947).

Lieberman, Sanford R., "Crisis Management in the USSR: The Wartime System of Administration and Control," in *The Impact of World War II on the Soviet Union,* ed. Susan J. Linz (Totowa: Rowman & Allanheld, 1985), 59-76.

Lomagin, Nikita, *Leningrad v blokade* (Moscow: Iauza, Eksmo, 2005).

———, "Spetsifika politecheskogo kontrolia v Leningrade v period blokady," in *The*

Soviet Union—A Popular State? Studies on Popular Opinion in the USSR, ed. Timo Vihavainen (St. Petersburg: Evropeiskii dom, 2003), 265–317.

————, *Neizvestnaia blokada (Dokumenty, prilozheniia)*, vol. 1 (St. Petersburg and Moscow: Dom "Neva" and "OLMA-PRESS", 2002). A second edition added a section on historiography and was published in 2004. The second volume of this work is a collection of documents. It is listed above under "Published Document Collections."

————, "Nastroeniia zashchitnikov i naseleniia Leningrada v period oborony goroda, 1941–1942 gg." in *Leningradskaia epopeia: Organizatsiia oborony i naselenie goroda*, ed. N. A. Lomagin et al. (St. Petersburg: Izdatel'stvo KN, 1995).

————, ed., *Bitva za Leningrad: Diskussionnye problemy* (St. Petersburg: Evropeiskii dom, 2009).

Lomagin, N. A. et al., eds., *Leningradskaia epopeia: Organizatsiia oborony i naselenie goroda* (St. Petersburg: Izdatel'stvo KN, 1995).

Magaeva, Svetlana, "Physiological and Psychosomatic Prerequisites for Survival and Recovery," in *Life and Death in Besieged Leningrad, 1941–44*, ed. John Barber and Andrei Dzeniskevich (Basingstoke: Palgrave Macmillan, 2005), 123–59.

Malkin, B. G., "Agitatsionno-propagandistskaia rabota Leningradskoi organizatsii KPSS v period oborony goroda (dekiabr' 1941—mart 1942 gg.)," *Vestnik Leningradskogo universiteta*, no. 2 (1964): 18–28.

Manakov, N. A., "Ekonomika Leningrada v gody blokady," *Voprosy istorii*, no. 5 (1967), 15–31.

Margolis, Iu. D. et al., *Leningradskii universitet v Velikoi Otechestvennoi voine* (Leningrad: Izdatel'stvo Leningradskogo universiteta, 1990).

Mawdsley, Evan, *The Stalin Years: The Soviet Union, 1929–1953*, 2d ed. (Manchester: Manchester University Press, 2003).

Medvedev, Roy and Zhores Medvedev, *The Unknown Stalin: His Life, Death, and Legacy*, translated by Ellen Dahrendorf (Woodstock: Overlook Press, 2003).

Meyerovich, I. G. and Ia. G. Okulov, *Meropriiatiia Leningradskoi partiinoi organizatsii po snabzheniiu trudiashchikhsia v period blokady, 1941–1942 gg.* (Leningrad, 1959).

Mikhel'son, V. I. and M. I. Ialygin, *Vozdushnyi most*, 2d ed. (Moscow: Izdatel'stvo politicheskoi literatury, 1988).

Miner, Steven, *Stalin's Holy War: Religion, Nationalism, and Alliance Politics, 1941–1945* (Chapel Hill: University of North Carolina Press, 2003).

Montefiore, Simon Sebag, *Stalin: The Court of the Red Tsar* (New York: Knopf, 2004).

Moskoff, William, *The Bread of Affliction: The Food Supply in the USSR During World War II* (Cambridge: Cambridge University Press, 1990).

Murphy, David E., *What Stalin Knew: The Enigma of Barbarossa* (New Haven: Yale University Press, 2005).

Overy, Richard, *Russia's War: A History of the Soviet War Effort, 1941–1945* (New York: Penguin, 1998).

Parrish, Michael, *The Lesser Terror: Soviet State Security, 1939–1953* (Westport: Praeger, 1996).

Pavlov, D. V., *Leningrad v blokade*, 6th ed. (Leningrad: Lenizdat, 1985).

————, *Leningrad 1941: The Blockade*, 2d ed., translated by John Adams (Chicago: University of Chicago Press, 1965).

Peris, Daniel, *Storming the Heavens: The Soviet League of the Militant Godless* (Ithaca: Cornell University Press, 1998).

Pohl, J. Otto, *Ethnic Cleansing in the USSR, 1937–1949* (Westport: Greenwood, 1999).

Putin, Vladimir, *First Person: An Astonishingly Frank Self-Portrait by Russia's President*

Vladimir Putin with Nataliya Gevorkyan, Natalya Timakova, and Andrei Kolesnikov (New York: PublicAffairs, 2000).

Pyzhikov, Aleksandr, "Leningradskaia gruppa: put' vo vlasti (1946-1949)," *Svobodnaia mysl'*, no. 2 (2001), 89-104.

Qualls, Karl, *From Ruins to Reconstruction: Urban Identity in Soviet Sevastopol After World War II* (Ithaca: Cornell University Press, 2009).

Rambow, Aileen, "The Siege of Leningrad: Wartime Literature and Ideological Change," in *The People's War: Responses to World War II in the Soviet Union*, ed. Robert W. Thurston and Bernd Bonwetsch (Urbana: University of Illinois Press, 2000), 154-70.

————, *Überleben mit Worten: Literatur und Ideologie während der Blockade von Leningrad, 1941-1944* (Berlin: Arno Spitz, 1995).

Reid, Anna, *Leningrad: The Epic Siege of World War II, 1941-1944* (New York: Walker, 2011).

Reznikova, I., "Repressii v period blokady Leningrada," *Vestnik "MEMORIALA,"* no. 4/5 (10/11) (1995), 94-111.

Rieber, Alfred J., *Zhdanov in Finland*, The Carl Beck Papers in Russian and East European Studies, no. 1107 (Pittsburgh: University of Pittsburgh Center for Russian and East European Studies, 1995).

Rollins, Patrick J., "Tarle, Evgenii Viktorovich," in *The Modern Encyclopedia of Russian and Soviet History*, ed. Joseph L. Wieczynski et al., vol. 38 (Gulf Breeze: Academic International, 1976), 179-81.

Roslof, Edward E., "Living Church Movement," in *Encyclopedia of Russian History*, ed. James R. Millar, vol. 2 (New York: Macmillan Reference USA, 2003), 866-67.

————, *Red Priests: Renovationism, Russian Orthodoxy, and Revolution, 1905-1946* (Bloomington: Indiana University Press, 2002).

Rossman, Jeffrey J., *Worker Resistance Under Stalin: Class and Revolution on the Shop Floor* (Cambridge, Mass.: Harvard University Press, 2005).

Rothstein, Robert A., "Homeland, Home Town, and Battlefield: The Popular Song," in *Culture and Entertainment in Wartime Russia*, ed. Richard Stites (Bloomington: Indiana University Press, 1995), 77-94.

Ruble, Blair, *Leningrad: Shaping of a Soviet City* (Berkeley: University of California Press, 1990).

————, "The Leningrad Affair and the Provincialization of Leningrad," *Russian Review* 42 (1983), 301-20.

Rubtsov, Iu. V. and V. M. Lur'e, "Blokada Leningrada: Vse li zhertvy uchteny?" *Voenno-istoricheskii zhurnal*, no. 3 (May-June 2000), 30-32.

Salisbury, Harrison, *The 900 Days: The Siege of Leningrad* (New York: Harper & Row, 1969).

Samsonov, A. M. et al., *Kratkaia istoriia SSSR*, vol. 2 (Moscow: Nauka, 1983).

Shkarovskii, M. V., *Iosiflianstvo: Techenie v Russkoi Pravoslavnoi Tserkvi* (St. Petersburg: Memorial, 1999).

————, "Religioznaia zhizn' Leningrada v gody voiny," in *Leningradskaia epopeia: Organizatsiia oborony i naselenie goroda*, ed. N. A. Lomagin et al. (St. Petersburg: Izdatel'stvo KN, 1995), 260-93.

Simmons, Cynthia and Nina Perlina, *Writing the Siege of Leningrad: Women's Diaries, Memoirs, and Documentary Prose* (Pittsburgh: University of Pittsburgh Press, 2002).

Sinitsyn, A. M., "Chrezvychainye organy Sovetskogo gosudarstva v gody Velikoi Otechestvennoi voiny," *Voprosy istorii*, no. 2 (1955), 32-43.

Sirota, F. I., "Voenno-organizatorskaia rabota Leningradskoi organizatsii VKP(b) v pervyi period Velikoi Otechestvennoi voiny," *Voprosy istorii*, no. 10 (1956), 16–31.

Skriabin, M. E. and I. K. Savchenko, *Neprimirimost': Stranitsy istorii Leningradskogo ugolovnogo rozyska* (Leningrad: Lenizdat, 1988).

Solomon, Peter H., Jr. *Soviet Criminal Justice under Stalin* (Cambridge: Cambridge University Press, 1996).

Sonner, Scott, "Scientists: Donner Family Not Cannibals," Associated Press Writer, *Yahoo News*, 13 January 2006.

Stites, Richard, ed., *Culture and Entertainment in Wartime Russia* (Bloomington: Indiana University Press, 1995).

Stremilov, V. V., "Leningradskaia partiinaia organizatsiia v period blokady (1941–1943 gg.)," *Voprosy istorii KPSS*, no. 5 (1959), 101–21.

Sutton, Antony C., *Western Technology and Soviet Economic Development*, vol. 1 (Stanford: Hoover Institution, 1968).

Titova, Irina, "Smiles and Sorrow as Veterans Recall End of War," *St. Petersburg Times*, 8 May 2003.

Tiul'panov, S. I., ed., *Industrializatsiia Severo-Zapadnogo raiona v gody vtoroi i tret'ei piatiletok (1933–1941 gg.)* (Leningrad: Izdatel'stvo Leningradskogo universiteta, 1969).

Tromly, Benjamin, "The Leningrad Affair and Soviet Patronage Politics, 1949–1950," *Europe-Asia Studies* 56, no. 5 (July 2004), 707–29.

Tskulin, V. A., *Istoriia gosudarstvennykh uchrezhdenii SSSR, 1936–1965* (Moscow, 1966).

Tucker, Robert C., *Stalin in Power: The Revolution from Above, 1928–1941* (New York: Norton, 1990).

Vazhentsev, I. A., *Vo glave geroicheskogo kollektiva* (Leningrad: Lenizdat, 1959).

Verkhovtsev, I. P., ed., *Gvardiia tyla* (Moscow: Izdatel'stvo politicheskoi literatury, 1962).

Viola, Lynne, *Collectivization and the Culture of Peasant Resistance* (New York: Oxford University Press, 1996).

Volkogonov, Dmitri, *Stalin: Triumph and Tragedy*, edited and translated by Harold Shukman (New York: Grove Weidenfeld, 1991).

———, *Triumf i tragediia: Politicheskii portret I. V. Stalina v 2-kh knigakh*, bk. 2, pt. 1 (Moscow: Izdatel'stvo Agentstva pechati Novosti, 1989).

Volkov, Solomon, *St. Petersburg: A Cultural History*, translated by Antonina W. Bouis (New York: Free Press, 1995).

Weiner, Amir, *Making Sense of War: The Second World War and the Fate of the Bolshevik Revolution* (Princeton: Princeton University Press, 2001).

Werth, Alexander, *Russia at War, 1941–1945* (New York: Carroll & Graf, 1964).

Zakharov, V. G. et al., *Ocherki istorii Leningradskoi organizatsii KPSS, 1918–1945* (Leningrad: Lenizdat, 1980.

Ziemke, Earl, "Battle for Moscow," in *The Oxford Companion to World War II*, ed. I. C. B. Dear and M. R. D. Foot (Oxford: Oxford University Press, 1995), 760–62.

———, "Siege of Leningrad," in *The Oxford Companion to World War II*, ed. I. C. B. Dear and M. R. D. Foot (Oxford: Oxford University Press, 1995), 685–86.

Zinich, M. S., *Trudovoi podvig rabochego klassa, 1941–1945* (Moscow: Nauka, 1984).

Zubkova, Elena, "Kadrovaia politika i chistki v KPSS (1949–1953)," *Svobodnaia mysl'* no. 4 (1999), 96–110.

PERIODICALS

Christian Science Monitor
Istochnik: Dokumenty russkoi istorii
Izvestiia TsK KPSS
Kritika
Ogonek
Moscow News
St. Petersburg Times
Voenno-istoricheskii zhurnal

DOCUMENTARY FILMS

Blokada, produced in 1994 by Fauna Films of St. Petersburg.
Program on the Siege of Leningrad and the Leningrad Affair, broadcast on the History Channel on 14 September 2003.
"The Donner Party," broadcast on the PBS television series "American Experience" on 21 July 2003.

INTERNET SOURCES

Criminal Code of the RSFSR (http://www.cyberussr.com/rus/uk-rsfsr.html).
Dexter, Keith and Ivan Rodionov, *The Factories, Research and Design Establishments of the Soviet Defence Industry: A Guide. Version 10.0* (University of Warwick: Department of Economics, April 2009), http://www.warwick.ac.uk/go/vpk.
Edeiken, Yale, "An Introduction to the Einsatzgruppen," www.holocaust-history.org.
Lorentz, George, "Mathematics and Politics in the Soviet Union from 1928 to 1953," www.math.ohio-state.edu/AT/LORENTZ/JAT02-0001_final.pdf.
Mezhdunarodnyi fond "Demokratiia," http://www.idf.ru. Subsequently changed to "Fond Aleksandra N. Yakovleva," http://www.alexanderyakovlev.org/fond/issues.

Index

Abakumov, V. A., *figure 40*
Abakumov, Viktor, 70, 74, 457 n. 32
"Activists" case, 372–76, 407
Adamiants, Matvei, 344
Adamovich, Ales, 6, 50–51, 323–24
Afanasiev, A. I., 81–82, 115
Afanasiev, V. V., 82
agriculture, 12, 15, 287–88
Akhmatova, Anna, 67–68
Akkerman (accused counterrevolutionary), 389
Akkonen (bakery worker), 245
Aladin (shipyard worker), 361
Aleksandr Nevsky (Eisenstein), 54
Alekseev (smith), 230
Aleksy (metropolitan), 167–70, 171, 174, 176–78, 179, 180, 181, *figure 59*
Altshuller, I. K., 390, 395, 396, 397, 398, 399
Amerlchenkov, Vasili, 151
Anashkina (factory worker), 363
Anatolevna, Olga, 340
Andreenko, I. A., 253, 300
Andreev, K. (religious leader), 173
Andreev (accused counterrevolutionary), 237, 238
Andreeva (factory worker), 235
Andreichik (bookkeeper), 233
Andropov, Yuri, 2
Anglicans, 180
Anokhina (factory worker), 243
Anti-Comintern Pact (1936), 19, 20

anti-Semitism, 57, 223–25, 332, 339–42
Antiufeev, L. M.: on German war crimes, 367; on mobilization, 187–88; on party membership, 259–60; public mood gauged by, 216, 226–33, 336, 338, 344, 346–47, 353–54, 356–64, 366; religious practices and, 179, 336
Antoniuk (military official), 107, 108
Antonov (NKVD official), 85, 150
Armenia, 209
arms production, 46, 66, 130–31, 140, 143, 187–92, 285–86, 348, *figures 59, 61;* battalions of workers in, 88, 186; employment in, 60, 299; evacuation of, 79–80, 84, 103; growth of, 17, 23, 48; mortality rate of workers in, 298; strains on, 133, 138, 405, 410
Artemiev, N. A., 394, 400
Artemov (KRO official), 394, 395
atheists, 30, 59, 165, 166, 171–72, 408
Averianova-Fyororova, Yelena, 281
Azerbaijan, 209

Badaev bakery and warehouses, 34, 45, 103, 262, 304, 309, 411
Baikov (academician), 399
Baimakov, Nikita, *figure 57*
Bakhvalov, G. A., 225
Bakshis, Maria, 72, 151–54, 407
Bakshis, Mstislav, 154, 407
Balashev (party official), 377

Balkars, 209
Baptists, 166
Baraiun (accused counterrevolutionary), 239
Baranov, B. P., 309
Baranov (janitor), 235
Barber, John, 10
bartering, 28, 292–93, 302, 304–5
Baskakov (party official), 375, 376–77
Basov, Mikhail, 138–40, 143, 188, 375, 376–77
Battle of Khalkin-Gol, 106, 125
Battle of Kursk, 140
Bazulitsky (factory worker), 235
Beaverbrook, Max Aitken, Baron, 348
belagerte Leningrad, Das (Ganzenmüller), 10
Belenky (pensioner), 215
Belous (*raiispolkom* chairman), 157–58, 173, 174
Berggolts, Olga, 213, 247–48, 290–91
Beria, Lavrenty, 74, 75, 79, 105–6, 116, 139, 140, 152, 162–63, 200; in "Activists" case, 374, 376; "Committee for Public Salvation" case and, 402; deportations and, 209, 212; dissent suppressed by, 205, 236; food supplies and, 136; as GKO member, 83; Kubatkin's communications with, 404; as NKVD chief, 20–21, 86, 134; reports to, 372, 373, 374, 380, 383, 405; security role of, 226; Stalin's fears exploited by, 72–73; Zhdanov vs., 69, 115, 158–59, 407
Beria, Sergo, 158–59, 400–402
Berlin Blockade, 73
Beskorovainaia, D. M., *figure 50*
Bettsikh (bookkeeper), 242
Bezhanov (railroad NKVD head), 162
Bezzubov, A. D., 281
Bialy (local official), 283
black market, 51, 154, 160, 255, 301–3, 309, 314
Blium (accused counterrevolutionary), 237
Blokadnaia kniga (Adamovich and Granin), 6, 50–51, 52, 323–24
Bobina, Aleksandra, 315
Bochagova (accused counterrevolutionary), 238
Bochkov, Viktor, 203
Boginsky, N. D., 398
Bogoliubov (shipyard director), 197
Bokshitskaia, Liudmila, 324
Bolotov (party official), 373, 375
Bolshevik arms plant, 19, 190, 196, 342, 344, 421 n. 2; mortality rate at, 298, 299; rebuilding of, 140; shortages at, 26, 28; workers mobilized at, 88, 139, 185
Bolsheviks, 15, 18, 88
Borisov, P., 248
Borshchenko (military official), 126–27
Bortnevsky, Viktor Georgievich, 441 n. 55

Boterbloem, Kees, 10, 21
Brandenberger, David, 75
Brauchitsch, Walther von, 36
Brezhnev, Leonid, 6
bribery, 161, 255, 310
Brooks, Jeffrey, 56
Bruk (bookkeeper), 357
Brun, I. V., *figure 41*
Brusilov, Aleksei, 55
Bubnov (government official), 175
Buddhists, 166
Bulgakov (party official), 356–58, 359–61
burials, 49, 52, 59, 173, 269–70, 273, 280–81, *figure 46*
Burmistrov (plumber), 243
Burtsev (factory worker), 235
Bushueva, Valentina, 296
Buzanova, Maria, 344
Byelorussia, 20, 180
Byrdina (party official), 356

cannibalism, 7, 161, 261, 309; arrests and prosecutions for, 48, 53, 254–55, 279, 315–16, 323; inconsistent data on, 321–22; official knowledge of, 134, 136, 226, 317–20, 405; taboo surrounding, 6, 314
Catholics, 171, 180, 205
censorship, 58, 67–68, 70, 93–94, 249, 257, 349–50, 409
Chaney, Otto, 108
Chanisev (professor), 381
Chanyshev, S. M., 394, 395, 398
Charushin (artist), 396
Chechens, 209
Chepko, Valia, 264–65
Cherepenina, Nadezhda, 272, 300
Cherniadiev (party official), 354
Chernorutsky, M. V., 325–26
Chistiakov (party official), 179
Chudin, Stepan, 333
Churchill, Winston, 114, 362–64
Churilovsky, V. N., 386, 392, 398–99
Cold War, 73
Comintern, 365
Counterespionage Department (KRO), 202, 379–80, 389–90, 392, 402, 403
cremation, 49, 60, 273, 282–83
Crimean Greeks, 209
Crimean Tatars, 209
Crimean War (Tarle), 382
Cripps, Stafford, 114
Cultural Revolution, 166
Czechoslovakia, 20

Danilov (factory worker), 343
Davies, Sarah, 29, 339
Davis, Nathaniel, 165

Dedijer, Vladimir, 74
Dedova (factory worker), 359–60
Defense of Leningrad, The (documentary film), 355
Dertin (propaganda official), 340
deserters, 122, 123, 125, 202, 244, 256, 286
Dimitrov, Gerogi, 75
Djilas, Milovan, 74–75
Dlugach, Moisei, 188
Dmitrichenko (blacksmith), 233
Dmitriev, Ivan, 427 n. 138
Domenenkov, A. D., 243–44
Donner Party, 314
Donskoy, Dmitry, 55, 176, 177
Dukhon (engineer), 381
Dzeniskevich, Andrei, 7, 10, 117, 316, 321

Eferiev (party official), 356
Efimova (factory worker), 235
Egkolm (engineer), 383
Eidelman (accused counterrevolutionary), 360
Eikhenbaum, Boris, 248
Eipshits (doctor), 154
Eisenstein, Sergei, 54
Eitingon, Leonid, 434 n. 178
electricity. *See* fuel and electricity
Elektrosila plant, 98, 138, 140, 185, 190, 193, 196, 240, 288
Eliasberg, Karl, 362
Eller (mechanic), 230
Emilianov, Antonia, 333
Emilianov, E. E., 333
Emilianov, Viktor, 333
Engels plant, 336, 343
Erenburg (military procuracy official), 224–25
espionage, 3, 75, 146, 151, 154, 202, 238, 370, 375
Estonia, 20, 22, 26, 27, 98
Etinger, Iakov, 427 n. 138

Federal Security Service (FSB), 12–13, 116
Fediuninsky, Ivan, 106, 127, 128, 405
Fedorov (physician), 237
Fedorov, A., 386–87, 388–89, 392
Fedorova, Maria, 288, 300–301
Fedorova (party official), 358
Fedoseev (scientist), 215
Filatov (health official), 363
Fillipov, Katia, 277
Fillipov, Vania, 277
Finland, 1, 22, 94, 105, 128, 134, 287, 366, 406; German alliance with, 62, 84, 393; Nonaggression Pact and, 20; Soviet invasion of, 21; territories reclaimed by, 35; ultimatums delivered to, 32, 67; Winter War against, 5
Finns, 195, 371; anti-Soviet sentiments among,

32; deportations of, 10, 45, 96, 204, 208, 209–15; executions of, 199, 208
First Siniavino Offensive, 108, 126
Fisak, E. A., 85
Fitzpatrick, Sheila, 163, 225
Fomina (factory worker), 235
Ford Motor Company, 421 n. 2
fortifications, 22, 40–41, 62, 66, 83–84, 87, 88, 105, 115, 121, 130, 159, 190, 195–96
France, 20, 21, 134
Franco, Francisco, 19
Frantsev (government official), 154
fraternization, 125
Frolov, I. M., 129–30
FSB (Federal Security Service), 12–13, 116
fuel and electricity, 26, 28, 48–49, 133, 138, 160–61, 187, 196, 293, 348, 405, 410; rationing of, 197; workers providing, 298
Furdman, E., 287

Gagarin, A. N., *figure 14*
Gagarina, D. M., *figure 14*
Galko (party official), 335
Ganichev (party official), 215
Ganzenmüller, Jörg, 10
gardening, 27, 60, 65, 288, 295, 306–8, *figures 50, 57*
GARF (State Archive of the Russian Federation), 12, 13
Garina, A. E., 242
Garold (informant), 389, 396
Garshin, Vladimir, 326
Geidina, V. V., *figure 13*
Georgia, 209
Getty, J. Arch, 200
Ginzburg, Lidia, 350
GKO. *See* State Defense Committee
Gladkikh, P. F., 284
Glantz, David, 84, 133
glasnost, 6, 69
Goncharov, Vladimir, *figure 11*
Gorbachev, Mikhail, 6, 69, 77, 183
Gorbovsky (accused counterrevolutionary), 385–86, 387–88
Gorlinski, N. D., 206–7
Goure, Leon, 8–9, 11, 87
Govorov, Leonid, 66, 147, 148, 171, 355, *figure 6*
Granin, Daniil, 6, 50–51, 52, 323–24
Great Britain, 2, 32, 70, 152, 207, 348, 353, 362; appeasement pursued by, 20; Finland warned by, 35; Molotov's pact with, 361
Great Northern War, 49
Great Terror (1937–38), 18, 29, 30, 73, 199–200, 248
Greek Civil War, 74
Greeks, 209

Griboedov (professor), 215
Grigoriev (metal worker), 342
Grigoriev, I. I., *figure 58*
Gross, Jan, 392–93
Grushko, E., 269–70, 311
Gul (professor), 373–74, 375–78
Guranda (factory worker), 229
Gusakova (factory worker), 364
Gusev, A. A., 40
Gusev, Sonia, 277
Gusev, Tania, 277

Halder, Franz, 35, 129
Hangö naval base, 21
Harriman, Averell, 348
Hermitage Museum, 299
Hitler, Adolf, 167, 169; Finnish alliance
    sought by, 95; ground assault rejected by,
    35–36, 38; Leningrad coveted by, 32, 34;
    Moscow targeted by, 61, 121, 127, 194,
    196, 334; northern region targeted by,
    84; Soviet power underestimated by, 21;
    Stalin's views of, 32; war on United States
    declared by, 406
hoarding, 287–88, 328, 331
Holocaust, 341
housing, 25–26

Iakovlev (blacksmith), 235
Ignatovskaia (accused counterrevolutionary),
    394, 398–99, 400
Ignatovsky, V. S., 237, 380, 381, 390, 393–96,
    398, 399
Iliashenko, Nikolai, 171
Iliushin-2 fighter, 23, 80
infectious diseases, 59–60, 281–82
inflation, 302
Ingush, 209
Inostrantsev, V. A., 411
Isakov, Ivan, 109, 111–13, 120–21
Istomina (informant), 377
Istoriia stalinskogo GULAGa, 12
Italy, 134
Ivanov (auto club head), 310
Ivanov (engineer), 234
Ivanov, A. S., 238
Ivanov, Evgeny, 150, 154–58
Ivanov, K. D., 129, 130
Ivanova (confectionery factory worker), 364
Ivanova (pneumatics factory worker), 356
Ivanova, Aleksandra, 336
Ivanova, Yevdokia, 352
Ivan the Great, 17
Ivan the Terrible, 17
Izhorsk plant, 26, 79, 104, 118, 190, 392
Izvekov, B. I., 386
Izvestiia TsK KPSS (journal), 6

Japan, 361; Manchuria occupied by, 19; Pearl
    Harbor attacked by, 48, 353; Soviet victory
    against, 38
Jews, 57, 166, 222–23, 332, 339–42, 343
Jodl, Alfred, 36
Jones, Michael, 9–10
Josephites, 181–82

Kachalin, V. I., 242
Kachalov, N. N., 381, 399
Kachanov (factory worker), 364
Kaganovich, Lazar, 99–100
Kaliada (factory worker), 179
Kalinin (shop foreman), 359
Kalinin, Mikhail, 341
Kalmyks, 209
Kalnin, A. G., 82
Kalugin (major), 369
Kamenev (accused counterrevolutionary),
    238
Kapustin, Yakov, 68, 150, 154–55, 163, 164,
    197, *figure 66*; archives evacuated by, 81;
    arrest and execution of, 69, 74, 157, 427
    n. 139; bread rations and, 229, 231; factory
    conversions and, 28, 159, 188; political
    ascent of, 18–19, 156; preferential treat-
    ment for, 285; reports to, 179, 229, 231,
    233, 338, 358, 359, 363
Karachays, 209
Karasev (government official), 139
Karasev, A. V., 4, 8
Karninsky (scientist), 215
Karpov, Georgy, 178, 179
Karpushenko (local official), 283
Katiusha rocket, 189, 190, 191, 192
Katsnelson (surgeon), 230, 299
Kazakov, Nikolai, 79
Kazan Cathedral, 172, *figure 24*
Kerensky, Aleksandr, 88
Ketlinskaia, Vera, 213, 215
Khaiponen (accused counterrevolutionary),
    239
Khanikainen (kolkhoz chairman), 239
Kharitonov, I. S., 68, 69, 155–58
Kharitonova, Anfisa, 352
Khemshils, 209
Khiankiainen (accused counterrevolution-
    ary), 239
Khlobystov (caretaker), 229
Khlusov (shop foreman), 296
Kholdin (professor), 215
Khozin, Mikhail, 128–29, 134–35, 233, 236,
    264, 407; deserters and, 122–23; dismissal
    of, 147–48; in First Siniavino Offensive,
    108; Frolov scapegoated by, 129–30; Mel-
    nikov lambasted by, 146, 148–49; military
    background of, 106–7, 144–45; military

control consolidated by, 143; Zaporozhets accused by, 148–49

Khropov (Osoaviakhim chairman), 310

Khrulev, Andrei, 103, 135

Khrushchev, Nikita, 4, 182–83, 379, 402

Khrustalev (inspector), 234

Kirillov (government official), 302

Kirov, Sergei, 18, 70, 72, 153, 158

Kirov works, 98, 189, 190, 288, 293, 341, 353, 370, 392, *figure 23;* evacuation of, 44, 79, 80, 104, 118, 188; as military target, 45, 118, 121–22, 295; mortality rate in, 298, 299; party organization at, 199, 336, 343, 351–52; production problems at, 24, 26, 405; rations at, 292, 354, 408; repairs and, 138, 305; service brigade at, 294; size of, 23, 88; volunteers from, 333, 334; workers mobilized at, 185, 193–94, 195–96

Kirschenbaum, Lisa, 4

Klebanov (party official), 227, 229, 233, 338, 362–64

Klimenko (local official), 283

Klimenko, L. V., 386, 400, 402

Klitny (naval officer), 120

Klykov, Nikolai, 105

Kniaz-Vladimirsky Cathedral, 166, 175–76

Kochina, Yelena, 264, 274, 286, 310, 312, 313, 321, 324, 350

Kollontai, Aleksandra, 35

Kolonitsky (accused counterrevolutionary), 237

Kolosov, P., *figure 25*

Kolosova (factory worker), 230

Kolosovsky, A. I., 242

Kolpakov, I. V., 135, 162–63, 211

Komissarova (housewife), 360

Kondratenko (factory worker), 344

Konenkov, V. I., 371–72

Kopokhnovskaia (factory worker), 230–31

Korchinskaia, Marianna Viktorovna, 447 n. 90

Kornilov, Boris, 248, 372

Korobenko, K., 238

Korolev, Leonid, 254

Koshliakov, N. S., 383, 384, 386, 391, 392, 393–94, 399–400, 401

Kostrovitskaia, Vera, 281

Kostygov (government official), 139

Kosygin, Aleksei, 19, 27, 95, 96–100, 136, 212, 275, 279, 286

Kotkin, Stephen, 11

Kotonov (factory worker), 350

Koval, George, 435 n. 178

Kovalchuk, Valentin, 50, 271

Kovalev, Nikolai, 458 n. 56

Kovriginaia, M. D., 394

Koyzova, Nina, 443 n. 110

Kozhemiakin, I. A., 395, 398, 399

Kozin, M. D., 118

Kozitsky radio factory, 291

Kozlov, Frol, 429 n. 141

Kozlov, S. K., *figure 26*

Kozlov, V. P., 8

KPK (Party Control Committee), 389–90, 393–401

Krasnaia Zaria plant, 189

Krasnogvardesik, 84, 86, 89, 91, 92, 93, 94

Krasny Oktiabr power plant, 138

Kravets (scientist), 399

Kresty Prison, 280

Krivoshlykov, H. F., 378

KRO (Counterespionage Department), 202, 379–80, 389–90, 392, 402, 403

Kronstadt naval base, 20, 32, 87, 96, 112

Krotov, E. G., 389, 390, 396, 397

Krotova, V. I., 400

Kruglov, Sergei, 69–70, 427 n. 140

Krupskaia candy factory, 289

Kruzhkov, N. F., 391–92, 394, 395, 397, 398

Kubatkin, Pyotr, 38, 117, 156, 158, 159–60, 162–63, 204, 206–8, 210, 272, 401, *figure 3;* arrest and execution of, 69, 74, 152, 157; Beria's communications with, 404; cannibalism reports of, 316–17, 318–22; deportations and, 212; on food shortages, 233–36; intellectuals targeted by, 380–81, 383–88, 390–91, 392; Melnikov and, 145–46; as NKVD chief, 96, 116, 150, 181, 203, 226, 227, 228, 248–49, 251, 255–57, 279, 340, 368–72, 373–74, 378; popular anger noted by, 346–47; skepticism of, 371; zealotry of, 202–3, 236–45; Zhdanov and, 406; Zhukov and, 125–26, 407

Kuchurenko (colonel), 310

Kudriavtsev (party official), 358

Kukushkina (sergeant), 311

Kulagin, Georgy, 293, 298, 305

Kulashkin, Shura, 277

Kulik, Grigory, 23, 104, 105, 107, 108

Kuplivatsky (commissar), 369

Kuprin, Pavel, 146, 149

Kupriyanova, Nadezhda, 324

Kurds, 209

Kutuzov, Mikhail, 55, 172

Kuzmin (military procurator), 321, 322, 323

Kuznetsov (factory worker), 235

Kuznetsov, A. A., 243

Kuznetsov, Aleksei, 38, 53, 122–23, 124, 131, 144, 145, 147, 149, 150, 163, 164, 333, 340, 379, 401, 405, *figures 2, 43, 66;* airlifts backed by, 103; arms production targets set by, 135, 138–39; demolitions and, 116, 117; documentary film and, 355, 356–58; evacuation orders to, 28, 127; execution

Kuznetsov, Aleksei (continued)
of, 69, 115, 140, 427 n. 139; food supplies and, 28, 136, 229, 231, 233, 264, 312;
fortifications built by, 83–84, 87, 115–16,
195; as information conduit, 85–86; Leningraders praised by, 71–72; Malenkov's
charges against, 74; political career of, 18,
39, 68, 69, 70, 75, 158; power shared with
military by, 150; preferential treatment for,
285; purge of, 3; reports to, 179, 229, 231,
233, 251, 317, 320, 338, 358, 359, 363, 380,
384, 385; security role of, 151–52, 226, 236,
251, 254; Stalin's discord with, 142; during
starvation winter, 275, 279; during Zhdanov's illnesses, 160
Kuznetsov, Nikolai, 95, 109–10
Kuznetsov, Valery, 115
Kuznetsov, V. I., *figure 11*
Kuznetsov, V. V., 244
Kuznetsov, Zinaida, 115
Kuznetsova, Alla, 71
Kuznetsova, M. I., 366
KV tank, 23, 79, 104, 105, 132, 133, 194

Ladoga ice road, 95, *figures 38–39;* control
of, 310; evacuations over, 49, 60, 97, 164,
273, 279, 294, 327, 353, 354, 410; food sent
over, 52, 292, 311; proposal for, 134–35;
significance of, 50, 406; Stalin's support
for, 72, 135, 137, 160, 285, 405; VSLF and,
135–36, 137, 212
Lapenkovnaia, Nadezhda, 249
Lapkin, A., 244
Lapkin, V., 244
Laptev (accused counterrevolutionary), 238
Larionov (accused counterrevolutionary), 244
Latintsev (factory worker), 235
Latvia, 20, 22, 98
Laursen (accused counterrevolutionary), 236–
37
Lazutin, Petr, 69, 264, 427 n. 139
League of Militant Godless (SVB), 166–67,
171–72, 335
Lebedev, V. A., 118–20
Leeb, Wilhelm, Ritter von, 32, 34, 35, 36, 38,
83
Lend Lease, 180, 361, 365
Lenenergo power plant, 48, 197
Leningrad Affair (1949–53), 3, 5, 6, 9, 11,
69–77, 140, 142, 156, 157, 401–2
Leningrad in Battle (documentary film), 3,
355–58
Leningrad Military Defense Council, 44, 85,
86–87, 89–93, 116
Leningrad Party Organization (LPO), 11, 68;
declining membership of, 56, 57–58, 199,
258–61, 300, 366, 407; NKGB monitor-
ing of, 151; recruitment by, 198–99, 258,
259–60, 407; resurgence of, 259, 365–66;
Stalin's reshaping of, 18; surveillance by,
199, 226
Leningrad Symphony (Shostakovich), 52–53,
305, 362
Leningradtsy v gody blokady, 1941–1943 (Kara-
sev), 4
Leningrad v blokade (Pavlov), 4
Leningrad v osade (Dzeniskevich), 7
Lenizdat (publishing house), 7
Lezhaeva, Elizaveta, 438 n. 231
Ligor, Pavel, 181
Likhachev, Dmitry, 50, 316
Lishina (bookkeeper), 354
Lithuania, 17, 20, 22, 151
Litvinov, Maxim, 382
Liubimstev, G. V., 82
Liubov, K. I., 394, 395, 400
Livonian Wars, 55
Livshits (factory worker), 235
Logunov, Sergei, 337
Lomagin, N. A., 13
looting, 53, 255, 286, 287, 312–13, 409
LPO. *See* Leningrad Party Organization
Luga Line, 34, 41
Lutherans, 166
Luzhkov, Sergei Vasilievich, 253–54
Lysenko, Ivan, 162–64, 408
Lysenko, Trofim, 68

Magaeva, Svetlana, 4, 297, 325, 326–27
Magnitogorsk steel plant, 12
Makhanov, A. I., 356, 359, 363
Maksimov (accused counterrevolutionary),
238
Mal (informant), 377
Malenkov, A. G., 109
Malenkov, Georgy, 72, 75, 101, 103, 115; anti-
party charges leveled by, 73–74; depor-
tations and, 212; on evacuation plan, 96,
97–98; as GKO member, 82, 95; on ration-
ing, 99–100; Zhdanov vs., 9, 69, 109, 404
Maltsev, Aleksandr, 458 n. 56
Malyshev, F. I., 400
Manchuria, 19
Manhattan Project, 435 n. 178
Mannerheim, Karl Gustav, 35, 67
Manstein, Erich von, 62
Marchuk (military tribunal official), 225
Markin (physician), 237
Markova (accused counterrevolutionary),
237–38
Marshall, George C., 361
Marshall Plan, 73
Martynov (professor), 215
Mashinostroitelny plant, 138

Maslov (naval officer), 120
Maslovskaia (factory worker), 240
Matus, Ksenia, 305
Mavrodin, V., 54–55
Medvedev, Dmitry, 8
Meier (accused counterrevolutionary), 388
Melnikov, N. D., 145–46, 147
Memorial (organization), 8, 422 n. 5
Mensheviks, 205, 247
Meretskov, Kirill, 66
Merkulov (accused provocateur), 389–90, 391–92, 395
Merkulov, Vsevolod, 178, 209, 372, 380, 383; demolitions planned by, 38, 114–17; deportations by, 209, 212; mass murders overseen by, 124–25; removal from office of, 70; security forces requested from, 158, 159, 160; security role of, 226, 236
Merzhvinsky (technician), 240
Meshketian Turks, 209
MGB (Ministry of State Security), 70
Mikhoels, Solomon, 458 n. 40
Mikoyan, Anastas, 74, 86, 159; food supplies and, 98, 100, 102, 103, 104, 134–35, 136
Mikoyan, Sergo, 72, 109
Mikulin (railroad worker), 234
Milinsky, V. I., 395, 400
Military Procuracy (VP), 201, 204, 207
Military Soviet of the Leningrad Front (VSLF), 76, 103–4, 109, 116, 121, 123, 142, 145, 146; creation of, 87; deportations by, 208–9; draconian policies of, 122, 125, 236–45; economy regulated by, 60, 141; food rations managed by, 154, 263–64, 292; fortifications built by, 105, 196; ice road and, 135–36, 137, 212; NKVD and, 126, 150; volunteers recruited by, 39
Military Tribunal (VT), 200, 201, 203–4
Miner, Steven, 176
Minichev, V. I., 373, 374, 377, 379
Minin, Kuzma, 55
Ministry of State Security (MGB), 70
Mirzakhanov (government official), 139
mobilization, of factory workers, 24, 42, 88, 138, 139, 141, 184–88, 193–94, 195–96
Mola, Emiliano, 440 n. 41
Molotov, Viacheslav, 21, 39, 78, 86, 96, 101, 108, 114, 129, 167, 178, 200; British pact with, 361; deportations and, 212; on evacuation plan, 97–98; food supplies and, 98–100; German atrocities detailed by, 351; German invasion announced by, 39, 54, 331, 333; as GKO member, 82, 95; Zhdanov vs., 9, 404; Zhukov threatened by, 125
Moscow, 1–2, 32, 35, 36, 38, 46, 58, 63; bombing of, 34; capital moved to, 70; looting

and panic in, 72; war materials sent to, 132–33
Moshnova (factory worker), 361
Mosolov (local official), 283
Munich Conference, 20
Muraviev (accused counterrevolutionary), 237
Muskaleva (accused counterrevolutionary), 239
Muslims, 166
Mutovkin, A. D., 225
Mytareva (building manager), 359

Napoleon (Tarle), 293, 382
Napoleon I, emperor of the French, 32, 54, 55, 167, 169, 382
NATO (North Atlantic Treaty Organization), 2, 73
Naumov, Oleg V., 200
Navalatsky (professor), 215
Nazarov (police chief), 311
Nechaeva (factory worker), 367
Nekliudova, Tamara, 306
Nekrasov (poet), 215
Nemkov, F. A., 82
Nevgvozd plant, 298
Nevsky, Aleksandr, 49, 55, 176
New Economic Policy, 15
Nicholas II, Czar, 18, 246, 382
Nikanorov, Shurik, 325
Nikiforov, A. I., 371, 373–74, 375–78
Nikiforov, A. P., 82
Nikitin, M. N., 210, 212, 214, 285
Nikolai (metropolitan), 178, 179
Nikolsky Cathedral, 171, 174–75
Nikonov (driver), 229
900 Days, The (Salisbury), 7, 9
NKGB (People's Commissariat of State Security), 12, 149, 201–2, 366, 406, 407
NKO (People's Commissariat of Defense), 138, 141, 143
NKVD. *See* People's Commissariat of Internal Affairs
Nonaggression Pact (1939), 5, 20, 22–23, 45, 165
Normandy invasion, 67
North Africa, 134, 362
North Atlantic Treaty Organization (NATO), 2, 73
Novikov (factory manager), 356
Nuremberg trials, 3, 21, 271

October Railroad, 161–62, 163
Ogoltsov, Sergei, 31, 202, 204–6, 228, 392, 395, 396, 397–98, 399
OGPU (United State Political Administration), 139, 158, 382
Old Believers, 166

Operation Barbarossa, 22, 24, 32, 39, 159, 351
Operation *Blau,* 61–62
Operation *Iskra,* 63
Operation Typhoon, 38, 127, 134, 334
Oppenheimer, Robert, 458 n. 50
Ordzhonikidze shipyard, 138, 295, 333, 334
Oreshina, G. V., *figure 50*
Orlova (medic's assistant), 352
Orlovskaia (factory worker), 359
orphans, 275
Orthodox Church, 11, 59, 164–83, 335, 365, 408–9
Osoaviakhim (Society for Air and Chemical Defense), 309–10
Ostroumova-Lebedeva, Anna, 290, 339–40

Palatkin (factory worker), 235
Panfilenko, A. I., 315, 316, 317–18
Pariisky (religious leader), 172–73
party committees, 198
Party Control Committee (KPK), 389–90, 393–401
Pashkovsky (factory manager), 240
Paulus, Friedrich, 62
Pavlenko, P. I., *figure 13*
Pavlov, Dmitry (commissar of trade), 4, 8, 84, 86, 102, 135, 154, 187, 271–72
Pavlov, Dmitry (general), 108
Pearl Harbor, 353
Pelevin, Mikhail, 292
People's Commissariat of Defense (NKO), 138, 141, 143
People's Commissariat of Internal Affairs (NKVD), 9, 89, 123, 126–27, 134, 146, 296; archives of, 12, 14, 80–81; censorship by, 58, 205, 257, 349–50, 409; churches monitored by, 172; "Committee for Public Salvation" case and, 393–403; conspiracies imagined by, 392–93, 407; crime combated by, 309, 310, 312, 313–14, 315, 330, 371; demolitions by, 38, 56, 116; deportations by, 45, 204, 208, 210–11, 213–15; executions by, 13, 21, 81; food supplies and, 48, 65, 268, 270, 407; internal review by, 201; leadership changes at, 69–70, 96, 116; Leningrad Regional Directorate of (UNKVD), 149–50, 154, 201, 202, 203, 301, 337; party's conflicts with, 149–50, 154–55, 373, 407; preferential treatment for, 51; property seized by, 254, 256–57; public mood monitored by, 11, 28, 57, 227, 246, 330, 344, 345–46, 365, 368, 372; stable membership of, 258, 407; Stalin's criticism of, 200; surveillance by, 30, 56, 151, 172, 198, 205, 225–26, 228–29, 245–49, 362, 406; underground section

of, 260–61; workers mobilized by, 24, 42, 138, 141
People's Commissariat of State Security (NKGB), 12, 149, 201–2, 366, 406, 407
Perfiryov (factory manager), 233
Perlina, Nina, 10
Peter the Great, 49
Petrograd, 246, 264, 423 n. 36
Petrov (electrician), 85
Petrov (VSLF official), 103
Petrov, N. N., 214
Petrova (factory worker), 364
Petrova, Tekia, 351
Petrovskaia, Kyra, 299, 308, 310–11, 325
Pevzner, Lev, 323, 325
Piletsky, F. I., 337
Pinchuk (party official), 377
Pivovarov, S. V., *figure 27*
Plakunova (party official), 363
Platonov, Mikhail, 378–79, 456 n. 18
Platonov, Sergei, 378
Podchasov, I. V., 395, 397, 398, 457 n. 31
Poland, 20–21, 393
Pomorsky (physicist), 234
Popkov, A., 386, 398
Popkov, Pyotr, 35, 59, 75, 83, 85, 150, 231, 269, 283, *figure 66*; anti-Soviet leaflets sent to, 253; documentary film denounced by, 355; execution of, 69, 427 n. 139; food supplies and, 161–62, 308; Kolpakov criticized by, 163; Leningrad's status promoted by, 71, 75; postwar career and purge of, 3, 68, 73, 74
Popov, Markian, 96, 100, 102, 105, 114, 204, 224, 225
Popov, N., 311–12
Popselova (government official), 234
Poretsky (manager), 234
Posadkov, K. F., 244
Poshibailov (store director), 231
Poskrebyshev, Aleksandr, 103, 382
Postoeva (professor), 394
Povaliaev (tram park worker), 344
Pozharsky, Dmitry, 55
prisons, 57, 204, 279–80, 315
Pronberg, Svetlana, 324
propaganda, 53–59, 199, 237–39, 293, 326, 333, 351, 354, 365–66, 408, *figures 66–70*; antireligious, 171–72; German, 202, 216–23, 250, 341, 342, 365; post-Marxist, 330; prewar, 335
Protestants, 171, 205
Provisional Government, 88, 246
public transportation, 26, 28, 161, 163, 293, 295, 296, *figure 34*
Pushkova (accused counterrevolutionary), 237
Putin, Vladimir, 4–5, 7–8, 76, 435 n. 178

Putitsin (factory worker), 229
Puzyrev, N. D., 194, 292, 334

Radeev, Evgeny, 174
Raevskaia, P. A., 332
Raevsky (supply chief), 310
railroads, 11, 65, 96, 98, 104, 133, 135, 136,
    202, 344; deportations by, 211; employ-
    ment by, 60; evacuations by, 268, *figure 54*;
    as fortifications, 121, 126, 196; October
    Railroad, 161–62, 163; severing of, 44, 84,
    187, 285; across Volga River, 49
Rakhmalev, Nikolai, 26
Rastorguev, F. F., 333
rationing, rations, 48–49, 53, 57, 96, 102, 164,
    229–31, 266, 302, *figure 33*; abuses of,
    154–57, 289, 300–301, 312, 408; of elec-
    tricity, 197; for factory workers, 291–92,
    297, 327, 408; insufficiency of, 45–46,
    50–51, 99, 227, 284, 311, 327, 405, 408;
    mismanagement of, 263; political attitudes
    shaped by, 353–54; prewar, 27, 29; as re-
    ward, 282; for soldiers, 304, 327; statistics
    on, 413–17; for youths, 286
Raus, Gerhard, 424 n. 65
Reagan, Ronald, 2
Red Chemist plant, 286
Reid, Anna, 10
Reingold, Ia. N., *figure 41*
religion, 29–30, 164–83, 335, 365
Renovationists, 180–81
Reshkin (local official), 283
Riabikov (government official), 139
Riabkov (accused counterrevolutionary), 251
Rodionov, Mikhail, 68, 73, 74, 76, 427 n. 139
Rodionova (factory worker), 179
Rogulin, D. Ya., 224
Romania, 20, 22
Romanov, B. I., 244
Romanov, G. V., 272
Rovinsky (factory director), 286
Roze, N. V., 383, 384, 385–86, 391, 398, 399,
    400
Rozhdestvensky (academician), 381, 399
Ruble, Blair, 71
Russian Civil War, 5, 15, 23, 143, 180, 196,
    258, 264, 423 n. 36
Russian Orthodox Church, 11, 59, 164–83,
    335, 365, 408–9
Ruzov, S. S., 386
Rybina, Anna, 193

Salambekov, B. K., 163
Salisbury, Harrison, 7, 9, 69, 70, 87, 108, 163,
    370
Samokhvalova (party official), 364
Sarosek, Dmitry, 254

Savinykh (factory worker), 231
Savucheva, Tania, 275
Second Siniavino Offensive, 61
Secret Political Department (SPO), 202, 247,
    250–51, 337, 342, 372–73, 380, 389
Sedyechenkov (professor), 456 n. 16
Semenov, Timofei, *figure 12*
Semenov (party official), 214
Semenova (yard-keeper), 359
Senichev, P. I., 98
Serdobintsev, B. A., 188
Sergeev, Nikolai, 289–90
Sergy (metropolitan), 167, 168, 176, 177, 178,
    179
Serov, Ivan, 427 n. 140
Serova, Tatiana, *figure 61*
Sevastopol naval base, 358
Seventh Day Adventists, 166
Seven Years' War, 55
Shabash (factory worker), 240
Shakh-Bazov, G. A., 381
Shapiro (banker), 238
Shaposhnikov, Boris, 94, 96, 106, 109, 125,
    137
Sharyov (engineer), 70
Shashkov (NKVD official), 150
Shazlinskaia (factory worker), 235
Shcherba, Fedor, 369
Shelkovnikov (caretaker), 229
Shemiakina (factory worker), 353
Shevelev (investigator), 392
Shilov (factory worker), 229
Shisheinina (cafeteria worker), 243
Shishkarev, N. M., 150
Shkarovsky, Mikhail, 182
Shneider (party official), 363–64
Shostakovich, Dmitry, 52–53, 305, 362
Shtern, Grigory, 108
Shtykov, Terenty, 83, 149, 150, 160, 285
Shubin (local official), 359
Shumilov, N. D., 216, 229, 231, 338
Shvyrkov (colonel), 151, 152–54
Silin (bakery worker), 354
Simmons, Cynthia, 10
Skorokhod plant, 138, 185, 189, 192, 195
Skriabina, Yelena, 266, 298
Skvortsov (accused counterrevolutionary), 237
Smirnov (professor), 397
Smirnov, G. L., 272
Smirnov, N. V., 371–72
Smirnov, P. L., 175
Smirnova (factory worker), 231
Smirnova (propaganda official), 356–57
Smolny (scientist), 215
Smolovik, V. I., *figure 53*
Sobchak, Anatoly, 437 n. 203
Sobolev, G. L., 271

Society for Air and Chemical Defense (Osoaviakhim), 309–10
Sokolov (accused counterrevolutionary), 238
Solo, A. A., 386
Solomon, Peter, 201
Solovev, N. V., 285
Solovieva, Aleksandra Ivanovna, *figure 18*
Solovyov, L. N., 118
Solovyov, N. V., 68, 69, 83, 160
Solzhenitsyn, Aleksandr, 12
Sorokin (writer), 240
Sorokovik (party official), 377
Spanish Civil War, 19, 130, 202
Spaso-Preobrazhensky Cathedral, 176, 181
SPO (Secret Political Department), 202, 247, 250–51, 337, 342, 372–73, 380, 389
spotted fever, 59–60
Sredneva (bakery worker), 245
Stakhanovite movement, 25
Stalin, Josef, 3, 28, 76, 143, 159; absolutism of, 78, 81, 88, 89, 90, 94; arms production demanded by, 131; Bakshis affair hidden from, 152; censorship by, 67; Churchill's visit to, 362–64; church's rapprochement with, 176–80; civilians disregarded by, 46, 79, 95, 101, 103, 111, 142, 404–5; demolitions ordered by, 114, 116, 118–20, 405; deportations and, 212; executions ordered by, 69, 108; food supplies and, 136, 262; German intentions misjudged by, 31–32, 82, 94; in German propaganda, 222; Great Terror launched by, 199–200; historical accounts of, 6, 8; ice road supported by, 72, 135, 137, 160, 285, 405, 411; industrialization drive of, 15; Kapustin and Kubatkin arrested by, 74; Khozin dismissed by, 147–48; Kuznetsov as threat to, 71–72, 100; Leningraders mistrusted by, 17–18, 70, 73; as military strategist, 15, 21, 22, 23, 38, 44, 56, 62, 95, 104, 109–12, 128–29, 134, 406; public statements of, 54, 55, 332, 334, 353; religious restrictions loosened by, 59; ruthlessness of, 123–24, 130; shortsightedness of, 132; Smolny's leaders vs., 11, 86, 89, 127, 142; Tarle and, 382; Tito vs., 75; Voroshilov mistrusted by, 63, 84, 85, 87, 101, 102, 105, 116; Voroshilov relieved of command by, 106–7, 108, 258
Stalingrad, 11, 62, 177, 365
Stalin metal works, 138, 139, 185, 189, 192, 196, 295, *figure 10*
Stashkevich (factory worker), 337
State Archive of the Russian Federation (GARF), 12, 13
State Defense Committee (GKO), 19, 81, 109, 111, 134, 204; arms production overseen by, 23, 46, 84, 130–32, 137–38, 140, 141,

188, 189–90, 198; commissars assigned by, 34, 83; demolitions ordered by, 114, 116; food supplies overseen by, 84, 103–4; Leningrad's defense planned by, 44, 95–97, 100, 101, 102, 114; membership of, 82–83; rail line built by, 136
Stelmakh, Grigory, 145, 148
Stelmakhovich (party official), 213–14
Stern (doctor), 266
Stolypin, Pyotr, 348
Storonkin (factory worker), 364
Strakhovich, K. I., 385, 390, 391, 394, 395, 396, 397, 398, 399
Strakhovich, S. I., 397
Streglo (engineer), 243
Streglo (inspector), 383, 384, 385–86
Stroganov, V. G., 386
Strunkin, A. T., 224
Struve (teacher), 240
Sudoplatov, Pavel, 146
Sukhov, Valery, 267–68
Superanskaia, E. M., 400
Superansky (accused counterrevolutionary), 384, 385–87, 389, 390, 391, 396, 397, 400, 402
Suslov, K. V., 395, 398, 399
Suslov, Mikhail, 271–72
Suvorov, Aleksandr, 55, 172
SVB (League of Militant Godless), 166–67, 171–72, 335
Sviataia Troitskaia (church), 181–82
Sviatokom (party official), 376–77
Sweden, 49
Sysoev, Tolia, 277

Taliush, P. T., 197
Tarle, Evgeny, 293, 381–83, 399
Tatarintsevaia, A. (government official), 172–73
Tatars, 209
Terentev (welder), 235
Tikhomirov, A. N., 244
Tikhon (patriarch), 181
Tikhonov (local official), 283
Timashuk, Lydia, 427 n. 138
Timofeev (factory worker), 359–60
Timofeev (professor), 394, 398, 399
Timoshenko, Semen, 82, 258
Tito, Josip Broz, 75
Titov, L. G., 381, 395, 398, 400
Tiunina, Ekaterina, 339
Tiurkin, P. A., 144, 145, 147, 149
Tolstoy, Leo, 293, 382
Tretiak, G. T., 398, 400
Treugolnik rubber plant, 45
Tributs, Vladimir, 118, 432 n. 98
Troshanov, N. S., 243

Trotsky, Leon, 18, 205, 258, 435 n. 178
Trotskyites, 30, 372
Tsirsh, V. E., *figure 58*
Tsivian, M. S., 244
Tsvetkov (party official), 375, 376–77
Tsyganov (chief of staff), 126, 218
Tucker, Robert, 54, 145
Tukhachevky, Marshal, 380
Tupolev ("Academician"), 250–51
Tur (professor), 396
Turks, 209
Tushina (factory worker), 347
typhoid fever, 59–60

Ukhtomsky (academician), 381
Ukraine, 20, 180, 406
Uniates, 180
United State Political Administration
    (OGPU), 139, 158, 382
United States, 70, 134, 152, 348; Finland
    warned by, 35; Japanese attack on, 48, 353;
    suspicions of, 361–62
UNKVD (Leningrad Regional Directorate of
    the NKVD), 149–50, 154, 201, 202, 203,
    301, 337
Ustinov, Dmitri, 19, 138, 140

Vaganov, Pyotr, 31
Vainshtein (planning official), 363
Vannikov, Boris, 19, 23
Vasilevsky, Aleksandr, 127–28, 147
Vasiliev, Lesha, 277
Vasiliev, Nikolai, 275, 277–78, 283
Vasiliev, N. N., *figure 58*
Vasilieva (factory worker), 357–58
Vavilov, Nikolai, 458 n. 56
Verkhovsky, David, 316
Verzhbitsky, B. D., 384, 391, 400
Viktorov (engineer), 363
Viktorov (informant), 389, 396
Viktorova (cafeteria director), 157
Vinogradov (government official), 215
Vinogradov, N. P., 386, 394, 397–98, 402
Vinokurov, Aleksei, 314
Vishniakov (engineer), 363
Vlasov, Andrei, 61, 144, 146, 147
Vlasov, Iakov, 339
Voinov, S. D., 114–15, 160
Volga German Autonomous Republic, 209
Volkhov power plant, 61
Volkogonov, Dmitry, 114
Volkov (factory worker), 235
Volkov, Aleksandr, 336–37
Volkov, V. P., 436 n. 197
Volodarsky print shop, 310
Volokh (engineer), 234
volunteers, 333–34

von Manteuffel, Baroness, 441 n. 55
Vorobev (accused counterrevolutionary), 238
Vorobiev (accused counterrevolutionary), 360
Vorobieva (factory worker), 359–60
Voronov, Nikolai, 95, 130, 131
Voropaev (factory worker), 235
Voroshilov, Kliment, 35, 78, 86, 88, 91, 100,
    114, 115, 160, 186, 204, 339, *figure 4;*
    alleged plot against, 369; civilians armed
    by, 89; defense council formed by, 44,
    87, 89–90, 92, 93; firing of, 23, 34; as
    GKO member, 82–83; military training
    lacked by, 143, 258; Northwestern Direc-
    tion commanded by, 34, 83; removal from
    command of, 106–7, 108, 146, 258, 407;
    Stalin's mistrust of, 63, 84, 85, 87, 101,
    102, 105, 116
Voznesensky, Aleksandr, 427 n. 139
Voznesensky, Maria, 427 n. 139
Voznesensky, Nikolai, 19, 28, 68, 69, 73, 74,
    79, 427 n. 139
VP (Military Procuracy), 201, 204, 207
VSLF. *See* Military Soviet of the Leningrad
    Front
VT (Military Tribunal), 200, 201, 203–4
Vudnov (physician), 237
Vulkan machine plant, 334

War and Peace (Tolstoy), 293, 382
Weiner, Amir, 425 n. 95
Werth, Alexander, 8, 106, 194, 334, 337
Wincott (writer), 154
Winter War, 5, 26, 29, 143
Writers' Union, 67

Yalta Conference, 70
Yanson (naval officer), 120
Yartsev, V. I., 82
Yegorenkov (party official), 254
Yegorova (student), 233
Yermakov, Vladimir, 348
Yershov (construction worker), 337
Yershov, Vasily, 249–50, 301, 321, 369, 370
Yershova (factory worker), 229
Yevdokimov, Aleksei, 65, 120, 267, 306
Yezhov, Nikolai, 199, 200–201, 371, 372
Yudenich (general), 196
Yugoslavia, 74–75, 169
Yukhnevich (hospital worker), 315, 318
Yurchenkova (accused spy), 238–39
Yushkov (professor), 394

Zaltsman, Isaak, 79, 118, 138, 139, 185, 189,
    192, 193–94, 195, 341
Zanin, S. F., 395, 397, 398, 399
Zaporozhets, Aleksandr, 144, 145, 146, 147,
    148–49

Zastrova (accused counterrevolutionary),
236–37

Zeits, F. A., 397

Zhdanov, Andrei, 10, 25, 28, 39, 74, 76, 81,
109, 134–35, 137, 144–45, 147, 148–49,
186, 204, 304, 405, *figures 1, 43, 66;* alleged plot against, 369; annexed territories overseen by, 20–21, 26; anti-Soviet
agitation seen by, 203; anti-Soviet leaflets
sent to, 252, 253; arms demanded by, 131;
Beria vs., 69, 115, 158–59, 407; censorship
by, 67–68, 93–94; "Committee for Public
Salvation" case and, 400–402; death of,
68, 70; defense council formed by, 44, 87,
89–90, 92, 93; demolition operations and,
116, 117; deportations and, 212; documentary film and, 355, 356–58; evacuations
and, 127, 141; failures acknowledged by,
107; food supplies and, 103, 136, 229, 231,
233, 264, 301; Frolov scapegoated by, 129–
30; grievances sent to, 30; ill health of,
72, 159–60; Khozin's deference toward,
146, 407; Kubatkin and, 406; Leningrad's
defenses overseen by, 34, 35, 78–79, 83,
84–85, 87, 88, 89–93, 96–100, 103, 108–9,
122–23, 124–25, 128–29; Malenkov vs.,
9, 69, 109, 404; as military strategist, 23;
Molotov vs., 9, 404; political ascent of, 18,
68, 158; post-siege activities of, 152; postwar visions of, 70–71; power shared with
military by, 150; reports to, 179, 229, 231,
233, 259, 320, 338, 358, 359, 363, 380, 384,
385; security role of, 226, 236, 251, 374;
Stalin's discord with, 84, 85, 100, 115, 142,
404; during starvation winter, 275, 279;
volunteer units formed by, 334

Zhdanov, Yuri, 68

Zhdanov shipyard, 138, 197, 333

Zhigarev, Pavel, 95

Zhukov (accused counterrevolutionary),
237–38

Zhukov, Georgy, 38, 108, 109, 145, 146, 159,
295, 407, *figure 5; Genshtab* led by, 82, 94;
Leningrad's defenses overseen by, 118–23;
memoirs of, 271; Voroshilov replaced by,
63, 106–7, 124–27, 407

Zhuravsky, A. M., 386, 393

Zinoviev, Grigory, 18, 70, 73

Zinoviev, Nikolai, 310

Zinoviev, Sasha, *figure 62*

Zinovievites, 372

Znamenskaia Church, 166

Zoshchenko, Mikhail, 67

Zotik, A. I., 214

Zozulia (KBF official), 120

Zviagin (party official), 377

BOOKS IN THE
ANNALS OF COMMUNISM SERIES

The Diary of Georgi Dimitrov, 1933–1949, introduced and edited by Ivo Banac

Dimitrov and Stalin, 1934–1943: Letters from the Soviet Archives, edited by Alexander Dallin and Fridrikh I. Firsov

Enemies Within the Gates? The Comintern and the Stalinist Repression, 1934–1939, by William J. Chase

The Fall of the Romanovs: Political Dreams and Personal Struggles in a Time of Revolution, by Mark D. Steinberg and Vladimir M. Khrustalëv

Gulag Voices: An Anthology, edited by Anne Applebaum

The History of the Gulag: From Collectivization to the Great Terror, by Oleg V. Khlevniuk

Katyn: A Crime Without Punishment, edited by Anna M. Cienciala, Natalia S. Lebedeva, and Wojciech Materski

The KGB File of Andrei Sakharov, edited by Joshua Rubenstein and Alexander Gribanov

The Kirov Murder and Soviet History, by Matthew E. Lenoe

The Last Diary of Tsaritsa Alexandra, introduction by Robert K. Massie; edited by Vladimir A. Kozlov and Vladimir M. Khrustalëv

The Leningrad Blockade, 1941–1944: A New Documentary History from the Soviet Archives, by Richard Bidlack and Nikita Lomagin

The Road to Terror: Stalin and the Self-Destruction of the Bolsheviks, 1932–1939, by J. Arch Getty and Oleg V. Naumov

The Secret World of American Communism, by Harvey Klehr, John Earl Haynes, and Fridrikh I. Firsov

Sedition: Everyday Resistance in the Soviet Union under Khrushchev and Brezhnev, edited by Vladimir A. Kozlov, Sheila Fitzpatrick, and Sergei V. Mironenko

Soviet Culture and Power, by Katerina Clark and Evgeny Dobrenko with Andrei Artizov and Oleg Naumov

The Soviet World of American Communism, by Harvey Klehr, John Earl Haynes, and Kyrill M. Anderson

Spain Betrayed: The Soviet Union in the Spanish Civil War, edited by Ronald Radosh, Mary R. Habeck, and G. N. Sevostianov

Stalinism as a Way of Life: A Narrative in Documents, edited by Lewis Siegelbaum and Andrei K. Sokolov

The Stalin-Kaganovich Correspondence, 1931–36, compiled and edited by R. W. Davies, Oleg V. Khlevniuk, E. A. Rees, Liudmila P. Kosheleva, and Larisa A. Rogovaya

Stalin's Letters to Molotov, 1925–1936, edited by Lars T. Lih, Oleg V. Naumov, and Oleg V. Khlevniuk

Stalin's Secret Pogrom: The Postwar Inquisition of the Soviet Jewish Anti-Fascist Committee, edited by Joshua Rubenstein and Vladimir P. Naumov

The Unknown Lenin: From the Secret Archive, edited by Richard Pipes

Voices of Revolution, 1917, by Mark D. Steinberg

The War Against the Peasantry, 1927–1930, edited by Lynne Viola, V. P. Danilov, N. A. Ivnitskii, and Denis Kozlov